THE COMPLETE LYRICS OF COLE PORTER

THE COMPLETE LYRICS OF COLE PORTER

EDITED BY
ROBERT KIMBALL

WITH A FOREWORD BY
JOHN UPDIKE

VINTAGE BOOKS
A DIVISION OF RANDOM HOUSE
NEW YORK

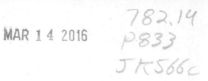

FIRST VINTAGE BOOKS EDITION,
November 1984

 Published in the United States by Random House, Inc., New York, and simultaneously in Canada by Random House of Canada Limited, Toronto. Originally published in Great Britain by Hamish Hamilton Ltd., London, and in the United States by Alfred A. Knopf, Inc. in 1983.

Library of Congress Cataloging in Publication Data

Porter, Cole, 1891-1964.
The complete lyrics of Cole Porter.

Includes index.
1. Musical revues, comedies, etc.—Librettos.
2. Music, Popular (Songs, etc.)—United States—Texts.
I. Kimball, Robert. II. Title.
[PS3531.0734125 1984] 784.5'05 84-40287

ISBN 0-394-72764-9 (pbk.)

Manufactured in the United States of America

PHOTO CREDITS

The Cole Porter Musical and Literary Property Trusts, Robert H. Montgomery, Jr., as Trustee: Frontispiece, 117, 157, 400

Courtesy of Culver Pictures: 150, 255, 294, 280

Courtesy of The Museum of Modern Art/Film Stills Archive: 197, 217, 453

Van Damn Photos, Theatre Collection, The New York Public Library, Astor, Lenox and Tilden Foundations: 237, 298

For my wife, Abigail,
and our children, Philip and Miranda,

and

In memory of Eubie Blake
and Ira Gershwin

CONTENTS

Foreword by John Updike xiii

Introduction xix

Chronology xxvii

Acknowledgments xxxiii

COLLEGE SONGS, 1909–1913 3

When the Summer Moon Comes 'Long · Bridget McGuire · Moon, Moon · Since Dolly's Come to Town · Mory's · Bingo Eli Yale · Hail to Yale · Eli · Bull Dog · The Motor Car · A Football King · If I Were Only a Football Man · I Want to Be a Yale Boy · I Want to Be a Prom Girl · It Pays to Advertise · When I'm Eating Around with You · Yellow Melodrama · Antoinette Birby

COLLEGE SHOWS, 1911–1912 10

CORA, 1911 Poker · Concentration · Saturday Night · Hello, Miss Chapel Street · Cora, the Fair Chorine · My Hometown Girl · Goodbye, Boys · The Old Rat Mort · Ninette · Far, Far Away · Rosebud · Rolling, Rolling

AND THE VILLAIN STILL PURSUED HER, 1912 We Are the Chorus of the Show · Strolling · The Lovely Heroine · I'm the Villain · Twilight · Llewellyn · That Zip Cornwall Cooch · Charity · Queens of Terpsichore · Leaders of Society · Submarine · Barcelona Maid · Silver Moon · Dear Doctor · Anytime · Come to Bohemia · Dancing · Fare Thee Well · When We're Wed

THE POT OF GOLD, 1912 At the Rainbow · Bellboys · Longing for Dear Old Broadway · When I Used to Lead the Ballet · My Houseboat on the Thames · She Was a Fair Young Mermaid · What's This Awful Hullabaloo? · What a Charming Afternoon · Since We've Met · Exercise · We Are So Aesthetic · Scandal · I Wonder Where My Girl Is Now · My Salvation Army Queen · It's Awfully Hard When Mother's Not Along · I Want to Be Married (to a Delta Kappa Epsilon Man) · Ha, Ha, They Must Sail for Siberia · I Love You So · Loie and Chlodo · So Let Us Hail

COLLEGE SHOWS, 1913–1914 25

THE KALEIDOSCOPE, 1913 At the Dawn Tea · We Are Prom Girls · Chaperons · In the Land Where My Heart Was Born · Meet Me Beside the River · Beware of the Sophomore · Rick-Chick-a-Chick · Goodbye, My True Love · On My Yacht · We're a Group of Nonentities · Flower Maidens · Absinthe · Absinthe Drip · Maid of Santiago · As I Love You · Duodecimalogue · Oh, What a Pretty Pair of Lovers · A Member of the Yale Elizabethan Club · Moon Man · My Georgia Gal

PARANOIA, 1914 Paranoia · Funny Little Tracks in the Snow · Innocent, Innocent Maids · Oh, What a Lonely Princess · Won't You Come Crusading with Me? · I Want to Row on the Crew · What Love Is · Down in a Dungeon Deep · Slow Sinks the Sun · The Prep School Widow · Idyll · I've a Shooting Box in Scotland · Down Lovers' Lane · The Language of Flowers · Dresden China Soldiers · Naughty, Naughty · Hail to Cyril

WE'RE ALL DRESSED UP AND WE DON'T KNOW HUERTO GO, 1914 Cincinnati

Craigie 404

SEE AMERICA FIRST, 1916 41

Badmen · Younger Sons of Peers · Greetings, Gentlemen · To Follow Every Fancy · See America First · Well, It's Good to Be Here Again · Hold-up Ensemble · Entrance of Indian Maidens · If in Spite of Our Attempts · The Social Coach of All The Fashionable Future Debutantes · Something's Got to Be Done · Pity Me, Please · I've Got an Awful Lot to Learn · Dinner · Hail, Ye Indian Maidens · Fascinating Females · Beautiful, Primitive Indian Girls · The Lady I've Vowed to Wed · Finale, Act I · Mirror, Mirror · Oh, Bright, Fair Dream · Ever and Ever Yours · Lady Fair, Lady Fair · Love Came and Crowned Me · Lima · When a Body's in Love · Revelation Ensemble · Step We Grandly · Buy Her a Box at the Opera · Sweet Simplicity · Je Vous Comprends

HITCHY-KOO OF 1919 61

When Black Sallie Sings Pagliacci · I Introduced · Hitchy's Garden of Roses · When I Had a Uniform On · I've Got Somebody Waiting · Peter Piper / The Sea Is Calling · My Cozy Little Corner in the Ritz · Old-Fashioned Garden · Bring Me Back My Butterfly · Another Sentimental Song · That Black and White Baby of Mine · You and Me · Since Ma Got the Craze Espagnole · Oh So Soon · Since

Little Baby Brother Became a Movie Star · China Doll · Tired of Living Alone

WAR SONGS AND OTHERS, 1915–1920 69

War Song · Katie of the Y.M.C.A. · It Puzzles Me So · Cleveland · Alone with You · I Never Realized · Washington Square · Widow's Cruise · Venus of Milo · You Make Up · A Table for Two · Oh, Honey

HITCHY-KOO OF 1922 75

Maryland Scene · Oh, Mary · Ah Fong Lo · My Spanish Shawl · In Hitchy's Bouquet · When My Caravan Comes Home · The American Punch · Play Me a Tune · Love Letter Words · The Bandit Band · The Sponge · The Harbor Deep Down in My Heart · The Old-Fashioned Waltz · Pitter-Patter · Twin Sisters · Jungle Rose · Curio Song *or* Old King Solly

GREENWICH VILLAGE FOLLIES, 1924 84

Brittany · Two Little Babes in the Wood · Broadcast a Jazz · Wait for the Moon · My Long Ago Girl · Make Every Day a Holiday · I'm in Love Again

LA REVUE DES AMBASSADEURS, 1928 90

Keep Moving · The Lost Liberty Blues · Omnibus · Do You Want to See Paris? · Pilot Me · In a Moorish Garden · Almiro · You and Me · Fish · Military Maids · Blue Hours · Alpine Rose · Gershwin Specialty · Boulevard Break · Hans · Baby, Let's Dance · An Old-Fashioned Girl · An Old-Fashioned Boy · Fountain of Youth

PARIS, 1928 100

Don't Look at Me That Way · Let's Do It, Let's Fall in Love · Vivienne · The Heaven Hop · Quelque-Chose · Let's Misbehave · Which? · Which Is the Right Life? · Dizzy Baby · Bad Girl in Paree · When I Found You

WAKE UP AND DREAM, 1929 107

Wake Up and Dream · I've Got a Crush on You · I Loved Him, But He Didn't Love Me · Looking at You · The Banjo That Man Joe Plays · Entrance of Emigrants · What Is This Thing Called Love? · Wait Until It's Bedtime · Operatic Pills · After All, I'm Only a Schoolgirl · I Dream of a Girl in a Shawl · Night Club Opening · I'm a Gigolo · I Want to Be Raided by You · The Extra Man · My Louisa

FIFTY MILLION FRENCHMEN, 1929 117

A Toast to Volstead · You Do Something to Me · The American Express · You've Got That Thing · Find Me a Primitive Man · Where Would You Get Your Coat? · At Longchamps Today · Yankee Doodle · The Happy Heaven of Harlem · Why Shouldn't I Have You? · Somebody's Going to Throw a Big Party · It Isn't Done · I'm in Love · The Tale of the Oyster · Paree, What Did You Do to Me? · You Don't Know Paree · I'm Unlucky at Gambling · I Worship You · Please Don't Make Me Be Good · The Queen of Terre Haute · Watching the World Go By · Down with Everybody but Us · Why Don't We Try Staying Home? · That's Why I Love You · The Heaven of Harlem · My Harlem Wench · Let's Step Out · The Boy Friend Back Home

MISCELLANEOUS, 1920s 130

A NIGHT OUT, 1920

MAYFAIR AND MONTMARTRE, 1922 Olga (Come Back to the Volga) · Cocktail Time · The Blue Boy Blues · Wondering Night and Day

PHI-PHI, 1922 Ragtime Pipes of Pan

OUT O' LUCK, 1925 Butterflies · Mademazelle · Opera Star

THE BATTLE OF PARIS, 1929 Here Comes the Bandwagon · They All Fall in Love

Love 'Em and Leave 'Em · Italian Street Singers · Poor Young Millionaire · Don't Tell Me Who You Are · The Scampi · I'm Dining with Elsa · That Little Old Bar in the Ritz · Sex Appeal · Hot-House Rose · Weren't We Fools? · The Laziest Gal in Town

THE NEW YORKERS, 1930 142

Go into Your Dance · Where Have You Been? · Say It with Gin · Venice · I'm Getting Myself Ready for You · Love for Sale · The Great Indoors · Sing Sing for Sing Sing · Take Me Back to Manhattan · Let's Fly Away · I Happen to Like New York · Just One of Those Things · The Poor Rich · We've Been Spending the Summer with Our Families · Where Can One Powder One's Nose? · It Only Happens in Dreams

GAY DIVORCE, 1932 150

After You, Who? · Why Marry Them? · Salt Air · I Still Love the Red, White and Blue · Night and Day · How's Your Romance? · What Will Become of Our England? · I've Got You on My Mind · Mister and Missus Fitch · You're in Love · Fate · A Weekend Affair · I Love Only You

NYMPH ERRANT, 1933 157

Experiment · It's Bad for Me · Neauville-sur-Mer ·

The Cocotte · How Could We Be Wrong? · They're Always Entertaining · Georgia Sand · Cazanova · Nymph Errant · Ruins · The Physician · Solomon · Back to Nature with You · Plumbing · Si Vous Aimez les Poitrines · You're Too Far Away · Sweet Nudity · French Colonial Exposition Scene

ANYTHING GOES, 1934 166

I Get a Kick Out of You · Bon Voyage / There's No Cure Like Travel · All Through the Night · There'll Always Be a Lady Fair · Where Are the Men? · You're the Top · Anything Goes · Public Enemy Number One · Blow, Gabriel, Blow · Be Like the Bluebird · Buddie, Beware · The Gypsy in Me · Waltz down the Aisle · What a Joy to Be Young · Kate the Great

ADIOS, ARGENTINA, 1934–1935 177

Adios, Argentina · The Chiripah · Don't Fence Me In · If You Could Love Me · The Side Car · Singing in the Saddle

JUBILEE, 1935 182

Our Crown · We're Off to Feathermore · Why Shouldn't I? · Entrance of Eric · The Kling-Kling Bird on the Divi-Divi Tree · When Love Comes Your Way · What a Nice Municipal Park · When Me, Mowgli, Love · Gather Ye Autographs While Ye May · My Loulou · Begin the Beguine · Good Morning, Miss Standing · My Most Intimate Friend · A Picture of Me Without You · Ev'rybod-ee Who's Anybod-ee · Aphrodite's Dance · Swing That Swing · Sunday Morning Breakfast Time · Mr. and Mrs. Smith · Gay Little Wives · To Get Away · Me and Marie · Just One of Those Things · There's Nothing Like Swimming · Yours · Sing "Jubilee"

BORN TO DANCE, 1936 197

Rolling Home · Rap Tap on Wood · Hey, Babe, Hey · Entrance of Lucy James · Love Me, Love My Pekinese · Easy to Love · I've Got You Under My Skin · Swingin' the Jinx Away · Goodbye, Little Dream, Goodbye

RED, HOT AND BLUE, 1936 204

At Ye Olde Coffee Shoppe in Cheyenne · It's a Great Life · Perennial Debutantes · Ours · Down in the Depths · Carry On · You've Got Something · It's De-lovely · A Little Skipper from Heaven Above · Five Hundred Million · Ridin' High · We're About to Start Big Rehearsin' · Hymn to Hymen · What a Great Pair We'll Be · You're a Bad Influence on Me · The Ozarks Are Callin' Me Home · Red, Hot and Blue · When Your Troubles Have Started · Bertie and Gertie · Who but You? · That's the News I'm Waiting to Hear · Where? · Lonely Star

ROSALIE, 1937 217

Who Knows? · I've a Strange New Rhythm in My Heart · Rosalie · Why Should I Care? · Spring Love Is in the Air · Close · In the Still of the Night · It's All Over but the Shouting · To Love or Not to Love · Opening, Romanza Sequence · Entrance of Prince Paul · I Know It's Not Meant for Me · A Fool There Was

YOU NEVER KNOW, 1938 224

I Am Gaston · Au Revoir, Cher Baron · Maria · You Never Know · What Is That Tune? · For No Rhyme or Reason · From Alpha to Omega · Don't Let It Get You Down · What Shall I Do? · At Long Last Love · Yes, Yes, Yes · Good Evening, Princesse · I'll Black His Eyes · I'm Yours · What a Priceless Pleasure · Just One Step Ahead of Love · Ha, Ha, Ha · By Candlelight · I'm Back in Circulation · I'm Going In for Love · It's No Laughing Matter

LEAVE IT TO ME, 1938 237

How Do You Spell Ambassador? · We Drink to You, J. H. Brody · Vite, Vite, Vite · I'm Taking the Steps to Russia · Get Out of Town · When All's Said and Done · Most Gentlemen Don't Like Love · Comrade Alonzo · Thank You · Recall Goodhue · From Now On · I Want to Go Home · My Heart Belongs to Daddy · Tomorrow · Far Away · To the U.S.A. from the U.S.S.R. · When the Hen Stops Laying · Just Another Page in Your Diary · Information, Please · There's a Fan · As Long As It's Not About Love · Why Can't I Forget You?

BROADWAY MELODY OF 1940, 1939 251

Please Don't Monkey with Broadway · Between You and Me · I've Got My Eyes on You · I Concentrate on You · I Happen to Be in Love · I'm So in Love with You

DU BARRY WAS A LADY, 1939 255

Where's Louie? · Ev'ry Day a Holiday · It Ain't Etiquette · When Love Beckoned · Come On In · Dream Song · Mesdames et Messieurs · But in the Morning, No · Do I Love You? · Du Barry Was a Lady · Give Him the Oo-la-la · Well, Did You Evah! · It Was Written in the Stars · Katie Went to Haiti · Friendship · What Have I? · In the Big Money

MISCELLANEOUS, 1930s 269

What's My Man Gonna Be Like? ·

STAR DUST, 1931 Auf Wiederseh'n · Mysteriously · Pick Me Up and Lay Me Down

EVER YOURS, 1933–1934 Gypsy Song · The Night of the Ball · Once Upon a Time · It All Seems So Long Ago · Coffee · It's Probably Just As Well

Miss Otis Regrets · Thank You So Much, Mrs. Lowsborough-Goodby

BREAK THE NEWS, 1938 It All Belongs to You

GREEK TO YOU, 1937–1938 Greek to You · Melos, That Smiling Isle · Wild Wedding Bells · It Never Entered My Head

River God · What Am I to Do? · At Last in Your Arms · Java · How Do They Do It? · Maybe Yes, Maybe No · The Upper Park Avenue · Dressing Daughter for Dinner

PANAMA HATTIE, 1940 280

A Stroll on the Plaza Sant' Ana · Join It Right Away · Visit Panama · My Mother Would Love You · I've Still Got My Health · Fresh as a Daisy · Welcome to Jerry · Let's Be Buddies · They Ain't Done Right by Our Nell · I'm Throwing a Ball Tonight · We Detest a Fiesta · Who Would Have Dreamed? · Make It Another Old-Fashioned, Please · All I've Got to Get Now Is My Man · You Said It · God Bless the Women · Here's to Panama Hattie · Americans All Drink Coffee

YOU'LL NEVER GET RICH, 1941 294

Dream-Dancing · Shootin' the Works for Uncle Sam · Since I Kissed My Baby Goodbye · So Near and Yet So Far · The Wedding Cakewalk

LET'S FACE IT, 1941 298

Milk, Milk, Milk · A Lady Needs a Rest · Jerry, My Soldier Boy · Let's Face It · Farming · Ev'rything I Love · Ace in the Hole · You Irritate Me So · Baby Games · Rub Your Lamp · I've Got Some Unfinished Business with You · Let's Not Talk About Love · A Little Rumba Numba · I Hate You, Darling · Get Yourself a Girl · Revenge · What Are Little Husbands Made Of? · Pets · Make a Date with a Great Psychoanalyst · Up to His Old Tricks Again · You Can't Beat My Bill

SOMETHING TO SHOUT ABOUT, 1943 312

You'd Be So Nice to Come Home To · I Can Do Without Tea in My Teapot · Through Thick and Thin · I Always Knew · Something to Shout About · Lotus Bloom · Hasta Luego · It Might Have Been · Couldn't Be · Take It Easy · Let Doctor Schmett Vet Your Pet

SOMETHING FOR THE BOYS, 1943 319

Announcement of Inheritance · See That You're Born in Texas · When My Baby Goes to Town · Something for the Boys · When We're Home on the Range · Could It Be You? · Hey, Good-Lookin' · He's a Right Guy · The Leader of a Big-Time Band · I'm in Love with a Soldier Boy · There's a Happy Land in the Sky · By the Mississinewah · Riddle-Diddle Me This · So Long, San Antonio · Washington, D.C. · Oh, How I Could Go for You · Texas Will Make You a Man · Well, I Just Wouldn't Know · Wouldn't It Be Crazy? · Carborundum

MISSISSIPPI BELLE, 1943–1944 334

Amo Amas · Close to Me · Hip, Hip, Hooray for Andy Jackson · I Like Pretty Things · I'm Not Myself at All · In the Green Hills of County Mayo · Kathleen · Loading Song · Mamie Magdalin · Mississippi Belle · My Broth of a Boy · School, School, Heaven-Blessed School · So Long · When a Woman's in Love · When McKinley Marches On · When You and I Were Strangers · Who'll Bid?

MEXICAN HAYRIDE, 1944 342

Entrance of Montana · Sing to Me, Guitar · The Good-Will Movement · I Love You · There Must Be Someone for Me · Carlotta · Girls · What a Crazy Way to Spend Sunday · Abracadabra · Count Your Blessings · Hereafter · It Must Be Fun to Be You · Here's a Cheer for Dear Old Ciro's · Tequila · We're Off for a Hayride in Mexico · He Certainly Kills the Women · A Humble Hollywood Executive · It's a Big Night · It's Just Like the Good Old Days · It's Just Yours · Octet · Put a Sack over Their Heads · A Sightseeing Tour · That's What You Mean to Me · I'm Afraid I Love You · I'm So Glahd to Meet You

SEVEN LIVELY ARTS, 1944 360

Big Town · Is It the Girl (or Is It the Gown)? · Everytime We Say Goodbye · Only Another Boy and Girl · Wow-Ooh-Wolf! · Drink · When I Was a Little Cuckoo · Frahngee-Pahnee · Dancin' to a Jungle Drum (Let's End the Beguine) · Hence It Don't Make Sense · The Band Started Swinging a Song · The Big Parade / Yours for a Song · Pretty Little Missus Bell · Dainty, Quainty Me · I Wrote a Play · If I Hadn't a Husband · Where Do We Go from Here? · Café Society Still Carries On

AROUND THE WORLD IN EIGHTY DAYS, 1946 375

Look What I Found · There He Goes, Mr. Phileas Fogg · Mee-rah-lah · Sea Chantey · Should I Tell You I Love You? · Pipe Dreaming · If You Smile at Me · Wherever They Fly the Flag of Old England · Missus Aouda · Slave Auction · Snagtooth Gertie

THE PIRATE, 1948 380

Mack the Black · Niña · Love of My Life · You Can Do No Wrong · Be a Clown · Voodoo · Manuela · Martinique

KISS ME, KATE, 1948 386

Another Op'nin', Another Show · Why Can't You Behave? · Wunderbar · So in Love · We Open in Venice · Tom, Dick or Harry · I've Come to Wive It Wealthily in Padua · I Hate Men · Were Thine That Special Face · I Sing of Love · Kiss Me, Kate · Too Darn Hot · Where Is the Life That Late I Led? · Always True to You in My Fashion · Bianca · Brush Up Your Shakespeare · I Am Ashamed That Women Are So Simple · Finale, Act II · It Was Great Fun the First Time · We Shall Never Be Younger · A Woman's Career · What Does Your Servant Dream About? · I'm Afraid, Sweetheart, I Love You · If Ever Married I'm

MISCELLANEOUS, 1940s 400

So Long, Samoa · Glide, Glider, Glide · Sailors of the Sky · The Gold Dusters Song · I Gaze in Your Eyes · Farewell, Amanda

OUT OF THIS WORLD, 1950 403

Prologue · I Jupiter, I Rex · Use Your Imagination · Hail, Hail, Hail · I Got Beauty · Maiden Fair · Where, Oh Where? · I Am Loved · They Couldn't Compare to You · What Do You Think About Men? · I Sleep Easier Now · Climb Up the Mountain · No Lover · Cherry Pies Ought to Be You · Hark to the Song of the Night · Nobody's Chasing Me · We're on the Road to Athens · From This Moment On · You Don't Remind Me · Hush, Hush, Hush · Away from It All · Midsummer Night · Oh, It Must Be Fun · To Hell with Ev'rything but Us · Tonight I Love You More · Why Do You Wanta Hurt Me So?

CAN-CAN, 1953 421

Maidens Typical of France · Never Give Anything Away · C'est Magnifique · Come Along with Me · Live and Let Live · I Am in Love · If You Loved Me Truly · Montmart' · Allez-vous-en · Never, Never Be an Artist · It's All Right with Me · Ev'ry Man Is a Stupid Man · I Love Paris · Can-Can · The Law · I Shall Positively Pay You Next Monday · A Man Must His Honor Defend · Nothing to Do but Work · Laundry Scene · Her Heart Was in Her Work · Who Said Gay Paree? · What a Fair Thing Is a Woman · Am I in Love? · To Think That This Could Happen to Me · I Do · When Love Comes to Call · I Like the Ladies

SILK STOCKINGS, 1955 437

Too Bad · Paris Loves Lovers · Stereophonic Sound · It's a Chemical Reaction, That's All · All of You · Satin and Silk · Without Love · Hail Bibinski · As On Through the Seasons We Sail · Josephine · Siberia · Silk Stockings · The Red Blues · Art · There's a Hollywood That's Good · Give Me the Land · If Ever We Get Out of Jail · Let's Make It a Night · The Perfume of Love · Under the Dress · What a Ball · Why Should I Trust You? · Bébé of Gay Paree

FILM VERSION, 1957 Fated to Be Mated · The Ritz Roll and Rock

HIGH SOCIETY, 1956 453

High Society Calypso · I Love You, Samantha · Little One · Who Wants to Be a Millionaire? · True Love · You're Sensational · Now You Has Jazz · Mind If I Make Love to You? · Caroline · Let's Vocalize · So What? · Who Has? · How Could I?

LES GIRLS, 1957 460

Les Girls · You're Just Too, Too · Ça, C'est l'Amour · Ladies-in-Waiting · Why Am I So Gone (About That Gal)? · Drinking Song · High-Flyin' Wings on My Shoes · I Could Kick Myself · My Darling Never Is Late · My Little Piece o' Pie · What Fun · You're the Prize Guy of Guys

ALADDIN, 1958 467

Trust Your Destiny to Your Star · Aladdin · Come to the Supermarket in Old Peking · I Adore You · Make Way for the Emperor · No Wonder Taxes Are High · Opportunity Knocks But Once · Wouldn't It Be Fun

Index 473

FOREWORD

You're the top!
You're the Colosseum.
You're the top!
You're the Louvre Museum.
You're a melody from a symphony by Strauss,
You're a Bendel bonnet,
A Shakespeare sonnet,
You're Mickey Mouse.

Could there be a love song more American than this?—this consumer's checklist, this breezy catalogue with its climactic, sublimely simple assurance to the beloved that she (or he) is Mickey Mouse. In the succeeding refrains, the Mickey Mouse line becomes "You're cellophane," "You're broccoli," "You're Camembert," "You're Pepsodent," "You're Ovaltine," and "You're stratosphere." Each time, whether we hear the words in the voice of Ethel Merman, who introduced the song fifty years ago in *Anything Goes,* or of Anita O'Day, who made a haunting croaky-voiced recording some decades later, something tender, solemn, nonsensical, and absolute seems to be being said. The song lyricist's task is to provide excuses for onstage demonstrations of energy and also, at the top of his craft, to provide new phrasings for the ineffable and virtually trite. How many times can the discovery and proclamation that one ersatz creature is in love with another be endured? Infinitely many, as long as real men and women continue to mate: popular composers from generation to generation, if they do not teach us how to love, do lend our romances a certain accent and give our courting rites and their milieux—proms, bars, automobiles with their dashboard moons—a tribal background, a background choir of communal experience. In the urbane, top-hat fantasy world wherein Fred Astaire and Cole Porter reign as quintessential performer and creator, love is wry, jokey, casual, and even weary but nonetheless ecstatic: you're Mickey Mouse. Not to mention, "You're romance, / You're the steppes of Russia, / You're the pants on a Roxy usher." One of the delights of this all-inclusive collection that Mr. Kimball has assiduously compiled from so many tattered sources consists of following half-recalled lyrics through their many ebullient refrains; we find, for instance, that Porter rhymed "top" not only with the expectable "flop," "pop," "hop," and "stop" but also with the more rakish "blop," "de trop," and "the G.O.P. or GOP."

He brought to the traditional and somewhat standardized tasks of songsmithing a great verbal ingenuity, a brave flexibility and resourcefulness (how many of these lengthy lyrics were discarded by showtime!), a cosmopolitan's wide expertise in many mundane matters including foreign lands and tongues, and a spirit that always kept something of collegiate innocence about it. The decade of the Depression, Porter's creative prime, maintained in its popular culture much of the Twenties' gaiety and bequeathed a surprising amount of it to the war-stricken Forties—the jauntiness of "Shootin' the Works for Uncle Sam" ("North, South, East, West, / All the boys are hep / To do their damndest (darndest) / To defend Miss Liberty's rep") on the eve of Pearl Harbor almost grates, and Porter's wartime musicals quaintly—it seems now —reassure the boys overseas that "Miss Garbo remains as the Hollywood Sphinx / Monty Woolley's still bathing his beard in his drinks" and that "Café Society still carries on." This lighthearted era was a heyday of light verse: there were book reviews in verse, and sports stories; there were droll ballades and rondeaux and triolets. The plenitudinous newspapers and magazines published Don Marquis, F.P.A., Louis Untermeyer, Arthur Guiterman, Christopher Morley, Dorothy Parker, Ogden Nash, E. B. White, Morris Bishop, and Phyllis McGinley, not to mention such clever curiosities as Newman Levy's rhyming versions of opera plots and David McCord's typographically antic "Sonnets to Baedeker." Song lyricists were of this ingenious company; William Harmon's *Oxford Book of American Light Verse* includes, with poems by all the above-mentioned, lyrics by Porter, Lorenz Hart, Ira Gershwin, Oscar Hammerstein II, and Johnny Mercer. Wit of a specifically literary sort lies behind Porter's sophisticated references and outrageous rhymes—"trickery / liquor we," "throws a / sub rosa," "presto / West, oh," "Siena / then a," and, famously from "Night and Day," "hide of me / inside of me" (which Ring Lardner parodied as "rind of me / mind of me" and "tegument / egg you meant.") Light verse seeks, though, to make its trickery seem unforced, and the peculiar grace of the form is well illustrated by the vivid refrain of "My Heart Belongs to Daddy," beginning:

> While tearing off
> A game of golf
> I may make a play for the caddy.
> But when I do
> I don't follow through
> 'Cause my heart belongs to Daddy.

And the next lines follow with another *double entendre* almost as elegant: "If I invite / A boy, some night, / To dine on my fine finnan haddie, / I just adore / His asking for more, / But my heart belongs to Daddy." The internal rhymes on the second and fifth syllable of the third line are a consummate prosodic trick, repeated without apparent effort, here and then twice more in the second refrain.

Yet how much, it must be asked, of our delight in these particular verses depends upon our memory of the melody, a melody that launched, Mr. Kimball confides in a headnote, the Broadway career of Mary Martin, a melody that has given dozens of thrushes excuse to pucker, pout, and prance, a melody of irresistible momentum and lilt? Very much, must be the honest answer. And where no tune comes to mind to fit the words, they spin themselves a bit vacuously down the page with their "honey / funny / sunny / money" cheer and relentless allusions to half-forgotten celebrities and publicly certified emotional states. Some of the love songs, I fear, put us in mind of that Ira Gershwin lyric that goes (in part):

Blah, blah, blah your hair,
Blah, blah, blah your eyes;
Blah, blah, blah, blah care,
Blah, blah, blah, blah skies.
Tra la la la, tra la la la la, cottage for two,
Blah, blah, blah, blah, blah, darling, with you!

Without music, one cannot really read (from Porter's "Why Should I Care?")

Tra, la, la, la,
La, la, la, la, la, la,
Tra, la, la, la,
La, la, la, la, la, la, la

or the thirty-four "again"s of "I'll Black His Eyes" or the one hundred eighty-four "ha"s of "Riddle-Diddle Me This." Without music, the simple lines of "I Love You" and "True Love" remain banal, daring parodies of banality, indeed; but alloyed with their enchanting tunes, and sung by Bing Crosby (in duet, for the sweet waltz of the second, with the delicate voice of Grace Kelly), the words become gold, affecting and unforgettable. The point scarcely needs making, least of all in the case of a composer like Porter who created his own melodies, that song lyrics are part of the whole, and that reading a book of them is a little like looking at an album of photographs of delicious food. The food looks good, but the proof is in the eating. The proof of Cole Porter's genius was in the stage shows and movies he made his crucial contributions to, and in the dozen or more standards—"Just One of Those Things," "I Get a Kick Out of You," "Begin the Beguine," "In the Still of the Night," "I've Got You Under My Skin," "It's De-Lovely," "From This Moment On," "You'd Be So Nice to Come Home To," "It's All Right with Me," "Night and Day," "My Heart Belongs to Daddy," "You're the Top," etc.—that are woven into the airwaves of these United States and familiar to all who have ears to hear.

Verse, including light verse, makes its own music. The tune is elusive but it requires no stage manager or electronic equipment; it hums and tingles up off the mute page. A light-verse writer is not constrained to extend his inspiration through enough refrains to exhaust the chorus, to shape his syllables toward easy vocalization by a possibly difficult star (Bert Lahr, we are told on page 262 herein, refused to perform a song composed for him because it rhymed "cinema" and "enema"), or to appeal to any store of shared information less vast than the language and its accumulated treasury of allusions. No doubt Cole Porter could have been such a writer, had the immeasurably wider audience for musical comedy not beckoned. Without any orchestral egging on we smile at such lines as

Your effect should be fantastic
In that pistache Perfolastic

and

Digging in his fertile glen,
Goldwyn dug up Anna Sten

and

Some folks collect paintings,
Some folks collect stamps,
Some are amassers
Of antimacassars
And other Victorian camps

and

If a lass in Michigan can,
If an ass in Astrakhan can,
If a bass in the Saskatchewan can,
Baby, you can can-can too.

Porter's transmogrification of Bob Fletcher's original lyric for "Don't Fence Me In," given on page 127, dramatically demonstrates his technical flair; almost every element in the rather staid, trite source is used in Porter's revision, but wonderfully loosened up with internal rhymes and a certain surreal humor—"Gaze at the moon till I lose my senses" has no corresponding sentiment in the original. True, we can hear the music, jingling and trotting along, and this greatly helps. The more of the music you can hear, the more you are apt to enjoy perusing this monumental omnium-gatherum; but even where the silence of your lonely room remains obdurate, something magical is apt to creep

Like the beat beat beat of the tom-tom
When the jungle shadows fall,
Like the tick tick tock of the stately clock
As it stands against the wall,
Like the drip drip drip of the raindrops
When the sum'r show'r is through.

—John Updike

INTRODUCTION

Goods, merchandise—that is what most songs were intended to be when Cole Porter was an aspiring composer-lyricist. The primary aim of popular music's songwriters and publishers then was unabashedly commercial. Songs were hustled, peddled, plugged in five-and-ten-cent stores and vaudeville houses across the land. Few people in America, including the creators of songs, thought of songwriting as one of the higher arts.

Yet some of what began as a "product," meant to become as automatically obsolescent as last year's fashions, emerged as enduring work. In many of these three-minute miniatures a whole age's exuberance and naïveté were captured, along with glimpses of truth, beauty, gaiety, and sorrow. Many of the most frivolous lyrics boast a craftsmanship and, at times, an artistry that command our respect and often engage our affections as well. This can be said of many of Cole Porter's early songs. The advice in "Exercise" of 1912—"For if you'd not neglect your / Figure's architecture"—was born of the same sophisticated talent that created "It's All Right with Me" in 1953.

Although Porter's youthful "merchandise" did not go unnoticed, his talent was slow to make its full impact; the classics or "standards" that he is best known for, such as "Love for Sale," "Night and Day," and "Begin the Beguine," were late offspring. Such contemporaries and younger colleagues as Irving Berlin, Jerome Kern, George Gershwin, Vincent Youmans, and Richard Rodgers achieved great success while in their twenties. Porter had written some two hundred songs (for Yale shows, for revues and book shows in New York, London, and Paris) by 1928, but he was nearly forty when *Paris* in that year and *Fifty Million Frenchmen* in 1929, with their candid, humorous treatment of love and sex, propelled him to the forefront of his profession.

Altogether, Porter wrote over eight hundred songs. More than half of his songs, however, have never been published. Of those that have been printed, some have appeared in curtailed or simplified or even censored versions. This book begins with Porter's earliest surviving lyrics, written in 1910 during his Freshman Year at Yale, and ends with his last score, completed in 1957 for the television production of *Aladdin.* Of course, it would have been desirable to have compiled the music along with the lyrics, especially since Porter almost always wrote both. But such a compilation would have run thousands of pages, and its cost would have been prohibitive. The task lies more properly in the domain of the music publishers.

Since Porter himself so avidly cultivated and celebrated "the top," shouldn't we be content with the best of his work, the "standards" that established and sustained his formidable reputation? But a "gems only" or a "greatest hits" approach encourages superficial and incomplete understanding of an artist's output. To know the best of Porter, even if we cannot agree on what it is, we must know all of Porter. His lesser work does not diminish his greater work.

It is reasonable to assume that Porter did not view all his songs as being of equal quality. Still, his youthful strivings, with their obvious shortcomings, are here, as they should be. Even these first efforts have special turns of phrase that are of interest. In some cases, where Porter used a theme or an idea more distinctively or adeptly in a later song, we have what can be considered works in progress or preparations for more mature and distinguished statements.

There are other reasons for this edition. A great many previously published songs are out of print and very hard to find. Publishing houses, aiming to achieve the widest possible dissemination of song hits, generally printed ballads and other numbers that could be easily performed by dance bands. Comedy songs, an area in which Porter excelled, were seldom printed because they were considered special material. Some songs were heard on recordings but were never printed. Only in a very few instances did the popularity of a show (*Anything Goes* in 1934, *Kiss Me, Kate* in 1948, and *Can-Can* in 1953) lead to the publication of a complete piano-vocal score.

Moreover, it is not always possible or advisable to regard popular published versions of Porter's songs—or anyone else's—as the final word on authenticity. Sometimes music was simplified in order to be playable and singable by large numbers of people. A lyric with more than two or three stanzas also suffered. Publishers could not fit so many words between the music staves and were apparently reluctant to substitute the additional lyrics for the time-honored advertisements for company products that adorned the back pages of printed songs.

In addition, quite often a song was published while a show was still in rehearsal or a film in the midst of production. The lyric might have changed for any number of reasons as the work progressed, but the song was already printed. It is helpful, perhaps, to think of a published song as offering a view of a lyric at one particular point in the creative process. A cast recording gives us another view at another stage in the process.

There were other elements of shows that publishers almost never concerned themselves with: lyrics to opening choruses, curtain-closers, scene-setters, and what might be described as filler material. Many of them, quite understandably, had no life outside the production for which they were written. But anyone interested in the complete lyrics of a show for research, revivals, or other purposes needs access to them.

Censorship was another problem that occasionally faced the songwriter; consequently, even some of Porter's most famous songs need to be re-examined. Consider, for example, the lines from "I Get a Kick Out of You" (*Anything Goes,* 1934): "Some get a kick from cocaine. / I'm sure that if I took even one sniff / That would bore me terrific'ly too . . ." Two rather frequently encountered variants are "Some like a bop-type refrain. / I'm sure that if I heard even one riff / . . ." and "Some like the perfumes of Spain. / I'm sure that if I took even one whiff / . . ." The "cocaine" lyric is Porter's original; the others, authorship unknown, were attempts to make the song more generally acceptable.

The lyrics for "But in the Morning, No" (*Du Barry Was a Lady,* 1939) and "By the Mississinewah" (*Something for the Boys,* 1943) were printed with only a single —and heavily laundered—refrain. Indeed, the laundering of Porter's lyrics for radio, television, and films was common practice, and it is well known that until a few years ago "Love for Sale" (*The New Yorkers,* 1930) could not be sung at all on radio or television. Instrumental versions were permitted, but the lyrics were considered too risqué.

Censorship forced Porter and other writers to increase, reluctantly, their own self-censorship and self-restraint. If one wanted approbation in the marketplaces of a mass society, one had to abide by the restrictions of that society. The atmosphere is healthier today for free expression by lyricists. It came too late for Porter to benefit very much. But Porter's willingness to dare, limited as it was, did help pave the way for today's more salubrious climate.

Inevitably, readers are going to wonder how Porter would have felt about having his entire surviving output held up to public scrutiny. In fact, Porter's own efforts to preserve his work suggest that he had an eye on posterity. Among the lyrics he saved was a fair sampling of songs from his college years that could be classified as juvenilia. He gave no instructions that this early work be destroyed after his death, and in his last years he had ample opportunity to throw out any other lyrics or material that he might not have wanted to leave behind.

His willingness to allow the *Yale University Library Gazette* to print in 1955 eight previously unpublished lyrics from *The Pot of Gold* (1912), a product of his college days, is strong evidence of a favorable attitude toward publication of his juvenilia. Porter's generous offering, near the end of his life, of unpublished songs to Ben Bagley for his show *The Decline and Fall of the Entire World As Seen Through the Eyes of Cole Porter* (1964) and his first *Cole Porter Revisited* recording hardly suggest that Porter was trying to keep his work from the public. His failure to retain much of his correspondence, on the other hand, implies different feelings in that area.

. . .

The man who is regarded as the most cosmopolitan of American composer-lyricists was born in Peru, Indiana, on June 9, 1891, of a well-to-do family. As a child, Cole Porter displayed an unusual interest in music and verse. As a Yale undergraduate, he wrote two of the school's most famous football anthems, "Bull Dog" and "Bingo." He was a gifted parodist and a singer-pianist of such imposing skills that many of his college friends thought he had all the makings of a future vaudevillian.

Yet, for all his precocity, he was dogged by a series of disappointments until fifteen years after his graduation from Yale in 1913. His first Broadway show, *See America First* (1916), was an inauspicious debut. Imagine, if you can, an attempt to Gilbert-and-Sullivanize the American musical by intermingling British peers and Indian maidens on an Arizona mesa. To produce an imitative, Anglophilic comic opera at a time when American vernacular tradition was emerging with the skilled and effervescent offerings of George M. Cohan, Irving Berlin, and the Princess Theatre shows of Guy Bolton, P. G. Wodehouse, and Jerome Kern was, to say the least, misguided. And *See America First,* except for a handful of songs, was not very good Cole Porter.

From World War I until the late 1920s, Porter lived primarily in Europe. There he gained a perspective, similar in many ways to that of the "lost generation" of literary exiles, that set him apart from the other great creators of American musical theater. His early passion for Tennyson, Browning, and Swinburne was mated to a familiarity with nineteenth-century art songs and the niceties of counterpoint, harmony, and orchestration that he sharpened during his studies at the Schola Cantorum in Paris. He absorbed the innovations of Stravinsky, the Gallic spirit of Milhaud and Poulenc, and American jazz. His ballet score, the satiric, jazz-influenced *Within the Quota* (1923), performed in Europe and the United States by the Swedish Ballet, predates Gershwin's *Rhapsody in Blue* by several months.

His travels and endless quest for new places and fresh experiences heightened his art and strengthened his individual voice. Actually, his years as a "playboy" expatriate, when many people thought he was doing little but giving and going to parties, afforded him both the distance and the stimulation to develop his distinctive style. But his career as a theater composer foundered. Some of his songs were presented in revues, but the response to his work was not encouraging, and he very nearly abandoned songwriting.

But at the end of the 1920s he came into his own. As post–World War I energy turned to frenzy, stock speculations went sour, Florida land booms fizzled, and the widespread belief that Utopia had a price tag was discredited by the Crash of 1929 and the Depression, Porter's lyrics became a heady tonic for a disillusioned age. His own world-weariness, shaped in part by the knowledge that his considerable wealth had not guaranteed him happiness or escape from boredom, was increasingly shared by others less affluent. Porter wrote tellingly of the pain and evanescence of emotional relationships. He gently mocked propriety and said that few things were simple or lasting or free from ambiguity. When America was in the depths of the Depression in the 1930s—Porter's most productive decade—his was a message of civilized cheer.

Even after the riding accident that crushed both his legs when a horse fell on him one October weekend in 1937, Porter continued to write his amusing, exhilarating, often poignant songs. Despite more than thirty operations over the years, and constant pain for the rest of his life, his courage remained enormous, his spirit indomitable, and his creative skill unimpaired. He finally lost the will to write, however, after the amputation of his right leg in 1958. He died in Santa Monica, California, six years later.

Porter's lyrics are presented here, for the most part, in chronological order and grouped according to the production for which he wrote them. Miscellaneous lyrics will be found at the end of the decade in which they were written.

The bulk of Porter's work was written for the stage. I have arranged the lyrics in the order in which they were sung in their respective shows, with the exception of his first Broadway show, the drastically altered *See America First.* I have used the opening-night programs as my guide, although they are not always completely accurate. Of course, songs were later deleted or added during a show's run and the order was sometimes changed. Lyrics for songs dropped from productions before openings follow the lyrics in the opening-night running order. These discarded lyrics are followed by those which were deleted during or prior to rehearsals.

When a lyric has more than one existing version, I have included the different versions. Although this book is not a variorum edition, I do indicate some alternative lines and lyric changes of particular interest.

In dealing with movie scores, I have also tried to present lyrics in the order in which the songs make their appearance. But film scores pose special problems. Sometimes, a song will be heard as underscoring or background music before it is sung. Or it may not be sung at all. Or the vocal might have been deleted from the film, leaving only an instrumental version. Even if the lyric is not heard in the film, I have included it in the spot in which the music is heard.

Brief headnotes accompany each production. In addition, almost all of the lyrics are supplemented by notes. While not exhaustive, these notes provide what I think is basic information—the date, when applicable, of a song's publication, the artists who introduced it, and its prior history in earlier productions or subsequent use in later productions.

Alternate titles are indicated. In cases where the music for a lyric has not survived, or where music survives but a lyric is lost, I have noted this information. Unless otherwise stated, the music for a lyric exists. Finally, if a song has an especially interesting history, I have related it.

My sources for this collection were manuscripts, printed songs, scripts, scrapbooks and other memorabilia, much of it collected by Porter himself.

Since Porter's mother, Kate Cole Porter, had introduced him to and nurtured his enthusiasm for music, it is not surprising that she was the person who saved his early efforts. She kept a scrapbook of his college years that included manuscripts (the earliest ones to survive) of songs and instrumentals that he wrote at Yale.

After Porter married Linda Lee Thomas in 1919, his wife put together scrapbooks for each of his productions, and also maintained general scrapbooks and photo albums that provide important glimpses into Porter's career. While some of Porter's music exercises from Yale, the Harvard Music School, and the Schola Cantorum in Paris have survived, there are, at this writing, no known pre-1936 notebooks containing music or lyric ideas for songs. The earliest existing notebook, in a loose-leaf binder that Porter labeled "Titles and Ideas," begins with a 1936 entry. Porter's oldest surviving music notebooks appear to date from 1940, when he was working on the score for *Panama Hattie.* I refer to these notebooks in the notes accompanying the lyrics.

Porter's secretaries, notably Margaret Moore and Madeline Smith, kept copies of the lyrics they typed as well as many music manuscripts. Madeline Smith, his secretary from 1947 until his death, deserves special praise for preserving Porter's work.

There are several repositories of Porter material today, and I have availed myself of them in assembling this collection. Copies of virtually all of Porter's songs are currently housed in the office of the Cole Porter Musical and Literary Property Trusts in New York City. Porter's two principal music publishers, Warner Brothers and Chappell, have some valuable material, while the Tams-Witmark Music Library, which licenses many Porter shows for production, has copies of important unpublished songs.

Only last year, an important discovery was made at the Warner Brothers Music warehouse in Secaucus, New Jersey. It turned out to be a treasure trove of music and lyrics, including manuscripts and previously unknown songs, by Porter and such illustrious colleagues as George and Ira Gershwin, Richard Rodgers and Lorenz Hart, and Vincent Youmans. News of this discovery made front page headlines in November 1982, an indication of the increasing value being placed on the distinguished body of work from the golden age of the American musical.

During his lifetime Porter made a large gift of published and unpublished materials, including manuscripts and sketches, to the Music Division of the Library of

Congress in Washington, D.C. This collection, buttressed by copies of all copyrighted Porter songs which are deposited at the Library of Congress, is a major source for any Porter scholar.

The largest collection is at Yale University, which was the recipient at Porter's death in 1964 of a substantial bequest of manuscripts, scrapbooks, and recordings. As curator of Yale's Collection of the Literature of the American Musical Theatre, which Porter and others helped to launch in 1954, I began organizing this material in 1966. The challenge of bringing together all known Porter lyrics aroused my interest when I started working on the Porter archives. From the beginning, my aim has been to seek out and preserve everything I could find. As editor, I have tried to reconstruct the lyrics, which sometimes survived in many versions, to correspond as closely as possible to what I believe were Porter's original intentions.

—Robert Kimball

CHRONOLOGY

1891

JUNE 9 Cole Porter born in Peru, Indiana, to Kate Cole and Samuel Fenwick Porter (married in April 1884). Two children born before Cole, Louis and Rachel, died in infancy.

1901

His first composition, the instrumental "Song of the Birds."

1902

OCTOBER Porter's composition "The Bobolink Waltz" published privately "for the author" by S. Brainard's Sons Co. in Chicago. Porter's mother arranges for its publication and the printing of one hundred copies.

1905–1909

Porter attends Worcester Academy, Worcester, Massachusetts, where he begins writing songs. None survive, but titles include "Fi, Fi, Fifi," "The Bearded Lady," "The Tattooed Gentleman," and "Class Song—1909." Porter graduates as valedictorian and spends the summer of 1909 on a tour of Europe, a graduation present from his grandfather.

1909–1910

Porter enters Yale College. He lives in a single room at Garland's lodging house, 242 York Street, New Haven, Connecticut. Member of the Freshman Glee Club. Writes earliest surviving songs, "When the Summer Moon Comes 'Long" and "Bridget McGuire."

JUNE 1910 "Bridget McGuire" printed as "Bridget," Porter's first published song.

1910–1911

Submits "Bingo Eli Yale" to Yale's 1910 football song competition.

OCTOBER 29, 1910 "Bingo Eli Yale" introduced at the Yale Dining Hall dinner concert by Eddie Wittstein and his orchestra. The words are later printed in the Yale *Daily News* and the song is tried out successfully at several football rallies.

During his sophomore year Porter is elected to the Delta Kappa Epsilon fraternity and becomes a member of the Yale Glee Club.

1911–1912

Junior year. Porter writes other Yale football songs, including "Bull Dog."

NOVEMBER 28, 1911 *Cora,* Porter's first musical comedy, presented for one performance at the Delta Kappa Epsilon fraternity house as the group's fall 1911 initiation play.

APRIL 24, 1912 *And the Villain Still Pursued Her,* Porter's second musical and his first Yale University Dramatic Association "smoker," is premiered at the New Haven Lawn Club. Second performance at the Yale Club of New York, May 10.

1912–1913

SUMMER 1912 Collaborates with Almet Jenks (Yale 1914) on the musical *The Pot of Gold.*

NOVEMBER 26, 1912 *The Pot of Gold* has first performance at Delta Kappa Epsilon. Second performance at the Hotel Taft, New Haven, December 4, 1912.

APRIL 30, 1913 *The Kaleidoscope* (Yale Dramat smoker) has first performance at the Hotel Taft, New Haven. Second performance at the Yale Club of New York, May 7, 1913.

During his senior year Porter is a football cheerleader; chairman of the Football Song Committee; member of: Hogans, Whiffenpoofs, Pundits, Mince Pie Club, Grill Room Grizzlies, and Scroll and Key; president of the University Glee Club.

SUMMER 1913 Tours Europe.

1913–1914

Attends Harvard Law School.

APRIL 24, 1914 First performance of *Paranoia* (Yale Dramat smoker), at the Hotel Taft, New Haven.

MAY 22, 1914 *We're All Dressed Up and We Don't Know Huerto Go* performed at the annual dinner of the Associated Western Yale Clubs in Cincinnati, Ohio.

JUNE 1914 Writes song for class reunion at Yale.

AUTUMN 1914 Transfers from Law School to the Harvard School of Music.

1915

Continues studies at Harvard School of Music.

JULY 22 New York opening of *Hands Up.* Interpolated in the score is "Esmeralda" (titled "As I Love You" in *The Kaleidoscope*). It is the first Porter song to appear in a Broadway show.

OCTOBER 15 "Two Big Eyes," music by Porter, is interpolated in the Broadway show *Miss Information.*

SUMMER–AUTUMN Porter and his collaborator on the book, T. Lawrason Riggs, work on the musical *See America First.*

1916

FEBRUARY 22 First performance of *See America First* at the Van Curler Opera House, Schenectady, New York. Tryout also includes performances in Albany, Rochester, New Haven, and Providence.

MARCH 28 *See America First* opens at the Maxine Elliott Theatre, New York; 15 performances.

1917

Porter studies music in New York with Pietro Yon.

SUMMER Sails for Europe, probably in July or August, to participate in the work of the Duryea Relief Organization in France.

1918

JANUARY Attached to American Aviation Headquarters in Paris.

JANUARY 30 Meets Linda Lee Thomas (born November 16, 1883) at a breakfast reception at the Ritz Hotel, Paris, following the marriage of Ethel Harriman and Henry Russell.

APRIL 20 Enlists in the First Foreign Regiment (Foreign Legion).

MAY 18 Song "Alone with You," co-author Melville Gideon, is introduced in the English production of *Very Good Eddie* at the Palace Theatre, London.

AUGUST 31 Song "Altogether Too Fond of You," co-authors Melville Gideon and James Heard, introduced in *Telling the Tale* at the Ambassador Theatre, London.

1919

APRIL Discharged from military service.

SPRING Returns to the United States. On ship he meets producer-comedian Raymond Hitchcock, presenter of the annual revue *Hitchy-Koo.* Hitchcock hears songs Porter has written during the war and takes most of them for the forthcoming 1919 edition of *Hitchy-Koo.* Asks Porter to write additional songs.

AUGUST 18 First performance of *Hitchy-Koo of 1919* at Nixon's Apollo Theatre, Atlantic City, New Jersey. Most of the songs are Porter's.

OCTOBER 6 *Hitchy-Koo of 1919* opens at the Liberty Theatre, New York; 56 performances. After New York engagement, *Hitchy-Koo* embarks on extended tour.

NOVEMBER 12 *The Eclipse,* with two songs co-authored by Porter, "I Never Realized" and "Chelsea" (original title: "Washington Square"), opens at the Garrick Theatre, London. "I Never Realized" is interpolated in New York production of *Buddies* and "Washington Square" in the New York production of *As You Were.*

DECEMBER 18 Porter marries Linda Lee Thomas in Paris. They honeymoon in the South of France and Italy and move into Linda's house in Paris.

1920

Porter studies counterpoint, harmony, and orchestration at the Schola Cantorum in Paris.

SEPTEMBER 18 *A Night Out,* which includes four songs with music by Porter (lyrics by Clifford Grey), opens at London's Winter Garden Theatre; 309 performances.

1921

FEBRUARY–MARCH The Porters, Howard Sturges, and Marthe Hyde charter a launch, the *Chonsu,* for a journey up the Nile. They visit the diggings of Howard Carter and T. Eric Peet with an introduction from Linda's friend Lord Carnarvon.

JULY The Porters rent a villa at La Garoupe near the beach of Antibes on the French Riviera, where they entertain, among others, Gerald and Sara Murphy and Sir Charles Mendl (the British press attaché in Paris).

1922

MARCH 9 The revue *Mayfair and Montmartre,* which includes three songs by Porter among the works of several other writers, opens at London's New Oxford Theatre; 77 performances.

AUGUST 16 The revue *Phi-Phi,* which includes one Porter song, "The Ragtime Pipes of Pan," opens at the London Pavilion Theatre.

SUMMER Porter returns to America to write songs for *Hitchy-Koo of 1922.*

OCTOBER 10 *Hitchy-Koo of 1922,* with words and music mostly by Porter, opens at the Shubert Theatre, Philadelphia, and closes there less than two weeks later. A few of Porter's songs, along with some of the skits and performers, are incorporated by the Shuberts into their revue *The Dancing Girl.*

1923

JANUARY 23 *The Dancing Girl* opens at the Winter Garden Theatre, New York; 123 performances.

FEBRUARY 3 Porter's grandfather, J. O. Cole, dies.

SUMMER Having received a portion of his grandfather's estate from his mother, Porter rents the Palazzo Barbaro in Venice, where Henry James wrote parts of *The Wings of the Dove.* Here and on the Lido, Porter and Gerald Murphy collaborate on the ballet *Within the Quota,* a satire on American life in the 1920s.

OCTOBER 25 World premiere of *Within the Quota* (libretto and decor by Murphy, music by Porter) by Les Ballets Suédois at the Théâtre des Champs-Elysées, Paris. Darius Milhaud's ballet *La Création du Monde* also has its premiere that night.

NOVEMBER, 28 American premiere of *Within the Quota* at the Century Theatre, New York. The company performs the ballet 69 times before disbanding in early 1925.

1924

SUMMER The Porters rent the Palazzo Papadopoli in Venice.

SEPTEMBER 8 First performance of the *Greenwich Village Follies* of 1924 at Nixon's Apollo Theatre, Atlantic City. Most of the songs are Porter's.

SEPTEMBER 16 *Greenwich Village Follies* opens at the Shubert Theatre, New York. During its run of 127 performances Porter's songs are gradually dropped from the production.

1925

SUMMER The Porters rent the Palazzo Rezzonico in Venice.

DECEMBER Porter contributes three songs to the Yale University Dramatic Association's production of *Out o' Luck,* written by Tom Cushing (Yale 1902) and directed by Monty Woolley (Yale 1911). The show is taken on tour by the Dramat during its 1925 Christmas vacation, performed twice at the Shubert Theatre, New Haven, on February 9, 1926, as the Dramat's annual prom offering, and reprised during the Dramat's 1926 Christmas tour.

1926

SUMMER The Porters rent the Palazzo Rezzonico in Venice.

1927

SUMMER The Porters' last summer at the Palazzo Rezzonico in Venice.

AUGUST 18 Porter's father, Samuel Fenwick Porter, dies.

NOVEMBER 21 Fanny Brice introduces Porter's song "Weren't We Fools?" at the Palace Theatre, New York.

1928

FEBRUARY 6 First performance of *Paris* at Nixon's Apollo Theatre, Atlantic City. Most of the songs are by Porter.

MAY 10 Opening of *La Revue des Ambassadeurs* at the Ambassadeurs Café, Paris.

OCTOBER 3 *Paris* opens at the Music Box Theatre, New York; 195 performances.

1929

MARCH 5 First performance of the revue *Wake Up and Dream* at the Palace Theatre, Manchester, England.

MARCH 27 *Wake Up and Dream* opens at the London Pavilion; 263 performances.

NOVEMBER 14 First performance of *Fifty Million Frenchmen* at the Colonial Theatre, Boston.

NOVEMBER 27 *Fifty Million Frenchmen* opens at the Lyric Theatre, New York; 254 performances.

NOVEMBER 30 *The Battle of Paris*, a Paramount Pictures film, with two songs by Porter, is released.

DECEMBER 30 American production of *Wake Up and Dream* opens at the Selwyn Theatre, New York; 136 performances. Last musical of the 1920s.

1930

JANUARY–MAY Trip to the Far East.

SUMMER Visits Venice and returns home to Paris (13 rue Monsieur).

NOVEMBER 5 Porter song "What's My Man Gonna Be Like?" sung by Evelyn Hoey in *The Vanderbilt Revue* at the Vanderbilt Theatre, New York; 13 performances.

NOVEMBER 12 First performance of *The New Yorkers* at the Chestnut Street Theatre in Philadelphia.

DECEMBER 8 *The New Yorkers* opens at B. S. Moss's Broadway Theatre, New York; 168 performances.

1931

Works on the score for *Star Dust*, an unproduced musical.

1932

NOVEMBER 7 First performance of *Gay Divorce* at the Wilbur Theatre, Boston.

NOVEMBER 29 *Gay Divorce* opens at the Ethel Barrymore Theatre, New York (transfers to the Shubert Theatre, January 1933); 248 performances.

1933

After returning to Paris, Porter meets Romney Brent and begins work on *Nymph Errant*.

SUMMER Travels on the Danube.

SEPTEMBER 11 First performance of *Nymph Errant* at the Opera House, Manchester, England.

OCTOBER 6 *Nymph Errant* opens at the Adelphi Theatre, London; 154 performances.

NOVEMBER 2 *Gay Divorce*, with three new songs by Porter, opens at the Palace Theatre, London; 180 performances.

1934

While staying in London, Porter writes the score for a musical variously titled *Yours*, *Ever Yours*, and *Once Upon a Time;* never produced.

SUMMER Boat trip on the Rhine.

OCTOBER 12 *The Gay Divorcée*, film version of *Gay Divorce*, released. The only Porter song used in the film is "Night and Day."

OCTOBER 26 Porter records piano-vocals of "Thank You So Much, Missus Lowsborough-Goodby" and "You're the Top."

NOVEMBER 5 First performance of *Anything Goes* at the Colonial Theatre, Boston.

NOVEMBER 21 *Anything Goes* opens at the Alvin Theatre, New York; 420 performances (longest-running Porter musical to date).

NOVEMBER 27 Porter records piano-vocals of "Anything Goes" and "Two Little Babes in the Wood."

DECEMBER Porter writes six songs for the Fox film *Adios, Argentina;* never produced.

1935

JANUARY 3 Porter records piano-vocals of "Be Like the Bluebird," "The Physician," "The Cocotte," and "I'm a Gigolo."

JANUARY 12 The Porters, Moss Hart, Monty Woolley, Howard Sturges, and William Powell sail from New York on an around-the-world cruise on the *Franconia*. Porter and Hart collaborate on *Jubilee* during the voyage.

MAY 31 Cruise ends in New York.

JUNE 14 *Anything Goes* opens at the Palace Theatre, London; 164 performances.

JUNE–JULY Porter and Hart go to Hollywood to audition and cast performers for *Jubilee*.

SEPTEMBER 21 First performance of *Jubilee* at the Shubert Theatre, Boston.

OCTOBER 12 *Jubilee* opens at the Imperial Theatre, New York; 169 performances.

DECEMBER Porter arrives in Hollywood with a twenty-week contract ($3,000 per week) to write the score for an untitled M-G-M picture.

1936

JANUARY–JUNE Writes score for *Born to Dance.* Film released in November 1936.

SUMMER Writes score for the stage show *Red, Hot and Blue.*

OCTOBER 7 First performance of *Red, Hot and Blue* at the Colonial Theatre, Boston.

OCTOBER 29 *Red, Hot and Blue* opens at the Alvin Theatre, New York; 183 performances.

DECEMBER 3 *O Mistress Mine,* with Porter song "Goodbye Little Dream, Goodbye," opens at the St. James Theatre, London. Porter returns to Hollywood to work on the score for the M-G-M film *Rosalie.*

1937

JANUARY–JULY At work on songs for *Rosalie.*

SUMMER While on vacation in Europe, writes two songs ("Don't Let It Get You Down" and "It All Belongs to You") for René Clair film tentatively titled *The Laugh of the Town,* released as *Break the News.*

SEPTEMBER Producer Vinton Freedley announces that Porter is writing the score for a musical, *Greek to You.*

OCTOBER 4 Porter returns to New York from Europe.

OCTOBER 24 Porter suffers the crippling riding accident in which both legs are crushed at the Piping Rock Club, Locust Valley, Long Island. During the next twenty years he undergoes over thirty operations to save his legs from amputation.

OCTOBER–DECEMBER Works on the score for *You Never Know.*

DECEMBER *Rosalie* is released by M-G-M.

1938

MARCH 3 First performance of *You Never Know* at the Shubert Theatre, New Haven, beginning a lengthy tryout that takes the show to several cities.

JUNE Vinton Freedley abandons *Greek to You* with only a few songs completed and no finished script.

JUNE 9 *The Sun Never Sets,* with Porter's song "River God," opens at the Drury Lane Theatre, London.

SEPTEMBER 21 *You Never Know* opens at the Winter Garden Theatre, New York; 78 performances.

OCTOBER 13 First performance of *Leave It to Me* at the Shubert Theatre, New Haven.

NOVEMBER 9 *Leave It to Me* opens at the Imperial Theatre, New York; 291 performances. Return engagement September 4, 1939; 16 performances. Total: 307 performances.

1939

SPRING–SUMMER Works on the score for the M-G-M film *Broadway Melody of 1939* (which becomes *Broadway Melody of 1940*).

OCTOBER 16 New York opening of the George S. Kaufman–Moss Hart play *The Man Who Came to Dinner,* with Porter's song "What Am I to Do?"

NOVEMBER 9 First performance of *Du Barry Was a Lady* at the Shubert Theatre, New Haven.

DECEMBER 6 *Du Barry Was a Lady* opens at the 46th Street Theatre, New York (transfers to the Royale Theatre, October 1940); 408 performances. Last full-length musical to open in New York during the decade.

1940

JANUARY 20 The Porters and several friends sail on the *Kungsholm* to Cuba, the Panama Canal Zone, Mexico, and the South Seas.

FEBRUARY 9 *Broadway Melody of 1940* is released.

FEBRUARY 25 Porter writes song "So Long, Samoa" or "Samoa, Samoa" on board the *Kungsholm;* it is later revised as "Farewell Amanda" and used in the film *Adam's Rib* (1949).

SUMMER Porters acquire Buxton Hill, a house near Williamstown, Massachusetts.

OCTOBER 3 First performance of *Panama Hattie* at the Shubert Theatre, New Haven.

OCTOBER 30 *Panama Hattie* opens at the 46th Street Theatre, New York; 501 performances (longest-running Porter show to date and the first "book" show to run over 500 performances since the 1920s).

1941

MARCH–MAY Works on the score for the Columbia film *You'll Never Get Rich.*

OCTOBER *You'll Never Get Rich* is released.

OCTOBER 6 First performance of *Let's Face It* at the Colonial Theatre, Boston.

OCTOBER 29 *Let's Face It* opens at the Imperial Theatre, New York; 547 performances (longest-running Porter musical to date).

NOVEMBER–DECEMBER Hospitalized for further surgery on legs.

1942

MARCH–MAY Completes most of the score for the Columbia film *Something to Shout About.*

SUMMER Writes most of the score for the show *Something for the Boys.*

NOVEMBER 19 *Du Barry Was a Lady* opens at the Hippodrome, London; 348 performances.

DECEMBER 18 First performance of *Something for the Boys* at the Shubert Theatre, Boston.

1943

JANUARY 7 *Something for the Boys* opens at the Alvin Theatre, New York; 422 performances.

FEBRUARY *Something to Shout About* is released.

FEBRUARY–JULY Works on the score for the Warner Brothers film *Mississippi Belle.*

AUGUST Begins work on the musical *Mexican Hayride.*

DECEMBER 29 First performance of *Mexican Hayride* at the Shubert Theatre, Boston.

1944

JANUARY 28 *Mexican Hayride* opens at the Winter Garden Theatre, New York; 481 performances.

April–June Continues work on the score for *Mississippi Belle*, but the film is never produced.

November 24 First performance of *Seven Lively Arts* at the Forrest Theatre, Philadelphia.

December 7 *Seven Lively Arts* opens at the Ziegfeld Theatre, New York; 183 performances.

1945
January–March Hospitalized for further surgery on legs.

March Warner Brothers sends Porter the script for a film biography of him which will be titled *Night and Day*.

1946
April 28 First performance of *Around the World in Eighty Days* at the Boston Opera House, Boston.

May 31 *Around the World in Eighty Days* opens at the Adelphi Theatre, New York; 75 performances.

August *Night and Day*, Porter film biography, has Hollywood premiere.

Summer Completes most of the score for the M-G-M film *The Pirate*.

1947
February–November Filming of *The Pirate*, for which Porter makes a few slight revisions in the songs. (This was generally a quiet year, as Porter had no contracts to fulfill for stage or screen scores.)

1948
February–May Writes most of the score for *Kiss Me, Kate*.

June *The Pirate* is released.

December 2 First performance of *Kiss Me, Kate* at the Shubert Theatre, Philadelphia.

December 30 *Kiss Me, Kate* opens at the New Century Theatre, New York; 1,077 performances (longest-running and most highly acclaimed of all Porter's shows).

1949
Summer Finishes most of the score for what is to become *Out of This World*.

Linda Porter, suffering from emphysema, is ill during much of the year.

1950
November 4 First performance of *Out of This World* at the Shubert Theatre, Philadelphia.

December 21 *Out of This World* opens at the New Century Theatre, New York; 157 performances.

1951
March 8 *Kiss Me, Kate* opens at the Coliseum, London; 400 performances.

Porter, severely depressed throughout much of the year, is hospitalized for a time for a mental breakdown.

1952
Summer Begins work on the score for *Can-Can*. Completes much of the score by August.

August 3 Porter's mother dies at the age of ninety after suffering a cerebral hemorrhage.

1953
March 23 First performance of *Can-Can* at the Shubert Theatre, Philadelphia.

May 7 *Can-Can* opens at the Shubert Theatre, New York; 892 performances (second longest-running Porter musical).

1954
May 20 Linda Porter dies at the age of seventy.

October 14 *Can-Can* opens at the Coliseum, London; 394 performances.

November 26 First performance of *Silk Stockings* at the Shubert Theatre, Philadelphia.

1955
February 24 *Silk Stockings* opens at the Imperial Theatre, New York; 477 performances.

February 19–June 7 Takes a long European trip with friends.

June 13 Receives Honorary Doctor of Music from Williams College.

July–November Works on the score for the M-G-M film *High Society*.

1956
February 19–June 5 Takes a long trip to Europe and the Middle East.

July–December Works on the score for the M-G-M film *Les Girls*. Writes two additional songs for the film version of *Silk Stockings*.

October *High Society* is released.

1957
January 8 Operated on for gastric ulcer.

April–June European trip (includes last visits to Paris and Venice).

July *Silk Stockings* is released.

August–November Works on the score for the television program *Aladdin*.

November *Les Girls* is released.

November 5 Completes the lyric for "Wouldn't It Be Fun," his last song, for *Aladdin*.

1958
February 21 *Aladdin* shown on CBS-TV as *The DuPont Show of the Month*.

April 3 Porter's right leg is amputated.

1960
June 9 Receives Honorary Doctor of Humane Letters from Yale University.

1960–1964
Frequently hospitalized.

1964
October 15 Dies at the age of seventy-three at St. John's Hospital in Santa Monica, California, of kidney failure and other complications. Buried in Peru, Indiana.

ACKNOWLEDGMENTS

My deepest gratitude to the late John F. Wharton and to Robert H. Montgomery, Jr., attorneys for Cole Porter and trustees of the Cole Porter Musical and Literary Property Trusts; to Florence Leeds, executive secretary of the Porter Trusts; to Joan C. Daly for legal advice; to Cole Porter's family, the Coles, and his longtime secretary, Madeline P. Smith; to Porter's music publishers, notably Chappell & Co., Inc. and Warner Brothers, Inc., for their participation in the preparation of this work; to the custodians of Porter archives, chiefly Yale University and the Library of Congress; to Porter's Yale classmates, particularly Arnold Whitridge and Sidney Lovett; to my Yale friends, Mr. and Mrs. Basil Duke Henning, Richard Warren, Jr., and Rutherford Rogers; to friends and collaborators Brendan Gill, William Bolcom, and Alfred Simon; to fellow musical theater historians Miles Kreuger and Stanley Green; to composer Leo Smit and musicologist Lynn Siebert, who graciously shared their knowledge of Porter's music; to Donald Smith for his unflagging devotion to Porter's legacy; to Bobby Short, who gave first performances of many previously unpublished Porter songs; to Mabel Mercer, Steve Ross, and others who lift our spirits with impeccable interpretations of Porter songs; to Porter's songwriting colleagues, above all to the most admired of all American songwriters and Porter's very close friend, Irving Berlin, who more than anyone else prodded Porter to find his own inimitable voice as a composer-lyricist and dispatched producer E. Ray Goetz to Venice in 1927 to bring Porter back to Broadway; to Porter intimates Jean Howard and Baron Nicolas de Gunzburg, who greatly enhanced my understanding of Cole and his wife, Linda; to original cast members and featured performers of Porter shows and films for their recollections of a rewarding association, principally Fred Astaire, Ethel Merman, Dorothie Bigelow, Betty Garrett, Paula Laurence, Alfred Drake, George Gaynes, Erik Rhodes, Celeste Holm, Gretchen Wyler, and Taina Elg; to Alan Williams, who launched this book nearly ten years ago; to Edwin Kennebeck for patient editorial help; to Robert Gottlieb, Martha Kaplan, John Woodside, Mary Maguire, Holly McNeely, Andy Hughes, and Robert Cornfield, who took charge and gently but firmly guided the book to completion; to others named in these pages and many more who unselfishly offered assistance along the way.

THE COMPLETE LYRICS OF COLE PORTER

COLLEGE SONGS

1909-1913

WHEN THE SUMMER MOON COMES 'LONG

"When the Summer Moon Comes 'Long" and "Bridget McGuire" are the oldest surviving songs for which Porter wrote music and lyrics. They were almost certainly composed during his freshman year at Yale (1909–1910), for the address on the first page of the holograph manuscripts is "242 York Street," which was where he first lived in New Haven. The manuscripts were discovered by this editor in a scrapbook which Porter's mother, Kate Porter, kept of her son's college years.

"Bridget McGuire" was copyrighted by Porter under the title "Bridget" on June 14, 1910. "When the Summer Moon Comes 'Long," which has the alternate title "Under the Summer Moon," was published in *The Unpublished Cole Porter.*

VERSE 1

If you want to wed a little girl,
Simply wild about her,
Couldn't live without her,
If your heart's completely in a whirl,
Just want to love and spoon,
Don't propose while wintertime is here.
Wait till stars are gleaming,
Winking, blinking, beaming,
Now's the time to ask your little dear,
Under the summer moon.

REFRAIN

First select a small canoe
Where there's only room for two.
You'll love her and she'll love you,
You could never get in wrong.
While the stars are shining bright
In the silv'ry, dreamy night,
You can hold her, fold her tight,
When the summer moon comes 'long.

VERSE 2

When you've popped the question to her too,
After you have kissed her,
She'll only be your "sister."
Then declare that you're completely through,
Paddle her back home soon,
Drift along until you've met a queen,
Someone who will marry,
Won't put off or tarry.
Take her to the spot where you've just been,
Under the summer moon.

BRIDGET MCGUIRE

VERSE 1

Bridget McGuire was a scullery maid,
And she worked in a home way uptown.
Patrick O'Brien was just simply dyin'
To marry and then settle down.
Most ev'ry night Pat on Bridget would call,
Thus he passed the long evenings away.
Soon Miss McGuire didn't mind it at all
Or the "blarney" when Patrick would say

REFRAIN

Bridget—Bridget,
Sweet Colleen Bawn!
Faith and I'm feelin' so sad and forlorn.
Won't you just smile at me,
Once in a while at me?
Sure! And my heart is on fire,
I never met a girl that I liked better.
Come on—Bridget,
Out for a lark,
We'll go meandering all through the park.
Ah! You're far too delicious
To wash and wipe dishes,
Miss Bridget, Bridget McGuire.

VERSE 2 (FIRST VERSION)

Pat struck it rich and the two were soon wed
In the church 'round the corner one day.
All was complete, when they moved to their suite
In a huge hotel down on Broadway.
'Most every night you can see them about,
For they go to the shows right along.
Perhaps that is Pat, who's asleep over there,
If it is, he'll wake up to this song.

VERSE 2 (SECOND VERSION)

Mister Pat had good luck, but to Bridget he stuck,
And he wedded her one day in May.
When they were married, Miss Bridget was carried
To a house of his own, people say.
Now she has steam yachts and motors galore,
And though happy she often will long
To hear Pat's "blarney," as in days of yore,
And to have him again sing that song—

MOON, MOON

This lyric appears in "Cole Porter: Some Unpublished Lyrics," edited by Shepard Krech, Yale 1913 (Privately printed, 1956). This compilation was assembled by some Yale classmates and by others who attended Yale between 1909 and 1914. No music survives.

Oh moon, moon shining up above her,
Moon, moon tell her I'll be true.
Moon, moon tell her I adore her.
Won't you take this message to her?
Moon, moon, moon.

SINCE DOLLY'S COME TO TOWN

This lyric appears to have been written during Porter's Yale years, 1909–1913.

Since Dolly's come to town
In a dainty, neat new gown,
All the men can see no other,
Each leaves home and wife and mother.
Dolly knows a thing or two,
How to use those eyes of blue,
And the next to lose a ring is you,
Since Dolly's come to town.

MORY'S

Louis Linder was the proprietor of Mory's Temple Bar. A music lover, he encouraged Yale singing groups to perform on his premises. The Whiffenpoofs began life at Mory's in February 1909. Porter was a Whiffenpoof and a member of The Hogan's, a group that met at Mory's to help Linder prepare and send out monthly bills. In 1912 Mory's Temple Bar was located at the corner of Temple and Center Streets. For a number of reasons, including Louis Linder's failing health (he died in October 1913) and a proposed redevelopment project, Mory's nearly closed. But by September 1912, the fall of Porter's senior year, it was saved, and a new home, its present splendid quarters, was found at 305 York Street. This lyric appears in Krech's compilation; no music survives.

Come on down to Mory's,
That's the place to be.
Happy home of friendship
And of jollity.
Now they're going to close it—
Louis Linder, change your mind!
When I'm lonely, one place only,
Mory's Temple Bar.

BINGO ELI YALE

This appears to be Porter's first Yale football song. It was written for Yale's annual football song competition in the fall of 1910 and introduced by Eddie Wittstein and his orchestra at the Yale Dining Hall dinner concert on October 29, 1910. It was copyrighted and published by Remick on November 5, 1910.

Bingo! Bingo!
Bingo! Bingo! Bingo! That's the lingo.
Eli is bound to win,
There's to be a victory,
So watch the team begin.
Bingo! Bingo!
Harvard's (Princeton's) team cannot prevail.
Fight! Fight!
Fight with all your might
For Bingo,
Bingo, Eli Yale!

HAIL TO YALE

Music by Arthur Troostwyck (class of 1912, Yale School of Music). Published in 1911 by Charles H. Loomis, New Haven, Connecticut.

Cheer, cheer for Eli today,
Alma mater true.
We are cheering, cheering, hearing once again
The story of the glory of the blue,
While down the field through poor Harvard we
go
And on to victory sail.
We'll break the ranks of Harvard's team
To win the game and Hail to Yale!

ELI

No music survives. The lyric was first printed in the New Haven *Register,* November 12, 1911.

E—li! E—li!
We are warriors ever glorious,
Leave the fray with hearts victorious,
Cheering for E—li! E—li!
Forever old Eli Yale!

BULL DOG

Porter's most famous Yale song was written in the fall of 1911. He is known to have written two other Yale football songs, "Beware of Yale" and "Fla-de-Dah" (according to the list of Yale Football Songs in *The Yale Book,* Spring Issue 1912), for which the music and lyrics have not survived.

During his senior year, 1912–1913, Porter was a cheerleader and chairman of the committee which sponsored the writing of new football songs.

VERSE

Way down, way down in New Haven town,
Lives Mister Yale,
Old Eli Yale.
No one ever cares to come around,
Just because of his pet "Bow-wow."
Poor old Harvard tries it once a year,
Always goes back,
Tied up in black,
For when old Yale sicks that big bull dog on,
He raises an awful row.

REFRAIN

Bull dog! Bull dog! Bow, wow, wow,
Eli Yale!
Bull dog! Bull dog! Bow, wow, wow,
Our team can never fail.
When the sons of Eli break through the line,
That is the sign we hail.
Bull dog! Bull dog! Bow, wow, wow,
Eli Yale!

THE MOTOR CAR

Written in either his sophomore or junior year and introduced by Porter with the Yale Glee Club in 1911. First published in *The New Yale Song Book.*

Off we go to take a ride, take a ride, take a ride,
All the fam'ly jam inside,
Mercy, what a clatter!
. . .
Something breaks and out gets Pa, out gets Pa,
out gets Pa.
Now he crawls beneath the car.
What can be the matter?

Oh! What was that awful crack, awful crack,
awful crack?
Hit the trolley in the back,
Trolley's system's twisted.

What makes Father look so queer, look so queer,
look so queer?
His nose is hiding behind his ear,
His whole expression's shifted.

Oh, the lovely motor car,
What a wreck it's made of Pa!
Over twenty doctor chaps
Worked on him in his collapse.
Mother wears a sickly grin
Where her face is dented in.
What do we care as long as we are
Having a ride in the motor car?

A FOOTBALL KING

Written in the summer of 1912. Original title was "If I Were Only a Football Man." Intended for the Delta Kappa Epsilon initiation play *The Pot of Gold* (first performed November 26, 1912), but not used in that show. Revised and sung by Porter with the Yale Glee Club during his senior year (1912–1913), when he was the club's president. First published in *The New Yale Song Book.*

VERSE

Now I'm in an awful condition,
Filled with a vaulting ambition.
While I rave on deliriously,
Please don't take me too seriously.
I merely want to say,
I'd like to shine in a physical way.

REFRAIN

If I were only a football King,
I'd go punting around all day,
Of every eye the apple,
When wearing my Y to chapel.
The girls would write for my autograph,
And all of that sort of thing,
Were I an oracular,
Very spectacular,
Regular football King.

PATTER

Now I'm sure that I should find it heaven
If I had a chance to make the Yale eleven,
With my only stunt to go around and punt the afternoon away.
The cynosure of ev'ry eye, whenever I should pass men,
I'd open up and show my Y to all the underclassmen.
For my autograph I'd charge a dollar,
And I'd be the title of an Arrow collar,
Such a very muddy sort of very bloody sort of thing.
My opponents I should give a scalding
That would make me rival Captain Jesse Spalding,
If they'd only realize that I'm a football King.

Early version for
THE POT OF GOLD (1912)

IF I WERE ONLY A FOOTBALL MAN

REFRAIN

If I were only a football man,
I'd go punting around all day,
Of every eye the apple
When wearing my Y to chapel.
My talk would be so corpuscular
My verbs would even be muscular,
And mine would be such downs
As to bring home the touchdowns
If I were a football man.

I WANT TO BE A YALE BOY

The lyrics for "I Want to Be a Yale Boy" and the corresponding "I Want to Be a Prom Girl" were recalled by the late Meade Minnigerode (Yale 1910), a founding member of the Yale Whiffenpoofs, to which Porter belonged during his senior year. The music does not survive.

I want to be a Yale boy,
A Yale boy tried and true.
I want to be a Yale boy,
Fighting for the Blue!
I want to beat old Harvard,
Princeton and West Point too.
Mother, if I can, when I grow to be a man,
I want to be a Yale boy too.

I WANT TO BE A PROM GIRL

I want to be a Prom girl,
A Prom girl through and through.
I want to be a Prom girl,
Dancing for the Blue.
I want to learn to tango,
Boston and two-step too.
Mother, if you can, introduce me to a man,
For I want to be a Prom girl too.

IT PAYS TO ADVERTISE

"It Pays to Advertise" and "When I'm Eating Around with You" were recalled by Porter's classmate and friend Arnold Whitridge, in a conversation with this editor in 1968. Both songs seem to have been written in 1912.

I'd walk a mile for that schoolgirl complexion,
Palmolive soap will do it every time.
Oh cream, oh best cigar!
Maxwell Motor Car!
Do you have a baby vacuum in your home?
Gum is good for you,
Try our new shampoo,
Flit will always free your home of flies.
If you travel, travel, travel at all,
You know, it pays to advertise.

WHEN I'M EATING AROUND WITH YOU

We'll have cocktails at Heublein's
And fish at Café Mellone.
If on an entree we can both agree
To the Heidelberg we'll roam.
We'll have salad at Hofbrau
And a bisque tortoni too.

To the Taft we'll stroll for a finger bowl,
When I'm eating around with you.

YELLOW MELODRAMA

Recalled by Whitridge and Basil Duke Henning (Yale 1932).

(SUNG) I'm so bored at going to the theater,
Modern drama isn't worth a penny.
Rostand has no charms for me,
Maeterlinck I cannot see—
Chanticleer and bluebirds are too many.
Oh, I know, it's hardly *comme il faut*
But a melodrama fills my soul with bliss.
My tastes may be plebeian
But efforts herculean
Can never change my taste for plays like this.

MAIDEN IN DISTRESS: (SPOKEN) Oh, picture me a poor girl alone in London;
Darkness, nightfall and not a sailor in sight.
Would that I were back in the United States of America,
Back among the cowboys, the buffaloes, and the families.
Hark! Someone is coming on horseback.
A knock at the door.
What if it were Victor Lambert?
Why, Daddy!

FATHER: (SPOKEN) Yes, my little girl, it is your dad.
For while hunting woodchucks in the south pasture,
I struck gold, and now I'm worth two thousand dollars.

DAUGHTER: (SPOKEN) Oh, Daddy, isn't it great to be rich?
And now that you have come to take me
Back to the portals and arms
Of my house and my mother respectively,
Let me tell you what it was
That dragged me from our home.
It was love—love for a dirty villain
Who called for me each afternoon
At the factory in a plush-lined barouche.
But he could not win me by his wiles,
For I had a far greater love—
A love for my own native country.

(SUNG) Oh, oh, that yellow melodrama,
Nowadays considered out of date.
I really fear that no more we'll hear
The distant mail train calling to its mate.
No more we'll see the villain cutting capers
With Lady Vere de Vere
Because he knows she has the papers.
They were grand old days,
They were wonderful plays,
Oh, that yellow melodrama for me.

ANTOINETTE BIRBY

Many who knew Porter recall this song. It was published in *Songs of Yale.* In the 1934 edition, it was printed under the title "Annabelle Birby." Whitridge believes that it was also known as "Sweet Alice Kirby." According to Lytton W. Doolittle (Yale 1913), an earlier version may have been known as "Naomi of Hartenstein's Restaurant."

VERSE 1

Miss Antoinette Birby lived way out in Derby,
A maid divinely fair.
She found it no heaven retiring at seven;
Her heart was filled with care.
'Twas truly a pity that a maiden so pretty
Should milk the cows all day,
So she took a notion to get into motion
And packed her trunk right away.
As the train pulled out of the station,
She gave forth this explanation:

REFRAIN 1

I'm off for New Haven, so long, goodbye,
I'm off for New Haven, I don't know why.
This leaving the family really makes me very sad,
For they are by far the best pa and ma I ever had.
But I've got to sling hash at the Taft Hotel,
As a waitress I never shall fail.
For I have a cravin' for dear old New Haven
And Yale, Yale, Yale.

VERSE 2

Arrived in the city, this maiden so pretty
Did walk down Chapel Street,
And then a young fellow to whom she said

"Hello"
Our heroine did meet.
Now he was a villain, but Nettie was willin',
She loved him right away.
Her scruples forsook her,
The villain he took her into a swell café.
As she took down her first few swallows,
She was heard to murmur rather incoherently as follows:

REFRAIN 2

I'm strong for New Haven, believe me, kid,
For this is the town where there ain't no lid.
The life in New Haven makes Derby seem so very tame,
I've learned sev'ral things that I never knew before I came.
I'm going to learn all that there is to know,
At least if I keep out of jail,
As a fountain of knowledge believe me some college
Is Yale, Yale, Yale.

VERSE 3

Next morn at eleven, instead of at seven,
She woke up in dismay.
Her bean it was addled, her brain had skedaddled,
For she had passed away.
The warden he brought her a pail of ice water,
Her thirst was so intense;
Her spirit was stricken, her conscience was pricken,
Her head it felt immense
As she left the police station,
She gave out this information:

REFRAIN 3

I'm going back to Derby, so long, goodbye,
I'm going back to Derby, you all know why.
When I came to New Haven I was so very good and sweet and true,
But I've done sev'ral things that a girlie shouldn't oughta do.
So it's back to the milking for Antoinette,
A sadder but wiser female.
No maiden that's pretty should come to the city
And Yale, Yale, Yale.

COLLEGE SHOWS

1911-1912

CORA, 1911

Produced by the Phi Opera Company as the fall initiation play at the Delta Kappa Epsilon fraternity house, November 28, 1911. One performance. Book by T. Gaillard Thomas II. Directed by Peter C. Bryce and Thomas. Cast, starring Cole Porter and Thomas, included Arnold Whitridge, L. C. Hanna, Jr., H. H. Parsons, J. Lytton, W. Doolittle, Reginald LeG. Auchincloss, and Fletcher Van W. Blood.

Of the thirteen surviving lyrics from *Cora*, all but "Far, Far Away" and "Hello, Miss Chapel Street" were included in a printed collection of lyrics from the show, a copy of which was preserved by Arnold Whitridge. Whitridge remembered the lyrics of "Far, Far Away" and "Hello, Miss Chapel Street," both of which he performed at several class reunions. He also recalled a couplet from "Queen of the Yale Dramat" ("Little Rufe King couldn't teach me a thing, / I'm the Queen of the Yale Dramat"). Rufus F. King (Yale 1914) was noted for his interpretations of ingenues in Yale musicals.

The lyrics to "We're Off," "Cablegram," "Le Rêve d'Absinthe," "Fair One," and "Mother Phi" have not survived. No music survives except through Whitridge's recollections.

POKER

"Poker," "Concentration," and "Saturday Night," which comprised *Cora*'s opening chorus, were introduced by the ensemble. No music survives.

Poker, poker forever,
That's a grand old game.
Of course it's rather hard on Father,
For sending checks is such a bother,
And we'll confess, yes,
Poker's expensive,
But we're not to blame.
Though it may be dissipation
We need our recreation,
So poker's the game.

CONCENTRATION

Oh, it's awfully hard to concentrate at college.
Oh, it's awfully hard to concentrate at Yale.
Though we came with the one idea to get some knowledge,
We seem to fail, fail, fail.
Now, our families never guess we have a snap-a.
They think we'll trap-a
Phi Beta Kappa.
But really that's too dumb,
For the extra curriculum
Makes the gay life at Yale.

SATURDAY NIGHT

Saturday night, Saturday night,
This is the one time we all get plenty of.
Liquor, liquor, just a wee flicker,
So order a gallon and don't stop to bicker.
We'll all sing something,
Any old tune's all right.
I love, I love the rest of the week,
But oh, you Saturday night!

HELLO, MISS CHAPEL STREET

Introduced by ensemble. Music and lyric recalled by Arnold Whitridge.

HE: Hello, Miss Chapel Street,
You look very sweet tonight.
SHE: Great damn,
I'm sweet as sugar jam,
And how is lovey-dovey,
Little Willie wise boy?
HE: I'm not so very well.
I'm low as hell,
For I can barely walk about a bit, dear.
Since we quit, dear,
I'm not feeling very fit.
SHE: Well-a, well-a, who's to blame?
I waited for an hour in the pouring rain.
HE: But you didn't wait 'til eight.
SHE: I had a date with a freshman.
HE: What's that you say,
That you had a date with a freshman?
SHE: Yesh, man.
HE: On my word,
But that's absurd.
SHE: That's enough funny stuff;
Cut the rough!
HE: When can we have a party for two, dear?
SHE: That's up to you, any time will do.
HE: Will you meet me tonight alone?

For I've an awful lot of love
That's simply hunting for a home.
SHE: Well, I'll be there,
A-waiting on the square.
HE: We'll have a drunken revel.
SHE: Good night, you little devil.
HE: We mustn't raise a riot.
SHE: Then kiss me on the quiet.
Bring a low-necked hack and a bottle of rye.
HE: Oh, won't I!
Goodbye.

CORA, THE FAIR CHORINE

Introduced by T. Gaillard Thomas, II. No music survives.

(They call her) Cora, the Fair Chorine,
(They call her) Cora, the Fair Chorine.
The way she hides her ankles when out walking makes me laugh,
For her legs appear each Sunday in the *Morning Telegraph.*
(The legs of) Cora, the Fair Chorine,
Known to fame as a Broadway queen.
When she saunters down the street,
Every person that you meet
Will exclaim,
What's the name
Of your daring little dame?
They call her Cora,
Cora,
Captivating Cora,
Cora, the Fair Chorine.

MY HOMETOWN GIRL

Introduced by Cole Porter. No music survives.

I'm lonesome,
I'm mighty lonesome
For my girl back home.
Without her,
I dream about her,
No matter where I roam.
Though my girl
Is just a shy girl,
She is as precious as a pearl.
Oh gee,
But she
Looks good to me,
My hometown girl.

GOODBYE, BOYS

Introduced by T. Gaillard Thomas II and Cole Porter. No music survives.

Goodbye, boys,
Goodbye, fare thee well.
(If you want a maiden from the Latin quarter
Only say the awful word and we'll export her.)
Goodbye, boys,
Goodbye, au revoir.
Though we'd like to go to France,
Still there's really not a chance,
So, so long, men—
Auf wiedersehen,
Goodbye, boys.

THE OLD RAT MORT

"The Old Rat Mort" and "Ninette" were introduced by the ensemble. Opening chorus, Act II. "Ninette" is listed in the program as "Ma Petite Ninette."

Marietta and sweet Babette,
We've got something wet
All for you.
Just to open your eye
Have some Mumm's Extra Dry,
And a bit of absinthe too.
But if you're very
Contrary,
We'll have to have some
Sherry,
For of liquor there's a store.
Allons vite,
Allons vite,
For a party complete,
At the old Rat Mort.

NINETTE

Ma p'tit' Ninette,
She's so coquette,

Why, when she does the can-can
Any little man can
Call her chérie.
She's so petite
You ought to meet her.
I never yet
Have met
A better
Petter
Than Ninette.
She's the one girl for me.

FAR, FAR AWAY

Introduced by Fletcher Van W. Blood and Arnold Whitridge. Music and lyric recalled by Arnold Whitridge. "Far Away" from *Leave It to Me* (1938) is an entirely different song.

Far, far away, dear,
In my cottage by the sea,
From the world secluded
We will live deluded
And we'll never disagree.
Maybe we'll have a baby
And a champagne fountain too;
And in my garden let's
Plant some cigarettes—
When I marry you.

ROSEBUD

Introduced by Fletcher Van W. Blood and ensemble. No music survives.

Rosebud,
My lovin' Rosebud,
I'm crazy 'bout you,
You're so divine.
I'm moanin' for you,
I'm groanin' for you,
And I never saw you
Lookin' half so fine.
When the moon shines brightly
I want you nightly
To hold me tightly
And I'll happy be.
Oh, hear me callin',
For you I'm fallin',
Oh, my lovin' Rosebud,
Come bloom for me.

ROLLING, ROLLING

Introduced by Cole Porter, Arnold Whitridge, T. Gaillard Thomas II, Fletcher Van W. Blood, and ensemble. No music survives.

Rolling, rolling
Over the crest of the sea
We've an awful mania
To slip
For a trip
On the *Lusitania,*
Back, back, back, back,
Back to the land of the free,
Back to footballing
And dear old Dwight-Halling
Far over the pounding
Sounding
Bounding
Over the bounding sea.

AND THE VILLAIN STILL PURSUED HER, 1912

Produced by the Yale University Dramatic Association at the New Haven Lawn Club, April 24, 1912, and at the Yale Club of New York City, May 10, 1912. Two performances. Book by T. Gaillard Thomas II. Staged by Messrs. Thomas and Porter. Cast, starring Monty Woolley, included Rufus F. King, Irving G. Beebe, Arnold Whitridge, Johnfritz Achelis, Hay Langenheim, Joseph Kelleher, and Lawrence M. Cornwall.

All lyrics from the show survive thanks to the memories of Johnfritz Achelis (Yale 1913), Arnold Whitridge, and others. Music manuscripts for "I'm the Villain," "Barcelona Maid" (also called "Barcelona") and "Any Time" were found by this editor among the manuscripts that Porter bequeathed to Yale University.

WE ARE THE CHORUS OF THE SHOW

"We Are the Chorus of the Show" and "Strolling," which comprised the opening chorus, were introduced by the ensemble. No music survives.

Hello, hello, listen to our bellow.
We are the chorus of the show.
Nimble and neat,
Light on the feet,
Dancing, prancing,
Beauties in a row.
We are getting sick of pirouetting
Everywhere we go,
For we are the well-appointed,
We are the double-jointed
Chorus of the show.

STROLLING

Strolling, just ambling up and down,
Posing just so,
Rolling, just rambling all around,
Keeping up the action of the show.
Turning and wandering toward the wings
When the song is nearly through,
Then tearing off a trick
By ending with a kick—
That's all we do.

THE LOVELY HEROINE

Introduced by Rufus F. King. No music survives.

VERSE

You see in me an innocent fleur-de-lis
So sweet and so simple
I'd blush at a dimple
On anyone else's knee.
That I am shy
Why nobody can deny,
For when a man passes
I don my dark glasses
And only open one eye.
This terrible clamor
To kill melodrama
I never could see at all.
For I'm so much prettier,
"Snowbound" like Whittier,
Wearing my old red shawl.

REFRAIN

Oh gee! It's heaven to be the lovely heroine.
All the men woo me
And try to undo me
But that's not in my line.
I live so far from New York
I faint dead away at the smell of a cork.
Why! I'm such a child I believe in the stork!
For I'm the heroine.

I'M THE VILLAIN

Introduced by Monty Woolley.

VERSE

Now, I'm the kind of villain that you hear about,
Why, Satan is a saint compared to me.
Now, I'm the kind of villain that you'd fear about,
As much as any other you could see.
I never seek the open when the stars are shining
  bright,
But only when the streets are dark and solemn,
So if you ever wander in the dead and stilly night
Beware, or I shall twist your spinal column!

REFRAIN

Oh, I'm the villain,
The dirty little villain;
I leave a pool of blood where e'er I tread,
I take delight
In looking for a fight
And pressing little babies on the head
Till they're dead.
I have gotten
A rep for being rotten,
I put poison in my mother's cream of wheat.
Tradition I base much on;
The family escutcheon
Is meat . . . raw meat.

TWILIGHT

Introduced by Irving G. Beebe and Hay Langenheim. No music survives.

My twilight sweetheart,
When day is dying
And winds are sighing,
Shadows whisper from above.
'Tis then my song, dear,
Will sadly long, dear,
For a smile from my twilight love.

LLEWELLYN

Introduced by Johnfritz Achelis. No music survives.

VERSE

Llewellyn was a girl from Wales
Who started o'er the sea
And fell in love with Patrick on the steamer.
Then in her simple fashion
She soon declared her passion
Was hotter than the light of his Fatima.
But not a word did Patrick say
But slowly went his way.
'Twas then she swore to win his love or die.
At once she took the notion
To leap into the ocean
And as she lost her balance she heard him cry:

REFRAIN

Oh, Llewellyn,
Come and share my dwellin',
Hear the love I'm tellin'
From my heart that's swellin'.
For my cutie,
For my pretty beauty,
And it's surely I love you.
Oh, my fairy,
Faith, and when we marry,
Then 'tis you I'll carry
Off to Tipperary.
Come and follow on my path,
I've got two rooms and a bath,
So come along, Llewellyn, do!

THAT ZIP CORNWALL COOCH

Introduced by Jack Stevens. No music survives.

Lawrence M. Cornwall (Yale 1912) was president of the Yale Dramat. He wore a mustache; his nickname was "Zip." Vanderbilt Hall was the residence of Yale College seniors. Cornwall told this editor by telephone in 1967 that Porter wrote the song as a result of a bet with a classmate.

VERSE

Now there's a rag that everybody's doin',
Now there's a rag that's everybody's ruin,
And it's called
Zip Cornwall Cooch.
That's what it's called.
Now there's a rag that's not to be forgotten,
There's a rag that Yale is turkey trottin',
And it's called
Zip Cornwall Cooch.
That's what it's called.
You can't deny
This latest cry
Is the favorite college sport.
You see it done
By everyone
In Vanderbilt court.

REFRAIN

That Zip Zip Cornwall Cooch,
That Zip Zip Cornwall Mooch,
Give it a dash,
Wear a mustache,
Everybody's fallin' for it.
Hear the college callin' for it.
Oh, that dramatic glide,
Aristocratic slide,
Gee, but it's great!
Leave it to fate,
Glide along the campus and
You'll never be late
When you do that Zip Cornwall Cooch.

CHARITY

"Charity," "Queens of Terpsichore," and "Leaders of Society" comprised the opening chorus, Act II. Introduced by ensemble. No music survives.

Charity, charity, everybody's doing it now.
Charity, charity, let the leading families teach
you how.
Just so many sit
At our benefit.
We are as successful as can be.
For we have no faith,

And there isn't any hope,
So we've got to have our charity.

QUEENS OF TERPSICHORE

We are the queens of Terpsichore,
We are given to trickery,
We drive many to liquor. We
Catch every man that we can.
Though we don't like to say it, we
Are so chuck full of gaiety,
Everyone knows
Anything goes
With Terpsichorean queens.

LEADERS OF SOCIETY

Rigid, frigid leaders of society,
Normal, formal ladies of propriety,
Always so smart,
Every single one of us a work of art.
Since New Haven functions are but rarities
We are forced to gad about in charities.
Filled with scorn, we
Lead a life of ennui,
Always so bored.

SUBMARINE

Introduced by Johnfritz Achelis. No music survives.

VERSE

HE: Now I have got a secret for you, my queen.
SHE: Sweet honey boy,
Fill me with joy.
HE: I own a beautiful submarine.
SHE: Hip, hip, hooray! Ship ahoy!
Huddled together, regardless of weather,
We'll shoot through our watery lane.
HE: That's all right, dear,
But what if I might, dear,
Get water on the brain?

REFRAIN

Down, down, down, in my lovely submarine,
Down, down, down, where the blue has turned to green,
We'll kiss and cuddle all day, and
We'll watch the sponges at play, and
As long as they've locked up us
We'll fear no octopus
Down in my submarine, marine,
Way down in my submarine.

BARCELONA MAID

Introduced by Irving G. Beebe. Also titled "Barcelona."

My little Barcelona maid
Was so entrancing.
Her charms were cleverly displayed,
Fandango dancing.
And when the moon is on the wane
I dream about her.
Oh! Would that I could see again
My Barcelona maid.

Barcelona maid entrancing,
Charms cleverly displayed by dancing,
And when the moon is waning I dream about her.
I would that I could see again my Barcelona maid.

SILVER MOON

Introduced by Gurney Smith. No music survives.

VERSE

Moon, moon, wandering nightly,
Moon, moon, floating so lightly,
Moon, moon, smile on me brightly,
Queen of skies above me.
Moon, moon, silently shining,
Moon, moon, ever declining,
Moon, moon, for you I'm pining,
So tell me that you love me.

REFRAIN

Moon, moon, silver moon.
Moon, moon, silver moon.
Only shine,

Luna mine,
Come back soon.
Moon, moon, when you die,
Moon, moon, then shall I.
Answer my longing, and grant me this boon,
Shine on, silver moon.

DEAR DOCTOR

Introduced by Monty Woolley. No music survives.

VERSE

Now when I was an undergrad,
And very bad,
Oh my!
I always was adorning
Some lamppost in the morning,
My taste for booze was infinite,
And ever lit was I.
So oft, in fact, I often lacked
The power to tie my tie,
But any time a recitation
Interfered with dissipation
To my little doctor I would cry:

REFRAIN

Dear Doctor, dear Doctor,
You've gotta
Concoct a
Remedy, some antidote,
'Cause I've got a funny little tickle in my throat.
So dear Doctor, dear Doctor,
Oh, hear my cry!
For you must produce me a sick excuse,
Or I'll wither up and die.

ANYTIME

Introduced by ensemble.

VERSE

HE: My life is done without a doubt.
SHE: Oh, don't be silly boy, Willy boy.
HE: I'm absolutely down and out.
SHE: Take a brace, hit the pace,
'Cause I love you more than ever,
We'll never sever.
HE: If you aren't sincere
Then it's clear
That you're clever,
For you put me on my feet again.
SHE: We'll meet again, but when?
HE: May I come around and call?
SHE: Yes, any time at all.

REFRAIN

(Boom, boom) Anytime you're feeling lonely,
(Boom, boom) Anytime you're feeling blue,
(Boom, boom) Anytime you have a longing
(Boom, boom) For a girl to woo.
(Boom, boom) Anytime you've got a feeling
(Boom, boom) That your heart is ever true,
(Boom, boom, boom) Anytime, any doggone time,
will do.

COME TO BOHEMIA

"Come to Bohemia," "Dancing," and "Fare Thee Well" comprised the finale of Act II. Introduced by ensemble. No music survives.

Let's all go and have a little party in Bohemia,
Bohemia.
Let's all go and have a little party in Bohemia,
Bohemia.
Hand in hand we'll make for the land
Where everyone's some other body's wife,
And each is able
To dance upon the table
And show some signs of life.

DANCING

Dancing, dancing,
Waltz entrancing,
Dark eyes glancing,
All the world romancing.
Slowly sliding,
Every heart confiding,
Won't you come to dear old Bohemia? Do!

FARE THEE WELL

Good night! Good night, everyone!
Good night! Good night, everyone!

We hate to leave you so,
But we've finished the whole damn show.
We are glad we met you all,
Rest in peace perpetual,
For you're immense as an audience;
So fare thee well!

WHEN WE'RE WED

This lyric appears among the miscellaneous lyrics in Krech's Yale compilation. In April 1974, Charles H. "Sparrow" Strange, a 1913 graduate of Yale's Sheffield Scientific School, sent Richard Warren, Jr., Curator of Yale's Historical Sound Recordings Collection, a manuscript of a Porter song, music and lyrics, as recalled and set down by Strange, virtually identical to "When We're Wed." Strange recalled the song's title as "Once We're Wed" and wrote (April 20, 1974) that it was performed in the Yale Lawn Club Smoker of 1912, the same show which included Porter's "Submarine." It is not listed in the program for *And the Villain Still Pursued Her.*

When we're wed, when we're wed,
You and I,
When we're wed, when we're wed,
We'll fly high.
I'll work all day, dear, and make you an heiress,
We'll water the garden with Appolanaris—
When we're wed, when we're wed,
By and by.

THE POT OF GOLD, 1912

Produced as the fall initiation play at the Delta Kappa Epsilon fraternity house, November 26, 1912, and at the Hotel Taft, New Haven, Connecticut, December 4, 1912. Two performances. Book by Almet F. Jenks, Jr. Staged by Messrs. Jenks and Porter. Cast, starring Cole Porter, included T. Gaillard Thomas II, Fletcher Van W. Blood, H. H. Parsons, Arnold Whitridge, and A. Clark.

In 1954, Jenks (Yale 1914) presented Yale with letters sent to him by Porter during the summer of 1912. The letters included early versions of eight lyrics from *The Pot of Gold.* They were printed with Porter's permission and an introduction by Robert Barlow (Yale 1933), founder and curator of Yale's Collection of the Literature of the American Musical Theatre, in the *Yale University Library Gazette,* July 1955, Vol. 30, No. 1. Jenks's effort inspired other Yale alumni of Porter's era to contribute what they had recalled or preserved, through programs and printed collections, of lyrics Porter wrote at Yale. Donaldson Clark (Yale 1914) made an a capella recording of some of the songs from *The Pot of Gold.*

But the most important, though unwitting, contribution came from Porter himself. On December 7, 1954, he had written to Yale University Associate Librarian John Ottemiller that "it will be perfectly all right for you to do whatever you wish with the lyrics of *The Pot of Gold.* Unfortunately, I have none of the music and none of the lyrics myself, for this composition." Yet in the large quantity of miscellaneous manuscripts that Porter bequeathed to Yale was an almost complete piano-vocal score of *The Pot of Gold,* making it the best-preserved of Porter's college shows.

AT THE RAINBOW

"At the Rainbow" and "Bellboys" comprised the opening chorus. Introduced by ensemble.

At the Rainbow, the Rainbow,
At last a life elixir at the Rainbow.
Some scandal seems approaching very hot on us
To thrill a spot that's otherwise monotonous.
At the Rainbow, the Rainbow,
Where Cupid used to shoot with but a vain bow,
We welcome all progression
In the line of indiscretion
At the Rainbow,
The Rainbow,
The Rainbow,
The Rain Rainbow Hotel.

BELLBOYS

Bellboys, bellboys,
Unenthusiastic bellboys.
Not a thing to drink but the mountain water,
Not a thing to love but the boss's daughter.
That old traitor
Can't afford an elevator,
So we climb the stairs, though tired and lame.
Truckhorse is our middle name.
And it's tough,
Rather rough,
For the bellboys are we.

LONGING FOR DEAR OLD BROADWAY

Introduced by Cole Porter. Published in *The Unpublished Cole Porter.*

VERSE

Gee what a place to waste a day in,
Gee what a place to fade away in.
Were I but free
Would I could be
Back where the world's alive.
Some people pine for mountain green'ry.
Never for mine this lonesome scen'ry.
I'd like to walk,
Start for New York,
Back where the lobsters thrive.

REFRAIN

For I'm longing for dear old Broadway,
Longing for dear old town.
Yes, I'm longing to stroll on Broadway,
Watching the world go 'round.
To be back where the boys all know me,
Back where the girls all bow,
For I'm lonesome, lonesome,
Longing for Broadway now.

WHEN I USED TO LEAD THE BALLET

Introduced by T. Gaillard Thomas II. Porter used this number later in his first Broadway show, *See America First* (1916), where it was introduced by Felix Adler and ensemble. Published February 1916. When the Yale Whiffenpoofs appeared in costumes for the Yale-Brown football game, 1912, Porter dressed as "Pavlova."

VERSE

Now you'd never infer
That as Premier Danseur
I was madly adored by the Russians
But when leading the ballet
My dance Bacchanale
Excited tremendous discussions.
With a negligee uniform
Over my puny form,
Thousands I made with delight rock!
In the get-up I had on
I looked like the "ad" on
A bottle of sparkling White Rock!

CHORUS: He was paid to say that,
He was paid to say that,
He was paid to say that about White Rock.

REFRAIN

When I used to lead the ballet,
When I used to lead the ballet,
In costume so scanty
The world dilettante
Pronounced me a perfect joy.
Those wonderful days are over
When I danced with the fair Pavlova.
For I was her lordkin,
Her lambkin, her Mordkin,
Her beautiful ballet boy.

MY HOUSEBOAT ON THE THAMES

Introduced by Humphrey Parsons.

VERSE

Now in life there's nought that's lower
Than the awful sort of bore
Who can rot around a place when uninvited
And in full appreciation
Of your cordial invitation
I've determined that it shan't be unrequited.
When in London and you're tired
And desire a little rest
I've a houseboat on the river
Only waiting for a guest.
Though it's quite dilapidated
In a harbor isolated
Still I think you'll like my houseboat
On the Thames.

CHORUS: When you think you'd like to float
On this silly sort of boat
Only send a little note,
For he's sure that you will dote
On his houseboat,
On his houseboat,
On his houseboat on the Thames.

REFRAIN

On my houseboat on the Thames,
On my houseboat on the Thames,
It's a jolly ripping vessel to relax on,
For it's deuced dull and deadly Anglo-Saxon.
We'll have Punch on board, I think,
One to read and one to drink,
But when you're bored and feeling undone
We can wander up to London
On my houseboat,
On my houseboat,
On my houseboat on the Thames

SHE WAS A FAIR YOUNG MERMAID

Introduced by Cole Porter.

VERSE

When a fellow immature,
I had one affaire d'amour
About as queer as e'er befell a man.
I was strolling by the tide
When I suddenly espied
A pretty dear—an Annette Kellerman.
She was sitting nonchalantly,
Quite undraped and all alone,
And I thought some debutante, she
Had escaped her chaperon.
But while gazing at her pulchritude celestial,
I perceived she was a girl—but not terrestrial.

REFRAIN

She was a fair young mermaid,
A debonair young mermaid.
As she gathered watercresses
Little wavelets combed her tresses,
For the sea was her maid.
And 'neath the moonlight shining
We rested, arms entwining,
For the queen of all her genus,
Yes, a veritable Venus,
Was my mermaid love.

WHAT'S THIS AWFUL HULLABALOO?

Introduced by ensemble. This number also included a reprise of "At the Rainbow."

What's this awful hullabaloo,
What's this awful hullabaloo,
Who are you and who are you,
What's this awful hullabaloo?
Why the girl in dress so vivid,
Why the youth in features livid,
What's the sheriff out to hinder,
Why the fainting Chlodoswinde,
What has caused this lamentation,
Why this heated conversation,
Whose mustache in conflagration,
Who has lost his reputation?
Who? Which? When? What? Why?

WHAT A CHARMING AFTERNOON

"What a Charming Afternoon," "Since We've Met," "Exercise," and "We Are So Aesthetic," which comprised the opening chorus of Act II and were introduced by the ensemble, were actually two "double" songs. Song A is sung, then song B, then A and B together. In this particular opening chorus, after "What a Charming Afternoon" and "Since We've Met" were sung, the pattern was repeated by "Exercise" and "We Are So Aesthetic."

LADIES: What a charming afternoon for exercise
is this.
Such a chance for sport we really can't
afford to miss.
If you want some golf sticks or a racquet,
ring the bell.
This hotel can give away what other
places sell.

SINCE WE'VE MET

BELLBOYS: Since we've met we've undergone a
metamorphosis.
In fact we've reached a paradise of
beatrician bliss,

Together with the renaissance of
Delor's bum hotel,
To *Police Gazettes* and cigarettes we've
made our last farewell.
LADIES: Oh, there's such a lot of game that
any sort of dub
Can fire at random in the woods and
interrupt a cub.
BELLBOYS: We shrink at any oath except a soft
"Beelzebub."
We're out-Elizabething the Elizabethan
Club.

EXERCISE

LADIES: Exer exer exer exer exer exercise!
We are going crazy over exer exercise.
If we had our pretty pink pajamas on
Each would be a perfect little Amazon.
Exer exer exer exer exer exercise!
Don't you think we members of our sex
are very wise,
For if you'd not neglect your
Figure's architecture
You've got to exercise,
You've got to exercise,
You've got to exer exer exer exercise.

WE ARE SO AESTHETIC

BELLBOYS: We are so aesthetic,
We are so poetic.
As a little baby has to have his bottle,
So we are dependent on our Aristotle.
We are so pedantic,
We are nearly frantic,
Searching every grammar
For the lost digamma.
Literary bellboys,
Literary bellboys,
Literary bellboys we,
Bellboys we!

SCANDAL

Introduced by Fletcher Van W. Blood and ensemble.

LOIE: Now here's some scandal I've just heard.
LADIES: We're on, we're on.
LOIE: You must promise on your honor
That you'll never say a word.
LADIES: We're gone, we're gone.
LOIE: Now you remember Missus Bear.
LADIES: That cross-eyed girl without the hair.
LOIE: Well, she drinks and she smokes
And you ought to hear her swear.
LADIES: Oh, how terrible.
BOTH: Oh, what scandal.
LOIE: Now you remember Mary Bell
And Charley Smith you know him well.
They say they're always stopping at the
same hotel.
LADIES: Oh, deplorable.
LOIE: No doubt you've met that Missus Best.
Now she's so rich and overdressed
They say she left her husband
'Cause he wouldn't wear a vest.
LADIES: Oh, how horrible.
BOTH: Oh, what scandal.
Tell me, have you heard the latest
scandal?
LOIE: Missus Hawes returned the parlor sofa
Just because it didn't suit her chauffeur.
BOTH: Oh, what scandal.
LOIE: There's an awful lot of it to handle.
BOTH: We can make you shake like gelatin
While we sit and calmly tell it on
Ev'ry person with a family skeleton.
Shh! Keep it dark.

I WONDER WHERE MY GIRL IS NOW

Introduced by T. Gaillard Thomas II. The only surviving music is a flute part from the orchestration of the score by Professor William Haesche.

VERSE

Now I met my girl on a roam through Prussia
And wooed her with some homemade caviar.
Then I led her back to my home in Russia
And taught her how to plot against the Czar.
When she lectured on the streets
She was so fiercely festic,

The crowd would all go crazy when they heard her.
She became so indiscreet,
So very anarchistic,
She even taught the baby how to murder.

REFRAIN

Oh, I wonder where my girl is now,
Yes, I wonder where my girl is now,
For she's so slender, tall and stately.
She's a most decided blonde, she just decided lately.
If you see her passing by,
Kindly tell her I'm the same old pal.
For even tho' she flirts a lot with other men,
She's a damned fine gal.

MY SALVATION ARMY QUEEN

Introduced by Cole Porter and ensemble. Music includes a brief snippet of "Onward, Christian Soldiers."

VERSE

Oh, Chlodo, Chlodoswinde,
How you alarm me
To know that you are in the
Salvation Army.
I stand and wait dejected
And rue the day
I see thee unprotected
Upon your way.
But why should I in tears despair,
Dreary tho' I be,
When I know my maiden fair
Must return to me?
My Salvation Army queen,
My goddess of love serene!

REFRAIN

My little Salvation Army Queen,
My little Salvation Army Queen.
She was so seraphic
That she blocked the traffic
When she beat that tambourine.
And like an angel, divinely tall,
She hollers, "Down with King Alcohol!"
So don't be disconcerted
If you find yourself converted
By my blue-eyed Christian soldier,
My Salvation Army Queen.

IT'S AWFULLY HARD WHEN MOTHER'S NOT ALONG

Introduced by Fletcher Van W. Blood.

VERSE

Now a maiden in my station
Has a life that's all temptation,
For the men think what we chorines do don't matter.
But I hate these midnight capers,
'Cause they're always in the papers
And my photographs were never said to flatter.
So I always bring Mamma along no matter where I go,
For she's really very thoughtful of her daughter.
When they ask us out to dine,
She insists that I have wine,
It's been years since I have touched a drop of water.

REFRAIN

But it's awfully hard when Mother's not along.
Yes it's awfully hard when Mother's not along.
Tho' my men friends may insist,
I object to being kissed,
For I always have considered kissing wrong.
Now I've often told my mother when alone
That I'm incomplete without a chaperon,
For when she is standing near
All the talk is fit to hear,
But it's awfully hard when Mother's not along.

I WANT TO BE MARRIED (TO A DELTA KAPPA EPSILON MAN)

Introduced by Cole Porter and ensemble.

VERSE

Now Harry was a Psi U sort of stoic
Who loved a girl as equally azoic.
He penned her panegyrics
And he'd send her pretty lyrics,
All in couplets that were nought if not heroic.

CHORUS: In couplets that were nought,
In couplets that were bought,

In couplets that were nought if not
heroic.
LARRY: But tried he all in vain the girl to marry
By sending her this brain confectionary,
For when his talk would tread upon
The day they were to wed upon,
She'd merely close her eyes and mutter
"Harry."
CHORUS: She'd merely close her eyes,
She'd merely utter sighs,
She'd merely close her eyes and mutter
"Harry."

REFRAIN

LARRY: I want to be married
To a Delta Kappa Epsilon man.
I never have varied
From the Delta Kappa Epsilon clan.
I've a friend or two in A. D. Phi,
And my mother's second cousin was a
Beta Theta Pi,
But I want to be married
To a Delta Kappa, Delta Kappa, Delta
Kappa,
Delta, Kappa, Delta Kappa Epsilon
man.
CHORUS: For they always are so jolly, oh so
jolly,
Oh so jolly.
LARRY: So I want to be married
To a Delta Kappa Epsilon man.

HA, HA, THEY MUST SAIL FOR SIBERIA

"Ha, Ha, They Must Sail for Siberia," "I Love You So," "Loie and Chlodo," and "So Let Us Hail" comprised the finale of Act II. Introduced by ensemble. "If I Were Only a Football Man" was not used in *The Pot of Gold,* although included in a letter from Porter to Jenks. Rewritten and used by Porter as Glee Club specialty during his senior year. See "A Football King" (page 5). A composition titled "That Rainbow Rag" was written for *The Pot of Gold* but not used. It survives as an instrumental. No lyric exists.

Ha, ha, they must sail for Siberia.
The thought makes us pale with hysteria.
To lands of the snow
The nihilists go.
In vain have they toiled,
Their plots have been foiled.
Fare thee well, fare thee well,
Fate has cast her dice.
Fare thee well, fare thee well,
Ever be on ice.

I LOVE YOU SO

LARRY: Now Chlodoswinde the fair and I
Are on our way to marry.
The quarrel which we've just
passed by
Was but a weird vagary.
This compact Delor made me
sign
Demanded efforts drastic,
So now that Chlodoswinde is
mine
Please be enthusiastic.
DELOR: Now pretty Miss Corotte and
I are running for the altar,
So join the bridal party and
You'll see her take the halter,
For she's my nucleus of life
And I'm her protoplasm.
Appreciate my darling wife
And show enthusiasm.
DELOR & THORNE: Lovey-dovey.
LOIE & CHLODO: You're all the world to me.
CHORUS: Her voice is like the whisper of
the seaweed to the sea.
DELOR & THORNE: Fairest, rarest.
LOIE & CHLODO: Our love can never die.
CHORUS: He's passionately fond of ev'ry
eyelash in her eye.
DELOR & THORNE: Cutey, beauty.
LOIE & CHLODO: My only earthly bliss.
CHORUS: He thinks he's getting Huyler's
when she's giving him a kiss.
I love you so
I'd like to show
How far I'd go
To let you know
I love you so,
I love you so,
I love you so.

LOIE AND CHLODO

Loie, Chlodo,
Our adorable Loie, Chlodo,
He is waiting to take you,
Make you ever his own.
You'll be his adorable Loie, Chlodo,
For he swears he will love you truly and alone.

SO LET US HAIL

So let us hail
To the love of the fair,
May it be true and forever
Strong to the end.
May they do all and dare,
Standing alone,
Ne'er to sever.
Seasons may change,
All the world may grow old,
Happy in love may they dwell.
So let us hail
Pot of Gold
At the foot of the Rainbow Hotel,
The Rainbow Hotel.

COLLEGE SHOWS

1913-1914

THE KALEIDOSCOPE, 1913

Produced by the Yale University Dramatic Association at the Hotel Taft, New Haven, April 30, 1913, and at the Yale Club of New York City, May 7, 1913. Two performances. Billed as "A Home Play in Two Acts." Cast, starring Newbold Noyes and Rufus F. King, included Archibald MacLeish, Howard T. Cumming, Arnold Whitridge, Johnfritz Achelis, Joseph Kelleher, and Hay Langenheim.

All lyrics have survived. With a few exceptions, the music has not survived.

AT THE DAWN TEA

"At the Dawn Tea," "We Are Prom Girls," and "Chaperons" comprise the opening chorus of Act I. Introduced by ensemble. No music survives.

At the dawn tea, at the dawn tea,
Disregarding the cold daybreak,
If you're then there
You'll see men there
All lit up like a birthday cake.

At the dawn tea, at the dawn tea,
It's a party
That is jaunty.
It's a place where they all talk
Conversational small talk—
The Prom dawn tea.

WE ARE PROM GIRLS

We are Prom girls.
Pretty little pink-cheeked Prom girls.
Gautier would swear that we're evil-eyed,
Browning would declare that we were ostrich-
  thighed.
We add pep to
Any tune that we one-step to.
You won't bore us
If you'll but adore us,
Pretty little Prom girls, we—
Pretty little Prom girls, we.

CHAPERONS

Chaperons, chaperons,
We are sporty,
Fat and forty,
Chaperons.
Very kind, very blind,
When we walk ahead,
We never lag behind.
College boys are our toys,
And the girls we protégé
Are mere decoys.
And if anybody throws a
Little kiss or two, sub rosa,
It is one, two, three, four, five, six, seven, eight,
Nine times out of ten the chaperon.

IN THE LAND WHERE MY HEART WAS BORN

Introduced by Hay Langenheim. No music survives.

VERSE

Now in every musical show
There's a song sentimental;
If it doesn't appear you may know
That it's purely accidental.
If your hungry heart yearns for a taste
Of a passionate saccharine sandwich,
Just imagine that you have been placed
In the highly improbable land which
Is covered with kisses
Of fair misses.
Oh, there's no other land such as this is!

REFRAIN

In the land of my heart,
Where the sea is sadly shining,
There's a breeze
Through the trees,
With another breeze entwining;
To the croon
Of the moon
Lies a maiden fair reclining,
And I nest
On her breast
In the land where my heart was born.

MEET ME BESIDE THE RIVER

Introduced by Joseph Kelleher. No music survives.

VERSE

Down by the river,
Dearie, shadowed by trees,
Where grasses shiver
At the tale of the breeze;
Down where the heavens are reflected
Over the stream,
There's a trysting place neglected
We must redeem—
The spot where Nature in her beauty lies
I think we really ought to utilize.

REFRAIN

Meet me beside the river,
'Neath the great big syc-ycamore,
You and I, dear,
On one night, dear,
And if your hat is off you're
Bound to muss your coiffure.
I love you so sincerely
That there's really nothing to fear.
And 'neath the moon
We'll steal a souvenir spoon,
When you meet me, dear.

BEWARE OF THE SOPHOMORE

Introduced by Rufus F. King. No music survives.

VERSE

SOLO: Have you ever heard the story of the Sophomore?
CHORUS: Oh, a fairy tale is always such a bore!
SOLO: Have you ever heard the war cry of a Sophomore?
CHORUS: Does it whistle, does it jibber, does it roar?
SOLO: A Sophomore is a creature full of concentrated gloom,
Who flitters through your window on a vacuum-cleaning broom,
And forces you to swear you'll not get up and leave the room.
CHORUS: Fearful, fearful!
Oh, what a terrible earful!
SOLO: Take care, take care,
For if a Sophomore is sitting over there
He'll beat you to a jelly.
CHORUS: Oh, you Pumpelly!

REFRAIN

Oh, beware of the Sophomore,
For he's rather apt to knock you 'round the block.
If you're yearning for position,
If you're burning with ambition,
Run for shelter, helter-skelter, to the Yale Hope Mission,
And prepare for the Sophomore,
Or he'll dislocate your window with a rock.
If his words you do shun
He'll wreck your institution.
Run, run, run, you son of a gun—
Here comes the militant Sophomore.

RICK-CHICK-A-CHICK

Introduced by Johnfritz Achelis. No music survives.

Rick-chick-a-chick, chick-a-chick, chick-a-chicken,
Little barnyard queen.
Rick-chick-a-chick, chick-a-chick, chick-a-chicken,
You're the best I've seen.
Rick-chick-a-chick, chick-a-chick, chick-a-chicken,
Any rainy day,
I might suggest, dear,
You'll find my nest, dear.
Rick-chick-a-chick, chick-a-chick, chick-a-chicken,
Well, upon my word,
Rick-chick-a-chick, chick-a-chick, chick-a-chicken,
You're a grand old bird.
If you'll be my little spouse, just say,
I'll let you lay around the house all day.
Rick-chick-a-chick, chick-a-chick, chick-a-chicken
Mine.

GOODBYE, MY TRUE LOVE

Introduced by Newbold Noyes. No music survives.

VERSE

Though Fate demands that I must leave you,
Though I may wander far away,
Let not the sands of time deceive you,
For I shall worship you for aye.
But ere we part grant one request, dear,
Come to my heart and find your nest, dear.

REFRAIN

Goodbye, my true love,
Fare thee well, mine own.
I'll dream of you, love—
None but you alone.
For you, my fair love,
No matter where, love,
My own, my rare love,
I bid thee goodbye.

ON MY YACHT

Introduced by Howard Cumming. No music survives for this, the finale of Act I.

Now, 'twas late last fall I bought a yawl
To take a trip of convalescence.
She was so ornate with nickel plate
I had to name her "Phosphorescence."
Now from that day on I've never gone
On any other sailing vessel;
For I find she's fast and not aghast
When with the sea she has to wrestle.
And it's really quite a comfort to have waiting in the harbor
Every possible convenience from a barmaid to a barber.
And I think it would be a unique end
To this party if we had a little week end
On my yacht—

CHORUS: On my yacht.
SOLO: On my yacht.
CHORUS: On my yacht.
SOLO: On my dressy yacht—
CHORUS: What?

REFRAIN (DOUBLE CHORUS)

On my yacht, on my yacht, on my dressy little yacht,
Will you not come and rot for a while?
O'er the foam we can roam 'neath the star-bedizened dome,
In a truly Ancient Mariner style.
If it's not very hot we can have a turkey trot,
And I wot that you'll like it a lot;
So, prepare for a rare little party in the glare
Of the moonlight.
On my yacht, on my yacht, on my dressy little yacht,
Eh what!

COUNTERMELODY TO REFRAIN (SECOND CHORUS)

On my yacht—on my yacht—
Will you not—come and rot for a while?
O'er the foam—we can roam—
In a tru—ly An—cient Mariner style.
If it's not—very hot—
Then I wot—that you'll like it a lot.
So prepare—for a rare—little smarty, little party
In the appetizing air.
On my yacht—on my yacht—
Eh what!

WE'RE A GROUP OF NONENTITIES

Opening of Act II, Scene 1. Introduced by ensemble. Music recalled by Arnold Whitridge.

(BOOM, BOOM) We're a group of nonentities,
(BOOM, BOOM) Can't you guess our identities?
We're but a fraction of a number graduated
Who found their abilities were underestimated,
And soon lost their jobs and (then) became intoxicated,
And so (diddle-dee-dum) sought the shelter of the street
(Be-boom boom boom)
(BOOM, BOOM) Known at Yale as the upper set,
(BOOM, BOOM) We were kings of the supper set,
Gorging at restaurants expensive and luxurious,
Racing to Wallingford in motors fast and furious,
And now, down and out, we must admit we're rather curious
To know (diddle-dee-dum)
Where to get a bite to eat.
(Be-boom-boom-boom)
(BOOM, BOOM) It's a hard life, (boom) it's a weary one
(BOOM) When the dogs begin to bark.
(BOOM, BOOM) It's a sad life, (boom) it's a dreary one,

(BOOM) When you're sleeping in the park.
Death hangs o'er us like the threatening sword of Damocles,
We're so poor we can't afford a box of Rameses.
(BOOM) It's a hard life, (boom) it's a weary one.
Damn! Damn! Damn!

FLOWER MAIDENS

Finale of Act II, Scene 1. Introduced by ensemble. No music survives.

Flower maidens, energetic,
So appealing, so pathetic,
Racing round from night till morning
Quite content with marathoning.
All we get's a mere existence,
Can't you lend us some assistance?
Cast your bread upon the waters,
It will float back home.
Flowers, flowers,
Nice ripe flowers.
The flower for the Senior
Is a pure mature gardenia.
The flower for the Junior
Is the frail and pale petunia.
The flower for the Sophomore kid
Is the all-important orchid.
For the Freshman silly
Here's a modest lily.
There's a flower for every year.
Won't you buy, won't you buy,
Won't you come along and try?

ABSINTHE

"Absinthe" and "Absinthe Drip" comprise the opening of Act II, Scene 2. Introduced by ensemble. The music for "Absinthe" was used later for the song "Two Big Eyes," lyric by John Golden. Published September 1915. Interpolated in the show *Miss Information* (1915), which had music by Jerome Kern. Introduced by Irene Bordoni.

Absinthe, absinthe, smile at me again,
Come devour the tissue of my weary brain.
Absinthe, absinthe, ever by my side.
Oh, you beautiful absinthe—my green-eyed bride.

ABSINTHE DRIP

As we drip, drip, drip, drip, drip along,
We can sip, sip, sip, sip, sip along;
And the feeling lingers,
Such a funny little tingle in the fingers.
As we swing, swing, swing, swing, swing along
We can sing, sing, sing, sing, sing a song.
Ah, you'd better take a trip
For a quiet little nip
Of our absinthe drip.

MAID OF SANTIAGO

Introduced by Hay Langenheim. No music survives.

VERSE

Down in Santiago town
Lived a maid of great renown.
In the land there was no sweeter
Than this brown-eyed señorita.
And every night a cavalier
'Neath her window would appear;
And as he touched his light guitar
This was the song that rang afar:

REFRAIN

Maid of Santiago, maid of my devotion,
Hear me calling,
Calling for you,
Let me sail you over the ocean.
Oh, my fair Fedora,
Come be my señora.
Don't decline,
You Santiago sweetheart of mine.

COUNTERMELODY

Santiago, Santiago,
I am calling, calling for you.
Let me sail you over the ocean.
High *ventana*,
My madonna.
Don't decline,
You Santiago sweetheart of mine.

AS I LOVE YOU

Introduced by Newbold Noyes. A partial manuscript of the music is at Yale. Retitled "Esmerelda," it was interpolated in the Broadway musical *Hands Up* (1915), music by Sigmund Romberg, lyrics by E. Ray Goetz, where it was introduced by Maurice and Florence Walton. It was Porter's first song to appear in a Broadway show (July 22, 1915) and was published in August 1915 by Irving Berlin, Inc. The programs spelled the title "Esmeralda."

VERSE

SHE: Now as long as we're united in the bonds of matrimony
You surely must have something to confess.
HE: To make the maxim suit the rhyme,
"Qui mal y pense soit honi,"
Of course there's naught to do but answer "Yes."
SHE: Now, before you popped the question weren't you something of a gadabout?
HE: My love affairs—well, let me see—I think I must have had about eleven.
SHE: Or a dozen.
HE: No, the twelfth one doesn't count—she was my cousin.
SHE: How I loathe them! How I hate them!
HE: Please control yourself and I'll enumerate them.

REFRAIN

Esmerelda,
Then Griselda,
And the third was Rosalie.
Lovely Lakme
Tried to track me,
But I fell for fair Marie.
Eleanora
Followed Dora,
Then came Eve with eyes of blue.
But I swear I ne'er loved any girl
As I love you.

DUODECIMALOGUE

Introduced by ensemble. No music survives.

MEN: Maiden, maiden, from the first
I have loved you madly.
GIRLS: If you don't control your thirst,
I'll tell Prexy Hadley.
MEN: Maiden, maiden, can't you see
I'm fidele semper.
GIRLS: Oh, sir, go, sir! Let me be!
I shall lose my temper.
MEN: Won't you come and fly with me?
GIRLS: Oh, sir, that could never be!

REFRAIN

HE: Maiden, pretty little maiden,
I love you so.
Come and fly away to lands afar,
In my big motor car.
SHE: Oh, sir, I could never go, sir,
I've no trousseau.
Don't you see that I really can't—
I'm not even a debutante.
BOTH: So, the whole case ends.
We'll just be friends.

OH, WHAT A PRETTY PAIR OF LOVERS

Introduced by Rufus F. King and Newbold Noyes. No music survives.

VERSE

HE: Let's live once more the day
Of warriors' surging fable.
SHE: When no one ran away,
And King Arthur ran a table.
HE: I love you so, my dear,
I swear I ne'er shall doubt you.
SHE: Alas, I greatly fear
I'm incomplete without you.
HE: My heart is out of key,
It yearns for you to tune it.
SHE: How happy we shall be
When once a perfect unit.
BOTH: Like lovers of the moyen-âge are we
Singing silly persiflage are we:

REFRAIN

BOTH: Oh, what a pretty pair of lovers
We two shall be!
Side by side
And always tied
In a true blue lover's knot we.
We don't care what the thoughts of the rabble are,
SHE: I'll be Eloise.
HE: I'll be Abelard.
BOTH: Words of love with hints interlinear,
HE: I'll be Paul,
SHE: And I Virginia.
BOTH: Climb the balcony by the trellis and

HE: I'll be Pelléas.
SHE: I'll be Mélisande.
BOTH: We don't care if the Round Table talks a lot.
SHE: I'll be Guinevere,
HE: I'll be Launcelot.
BOTH: So cemented, quite unprecedented,
Oh, what a pretty pair of lovers
We two shall be!

A MEMBER OF THE YALE ELIZABETHAN CLUB

Introduced by Arnold Whitridge. The music is published under the title "The Yale Elizabethan Club" in *Songs of Yale.*

VERSE

I'm a member very noted
Of a club that's often quoted
As the most exclusive club in college.
My medulla oblongata
Has an awful lot of data
On the sources of our springs of knowledge.
I delight in being chatty
With New Haven's literati
On the subject of a brand-new binding.
All the critics sing my praises
In illuminated phrases;
As a literary light I'm blinding.

CHORUS: As a literary light, as a literary light,
He's blinding!
Did you get that metaphor?
I confess I could do better for—

REFRAIN

I'm a member of the Yale Elizabethan Club
In a very hypocritical way.
By belonging to the Yale Elizabethan Club
I've a terrible political sway.
I convert New Haven
To the bard of Avon,
And a highbrow must I be;
For I give support
To the latest college sporto,
Tea by the quart
And editions by the quarto.
Good gadzooks! But I love those books.
With a fol, with a fol,
With a hey, with a hey,
With a toureloure tourelourelay,
With a tralalalala,
With a tralalalala,
And a noney, noney, noney noney, ney,
For a member of the Yale Elizabethan Club am I!

MOON MAN

Introduced by Joseph Kelleher. No music survives.

VERSE

There's a myth about a maiden called Urania,
With a terrible attack of moonamania,
Who would sit on her steps
With her heart in the depths
Of despair
For her love.
Now you'll have to grant me it's a rare amour
When a maiden wants a planet for a paramour,
But it's true just the same,
That the girl found a flame
In the fair
Moon above.
As he sailed across the sky in all his glory,
She would warble from her small observatory:

REFRAIN

Moon man, won't you cast your eyes on
Someone with a heart that's true?
Moon man, seek the far horizon,
I'll be waiting there for you,
My big red
Moon man, can't you hear me calling?
Won't you listen to my tune?
When those thunderclouds come rumbling 'roun',
Won't you please come tumbling down,
My man moon.

MY GEORGIA GAL

Introduced by Johnfritz Achelis. No music survives.

Oh, my gal in Georgia,
My maid of Southern clime,
Like Lucretia Borgia
She makes a killing every time.
My blue-eyed belle, she is my one flower—
My fairest summer sunflower—
When those banjos start to play,

When her shoulders start to sway,
She's petite, she's my lamb,
She's my sweet, sugar jam,
She's my pal—
My doggone Georgia gal.

PARANOIA, 1914

Produced by the Yale University Dramatic Association at the Hotel Taft, New Haven, April 24, 1914. One performance. Book, music, and lyrics by Thomas Lawrason Riggs and Cole Porter. Directed by Monty Woolley.

Written during Porter's year at the Harvard Law School (1913–1914), *Paranoia* was subtitled *Chester of the Yale Dramatic Association.* Its original title was *Belle of the Balkans.* All of the music and virtually all of the lyrics were by Porter. A copy of the book is in the Yale University Library's Historical Manuscripts Collection.

PARANOIA

Introduced by ensemble. No music survives.

ONSTAGE: Paranoia!
OFFSTAGE: Paranoia!
ONSTAGE: It's a kingdom behind the Beyond!
Paranoia!
OFFSTAGE: Paranoia!
ONSTAGE: Where the ladies are famously fond.
Paranoia!
OFFSTAGE: Paranoia!
ONSTAGE: It's a beautiful spot you'll agree,
From the lowland, to the highland,
A unique sort of an island—
Paranoia.
OFFSTAGE: Paranoia.
ONSTAGE: By the sea.
SECONDS: This day is a holiday,
This day is a jolly day,
This is a fun and folly day,
When you throw your cares away.
FIRSTS: This day is a holiday,
This day is a jolly day,
This is a fun and folly day,
When you throw your cares away.
ALL: Away, away, away, away.
ONSTAGE: La la la—la la la la la la la
OFFSTAGE: La la la—la la la la la la la
ONSTAGE: La la la—la la la la la la la la.

FUNNY LITTLE TRACKS IN THE SNOW

Introduced by William S. Innis and ensemble. No music survives.

Oh, those funny little tracks in the snow!
How I wonder what they are and where they go!
I saw a bunny rabbit white,
Hop across the snow last night.
Oh, what funny little tracks in the snow!
Oh, those funny little tracks!

INNOCENT, INNOCENT MAIDS

Introduced by ensemble. No music survives.

VERSE

Kindly adjust your opera glasses—
We are a group of village lasses,
Sprung from the very lowest classes.
We're very far from frisky fillies;
When we are met by wayside Willies,
We droop our heads like modest lilies.
Like demure girls
We coyly dimple,
Simply pure girls,
Not purely simple.

REFRAIN

For we're such innocent, innocent, innocent,
We're such innocent maids!
Like dear old Lillian Russell,
Our springtime never fades.
Why, we don't know what they mean by vice;
We do know though that it's not quite nice;
And spite of tempers' efforts strenuous,
We remain such damned ingenuous
Innocent, innocent maids.

OH, WHAT A LONELY PRINCESS

Introduced by Rufus F. King and ensemble. No music survives.

VERSE

PRINCESS: Everyone knows, when a maiden is beautiful
No one presumes to be dutiful.
CHORUS: Dutiful.
PRINCESS: But in a frenzy of filial loyalty
I told Papa I'd wed royalty.
CHORUS: Royalty.
PRINCESS: But in my suitor, before I to wed agree,
There must be more than a pedigree.
CHORUS: Pedigree.
PRINCESS: Years have I waited for someone adorable;
So far my luck is deplorable.
CHORUS: Deplorable.
PRINCESS: Tristam's love potion appears a sweet cup to be,
Blushing unseen is not all it's cracked up to be.
CHORUS: Poor little girl doesn't like it at all,
Being a "Flower in a Crannied Wall."

REFRAIN

Oh, what a lonely princess is she!
Oh, what a lonely princess is she!
Nobody cares what her fate may be.
Nobody cares if it's grief or glee.
Pining away in her own countree
Oh, what a lonely princess is she.

WON'T YOU COME CRUSADING WITH ME?

Published February 1916 as "Prithee, Come Crusading with Me." Rewritten and used in Porter's first Broadway show, *See America First.* Both versions are included here. Some *See America First* programs list the title as "Damsel, Damsel." Introduced in *Paranoia* by Newbold Noyes and Rufus F. King. Introduced in *See America First* by Dorothie Bigelow and John Goldsworthy.

VERSE

HE: Let's pretend we lived of old
In some early Louis' reign.
SHE: You're Sir Floris, hight "The Bold,"
I'm yclept Fair Yglavaine.
HE: Far below your casement high
I conduct my nightly wooing.
SHE: I have more than half an eye
To observe what you are doing.
HE: In the tongue of fair Provence
I implore your condescension.
SHE: My apparent nonchalance
Need not cause you apprehension.
HE: As I strum my sweet citole,
Hear this outburst of my soul:

REFRAIN 1

HE: Damsel, damsel, dainty little damsel,
Won't you come crusading with me?
I've a palfrey, waiting all free,
Champing at the bit for thee.
Lily flower, leave your fragrant bower,
Lay aside your dull embroiderie.
Come put color in the Red Sea,
Come put life into the Dead Sea.
When we meet a big black paynim
You'll entice him, I shall brain 'im;
Mon joie, Saint Denis!
Won't you come crusading with me?

SHE: True love, true love,
An it list you,
Marry I should love to go
Crusading,
Escapading,
To Jerusalem or Jericho.
Leagues with you, love,
Close behind you
So, on my pillion seated,
We'll put red in the Red Sea,
We'll put life in the Dead Sea.
Foes will bellow, when you yell oh!
Mon joie, Saint Denis!
I shall go crusading with thee.

Version used in SEE AMERICA FIRST (1916)

VERSE 1

CECIL: Let's pretend we lived of old
In some early Louis' reign.
POLLY: You're Sir Floris, hight the Bold,
I'm yclept Fayr Yglavaine.
HE: Far below your casement high
I conduct my knightly wooing.
SHE: I have more than half an eye
To observe what you are doing.
HE: In the tongue of fair Provence
I implore your condescension.
SHE: My apparent nonchalance
Needn't cause you apprehension.
HE: As I strum my sweet citole
Hear this outburst of my soul:

REFRAIN 1

HE: Damsel, damsel, dainty little damsel,
Won't you come crusading with me?
SHE: Marry, I should love to go crusading.
HE: I've a palfrey, waiting all free,
Champing at the bit for thee.
SHE: Tirra, lirra, lirra!
HE: Lily flower, leave your fragrant bower,
Lay aside your dull embroideree.
SHE: What! my pretty dull embroideree?
HE: Come add color to the Red Sea.
SHE: To the Red Sea.
HE: Come put life into the Dead Sea.
SHE: In the Dead Sea.
HE: When we meet a big black paynim
You'll entice him, I shall brain 'im
Mon joie, Saint Denis
Won't you come crusading with me?

VERSE 2

POLLY: And I may not say thee nay,
Let's be wed on Whit-sun-feast.
CECIL: In a gothic minster gray
By a most imposing priest!
POLLY: In my sire's tusseted pile
On a dais proudly seated.
CECIL: Thou shalt smile a stained-glass smile,
As with cheers thou art greeted.
POLLY: Then the moments I shall count
Till the feasters we've eluded.
CECIL: Ah, behold each trusty mount
At the postern gate secluded.
POLLY: As we swiftly ride away,
I shall chant this rondelay—

REFRAIN 2

POLLY: True love! True love, summer skies are blue love,
As I go crusading with thee.
CECIL: Marry! 'Tis a joy to go crusading,
POLLY: Larks are trilling, [*illegible*] is shrilling,
Hark their merry minstrelsy.
CECIL: Tirra, lirra, lirra,
POLLY: True love, true love, let us bill and coo love
All the way to sunny Arabie.
CECIL: All aboard for sunny Arabie.
POLLY: We'll add color to the Red Sea.
CECIL: To the Red Sea.
POLLY: We'll put life into the Dead Sea!
CECIL: In the Dead Sea!
POLLY: When we meet a big black paynim
I'll entice him,
Thou shalt brain 'im
Mon joie, Saint Denis
Thus, I'll go crusading with thee!

I WANT TO ROW ON THE CREW

Published under the title "The Crew Song" in *Songs of Yale.* Introduced in *Paranoia* by Newbold Noyes.

VERSE

Now when Willie was still an obtuse Montessori-an,
Having heard of Yale victories early Victorian,
He was mad to show oarsmanship ichthyosaurian,
On the Yale University Crew.
What a "Bright College Years" thing to do!
Though his mother regarded his scheme as chimerical,
And referred to his prospects in accents satirical,
Little Willie would chant in apostrophes lyrical
To the Yale University Crew.
Swing, swing, together!
In a voice that might rival Apollo's,
He expressed his intentions as follows:

REFRAIN

I want to row on the crew, Mama.
That's the thing I want to do, Mama.
To be known throughout Yale when I walk about it,
Get a boil on my tail and then talk about it.
I want to be a big bloke, Mama,
And learn that new Argentine stroke, Mama.
You'll see your slim son putting crimps in the crimson,
When I row on the (Brek-ek-co-ax-co-ax
Brek-ek-co-ax-co-ax Parabalou)
When I row on the Varsity Crew.

WHAT LOVE IS

Introduced by Hay Langenheim. No music survives.

Love is a pure and purple fire.
Love is the crown of wan desire.
Love is the bloom of tomorrow.
Love is an ivory sorrow.
Love is the glint in beryl eyes.

Love is the musk of fragrant sighs.
Love is a velvet paradise.
Love is the lotus of life.
Ah! Ah!
Love is the lotus of life!

DOWN IN A DUNGEON DEEP

Introduced by ensemble. No music survives.

Down in a dungeon deep!
Down in a dungeon deep!
Down where the light of day ne'er approaches,
Down with the bats and the rats and the roaches,
Down in a dungeon deep!
Down in a dungeon deep!

SLOW SINKS THE SUN

Published February 1916. Also intended for *See America First*, but dropped from that show before the New York opening. Introduced in *Paranoia* by ensemble. The music parodies Claude Debussy's Prelude to *The Afternoon of a Faun*.

Slow sinks the sun like a big Bunsen burner,
Rather suggestive of something by Turner.
Purple the sea as the Lago di Como,
Trying to look like a postal-card chromo.
Lo! The moon's horn that you read about in Burns
Wakes the brown nightingale sweeter than Swinburne's.
Zephyrs that sway the tall cypresses, you see,
Murmur whole tones in the mode of Debussy:
Midsummer nights—when your years are but twenty—
Provide the perfection of dolce far niente.
Slow sinks the sun like a big Bunsen burner,
Rather suggestive of something by Turner.
Purple the sea as the Lago di Como,
Trying to look like a postal-card chromo.
Lo! The moon's horn that you read about in Burns
Wakes the brown nightingale sweeter than Swinburne's,
Swinburne's,
A. C. Swinburne's!

THE PREP SCHOOL WIDOW

Introduced by Rufus F. King. No music survives.

VERSE

In counting up celebrities,
From Michigan to Hebrides,
The college widow always is included.
You'll find her at Decennial—
She's what you might call perennial—
And freshmen love her just as much as you did.
I find that school boys offer more
Than many a college sophomore,
Their tender hearts I'm almost always catching.
In me, a youth's precocity arouses no animosity,
Though horrid people call it cradle snatching!

REFRAIN 1

I loved a boy from Groton
And he gave me quite an awful thrill,
And when over this I'd gotten,
I'd a terrible affair at Hill.
Then I found a youth at Hotchkiss
With an, oh! such a very butterscotch kiss;
And I must confess they loved me more or less—
These prep school boys.

REFRAIN 2

I loved a boy at Pomfret.
"Now he's mine. Ha, ha, ha, ha," I laughed.
But it made my pop and mom fret,
So I chucked him for a chap from Taft.
And if ever I'm a spinster,
Well, you can't blame that fellow from Westminster.
For I must confess they loved me more or less—
These prep school boys.

PATTER

I loved a boy from Groton
And when weary of that I'd gotten,
I'd a dramatical, rather ecstatical time at Hill.
Then I found a youth at Hotchkiss,
With a more or less butterscotch kiss
And a sensational, quite educational kind of a thrill.
Then I tried a lad at Pomfret,
But his methods made my pop and mom fret.
So when they chided, I quickly decided to end his joys.
Though that Taft fellow made me within stir

Since I went to the play at Westminster,
Well, there is little I haven't seen of prep school boys.

IDYLL

Introduced by Hay Langenheim. No music survives. It appears to be an early version of "Love Came and Crowned Me," intended for *See America First.*

Still do I mind me
How love did start.
Lone did he find me
Dreaming apart,
Left hope to bind me—
Ah, how I mind me
When we did part.
Nay, peace, weary, weary heart!

Trust thou and let not
Doubtings arise;
Love and forget not
Vows in his eyes.
Tears—oh, regret not,
Shed them but let not
Fear cloud thy skies,
For hope never, never dies.

I'VE A SHOOTING BOX IN SCOTLAND

Published February 1916. This was the first Porter song to have a commercial recording (Joseph C. Smith and his orchestra recorded it). Introduced in *Paranoia* by Newbold Noyes and Rufus F. King. Appeared with revised lyric in *See America First,* where it was presented by Dorothie Bigelow and John Goldsworthy. The parody version was recalled by Porter's friend Lieutenant Colonel Sir Rex Benson, who enclosed a copy of it in a letter to Yale University Librarian James T. Babb (November 2, 1967). Dorothie Bigelow, confirming Benson's recollection, said that Porter often humorously referred to the song as "Shooting Pains in Scotland."

VERSE 1

Nowadays it's rather nobby
To regard one's private hobby
As the object of one's tenderest affections;
Some excel at Alpine climbing,
Others have a turn for rhyming,
While a lot of people go in for collections.

Such as prints by Hiroshigi,
Edelweiss from off the Rigi,
Jacobean soup tureens,
Early types of limousines,
Pipes constructed from a dry cob,
Baseball hits by Mister Ty Cobb,*
Locks of Missus Browning's hair,
Photographs of Ina Claire,
First editions still uncut,
Daily pranks of Jeff and Mutt,
Della Robbia singing boys,
Signatures of Alfred Noyes,
Fancy bantams,
Grecian vases,
Tropic beetles,
Irish laces,
But my favorite pastime
Is collecting country places.

REFRAIN 1

I've a shooting box in Scotland,
I've a château in Touraine,
I've a silly little chalet
In the Interlaken Valley,
I've a hacienda in Spain,
I've a private fjord in Norway,
I've a villa close to Rome,
And in traveling
It's really quite a comfort to know
That you're never far from home!

VERSE 2

Now it's really very funny
What an awful lot of money
On exorbitant hotels a chap can squander;
But I never have to do so,
Like resourceful Mister Crusoe,
I can find a home however far I wander.

REFRAIN 2

I've a bungalow at Simla,
I've an island east of Maine,
If you care for hotter places,
I've an African oasis
On an uninhabited plain;
I've a houseboat on the Yangtse,
I've an igloo up at Nome,
Yes, in traveling

**Original version:*
Priceless sets of Pepys and Evelyn, Footballs kicked by Tommy Shevlin.

It's really quite a comfort to know
That you're never far from home!

VERSE 3

Having lots of idle leisure
I pursue a life of pleasure,
Like a rolling stone in constant agitation
For tho' stay-at-homes may cavil,
I admit I'd rather travel,
Than collect a crop of mossy vegetation!

REFRAIN 3

I've a shanty in the Rockies,
I've a castle on the Rhine,
I've a Siamese pagoda,
I've a cottage in Fashoda,
Near the equatorial line!
On my sable farm in Russia
O'er the barren steppes we'll roam,
And in traveling,
It's really quite a comfort to know
That you're never far from home.

Parody

I've had shooting pains in Scotland,
I've had measles in Touraine,
I've had horrible malaria
When going through Bavaria
That suddenly turned to ptomaine;
I've had Bright's disease in Denmark,
I've had whooping cough in Rome,
But when traveling the Continent
It's pleasant to know
That there's leprosy at home.

DOWN LOVERS' LANE

Introduced by ensemble. No music survives.

VERSE

MAIDENS: Every summery night,
'Neath the loony moonlight,
We appear in the park,
Quite prepared for a lark.
Don't receive any wrong impression,
We are ladies of strong discretion;
But we'd rather go out and tramp,
Though they tell us the nights are damp,
Than remain by the parlor lamp,
Sticking around like a postage stamp.

REFRAIN 1

MAIDENS: We're suitably attired tonight,
We think we'd be inspired tonight,
Were we to be admired tonight
By quite the proper swain.
We're not inclined to balk tonight,
If any one should talk tonight
About a little walk tonight
Down lovers' lane.

REFRAIN 2

SOLDIERS: As Cupid's students
We won't be too dense;
Shyness and prudence
Proffer no gain.
Don't stop to ponder,
Come, let us wander,
Way, way down yonder,
Down lovers' lane.

THE LANGUAGE OF FLOWERS

Published February 1916. "Flower Song" in *Paranoia*, introduced by Stoddard King and Percival Dodge, became "The Language of Flowers" in *See America First*, where it was sung by Clifton Webb and Jeanne Cartier.

VERSE 1

HE: Lovers are a funny lot
When they deal in conversation.
SHE: Language doesn't help a jot
To express infatuation.
HE: Winking is an old device
When to talk you are unable.
SHE: Kicking isn't quite so nice
'Neath an unsuspecting table.
HE: An inverted stamp on a billet-doux
May be more than half the letter;
SHE: But we don't much care what the silly do,
We shall go them all one better.
BOTH: The code that is ours is the language of the flowers:

REFRAIN

HE: Hyacinth and violet,
SHE: Marigold and mignonette.

HE: Lily of the valley, eglantine!
SHE: Canterbury bell and columbine!
HE: Peony and hollyhock.
SHE: Clematis and four-o'clock?
HE: Lady slipper, larkspur, feverfew!
SHE: Honeysuckle, aster, phlox and rue!
HE: Cyclamen, azalea.
SHE: Heliotrope and dahlia.
HE: Daffodilly.
SHE: Pansy.
HE: Tiger lily.
SHE: Tansy.
HE: That's how I love you, dear!
SHE: That's how I say I love you!
BOTH: That's how I love you, dear.

VERSE 2

SHE: Fond ones in dejection drift
When relentless fate divides them.
HE: Postcards are a sorry shift,
As you find when you have tried them.
SHE: Danger in a letter lies
If a lady chance to lose it.
HE: Scandal will at once arise
If an eye profane peruse it.
SHE: When a tender thought I convey to you
I shall write in floral fashion.
HE: Not a soul shall know what I say to you
If a nosegay tells my passion.
BOTH: A secret of ours is the language of flowers.

DRESDEN CHINA SOLDIERS

Introduced by William S. Innis and ensemble. No music survives.

SOLO: I'm the Gen.
I'm the Gen.
I'm the General.
CHORUS: We're his men,
We're his men,
At his beck and call.
SOLO: I'm a Hanni-
I'm a Hanni-
I'm a Hannibal at scheming.
CHORUS: He's uncanny,
He's uncanny,
When Bellona starts a-screaming.
SOLO: At the fighting game
I've a lot of fame,
And I've never been defeated.
CHORUS: At the warrior's art
He's a Bonaparte,
So he's more or less conceited.
SOLO: I am always covered o'er
With coagulated gore,
When I struggle from the battlefield of glory.
CHORUS: He is really such a Mars,
That his catalogue of scars
Would be longer than the new De Morgan story.
SOLO: Attention!
Present arms!
Drill!
CHORUS: Shall we drill?
Shall we drill?
Shall we go through a dressy little drill?
Let us drill. Let us drill.
Let us go through a dressy little drill.

REFRAIN

We are Dresden china soldiers,
Ballroom pirates in disguise.
With all our skill and fitness,
We've no desire to witness
The whites of the enemy's eyes.
We don't care for bloody battle,
War is hell we all agree.
The type of man we class a cur
Is one that likes to massacre,
For Dresden china soldiers are we.

NAUGHTY, NAUGHTY

Introduced by ensemble. No music survives.

Oh, what terrible suspense,
Like a shock of electricity,
Makes the atmosphere intense,
Shattering our domesticity.
Slapdash, horrible to say,
Plans an absolute dictatorship.
We would try to sail away
If we could only locate a ship.
Where is that competent young man,
In this, our unforeseen emergency?
He will protect us if he can
From totally depraved insurgency.
What's that?
Can it be Cyril?
Has he conquered?
Brek-ek-ke-kex
Coax-coax

O-op, O-op
Parabalou Yale
Cyril, Cyril, Cyril!

SOLO: Your majesty, here are the traitors.
CHORUS: Naughty, naughty, fie for shame!
Badness hurts you when you play with it,
Those whose conduct merits blame
Very seldom get away with it.
Since your actions are amiss,
We express contempt like this—
Hiss, hiss, hiss, hiss, hiss, hiss, hiss,
Hiss!

HAIL TO CYRIL

Introduced by ensemble. No music survives.

Hail, hail to Cyril,
Unconquerable king!
Hail, hail to Vodka,
Her praises loudly sing!
Hail to the monarchs both,
Ne'er be their sway despotic.
Hail to their royal troth,
In greetings polyglotic.
CHAIRE! CHAIRE! CHAIRE!
EVVIVA!
HOCH!
HAIL!

WE'RE ALL DRESSED UP AND WE DON'T KNOW HUERTO GO, 1914

Produced by members of the Yale University Dramatic Association at the Hotel Gibson, Cincinnati, May 22, 1914, for the annual dinner of the Associated Western Yale Clubs. The songs, with the exception of "Cincinnati," are unknown and presumed lost.

CINCINNATI

The lyric was recalled by Johnfritz Achelis. The music had been preserved by Clifford Wright.

VERSE

There's a place that I want to G-O
On the banks of the O-H-I-O.
What's the name of the C-I-T-Y?
C-I-N, C-I-N, N-A-T-I.
Let's go off for a T-R-I-P
'Neath the flag that is B-L-U-E,
To the town that is not D-R-Y,
C-I-N, C-I-N, N-A-T-I.
There you'll probably S double E
Every drunken old G-R-A-D,
Get it way up his N-O-S-E.
S-O-S, P-D-Q, R-S-V-P.

REFRAIN

In Cincinnati, in Cincinnati,
From hill and dale
Gathers Yale
To develop tissue fatty,
On the beer here, beer there, beer everywhere,
Flowing from the fountain in the public square.
In Cincinnati, in Cincinnati,
The way they sing,
Everything
Would make Adelina Patti
Give the kitchen stove and the derby of brown
To that Ohio town.

Porter wrote many other songs as a Yale undergraduate for which music and lyrics are lost. The titles of some of Porter's Yale songs are known and include "Perfectly Terrible," "Mercy Percy," "No Show This Evening," "Music with Meals," and "The Talk You Hear at the Prom." Porter also wrote a Class of 1913 song for his first reunion in 1914, but no copy has come to light. A few of Porter's classmates from his senior society, Scroll and Key, have told this editor that Porter wrote at least one song for the society. But members of Scroll and Key, who have searched the society's records, have failed to turn up a copy.

CRAIGIE 404

Porter roomed at 404 Craigie during his year at the Harvard Law School, 1913 to 1914. Music survives.

In four-o-four
On the second floor
Lives a crazy Craigie crowd.
They play all day,
All night they play.

No work is there allowed.
Away with law.
It's an awful bore
Their war cry rings out clear.

(Lyric breaks off here.)

SEE AMERICA FIRST

1916

Tryout: Van Curler Opera House, Schenectady, New York, February 22, 1916; Harmanus Bleecker Hall, Albany, New York, February 24, 1916; Lyceum Theatre, Rochester, New York, February 28, 1916; Shubert Theatre, New Haven, Connecticut, March 22, 1916; Grand Opera House, Providence, Rhode Island, March 23, 1916. Produced by Miss Elisabeth Marbury at the Maxine Elliott Theatre, New York, March 28, 1916. 15 performances. A comic opera with book, music, and lyrics by T. Lawrason Riggs and Cole Porter. Staged by Benrimo. Cast, starring Dorothie Bigelow and John Goldsworthy, included Clifton Webb, Jeanne Cartier, Clara Palmer, Sam Edwards, and Felix Adler.

This editor spent more time locating and organizing lyrics, music, programs, reviews, and other information for *See America First* than for any other Porter musical. Porter gave portions of the piano-vocal score (his manuscript) to the Music Division of the Library of Congress. Other material from the show was part of his bequest to Yale.

When I examined the Yale manuscripts in the spring and summer of 1966, I found them in considerable disarray. The manuscripts were scattered about, and often in no particular order. A special problem involved separating out manuscript material from *The Pot of Gold* which had been included among the *See America First* manuscripts. The most frequently encountered and vexing problem was reassembling songs. A twenty-page manuscript, for example, might have been dismantled into bits and pieces, each only one or two pages long.

After reconstructing all the Yale material, I still found that a number of pages were missing from several manuscripts. This problem was largely solved by comparing the Yale material with the manuscripts at the Library of Congress. In a number of instances, complete songs were reconstructed by bringing together the segments from each collection. For example, pages 1–4 of a song might be at Yale, pages 5–8 at the Library of Congress, pages 9–12 at Yale, and so on.

Fortunately, the combined material of the two libraries led to the reassembling of an almost complete score of *See America First.*

Certain numbers are still missing and presumed lost, including "Dawn Music" and "Woodland Dance" (neither of which had lyrics), "Serenade" (unless it is an alternate title of another number), "Bichloride of Mercury," "Wake, Love, Wake," and "Finale, Act II." "Will You Love Me When My Flivver Is a Wreck?" was probably not written by Porter. It, too, is missing.

All manuscript material has been copied and put in order. It can be examined at the Cole Porter Trusts office.

See America First went through many changes between its completion in the autumn of 1915 and its New York opening. Most of the score was composed during the summer of 1915 at Riggs's family home in New London, Connecticut. The programs, gathered over a three-year period, help chart the changes in the score, which were more extensive than for any other Porter musical. But, as theater historians know, program lists are not always complete, accurate, or up to date.

In presenting the lyrics of *See America First* in this collection, I have departed from my usual practice of listing them in the show's running order. What I have tried to do is reconstruct as closely as possible the original sequence of numbers. When one number was deleted in favor of a second or even a third, I have attempted to put the two or three together. However, lyrics written originally for *The Pot of Gold* ("When I Used to Lead the Ballet") and *Paranoia* ("Prithee, Come Crusading with Me," "Slow Sinks the Sun," "I've a Shooting Box in Scotland," and "The Language of Flowers") will be found in this collection with the lyrics for the shows in which they were first performed. It is interesting to note that five of *See America First*'s thirteen published songs had been written for earlier productions.

BADMEN

The original opening chorus. Manuscript in the Music Division of the Library of Congress. Introduced by ensemble. No. 1 in the original sequence.

TENORS: A thoro'ly roaring reckless lot in us
you see.
We're everything that you would not
desire to be.
All moral maxims we defy.
We gamble, swear and guzzle rye.
We are the pink of impropriety-ety-ety.

BASSES: Ha-ha! Ho-ho! What very wild oats we
sow.
Ho-ho! Ha-ha! What terrible brutes we
are.
Unheeding possible dangers,
We plunder innocent strangers.
Ha-ha! Ho-ho! Ha-ha! Ho-ho! Ha-ha!

TENORS
& BASSES: Badmen, badmen, picturesquely clad
men.
Badmen, badmen, dangerous as
madmen.
Badmen, badmen, the world has
seldom had men
So likely to hurt you,
So void of all virtue as we.
The very pink of impropriety are we.

YOUNGER SONS OF PEERS

This number, the Revelation Chorus of Badmen, might have been the second part of the original opening chorus. Manuscript at the Library of Congress. It might have been deleted before the New York opening. No. 2 in the original sequence.

We've a little secret to confess to you.
What we've been asserting isn't strictly true.
Don't be disappointed when you hear us say
That we are late arrivals in the U.S.A.
Don't be too surprised
When we say we're aristocracy disguised.
Please believe your ears
When we tell you we are younger sons of peers,
Sons of houses dated
From medieval years.
In Burke you'll find us rated
As younger sons of peers.
We're second, third, fourth, fifth, sixth, seventh,
Eighth, nine sons of peerless peers.
We're younger sons of England's most eminent
peers,
Younger sons of English peers,
Younger sons of English peers.
Three cheers!

GREETINGS, GENTLEMEN

This is almost certainly the recitative of "To Follow Every Fancy." Manuscript in Porter Collection at Yale. Not listed in the New York program. No. 3 in the original sequence.

CECIL: Greetings, gentlemen,
MEN: 'Tis Cecil! Let us maintain a dignified
reserve.
CECIL: It is a splendid morning, you will note.
MEN: We had not noted. No doubt it is.
CECIL: The birds are singing merrily.
MEN: Merely because they persist in ignoring
life's tragedy.
CECIL: The view could scarcely be surpassed!
MEN: Possibly not.
CECIL: Come, come! Your singular
unresponsiveness
Forces my unwilling attention.
MEN: That was exactly what we wanted.
CECIL: Patience! Courage!
I've done my best to help you make your
fortunes
Here, in this great unmoral, untrammeled,
Unmanicured West.
Tho' we may not be surrounded by the
luxuries
Of an effete civilization,
Yet at least we are free, free, free
To follow ev'ry fancy that occurs to us.

TO FOLLOW EVERY FANCY

Manuscript at the Library of Congress. No. 4 of original sequence. Introduced in New York by John Goldsworthy and ensemble.

VERSE 1

My childhood's happy hours were spent in ducal
towers
Midst luxuries that seemed almost absurd to me.
My noble parents tried to keep me satisfied,
In whims and peccadillos they deferred to me.
When I became a duke, 'twas not without rebuke,
For the bally party leader said, "My word!" to me.
That I left the House of Lords and all that it
affords
To follow ev'ry fancy that occurred to me.

REFRAINS 1 AND 2

To follow, follow, follow,
O'er hillock and o'er hollow,
O'er continents and oceans,
In search of new emotions,
He left the House of Lords and all that it affords
To follow ev'ry fancy that occurred to he.

VERSE 2

I toyed with winter sports in crowded Swiss
resorts
Where medal-covered skiers had to yield to me.
Those Monte Carlo chaps beheld their bank
collapse
When louis' by the wagonload were wheeled to
me.
I led exploring bands thru hot Brazilian lands
Where highly doubtful rivers were revealed to
me.
I roamed this earthly ball, the victim of a call
To follow ev'ry fancy that appealed to me.

VERSE 3

One afternoon I met these fellows of my set
And rather tough conditions they had lit upon,
For younger sons are poor by primogeniture,
They have no seats manorial to sit upon,
And so, I thought it best to lead them to the
West
To quite a peerless place, if you'll permit a pun.
But now, to my dismay, they find it doesn't
pay
To follow ev'ry fancy that I hit upon.

REFRAIN 3

To follow, follow, follow,
O'er hillock and o'er hollow,
Thru sundry tribes and nations,
In search of new sensations,
He roamed this earthly ball,
A victim of the call
To follow ev'ry fancy that appealed to *him.*

SEE AMERICA FIRST

Second version published March 1916. No. 5 in the original sequence. Act I, No. 8 in New York program. Manuscript at the Library of Congress and Yale. Introduced in New York by Sam Edwards.

Version 1

Of European lands effete,
A most inveterate foe,
My feelings when my camp I greet
Are such as patriots know.
Condemning trips across the blue
As dollars badly dispersed,
I hold that loyal men and true,
Including in the category all of you,
Should see America first,
Should see America first.

All hail salubrious sky,
All hail salubrious sky.
Observe when I invoke the sky
It echoes reassuringly
That one should try to see America first,
To see America first.

Of course, it's really not the sky,
But just a repetition of his battle cry,
To see America first,
To see America first,

. . .

So ev'ry true American,
Whether white or red or black or tan,
Should push this patriotic plan
To see America first.

This version was discarded and an entirely new title song was substituted, one with a distinctly Cohanesque quality.

Version 2 (published)

VERSE

HUGGINS: Of the sturdy Middle West I am the
patriotic cream,
I'm the enemy of European Kings,
On the slightest provocation I can make
the eagle scream,
When the Senate to my oratory rings.
BADMEN: He can talk for a week—
When he once starts to speak!
HUGGINS: And I've thundered many times
That a trip to foreign climes
Is a thing no true American will seek.

REFRAIN

Don't leave America,
Just stick around the U.S.A.
Cheer for America
And get that grand old strain of Yankee Doodle
In your noodle;
Yell for America,
Altho' your vocal cords may burst;
And if you ever take an outing,
Leave the station shouting:
"See America First!"

WELL, IT'S GOOD TO BE HERE AGAIN

This soliloquy preceded the "Hold-up Ensemble," but might have been deleted before the New York opening. Manuscript at the Library of Congress. No. 6 in the original sequence.

Well, it's good to be here again,
Miles away from any human being,
Alone in the silent forest.
I'm getting sleepy.
It must be the altitude.

HOLD-UP ENSEMBLE

Manuscript at the Library of Congress and Yale. No. 7 in the original sequence, also No. 7 in Act I of the New York production. Introduced by John Goldsworthy, Sam Edwards, Clara Palmer, and ensemble. No. 8 in the original sequence was "The Language of Flowers" (see *Paranoia*, 1914). In New York it was Act I, No. 9.

BADMEN: Up with your hands, do not attempt resistance.
Up with your hands, you're far from all assistance.
Something stirred, it must have been a bird.
Up with your hands, no further hesitation.
Up with your hands or suffer perforation.
HUGGINS: Mercy me, some little buzzing bee.
BADMEN: Up with your hands, up with your hands,
Up with your hands, up with your hands,
Up with your up with your hands,
Up with your up with your hands.

SARAH: Desist, forbear, refrain,
Release your portly victim.
I will not see him slain
Tho' foully you have tricked him.
Was ever man so handsome
In such distressful woe?
Oh, let me be his ransom
Because I love him so,
I love him so.
HUGGINS: She loves me so.

SARAH: I love him with a passion so intense,
So poetic, energetic and immense,
So amusingly exotic,
So confusingly chaotic,
That it's quite beyond the bounds of common sense.

CECIL: Fair lady, hark to me
Without an introduction.
In rules of chivalry
I do not need instruction,
For tho' our sense of duty
Be shady now and then,
We yield to pleading beauty
Like Nature's gentlemen,
Like Nature's gentlemen.
HUGGINS: Like Nature's gentlemen.

BADMEN: This is very sensational.
This is very sensational.
And to listen to the ravings of a love like this
Is truly educational.
What idyllic simplicity!
What idyllic simplicity!
To conduct a highly intimate affair like this
With such appalling publicity.
This is very embarrassing.
This is very embarrassing.
Tho' some deem it delectable
It's our personal opinion
That a scene like this
Cannot be wholly respectable.

Moral inclinations, when we're suddenly confronted
With rhetorical effusion on the duties of a
Gentleman, are far from being respectable.
This is very sensational.
This is very sensational.
A rhetorical effusion from a man like this
Is truly educational.
What idyllic simplicity!
What idyllic simplicity!
Such apologetic polish in an age like this
Deserves the widest publicity.
This is very embarrassing.
This is very embarrassing.
Tho' some deem us delectable,
Tho' some deem us delectable,
Yet our personal opinion is
That a scene like this
Cannot be wholly respectable.

Moral inclinations, when we're suddenly confronted
With rhetorical effusion on the duties of a
Gentleman, are far from being respectable.

ENTRANCE OF INDIAN MAIDENS

Manuscript at the Library of Congress. No. 9 in the original sequence. This might be the number titled "Indian Girls' Chant" listed in New York program as Act I, No. 1b.

Indian maidens slouching o'er the hills and plains,
Nature's children undisturbed by lack of brains,

Stalking frisky fauna through the craggy rocks,
Dressed in brownish out-of-townish buckskin
frocks,
In the campfire's trying tho' romantic glare,
Munching juicy haunches of the grizzly bear.
Swaying in this simple but effective dance,
Singing slowly melancholy tribal chants.
Tribal chants,
Tribal chants,
Singing slowly melancholy chants.
Onandaga
Lackawanna
Oneonta
Ticonderoga
Canandaigua
Tonawanda
Geneseo
Tuscarora
Oneida
Oswego
Chautauqua.

IF IN SPITE OF OUR ATTEMPTS

Manuscript at Yale. This might be the "Indian Maidens' Chorus" listed as Act I, No. 3 in the New York program. No. 10 in the original sequence.

If in spite of our attempts
You have all surmised
That for Indian maids
We seem rather civilized,
Yet we beg you let politeness rule
And refrain from vulgar ridicule
Of our highly novel training school,
Of our most exclusive training school,
For tho' Indian lingo we repeat
In a quite realistic way,
Nonetheless we come from towns effete,
Where our mothers' rule the top elite
With a cold autocratic sway,
With a cold autocratic sway.
So we'll each appear as a bud next year
In the social garden gay.

So if in spite of our attempts
You have all surmised
That for Indian maids
We seem rather civilized,
Yet we beg you let politeness rule
And refrain from vulgar ridicule
Of our highly novel most exclusive school,
Our summer training school,
Our school that's highly novel,
Our school that's most exclusive,
Our unprecedented training school.

THE SOCIAL COACH OF ALL THE FASHIONABLE FUTURE DEBUTANTES

Manuscript at Yale. Probably intended to follow "If in Spite of Our Attempts," but dropped and replaced by "Something's Got to Be Done" before the show went into production. Almost certainly No. 11 in the original sequence.

Since first I left my native France
About a dozen years ago
As social coach for debutantes
I've run a thriving business.
When somebody suggested it
I cried, "Sapristi, here's a go!"
Since then my yearly profit
Makes me totter with a dizziness divine.
In educating ingenues I've famous ingenuity.
Each year a host of fond mammas
Endeavor to enlist their girls
But if they haven't beauty, birth and wealth in
superfluity
I stubbornly refuse their supplications
To assist their girls to shine.

CHORUS: Such a thriving business
Staggers her with dizziness.
Wealth in superfluity
Proves her ingenuity.
We're the illustrations of her altogether
pardonable vaunts
And she's the social coach of all the
fashionable future debutantes.

SOMETHING'S GOT TO BE DONE

Published February 1916. Manuscript at Yale. No. 12 in the original sequence. Act I, No. 4 in the New York production. Introduced by Felix Adler and Clara Palmer.

PART 1

BLOOD-IN-HIS-EYE: The girl who "comes out"
Requires, no doubt,
Far more than a lot of dresses;
It's perfectly plain
If she would attain
Society's chief successes,
MAIDENS: Something's got to be done!
Something's got to be done!
BLOOD: On cutting a dash
And making a splash
Each innocent has her heart set
But finds as a rule,
That lessons in school
Don't help her to meet the smart set.
MAIDENS: So something's got to be done!
BLOOD: Something's got to be done!
Supposing your daughter possesses a mind
Devoted to Browning with passion refined.
To stifle regrettable tastes of the kind
MAIDENS: Something's got to be done!
BLOOD: Or say she wears spectacles perched on her nose,
Would rather see Ibsen than musical shows,
To lectures on Maeterlinck eagerly goes,
MAIDENS: Something's got to be done!
BLOOD: For daughters enamour'd with lore astronomical,
Classic philology, social research,
Among the Four Hundred appear rather comical,
Terribly prone to be left in the lurch!
Tho' they may revel in Byzantine art,
Know all the sonnets of Shelley by heart,
Learning is trash in the marital mart.
MAIDENS: Something's got to be done!
ALL: Something's got to be done!
Something's got to be done on the spot!
Something's got to be, got to be, got to be done!

PART 2

BLOOD: If daughter appears
To envy careers
Of "love in a cottage" blisses,
Would walk on the air
With no better fare
Than crackers and cheese and kisses,
MAIDENS: What on earth can be done?
BLOOD: What on earth can be done?
Endeavor with haste
To foster a taste
For truffles and hothouse peaches.
Show money's to burn
By letting her learn
How charming a place Palm Beach is.
MAIDENS: That's what's got to be done.
BLOOD: That's what's got to be done.
If Alice a love for the fireside shows
And beats a piano so Grandma can doze,
And often forgets to put powder on nose,
MAIDENS: What on earth can be done?
BLOOD: Her nature domestic she'll have to conceal,
At marathon dances no weariness feel,
Nor look upon home as a place for a meal.
MAIDENS: That's what's got to be done!
BLOOD: A damsel adapted to ways of modernity
Never should marry a miserly Scrooge.
Tho' Hubby inherit, or steal it, or earn it,
He must have an income incredibly huge,
Who's to make sure that she's perfectly clad?
Who'll pay the bill if her "Auction" is bad?
Surely she can't put it all up to Dad.
MAIDENS: Something's got to be done!
ALL: Something's got to be done!
Something's got to be done on the spot!
Something's got to be, got to be, got to be done!

PITY ME, PLEASE

Published February 1916. Manuscript at Yale. No. 13 in the original sequence. Dropped just before the New York opening. Sung on pre-Broadway tour by Dorothie Bigelow and ensemble. Replaced in the show by "I've Got an Awful Lot to Learn."

VERSE 1

Now when I was an infant exceedingly young
I heard "God Save the King" so impressively sung
That my sensitive soul was incurably stung
By the microbe of Anglomania.

. . .

I began saying Hyde when I meant Central Park
And I strolled into Macy's and called for a clark
And when people said "Punch" was composed in the ark
It offended my Anglomania.

REFRAIN 1

Pity me, pity me, pity me, please,
Hopelessly cursed with this mental disease,
Waiting in vain for a trip overseas,
Pity me, pity me, pity me, please,
Longing for dear old London.

VERSE 2

Now the climax occurred on an Arkansas train
When I tried to book luggage but had to explain
Till the dear old pater was almost profane
At my virulent Anglomania.

So a journey to England he never allows
But a love for the West he attempts to arouse
While I'm yearning for Mayfair and Ascot and Cowes
With unsatisfied Anglomania.

REFRAIN 2

Pity me, pity me, pity me, please,
Bored by the hopeless profusion of trees,
Bored by the mountains and bored by the breeze,
Pity me, pity me, pity me, please,
Longing for dear old London.

I'VE GOT AN AWFUL LOT TO LEARN

Published March 1916. Act I, No. 5 in the New York production. Added to show in place of "Pity Me, Please" just prior to the New York opening. Introduced by Dorothie Bigelow and ensemble.

VERSE

POLLY: Hello, girls! How d'ye do?
MAIDENS: This is such a pleasant shock, dear!
POLLY: Hello, girls! How are you?
MAIDENS: What a fascinating frock, dear!
POLLY: Aren't you at lessons zealous, girls?
Aren't they the least bit slow?
Pray, can the schoolbooks tell us, girls,
All that there is to know?
MAIDENS: Oh, beauteous maiden!
You excite our grave concern,
For we fear you've got an awful lot to learn!

REFRAIN

POLLY: Yes, I've got an awful lot to learn, girls,
Oh! Such an awful lot to learn!
I'm as guileless as a dove,
And I've never been in love,
So you'll grant me
I've an awful lot to learn!

DINNER

Manuscript at Yale. No. 14 in the original sequence. Dropped just before the New York opening.

VERSE 1

When the time arrives for dinner
In this bracing mountain air
Waiving hopes of getting thinner
We attack our bill of fare.
Showy silver, costly china
From the board are absent quite
Yet we show when e'er we dine a
Most enormous appetite.
A most enormous appetite.

VERSE 2

First we're rather busy stacking
Brittle firewood free from wet.
Soon the fire starts a-cracking
In our rural kitchenette.
Hear the kettle boil and bubble
With a short asthmatic breath.
Double double toil and trouble,
Vide witches in *Macbeth,*
Vide witches in *Macbeth.*

GWENDOLIN: Someone must be sitting on the plates.
MURIEL: I hope the percolator percolates.
ETHEL: Oh, how good that flapjack looks.
MURIEL: This is just like Rex Beach's books.

Welcome, toothsome dinner,
Gastronomic winner,
Tho' we ne'er grow thinner
Than the fat Berliner.
Clothe, fateful spinner,
Grant each hungry sinner

Consolation inner
From this toothsome dinner.

Dinner dinner dinner dinner dainty dinner
Dinner dinner dinner dinner charming dinner.

HAIL, YE INDIAN MAIDENS

Manuscript at Yale. No. 15 in the original sequence. It is difficult to know whether this recitative and "Fascinating Females" were in the show along with "Beautiful, Primitive Indian Girls."

ALGERNON: Hail, ye Indian maidens.
INDIAN MAIDENS: Gracious, the badmen.
PERCY: Calm yourselves.
We are positively lamblike in the presence of the fair sex.
MAIDENS: Ah, gallant one.
MARMADUKE: My word, they're eating dinner.
At last a good square meal.
TENORS: We've had no experience in conversing with savage damsels,
But here goes.
ALTOS: We've no idea how to talk to desperadoes,
But we'll do our best.

FASCINATING FEMALES

Manuscript at Yale. Lynn Siebert feels this is a separate number and should stand on its own.

BADMEN: Ah there! Fascinating females,
Probably you'll suffer us to stay a while.
MAIDENS: Though we're terrified to see males,
Possibly we'll let you if we like your style.
TENORS: Was each of you once an entrancing papoose?
SOPRANOS: We were strapped to our mothers and couldn't get loose.
TENORS: And what were your toys in these desolate Alps?
ALTOS: We played with the palefaces' scalps.

BEAUTIFUL, PRIMITIVE INDIAN GIRLS

Manuscript at Yale. No. 16 in the original sequence. Act I, No. 6 in the New York production. Introduced by Clifton Webb, Roma June, Betty Brewster, Gypsy O'Brien, and ensemble.

BADMEN: Beautiful, primitive Indian girls.
MAIDENS: Primitive, beautiful badmen.
BADMEN: Barbarous, ravishing Western pearls.
MAIDENS: Ravishing, barbarous madmen.
BADMEN: Wonderful, terrible redskin belles.
MAIDENS: Terrible, wonderful rangers.
BOTH: Isn't it queer how politeness tells
When one gets chatty with strangers.

MAIDENS: Beautiful, primitive Indian girls
Love to eat their dinner.
BADMEN: All aboard for dinner,
Primitive, beautiful badmen.
MAIDENS: Barbarous, ravishing Western pearls
Need not get much thinner.
BADMEN: Cling to comfort inner,
Ravishing, barbarous madmen.
MAIDENS: Wonderful, terrible redskin maids.
BADMEN: Feed each hungry sinner.
MAIDENS: Seek nutrition inner.
BADMEN: Wonderful, terrible rangers.
BOTH: Isn't it queer how refreshment aids
When one gets chatty with strangers.

THE LADY I'VE VOWED TO WED

Also titled "Announcement Ensemble" and "Engagement Ensemble." Together this material comprises Nos. 17 and 18 of the original sequence. This ensemble number (manuscript at Yale and the Library of Congress) was Act 1, No. 11 in the New York program. No 19 in the original sequence, listed as "Damsel, Damsel" in the program, is also titled "Prithee, Come Crusading with Me" and "Won't You Come Crusading with Me?" (see *Paranoia*, 1914).

CHORUS: Don't talk loud,
Please don't crowd,
Enter hero to gain his prize.
Pale but proud,
Far from cowed,
Enter heroine with flashing eyes.

Hero notes the time is near
As a lump in his throat he swallows.
Heroine wipes away a tear,
Then they both speak as follows.

MAIDENS: Then they both speak as follows.
BADMEN: Then they both speak as follows.

POLLY & CECIL: I'm thoroughly perplexed,
I'm also rather vexed
At this extraordinary performance
Which is coming next.
I may be forgiven for being in
Something of a pet.
I have no essential objection
To the institution of matrimony and yet
It is a little disconcerting to be engaged
In this arbitrary manner to a person
You've never met.
If I were asked to give my opinion on this whole affair
I should regard it as a most annoying quiz,
Especially as my fiance may turn out
In spite of high moral qualities to be
Characterized by a most unattractive phiz,
Not to mention an inability to talk the English language correctly,
Deficiencies in table manners, gold teeth, a habit of
Chewing gum and—good heavens, there she (he) is.

CECIL: So you're the lady I've vowed to wed.
POLLY: I am.
CECIL: Perhaps you're sorry I'm not well bred.
POLLY: I am.
CECIL: A first impression, as you'll agree,
Is sometimes only a sham,
But you look much nicer than I thought you'd be.
POLLY: I am. I am.
MAIDENS: She am.

BADMEN: So she's the lady he's vowed to wed.
MAIDENS: She am.
BADMEN: Perhaps she's sorry he's not well bred.
MAIDENS: She am.
BADMEN: A first impression, as you'll agree,
Is sometimes only a sham,
But she looks much nicer than we thought she'd be.
MAIDENS: She am. She am.

HUGGINS: Now look and listen raptly
Before you give three cheers.
As Shakespeare puts it aptly,
Kindly lend your ears.

POLLY: My boredom is intense
At this unseemly caper.
Since Father won't talk sense,
I think I'll read the paper.

BLOOD: Tho' others might be tricked
By threats to read the paper,
I venture to predict
That nothing will escape her.

HUGGINS: Ladies and gentlemen,
POLLY: "Skirts Are Getting Wide."
"Attempted Suicide."
HUGGINS: I take great pleasure
POLLY: "Clubman Wins Divorce." "Caruso Rather Hoarse."
HUGGINS: In announcing to all of you
POLLY: "Kitten with the Rabies Snaps at Seven Babies."
HUGGINS: The engagement of my daughter to Mister Peppery.
POLLY: Father, this tyrannical proceeding must cease at once!
Look what I've found! Look what I've found!
"Victory for Women. Sensational Scenes in the
Legislature. Capitol City, July 20th.
The Governor, under threats of being tarred and
Feathered by the League for the Supremacy of Women,
Signed a bill at noon today, to take effect at once,
Forbidding any man to marry
Without the consent of his nearest female relative."

DIVIDED ENSEMBLE: His nearest what? His nearest what?
His nearest female relative!
His nearest what? His nearest what?
His nearest female relative.
Well goodness gracious sakes above,
His nearest female relative.
(He has no)
His nearest, dearest female relative.
(He has no female relative, alive.)
Now what do you think of that?
Now what do you think of that?
Now what do you think of that?
Now what do you think of that?

We never thought the moment would arrive
When a man should want a female relative.

Unless a female relative can first be found,
In fetters matrimonial
He can't be bound.
Of conjugal bliss
The drastic law will thus deprive the suitor
Who can't produce a female relative.

CECIL: Since in these conditions the law is plain
I'll vent my emotions in a lyric vein.
When first I saw you, radiant one,
Hope was born and soared to the sun,
But an infant so daring ne'er could thrive
Hurled from Fate from ether on high.
Never more exultant to fly,
Wounded hope must sicken and die,
For I have no female relative.

ENSEMBLE: He has no what? He has no what?
He has no female relative.
He has no what? He has no what?
He has no female relative.
Well, now what do you think of that?
Now what do you think of that?
Now what do you think of that?
Now what do you think of that?
However did the gentleman contrive
To be without a female relative?
Unless a female relative can first be found,
In fetters matrimonial he can't be bound.
Of conjugal bliss the drastic law will thus deprive
The suitor who can't produce a female relative,
A female relative, a relative,
For he has no female relative, alive.

FINALE, ACT I

Manuscript at Yale and the Library of Congress. No. 20 in the original sequence. There are two or more versions for this extended ensemble number and several missing pages. Some of the material at the end of the number is missing and presumed lost.

Strolling quite fancy free in maiden meditation,
Praising the beauties of this airy situation,
Ever cheery, never weary,
We have nought else to do
But contemplate the view.
So we continue in our circumambulation.
Really we think it is a harmless occupation,
Thus to stray
To and fro,
All the day
On the go.

[*Repeat against countermelody:* Ceasing *etc.*]

Ceasing for a while our course of depredation,
Leisure we beguile with careless recreation,
Singing idly, wan-d'ring widely,
We condescend
Our time to spend
Cruising like a fleet in circumnavigation,
Following our feet in aimless circulation.
And so we stray
The livelong day,
Thus to and fro
We go.

Raise the swelling chorus
As we fling before us
Tributary flowers to the female relative.
Tread the joyful measure
Welcoming our treasure,
Seldom does so bright a day of merriment arrive.
Now to joy give glad vent,
Let your rapture thrive.
Celebrate the advent
Of the relative.
Her cooperation
Saves the situation.
Nuptial celebration
They can thus contrive.

Raise the swelling chorus
O'er we fling before us
Tributary flowers to the female relative.
Tread the joyful measure
Welcoming our treasure,
Seldom does so bright a day of merriment,
Seldom does so bright a day of merriment,
Seldom does so bright a day of merriment,
Merriment merriment merriment merriment
Arrive.

MEN'S CHORUS: Shout, joyous throats
As we attend her progress festive.
Sound all the notes
Which are of jubilee suggestive.
Fate that frowned but lately
Favors lovers greatly,
So hail her who comes sedately.
The female relative.
Hail the female relative.
Hail the female relative.

. . .

SOPRANOS
& ALTOS: [*Repeat:* Raise the swelling chorus
etc.]

TENORS &
BASSES: [*Repeat:* Shout, joyous throats *etc.*]

ALL: Hoorah! Hoorah! Hooray!
SARAH: My long-lost nephew!
CECIL: My long-lost aunt!
Oh, beautiful moment of meeting
SARAH: When kin long apart are united.
CECIL: Oh, tender affectionate greeting
SARAH: When sad separation's requited.
CECIL: No pleasure more soothing you could
buy,
SARAH: Tho' monarchs with riches enfeoff you,
CECIL: Than when after bidding him goodbye
SARAH: An aunt meets her favorite nephew.
CECIL: Dear aunt that I fancied had perished.
SARAH: Dear nephew from infancy cherished.
SARAH &
CECIL: Oh, in life there's naught more gentle,
More sublimely sentimental.
You may try your best to beat it
But you can't.
SARAH: You certainly can't.
SARAH &
CECIL: For there's nothing more appealing,
More replete with tender feeling,
Than the sight of a long-lost nephew
Meeting his long-lost aunt,
Than the sight of a long-lost nephew
Meeting his long-lost aunt.

INDIAN
MAIDENS: How anguishing!
BADMEN: How emotional!
MAIDENS: How languishing!
BADMEN: How devotional!

SARAH &
CECIL: Is the sight of a long-lost nephew
Meeting his long-lost aunt.

POLLY: Now to business.
The law inspired by ladies influential
As you're aware regards it as essential
That ev'ry man on matrimony bent
Should get some female relative's
consent.
So now conforming to the regulation
Please take this pen and write at my
dictation.

POLLY &
SARAH: Since Pete would wed
That he should wed
Makes his fond aunt quite content.
Know all men now
That this pen now
Marks my full and free consent.

POLLY:	Ah————	Ah————
SARAH:	I give my consent.	I give my consent.
MAIDENS:	She gives her consent.	She gives her consent.
CECIL, HUGGINS, & BADMEN:	She gives her consent.	She gives her consent.
	She gives her consent.	She gives her consent.
POLLY:	She gives her consent.	She gives her consent.
SARAH:	I give my consent.	I give my consent.
	I give my consent.	
CECIL:	She gives her consent.	She gives her consent.

MAIDENS
& BADMEN: She gives, she gives her full
and free consent.

POLLY & MAIDENS:	She gives	She gives
	She gives	She gives
SARAH:	I give	I give
	I give	I give
CECIL:	She gives her consent.	She gives her consent.
BADMEN:	She gives her consent.	She gives her consent.

SARAH: I give, I give my consent.
ALL OTHERS: She gives, she gives her fond
consent.

MEN:	She gives her consent.	She gives her consent.
	She gives her consent	She gives her fond consent.

[*All end together on:* consent]

BLOOD: Hold, sir!
This hill contains an aunt of yours
no more than does the
Capitoline
Palatine
Esquiline
Quirinal
Or Viminal.
So your attempt at palming off this
woman is an act distinctly
Shady
Crooked
Illegal
Felonious

And criminal.
Though she were disguised in twice as many
Wigs
Chignons
Toupées
Transformations
Or Early English merkins,
My eagle eye would have no difficulty in detecting her as being
none other than Sarah Perkins.

MAIDENS: Horror! Horror! Horror!
BLOOD: I am the county sheriff sly and keen.
POLLY: Don't shout!
HUGGINS: Here's lip and cup but there's a slip between.
CECIL: No doubt!
BLOOD: I'd like to have a jail to lock you up.
POLLY: I plead!
HUGGINS: It looks as though the lip had slipped the cup.
CECIL: Indeed!
BLOOD: These little trinkets on you I shall slip.
POLLY: No! No!
HUGGINS: And that's the slip between the cup and lip.
CECIL: Ah, woe!
BLOOD: I think you'd better come along with me.
POLLY: Boo-hoo!
HUGGINS: A pretty fatal slip it seems to be.
CECIL: I'm through!

CECIL: From rapture rudely torn
I go to suffer scorn,
And a desolate future is mine, dear.
But far more potent bands
Than these that bind my hands
Have fettered my heart to thine, dear,
Have fettered my heart to thine.

MAIDENS: Come along,
Don't you dare make light of us.
You shall not wander out of sight of us.
BADMEN: We object,
We object censoriously.
MAIDENS: With vigilance conscious and subliminal
Night and day we shall guard the criminal.
BADMEN: We protest,
We protest uproariously.
BLOOD: Ah, don't protest.
He merely gets his due.
BADMEN: Oh, that's not the point!
We want to be arrested too.

MAIDENS: This is very embarrassing,
This is very embarrassing.
To be suddenly confronted
With a plea like this
Is altogether too harassing.
Tho' some deem it delectable,
Tho' some deem it delectable,
It is our personal opinion
That a scene like this
Cannot be wholly respectable.

BADMEN: Oh, won't you please arrest us?
To share his fate we long.
MAIDENS: For shackles why request us
Since you have done no wrong?
BADMEN: Our guilt has quite obsessed us.
MAIDENS: Our hearts are not asbestos.
BADMEN: As convicts kindly test us.
MAIDENS: Oh, well then, come along.
Come along.
Don't you dare make light of us.
You shall not wander out of sight of us.
BADMEN: On we go
Led away ingloriously.
MAIDENS: With vigilance conscious and subliminal,
Night and day we shall guard each criminal.
BADMEN: On we go marking time laboriously.

CECIL: From rapture rudely torn
I go to suffer scorn,
And a desolate future is mine, dear.
But far more potent bands
Than these that tie my hands
Have fettered my heart to thine.
From rapture rudely torn
I go to suffer scorn,
From rapture rudely torn
I go to suffer scorn, [*unfinished*]

POLLY: Pity me. Pity me. Pity me, please.
Rashly presuming love's bounty to seize,
Brutally blighted by cruel decrees.
Pity me. Pity me. Pity me.
Torn from my [*unfinished*]

SOPRANOS: Come along, don't you dare make light of us.
You shall not wander out of sight of us.
Come along, led away ingloriously.
With vigilance conscious and subliminal,
Night and day we shall guard each criminal.
Come along, marking time laboriously.
ALTOS: Left Left Left Left Left Left Left Left Left

BASSES: Left Left Left Left
[*Repeat 20 times*]
TENORS: On we go. Let us not make light of them.
We shall not wander out of sight of them.
On we go, led away ingloriously.
With vigilance conscious and subliminal,
Night and day they shall guard the criminal.
On we go marking time laboriously.
ALTOS: Come a-long.
BASSES: On we go.
ALTOS: Don't you dare make light of us.
BASSES: Let us not make light of you.
ALTOS: You shall not wander out of sight of us.
BASSES: We shall not wander out of sight of them.
ALTOS: Come along. Come along.
BASSES: On we go. On we go. On we go. On we go.
MAIDENS & BLOOD: Come along, don't you dare make light of us.
You shall not wander out of sight of us.
With vigilance conscious and subliminal,
Night and day we shall guard each criminal.
BADMEN: On we go. Let us not make light of them.
We shall not wander out of sight of them.
ALL EXCEPT CECIL & POLLY: With vigilance conscious and subliminal
Night and day they shall guard each criminal [*Unfinished*]

MIRROR, MIRROR

Manuscript at the Library of Congress. This is the opening chorus of Act II. It was presented in the New York production by the ensemble.

SOPRANOS: Mirror,
Harmless necessary glass,
Wonder-working fairy glass,
Mirror.
ALTOS: Clear or cloudy though the weather be
We shall e'er together be,
Mirror.
SOPRANOS: We guard thee with affection
ALTOS: Just like the Lady of Shalott.
SOPRANOS: To act without reflection
ALTOS: Would be improper, would it not?
ALL: Mirror,
Follies in forsaking thee,
Dreadful doom in breaking thee,
Oh, Mirror.
1ST SOPRANO: Our interest aesthetic
Is chiefly cosmetic.
1ST ALTO: Nor could it well be otherwise.
2ND SOPRANO: Devotion to beauty
We hold as a duty.
3RD SOPRANO: Instructed by each mother wise.
ALL: Mirror,
Harmless necessary glass,
Wonder-working fairy glass,
Mirror.
Clear or cloudy though the weather be
We shall e'er together be,
Mirror,
Mirror,
Mirror.

OH, BRIGHT, FAIR DREAM

Published March 1916. This was Act II, No. 2 in the original sequence. It was replaced during the pre-Broadway tryout by "Ever and Ever Yours."

VERSE

CECIL & MAIDENS: I roam thro' darkest night,
Tho' sunniest noon be shining!
Ah, worse than death the plight
Of heart for heart repining!
But like a starbeam cleaving the storm
A vision pure, a virginal form,
My desolate longing allays
With its heav'n-sent rays.

REFRAIN

Oh, bright, fair Dream!
Around me gently hover!
Oh, bright, fair Dream!
Console this yearning lover.

. . .

CHORUS: Oh, bright, fair Dream!
His lonely heart thou cheerest.
CECIL: From far thou dost bring
On magical wing
A memory ever dearest.
Oh, bright, fair Dream!
ALL: Oh, bright, fair Dream!

EVER AND EVER YOURS

Published March 1916. Added just before the New York opening and introduced by Dorothie Bigelow and John Goldsworthy.

VERSE

POLLY & CECIL: Naught shall sever us now,
That is my vow most true;
When you gaze in my eyes,
My heart replies to you!

REFRAIN

I must go where you lead me,
I must come when you need me
I must yield to your lips' caress.
When you plead, I must answer "Yes!"
Though the years pass us by, love,
Time and change we'll defy, love!
I am yours till I die, love,
Ever and ever yours!

LADY FAIR, LADY FAIR

Manuscript at the Library of Congress. This sextet was Act II, No. 3 in the original sequence. It was dropped before the New York opening. For a portion of the tryout it followed "Wake, Love, Wake," a lost number.

MARMADUKE: Lady fair, Lady fair,
I have an intellect absurdly rare.
Unsurpassed I am
At an epigram
And my verses have a note that's new.
People weigh what I say
Posing as the critic of a book or play.
On the whole it's plain
I've a brilliant brain,
So I ought to be the man for you.

ETHEL: Gentle Sir, gentle Sir,
Culture is a quality I much prefer.
I have always frowned on the sentimental sort,
For I'm Queen uncrowned of a literary court
In that learned Massachusetts city
Where the stockings all are blue,
So I'm sure I'd get along with you.

ALGAE: Lady fair, Lady fair,
I am a victim of the open air.
I have cups galore
For my golfing score,
For I always do a hole in two.
Cheers I catch when I snatch
Goals by the dozens at a polo match.
All the world agrees I'm a Hercules,
So I ought to be the Man for you.

MURIEL: Gentle Sir, with your notions I concur,
For I love to be a stir
In some dashing sort of a sport.
For pleasures athletic, peripatetic,
I excel in
Ev'ry game I figure well in,
And you'll find very few
So competent to get along with you.

PERCY: Lady fair, Lady fair,
I tell the tailors "what the men will wear."
In the swagger set
I'm a pampered pet,
For my dancing is a joy to view.
Fashion's knee bends to me
Begging for the pleasure of my company.
Unapproached am I
As a butterfly,
So I ought to be the Man for you.

GWENDOLIN: Gentle Sir,
I've a tender passion for expensive Paris frocks.
Gentle Sir,
No one sees the Opera when I am in my box.
Though its demands are not light
I love the social spotlight.
You must admit it's very true
I'd get along with you.

MEN & GIRLS: Please give a quick consent.
Thanks for the compliment.

But though it could never be
disputed
Each to each is beautifully suited,
Life would be very very dull.
MEN: Very very dull.
GIRLS: Very very dull.
Why not try this obvious solution?
Let's attempt a little substitution.
I'll take you.
MEN: You'll take me.

ALL: Oh, how much more interesting life
will be!
Oh, how much more interesting life
will be!

LOVE CAME AND CROWNED ME

Manuscript at the Library of Congress. This was Act II, No. 4 of the original sequence. This number was a revision of "Idyll" from *Paranoia*, although its lyric is substantially different. It was dropped from the show just before the New York opening.

Love came and crowned me
Queen of his quest,
Dreaming he found me,
Woke me and blessed.
Tears now surround me,
Love came and crowned me
Only in jest.
Nay, peace,
Love is always best!

Bide thou his greeting,
Doubts are but lies,
Promise of meeting
Shone in his eyes.
Dear vows repeating,
Bide thou his meeting,
Dark tho' the skies,
For love never never dies.

Ah, how I mind me
When Love did start,
Lone did he find me
Dreaming apart.
Left Hope to bind me,
Ah, how I mind me
When we did part.
Nay, peace,
Weary weary heart!

LIMA

Published March 1916. Added to the show just before the New York opening. Introduced by Clara Palmer. Porter's home town was Peru, Indiana. His use of the Wabash River town of Lima (pronounced "Lye-ma") was obviously meant as a joke on the Indiana Peru rather than the South American Peru.

VERSE

Other towns you may boast of,
Other towns may have style.
But the town I know most of
Has 'em all beat—a mile;
You may think you live well in
Budapest or Bagdad,
But the town that—I dwell in
Makes the others—look sad.
Lima's the place
And I'd give a lot, I guess,
Back there to race
On a Limited Express!

REFRAIN

Li—ma! Li—ma!
Ease my pain for me, send a train for me, do!
Li—ma! Li—ma!
Hear me callin', for I'm a-fallin' for you!
I simply quiver—to drive my flivver
Along that lazy hazy crazy Wabash River
And if I ever, ever get home again,
Why, I never, never shall roam again,
For I'm madly in love with that Li-ma town.

WHEN A BODY'S IN LOVE

Manuscript at the Library of Congress. Act II, No. 5 in the original sequence. It was dropped during the pre-Broadway tryout.

POLLY: When a body's in love
Existence is a question.
BLOOD: When a body's in love
It ruins his digestion.
SARAH: When a body's in love
The world's a garden blooming.
HUGGINS: When a body's in love,
His stock is always booming.
SARAH: You soar on high!

POLLY: You droop and sigh!
HUGGINS: You swell with hope!
BLOOD: You moan and mope!
SARAH: You bill and coo!
POLLY: You fret and stew!
HUGGINS: You laugh and shout!
BLOOD: You're down and out!
BLOOD & POLLY: You waste your time
In hopeless sorrow and yearning.
SARAH & HUGGINS: With flame sublime
The joyful moments are burning.
ALL: It's evident we can't agree
On what this thing called love may be
Which often blights sweet youth's delights
Yet sometimes cheers maturer years.
It's heaven! It's, well,
In short you never can tell
What merriment magic
What turbulence tragic
You suffer 'neath Cupid's spell.
HUGGINS: Whether you're fifty,
SARAH: Whether you're forty,
BLOOD: Whether you're thirty,
POLLY: Whether you're twenty,
ALL: It is undeniable
That love is never reliable.
It is undeniable
That love is never reliable.

REVELATION ENSEMBLE

Manuscript at the Library of Congress. Act II, No. 6 in the original sequence, it too was dropped from the show during its pre-Broadway tryout. The published "Slow Sinks the Sun" (see *Paranoia*) was also dropped before the New York opening. It might have been Act II, No. 7 or 8.

PART 1

4TH OF WOMEN'S CHORUS: Peer! Stare! Step slow!
Here, there, shades grow.
Pale day, dim gray,
Wanly lights the ground.

4TH OF MEN'S CHORUS: Stop! Hark! Pause! Hist!
Stay! Mark! Hush! List!
Hearts thrill, stand still—
Heard you not a sound?

ANOTHER 4TH OF WOMEN'S CHORUS: Mutt'ring breeze! Ruffled lake!
Moaning trees! Earth-a-quake!
Cries of birds, plaintive thirds,
Echo through the air!

ANOTHER 4TH OF MEN'S CHORUS: Ghostly gloom! Squinting light!
Clouds that loom! Gleams that fright!
Vague suspense! Breathing tense!
Omens ev'rywhere.

ANOTHER 4TH OF WOMEN'S CHORUS: Nature's voices groan portentous
Prophesying things momentous;
Secrets fateful, bright or hateful
Tease the tortured ear.

ANOTHER 4TH OF MEN'S CHORUS: Hidden sagas, riddles cryptic,
'Mid these signs apocalyptic;
Seem to quiver, start and shiver
Ere their sense appear!

ANOTHER 4TH OF WOMEN'S CHORUS: Terrible enigmas,
Crushing revelations,
Legendary stigmas,
Blighted generations,
Sanguinary curses,
Hideous reverses
Tow'ring Fate may show.

ANOTHER 4TH OF MEN'S CHORUS: Destiny tremendous
Quickly be enacted!
Shatter or befriend us,
Keep us not distracted!
If a cry can reach thee,
Tell us, we beseech thee,
Bringst thou weal or woe?

ENTIRE CHORUS: Terrible enigmas,
Crushing revelations,
Legendary stigmas,
Blighted generations,
Sanguinary curses,
Hideous reverses
Tow'ring Fate may show!
Destiny tremendous
Quickly be enacted!
Shatter or befriend us,
Keep us not distracted!
If a cry can reach thee,
Tell us, we beseech thee,
Bringst thou weal or woe?
Weal or woe?
Weal or woe?
Weal or woe?
Weal or woe?

Weal
Weal
Weal or woe?

PART 2: GREEK CHANT

GWENDOLIN: We proceed to portray emotion,
Our manner of dancing is Greek,
Its significance couldn't be
darker.
PERCY: For the sake of exact description
Perhaps it is better to speak
Of the manner of Granville
Barker.
INDIAN MAIDENS: Hoi polloi,
Don't make fun of us, if you
please.
BADMEN: Hoi polloi,
We're only acting Euripides.
GWENDOLIN: Oh, favor of fate unexpected,
Oh, highest of rapture's decrees,
No climax of bliss could be
gayer.
PERCY: Which doubtless explains his
behavior
In suddenly tackling her knees
Like a varsity football player!
INDIAN MAIDENS: Hoi polloi,
That's a most improbable touch!
BADMEN: Hoi polloi,
That undoubtedly beats the
Dutch!

PART 3

INDIAN MAIDENS: Calisthenic maids Hellenic,
Types of beauty, grace and ease,
Moving Greekly, most antiquely
Like the Parthenonian frieze!
How the world advances,
Those were funny dances.
Melodies demented
Hadn't been invented.
Festivals bacchantic
Never could have been as frantic
As the rags are today.
Happy generation,
Free from syncopation,
Ere the days of plotting,
Diff'rent ways of trotting,
You were not the vassals
Of the plutocratic Castles
On the Gay White Way!

STEP WE GRANDLY

Manuscript at Yale. Act II, No. 9 in the original sequence. Dropped before the Broadway opening. "I've a Shooting Box in Scotland," originally slated for either the 7th or 8th spot in Act II, can be found with the lyrics for *Paranoia.*

Step we grandly,
Smile we blandly,
Our rejoicing
Calmly voicing.
Proudly and correctly,
Very circumspectly
We proceed to execute a dance,
Fragrant with the breath of old romance,
Mad exaltation,
And joyous elation.
We find it essential to modify
Lest we be taken for odd if i-
Ronical people should see.
Persons of breeding
Are never unheeding
Of showing emotion with reticence.
Shy as a bride who confetti scents,
Fearful of frolic are we.

This gavotte
Shows a lot
Of determined self-control,
Does it not?

BUY HER A BOX AT THE OPERA

Published March 1916. This late addition to the score was introduced by Dorothie Bigelow and ensemble. It was a replacement for both "Step We Grandly" and "Sweet Simplicity."

VERSE

Wise young fellows when they marry,
Of extravagance are wary.
Costly pleasures, full of ostentation,
Hollow satisfaction give.
If your wife all frivolous display shuns,
Happy as a lark she'll live.
Just a few slight toys are ample;
For example:

REFRAIN

You should buy her a box at the opera,
And a motor to match ev'ry gown,
She must cruise quite a lot
On a record-breaking yacht
When she wearies of the whirl of town:
With a new string of pearls ev'ry week or so,
Of her marriage she'll never repent.
If she only gets these simple little comforts,
She'll be quite content.

SWEET SIMPLICITY

Manuscript at Yale. Act II, No. 10 in the original sequence. Dropped during the pre-Broadway tour. "When I Used to Lead the Ballet" was the next-to-closing number in both the original sequence and the New York production. For its lyric, see *The Pot of Gold*, 1912. I do not know what the finale of Act II was. It might have reprised previous numbers.

POLLY: Some ladies live in extravagant style,
Doting on vain display.
Happy with little, I cheerfully smile.
Isn't a pittance as good as a pile?
That's what I always say.
A string of pearls refined and chaste,
With one tiara in perfect taste,
For any young girl should suffice.
Why, I once wore a ball gown twice!
CHORUS: Fancy, she once wore a ball gown twice!
POLLY: For I revel in sweet simplicity,
I flourish on sweet simplicity,
Refreshingly fresh rusticity
To follow I've always tried.
Extravagance means banality.
I'm all for refined frugality,
Arcadian pastorality,
True happiness will provide.
And as long as I have simplicity
I'm perfectly satisfied.

POLLY: I revel in sweet simplicity.
SOPRANOS: She revels in sweet simplicity.
ALTOS & BASSES: Oh, sweet, sweet simplicity.

. . .

POLLY: I flourish on sweet simplicity.
SOPRANOS: She'd flourish on sweet simplicity.
ALTOS & BASSES: She worships sweet simplicity.

POLLY: Refreshingly fresh rusticity
SOPRANOS: Refreshingly fresh rusticity
ALTOS & BASSES: Refreshingly fresh rusticity

POLLY: To follow I've always tried.
SOPRANOS: To follow she's always tried.
ALTOS & BASSES: To follow she's always tried.

POLLY: Ah——
SOPRANOS: Extravagance spells banality.
ALTOS & BASSES: Averse to banality.

POLLY: Ah——
SOPRANOS: She's all for refined frugality,
ALTOS & BASSES: She loves pastorality,

POLLY: Ah——
SOPRANOS: Arcadian pastorality,
ALTOS & BASSES: Austere pastorality,

POLLY: Ah——
SOPRANOS: True happiness can provide.
ALTOS & BASSES: True happiness can provide, provide.

POLLY: Ah——
SOPRANOS: And as long as she has simplicity
ALTOS & BASSES: With sweet, sweet simplicity

POLLY: I'm perfectly satisfied.
SOPRANOS: She's perfectly satisfied.
ALTOS & BASSES: She's perfectly satisfied.

JE VOUS COMPRENDS

By Cole Porter and T. Lawrason Riggs. A copyist ink score (music and lyrics) was found at the Warner Brothers Music warehouse in Secaucus, New Jersey. There is no evidence that this song was intended for *Paranoia* or *See America First*, but, almost certainly, it was written no later than 1916.

HE: Belle en-chan-te-ress-e!
SHE: I do not quite comprehend.
HE: Vous êtes wa-de-ess-e!
SHE: Try to be plainer, my friend.
HE: Douce lée char-man-te!

SHE: Tell me in some other way.
HE: Beau-té ra-vis-san-te!
SHE: What are you trying to say?
HE: Dan -sous je vous sup-plie
SHE: You want to dance—I see!

REFRAIN

SHE: Hin Hin Hin Hin
HE: Hin Hin Hin Hin Hin
SHE: That's a soothing canto
HE: Que c'est cares-sant'
SHE: Hin Hin Hin Hin
HE: Hin Hin Hin Hin Hin
SHE: We don't need esper-an-to!
HE: Je vous com-prends!

HITCHY-KOO OF 1919

Tryout: Nixon's Apollo Theatre, Atlantic City, August 18, 1919; Colonial Theatre, Boston, September 1, 1919. Produced by Raymond Hitchcock at the Liberty Theatre, New York, October 6, 1919. 56 performances. Book by George V. Hobart. Staged by Julian Alfred. Cast, starring Raymond Hitchcock, included Lillian Kemble Cooper, Ruth Mitchell, Joe Cook, and Florence O'Denishawn.

WHEN BLACK SALLIE SINGS PAGLIACCI

The New York program lists "Pagliacci" as the opening number. It was introduced by Lillian Kemble Cooper, Elaine Palmer, Ursula O'Hare, and ensemble. No music or lyrics are known to survive. The lyric printed here of the show's second number exists in an incomplete holograph sketch in the Cole Porter Collection at Yale. It is impossible to know how closely it resembles the version sung in the show. No music survives. Introduced by Ruth Mitchell and ensemble. No music or lyrics have turned up for "I'm an Anesthetic Dancer," introduced by Sylvia Clark.

Oh, way down in Coontown Alley!
Where's it at?
Where's it at?
Where's it at?
Lives a gal they call "Black Sallie."
What of that?
What of that?
What of that?
Well, the funny part of that
Is she's a human nightingale.
Well I never!
Now did you ever!
Talk of Tetrazzini's trilling
What d'you mean?
What d'you mean?
What d'you mean?
Or maintain that Farrar's thrilling
Geraldine
Geraldine
Geraldine
When you hear Black Sallie's wail.

I INTRODUCED

Published August 1919. Introduced by Raymond Hitchcock and ensemble. Boston program lists title as "I Presented."

VERSE

Though it's not quite generally known
That I'm a one-horse power behind the throne,
Yet lots of people are in clover,
Simply due to things that I've put over.
Just pick up your fav'rite magazine,
Peruse the ads and you'll see what I mean,
For ev'ry partnership you see is wholly owing to
me.

REFRAIN

For I presented Mister Morgan to Mister Harjes,
I presented Mister Peet to Mister Rogers,
I introduced Mister Cross to Mister Mark,
Mister Lord to Mister Taylor,
Mister Tilford to Mister Park.
It's entirely thanks to me,
Though few people know it,
That that dear old Mister Chandon
Met that dear old Mister Moët,
But the greatest introduction that I ever put
through
Was when I presented myself to you.

HITCHY'S GARDEN OF ROSES

Published August 1919. The program lists this as "Hitchy's Garden of Roses." The title on the published version is "In Hitchy's Garden." Introduced by Lillian Kemble Cooper and ensemble.

VERSE

Humbly begging your pardon,
Let me show you the way
To the sort of a garden
You don't see ev'ry day.
Where each flower a rose is,
And each rose a maid,
So rare, so fair,
You'll be dismayed.

REFRAIN

In Hitchy's garden of roses
You'll meet the sweet wild rose.
In Hitchy's garden of roses
The white rose gently blows.
There grows the rose of Killarney
With her Irish eyes of blue.
And for some nice young fellow

There's a rose of yellow
Simply longing to be true.
And if you're one of those heroes
Accustomed to be kissed,
You'll find that Japanese tea rose
Is something to resist.
And you'll forget your trials
When that American Beauty smiles
In Hitchy's garden of roses
In Hitchy-Koo.

WHEN I HAD A UNIFORM ON

Published August 1919. This is one of the numbers Porter played for Hitchcock which persuaded him to ask Porter to write the score for the 1919 edition of *Hitchy-Koo.* Introduced by Joe Cook, Eleanor Sinclair, and ensemble. Some post-Broadway programs list it as "Demobilization Song."

VERSE

Now since the Allied banners
Gave a lesson in good manners
To the Kaisers and crown princes,
And von Hindenburgs, von Ludendorffs,
Von Falkenhayns, von Mackensens,
Von Tirpitzes, von Klucks,
The youth of all the nations
Finds its greatest recreations
Drinking Pol Roger and Pommery,
Veuve Clicquot, Louis Roederer,
Ruinart, Piper Heidsieck,
Montebello, Mumm's and Cook's,
But while I watch the other fellows throwing up their hats,
And crying that at last the world's made safe for democrats,
For me the road seems rocky,
For they've stripped me of my khaki,
And since I've been demobilized

REFRAIN

I find that life's not what it used to be
When I had a uniform on,
For all the lovely ladies fell for me
When I had a uniform on.
And in those days of glory I was the beau
Of ev'ry doggone musical show.
Each night you'd see me supping somewhere
With a dainty little star upon my Croix de Guerre.
Into their inmost hearts they'd let me strike
When I had a uniform on.
But now the war is o'er
They don't quite like me anymore,
And it's a bore.
For they used to bound around me in millions,
But now, somehow that I'm in civilians,
They pass me by.
Gee, I wish I
Could start another war.

I'VE GOT SOMEBODY WAITING

Published December 1919. Introduced by Ruth Mitchell and ensemble.

VERSE

I used to be the type of mouse
That sort of creeps about the house.
I used to go from room to room,
And spread an atmosphere of gloom,
Until the day I happened to meet
Somebody who became my slave;
Somehow since then the change is complete
And I'm on the crest of a wave
'Cause

REFRAIN

I've got somebody waiting,
Waiting for me.
Somebody radiating
Love and devotion,
I've half a notion
That she (he) knows I adore her (him) madly.
Gee!, she's (he's) sublime!
But lest her (his) hopes overleap her (him),
I think I'll keep her (him)
Waiting a long, long time,
Waiting a long, long time.

PETER PIPER / THE SEA IS CALLING

Published August 1919 as "Peter Piper." The sheet music includes the song "The Sea Is Calling" as well. They were separate songs sung in counterpoint. "Peter Piper" was introduced by Raymond Hitchcock and ensemble. "The

Sea Is Calling" was introduced by Ruth Mitchell and ensemble.

VERSE

It seems to me that human history
Is but a subject sadly overrated.
Just take a look at any hist'ry book
Why, ev'ry tale you read is expurgated.
For instance, take the case of Peter Piper, it's absurd,
For the unimportant half of it is all you ever heard.

REFRAIN 1

The sea is calling for you,
The sea is calling for you,
Neptune commands you leave these lands
And sail o'er the blue.
The mermaids are praying for you,
The sirens are laying for you,
So lend an ear and cry
"I hear you calling me!"

REFRAIN 2

For when Peter Piper picked a peck of peppers,
Peter Piper picked a pippin too,
A perfect pearly of a pretty girlie
With big eyes of baby blue.
And by the pace they're setting
Everybody's betting
That they'll soon have something to predict.
I know piles of people who would climb a steeple
Just to pipe the pippin Peter picked.

MY COZY LITTLE CORNER IN THE RITZ

Published August 1919. Introduced by Raymond Hitchcock and ensemble.

VERSE

Now, when I was but a baby
Father took me upon his knee.
Saying, "Son, you must let Town Topics be your Bible,
For I want my little boy to be
As well brought up as he can be.
Yet never, never, never brought up for libel."
So under the eye of Mother
I was taught all my childhood games,
Such as betting with baby brother
As to dowagers' maiden names.
From then on I've followed the same old plan
Of spotting the real "Who's Who's,"
But it wasn't Town Topics that made me a man,
For now when I want the news:

REFRAIN

I simply adorn a secluded corner,
A cozy corner in the Ritz Hotel.
When I wander each afternoon for tea,
'Cause I like to see the kings
And let the queens see me
In my corner, my dear little corner
Where I gather up the spicy bits.
And if you want to meet the girl
That's got the latest complexion on her;
If you'd like to see the fellow
That your favorite prima donna
Cashes checks on,
Just put your specks on
And try my cozy little corner in the Ritz.

OLD-FASHIONED GARDEN

Published August 1919. This was the first Porter song to gain wide popularity. Introduced by Lillian Kemble Cooper and ensemble. Programs list the title as "An Old-Fashioned Garden."

VERSE

One summer day I chanced to stray
To a garden of flow'rs blooming wild,
It took me once more to the dear days of yore
And a spot that I loved as a child.
There were the phlox,
Tall hollyhocks,
Violets perfuming the air,
Frail eglantines,
Shy columbines,
And marigolds everywhere.

REFRAIN

It was an old-fashioned garden,
Just an old-fashioned garden,
But it carried me back
To that dear little shack
In the land of long ago.
I saw an old-fashioned missus
Getting old-fashioned kisses,

In that old-fashioned garden
From an old-fashioned beau.

BRING ME BACK MY BUTTERFLY

Published August 1919. Introduced by Lillian Kemble Cooper and ensemble.

VERSE

I was still the mild, money-wild type of child
 that's styled "commuter,"
When I fell as the suitor for a butterfly,
One of those sweet peace-loving geese that police
 Maurice's Biltmore.
No one ever loved gilt more than my butterfly,
So when I'd got her tied as a bride with pride
 a-blushing,
I chose one of those bungalows God grows in
 Flushing.
Then try picture my surprise the other night
When I got to the spot and found she'd taken
 flight.

REFRAIN

Oh, bring, oh, bring me back my butterfly,
She simply wrote me
"Goodbye, I've found the man of my choice
And he's got a Rolls-Royce."
Oh, send her home or else I'll surely die,
Oh, won't you please, please bring me back my
 butterfly.

ANOTHER SENTIMENTAL SONG

Published October 1919. I believe this song was dropped before the New York opening.

VERSE

When people contend
That we'll soon see the end
Of the dear old sentimental song,
Don't trouble your brain
But just learn this refrain,
For it proves that they're completely wrong:

REFRAIN 1

As long as "spoon" rhymes with "night in June"
And "meet me soon" rhymes with "honeymoon,"
As long as "heart's a-whirl" rhymes with "a
 pretty girl,"
As long as "stars up above" rhymes with "falling
 in love,"
As long as "true" rhymes with "eyes of blue"
And "room for two" rhymes with "I love you,"
As long as such rhymes endure
You could always be sure
Of another sentimental song.

REFRAIN 2

Come out and spoon 'neath this night in June,
Oh, meet me soon 'neath our honeymoon.
You've got my heart a-whirl,
You're such a pretty girl,
And all the stars up above
Know I'm falling in love.
I will be true, dear, to eyes of blue,
There's room for two, dear, and I love you.
As long as such rhymes get by
Why don't you go home and try
To write another sentimental song.

THAT BLACK AND WHITE BABY OF MINE

Published August 1919. I believe this song was dropped before the New York opening.

VERSE

Now since my sweetheart Sal met Miss Elsie de
 Wolfe,
The leading decorator of the nation,
It's left that gal with her mind simply full'f
Ideas on interior decoration.
For instance, she assumes
That the colors of our rooms
Are a most important factor in our lives
And that if a lot of bedrooms
Were pink instead of red rooms
There might be many more contented wives.
And so she's put all color from her sight
And ev'rything she owns is black and white.

REFRAIN

She's got a black and white dress, a black and
 white hat,

A black and white doggie and a black and white
cat.
Why, she's gone so far that she's started to look
Thro' the daily advertisements for a black and
white cook.
She's got a black and white shack
And a new Cadillac
In a black and white design.
All she thinks black and white,
She even drinks Black and White,
That black and white baby of mine.

YOU AND ME

This song appears to have been a forerunner of "I Introduced." Porter later wrote a song with the same title for *La Revue des Ambassadeurs* (1928). It is a different song.

VERSE

If you're a reader of the daily news
You know a lot of names that go in twos.
There's Haig and Haig and there's Taylor and Lord.
There's Siegel, Cooper, Montgom'ry and Ward.
The name of Tilford always follows Park.
You never see the Cross without the Mark.
They're linked together,
I wonder whether,
As close as you and me.

REFRAIN

You and me,
Oh, what a combination.
You and me,
The closest corporation,
Starting from a brilliant career,
Adding to our production each year.
When we're
You and me
The world can never sever
You and me.
Forever and forever
Rolling down through posterity
As the partnership of you and me.

SINCE MA GOT THE CRAZE ESPAGNOLE

Porter's original title for this song was "Since Ma Got the Grippe Española," a reference to the severe epidemic of Spanish influenza that raged during the winter of 1918–1919.

VERSE

Now I've always known that dear Mother was
prone
To be rather too ultra-progressive.
Her one idea was to go in for everything new.
However, of late it's approaching a state
When her fads are becoming excessive.
Really, my dear, I don't quite see what we're
going to do
To show to what limits our nerves have been
taxed.
Why, she just had the bathroom done over by
Bakst.
And, for instance, tho' only two servants we have
Yet the cook's Czecho-Slovak, the maid's
Yugoslav.
Why, in order to cure Father's stroke of
paralysis,
She chucked Christian Science for psychoanalysis.
But the fad she's got now makes all hope for her
vanish,
For she's taken a fancy for anything Spanish.

REFRAIN 1

And since Ma got the craze Espagnole
It's impossible quite to control her,
For she races the heath
With a rose in her teeth
Crying, "Please find me some beau
Like Christy Columbo!"
O'er the Fandango she's gone so silly
That the parlor floor's getting all hilly,
And in order to practice that bullfighting game,
Why, she fights with our cow which is almost the
same.
And the way that poor cow looks today is a
shame
Since Ma got the craze Espagnole.

REFRAIN 2

Since Ma got the craze Espagnole
It's impossible quite to control her,
For she rants 'round the home
Simply clad in a comb
Shouting, "I'm Isabella,
Where's that Ferdinand fella?"
She's learning the *Carmen* libretto,
So we all have to dodge her stiletto.
And old Granny sits over her porridge and frets,
For she's tied all the spoons up to make
castanets.

Even small Baby Jane rolls her own cigarettes
Since Ma got the craze Espagnole.

OH SO SOON

Gilbert Seldes, who wrote with such engaging insight about Porter and other American songwriters in his pioneering study of popular culture, *The Seven Lively Arts* (1924), referred (pp. 93–94) to a song of Porter's titled "Soon." For years I had been baffled by this reference, as I had never heard of or seen any other reference to a Porter song by this title. Yet the specificity of Seldes' reference, his obvious familiarity with the song, and my thoroughgoing trust in the accuracy of his observations led me to hope that someday the mystery of Porter's "Soon" would be solved. Seldes wrote of it as follows:

> The song "Soon," for example, is a deliberate annihilation of the Southern negro sentiment carefully done by playing Harlem jazz, with a Harlem theme, mercilessly burlesquing the clichés of the Southern song—the Swanee-Mammy element—in favor of a Harlem alley. Porter's parody is almost too facile; "Soon" is an exasperatingly good piece of jazz in itself. He is a tireless experimenter, and the fact that in 1923 others are doing things he tried in 1919 makes me wonder whether his excessive intelligence and sophistication may not be pointing a way which steadier and essentially more *native* jazz writers will presently follow.

In early 1978 a visit to a private collection, whose owners have requested anonymity, led to my discovery of the lyric for "Oh So Soon," which is printed here. This clearly is the song Seldes is describing. He never said where he heard it, but he refers to its being written in 1919. I'm quite convinced by evidence on the manuscript itself that it was one of many songs Porter submitted to Hitchcock for his 1919 revue. It is also quite likely that Porter played it for friends at private parties.

VERSE

Now as Sam was traveling from Harlem to
 Tennessee
He cried, "I'se home and now oh happy I'se
 goin' to be.
I'll spend from night to dawn
Sittin' on
Mammy's knee."
But after two weeks livin'
With the folks in the Southern wilds
He found that homemade waffles
Weren't as good as the cakes at Child's,
I mean those red-hot wheat
Cakes you eat
'Round at Child's.
He missed the great big tall skyscrapers
And the elevated's roar,
And he longed for morning papers
That come out the night before.
But he never told nobody nothin'
Until one day
When someone asked how long he was going to
 stay
He answered:

REFRAIN

Soon, oh so soon
This here coon
Is goin' to mosey from the land of cotton
Back to ole Manhattan
Where he's not forgotten.
Walk to Noo York
And jest stalk
Along to Harlem and its coontown alleys
Till I find the number where my yaller gal is.
Choose me some shoes,
I need some booze
So awfully bad I simply shake and shiver,
For there's nothing flowing but the Swanee River.
I'se hummin'
I'se comin'
Back to you Manhattan, mighty doggone soon.
Oh so soon.

PATTER

Soon when I get back to town,
Soon I'll find Miss Liza Brown,
Soon she'll see my face and then
My ever-lovin' used-to-be'll be it again.
Soon I'll take her on a search,
Soon I'll find a Baptist church,
Soon she'll hear the parson say,
"Promise that you'll love him, honor and obey."
Soon I'll give my dusky queen,
Soon a flivver limousine.
Soon we'll have a residence
And something to run around the house besides
 the fence.

SINCE LITTLE BABY BROTHER BECAME A MOVIE STAR

The reference to Theda Bara, who was a top cinema star in 1919, and the fact that a manuscript of this lyric was found among other Hitchcock material suggest that it, too, was a contender for inclusion in *Hitchy-Koo of 1919.*

VERSE

Since little baby brother became a movie star,
He makes so darn much money we don't know
  where we are.
If Theda Bara heard of his pay,
It's the one thing that would shock her.
So just for fear she'll steal him away,
We keep him locked in the liquor locker.

REFRAIN

And though we live in the grandest kind of style,
It's hard to be dependent upon a baby's smile.
For every time he hollers
We lose a thousand dollars,
Since little baby brother
Deserted home and mother
And went to work as a movie star.

CHINA DOLL

Appears to have been written for *Hitchy-Koo of 1919.* Pages 5 to 8 of a manuscript (music and lyric) survive.

. . . Don't hide it from me.
It's just as plain as can be
So do I,
'Cause I never saw a finer
China doll, China doll, China doll.

TIRED OF LIVING ALONE

This number also appears to have been a possible candidate for inclusion in *Hitchy-Koo of 1919.* No music survives.

The first time I told him
By simply singing that old hymn
"I'm Tired of Living Alone."
When I'd hear him coming
I'd start immediately humming.
But since his silence continued
I took him to church.
'Twas the best plan I've ever known,
For sure enough he told me he loved me
While the choir was singing above me
"I'm Tired of Living Alone."
There's someone over the sea
You're dreaming of,
There's somebody waitin' for you.
China doll, China doll,
Why aren't you bolder?
Please be bold, please be bolder.
Rest your head upon my shoulder.
I know well that you, dear,
Feel awfully blue, dear.

WAR SONGS AND OTHERS

1915-1920

WAR SONG

This is a parody of the Jerome Kern–Herbert Reynolds (M. E. Rourke) classic song "They Didn't Believe Me." Years later, when it was included in Joan Littlewood's revue *Oh, What a Lovely War,* the author of the words was listed as "unknown." When this editor was looking through the oldest compilation Porter had preserved of his work, a set of typed miscellaneous lyrics, he was startled to discover that here indeed was the "unknown" who wrote this skillful parody. One wonders how many other Porter parodies—his friends say he composed many—might survive.

And when they ask us how dangerous it was
We never will tell them, we never will tell them.
How we fought in some café
With wild women night and day—
'Twas the wonderfulest war you ever knew.
And when they ask us, and they're certainly
going to ask us,
Why on our chests we do not wear the Croix de
Guerre,
We never will tell them,
We never will tell them,
There was a front, but damned if we knew
where.

KATIE OF THE Y.M.C.A.

The lyrics for "Katie of the Y.M.C.A." and "It Puzzles Me So" were recalled by Lieutenant Colonel Sir Rex Benson, a friend of Porter's, in a letter (November 2, 1967) to Yale University Librarian James T. Babb:

> I met Cole for the first time when I was a subaltern in the 9th Lancers and very occasionally was given a day or two's leave from the north to go to Paris. I saw a good deal of Cole, particularly in late 1917 and throughout 1918, when I was Liaison Officer between Sir Douglas Haig and Marshal Pétain. This enabled me to get to Paris fairly often and we had a little coterie of friends consisting of Cole, Alan Graham (an English officer), the Kingsland brothers, Count Antoine Sala, Monty Woolley, and Howard Sturges, who used to meet frequently at 22 Place Vendôme or latterly at Linda's house, and listen to Cole playing the piano and writing his songs.

Katie
That dainty little creature from the Y.M.C.A.
Katie, such a captivating creature, giving suppers
away.
I'll ne'er forget that time we met
She asked me if I wanted doughnuts
And although I hate 'em
All the same I ate them
Simply because I was so nuts
On Katie
That willing little worker with the wile in her
smile.
Katie
[. . .]
And when this doggone war is through,
I'll build an all-night canteen for two.
So that's of course why I am for the Y.M.C.A.

IT PUZZLES ME SO

Who on earth was Mr. Pankhurst?
Who is Mr. Humphrey Ward?
Oh, I'd like to know, 'cause it puzzles me so.

Who is Duff Cooper?
Not Lady—but Lord.
Who was Mr. Langtry?
Yes, I'd like to know, for it puzzles me so.
Who will I be if I marry you?

CLEVELAND

Johnfritz Achelis (Yale 1913), president of the Dramat during Porter's senior year and the classmate with the most complete recall of Porter's college songs, remembered this one. No music survives.

VERSE 1

Listen, my dearie,
Out on Lake Erie
I know the grandest town,
Cleveland, Ohio,
Oh me oh my-oh,
A place of great renown.
Cleveland—that's the title of my ditty.
Cleveland—it's the famous Forest City,
Cleveland—where they have the ammunition,
Cleveland—to prohibit Prohibition.
Cleveland—praise the Lord and sing Hosannah.
Cleveland—it's the home of Hoyt and Hanna.
Cleveland, Cleveland, Cleveland, Cleveland,
Cleveland!

REFRAIN

Oh, Cleveland—let's make it Cleveland,
It's such a gay old town,
Chock full of real he-men
Y-A-L-E men,
The kind who drink it down, way down.
They're slicker at drinking liquor
Than any men I know,
So we won't go beggin'
When we go bootleggin'
Out in Cleveland, O-hio.

VERSE 2

Some say Toledo
Is full of speed-o
And rate Alliance
By quarts and pi-ants.
In Marietta
Folks who know better
Are growing wetter and wetter and wetter.
The wine in Akron
Is full of saccharin.
The beer is cooler
In Ashtabula.
The drinks in Dayton
More stimulatin'.
But just you wait an' see.

ALONE WITH YOU

Published July 1918. Porter's co-author was Melville Gideon. There is no way of knowing exactly what Gideon's contribution to the song was. Interpolated in the English production of *Very Good Eddie* (opened at the Palace Theatre, London, May 18, 1918). Sung by Nelson Keys. A copy was preserved in Porter's set of typed versions of early lyrics. Alternate title: "All Alone."

Also with Melville Gideon, Porter is credited as co-author of "Altogether Too Fond of You," published in 1918, though his contribution is almost certainly to the music and not the lyric.

VERSE 1

When I left this great big town,
Mother remarked to me:
"Never rise till the sun goes down,
You've got a lot to see."
So each night when the clock strikes twelve,
Gaily I prepare to have a time,
Waiting and willing to
Start something thrilling.
But how can this be done
When I'm

REFRAIN

All alone,
I get so tired of sitting
All alone.
I want to go a flitting
Here, there, everywhere.
Dancing to bright lights,
Stay out all night lights.
Won't you show a little pity for me,
I don't know what to do.
I feel left on the shelf
All alone with myself,
When I might be all alone with you.

VERSE 2

I once went to a cabaret.
Heard it would be great fun.
Thought I'd stay up till break of day—
My life had just begun.
Though I asked many girls to dance,
Each of them received me with rebuff;
I was quite willing to start something thrilling,
But one rebuff was quite enough.

I NEVER REALIZED

Published February 1921. It was first sung in the London production of *The Eclipse* (opened at the Garrick Theatre, November 1919) by Nancy Gibbs and F. Pope Stamper. It was later interpolated in the New York run of *Buddies* (1919).

VERSE 1

Many girls I've met
I've forgotten quite,
You I can't forget
Any day or night,
Since you came my way,
Others seem just a dream.
Now I say—

REFRAIN

I never realized
That you cared for me.
I never realized
That such a thing could be.
And when you went away, dear,
I never guessed the cause,
I never realized
What a fool I was.

VERSE 2

When you were not there
Other girls were by.
But I did not care,
And I wonder why.
When I dream today
You were all I recall,
So I say—

WASHINGTON SQUARE

Published March 1920. The lyric is credited to Porter and E. Ray Goetz, the music to Melville Gideon. "Washington Square" was the original title. It was changed to "In Chelsea Somewhere" when the song was presented in the London production of *The Eclipse.* Under the title "Washington Square," it was presented in the New York production of *As You Were* (1920). "Chelsea" and "I Never Realized" were the first Porter songs to receive original cast recordings. They were sung by Nancy Gibbs and F. Pope Stamper (English Columbia F-1033).

VERSE 1

I'm feeling very happy for the future's that's in
  store for us,
When you and I together quietly settle,
I never will be snappy and all troubles are no
  more for us,
I've started furnishing, I've bought a kettle,
I've settled all my plots and plans
And gone and purchased pots and pans,
A sofa and a chair for two,
The bedroom suite's my favorite,
I don't know how I'll pay for it,
But I don't mind if I've got you.

REFRAIN 1

We'll take a trip to Washington Square,
And hire a nice, old studio there,*
A room with a skylight,
Where we can try light-
House keeping
Free from care.
We'll take the world of art as our aim
And keep the "Victor" playing *Bohème,*
And life will be ecstatic, dear,
So melodramatic, dear,
Just we two in our attic, dear,
In Washington Square.†

VERSE 2

Within our sanctuary, although wealth may be
  evading us,
We'll wear a pair of smiles quite optimistic,
Our views we'll never vary, that mere money is
  degrading, thus
We'll live a life that's almost socialistic.
Your smocks I will "batik" for you,
No frocks or shirtwaists, peek-a-boo
Will ever mar your classic skin,
Each Shaw and Ibsen matinee
We'll see and ev'ry Saturday
We'll dine out at the Village Inn.

REFRAIN 2

We'll settle down in Washington Square
And try out each "New Thought" bill of fare,
We'll eat and grow thin, there
Down at each inn, where everyone "bobs" their
  hair.
"The Pig and Whistle" and "The Pink Prune"
We'll try them all to prove we're immune.
Though the food may be erratic, dear,
We'll be democratic, dear,
When we settle in our attic, dear,
In Washington Square.

WIDOW'S CRUISE

No music is known to survive for "Widow's Cruise," "Venus of Milo," "You Make Up," and "A Table for Two." These numbers were located in Porter's oldest surviving typed lyric compilation. The dates of composition are unknown, but 1919 seems reasonable.

VERSE

How dare you issue such an order.
Your boat has put to sea with us aboard her.
Give us quick an explanation.
Not a moment's hesitation.
You surely will admit as man to man, sir.
The least that you can do is give an answer.

**Published version:*
Let's settle down in Washington Square,
We'll find a nice old studio, there.

†*Or:*
We'll have to live on love and fresh air,
We'll have to cook and cut off our hair,
And life will be exquisite, dear,
No relations to visit, dear,
So delightful too—is it, dear?
In Washington Square.

The situation's agonizing.
Why be so antagonizing?

REFRAIN

Oh, it really is confusing
To be forced to go a-cruising.
When we'd infinitely rather stay at home.
And we have no way of knowing
If the place to which we're going
Is Odessa, Minneapolis or Rome.
If we didn't fear a rumpus
We should monkey with the compass,
Or at least do something funny with the screw.
But we'd hardly like to wrestle
With the captain of the vessel,
Not to mention all the members of the crew.

VENUS OF MILO

VERSE

A lonely young student once loved, they say,
The beautiful Venus of Milo.
And so he would go to the Louvre each day,
And sit in a corner and lie low,
Till all the Cook's tourists had gone away.
And then he would whisper and sigh low
In the following foolish fashion,
To the object of his passion.

REFRAIN

Venus of Milo,
Love once more.
Give me a smile, oh,
I implore.
Just forget you're of stone,
And descend from your throne.
For it's you, you alone
I adore.
Fairest creation
Known to art.
Give consolation
To my heart.
Tho' you be armless,
Why should you be charmless?
Venus of Milo,
I love you.

YOU MAKE UP

VERSE

Since the day I succumbed to your fatal charms,
The day has seldom shone.
For each time I think you've found my arms,
Why, suddenly you're gone.
All the faults of an undecided weather vane
  you've got
And one little question I just must ask you,
Whether vain or not.

REFRAIN

You make up your face, dear,
For me to embrace, dear.
You make up a party
But leave just after we've dined.
Then when the next morning you wake up,
Our quarrel you make up,
So tell me,
Why can't you make up your mind?

A TABLE FOR TWO

VERSE

HE: Hello, Mabel, how are you?
SHE: I'm all right.
HE: What are you doing tonight?
SHE: I've got nothing in sight.
HE: Hooray, Mabel, then you're dining with me.
SHE: If I'm invited to,
I'd be delighted to.
We'll make it a spree.

REFRAIN

HE: I've got a table for two.
SHE: One place for me, one for you.
HE: Over a chicken,
The love plot will thicken,
And when we've done drinking wine,
We'll be one, 'cause you'll be mine.
SHE: After the dinner is through.
We'll have a nice bill and coo.
HE: Don't fail me, Mabel.
SHE: I'll come dressed in sable
HE: But come dressed in sable.
SHE: If you've got a table for two.
HE: 'Cause I've got a table for two.

OH, HONEY

Recalled by Lieutenant Colonel Sir Rex Benson in his November 2, 1967, letter to Yale University Librarian James T. Babb. No music survives.

Oh, Honey—Oh, Honey,
Now I know you've got money
I love you better than other girls.
Your gauche way of dancing
Is positively entrancing.
You've got me on a string,
You funny little thing,
You've strings of pearls.
For five million yearly
I feel I'd love you dearly.
So somehow some way must be found.
So don't be resistant,
For I know you need an assistant
To help you throw your money around.

HITCHY-KOO OF 1922

Porter wrote most of the score for this show, which opened at the Shubert Theatre in Philadelphia on October 10, 1922, and closed there less than two weeks later. As far as I know, this is the only Porter musical which expired between its tryout and its New York opening. Produced by Lee and J. J. Shubert. Directed by J. J. Shubert. Book by Harold Atteridge. The cast, headed by Raymond Hitchcock, included Benny Leonard, May Boley, Jack Pearl, and Edythe Baker.

MARYLAND SCENE

No music survives. The lyrics included here were probably presented in Scene 2, "My Maryland."

VERSE

Ladies and gentlemen, if you care for
 syncopation,
Stop your fuss and come with us to the old
 plantation
Down where the old Potomac flows
Through its sleepy hills and hollows,
Down where its Pickaninny grows
And spends its time as follows.

REFRAIN

Southern belles—We're famous.
Southern belles—Don't blame us
If we hold our little heads too high.
It's because we're thoroughbreds—that's why.
Damozels delightful,
We're frightful
Swells,
And if you're the kind of fellow who wishes
For a garden full of Lillian Gishes
Then you must admit, we're rather delicious
Little Southern belles.

INTERLUDE

ALL: Good evenin', honey,
It sure is grand
To welcome you to Maryland.

MAMMY: I'se ole Mammy, black Mammy,
Mammy that's just the best of all
 critters.
Mammy that makes the cakes and corn
 fritters
Ole Mammy, plain Mammy,
Mammy, the queen serene of sweet
 harmony.
In all the songs they use in jazz revues
Those singers always talk
'Bout goin' back to Mammy's shack,
But they never leave New York
'Cause tho' I'se ole Mammy, plain
 Mammy,
Most of the shows would close if it
 weren't for me.

FINALE

CHORUS: Roll your bones,
Roll 'em seven, eleven, honey.
Roll your bones,
Roll 'em all of the day.
Roll your bones
Till you're ready for heaven
And the good Lord comes to roll your
 bones away.
Put those bones away, hide your dice.
Who's that comin' along?
Why, it's Mammy, Mammy,
And we'll make her sing us a song.
Oh, Mammy, if you're willin'
For a sentimental song we sigh.

MAMMY: Now if you'll listen to me, chillun,
I'll sing a Prohibition lullaby.

Hushabye, my baby, you
Must stop your beggin',
No more rum to be had.
When you're older, maybe you
Can start bootleggin'
Just like your dear old dad.
No more juleps,
So hush dem two lips
And close those poor heavy eyes.
If you want to go to heaven, you
Be quiet, or the revenue
Agents'll sure get wise.

Come on, my dear,
The choo-choo's at the station,
Away, away.
Come on and hear
Some Southern syncopation,
Away, away.

CHORUS: Roll your bones,
Roll 'em seven, eleven, honey.
Roll your bones,
Roll 'em all of the day.
Roll your bones
Till you're ready for heaven
And the good Lord comes to roll your
 bones away.
Roll your bones,
Roll your bones,
Roll your bones,

And the good Lord comes to roll your
bones away.

OH, MARY

Not listed in the program, but probably in the show.

VERSE

Listen, listen, Mary,
Hear the military
Band attack that tune.
Watch the trumpets blarin'
Then begin preparin'
For a honeymoon.
I've got the parson by my side,
So come along, my bonny bride,
And settle down in Dixie,
In the heart of Maryland.

REFRAIN

Oh, Mary, oh, Mary,
Come to Maryland.
Make it Fairyland,
You're very contrary,
Won't you give me a sign?
For you're the only girl that I adore.
Let me make you queen of Baltimore.
Oh, Mary, don't tarry,
Come on, Mary, be mine.

AH FONG LO

Sung by Llora Hoffman. No music survives. Lyric is at the Cole Porter Trusts office. Originally slated for *Hitchy-Koo of 1919*, but dropped before the New York opening.

VERSE

The moon looking down over London town,
Sees a coster lad singing 'neath a window
His love song to a China girl,
Who smiles as he whispers her name.

REFRAIN

Ah Fong Lo,
Ah Fong Lo,
In the streets forsaken,
Ere the town awaken,
Ah Fong Lo,
Ah Fong Lo,
Over London's droning,
Can't you hear me moaning?
Far away the sun of summer blazes,
Leave behind the city's sullen hazes,
Ah Fong Lo,
Ah Fong Lo,
I am waiting for you,
Ah Fong Lo.

MY SPANISH SHAWL

Introduced by Conchita Piquer. Later intended for the *Greenwich Village Follies* (1924). Revised and included as part of "I Dream of a Girl in a Shawl" in *Wake Up and Dream* (1929).

VERSE

Shawl, though the swallow has taken to wing
Since first I found you,
Yet the scent of Granada in spring
Still lingers 'round you.
Ah, what beautiful nights you have known,
What glory.
Won't you whisper to me while we're alone,
Your story?

REFRAIN

What secrets hover
Beneath your cover?
What are the memories you recall,
Wonderful silken shawl?
What tale reposes
Among your roses?
What were your moments divine within love's
thrall?
I hear a distant guitar
And see you afar
Revealing a maiden's charms,
Swaying before
A toreador
Then falling into his arms,
At last reclining
'Neath moonbeams shining.
Don't you remember it all,
My Spanish shawl?

IN HITCHY'S BOUQUET

Introduced by Edythe Baker and ensemble.

VERSE

Now a lot of people say
Hitchy
Has a buttonhole bouquet
Which he
Always wears when lights are shining out
And he's dining out
Somewhere.
It's composed of fragrant spring
Flora
And it's quite the smartest thing
For a
Man as fond as he of botany
Who's got any
Time to spare.

REFRAIN

In Hitchy's bouquet the pansy
May strike you as naughty.
Lily is there
Divinely fair,
Stately and haughty.
Primrose you'll see,
Prim as can be,
Come up and meet the daffy-down-dilly.
Isn't she sweet, but isn't she silly?
Chrysanthemum is hunting somebody to pet her.
Forget-me-not is wondering what makes 'em
forget her.
Daisy appears and she's selected.
Then add the sweet and unaffected
Rose for a star and there you are—
Hitchy's bouquet.

Earlier version of refrain

In Hitchy's bouquet you'll find a gay
Party of flowers.
Each one a gem and all of them
Fresh from their bowers.
Primrose you'll see,
Prim as can be,
Snowdrop awakes and makes the air chilly
Spite of the laugh of daffy-down-dilly.
Forget-me-not is wond'ring what makes 'em forget
her
Poor buttercup is looking up someone to pet her.
You've never known
What indoor sport meant
'Til you've been shown
The choice assortment
Of flowers galore collected for
Hitchy's bouquet.

WHEN MY CARAVAN COMES HOME

Published October 1922. Listed in the program as "My Caravan." Introduced by Jack Squires and ensemble.

VERSE

Queen of my heart,
Should we part and years roll away,
Trust in our fate
And wait for the wonderful day

REFRAIN

When my roving caravan
Comes to offer sacrifices,
Bearing silks from far Japan,
Bringing Java's scented spices,
Rings of gold from Hindustan,
Beads from Burma's amber foam,
At your feet I'll fawn,
When out of the dawn
My caravan comes home.

THE AMERICAN PUNCH

Published November 1922. Introduced by Raymond Hitchcock, Benny Leonard, and ensemble as the Act I finale. Listed in the program as "It's the Punches." It was also featured in *The Dancing Girl* (Winter Garden, New York, January 24, 1923, 136 performances), where, once again, it was presented as the Act I finale by Benny Leonard and ensemble. Most of the music in *The Dancing Girl* was by Sigmund Romberg. There were several lyricists.

VERSE

Tell me what makes the U.S.A.
The grandest land in the world today?
You'll agree when you hear me say
It's the punch—It's the punch—It's the punch!
What's the sure way to happiness?
What's the one thing that spells Success?
Think it over, and you'll confess
It's the punch—It's the punch—It's the punch!

REFRAIN

It's the punch of old George Washington,
It's the punch of Grant and Lee,
It's the punch that you felt
When Ted Roosevelt went riding to victory.
It's the punch that Gen'ral Pershing had
When he led our doughboy bunch.
It's the punch full of hustle, the punch full of muscle,
The grand old American punch!

PATTER

COUNT ONE: Oh, what an awful punch in the eye.
COUNT TWO: He looks as if he's going to die.
COUNT THREE: He's lying on the floor in a heap.
COUNT FOUR: He's dead or else he's fallen asleep.
COUNTS FIVE & SIX: You hear the referee call.
COUNTS SEVEN & EIGHT: Perhaps he'll live after all.
COUNT NINE: He knows he's down and out when it's ten.
COUNT TEN: Why, look, he's up and at it again.

PLAY ME A TUNE

Porter told several interviewers that he had a special fondness for this song. Yet it remained lost for many years. An article on Porter in *The New York Times Magazine*, by Richard Severo, revived a memory of veteran newspaperman Arthur Krock, who wrote Severo that he believed Porter wrote "Play Me a Tune" in the 1920s for his friend, the illustrator Neysa McMein. Krock recalled the following lines:

Play me a tune, my dearie,
Play me a tune, I'm weary,
Weary for the days of long ago.
Ah, how my mem'ry lingers
And I can see your fingers
Flickering o'er the Chickering
In the days gone by.

The lyric reprinted here comes from a private collector who has requested anonymity. No music is known to survive. The song became a specialty for singer-pianist Edythe Baker. After introducing it in the brief run of *Hitchy-Koo of 1922*, she presented it again in *The Dancing Girl* (as a duet with Teddy Doner). Miss Baker also sang it in the 1927 London revue *One Dam Thing After Another* under the title "Play Us a Tune."

VERSE

Don't you remember, darling,
In that old New England town,
Whenever I came to call on you,
You used to play the piano in your little gingham gown,
While I gazed in your eyes of blue,
And though it's quite a while since last we met
You looked so sweet I never can forget.

REFRAIN

Play me a tune, my dearie,
Play me a tune, I'm weary
Waitin' for the dreamy look in your eye.
Every mem'ry lingers
And I can see your fingers
Flickering on the Chickering in the days gone by.
Play an old-fashioned song
That's full of wonderful harmonies,
You don't know how I long
To hear you tickle the ivories.
Play me a tune, I say, you
Play me a tune the way you
Used to back in the good old days.

PATTER 1

C See if you can play the melo-
D Dy I want to hear,
E Even though you find that it's an
F Effort for you, dear. You were a
G Genius when you dressed in abbrevi-
A Ated gingham frocks. So
B Be a good little girl and let me
C See you beat the box,

Go on and play

SHE: Is this the tune?
HE: Yes, that's the tune you used to play there.
It made me stay there
All afternoon.
SHE: You like it still?
HE: I feel a thrill in every phrase, dear,
What happy days, dear,
Oh, what a song!
Come along and
[*Repeat refrain*]

PATTER 2

I'll
C See if I can play the melo-

D Dy you want to hear,
E Even though it means a lot of
F Effort for me, dear. You thought me a
G Genius when I dressed in abbrevi-
A Ated gingham frocks. So I'll
B Be a good little girl and let you
C See me beat the box.
[*Repeat refrain*]

LOVE LETTER WORDS

Published October 1922. Introduced by Joyce Maple and ensemble.

VERSE

When somebody writes you a letter
In the style that you've always admired,
You say, "This could never be better,
It's something that love has inspired."
Then you read through the lines and discover
Many words that you already know,
For the phrases you find in the letter,
Were first uttered ages ago.

REFRAIN

Oh, the wooing words in a love letter
Are the dearest words ever known,
For the cooing words in a love letter
Are as old as the Blarney Stone.
They are always the same
Just a part of the game,
And you've heard them so often before.
Yet how sweet they sound in a love letter
When you read them over once more.

THE BANDIT BAND

Published November 1922. Introduced by Llora Hoffman and ensemble. The earlier version was intended for *Mayfair and Montmartre* (March 1922).

Early version

VERSE

Across the Rio Grande
I know a bandit band
That captures everyone who passes.
It's not the kind of band
That robs the overland.
But just a band composed of brasses.
And when it starts to croon
Some syncopated tune,
It twists your heart and clings on,
And when you've heard it play
You throw your cares away
And put a pair of wings on.

REFRAIN

Oh boy, that bandit band!
It beats the band of any land.
Demand it and you'll understand.
The kind of jazz it has will make you feel as
  happy as a bandit,
For it's simply grand.
It doesn't hold you up like most robber bands,
By shooting guns and shouting "Up with your
  hands."
It simply plays until you take your only dollar
  bill,
And hand it to the bandit band.

Published version

VERSE

Throughout this mighty land
There is a bandit band
That's raising quite a lot of Hades.
It's not the kind of band
That you can reprimand,
For it's a band composed of ladies.
No matter where you go
They always get your dough
And leave you nothing but your sorrows.
You often hear the phrase
"The woman always pays"
But what she pays, she borrows.

REFRAIN

Oh boy, that bandit band!
It beats the band in any land,
Withstand it, and I'll say you're grand.
Gold-digging is it's game,
And woman's just another name
For bandit, but a diff'rent brand.
She doesn't hold you up like most robber
  bands
By shooting and shouting
"Up with your hands."
She gives you one sweet look,
And then you take your pocketbook
And hand it to the bandit band.

THE SPONGE

Introduced by Helene Dahlia.

VERSE 1

Down in the depths of the water
Lived Old Mother Sponge and her daughter,
Such a nice young child
But extremely wild
In every way.
She had a longing to try spots
More lively where folks hit the high spots,
But each time a diver
Would arrive her
Mother would say:

REFRAIN 1

I think we'd better go, better go, better go.
There's a diver not far.
He simply mustn't know, mustn't know, mustn't know,
What a nice sponge you are.
Or he'll carry you away,
Where you'd find it hard to stay
On the straight and narrow path,
And I'd rather see you drowned
Than to have you floatin' round
In somebody's bath.

VERSE 2

This good advice from her mother
Went in one ear and then out the other.
And soon she sat in an artist's flat
In Washington Square,
Leading a life that annoyed her,
As nobody ever employed her.
She faced this disaster
Till at last her
Voice filled the air.

REFRAIN 2

I think I'd better go, better go, better go,
This is no place for me.
The water doesn't flow, doesn't flow, doesn't flow
As it did in the sea.
Simply hanging on a wall
Isn't any fun at all,
When the bathtub's so nice.
And I'll say to any sponge,
Who's about to take the plunge:
Take mother's advice.

THE HARBOR DEEP DOWN IN MY HEART

Published October 1922. Probably dropped before the Philadelphia opening. It appears to have been intended for Llora Hoffman and members of the ensemble for something called "The Harbor Scene."

VERSE

When the right man comes my way
I know precisely what to say.
When I want him to know I want him to stay
I shall murmur musingly:
"Young man, if you're a ship at sea
Vainly hunting a haven,
Lay your course for me,
For

REFRAIN

"I've got a harbor
Deep down in my heart,
Sheltered from every danger
Waiting for some little stranger.
When you're weary
Sailing the ocean blue,
Merely make for my harbor,
I'll make room for you."

THE OLD-FASHIONED WALTZ

Apparently dropped before the Philadelphia opening. Music for a verse survives, but no verse lyrics. Lynn Siebert in her Porter Thematic Catalogue says that "except for slight rhythmic differences, the melody of this song is identical with that of 'Auf Wiederseh'n' from *Star Dust* (1931)."

Come with me and waltz once more,
The way they did in the days of yore,
We'll sing the rhymes of olden times,
When all lovers were gay.
The stars are twinkling merrily,
They're dancing, darling, for you and me,
Tonight's the night,
So hold me tight,
And waltz our troubles away.

PITTER-PATTER

Apparently dropped before the Philadelphia opening. The Yale manuscript bears the notation "Copyright Harms, 1922," but it was not copyrighted at that time.

VERSE

When you feel your heart go pitter-patter,
There's no reason why your teeth should
chatter,
For it's just the usual thing
That attacks one in the spring.
I've a case, in case you'd like to try it,
But we'd have to find some spot more quiet,
Where the breezes gently moan,
And there is no chaperon,

REFRAIN

If you've
Got that pitter-patter in your heart,
I can tell you what's the matter from the start.
All you need is a notion
Of true devotion.
Don't get a doctor to concoct a remedy,
Come to me,
And I'll make you feel much better very soon.
If you'll only try my treatment 'neath the
moon,
You'll admit once you've been kissed,
I'm the greatest specialist
For that little pitter-patter in your heart.

TWIN SISTERS

Music exists in the Porter Collection at Yale for the finale and for sections titled "Scotch Twins," "South Sea Isles," and "Twin Sisters (Egyptian)." This editor located the lyrics for the number in a private collection. Only the Scotch portion was missing. Porter seems to have worked hard on "Twin Sisters," but there is no evidence that it was actually sung in the show. It must have been intended for the Swansons and other sisters whom the Shuberts recruited for the production.

DUTCH: Mr. Shubert, J. J.,
Said to Hitchy one day,
I have lately discovered the fact
That the one thing that pays
In a show nowadays
Is a nice little twin sister act.
Go and find us some twins,
Whether Zulus or Finns
I don't care, if they'll make millionaires
of us.
And so just to make sure
Hitchy went on a tour.
He came home with six little pairs of
us.
The first pair of twins are we
And straight from the Zuider Zee.
RUSSIAN: Hi hi hi, we're Sonia and Olga.
Hi hi hi, twins from the Volga.
If you're who's who, and know what is
whatski,
Watch us do the new Russian Trotski.
EGYPT: The Nile twins are gay little minxes,
Two rowdy Rebeccahs at the well.
We know what the secret of the Sphinx
is
But it is much too awful to tell.
We don't much resemble each other
And often wondered why it was,
For I look exactly like my mother
While I take after a friend of Pa's.
FRENCH: Here are we, from Paree.
The elite declare we're sweet and très
jolie.
We are both much fairer than Venus
But we've only one brain between us.
We've agreed to exceed
So in case we try to shock you,
It's a nice catastrophe
For the two little girls from Paree.
SOUTH
SEA
ISLES: Far from Tahiti twin maidens are we.
We know what to do and do it daily.
So if you're looking for good company
We'll accompany you on the ukulele.
SPANISH: We're two little dark-eyed sisters from
Andalusia,
Two little tummy twisters who might
amuse yuh.
We haven't the slightest notion of what
dramatics are
And so we'll show you what Spanish
acrobatics are.

SISTER ACT—REFRAIN

Everything's twins,
Everything's twins,
Everything's twins nowadays,
Everything's twins,
Everything's twins,
Everything's twins, it's the craze.
Take the fellow who picks
Out a Packard twin-six

And the wife who wants someone to sweep away the old dust
Always gets those twins called Gold Dust.
Everything's twice,
Everything's twice,
Everything's twice what it was.
This is the price
A modern person pays
Yet, at night, it's good to get in bed,
And know you're next to a twin bed,
For ev'rything's twins,
Ev'rything's twins nowadays.

ADDITIONAL SECTION

The twins from the town of Manhattan
Are swifter than all other pairs.
When not dressed in silk, we're in satin,
So, no wonder we put on airs!
We don't much resemble each other
And often we've wondered why it was,
For I look exactly like Mother
While I take after a friend of Pa's.

JUNGLE ROSE

Apparently dropped before the Philadelphia opening.

VERSE

A sailor lost in the jungle wild
Found a rose of deepest red,
A flower who gazed like a trusting child
When he raised her drooping head.
The breeze hushed its refrain.
The moon, still on the wane,
Lingered longer and sadly smiled
As the sailor softly said:

REFRAIN

Oh, sweet Jungle Rose,
Nobody knows
How I worship and adore you.
Don't you realize
That in any flower show you'd win the prize?
So come bloom for me over the sea,
I've a garden waiting for you.
Twine round my heart,
Never to part,
My shy little Jungle Rose.

CURIO SONG or OLD KING SOLLY

Unused, but almost certainly by Porter. I have not included "Dancing Shoes" (introduced by Alice Ridnor and girls), "Daughters of Satan" (Llora Hoffman and ensemble), "Under a Pretty Hat" (Jack Squires, the Swanson sisters, and ensemble), or even the number "Versailles" (Llora Hoffman, Martha Mason, and Louis Hector), because I have no conclusive evidence that they were written by Porter.

VERSE

I'm a dealer in antiques,
In old curios and freaks,
In furnitures and tapestries so rare.
They all bring out the past to me
And I know their history.
That makes me feel that I am living there.
For instance, if I put on Nero's crown,
I'm back in Rome and see it burning down.

REFRAIN 1

I sat in old King Louis' chair one night in sunny France
And saw Du Barry wink her other eye.
I wore the coat of Bonaparte and went into a trance
And saw the Empress Josephine go by.
I saw Egyptian dancing girls along the river Nile
When I put Pharaoh's crown upon my head.
And I learned a lot of things
About those queer Egyptian kings
The night I slept in Cleopatra's bed.

REFRAIN 2

I took the sword of Joan of Arc and held it in my hand
And saw her leading France to victory.
I held a seashell to my ear that I found on the sand
And I saw Venus rising from the sea.
I found the jug of Omar in far-off Hindustan
And pictured him beneath the crescent moon.
And a thousand wives, it seems,
Rushed in and woke me from my dreams
The night I slept in old King Solly's room.

GREENWICH VILLAGE FOLLIES

1924

Tryout: Nixon's Apollo Theatre, Atlantic City, September 8, 1924. Produced by A. L. Jones and Morris Green at the Sam S. Shubert Theatre, New York, September 16, 1924. Also played Winter Garden Theatre. 127 performances. The entire production devised and staged by John Murray Anderson. Cast included the Dolly Sisters and George Hale.

Porter wrote most of the original score, but his songs were dropped at different points in the New York engagement, and by the time the production began its post-Broadway tour in early 1925, all of Porter's songs had been deleted.

Many were missing and presumed lost until February 1982, when musical comedy songs and orchestrations were rediscovered at the Warner Brothers Music warehouse in Secaucus, New Jersey. The find included considerable material from this show, much of it shedding light on Porter's evolution toward the simpler, more accessible style that achieved success for him in the late 1920's.

BRITTANY

Published September 1924. Introduced by George Hale. Dropped before December 1, 1924. A much more detailed and intricate version of this song, including additional lyrics and countermelodies, surfaced in the Warner Brothers Secaucus material. The "Hackensack Version" and "Brittany Girl" were not in the published version.

VERSE

Night time and day time,
My thoughts turn to France,
Back to my play time
And its May time romance.
Once again the shy nightingale trills
Where surrounded by flowering hills:

REFRAIN

There's a town in Brittany
By the side of the sea.
There's a girl in Brittany
At a cottage door, waiting for me.
There's a boat for Brittany
And the only thing I'm dreaming of
Is to sail for Brittany
And the little girl I love.

Hackensack Version

Why not stay back in Hackensack?
You've got a perfectly good girl there.
I feel so blue that due to you
I'm a vision of deep despair.
If you make me countermand my wedding gown,
I will leave my native land and track you down
And carry you back to Hackensack.
You've got a perfectly good girl there.

Brittany Girl

I'm that charming maiden of Brittany
Mentioned in the song before.
I'll go mad if I have to sit any
Longer at my cottage door.
When shall I see
That man I miss?
When will there be
An end to this
Everlasting waiting in Brittany?
Gee, but it's an awful bore.

TWO LITTLE BABES IN THE WOOD

Published February 1928, with other songs from *Paris* (1928). Introduced by Julia Silvers and George Hale. Dropped from the *Greenwich Village Follies* before October 13, 1924. Porter made a piano-vocal recording for Victor (24825) on November 27, 1934. Irene Bordoni, who sang it in *Paris,* recorded it on May 3 and June 24, 1928, but neither recording was released.

The version printed here was found at the Warner Brothers Music warehouse in Secaucus, New Jersey. It includes the words and music for the two announcements that precede the two verses. The announcements were dropped from the 1928 *Paris* version.

PART I. ANNOUNCEMENT.

Listen, my children, and don't say a word.

Now, you'll grant me that Denmark has ne'er had
a grander son,
Than her great author, old Hans Christian
Andersen.
All of you know him, so just to be good to you,
I'll tell his tale of the Babes in the Wood to you.

VERSE 1

There's a tale of two little orphans who were left
in their uncle's care,
To be reared and ruled and properly schooled
Till they grew to be ladies fair.
But, oh, the luckless pair!
For the uncle, he was a cruel trustee,

And he longed to possess their gold;
So he led them thence to a forest dense,
Where he left them to die of cold.
That, at least, is what we're told.

REFRAIN 1

They were two little babes in the wood,
Two little babes, oh, so good!
Two little hearts, two little heads,
Longed to be home in their two little beds,
So—two little birds built a nest
Where the two little babes went to rest,
While the breeze, hov'ring nigh,
Sang a last lullaby
To the two little babes in the wood.

PART II. ANNOUNCEMENT.

Listen, my children, and don't say a word.

Now in spite of all efforts to strengthen and
  quicken it,
Andersen's tale never had any kick in it.
So his descendant, John Murray, in fantasy,
Added a scene for the tired businessman to see.

VERSE 2

They were lying there in the freezing air,
When fortunately there appeared
A rich old man in a big sedan,
And a very, very fancy beard.
He saw those girls and cheered,
Then he drove them down to New York town,
Where he covered them with useful things,
Such as bonds, and stocks, and Paris frocks,
And Oriental pearls in strings,
And a showcase full of rings.

REFRAIN 2

Now those two little babes in the wood,
Are the talk of the whole neighborhood,
For they've too many cars, too many clothes,
Too many parties, and too many beaux,
They have found that the fountain of youth
Is a mixture of gin and vermouth,
And the whole town's agreed
That the last thing in speed
Is the two little babes in the wood.

BROADCAST A JAZZ

Introduced by Bobbe Arnst. Dropped soon after the New York opening. The music is lost.

The following note was found with the refrain at the Cole Porter Trusts. It was probably part of a letter from Cole to Linda:

> I've just finished a first act finale called "Broadcast a Jazz," which, between ourselves, is a knockout. It is in an entirely new rhythm, which only the blacks have used so far. It is a conversation between Lopez' band and the company. The band has announced that it's time to broadcast a tune, and asks the company what to play. The decor behind is two huge screens on which are painted old-fashioned maps of the two hemispheres, and as the company mentions a country, a figure representing the country appears on the map.

Come on you
Syncopatin' band
Broadcast a jazz,
Let old Yankee land
Show what she has.
Make Hawaii strut her
Meanest stuff.
Play until Calcutta
Cries, "Enough."
Go thru China, Japan,
And Siberia,
Drive all Turkey insane.
Travel from the Sudan
To Algeria,
Fly on over to Spain.
Spread thru Europe in-
Jecting a thrill.
After that begin
Shockin' Brazil.
Teach the world to love
To the rhythm of
Jazz, broadcast a jazz.

WAIT FOR THE MOON

Published September 1924. Introduced by Jennie Dolly and George Rasely. Dropped in November 1924.

VERSE

Pierrot fondly lingers
Beside his lady love
Awaiting fairy fingers
To light the moon above.
To this fair one near him
He softly hums a strain
But all true lovers hear him
And sing the same refrain.

REFRAIN

Wait for the moon,
The moon of your dreams,
Wait for the moon,
And bathe in her beams,
Wait while she charms
Our last night in June,
Just stay in my arms
And wait for the moon.

MY LONG AGO GIRL

Published September 1924. Introduced by George Rasely. Dropped in November 1924. Also titled "My Long, Long Ago Girl." A version found at Warner Brothers Music warehouse in Secaucus, New Jersey, in February 1982 includes music for Thomas Haynes Bayly's nineteenth-century song "Long, Long Ago!" deployed as a countermelody to "My Long Ago Girl." Obviously, Porter wrote his song as a countermelody to Bayly's.

VERSE

Gone are the roses that grew down the lane,
The lane of our sunny September,
Still, proudly blooming I see once again
The one rose to make me remember.

REFRAIN

Long, long ago,
Long, long ago
Under a sycamore tree,
A maiden said she could grow
Fond of me,
But one summer day,
She went away,
Leaving my heart in a whirl,
And there's only one love I know,
My long ago girl.

MAKE EVERY DAY A HOLIDAY

Published September 1924. Introduced by Julia Silvers. Later sung by Polly Williams. It seems to have been dropped from the show in December 1924 and replaced by a song with the title "Let Every Day Be a Holiday," sung by Rosalie Claire. This new song was probably not Porter's.

VERSE 1

We all know life is short,
It's soon over, so be a sport,
Don't be blue, simply do
Exactly what I tell you to.

VERSE 2

Troubles end, never last,
So start laughin' and make it fast,
Leave those blues, hunt good news,
And when you've got your dancin' shoes

REFRAIN

Make ev'ry day a holiday
And ev'ry moment sublime.
Pick out a dainty doll a day
And give yourself a good time.
If troubles come, a dash of rum
Will do the trick for you,
So order service.
Open a nice
Bottle or two, till you
Forget you're blue.
Don't be afraid to leave the shade
And take your place in the sun,
Go runnin' wild, remain a child
Until you've had some good fun.
Before you say, "I'm on my way
To hit the hay,"
Play "Cabaret"
And make the day a holiday.
O.K.
Hip! Hip! Hooray!

I'M IN LOVE AGAIN

Published June 1925. Added to the show after the New York opening. Introduced by Rosie and Jennie Dolly. Later sung by Marjorie Alton and Bobbe Arnst and then by Margaret and Elizabeth Keene. Porter's account of its early history, included in a letter he sent his mother (February 2, 1927), erroneously states the song was not in the *Greenwich Village Follies.* Recordings made in 1927 by Paul Whiteman, Aileen Stanley and Billy Murray, and the Revellers helped ensure its success after it was published.

Mammammamma,

I want to tell you a curious story.

Three years ago, when I was writing the *Greenwich Village Follies,* I gave them a tune called *I'm in Love Again.* This tune I had written before and had sung it around Paris, and always with howling success, as the melody was very simple and the sentiment appealed to everyone.

The great powers of the *Greenwich Village Follies* thought less than nothing of this song, and never would allow it in the show. So it lay in a drawer at Harms, and I thought it was dead forever. But one thing very funny about that little song, no matter where I traveled to, I'd always hear someone singing it. Last year, in New York, I heard it at Maurice's cabaret. They played it over and over again, simply the one refrain, as no one knew the verse. I went to the band leader and asked him who wrote it, and he said, "Oh, a Harlem nigger wrote it." Everybody in Paris knows it, and it's almost as well known in London and in Rome. But practically no one knows that I wrote it.

Now, suddenly out of a clear sky, comes a wire from Harms, offering me an excellent royalty to publish this song and do everything they can to make a big hit out of it. And I have sent them a verse and a second refrain, and its coming out immediately as a popular song. As Harms usually only publish songs in productions, and never launch a song unless they make a big hit of it, I shall be surprised if I don't make a lot of money out of it.

Don't you think its a funny story, that poor little deserted song suddenly landing on her feet.

VERSE 1

Why am I
Just as happy as a child?
Why am I
Like a racehorse running wild?
Why am I
In a state of ecstasy?
The reason is 'cause
Something's happened to me.

REFRAIN 1

I'm in love again
And the spring is comin',
I'm in love again,
Hear my heart strings strummin',
I'm in love again,
And the hymn I'm hummin'
Is the "Huddle Up, Cuddle Up Blues!"
I'm in love again,
And I can't rise above it,
I'm in love again,
And I love, love, love it:
I'm in love again,
And I'm darn glad of it,
Good news!

VERSE 2

Someone sad,
Had the awful luck to meet,
Someone bad,
But the kind of bad that's sweet.
No one knows
What a glimpse of paradise,
Someone who's naughty
Showed to someone who's nice.

REFRAIN 2

I'm in love again,
And with glee I bubble.
I'm in love again,
And the fun's just double.
I'm in love again.
If I got in trouble,
I'll be cursin' one person I know.
I'm in love again,
I'm a lovebird singin',
I'm in love again.
I'm a spring lamb springin',
I'm in love again,
Weddin' bells are ringin',
Let's go.

Music, but no lyrics, were found at the Warner Brothers Music warehouse in Secaucus, New Jersey, February 1982, for the following previously "lost" songs from the *Greenwich Village Follies* of 1924.

"Understudies"—Dropped before New York opening.
"I Want Twins"—Dropped during New York run.
"Bring Me a Radio"—Dropped from the New York run. Bandleader Vincent Lopez claimed that he composed this song, but Porter's name is on the copyist ink score found at the Warner Brothers warehouse in Secaucus.
The Dollys and Their Collies"—Dropped during New York run. Retitled "The Follies Girls and Their Collies."

Music, but no lyrics, was also found for the following numbers, which appear to have been dropped from the show before its pre-Broadway tryout.

"I've Got Quelque Chose"—See "Quelque Chose" in *Paris,* 1928.
"I Love a Girl in a Shawl"—See "I Dream of a Girl in a Shawl" in *Wake Up and Dream,* 1929. The Secaucus score has music of original (Spanish) and of Italian, Chinese and Chicago versions.
"Greenwich Village Ladies' Barber Shop"—Title

previously unknown.
"Opening Act I"—This includes music for a number entitled "Gibson Girls' Entrance."
"Untitled waltz"

Lyrics and music for the following songs are still lost.

"The Life of a Sailor"—Dropped before New York opening.
"Toy of Destiny"—Dropped during New York run.

"Syncopated Pipes of Pan" is the same song with a slightly altered lyric as "Ragtime Pipes of Pan" (see "Miscellaneous Songs, 1920s.")

LA REVUE DES AMBASSADEURS

1928

Produced by Edmond Sayag at the Ambassadeurs Café, Paris, May 10, 1928. Number of performances unknown. Directed by Bobby Connolly. Cast, starring Buster and John West and Fred Waring's orchestra, included Evelyn Hoey, Mary Leigh, Carter Wardell, Morton Downey, Katheryn Ray, Frances Gershwin, the Pearson Brothers, Eleanor Shaler, Basil Howes, Muriel Harrisson, and the Three Eddies.

On the program this revue was titled *Troisième Ambassadeurs—Show of 1928.* In a printed book of lyrics it was called *In the Old Days and Today.* Many of the songs were printed in a single volume by Francis Salabert in August 1928. Five of those songs were also published individually in May 1928.

KEEP MOVING

No music survives. Introduced by Muriel Harrisson.

Oh, ladies and gentlemen,
Especially gentlemen,
And other incidental men,
We've got some good news,
If you want to skip with us,
And take a nice trip with us,
We'll ask you on the ship with us,
To make a big cruise.
We don't know where
We're gonna go.
We wouldn't care,
We wouldn't know.
But if you're
Blue, and need a cure,
Then you'd better come along.
We'll do everything for you
To make the bells ring for you
And to prove it, we'll sing to you
Our traveling song.

Keep moving, keep moving,
Don't stand around.
Keep moving, keep moving, and cover ground.
If you meet disaster,
Step lively, get past her,
Go faster and faster
And put a bit more pep in your step.
Lay on it, go-getter,
Don't let her pass.
Doggone-it, you'd better
Step on the gas.
No dropping, no stopping,
Or you'll get in wrong,
Keep moving, keep moving along.

. . .

All aboard for over-there.
All aboard for God-knows-where.
All aboard, goodbye, Uncle Sam.
Give our love to the family Ford.
All aboard, and let's vamoose.
All aboard and raise the deuce.
All aboard, we're off on the loose,
So turn on the juice,
All aboard.

THE LOST LIBERTY BLUES

Published August 1928. Introduced by Evelyn Hoey.

VERSE

THE STATUE OF LIBERTY: As you sail away
On your holiday,
Take a last little look at me.
GIRLS: Who are you?
STATUE: I'm an innocent
Public monument
Called the Statue of Liberty.
GIRLS: How do you do.
STATUE: And I'm a slave
In the home of the brave
And the land of the free.
GIRLS: Poor girl, she's feeling mighty blue.
STATUE: Once, my country, France,
Had a Yank romance,
So she gave me to Uncle Sam.
GIRLS: Such an affair.
STATUE: But he's changed me so
That I hardly know
What I'm meant for or who I am.
GIRLS: What do we care.
STATUE: He's made a mess
Of my chance for success,
And I'm not worth a damn.
GIRLS: A perfect lady doesn't swear.

REFRAIN

STATUE: I've got the lost liberty blues.
Those lost liberty blues.
With a pair of handcuffs on my wrists.
And padlocks on my shoes.
Can you expect me to be gay
Or ask me to enthuse?
While reformers lead 'em
From the battle cry of freedom
To the lost liberty blues.

PATTER

They're gonna abolish drinks, abolish
smokes,
Abolish sports, abolish jokes,
Abolish rouge for frivolous frails,
And abolish the polish for their fingernails.
They're gonna abolish jazz, abolish plays,
Abolish dances and cabarets.
And I warn you now that before you're dead,
If you're not careful, they'll abolish bed.

OMNIBUS

The revised version, titled "Do You Want to See Paris?," was used in *Fifty Million Frenchmen* (1929). Introduced here by Eleanor Shaler, Jack Pearson, and ensemble, and in *Fifty Million Frenchmen* by William Gaxton and ensemble.

GUIDE: Do you wanna see Paris?
Do you wanna see Paris?
If you wanna see Paris,
You'd better come with me.
FLAPPERS: We wanna see Paris.
We wanna see Paris.
MILLIONAIRE: And see how Paris
Compares with Kankakee.
GUIDE: Then get aboard my omnibus.
FLAPPERS: First, how much is it, sonny?
GUIDE: It's only fifty francs apiece.
MILLIONAIRE: What's that in American money?
GUIDE: Well, fifty francs, divided by
three,
And multiplied by seven
Makes let me see, let me see.
MILLIONAIRE: Why, you damn fool, eleven.
FLAPPERS: Is that all? Is that all?
You're talking through your hat.
MILLIONAIRE: You couldn't get a ride in a baby
carriage in the U.S.A. for that.
GUIDE: We now are going up the Champs
Elysées, if you please.
You see those poles sticking out the
ground, those are trees.
FLAPPERS: Poor little trees, they've got some
awful disease.
GUIDE: That building there, upon the
right,
Is the famous Hotel Claridge.
It's where the ladies go at night,
When they get fed up with
marriage.
FLAPPERS: Hurrah for the Claridge, and down
with marriage.
GUIDE: And now, before you, straight
ahead, the Arc de Triomphe
stands,
To commemorate the victories of
France in many lands.
It was built in eighteen hundred
and five by Napoleon the Great.
FLAPPERS: 'Swonderful. 'Smarvelous. It'd make
such a nice front gate.
GUIDE: It's a hundred and sixty-four feet
high, and a hundred and fifty
wide,
And exactly seventy-two feet deep.
FLAPPERS: Well, we'll say you're some guide.
GUIDE: This great arcade
Sits all alone,
But unafraid.
A flower full-blown,
Entirely made of
Of solid stone.
MILLIONAIRE: I'll buy it.
GUIDE: Before you stands the Eiffel Tow'r,
a monument adored.
MILLIONAIRE: Then what does that sign mean,
Citroën?
GUIDE: Citroën is French for Ford.
FLAPPERS: Aux armes, Citroën.
Citroën is French for Ford.
GUIDE: Do you realize this famous tow'r
Will be all lit up, in another hour,
By a light of a million candlepow'r?
MILLIONAIRE: I'll buy it.
GUIDE: Kneel in pray'r
And doff your hat
And cease your remarks profane.
The building there
You're looking at
Is the famous Church of the
Madeleine.
FLAPPERS: Hallaluyah, Hallaluyah.
It's the famous Madeleine.
MILLIONAIRE: We've got a church in Kankakee,
But this one is a riot.
So if you'll send it C.O.D.
I'll buy it.
GUIDE: If you're really connoisseurs,
I've got a treat for you.
We're now at the Ambassadeurs,
To see the new Revue.
FLAPPERS: Oh, this is swell.
Is this the Ambassadeurs?
GUIDE: Yes, this is the reason why Chanel
Invented summer furs.
FLAPPERS: And who's that little lonely
Fellow sitting down?
GUIDE: Why, that man is the only
Frenchman left in town.

You see that lovely lady with a young man sitting by 'er?
Well, she's a famous beauty here, that all the men admire.
They tell me she has ev'rything a lover could require.

MILLIONAIRE: I'll buy her.

ALL: Now that we've seen Paris, it's time that we begin
To pack our trunks and buy our bunks on a fast train to Berlin.
The next day to Vienna, and then a day in Rome.
And after that we'll hurry back to home, sweet home.

Revised version from FIFTY MILLION FRENCHMEN (1929)

DO YOU WANT TO SEE PARIS?

GUIDE: Do you want to see Paris?
Do you want to see Paris?
If you want to see Paris,
Then come along with me.

GIRLS: We want to see Paris,
We want to see Paris
And see how Paris
Compares with Kankakee.

GUIDE: Then hop aboard my omnibus.

GIRLS: First, how much is it, sonny?

GUIDE: It's only fifty francs apiece.

FATHER OF GIRLS: What's that in American money?

GUIDE: Well, fifty francs divided by three
And multiplied by seven
Makes let me see, let me see—

FATHER: You damn fool, eleven.

GIRLS: Is that all, is that all? You're talking through your hat.

FATHER: You couldn't get a ride in a baby carriage in the U.S.A. for that.

GUIDE: We're on the Champs Elysées now, a street of great renown.
You see that fellow there, he's the only Frenchman left in town.

GIRLS: Oh, what a face.
He looks so out of place.

GUIDE: That building there, upon the right, is the famous Hotel Claridge.
It's where the ladies go at night, when they get fed up with marriage.

GIRLS: Hurrah for the Claridge.
And down with marriage.

GUIDE: And now before you straight ahead, the Arc de Triomphe stands
To commemorate the victories of France in many lands.
It was built in eighteen hundred and five by Napoleon the Great.

GIRLS: 'Swonderful. 'Smarvelous. It'd make such a nice front gate.

GUIDE: It's a hundred and sixty-four feet high, and a hundred and fifty wide.

GIRLS: And exactly seventy-two feet deep.
Well, we'll say you're some guide.

GUIDE: This great arcade
Stands, all alone
But unafraid,
Upon her throne,
Entirely made of solid stone.

FATHER: I'll buy it.

GUIDE: Before you stands the Eiffel Tower, a monument adored.

FATHER: Then what does that sign mean—Citroën?

GUIDE: Citroën is French for Ford.

GIRLS: Aux armes, Citroën. Citroën is French for Ford.

GUIDE: Do you realize this famous tower
Will be all lit up in another hour,
With a light of a million candlepower?

FATHER: I'll buy it.

GUIDE: Kneel in prayer and doff your hat
And cease your remarks profane.
The building there you're gazing at
Is the famous Church of the Madeleine.

GIRLS: Hallaluyah, Hallaluyah,
It's the good old Madeleine.

FATHER: We've got a church in Kankakee
But this one is a riot
And if you'll send it C.O.D.
I'll buy it.

GUIDE: We are now in the theater called the Moulin Rouge,
An old Parisian pet
Where the men that girls remember meet the girls that men forget.
Its promenade is an ideal spot
For a man whose French is not so hot
To improve his French with a French cocotte.

FATHER: I'll buy it.

GUIDE: Good night, everybody.

ALL: Good evening, Mr. Guide.
We're glad that we have seen Paree
And thanks for the buggy ride.

GUIDE: But please before you leave me
And go back to your huts

Will you kindly tell me what you think of Paris?
CHORUS: It's the nuts.
GUIDE: Do you want to see Paris, do you want to see Paris? Do you want to see Paris? I thank you.

PILOT ME

Published August 1928. Introduced by Muriel Harrisson, Carter Wardell, and ensemble.

VERSE

I've got an aeroplane,
Entirely new,
A cozy, narrow plane,
Just built for two.
I'll let you drive it, dear,
And when you do,
Up where it's private, dear,
We'll bill and coo.

REFRAIN

Pilot me,
Pilot me,
Be the pilot I need.
Please give my ship
A maiden trip,
And we'll get the prize for speed.
So cast away your fears,
Strip my gears,
Let me carry you through.
And when afraid you are
Of going too far,
Then I'll
Just pil-
Ot you.

IN A MOORISH GARDEN

Published August 1928. Introduced by Morton Downey.

VERSE

One night, in Marrakesh,
A rose, in bloom,
Made all the evening fresh
With her perfume.
But when I searched the glade
To find her bow'r,
I found the flow'r
Was a maid.

REFRAIN

In a Moorish garden,
One night in June,
Beneath the moon,
I found her.
In a Moorish garden
I saw her charms
And put my arms
Around her.
As we sat there, clinging,
A swallow
Who was winging
Through the hollow
Started singing
A serenade.
When I see a swallow
And hear his song,
I always long
For that maid.

ALMIRO

Published May and August 1928. Introduced by Basil Howes.

VERSE 1

Almiro was a dancer who came from far Brazil,
And got his rep
From doing a step
That gave the girls a thrill.
He started giving lessons to all the dizzy blondes,
And soon he'd got
A beautiful yacht,
And flocks of stocks and bonds.
Ah! Ah!

REFRAIN 1

Almiro
Brought a step from Rio Janeiro.
People cheered whenever Almiro
Started dancing it up and down.
And though Almiro,
As a lover equaled a zero,
All the ladies called him the hero
Of Rio Janeiro
Town.

VERSE 2

One fatal night, Almiro
Was resting on his fame,
When suddenly,
From over the sea,
A Broadway dancer came.
And when they saw the dance of this jazzing acrobat,
The girls about
All followed him out,
And left Almiro flat.
Ah! Ah!

REFRAIN 2

Almiro
Traveled back to Rio Janeiro,
Where that former fabulous hero
Bought a cottage and settled down.
There lived Almiro
Till his bank account was a zero
And he got a kick in the rear-o
From Rio Janeiro
Town.

YOU AND ME

Published May and August 1928. Introduced by Mary Leigh and Basil Howes.

VERSE 1

HE: Jazz may
Be other folks' diet,
I like the quiet
Life.
SHE: We'll play
To music more measured,
Once I'm your treasured wife.
Just think of us two,
The wedding is through,
The hullabaloo
Is past.
We're suddenly shown
A home of our own,
And we are alone
At last.

REFRAIN 1

BOTH: Just you and me
HE: We'll be so clever
Nothing can sever
BOTH: You and me.
SHE: Ever in harmony.
HE: Oh, what a rosy
Future to view.
SHE: Think of that cozy
Cottage for two.
HE: There we'll be,
BOTH: Nobody but you and me.

VERSE 2

SHE: Oh boy,
I dream such a lot of
Our little plot of
Ground.
HE: What joy
To sit on a v'randa,
Where there's no band around.
SHE: And when like a thrall,
A whip-poor-will call
Announces the fall
Of night,
HE: Some zephyr, no doubt.
Who's breezing about,
Will come and blow out
The light.

REFRAIN 2

BOTH: For you and me
SHE: Are those pajamas
Papa's or Mamma's?
BOTH: You and me
HE: Sleeping so peacefully.
SHE: One night, a curs'ry
Stork may suggest
HE: Making a nurs'ry
Out of his nest.
SHE: Who'll agree?
BOTH: Nobody but you and me.

FISH

Published August 1928. Introduced by Carter Wardell.

VERSE 1

There was once a staid
Little fisher maid,
And she lived beside the shore.
Her only wish
Was to catch enough fish
To keep the wolf from the door.
So on the sand
With a pole in her hand,

She would linger all the day long,
And the fish would curse
When she'd start to rehearse
This song.

REFRAIN

Fish, fish, stop and take a look.
Whet your appetite.
I've got something on my hook.
Won't you take a bite?
Don't be so suspicious,
Sample my line.
All the other fishes
Say it's delicious.
Fish, fish, won't you grant my wish.
Don't be so noncommittal,
Little
Fish.

VERSE 2

Not a single fish
Would grant her wish,
And her income equaled nought.
So off went she
To that city, Paree,
Where even wise fish get caught.
And I've no doubt,
If tonight, you went out,
You would see her strolling along.
She has changed her game,
But she's singing the same
Old song.

MILITARY MAIDS

Published May and August 1928. Introduced by Evelyn Hoey and ensemble.

VERSE

It is Hades
To be ladies
Whose hearts have never been warmed.
That's the reason
Why, this season,
Our regiment has been formed.
We are waging war
On the bachelor
And in victory we trust,
For the sole intent
Of the regiment
Is to get married or bust.

REFRAIN

Military maidens,
Amorous females
Hunting for he-males,
Unafraid.
Ev'ry little flapper
Is a good scrapper,
And you'll admit we're rather dapper
On parade.
Listen to the rattle
Of that drum,
If you want a battle
Here we come.
Unless you want to play, boys
You'd better run away, boys,
For we're underheated,
Cheated,
Military maids.

BLUE HOURS

Published August 1928. Introduced by Morton Downey. This number originally was intended for *Paris.* A copy of it with virtually the same lyric was found at the Warner Brothers Music warehouse in Secaucus, New Jersey.

VERSE

I feel so blue,
When I think of you,
Every moment seems harder to bear.
And since the day
When you went away,
I've been spending
Hours unending.

REFRAIN

Blue hours,
Missing you, dear.
Blue hours,
Wanting you near.
Hours rent
By memories too
Of hours spent
Together with you.
In the blue dell,
We used to adore,
The bluebell
Is blooming once more,
But the bluebird
Won't sing his song,
Till you've ended my long
Blue hours.

ALPINE ROSE

Published August 1928. Introduced by Eleanor Shaler.

VERSE

Just look at this miss,
And hear my voice.
I am a Swiss miss,
But not from choice.
So high in Switzerland
My homestead lies
That though my yodel's grand,
No one replies.

REFRAIN

I'm an Alpine rose, just an Alpine rose,
And I live up there in one of those bungalows.
I'm a Swiss Bo-Peep,
And I've lost my flock,
So my only boon companion is a cuckoo clock.
When the winter comes, it begins to storm,
And I have to get my Saint Bernard to keep me
warm.
But I've got no choice,
As I've got no beaux,
And I'm nothing but an Alpine rose.

PATTER (WITH APOLOGIES TO LONGFELLOW)

The shades of night were falling fast,
As through an Alpine village passed
A maid who bore, 'mid snow and ice,
A banner with the strange device,
Excelsior.

"Try not the pass," the old man said,
"Dark lowers the tempest overhead,
The roaring torrent is deep and wide,"
And loud that clarion voice replied,
Excelsior.

"Beware the pine tree's withered branch,
Beware the awful avalanche."
This was the peasant's last good night,
A voice replied far up the height,
Excelsior.

There in the twilight cold and gray,
Lifeless, but beautiful she lay,
And when she rose and tried to stir,
She tripped and landed flat on her,
Excelsior.

GERSHWIN SPECIALTY

Porter wrote this brief introduction to a medley of Gershwin songs sung by George and Ira Gershwin's sister Frances. No music survives.

I happen to be the sister
Of a rhythm twister.
No doubt you know him as Mister
George Gershwin.
If you're prepared for an orgy
Of music written by Georgie,
I'll try to sing you some fav'rites of
The man I love.

BOULEVARD BREAK

No music survives. Introduced by Frances Gershwin, the Pearson Brothers, and ensemble.

VERSE

Come on, you poor ungodly sinners,
Get up and leave your heavy dinners,
The hour has come for you to pull a
Dance on the boule-
Vard.
You can't fool
Around on a bench,
In my school,
To improve your French.

REFRAIN

You do the boulevard break,
Do that boulevard break,
Get that boulevard shake
In your shoes.
All the boulevard gals,
With their boulevard pals,
Throw the boul, boul, boul, boulevard blues.
And ev'ry boulevard vamp,
'Neath a boulevard lamp,
Does that boulevard stamp
To keep awake.
If you're a boulevard hound,
And you're boulevard bound,
Do that boul, boul, boul, boulevard break.

HANS

Published May and August 1928. Introduced by Katheryn Ray, Jack Pearson, and ensemble.

VERSE

When Hansel and Gretel had grown up,
They lived on the Zuider Zee.
Though Hansel already had slown up,
His wife still enjoyed a spree.
So when in the neighboring village,
The music would start to play,
She'd straighten her little backbone up,
And say: Oh,

REFRAIN

Hans, Hans, let's go to the dance.
The others all have gone.
The sweet summer breeze is
So fragrant with cheeses
There must be a party on.
Hans, Hans, one night of romance
Would fill my heart with joy,
But a much longer wait'll
Prove fatal
To Gretel,
So hurry, Hans, my boy.

BABY, LET'S DANCE

Published August 1928. Introduced by Buster West and ensemble.

VERSE

Come, baby, wake up.
Put on your make-up.
It's time to take up
Your bottle, baby.
So dry your eyes up,
And hush those cries up,
Or Poppa'll rise up
And throttle baby.
Turn on the Victor,
Please me to death.
Be a boa constrictor,
Squeeze me to death.

REFRAIN

Take hold of my hand, baby,
Just listen to that band, baby,
Oh, isn't it just grand, baby,
Let's dance.
I've got a new step, baby,
So come on and get hep, baby,
We'll turn on the old pep, baby,
Let's dance.
Just put your head on my heart,
And we'll start
Shakin' the shoes,
Wakin' the blues,
Breakin' the news.
Hang on and hold tight, baby,
I feel like a big night, baby.
So give me a kick
Out of a quick
Dance, baby, let's dance.

AN OLD-FASHIONED GIRL

"An Old-Fashioned Girl" and "An Old-Fashioned Boy" were published May and August 1928. Introduced by Mary Leigh, Basil Howes, and ensemble.

VERSE

HE: Today I find
The modern flapper
Is but a kind
Of whippersnapper.
She plays no part
Within my heart
However smart
She may be.
The type of blond
I long to treasure
Is one who's fond
Of homemade pleasure,
And likes to sit
Around and knit
A little kit
For baby.
Won't you find her for me?
Where on earth can she be?

REFRAIN 1

For I'm looking for an old-fashioned girl.
I want to marry a type,
Like some daguerreotype,
Some fair maiden
With an old-fashioned curl,
Somebody sweet and demure,
And as pure as a pearl.
The very moment that I've found her,
I'll take her with me,

Build a bungalow around her,
And throw away the key.
There, protected from the world's endless whirl,
I'll be happy with my old-fashioned girl.

REFRAIN 2

SHE: If you're looking for an old-fashioned girl,
I'm just the lady for you,
To find Arcady for you.
By the length, sir, of my old-fashioned curl,
You can be perfectly sure
I'm as pure
As a pearl.
If, as a husband, you will play up
I never will roam,
And we'll always wind the day up
By singing "Home, Sweet Home."
There, protected from the world's endless whirl,
You'll be happy with your old-fashioned girl.

AN OLD-FASHIONED BOY

VERSE

I'm a girl out of fashion
Full of old-fashioned passion,
And I know whereof I speak.
All these new-fashioned lassies
May have new-fashioned chassis,
But they lack old-fashioned technique.
I have old-fashioned notions
Of those old-fashioned motions
For those old-fashioned moments sublime.
If you know where I live, you
Come around and I'll give you
Just a hell of an old-fashioned time.

REFRAIN

For I'm looking for an old-fashioned boy,
Some dear delicious old thing,
Some slightly vicious old thing,
Just a fellow full of old-fashioned joy,
Who'll let me make him my slave
And my fav-
Orite toy.
The very moment I discover
The man of my prayers,
I will claim him as my lover
And carry him upstairs.
There, secluded from the rude hoi polloi,
I'll be naughty with my old-fashioned boy.

FOUNTAIN OF YOUTH

Published August 1928. Introduced by Buster West and ensemble.

VERSE

Though your age
Be eighty-seven,
Don't engage
In thoughts of heaven,
Until you've heard the wonderful truth.
Very high,
There, where the mountain
Hits the sky,
There is a fountain
That's called the magic fountain of youth.
Just give it a try,
And you won't be put on the shelf,
I know it, for I
Was once eighty-seven myself.

REFRAIN

If you're depressed,
And you're not at your best,
Go and put on your hat,
Hurry to that
Fountain of youth.
When all the pleasures of life
Start to roll off your knife,
And you feel like a fool,
Jump in the cool
Fountain of youth.
Continue swimming about
Till your gray has turned to gold,
And you'll come out
Just a gay young two-year-old.
Do what I say,
Try that cure right away.
'Stead of falling asleep,
Dive in the deep
Fountain of youth.

PARIS

1928

Tryout: Nixon's Apollo Theatre, Atlantic City, February 6, 1928; Adelphi Theatre, Philadelphia, February 13, 1928; Wilbur Theatre, Boston, May 7, 1928; Poli Theatre, Washington, D.C., September 30, 1928. Produced by Gilbert Miller in association with E. Ray Goetz at the Music Box Theatre, New York, October 8, 1928. 195 performances. Staged by William H. Gilmore. Cast, starring Irene Bordoni, included Arthur Margetson, Louise Closser Hale, and Irving Aaronson and his orchestra, The Commanders. A comedy with music, *Paris* was called a "musicomedy" in the show's program.

DON'T LOOK AT ME THAT WAY

Published February 1928. A copy at the Porter Trusts office bears either an earlier or an incorrect title, "Don't Look at Me Like That." Introduced by Irene Bordoni.

VERSE

Oh, I'm so mad about a lad,
It's too deep to express!
And when he tries to use his eyes,
They have instant success.
So full of passion, these pupils are,
That girls forget what their scruples are;
So when he turns them on me, I murmur tenderly:

REFRAIN 1

I think you're great,
I think you're grand,
And I don't mind if you hold my hand,
But don't look at me that way!
Your kisses, too, are heavenly;
And oh, so full of variety,
But don't look at me that way!
When you tell me sweetly you're mine completely,
I always give a long cheer;
But those sudden flashes behind your lashes
Are nobody's business, dear.
Since you began to play your role,
I've lost my heart and I've lost my soul
But as for losing my self-control,
Don't look at me that way!

REFRAIN 2

I just adore your loving arms,
In fact, they're two of your greatest charms
But don't look at me that way!
I'm very mild, I'm very meek,
My will is strong, but my won't is weak;
So don't look at me that way!
When that strange expression of indiscretion
Begins to show in your stare,
There's a hocus-pocus about your focus
That gives me a terrible scare.
I feel a thrill when you arrive,
And while you're near me I simply thrive,
But if you want to get home alive,
Don't look at me that way!

LET'S DO IT, LET'S FALL IN LOVE

Published October 1928. It replaced "Let's Misbehave" before the New York opening and was used later in the English production of the revue *Wake Up and Dream* (1929). The opening lines of refrain 1 were changed to the familiar "Birds do it, bees do it," etc., when Porter realized that many would find the words "Chinks" and "Japs" offensive. Introduced by Irene Bordoni and Arthur Margetson.

VERSE

When the little bluebird,
Who has never said a word,
Starts to sing "Spring, spring,"
When the little bluebell,
In the bottom of the dell,
Starts to ring "Ding, ding,"
When the little blue clerk,
In the middle of his work,
Starts a tune to the moon up above,
It is nature, that's all,
Simply telling us to fall
In love.

REFRAIN 1

And that's why Chinks do it, Japs do it,
Up in Lapland, little Lapps do it,
Let's do it, let's fall in love.
In Spain, the best upper sets do it,
Lithuanians and Letts do it,
Let's do it, let's fall in love.
The Dutch in old Amsterdam do it,
Not to mention the Finns,
Folks in Siam do it,
Think of Siamese twins.
Some Argentines, without means, do it,
People say, in Boston, even beans do it,
Let's do it, let's fall in love.

REFRAIN 2

The nightingales, in the dark, do it,
Larks, k-razy for a lark, do it,
Let's do it, let's fall in love.
Canaries, caged in the house, do it,
When they're out of season, grouse do it,
Let's do it, let's fall in love.
The most sedate barnyard fowls do it,
When a chanticleer cries,
High-browed old owls do it,
They're supposed to be wise,
Penguins in flocks, on the rocks, do it,
Even little cuckoos, in their clocks, do it,
Let's do it, let's fall in love.

REFRAIN 3

Romantic sponges, they say, do it,
Oysters, down in Oyster Bay, do it,
Let's do it, let's fall in love.
Cold Cape Cod clams, 'gainst their wish, do it,
Even lazy jellyfish do it,
Let's do it, let's fall in love.
Electric eels, I might add, do it,
Though it shocks 'em, I know.
Why ask if shad do it?
Waiter, bring me shad roe.
In shallow shoals, English soles do it,
Goldfish, in the privacy of bowls, do it,
Let's do it, let's fall in love.

REFRAIN 3 (ENGLISH PRODUCTION)

Young whelks and winkles, in pubs, do it,
Little sponges, in their tubs, do it.
Let's do it, let's fall in love.
Cold salmon, quite 'gainst their wish, do it,
Even lazy jellyfish do it,
Let's do it, let's fall in love.
The most select schools of cod do it,
Though it shocks 'em, I fear,
Sturgeon, thank God, do it,
Have some caviar, dear.
In shady shoals, English soles do it,
Goldfish, in the privacy of bowls, do it,
Let's do it, let's fall in love.

REFRAIN 4

The dragonflies, in the reeds, do it,
Sentimental centipedes do it,
Let's do it, let's fall in love.
Mosquitoes, heaven forbid, do it,
So does ev'ry katydid, do it,
Let's do it, let's fall in love.
The most refined lady bugs do it,
When a gentleman calls,
Moths in your rugs, do it,
What's the use of moth balls?
Locusts in trees do it, bees do it,
Even overeducated fleas do it,
Let's do it, let's fall in love.

REFRAIN 5

The chimpanzees, in the zoos, do it,
Some courageous kangaroos do it,
Let's do it, let's fall in love.
I'm sure giraffes, on the sly, do it,
Heavy hippopotami do it,
Let's do it, let's fall in love.
Old sloths who hang down from twigs do it,
Though the effort is great,
Sweet guinea pigs do it,
Buy a couple and wait.
The world admits bears in pits do it,
Even pekineses in the Ritz, do it,
Let's do it, let's fall in love.

VIVIENNE

Published October 1928. Apparently added to the show just before the New York opening. Introduced by Irving Aaronson and the Commanders.

VERSE

Vivienne's the sweetest little creature,
Simply heaven-sent.
Vivienne's so fair in ev'ry feature,
She's a big event.
From the start, it's inconceivable,
How we both agree,
And the part that's unbelievable,
She loves me.

REFRAIN

Who first made my heart stand still?
Who did it and always will?
Vivienne, Vivienne.
Who's promised that she'll be mine,
And sign on the dotted line?
Vivienne, Vivienne.
Who is the one and only,
That I'm waiting for?
I'm so lonely,
When I'm in bed,
In my twin bed.
Who'll be in the other one,

As soon as the wedding's done?
Vivienne, Vivienne.*

THE HEAVEN HOP

Published October 1928. Apparently added to the show just before the New York opening. Introduced by Irving Aaronson and the Commanders.

VERSE

Up at heaven's happy portals,
Where the parties never stop,
All the debonair immortals
Do a dance called the Heaven Hop.
In this big celestial center
It's the only dance they do.
So before you try to enter,
You'd better start doing it too.

REFRAIN

Spread your wings and start them flapping,
Lift your feet and set them tapping,
Start right now and do that Heaven Hop,
Hop, the Heaven Hop!
Wag your ankles to that meter,
Let your shoulders gently teeter,
If you want to please Saint Peter,
Take up the Heaven Hop.
When the angels play low
On their harps of gold,
Kneel and pray low,
Then get up and shake your halo.
Let that rhythm filter through yuh
Till you holler "Hallelujah."
Start right now and do that Heaven Hop,
That Heaven Hop!

QUELQUE-CHOSE

Published February 1928. Also titled "I've Got Quelque-chose." It was deleted before the New York opening. Introduced by Irene Bordoni during the tryout. Music found at Warner Brothers Music warehouse in Secaucus, New Jersey, February 1982, indicates that this number was written for *Greenwich Village Follies*, 1924, but not used in that show.

VERSE 1 (PUBLISHED VERSION)

When men declare
Some lady fair
Has "something," I suppose
They mean that she
Has got what we
In France call "quelque-chose."
That charm one can't define,
That certain something as you say,
That quelque-chose
That gets the beaux
And makes them stay.

VERSE 1 (ORIGINAL)

Now, Mrs. Nash
May have more cash,
And Peggy Joyce, more clo'es,
But while they sit
At home and knit,
I entertain their beaux.
For I can give them something
That those other ladies lack,
And once they've come
And sampled some,
They all come back.

REFRAIN 1

I've got quelque-chose,
Something very rare,
Quelque-chose
That brings me beaux
From ev'rywhere.
Quelque-chose inviting,
Quelque-chose exciting,
And if I'm a belle,*
It's due to that quel-
Que-chose.

VERSE 2

This quelque-chose
Gets all my beaux
In such a state of haze
That some who call
Won't leave at all,
But stay for days and days.
There's such a great demand for it
That life becomes a bore,
For even though
I say "No, no,"
They all take more.

**Ending to refrain 2:*
Who's given her solemn oath
That someday she'll fill them both?
Vivienne, Vivienne.

**Or:*
And if I've done well,

REFRAIN 2

I've got quelque-chose
I can count upon,
Quelque-chose
That makes my beaux
Stay on and on.
If you're feeling lifeless,
Weary, wan, and wifeless,
Come up where I dwell
And ask for that quel-
Que-chose.

VERSE 3

Lest you suppose
This quelque-chose
Be something too bizarre,
I'll hasten to
Enlighten you,
It's nothing but a bar,
A little private bar of mine
Where all the fellows flock
And have a try
At my supply
Of pre-war stock.

REFRAIN 3

I've got quelque-chose,
Something hard to find,
Quelque-chose
That gets my beaux
Completely blind.
Though it's compromising,
It's so appetizing,
That ev'ry old elk
Goes after that quelqu-
E-chose.

LET'S MISBEHAVE

Published June 1927. Introduced by Irving Aaronson and the Commanders at the Ambassadeurs Café, Paris, in the summer of 1927. It was dropped before the New York opening of *Paris* and replaced by "Let's Do It, Let's Fall in Love."

VERSE

You could have a great career,
And you should.
Only one thing stops you, dear,
You're too good.
If you want a future, darling,
Why don't you get a past?
'Cause that fatal moment's coming,
At last.

REFRAIN 1

We're all alone
No chaperon
Can get our number,
The world's in slumber,
Let's misbehave.
There's something wild
About you, child,
That's so contagious,
Let's be outrageous,
Let's misbehave.
When Adam won Eve's hand,
He wouldn't stand for teasin',
He didn't care about
Those apples out of season.
They say that spring
Means just one thing
To little love birds,
We're not above birds,
Let's misbehave.

REFRAIN 2

It's getting late
And while I wait,
My poor heart aches on,
Why keep the brakes on?
Let's misbehave.
I feel quite sure,
Un peu d'amour
Would be attractive,
While we're still active,
Let's misbehave.
You know my heart is true,
And you say, you for me care;
Somebody's sure to tell,
But what the hell do we care?
They say that bears
Have love affairs,
And even camels;
We're merely mammals,
Let's misbehave.

WHICH?

Published February 1928. Probably written for Irene Bordoni to sing in *Paris,* but it is not listed in any playbills and was either dropped in rehearsal or introduced and dropped before the New York opening. It was introduced under the title "Which Is the Right Life?" in a revised version by Jessie Matthews in the English and New York productions of *Wake Up and Dream* (1929).

Which is the right life,
The simple or the night life?
When, pray, should one rise,
At sunset or at sunrise?
Which should be upper,
My breakfast or my supper?
Which is the right life,
Which?
If the wood nymph left the park,
Would Park Avenue excite her?
Would the glowworm trade her spark
For the latest Dunhill lighter?
Here's a question I would pose,
Tell me which the sweeter smell makes,
The aroma of the rose
Or the perfume that Chanel makes?
Which land is dreamier,
Arcadia or Bohemia?
Who'll tell the answer,
The daisy or the dancer?
Which life is for me,
The peaceful or the stormy?
Which is the right man,
Walt Whitman or Paul Whiteman,
Which?
Should I read Euripides or continue with the
Graphic?
Hear the murmur of the breeze or the roaring of
the traffic?
Should I make one man my choice
And regard divorce as treason,
Or should I, like Peggy Joyce,
Get a new one ev'ry season?
Which is the right life,
The simple or the night life?
When, pray, should one rise,
At sunset or at sunrise?
Which should be the upper,
My breakfast or my supper?
Which is the right life,
Which!

Version used in WAKE UP AND DREAM (1929)

WHICH IS THE RIGHT LIFE?

VERSE

As a cloak room girl befitting,
I spend hours and hours in sitting,
And I must say that the mental strain is great.
I have looked in vain for solace
In the books of Edgar Wallace,
So I simply sit and look and contemplate.
As I watch the fash'nables turning day into
night
I just wonder whether they're wrong or whether
they're right.

REFRAIN

Which is the right life,
The simple or the night life?
When, pray, should one rise,
At sunset or at sunrise?
Which should be upper,
My breakfast or my supper?
Which is the right life,
Which?
Does the wood nymph in the park
Long for painted lips that pucker?
Would the little meadowlark
Like to sing like Sophie Tucker?
Here's a question I would pose,
Tell me which the sweeter smell makes,
The aroma of the rose or the perfume that
Chanel makes?
Which land is dreamier,
Arcadia or Bohemia?
Who'll tell the answer,
The daisy or the dancer?
Which man's the right man,
Walt Whitman or Paul Whiteman?
Which is the right life,
The simple or the night life,
Which?

DIZZY BABY

Dropped during rehearsals. Introduced forty-six years later in the Mermaid Theatre's City of London Festival production of *Cole* in July 1974, where it was sung by Una Stubbs, Rod McLennon, and Kenneth Nelson.

VERSE

Sweet baby, you're a saint,
I've only one complaint,
You go so fast I can't keep up with you.
I'm tired of op'ning plays,
And closing cabarets,
I'd rather breakfast, dear, than sup with you.
Why don't you let me make a bride of you,
And stop that dynamo inside of you?

REFRAIN

Dizzy baby, dizzy baby,
Won't you please slow down?
Can't you find one moment to relax?
Look behind, I'm falling in your tracks.
You're so busy being dizzy
I get dizzy too.
Still it may be
Because you're
Dizzy baby
I love you.

BAD GIRL IN PAREE

Music and lyrics found with *Paris* material at Warner Brothers Music warehouse, Secaucus, New Jersey, February 1982. A copy had been in the files of the Cole Porter Musical and Literary Property Trusts, but it gave no indication for which show the song was written.

VERSE

I used to be twice as shy as a lily.
Oh, such an innocent lamb.
Ladies who met me would say "Listen Willy,
You're just as cold as a clam."
Till, one night,
In Paris France—
I saw the light
And found romance
Through one certain person who knocked me
so silly
I don't know yet where I am.

REFRAIN

I never will forget
The night I met
That girl in Paree.
She had the kind of eyes
That advertise,
That girl in Paree.
She gave me one long look
And I understood.
That was about all it took
To forget to be good.
So if I'm not the same,
Please put the blame
On that girl in Paree.

WHEN I FOUND YOU

Music and lyrics were found at the Warner Brothers Music warehouse in Secaucus, New Jersey, February 1982. Although "When I Found You" was written for *Paris,* there is no evidence it was ever in the show.

VERSE

I used to mourn
The day I was born,
For life seemed so empty to me.
Then I came upon you
And suddenly knew
How wonderful life could be.

REFRAIN

I found romance
Within your glance
When I found you.
You touched my hand
And I found the land
Of castles-in-air built for two.
You put your arms around me.
And I found my dreams come true.
But all else above,
I discovered love,
When I found you.

WAKE UP AND DREAM

1929

Tryout: Palace Theatre, Manchester, England, March 5, 1929. Produced by Charles B. Cochran at the London Pavilion, March 27, 1929. 263 performances. Book by John Hastings Turner. Staged by Frank Collins under the personal direction of Charles B. Cochran. Cast, starring Jessie Matthews, Sonnie Hale, Tillie Losch, and George Metaxa, included Toni Birkmeyer, Douglas Byng, William Stephens, Moya Nugent, Tina Meller, Elsie Carlisle, and Chester Fredericks.

The American production was presented by Arch Selwyn at the Selwyn Theatre, New York, December 30, 1929. 136 performances. Cast starred Jack Buchanan, featured Jessie Matthews and Tilly Losch, and included many members of the original English production.

In Manchester the show was titled *Charles B. Cochran's 1929 Revue.* The title was changed before the London opening.

WAKE UP AND DREAM

Published March 1929. Introduced by George Metaxa in England and by Jessie Matthews in New York.

VERSE 1

When you grumble and sigh,
And you ask yourself why
You've the weight of the world on your mind,
Did you ever reflect
It's because you neglect
The dreams that you've left behind?
They were gay, they were mad,
Those dreams you had,
And you welcomed them all with open arms.
But in giving your life
To the world and his wife,
You have fallen asleep to their charms.

REFRAIN

Wake up and dream,
It's so easy to dream,
Things are really not what they seem.
Wake up and dream.
Open your eyes,
Take a look at the skies,
Where the stars so romantic'lly gleam.
Wake up and dream.
Ev'ry moment you're bored is a sword
Of hari-kari in you.
If you wake up, you'll find you've the mind
Of Master Barrie in you.
Listen, young man,
You were once Peter Pan
And you've simply forgotten your theme,
Wake up and dream.

VERSE 2

When you're conscious that you've
Simply got in a groove,
And you've lost all desire for a spree,
If you wake up and dream,
Life will suddenly seem
As gay as it used to be.
And though any amount
Of men who count
Will maintain that you've quite gone off your
head,
Never mind what they say,
Let your dreams dream away,
And you'll still be alive when they're dead.

I'VE GOT A CRUSH ON YOU

Introduced in England by Margie Finley, Chester Fredericks, and ensemble. Not presented in New York.

VERSE 1

HE: Ever since that fatal moment
When I found your "no, no, no" meant
"yes,"
I've become a mess.
Ever since you, Amazon-like,
Threw your arms around my swanlike neck,
I'm a total wreck.
I always was a fool, but you've made me
worse.
I really should engage a nurse.

REFRAIN 1

I've got such a crush on you,
My heart's in a state of stew.
You've got me so up in the air
My brain, sister,
Won't register.
Half-witted we were in fits
But now we're quarter-wits,
You know, dear, to what it is due,
I've got a crush on you.

VERSE 2

SHE: Ever since that night electric,
When you did your famous neck trick,

I've
Just become alive.
Ever since that final grapple,
Eve's so fond of Adam's apple,
She
Wants his apple tree.
This ship was heading for a watery grave,
But now she's riding on a wave.

REFRAIN 2

I've got such a crush on you,
My heart's in a state of stew.
You've got me so up in the air
My brain, mister,
Won't register.
Thought I'm not a girl who sews,
I've made mental baby clo'es,
You know, dear, to what it is due,
I've got a crush on you.

I LOVED HIM, BUT HE DIDN'T LOVE ME

Published March 1929. Introduced in England by Jessie Matthews. Not presented in New York.

VERSE 1

The gods who nurse
This universe
Think little of mortals' cares.
They sit in crowds
On exclusive clouds
And laugh at our love affairs.
I might have had a real romance,
If they'd given me a chance.

REFRAIN 1

I loved him,
But he didn't love me.
I wanted him,
But he didn't want me.
Then the gods had a spree,
And indulged in another whim.
Now he loves me,
But I don't love him.

VERSE 2

I told this tale
With its weary wail
To sev'ral devoted wives.
They said, "You're young,
You have simply sung
The story of all our lives."
So maybe there are couples here
Who have had the same career.

REFRAIN 2

You loved him,
But he didn't love you.
You wanted him,
But he didn't want you.
Then the gods saw you two,
And indulged in another whim,
Now he loves you,
But you don't love him.

REFRAIN 3

You loved her
But she didn't love you.
You wanted her,
But she didn't want you.
Then the gods saw you two,
And you both felt a change occur.
Now she loves you,
But you don't love her.

LOOKING AT YOU

Published March 1929. Introduced in England by Jessie Matthews, Sonnie Hale, and ensemble and in New York by Miss Matthews, Dave Fitzgibbon, and ensemble. It was first sung by Clifton Webb and Dorothy Dickson with Noble Sissle's orchestra at the Ambassadeurs Café, Paris, 1928.

VERSE

I've gone afar,
Collecting objets d'art,
I know the whole game by heart.
Why, Joe Duveen
Will tell you what I mean,
'Twas I who gave him his start.
But since I looked, dear, in your direction,
I've quite forgotten my art collection.
To be exact,
You simply prove the fact
That nature's greater than art.

REFRAIN

Looking at you,
While troubles are fleeing.

I'm admiring the view,
'Cause it's you I'm seeing.
And the sweet honeydew
Of well-being settles upon me.
What is this light
That shines when you enter?
Like a star in the night,
And what's to prevent 'er
From destroying my sight,
If you center all of it on me?
Looking at you,
I'm filled with the essence of
The quintessence of
Joy.
Looking at you,
I hear poets tellin' of
Lovely Helen of
Troy, darling.
Life seemed so gray
I wanted to end it,
Till that wonderful day
You started to mend it.
And if you'll only stay,
Then I'll spend it looking at you.

THE BANJO THAT MAN JOE PLAYS

Published March 1929. Introduced by William Stephens in both England and New York.

VERSE 1

Joe plays the banjo and plays ev'ry night,
Under a lazy moon.
I know what Joe's gonna play, all right.
He only knows one tune.
It may be a limited repertory.
Still ev'ry note of it tells a story.

REFRAIN

When that man Joe
Makes that banjo
Play that old tune I adore,
San Francisco,
Dear old Frisco,
Calls me 'cross the prairies once more.
Something lingers
In his fingers
That reminds me of early days.
And I'm back with my Amanda,
On that old-fashioned veranda.
That's why I make propaganda
For the banjo that man Joe plays.

VERSE 2

Whenever Joe starts that old song of mine,
Somehow my mem'ry strays
Back to the Gold Coast in forty-nine,
Back to those good old days.
A banjo is playing and there's Miss Mandy
Strumming that tune for her fav'rite dandy.

ENTRANCE OF EMIGRANTS

Introduced by members of the ensemble in England and New York, it was also sung by the ensemble in the Boston performances of *Fifty Million Frenchmen* in November 1929, under the title "The Emigrants." Manuscript copy lists the title as "The Emigrants' March." It is almost certain that Porter included it in *Frenchmen* before he knew there would be a New York production of *Wake Up and Dream.* Once he knew, he dropped it from *Frenchmen.*

VERSE

We were simple Europeans,
Inveterate plebeians,
When fortunately we were told
An authenticated story
That in this territory
Somebody had discovered gold.
So we hopped aboard a clipper,
And simply told the skipper
To take us to the Golden Gate.
We have all been rather seasick
(It isn't fun to be sick)
But otherwise the trip was great.

REFRAIN

As we're poor pioneers, in a bad financial fix,
We'd appreciate your extra dimes.
We're the Astors, the Vanderbilts, the Morgans and the Fricks,
The Mackays and the Guggenheims.
Though today we may look like an awful lot of hicks,
We'll be photographed in future times,
As the Astors, the Vanderbilts, the Morgans and the Fricks,
The Mackays and the Guggenheims.
We'll dispense with collars

Until we get the dollars
That all the daily papers discuss,
So that our descendants
Can cheer for independence
And cut the folks who used to cut us.
For the great day will come when you'll all be
glad to mix,
If you live until the market climbs,
With the Astors, the Vanderbilts, the Morgans
and the Fricks,
The Mackays and the Guggenheims.

Verse for version intended for FIFTY MILLION FRENCHMEN

We were simple Europeans,
Quite content to be plebeians,
Sitting calmly 'round the kitchen range,
Till we heard how in Manhattan
All our friends get rich and fatten
On the New York Stock Exchange.
At the thought of sitting pretty
On the top of New York City,
We resolved to take the nearest ship
With the hope that, on our landing,
Mayor Walker will be standing
To receive us with an inside tip.

WHAT IS THIS THING CALLED LOVE?

Published March 1929. Introduced by Elsie Carlisle in England and by Frances Shelley in New York.

VERSE 1

I was a humdrum person,
Leading a life apart,
When love flew in through my window wide
And quickened my humdrum heart.
Love flew in through my window,
I was so happy then.
But after love had stayed a little while,
Love flew out again.

REFRAIN

What is this thing called love?
This funny thing called love?
Just who can solve its mystery?
Why should it make a fool of me?
I saw you there one wonderful day.
You took my heart and threw it away.
That's why I ask the Lord in heaven above,
What is this thing called love?

VERSE 2

You gave me days of sunshine,
You gave me nights of cheer,
You made my life an enchanted dream
Till somebody else came near.
Somebody else came near you,
I felt the winter's chill
And now I sit and wonder night and day
Why I love you still.

WAIT UNTIL IT'S BEDTIME

Introduced by Jessie Matthews in England. Not presented in New York.

VERSE

When I started my married career, I confess,
I was an unsuccessful wife,
In persuading my husband to give me the nec-
Essary luxuries of life.
Till one lucky night,
I turned out the light,
And found the secret of success.
And so now when I ask him for something,
He always says "yes."

REFRAIN

Wait until it's bedtime
If you've an ax to grind.
Wait until it's bedtime
And he'll be much more kind.
If he loves you dearly,
You can ask him for the moon,
If you merely
Wait until it's time for bed.

OPERATIC PILLS

Introduced by Sonnie Hale and ensemble in England and by Jack Buchanan and ensemble in New York. The alternate title on manuscripts is "If You Take One Pill." A note in the New York program said: "Sir Thomas Beecham is at present fighting an intensive battle for Grand

Opera in England. His father, Sir Joseph Beecham, was, too, the father of the world-famous pills. Musically, therefore, and medicinally, their countrymen are greatly in their debt."

Three years earlier, in 1926, the Porter-Beecham "feud" had produced Beecham's privately printed pamphlet, "The Tragical History of Young King Cole," under the authorship of Didymus Belcampus. At the conclusion, Young King Cole was swept out to sea and drowned for having brought jazz and a cocktail barge to Venice. See also "Italian Street Singers" (page 96).

VERSE

I've begged all of England's classes
To invest in op'ra glasses,
But in spite of my insistence, they refuse.
'Twould be infinitely prop'rer
If they went to hear the op'ra
'Stead of going to these barbarous revues.
So, convinced that the British nation
Cares for nothing but syncopation,
I have sworn that their education
Somehow I will form.
I'm determined that I shall teach 'em,
And decided the way to reach 'em.
As a dutiful son of Beecham
Is in pill form.
That is why, to cure the public of its ills,
I am off'ring you my operatic pills.

REFRAIN

If you take one pill,
You'll hear the Barber of Seville.
If you take two pills, you'll hear Louise.
If you take one more,
The Song of the Toreador
Will come thund'ring over the breeze.
If a fourth you try,
You'll hear Madame Butterfly.
Take a fifth, and Lohengrin's wedding bell'll
ring.
And if your fears you throttle,
And you take a whole bottle,
You'll hear the angels sing.

AFTER ALL, I'M ONLY A SCHOOLGIRL

Published in *The Unpublished Cole Porter.* Introduced by Jessie Matthews and ensemble in both England and New York.

VERSE 1

My mama says that ev'ry girlie
Ought to marry and marry early.
So she found a tutor
To prepare me for a suitor.
Making love is the art he teaches,
And as he practices what he preaches,
I'm very busy learning
How to keep the home fires burning.
He's an expert regarding marriage
And teaches me a lot too—
When to order a baby carriage,
And better still, when not to.

REFRAIN 1

After all, I'm only a schoolgirl.
What they call an innocent dove.
After all, I'm only a fool girl,
Simply studying
That funny thing
Called love.

VERSE 2

First we started by reading over
Sev'ral memoirs by Casanova,
A midnight guide to Paris,
And the life of Frank B. Harris.
Then to prove he deserves his sal'ry,
He took me off to a picture gallery,
To see how Aphrodite
Kept so warm without a nightie.
I suppose that we've seen between us,
Most ev'ry exhibition.
'Cause he wants me to study Venus
In ev'ry known position.

REFRAIN 2

After all, I'm only a schoolgirl
What they call an innocent dove.
After all, I'm only a fool girl,
Just a clinging vine
On the holy shrine
Of love.

I DREAM OF A GIRL IN A SHAWL

Published April 1929. During the Manchester performances, this number was presented in four parts. The order was: "Venice" (George Metaxa and Alanova),

"China" (William Stephens and Tilly Losch), "Chicago" (Sonnie Hale and Polly Ward), and "Spain" (George Metaxa, Tina Meller, and Antonio Rodriguez). Before the London opening, the "Venice" section was dropped.

Porter's manuscripts contain the notation "Greenwich Village Follies," indicating this number may have been intended for the 1924 production. The Manchester and London programs for *Wake Up and Dream* list the title as "A Girl in a Shawl." The music manuscripts, in four distinct sections, bear the titles "Italian Shawl," "Chinese Shawl," "Chicago," and "Spanish Shawl." No lyric survives for the refrain of "Italian Shawl."

The "China" section was presented in New York by Mr. Stephens and Miss Losch. The other parts were omitted.

VERSE

Life at its best is a puzzle
But I haven't lived in vain.
For any time I get
With worldly cares beset,
I dream of a girl I met
In Spain.

REFRAIN

At evening, when night starts to fall
I dream of a girl in a shawl.
I'm back in Granada, and watching her dance
With the shadows that played on the wall.
A distant guitar twanged a tune,
As we wandered along 'neath the moon,
And when I feel that I'm
Simply wasting my time,
I dream of a girl in a shawl.

Italian Version

Baccia mi, baccia mi con passione,
Stringi mi, stringi mi con adore,
Prende mi, la mia vit'e com'un fiore.
Che fiorisce presto, presto muore,
E sol per te, il mio cuor'.

Chinese Version

Though very humbly born I must confess
I love a little Manchu marchioness.
And since the moment when first I found her,
I sit and envy the shawl around her.
She doesn't even know that I exist.
She doesn't realize how much she's missed.

My lovely Manchu marchioness wears a shawl,
Made of flowers that grow by her garden wall.
Sweet-scented cherry blossoms and fragrant lotus blooms,
Favor the rarest, fairest flower of them all.
I long to tell the lady how much I care.
But she's so well connected that I don't dare.
So very soon I'll have to begin a
Lesson in love, and learn how to win a
Blue-blooded Manchu marchioness in a
Shawl.

Chicago Version

When from London I came to Chicago
I was awfully indiscreet.
I picked up a little virago
I met on a quiet street.
I started at once to caress her,
When a gun fell out of her shawl.
I trembled with fear
Till she said to me, "Dear,
I'm a gangster's daughter, that's all."

I don't care for human slaughter,
Not at all.
But I love a gangster's daughter
In a shawl.
She thinks it's frightful fun
To pop me with a gun.
I twice have been hit
In the place where I sit,
Though she knows it isn't done.
Each time we meet, I'm feted by her smiles,
But, alas, I'm from those hated British Isles.
So the Mayor of Chicago
Won't let this poor papa go
With that charming,
If though alarming,
Girl in a shawl.

Spanish Version

What shadows hover
Beneath thy cover?
What are the memories you recall,
Wonderful silken shawl?
What tale reposes
Among thy roses?
What were your moments divine
Within love's thrall?
I hear a distant guitar,
And see you afar,
Revealing a maiden's charms.
Swaying before
A toreador,
Then sinking into his arms.
At last reclining
'Neath the moonbeam's shining.
Don't you remember it all,
My Spanish shawl?

NIGHT CLUB OPENING

Also titled "Night Club Quartet" and "The Night Club." Introduced in London by Sonnie Hale, George Metaxa, William Stephens, and Chester Fredericks. Not presented in New York.

If you've ever been to a night club
And we know you all have done it.
Then we trust
You surmise
That we must
Be the guys
Who run it.
When you've said good night to your night club
And your homeward tracks you've beaten,
In this room,
So bereft,
We consume
What you've left
Uneaten.

HOSTESS: I'm the shady night club hostess
With a shady night club brain.
CLOAK ROOM GIRL: I'm the cloak room girl you curse
just before you go.
WAITER: I'm the wild Italian waiter who
upsets your fresh champagne.
GIGOLO: And I'm the lamented, scented
dancing pro, the gigolo.

I'M A GIGOLO

Published May 1929. Not listed in the London opening-night program, it was introduced during the run there by William Stephens and in New York by Jack Buchanan and after two weeks by Mr. Stephens.

VERSE

I should like you all to know,
I'm a famous gigolo.
And of lavender, my nature's got just a dash in
it.
As I'm slightly undersexed,
You will always find me next
To some dowager who's wealthy rather than
passionate.
Go to one of those night club places
And you'll find me stretching my braces
Pushing ladies with lifted faces 'round the floor.
But I must confess to you
There are moments when I'm blue.
And I ask myself whatever I do it for.

REFRAIN

I'm a flower that blooms in the winter,
Sinking deeper and deeper in "snow."
I'm a baby who has
No mother but jazz,
I'm a gigolo.
Ev'ry morning, when labor is over,
To my sweet-scented lodgings I go,
Take the glass from the shelf
And look at myself,
I'm a gigolo.
I get stocks and bonds
From faded blondes
Ev'ry twenty-fifth of December.
Still I'm just a pet
That men forget
And only tailors remember.
Yet when I see the way all the ladies
Treat their husbands who put up the dough,
You cannot think me odd
If then I thank God
I'm a gigolo.

I WANT TO BE RAIDED BY YOU

Published April 1929. Not listed in the London opening-night program, but introduced by Sonnie Hale during the run there. Not presented in New York. Published copies of this song are very rare; I have never seen one. A music manuscript and a typed lyric are at the Porter Trusts office.

VERSE

There's a p'liceman on my street,
And he's oh so sweet.
And when he shakes his stick,
I get a kind of kick
I thought was obsolete.
Ev'ry time he passes by,
With his roving eye,
I get such heart disease
I sink upon my knees,
And I cry:

REFRAIN

Dear bobby,
Come here, bobby,
And change my point of view.

People say that I'm
A daughter of crime,
And I want to be raided by you.
Brave bobby,
Behave, bobby,
The way I want you to.
I could call, of course,
On the rest of the force,
But I want to be raided by you.
I've prayed and prayed
And prayed for a raid,
But no one ever calls my bluff.
So step right in
And kindly begin,
To do, do, do your stuff.
Divine bobby,
Be mine, bobby,
And thrill me through and through.
I'm a night club queen
And rather obscene,
And I want to be raided by you.

THE EXTRA MAN

Apparently unused in *Wake Up and Dream.* A possible forerunner of "I'm a Gigolo." A clipping titled "A Paris Dinner-Party" kept by Porter from an untitled, undated publication has the following information about this song:

> An especially delightful Paris dinner-party was given recently by Mrs. Toulmin. After dinner, Miss Elsa Maxwell and Cole Porter played and sang some of Mr. Porter's songs—songs with clever lyrics that really should be published as a document of the European drawing-room of 1927. The music is charming and well-composed, but the lyrics are even better. One of the latest of these is "The Extra Man," an amusing but almost wistful picture of those odd men whom one meets casually and continually wherever one dines.

This song also was intended for *9:15 Revue,* 1930, and *The New Yorkers,* 1930.

VERSE

In the infinite variety
Of men who make up society,
I'm quite the most pathetic of all the clan,
For among the gay unthinking set,
The heavy eating and drinking set,
I'm commonly known as an extra man.
If a hostess's voice is hearty
When inviting me to a party,
I accept although I know what it's all about,
For I realize I'm the buddy
Who's elected to understudy
Some boy friend who's suddenly given out.

REFRAIN

I'm an extra man, an extra man,
I've got no equal as an extra man,
I'm handsome, I'm harmless, I'm helpful, I'm
able,
A perfect fourth at bridge or a fourteenth at
table.
You will find my name on ev'ry list,
But when it's missing, it is never missed.
And so I'll live until that fatal day,
The press will tell you that I've passed away,
And you will feel sad as the news you scan,
For that means one less extra man.

MY LOUISA

Apparently unused in *Wake Up and Dream,* but quite possibly intended for George Metaxa to sing in the "Night Club Scene." Later earmarked for *The New Yorkers* (1930) and *Nymph Errant* (1933), but not used in either production.

VERSE

As a waiter
Of course I have to cater
To a worthless lot
Who are not
Worth thinking of.
Still while serving
A public undeserving
It's the cross I bear
For a fair
Young maid I love.
For Louisa says she'll be my bride
Just as soon as I've put enough cash aside.

REFRAIN

So while I'm counting my tips
I dream of the lips
Of my Louisa.
My Louisa lives in Pisa
Down in sunny Italy.
When I've enough in the bank
I'll buy me a swank
Hispano-Suiza.

And go motoring back to Pisa,
Where my Louisa waits for me.
No one has the least idea
How I love my Louisa mia.

ALTERNATE VERSE

As a doorman
I have to be polite
To a useless lot
That is not worth thinking of.
Yet in serving these children of the night
It's the cross I bear,
For a fair
Young maid I love.
For Louisa says she'll be my bride
Just as soon as I've put enough cash aside.

Music survives for a song titled "The Lady I Love," but the lyric is lost. Porter's "Agua Sincopada Tango," music only, was published in April 1929. It was danced in the English production by June Roper and Jack Kinney. "Let's Do It, Let's Fall in Love," first sung in *Paris* (1928), was introduced in the English production of *Wake Up and Dream* by Jessie Matthews and Sonnie Hale. "The Tale of an Oyster" (See *Fifty Million Frenchmen*) was also earmarked for *Wake Up and Dream* but was not used in the show.

FIFTY MILLION FRENCHMEN

1929

"Fifty Million Frenchmen," 1929; William Gaxton and Girls

Tryout: Colonial Theatre, Boston, November 14, 1929. Produced by E. Ray Goetz at the Lyric Theatre, New York, November 27, 1929. 254 performances. Book by Herbert Fields. Directed by Monty Woolley. Cast, starring William Gaxton and Genevieve Tobin, included Helen Broderick, Evelyn Hoey, Betty Compton, and Jack Thompson.

A letter from Goetz to Porter, November 16, 1928, says that this show was to have been co-produced by Goetz and Irving Berlin.

A TOAST TO VOLSTEAD

Alternate title found on manuscripts is "Opening, Ritz Bar." This male ensemble number, the show's opening chorus, was dropped from *Frenchmen* five weeks after the New York opening.

ROTARIAN: Step right up to the bar, gentlemen,
And have a drink on me.
BARMAN: Step right up to the bar, gentlemen,
What will your pleasure be?
1ST MAN: A martini.
2ND MAN: A manhattan.
3RD MAN: A gin ricky.
4TH MAN: A gin fizz.
5TH MAN: A mint julep.
6TH MAN: A Tom Collins.
7TH MAN: Give me the same thing, whatever it is.
ROTARIAN: Just step right up to the bar,
gentlemen,
And don't forget I'm host.
Raise your glasses high
And pause while I
Propose a little toast.

Here's a long life to Volstead,
Our senator from heaven sent.
Let us give our endorsement
To his act of enforcement,
What a noble experiment!
Let's sing a swan song to liquor
That blight with which we once were
cursed.
Here's a long life to Volstead,
And I hope he dies of thirst.

Bonsoir, ma chérie,
Comment allez-vous?
Bonsoir ma chérie,
Je vous aime beaucoup.
Avez-vous un fiancé?
Ça ne fait rien.
Voulez coucher avec moi
Ce soir?
Oui, oui, combien?

YOU DO SOMETHING TO ME

Published November 1929. *Frenchmen*'s most famous song was introduced by Genevieve Tobin and William Gaxton.

VERSE 1

I was mighty blue,
Thought my life was through,
Till the heavens opened,
And I gazed at you.
Won't you tell me, dear,
Why, when you appear,
Something happens to me
And the strangest feeling goes through me?

REFRAIN

You do something to me,
Something that simply mystifies me.
Tell me, why should it be
You have the pow'r to hypnotize me?
Let me live 'neath your spell,
Do do that voodoo that you do so well,
For you do something to me
That nobody else could do.

VERSE 2

If I seem to stray
When you talk this way
It's because I'm wondering
What I ought to say.
I could cry, please don't,
But I believe I won't,
For when you talk to me
Such a soothing feeling goes through me.

THE AMERICAN EXPRESS

Alternate title found on manuscripts is "Opening, American Express Scene." Introduced by ensemble.

ALL: To the dear old American Express
Each morning we roam,

It's the only place a tourist in distress
Gets that atmosphere of home.
For there's such a crowd and such a crush,
And ev'rybody's in such a rush.
That is why the American Express
Is oh such a big success.

MRS. DE VERE: Can you give us an outside cabin on the—*
1ST CLERK: Sorry, madam, nothing.
MRS. DE VERE: Can you give me a first-class ticket on the—
2ND CLERK: Sorry, madam, nothing.
MRS. DE VERE: Will you see if you've got a letter there for—
3RD CLERK: Sorry, madam, nothing.
MRS. DE VERE: What's the best exchange for a million rubles?
4TH CLERK: Sorry, madam, nothing.

*Originally there were four tourists and four clerks.

YOU'VE GOT THAT THING

Published December 1929. A manuscript found at Tams-Witmark included the lyric for the previously unknown third refrain. Introduced by Jack Thompson and Betty Compton.

VERSE

Since first you blew in like a boisterous breeze
I often have wondered, dear,
Why gentlemen all seem to fall on their knees
The moment that you appear?
Your fetching physique is hardly unique,
You're mentally not so hot;
You'll never win laurels because of your morals,
But I'll tell you what you've got

REFRAIN 1

You've got that thing, you've got that thing,
That thing that makes birds forget to sing.
Yes, you've got that thing, that certain thing.
You've got that charm, that subtle charm
That makes young farmers desert the farm,
'Cause you've got that thing, that certain thing.
You've got what Adam craved when he
With love for Eve was tortured,
She only had an apple tree,
But you, you've got an orchard.
You've got those ways, those taking ways
That make me rush off to Cartier's
For a wedding ring,
You've got that thing.

REFRAIN 2

You've got that thing, you've got that thing,
That thing that makes vines prefer to cling.
Yes, you've got that thing, that certain thing.
You've got those looks, those fatal looks.
That make book censors enjoy their books,
'Cause you've got that thing, that certain thing.
Just what made Samson be, for years,
Delilah's lord and keeper?
She only had a pair of shears.
But you, you've got a reaper.
You've got that pow'r, that pow'r to grip
That makes me map out a wedding trip
For the early spring,
You've got that thing.

REFRAIN 3

You've got that thing, you've got that thing,
That thing that makes bees refuse to sting.
Yes, you've got that thing, that certain thing.
You've got that kiss, that kiss that warms,
That makes reformers reform reforms,
'Cause you got that thing, that certain thing.
They tell us Trojan Helen's lips
Made ev'ry man her slavey.
If her face launched a thousand ships
Well, yours could launch a navy.
You've got that love, and such a lot*
It makes me think you're prepared for what
Any stork might bring.
You've got that thing.

FIND ME A PRIMITIVE MAN

Published December 1929. The French version was probably written by Porter. Introduced by Evelyn Hoey, Billy Reed, Lou Duthers, and ensemble.

VERSE

Now before this modern idea had burst
About the women and children first,

*You've ideas inside your head
That make me order an extra bed
With an extra spring.
You've got that thing.

The men had much more charm than they have
today.
And if only one of that type survived,
The very moment that he arrived
I know I'd fall in love in a great big way.
I can't imagine being bad
With any Arrow collar ad,
Nor could I take the slightest joy
In waking up a college boy.
I've no desire to be alone
With Rudy Vallee's megaphone,
So when I'm saying my pray'rs I say:

REFRAIN

Find me a primitive man
Built on a primitive plan,
Someone with vigor and vim,
I don't mean the kind that belongs to a club,
But the kind that has a club that belongs to him.
I could be the personal slave
Of someone just out of a cave.
The only man who'll ever win me
Has gotta wake up the gypsy in me.
Find me a primitive man,
Find me a primitive man.

Trouve moi un homme primitif.
Trouve moi un garçon naïf.
Quelqu'un tout plein de vigeur,
Ces p'tits maquereaux qu'on appelle gigolos ne
Pourraient jamais me donner le vrai bonheur.
J'ai besoin d'un bel animal
Pour regeler mon chauffage centrale.
Et l'homme qui me veut pour capitane
Devrait reveiller mon sang tzigane.
Trouve moi un homme primitif, vif.
Trouve moi un homme primitif.

WHERE WOULD YOU GET YOUR COAT?

Possibly intended for *Wake Up and Dream.* Introduced by Helen Broderick.

VERSE

As a buyer for a firm that deals in ladies' fur
coats
I get sort of pessimistic now and then
'Cause so many women who invest in our coats
Spend so many evenings out with other men.
I wish they'd simply take a few notes
From the animals who make their coats.

REFRAIN 1

For if dear little ermines in Siberia
On their dear little husbands didn't dote,
If the dear little 'possum
Didn't let their husbands boss 'em,
Tell me where would you get your coat?
If the dear little caraculs in Syria
All their time to their mates did not devote,
If the dear little sables ever told their husbands
fables,
Tell me where would you get your coat?
If you modern wives led more domestic lives
And started singing "Home, Sweet Home"
There'd be no more divorce in Paris and
Of course there'd be no more annulments in
Rome.
For if the dear little foxes had hysteria
When their mates fondly grabbed them by the
throat,
If the dear little rabbits weren't so bourgeois in
their habits,
Tell me where would you get your coat?

REFRAIN 2

If the dear little lamb in Lithuania
Ever had a flirtation with a goat,
If home life didn't thrill a South American
chinchilla,
Tell me where would you get your coat?
If the dear little skunk in Pennsylvania
Over her dear little husband didn't gloat,
If the dear little beaver
Were in birth control a believer,
Tell me where would you get your coat?
Now if each wife I see
Would only try to be
Content to make her husband's bed,
Cholly Knickerbocker might have nothing more
to write
And Town Topics would cease to be read.
For if the dear little mink should get a mania
For some hell-raising gigolo of note,
If the dear little squirrel
Quit her mate
'Cause he was virile,
Tell me where would you get your coat?

AT LONGCHAMPS TODAY

Alternate title is "Opening, Longchamps Scene." Introduced by ensemble.

CROWD: Ev'rybody who's anybody's at Longchamps today.
They're all so busy they're simply dizzy throwing money away.
The Prince of Wales is here,
And Mabel Boll is here,
And that delightful very merry Berry Wall is here,
For ev'rybody who's anybody's at Longchamps today.

MANNEQUINS: Comme mannequins, nous sommes charmantes,
Comme filles, tres provoquantes.
Nous portons des robes élégantes,
Qui rendent les femmes du monde ga-ga.
Peut-être vous, les touristes,
Trouvez que nous avons l'air triste,
Mais si nous avons l'air
La raison est clair,
Nos robes ne nous n'appartiennent pas.

MEN IN THE CROWD 1: Oh, what a swell little girl from Chanel.
2: Oh, what a pippin from Paquin.
3: I'm rather strong for the lass from Lelong.
4: As for me, give me Miss Lanvin.
5: Just get a view of that peach from Patou.
6: I like Miss Molyneux there.
ALL: Oh, isn't it, buddy,
Instructive to study
What the woman will wear?

YANKEE DOODLE

Although not listed in any programs, this number almost certainly followed "At Longchamps Today." Introduced by ensemble.

JULIA & MAY: Come on and take your places,
Before the race begins,
And pray the gods
Who make the odds
That Yankee Doodle wins.

They're off
CROWD: Come on, Yankee Doodle.
JULIA & MAY: He's gaining.
CROWD: Hurrah, Yankee Doodle.
JULIA & MAY: He's neck and neck with the second.
CROWD: Good old Yankee Doodle.
JULIA & MAY: He's passing the second.
CROWD: Go to it, Yankee Doodle.
JULIA & MAY: He's just behind the leader.
CROWD: After him, Yankee Doodle.
JULIA & MAY: He's level with the leader.
CROWD: Pass him, Yankee Doodle.
JULIA & MAY: He's passing the leader, they've ten lengths to go.
CROWD: Step on it. Step on it. Step on it. Step on it.
Step on it. Step on it. Step on it. Step on it.
JULIA & MAY: Yankee Doodle wins.
CROWD: Yankee Doodle wins.
Yankee Doodle, Yankee Doodle wins.

THE HAPPY HEAVEN OF HARLEM

Published December 1929. Listed in the programs as "The Heaven of Harlem," but "The Happy Heaven of Harlem" title is correct. Introduced by Billy Reed.

VERSE

I think I've gained enough renown
To take a wife and settle down,
But first I've got to go to Harlem town.
And right away,
For there I have a gloomy friend
Who thinks he's reached his journey's end.
That's why my homeward way I'm going to wend,
So I can say:

REFRAIN

There's a happy heaven of Harlem
In a country over the sea
Where there ain't no rule
Against white mule
And all lovin' is free.
There's a happy heaven of Harlem,
Twice as nice as heaven above,
Where you're never blue
'Cause all you do
Is eat, sleep and make love.
I ain't your redeemer, but one thing I do know,
That if you take a steamer, and tell the captain to go
To that happy heaven of Harlem, then I know that you will agree
If a heaven's planned

For Dixieland,
The heaven is Paree.

WHY SHOULDN'T I HAVE YOU?

Replaced "Down with Everybody but Us" before the New York opening. Introduced by Betty Compton and Jack Thompson.

VERSE

Every time that I feel the way of all flesh,
I proceed to congeal and tell you you're fresh.
All that I am demanding, dear, are my rights
But I don't like Arabian knights.

REFRAIN 1

Every law-abiding jurist
Has at least a manicurist
Who can show him how to have fun and still be legal.
Every king aristocratic
Has a wife who's morganatic
He can call upon when the queen becomes too regal.
Every cowboy in the canyon
Has a little home companion,
Every Turk who loves his work has one or two.
Every human thing and dumb thing
Has at least someone or something,
So why shouldn't I have you?

REFRAIN 2*

Every self-respecting grocer
Has a girl who won't say no, sir,
Any time he feels that he'd like to play and trifle.
In the Andes every llama
Has its fav'rite llama mamma,
Every ram that's fond of lamb at least has two.
Every armored armadillo
Has a mate who shares its pillow,
So why shouldn't I have you?

*Lines 1–3 of refrain 2 are instrumental.

SOMEBODY'S GOING TO THROW A BIG PARTY

"Somebody's Going to Throw a Big Party" and "It Isn't Done" made up "Opening, Claridge Scene." The programs list "It Isn't Done," but not "Somebody's Going to Throw a Big Party," although it is a separate number. Both introduced by ensemble.

SERVANTS: Somebody's going to throw a big party,
Somebody's going to have a big bust,
Somebody's going to break some more china,
Somebody's going to raise some more dust.
Somebody's just delighted
'Cause they've invited
The upper supper set to sup.
Somebody's going to pay the check,
Somebody's going to leave a wreck
For somebody else to clean up.

IT ISN'T DONE

VERSE

PROPRIETOR: My dutiful servants, I come to you
On a matter extremely vital.
A certain American parvenue
Has a daughter who needs a title.
I've hunted all over and finally met
A prince who desires to win her,
And so as a matter of etiquette,
Her ma's giving a dinner.

SERVANTS: To celebrate her daughter's fate,
Mamma's giving a dinner.

PROPRIETOR: The people she told me I should invite
Have all been engaged for ages,
So if you masquerade as the guests tonight
I promise to raise your wages.
But as about your behavior,
I'm still in a state of doubt,
I want to give you several rules
For dining out.

SERVANTS: As we've been waiting for ages
To get a raise in our wages,

We're nat'rally perfectly willing to listen
To several rules for dining out.

REFRAIN

PROPRIETOR: Don't start the dinner with saying grace, it isn't done.
Don't wrap the napkin 'round your face, it isn't done.
If you see the man who's next to your wife
Giving her the time of her life,
Don't begin to sharpen your knife, it isn't done.
Don't hit the person across from you with bits of toast,
And don't, when dinner is nearly through, say "Who's the host?"
You may be tempted to steal a bit of the silver just for fun,
But the fact remains it simply isn't done.

VERSE (IN SCRIPT)

BOYS: Although as perfect servants you may say we're not so hot,
We know exactly who is who and also what is what,
So if your social position is still in a state of doubt,
We're glad to give you several rules for dining out.

I'M IN LOVE

Published December 1929. Added to the show after the Boston opening. Introduced by Genevieve Tobin and ensemble.

VERSE

At boarding school I was always taught,
Not to reveal what I really thought,
Nor ever once let my eyes betray
The dreadful things that I longed to say.
And though no longer at boarding school,
I've always tried to obey this rule,
But now a certain exciting event
Is about to make me disobedient.

REFRAIN

I'm in love, I'm in love.
Life seems sweet since I've
Become the luckiest girl alive,
For strange to say,
It simply happens to be
That I'm in love with someone
Who's in love with me.

THE TALE OF THE OYSTER

Published in *The Unpublished Cole Porter.* Added to *Frenchmen* before the New York opening to give comedienne Helen Broderick another song. An earlier version with a different lyric was called "The Scampi" (see page 97). After amusing the Venice social set, the lyric was rewritten, and the song, after first nearly going into *Wake Up and Dream,* had a brief life in *Frenchmen.* When *Frenchmen* opened in New York, some people, including the noted critic Gilbert Seldes, found the song offensive. The program for the week of January 6, 1930, shows that "The Tale of the Oyster" (listed in the program as "The Tale of an Oyster") had been deleted from the show.

The song was rescued from oblivion by Ben Bagley and recorded by Kaye Ballard on Bagley's *Cole Porter Revisited* album.

Down by the sea lived a lonesome oyster,
Ev'ry day getting sadder and moister.
He found his home life awf'lly wet,
And longed to travel with the upper set.
Poor little oyster.
Fate was kind to that oyster we know,
When one day the chef from the Park Casino
Saw that oyster lying there,
And said, "I'll put you on my bill of fare."
Lucky little oyster.
See him on his silver platter,
Watching the queens of fashion chatter.
Hearing the wives of millionaires
Discuss their marriages and their love affairs.
Thrilled little oyster.
See that bivalve social climber
Feeding the rich Mrs. Hoggenheimer,
Think of his joy as he gaily glides
Down to the middle of her gilded insides.
Proud little oyster.
After lunch Mrs. H. complains,
And says to her hostess, "I've got such pains.
I came to town on my yacht today,
But I think I'd better hurry back to Oyster Bay."
Scared little oyster.
Off they go thru the troubled tide,
The yacht rolling madly from side to side.
They're tossed about till that poor young oyster
Finds that it's time he should quit his cloister.
Up comes the oyster.

Back once more where he started from.
He murmured, "I haven't a single qualm,
For I've had a taste of society
And society has had a taste of me."
Wise little oyster.

PAREE, WHAT DID YOU DO TO ME?

Published November 1929. In Boston it was sung by Betty Compton, Evelyn Hoey, Jack Thompson, and Lester Crawford; in New York by Miss Compton and Mr. Thompson. The opening words of the refrain, "Paree, Paree," furnished the title for the 1934 Vitaphone two-reel film which introduced Bob Hope to the movies. A sharply condensed version of *Frenchmen, Paree, Paree* retained only a few of the best-known songs.

VERSE

HE: Until I came to Paris,
I was such a very serious guy,
My only thought in life was how to succeed.
SHE: Until I hit the Boulevard,
I played croquet in my own little yard,
And thought that I had reached the limit of speed.
HE: Before "La Vie Parisienne" had made me such a fool,
I was a hard-boiled go-getter, and how!
SHE: Just think that not so long ago I went to Sunday school,
Then simply take one long look at me now.

REFRAIN

Paree, Paree,
Oh, what did you, what did you, what did you do to me?
Paree, Paree,
I'm not the respectable person I used to be.
I've ceased to care what my troubles are,
If I can get into a bottle where the bubbles are.
Paree, Paree,
Oh, what did you, what did you do to me?

YOU DON'T KNOW PAREE

Published December 1929. Added to *Frenchmen* after the first Boston performance but before the New York opening. Introduced by William Gaxton.

VERSE

You come to Paris, you come to play;
You have a wonderful time, you go away.
And, from then on, you talk of Paris knowingly;
You may know Paris, you don't know Paree.

REFRAIN

Though you've been around a lot,
And danced a lot, and laughed a lot,
You don't know Paree.
You may say you've seen a lot,
And heard a lot, and learned a lot;
You don't know Paree.
Paree will still be laughing after
Ev'ry one of us disappears,
But never once forget her laughter
Is the laughter that hides the tears.
And until you've lived a lot,
And loved a lot, and lost a lot,
You don't know Paree,
You don't know Paree.

I'M UNLUCKY AT GAMBLING

Published December 1929. Alternate title is "I'm Unlucky in Gambling." The Boston program lists it as "Unlucky in Gambling." The second verse, though sung in the show, was not included in the published sheet music. Introduced by Evelyn Hoey and Larry Ceballos' Hollywood Dancers.

VERSE 1

I went to Monte Carlo the other day,
I went to Monte Carlo to have some play;
I went to Monte Carlo and, straightaway
I went and fell in love with a croupier.
The croupier advised me to back the red,
The croupier was handsome, I lost my head;
And when the game was over and love was dead,
I realized I'd played on the black instead.

REFRAIN

For I'm unlucky at gambling,
And I'm unlucky in love.
Why should I go on scrambling
To get to heaven above?
It's bad enough to lose your purse
But when you lose your heart, it's even worse.
Oh, I'm unlucky at gambling
And I'm unlucky in love.

VERSE 2

I took the croupier to a picture show,
I took the croupier to a picture show,
And though I snuggled close when the lights
were low,
The croupier impressed me as rather slow.
I said I like John Gilbert a lot, don't you?
I said I like John Gilbert a lot, don't you?
He didn't answer but when the show was through
I realized that he liked John Gilbert too.

I WORSHIP YOU

Published November 1929. Dropped before the New York opening. Intended as a kind of theme song for the show. First sung by William Gaxton to Genevieve Tobin, it was reprised twice during the second act while the production was playing the Colonial Theatre in Boston. There it shared the critical spotlight with "You Do Something to Me," "Find Me a Primitive Man," "Where Would You Get Your Coat?" and "Please Don't Make Me Be Good." Porter had a special fondness for the song, for after it was dropped from *Frenchmen* (it is difficult to know why), it was resurrected for *Star Dust,* a show Porter was planning with Goetz and Fields in 1931 but which was never produced. Years later Hildegarde recorded it for Decca and Ben Bagley included it in his *Cole Porter Revisited* album and his *Decline and Fall* revue.

VERSE

Back in the days when Greece was mighty,
Men used to worship Aphrodite.
When the Phoenicians threw a party,
The driest host drank a toast to Astarte.
The big Egyptian sacrifices
Were made to please the goddess Isis,
And one of my most ancient vices
Is my worship of you.

REFRAIN

I don't love you, dear,
I swear it's true,
I don't love you, dear,
I worship you.
Must I modify
My point of view?
Why should I be odd if I
Worship you?
On that sacred day
When you become mine,
Somewhere far away
I'll build you a shrine.
There I'll put you, dear,
And when I do,
I'll get on my knees
And worship you.

PLEASE DON'T MAKE ME BE GOOD

Published November 1929. Performed by Evelyn Hoey and Larry Ceballos' Hollywood Dancers at the Colonial Theatre, Boston. Dropped from the show before the New York opening either to shorten the second act, which all Boston critics said was too long, or to placate cast members who felt that Miss Hoey had too many songs.

VERSE

I've wasted years enslaving myself
By behaving myself.
I've wasted tears consoling myself
For controlling myself.
But when the right man arrives
It's a question of our two lives,
So that's when I'll start undressing myself
By confessing myself.
I'll say to him:

REFRAIN

I'm so awfully weary
Doing just what I should.
I'm getting so bored
With virtue's reward,
So please don't make me be good.
Gee, but life can be dreary
When you're misunderstood.
In spite of my rep,
I'm all full of pep,
So please don't make me be good.
Though heaven may
Be okay,
When life's long journey ends,
I'd rather go
Down below

And be with my intimate friends (God bless 'em).
I could love you, my dearie,
More than anyone could,
You can make me, sweetheart,
But please don't make me be good.

THE QUEEN OF TERRE HAUTE

Published November 1929. Sung in the Boston tryout by Bernice Mershon, who played the role of the ingenue's mother, it was dropped before the New York opening.

VERSE

My mother and father
Once went to a lot of bother
To make me the happiest of girls.
To better my station*
They gave me an education,
Not to mention a string of pearls.
But in spite of my backing,
I still feel there's something lacking,
And that fate has rather let me down,
For instead of being famous
I'm an unknown ignoramus
From a small Middle Western town.

REFRAIN

Why couldn't I have been Salome,
Or Mary Pickford,
Or Joan of Arc?
If I were El'nor Glyn,
Or even Anne Boleyn,
The future wouldn't look half so dark.
Why couldn't I be Whistler's Mother?
Or any other woman of note?
Why did the gods decree
That I should only be
The Queen of Terre Haute?

*My string of Rolls-Royces
Is longer than Peggy Joyce's,

WATCHING THE WORLD GO BY

Sung by the tourists at the opening of the "Café de la Paix Scene" in Act I while the show was in Boston, it was dropped before the New York opening.

Watching the world go by,
It's fascinating, watching the world go by.
When you've some spare time to while away,
We highly recommend this decayed café,
For tho' you may not be one of them
Who care for brioche and café-crême,
And tho' the sole drinks that you can get,
Can only be described as wet,
Still at best, you can feast the eye,
Just sitting with us,
Watching the world go by.

DOWN WITH EVERYBODY BUT US

Sung during the Boston performances by Betty Compton and Jack Thompson but dropped before the New York opening and replaced by "Why Shouldn't I Have You?"

VERSE

Mother Earth would be a charming place
If it weren't for the boring human race.
Only think how nice this world would be
If the sole inhabitants were you and me.
We could live and laugh and love and sin
With no fear of someone butting in.
As it is, what chances have a simple man and
wife
What with all those folks who take the joy out of
life?

REFRAIN

Down with the legislators,
Down with the agitators,
Down with ev'rybody but us.
Down with the tax collectors,
Down with the p'lice inspectors,
Down with ev'rybody but us.
Why should we trouble and trifle
With people we dread?
Let's buy a Remington rifle
And shoot 'em all dead.
Down with the folks who bore us,

Up with the Anvil Chorus,
Down with ev'rybody but us.

WHY DON'T WE TRY STAYING HOME?

Published 1975 in *The Unpublished Cole Porter.* Dropped from *Frenchmen* during rehearsals and replaced by "Down with Everybody but Us," which, in turn, was replaced by "Why Shouldn't I Have You?"

VERSE 1

Since first we started out, we've simply run about,
And life's been one long rout unending.
We're always op'ning plays,
Or closing cabarets,
It seems to me our ways need mending.
Let's let the dressy dames with hyphenated names
In search of faster games fly by.
Content with being slow,
We'll never let them know.
The nicest place to go is bye-bye.

REFRAIN 1

Why don't we try staying home?
Why don't we try not to roam?
What if we threw a party or two,
And asked only you and me?
I long to sit by the fireside,
My girl, with me sitting by 'er side,
Wouldn't that be nice?
We've tried ev'ry thing else twice,
So why don't we try staying home?

VERSE 2

Let us begin to cut the folks who merely strut
And talk of nothing but their incomes.
Let's have no further use,
For going on the loose,
The moment orange juice and gin comes.
Our little love affair will make us cease to care
How many parties they're giving.
We're done with being smart,
And so we're goin' to start
To learn the gentle art of living.

REFRAIN 2

Why don't we try staying home?
Why don't we try not to roam?
What if we threw a party or two,
And asked only you and me?
Though all the home folks that we know
Pay for it later in Reno,
Just being still
Might give us a brand-new thrill,
So why don't we try staying home?

THAT'S WHY I LOVE YOU

This song bears some resemblance to "You've Got That Thing" and may have been replaced by it during rehearsals. Another Betty Compton–Jack Thompson song, it was dropped before the Boston opening.

REFRAIN 1

I don't like men who take you off
And give you talks on their game of golf.
You don't know how to play golf,
That's why I love you.
I don't like men of great renown
Who tell you how much they made downtown,
You lost a fortune downtown,
That's why I love you.
That's why I love you, dear,
Why the others won't do,
It's not what you do, dear,
It's what you don't do.
I don't like men who corner folks
And fill them up with the latest jokes.
You only tell me old jokes,
That's why I love you.

REFRAIN 2

I don't like girls who make a date
But when they keep it they're three hours late.
You're only half an hour late,
That's why I love you.
I don't like girls who talk with glee
Of other men when they're out with me.
You only talk about me,
That's why I love you.
That's why I love you, dear,
Why the others won't do,
It's not what you do, dear,
It's what you don't do.
I don't like girls who wander in
And calmly drink up your finest gin.
You always bring your own gin,
That's why I love you.

THE HEAVEN OF HARLEM

Only the lyric survives from Porter's first attempt to write a Harlem song for the show. The lyric was located in a Porter notebook at the Porter Trusts office.

VERSE

Listen here, baby dear,
If you're longing to dance,
Why not take a quick glance
At that country called France?
They tell me Gay Paree
Wants to hear a new tune.
Go sing in Paris,
You'll be an heiress
Soon,
Coon.

REFRAIN

For your thrills
Follow Florence Mills
To the heaven of Harlem,
For the heaven of Harlem has been moved to
   Paris, France.
All the swells
Love the Lulu belles
In the heaven of Harlem,
And you're sure to ensnare 'em if you ask 'em
   for a dance.
Since Josephine Baker started to shake her
   bones,
No cabaret lacks a chorus of saxophones.
Holy Palmer Jones
Syncopates
At the pearly gates
Of the heaven of Harlem,
For the heaven of Harlem is Gay Paree.

MY HARLEM WENCH

A second try at a Harlem song. Musically it resembles "The Happy Heaven of Harlem." It was found in the Tams-Witmark material.

As a Romeo I'm a wonder
And I've studied lovin' in French,
But the more I learn,
The more I burn
For my Harlem wench.
All the girls I meet in the moonlight
Say that I'm just great on the bench,
But the more they fall,
The more I call
For my Harlem wench.
These vampires you read of are all right in their
   line
But they ain't got the speed of that high-powered
   mamma of mine.
When for red-hot kisses I'm thirsty
Then my thirst I just gotta quench
But the more I take,
The more I ache
For my Harlem wench.

LET'S STEP OUT

Published April 1930. The program for the Lyric Theatre for March 24, 1930, lists a number titled "Stepping Out," sung by Evelyn Hoey and Gertrude McDonald. A March 13, 1930, story in the Cleveland *Plain Dealer* said that "unable to amuse himself much in Africa, Cole Porter, loafing his way around the world, sat himself down and composed a new song, called 'Stepping Out.' " Introduced by Evelyn Hoey and Gertrude McDonald. Published as "Let's Step Out," it became the twelfth published song from *Frenchmen.*

VERSE

Up to now we've been two shy young things,
Always tied to our mothers' apron strings,
Merely maids uncouth, simply throwing our youth
   away.
But tonight we must confide in you,
We've decided to change our point of view,
Take a brand-new pose,
Find a couple of beaux,
And say:

REFRAIN

Let's step out, let's step out,
Let's go somewhere and dance about,
We're all set for a rout,
C'mon, let's step out.
People say France is hot,
We're beginning to fear it's not.
Please, don't leave us in doubt,
C'mon, let's step out.
Life's a bore when you simply jog on
And never show your pep.
I confess that I'm getting doggone
Tired watching my step.
Let's run wild, let's be fools,

Let's go crazy and break the rules,
Fall in line when we shout,
"C'mon, let's step out."

THE BOY FRIEND BACK HOME

The program for the Lyric Theatre for December 16, 1929, lists "The Boy Friend Back Home" for the first time. It was sung by Evelyn Hoey and thus became a belated replacement for "Please Don't Make Me Be Good." It, in turn, was replaced by "Let's Step Out" in March 1930.

VERSE

If I didn't belong to a nation
Where people go from Poland to polo in one generation,
Then I might not slight so many parlor pets for my boy friend back home.
He's a coin-fed collegiate from Yonkers
And yet he has the kind of persuasion that goes out and conquers.
That is why that I am placing all my bets on the boy friend back home.
Although I know a lot more prominent men
My Bill is still my one particular yen—when

REFRAIN 1

I went to London I met the King.
I grant you that the King is quite a sweet old thing,
But he's not as sweet as the boy friend back home.
I spent the winter in Italy.
I looked at Mussolini and he looked at me,
But he didn't look like the boy friend back home.
My boy friend may not be a perfect sheik
But he's got what Mae West calls neck technique,
And although Maurice Chevalier may
Be a good performer in a certain way,
Still he can't perform like the boy friend back home.

REFRAIN 2

I went to Ireland, where friends I'd known
Persuaded me to go and kiss the Blarney Stone,
But I missed the kiss of my boy friend back home.
The King of Spain I idolized
And once he let me see the Spanish in his eyes,
But they weren't the eyes of my boy friend back home.
My boy friend's low brow, doesn't understand
But somehow his supply meets my demand.
And although dear Mr. Ziegfeld may
Be quite a good producer in a modest way,
Still he can't produce like the boy friend back home.

Piano copies of the overture, entr'acte, and much incidental music from *Frenchmen* also survive. So does the ballet music for *The Snake in the Grass,* which was staged for the Boston performances by Leonide Massine. It is approximately five to six minutes long and is divided into three sections. The scene is the Bois de Boulogne. In the first part a young girl dances alone. In the second section she is joined by a young man. The final segment begins with the entrance of a contortionist carrying a basket, from which a snake emerges. The piece ends with boy and girl together longing to leave Paris and return to America. The ballet was dropped from the show before the New York opening and replaced by "You Don't Know Paree." Considerable material from *Fifty Million Frenchmen* was discovered at the Warner Brothers Music warehouse in Secaucus, New Jersey, February 1982. There was an earlier version of music for "Find Me a Primitive Man," much hitherto unknown incidental music including Act II, Scene I ("Classique"), Act I, Scene II (Special Dance with conductor's score and instrumental parts), an earlier version of "The Queen of Terre Haute," titled "A Girl from Terre Haute," and music, but no lyrics, for an unused second act song, "Let's Turn On the Love Interest."

MISCELLANEOUS

1920s

A NIGHT OUT, 1920

Porter wrote the music to four numbers from the English production of *A Night Out*, which opened at the Winter Garden Theatre, London, September 18, 1920, and ran for 309 performances. But the lyrics are by Clifford Grey. The titles are: "Look Around," "Why Didn't We Meet Before?," "Our Hotel," and "Finale, Act II, Scene 1" (a reprise with a different lyric of "Our Hotel").

MAYFAIR AND MONTMARTRE, 1922

Tryout: no information. Produced by Charles B. Cochran at London's New Oxford Theatre, March 9, 1922. 77 performances. A revue by John Hastings Turner to which Porter contributed some songs. The cast starred Alice Delysia and included Nikitina, Nellie Taylor, and Joyce Barbour.

OLGA (COME BACK TO THE VOLGA)

Published March 1922. Introduced by Nikitina.

VERSE

Olga from the Volga
Made the whole of London moan,
Chanting that Volga ballad,
Dressed like a Russian salad.
No one knew that Olga
Had a husband of her own.
She'd cut her heart to pieces
And only took beaux on leases,
But one night when the lights were bright
And the cheering began to subside,
There appeared such a bushy beard
And behind it a voice that cried:

REFRAIN

My beautiful Olga,
Come back to the Volga—
Instead of your dancing like a star,
You should be catching caviar
For Lenin and Trotsky,
They eat such a Lotski.
I'll jump in the Volga, Olga,
If you don't come home.

COCKTAIL TIME

Published March 1922. Introduced by Joyce Barbour.

VERSE

GIRL: I must be on my way,
I haven't time to stay.
MEN: Ah, linger longer, pretty maiden,
We pray!
GIRL: I really must be gone,
I've got a party on.
MEN: Fairest flower,
Oh, grant us but an hour.
GIRL: Alas, I cannot pause;
The reason is because

REFRAIN

GIRL: It's cocktail time!
MEN: Cocktail time!
GIRL: Cocktail time!
MEN: Maybe it's so, but we should rather doubt it.
GIRL: Cocktail time!
MEN: Cocktail time!
GIRL: Cocktail time!
MEN: Surely you know we'd like to hear about it.
GIRL: That's the time when all youth
Goes to see the gin attack the French
vermouth.
Never a single word.
MEN: No!
GIRL: Am I mistaken?
Thought I heard
MEN: Oh!
GIRL: The shaker shakin'.
If your girl's a quiet pussy-footer,
You should quickly put her out of sight.
And when you've found some flapper full
of frolic,
With an alcoholic appetite,
Never mention apple-blossom time
MEN: In Normandy

GIRL: Or even tulip time
MEN: Beside the Zuider Zee;
GIRL: But if you want
MEN: What?
GIRL: To win a victory,
Make it to the Ritz at cocktail time!

THE BLUE BOY BLUES

Published March 1922. Introduced by Nellie Taylor.

Two other Porter songs, "The Bandit Band" and "The Sponge," are listed among the published songs from *Mayfair and Montmartre,* but neither is listed in the London opening-night program. Both songs, which were probably dropped before the London opening, turned up in a later show, *Hitchy-Koo of 1922.* Further information on them can be found with *Hitchy-Koo.* Like "Olga," "Cocktail Time," and "The Blue Boy Blues," they were copyrighted on March 3, 1922, further proof that they were originally part of *Mayfair and Montmartre.*

VERSE

As a painting you must have heard a lot about me,
For I lived here for many happy years;
Never dreaming that you could ever do without me
Till you sold me in spite of all my tears.
It's a long way from gilded galleries in Park Lane
To the Wild West across the winter sea.
If you don't know quite what I mean,
Simply ask Sir Joseph Duveen
And he'll tell you what he gave 'em for me.

REFRAIN

For I'm the Blue Boy;
The beautiful Blue Boy;
And I am forced to admit
I'm feeling a bit depressed.
A silver dollar took me and my collar
To show the slow cowboys
Just how boys
In England used to be dressed.
I don't know what I shall do
So far from Mayfair;
If Mister Gainsborough knew,
I know he'd frown.
As days grow fewer,
I'm bluer and bluer;
For I am saying goodbye to London town.

CHORUS: We've got those Blue Boy blues,
We've got the doggone Blue Boy blues.
We fairly feel it oozing from our heads
Down to our shoes.
So won't you tell us what to do, boy?
We've got the Blue Boy blues.
We've got those Blue Boy blues.
We've got those doggone Blue Boy blues.
We fairly feel it oozing from our heads
Down to our shoes.
So won't you tell us what to do, boy?
We've got the Blue Boy blues.

ENCORE

CHORUS: Don't be so blue,
Always so blue,
We never saw such a crybaby, crybaby,
Why don't you smile
Once in a while?
Say, Willie, what silly book ever sold
you that collar?
Boo-hoo! Boo-hoo!
That's all you know to do.
Boo-hoo! Boo-hoo!
Why don't you try something new?
Powder your nose,
Buy some new clothes,
And stop longing for London town.

WOND'RING NIGHT AND DAY

I have never seen a published copy of this song, but the Copyright Office says it was published, listing the copyright day as March 16, 1922. Is it possible that it was interpolated into *Mayfair and Montmartre?* I have no evidence that it was. There are manuscript copies of this song at the Porter Trusts office and Yale.

VERSE

By the fire
I watch each dying ember
And remember
Those dear days of yore
Before the June of our love
Became September
And I'm gazing in your eyes
Once more.

REFRAIN

Won'dring night and day
Why you went away,
Won'dring too
Whether you
Forget our spooning

And honeymooning.
Won'dring if your kiss
Really meant goodbye,
All alone
I'm still your own,
I wonder why.

PHI-PHI, 1922

Porter had one song in this Charles B. Cochran revue, which opened at the London Pavilion Theatre on August 16, 1922.

RAGTIME PIPES OF PAN

Published September 1922. Introduced by Clifton Webb, this is the same song musically as "Syncopated Pipes of Pan," which appeared in the *Greenwich Village Follies* (1924). The only difference in the lyrics is the substitution of the word "ragtime" for "syncopated."

VERSE

People who dwell
Down in the dell,
Tell of a rustic cabaret.
Where all the good folk of the wood go each night.
Old Mister Pan
Gathers the clan,
And makes his ragtime pipers play
Wonderful tunes, under the moon's
Silv'ry light.
Songs sentimental,
Melodies gentle,
Scurry aloft
To join the soft summer breeze.
While all the fauna
Dance gaily on a flowery heath,
Stretching beneath shady trees.

REFRAIN

Play on, pipes of Pan,
Lay on all you can.
Rush out of your rushes,
Beavers and ducks,
Woodpeckers and thrushes.
Hurry aboard and order your tables.
Fireflies, fly this way.
Woodchucks, chuck your play.
Bullfrogs and crickets,
Come buy your tickets.
We'll undertake
To make the snake shake,
To the ragtime pipes of Pan.

PATTER

Trot like a fox,
Strut like a cock.
Twist like a turtle on a sunny rock.
Hop like a magpie,
Tremble like a 'possum.
Bounce like a butterfly upon a blossom.
Squirm like a worm
When the leaf begins to quiver.
Swish like a fish
Thru the ripples in the river.
Jump like a hare,
Hug like a bear,
What could be sweeter
Than the syncopated meter?

OUT O' LUCK, 1925

Produced in 1925 and 1926 by the Yale University Dramatic Association. Directed by Monty Woolley.

BUTTERFLIES

Lyrics for "Butterflies," "Mademazelle," and "Opera Star" were recalled by the well-known stage and screen director the late Henry C. Potter in a letter to this editor dated December 18, 1968. His letter included the following information on *Out o' Luck*'s three Porter songs.

> Cole's songs were sandwiched into Act II, during an impromptu "show" being put on by some of the soldiers, dressed in spangled, chorus-girl "tutus" (but still wearing their GI boots). There were three of them:
> *Butterflies*—an "opening Chorus,"
> *Mademazelle*—comedy love-song,
> *Opera Star*—a "special material" comedy song.
> I played the lead and sang the first two. The third, *Opera*, was especially written for John Hoysradt, '26, president of the Dramat, who did his very funny and adroit falsetto burlesques of current divas for Cole one day at rehearsal; within a week Cole delivered

Opera, incorporating John's burlesques; *Opera* proved to be what used to be called "a wow."

The two songs that I sang, while great for the show and the period, and while perfectly good examples of 1925 "pop" songwriting, have no lasting value—as I am sure Cole would have been the first to admit, and as one can see from the lyrics themselves—except that they do possess, here and there, that Cole Porter flip of phrasing and rhyming that was so uniquely his. *Opera* lived a little longer: John Hoysradt (today John Hoyt—at the request of Paramount Pictures which insisted that "Hoysradt" would get him nowhere) used it for several years in his night-club act.

The music does not survive. Potter told me he would have been willing to record the songs, but he did not think the music represented Porter at his best.

VERSE

Hello, hello, hello!
We want you all to know,
That we are young ladies
Who'll be at home in Hades
In less than a year or so!
We've done the best we could,
To shock the neighborhood.
So don't try to storm us
With reasons to reform us
'Cause we don't want to be good!

REFRAIN

We're butterflies,
Gay butterflies,
Bad butterflies, that's all.
We've nothing much
Inside the dome
'Cept a rare old flair for wrecking a home!
Each time we think
We meet a gink
We simply wink
One eye,
And if every go-getter
Were not such a petter
We'd be much better
Butterfli . . . ies,
Much better butterflies!

MADEMAZELLE

VERSE

I'm in love with the nicest doughboy
And I'll say that there's simply no boy,
Quite as "gentil,"
As he
Is to me,
Why, the first time he took me walkin'
He began right away to talk in
Terms of l'amour,
And this
Was his overture: Oh,

REFRAIN

Mademazelle, please marry me,
Mademazelle, oh, say "oui oui,"
I'm just as glad as I can be
I found you.
After the war we're gonna go
Back to my home in Kokomo.
I want to build a bungalow
Around you.
We'll have a slick life
Leading a hick life
Out in a one-horse town.
Think of it maybe
You will someday be
Bouncing a Franco-Yanko baby!
Mademazelle, don't say nay-nay
'Cause I know you'll think that it's swell,
As we go walking down Main Street,
Me and Mademazelle,
Oh la-la,
Me and Mademazelle!

OPERA STAR

VERSE

If the critics have dominion
Over popular opinion
I'm the opera's most sensational soprano.
It's because I have a fashion
Of my own for putting passion
In the roles that I portray for Otto Kahn-o.
All the smart set go as far as
Wearing top hats and tiaras
Every time they come to see me do a rave.
And commuters enter rushing
From their furnished flats in Flushing,
To encourage me to mis . . . be . . . have.
As an opera vamp I've reached the very top,
But in private life my technique is a flop:

REFRAIN

I'm a great success making love on the stage,
But a terrible failure at home.

I can find a nice fellow once in an age
But in no time he starts in to roam.
'Round the fireside I'll admit I'm much too tame
But they call the fire department when I sing
Bohème:
[*Burlesqued bit from the opera*]
I'm a great success making love on the stage
But a terrible failure at home.

THE BATTLE OF PARIS, 1929

A film produced by Paramount Pictures. Released November 30, 1929. Screenplay by Gene Markey. Directed by Robert Florey. Cast, starring Gertrude Lawrence, included Charles Ruggles, Walter Petrie, Gladys Du Bois, Arthur Treacher, and Joe King.

Porter wrote two songs for the film.

HERE COMES THE BANDWAGON

"Here Comes the Bandwagon" and "They All Fall in Love" were published in November 1929 and were introduced by Gertrude Lawrence.

VERSE

If you look your childhood over,
There was nothing half so grand,
As the old-fashioned circus parade.
And the greatest thing about it
Was the
Oom-pah, oom-pah band!
And the heartbreakin' music it played.
And when you'd hear it drawing near
You'd get so awf'ly upset,
You'd rush about and wildly shout
To ev'rybody you met:

REFRAIN

Here comes the bandwagon!
Here comes the bandwagon!
Listen to that rat-tat-a-tat,
Rat-tat-a-tah!
Those vo-de-o brasses,
Sweeter than molasses,
Make me so gay,
I want to say, "Hip hip hoorah!"
As they float gaily by,
Ev'ry note seems to cry,
"If you wait you'll be late for the show."
Oh, no!
Here comes the bandwagon!
Don't simply stand laggin'!
Here comes the bandwagon,
Let's go!

THEY ALL FALL IN LOVE

VERSE

Each year, when spring, quite uninvited,
Gives a garden party to the world united,
Ev'ryone gets so excited
They don't know what they're thinking of.
Folks who've spent the winter freezin',
Whiff the balmy breeze and simply lose their
reason,
They know it's the open season,
For falling in love.

REFRAIN 1

The young fall, the old fall,
The red-hot mammas, and the cold fall,
From the lily white to the black as night,
They all fall in love.
The fools fall, the wise fall,
The wets, the sprinkled, and the drys fall,
From the men who drink
To the men who wink,
They all fall in love.
You may believe your broker is very mediocre
At playing with your stocks and bonds,
At business he may blunder,
Yet he's a perfect wonder,
When he plays with blondes.
Old maids who object fall,
Old men you never would suspect fall,
Even babies, who can hardly crawl, fall,
'Cause they all fall in love.

REFRAIN 2

The wags fall, the boobs fall,
The gold-brick sellers and the rubes fall,
From the underbred to the overfed,
They all fall in love.
The good very oft fall,
The hard-shelled Baptists and the soft fall,
Just to prove they believe,
In the fall of Eve,
They all fall in love.

The solemn undertaker is shyer than a Quaker,
As long as he is filling graves,
But let him meet a missus
Who hasn't prejudices,
And he misbehaves.
The angels on high fall,
And men like Lindbergh who can fly fall,
Even boxers much too pure to fall, fall,
'Cause they all fall in love.

REFRAIN 3

The pet parakeets fall,
The English sparrows in the streets fall,
From the doves of peace to the wildest geese,
They all fall in love.
Small bookworms on the shelves fall,
Amoebas even for themselves fall.
From the early worms to the latest germs,
They all fall in love.
When strolling in a thicket, if you pick up a
cricket
And put him in a shady tree,
You'll find a little later
That he's become the pater
Of a family.
The pigs fall, the sows fall,
The bull walks in and all the cows fall,
Even mules that never fall at all, fall,*
'Cause they all fall in love.

LOVE 'EM AND LEAVE 'EM

Written in the early 1920s or perhaps earlier.

VERSE

I still was a dumb child
When Mother said: Come, child,
The moment's arrived
When you should roam.
But before you go, dear,
I want you to know, dear,
The best way to bring the bacon home.
If you want ev'rything in the world that's nice,
You'll succeed if you follow your ma's advice.

REFRAIN

Love 'em and leave 'em
And leave while the leavin' is good.
Love 'em and leave 'em
And say that you misunderstood.
When you've had your innings,
Prepare to fly,
Just pack up your winnings,
And say goodbye.
Pet 'em and please 'em
And swear that you love 'em a lot.
Get 'em and tease 'em
And get everything that they've got.
When they start to "sex" it
Be quick and choose the nearest exit,
Love 'em and leave 'em high and dry!

Or:
Even bearded goats in Donegal fall,

ITALIAN STREET SINGERS

I was able to reconstruct a holograph manuscript (music and lyrics) from the miscellaneous material Porter bequeathed to Yale. Written, I believe, in Venice about 1926.

We are a trio of cantanti,
And like all the best baccanti,
Very fond of good Chi-anti
And spaghetti.
Viva spaghetti.
Under the heavens bright and starry,
On we wander, near and far-y,
Gaily singing popolari
Canzonetti,
Canzonetti.
Tho' perhaps you be a scorner
Of our concerts on the corner,
Yet we know that they would please Sir Thomas
Beecham,
For since London music lovers
Can't be pulled from out their covers,
It's the only way in which to reach 'em
Tutti tutti.

I'll admit, in case you're a connoisseur of
col'ratura,
As a singer I shall never very far go.
Yet you'd be more interested
If my name I once suggested,
For it's known to ev'ry tongue and ev'ry argot.
And so long as I've this to work with
And my dear little voice to ask with
I'll continue this till I'm a millionaire.
Then I'll chuck my bad Italian,
Find myself a snow-white stallion
And Godiva thru Trafalgar Square.

GIRL: Piano, piano

MEN: Forte, forte, forte, fortissimo
GIRL: Piano, piano
MEN: Forte, forte, forte, fortissimo
GIRL: Crescendo, crescendo
MEN: Poco a poco a poco a poco
GIRL: Diminuendo, endo
MEN: Non troppo, non troppo, non troppo, non troppo
GIRL: Legato, legato
MEN: Staccato, staccato
GIRL: Maggiore, maggiore
MEN: Minore, nore, nore, minore
GIRL: Più lento, più lento
MEN: Uno momento, momento, momento, momento, momento
GIRL: Una cadenza
Tra-la-la, tra-la-la
In the meantime . . . Ain't we got fun . . .
Down on the Swanee River.

POOR YOUNG MILLIONAIRE

Porter's music is lost. The lyric was found in a Porter lyric notebook at the Porter Trusts office. A new musical setting was made for it by Peter Bogdanovich and Artie Butler for Bogdanovich's film *At Long Last Love* (1974). That version was introduced in the film by Burt Reynolds.

After hunting all over for pleasure
With some measure of success,
I've decided the pace known as rapid
Leads to vapid nothingness.
And I'm tired of betting,
Tired of sporting,
Tired of flirting,
Tired of courting,
Tired of racing,
Tired of yachting,
Tired of loafing,
Tired of rotting,
Tired of dining,
Tired of wining,
Tired of teaing,
Tired of being
Tired, tired, tired.
Oh, won't somebody care
For a poor young millionaire?
If you knew what blues meant
You'd find me amusement.
I've had every thrill
From a Rolls-Royce to a Ford.
And there's no concealing
The fact I'm feeling
Bored, bored, bored.

DON'T TELL ME WHO YOU ARE

The music is lost. Probably written in the early 1920s.

VERSE 1

A fiddler was fiddling a wonderful tune,
A sweet serenade to the maid in the moon.
It woke up a singer who longed for a fling,
So she went to her window and started to sing:

REFRAIN 1

Don't tell me who you are, dear. Don't let me ever know.
Make this a rare,
Romantic affair,
And keep your incognito.
I want to think, all through life, it's
Been Jascha Heifetz
Playing to me from afar.
But if I knew your name,
It would spoil the whole game,
So don't tell me who you are.

VERSE 2

The fiddler decided to enter the game,
And promised he never would tell her his name.
She started to throw him her visiting card,
But the fiddler replied, as he stood in the yard:

REFRAIN 2

Don't tell me who you are, dear. Don't let me ever know.
Make this a rare,
Romantic affair,
And keep your incognito.
I want to think, dear, that it's a-
Lluring Jeritza
Singing to me from afar.
If you give me a smile,
I'll come up for a while,
But don't tell me who you are.

VERSE 3

The singer was willing to give him a smile,
So up went the fiddler and stayed for a while.

He taught her to fiddle, she taught him to sing,
And they sang this refrain when they'd finished their fling:

REFRAIN 3

Don't tell me who you are, dear. Don't let me ever know.
Make this a rare,
Romantic affair,
And keep your incognito.
You're quite the best bet I've met yet,
In a duet, yet
Why trust each other too far?
I might get you in deep,
If I talked in my sleep,
So don't tell me who you are.

THE SCAMPI

Written in Venice to amuse his friends, including the Queen of the Lido, the Princess San Faustino, the former Jane Campbell of New Jersey. The music is the same as the music for "The Tale of the Oyster" (see page 87), which was written after "The Scampi."

Once there lived a nice young Scampi
In a canal that was dark and damp, he
Found his home life much too wet,
And longed to travel with the supper set.
Poor little Scampi.
Fate was kind, for very soon a-
Long came the chef from the Hotel Luna,
Saw that Scampi lying there,
And said, "I'll put you on my bill of fare."
Lucky little Scampi.
See him on his silver platter,
Hearing the Queens of the Lido chatter,
Getting the latest in regard
To Elsa Maxwell and Lady Cunard.
Thrilled little Scampi.
See that ambitious Scampi we know
Feeding the Princess San Faustino.
Think of his joy as he gaily glides
Down to the middle of her Roman insides.
Proud little Scampi.
After dinner the Princess Jane
Said to her hostess, "I've such a pain.
Don't be cross, but I think I shall
Go for a giro in a side canal."
Scared little Scampi.
Off they went through the troubled tide,
The gondola rocking from side to side.
They tossed about till that poor young Scampi
Found that his quarters were much too crampy.
Up comes the Scampi.
Back once more where he started from,
He said, "I haven't a single qualm,
For I've had a taste of the world, you see,
And a great princess has had a taste of me."
Wise little Scampi.

I'M DINING WITH ELSA

The song was a surprise birthday present from Porter at a party for Elsa Maxwell in Paris in the late 1920s. The music may exist, but I have never seen a copy of it.

I met a friend of mine a week or two ago,
And he was all togged out.
I said, "Excuse me, but I'd really like to know
What this is all about.
You're over-dressed, you're absurd!"
He answered, "Haven't you heard?

I'm dining with Elsa, with Elsa, supreme.
I'm going to meet princesses
Wearing Coco Chanel dresses
Going wild over strawberries and cream.
I've got Bromo Seltzer
To take when dinner ends,
For I'm dining with Elsa
And her ninety-nine most intimate friends!"

Last night I met that little friend of mine once more
Dressed like a bold apache.
I hardly knew him, for across his face he wore
A very false mustache.
I said, "But why this disguise?"
He whispered, "Don't put them wise—

I'm dining with Maxwell, with Maxwell, my dear.
She's tired of princesses
In their Coco Chanel dresses,
And she's longing for sausages and beer.
I've covered our tracks well,
For I'm saving Miss Maxwell
From her ninety-nine most intimate friends."

THAT LITTLE OLD BAR IN THE RITZ

No music survives. This lyric was found in one of the Porter scrapbooks at Yale and may have been printed in a magazine article during the late 1920s.

When the day's business battle is won,
And your spirits have sunk with the sun,
And again you're aware
That it's time to prepare
For that dinner that's got to be done,
There's a place in the center of town
That can give the required benefits.
So if lacking in pep,
I advise you to step
To that little old bar in the Ritz.

There, Americans, Germans and Greeks
Mix with Arab and Argentine sheiks.
There's a man on one bench
Who's undoubtedly French,
For the waiters all blush when he speaks.
There, where fizzes and punches and grogs
Mix with cocktails and Pommery splits,
International thirst
Can be seen at its worst
At that little old bar in the Ritz.

When your heart has been broken in two,
And you're battered, embittered and blue,
Or when weary you get
Of the same cinq à sept,
And you haven't another in view,
You will find, once you get to this spot,
Far away from the chatter of chits,
You'll thank God that you're male
As you cling to the rail
Of that little old bar in the Ritz.

SEX APPEAL

The music is lost. An article about Porter in an undated issue of a publication called *The Boulevardier* mentions the song, suggesting that it was sung at the Ambassadeurs Café in Paris in the summer of 1927.

VERSE

Mary isn't a youngster, Mary hasn't a bob,
But girls much younger,
Drop dead from hunger
While Mary's ordering squab.
Mary's covered with sables, Mary's got a new car.
If you've missed her,
I'll tell you, sister,
Why Mary went so far.

REFRAIN

It's sex appeal, it's sex appeal, it's sex appeal,
  that's all.
That certain something, that yummy-yum thing
That makes gentlemen fall.
When she's around, the hes around all breeze
  around and call,
She's got no beauty, she's nearly plain,
And heaven made her without a brain.
I know her heart is as hard as steel,
But, oh boy, she's got sex appeal.

HOT-HOUSE ROSE

Published November 1927. This parody of "Second-Hand Rose" was written for Fanny Brice during the summer of 1927. Porter recalled the song in a 1953 letter to entertainer George Byron:

> Fanny Brice visited Venice in 1926, when my wife and I were living in the Palazzo Rezzonico. At this time in my life I had given up all hope of ever being successful on Broadway and had taken up painting, but Fanny, whom we grew to know very well, asked me to write a song for her. This was the reason for *"Hot-House Rose."* When I finished it, I invited her to the Rezzonico to hear it and afterwards she always told friends how wonderfully incongruous it was, that I should have demonstrated to her this song about a poor little factory girl as she sat beside me while I sang and played it to her on a grand piano that looked lost in our ballroom, whose walls were entirely decorated by Tiepolo paintings and was so big that if we gave a ball for less than a thousand people they seemed to be entirely lost. She never sang the song.

VERSE

No wonder that the rose to me's
The fairest flow'r that grows;
My fam'ly name is Rosenbaum,
My other name is Rose.
So yesterday
When I got my pay
I went to a park I know,
And walked around
Till I fin'lly found

The place where the roses grow.
When I saw those flowers all in bloom,
I almost forgot my basement room.

REFRAIN 1

I'm hot-house rose from God knows where,
The kind that grows without fresh air.
The whistle blows and work is done
But it's too late for me to get the sun.
They say that when you dream a lot,
You always dream of what you haven't got.
That's why I dream of a garden, I s'pose,
'Cause I'm only a hot-house rose.

REFRAIN 2

I'm hot-house rose from God knows where,
The kind that grows without fresh air.
A summer breeze I never get,
The morning dew has never kissed me yet.
I bought an ounce of nice perfume
And now I smell just like a rose-in-bloom.
But why take trouble when ev'ryone knows
That I'm only a hot-house rose.

WEREN'T WE FOOLS?

Published November 1927. Written for Fanny Brice and performed by her during her vaudeville act at New York's Palace Theatre beginning November 21, 1927. On the second night of the famous singing comedienne's week-long engagement, she learned that her former husband, Nicky Arnstein, was in the audience and so she dropped "Weren't We Fools?" for that evening's performance. Porter told a reporter for the New York *Telegram* (November 22, 1927) that the song had been composed long before Miss Brice's divorce.

VERSE 1

Ev'ry time I see you, dear,
I think of days when you were near,
And I held you close to my heart.
Life was like a perfect dream
And yet so real it didn't seem
That we two could ever drift apart.
I know that all you said to me was true,
And you love me still
As I love you.

REFRAIN

Weren't we fools to lose each other?
Weren't we fools to say goodbye?
Tho' we knew we loved each other,
You chose another.
So did I.
If we'd realized our love was worth
defending
Then the story's broken threads we might be
mending
With perhaps a diff'rent ending,
A happy ending.
Weren't we fools?
Weren't we fools?

VERSE 2

Think of all the plans we made,
The schemes we had,
The plots we laid,
To work out a life of our own.
All of them were thrown away,
Yet when we meet again today,
The crowd disappears and we're alone.
I long to put my arms around you now!
But it wouldn't be the same, somehow.

THE LAZIEST GAL IN TOWN

Published June 1927. This song was probably written for a summer show at Edmond Sayag's Ambassadeurs Café. It was made famous by Marlene Dietrich in Alfred Hitchcock's film *Stage Fright* (1950) and became part of Miss Dietrich's repertoire.

VERSE

I've a beau, his name is Jim,
He loves me and I love him,
But he tells me I'm too prim,
That means I'm too slow.
I let him rant, I let him rave,
I let him muss my permanent wave,
But when he says "Let's misbehave,"
My reply is "No!"

REFRAIN

It's not 'cause I wouldn't,
It's not 'cause I shouldn't,
And, Lord knows, it's not 'cause I couldn't,
It's simply because I'm the laziest gal in
town.
My poor heart is achin'
To bring home the bacon,
And if I'm alone and forsaken,

It's simply because I'm the laziest gal in
town.
Though I'm more than willing to learn
How these gals get money to burn,
Ev'ry proposition I turn down,
'Way down,
It's not 'cause I wouldn't,
It's not 'cause I shouldn't,
And, Lord knows, it's not 'cause I couldn't,
It's simply because I'm the laziest gal in
town.

VERSE SUNG BY MARLENE DIETRICH

Nothing ever worries me,
Nothing ever hurries me.
I take pleasure leisurely
Even when I kiss.
But when I kiss they want some more,
And wanting more becomes a bore,
It isn't worth the fighting for,
So I tell them this:

THE NEW YORKERS

1930

Tryout: Chestnut Street Opera House, Philadelphia, November 12, 1930; Shubert Theatre, Newark, New Jersey, November 24, 1930. Produced by E. Ray Goetz at B. S. Moss's Broadway Theatre, December 8, 1930. 168 performances. Book by Herbert Fields, based on a story by E. Ray Goetz and Peter Arno. Directed by Monty Woolley. Cast, starring Hope Williams, Charles King, and Jimmy Durante, included Ann Pennington, Frances Williams, Marie Cahill, Lou Clayton, Eddie Jackson, Richard Carle, and Fred Waring and his orchestra.

GO INTO YOUR DANCE

Porter sent most of the surviving music from *The New Yorkers,* including "Go into Your Dance," to the Music Division, Library of Congress, Washington, D.C., in November 1963. Introduced by Frances Williams and ensemble.

VERSE

I gotta swell idea
To put you on your toes.
I gotta panacea
That will cure all your woes.
So if you're sad and gloomy
And want to end it all,
Don't even stop to think twice,
Just follow this good advice:

REFRAIN

When you find that old man Trouble
Has you by the pants,
Don't yelp and cry for help,
Go into your dance.
When you get the cross that's double
From your pet romance,
Don't swear and tear your hair,
Go into your dance.
When those old blues come
To lead you astray,
You'll make good news come
If you dance, dance 'em away.
When your life's a busted bubble
And you've lost your chance,
Don't run and get your gun,
Go into your dance.

WHERE HAVE YOU BEEN?

Published November 1930. Introduced by Charles King and Hope Williams.

VERSE

If ever you love again,
If such luck could be,
You must fall in love again
With nobody but me;
For now that I see you, I know
That we should have met long ago.

REFRAIN

Where have you been?
I want to know where have you been?
My life was a losing fight
Till the lucky night,
Baby, you happened in.
From what I had heard about love,
I thought it was all sorrow and sin,
But now that we meet at last,
I forget the past.
Baby, where have you been?
I was alone, unbefriended,
In the depths of despair,
When out of the blue you descended
And somehow ended ev'ry care.
So if you will give me a break,
And order the love scene to begin,
So close to your side I'll stay
You can never say,
"Baby, where have you been?"

SAY IT WITH GIN

Also titled "Opening Chorus to Bootleg Scene." Introduced by ensemble.

Don't say it with candy,
Don't say it with flow'rs.
Don't give her something high-brow to read,
Maybe she doesn't know how to read.
Don't say it with music,
It's early Irving Berlin.
But if you want to woo her,
And get a lot closer to her,
Say it with
Gordon's and Gilbey's and High and Dry and
  Plymouth,
Just step right up and kindly give your order.

A brand-new consignment of very great
  refinement
Has just come in today across the border.
In case to make your sweetie fall,
You find you're unable,
Our gin is guaranteed to put her under the table,
But if we shouldn't have on hand
The special brand that you demand,
Just give us thirty seconds and
We'll change the label.

[*Repeat first eight lines*]
Say it
Say it
Say it with gin.

VENICE

No music survives. Introduced by Hope Williams, Jimmy Durante, Lou Clayton, and Eddie Jackson.

DEEGAN: It must be a menace to those who
    play tennis in Venice.
GREGORY & MONAHAN: Where's Venice?
ALICE: In Venice—
DEEGAN: She knows—
  For the lack of dry land,
  There's no place to stand
  In Venice—
GREGORY & MONAHAN: Where's Venice?
ALICE: In Venice—
DEEGAN: She's marvelous—
ALICE: Stop all this nonsense.
  Do you realize that water when
    frozen makes ice?
  Do you realize that chickens lay
    eggs?
ALL THREE: *No—*
ALICE: Do you realize that all the best
    oysters have pearls,
  And that now and then diamonds
    have legs?
  Do you realize that hydrogen and
    oxygen make air,
  And that six minus two equals four?
ALL THREE: No—
ALICE: Well, whenever you're blue and
    you've nothing to do
  Come around, mugs, and I'll tell you
    some more.
DEEGAN: Why, we knew it all the time.
ALICE: Why, it's marvelous—
DEEGAN: Wait a minute—wait a minute—
  I've been all over this continent,
  I've been from coast to coast,
  I've even been up as far as Quebec
    Mass,
  I've swum the muddy waters of the old
    Lafayette Baths,
  I've even swallowed Chile in Chiam,
  I've had the yellow jack,
  I've been shot full of holes,
  I've even grabbed an army mule plump
    by the plumper,
  But I've never been so rip-snortin'
    hifalutin mad
  When she ups and says I've got perfume
    on my kercherfer—
  [*Lyric breaks off here*]

I'M GETTING MYSELF READY FOR YOU

Published November 1930. Introduced by Frances Williams, Barrie Oliver, Ann Pennington, and Maurice Lapue.

VERSE

HE: Gee, I'm lucky to get you here,
  What a wonderful treat!
  Just look over the menu, dear,
  And say what you'll have to eat.
SHE: If I say I'll have nothing, dear,
  Please don't think me extreme,
  But since we've met,
  I'm so upset
  I've gone on a regime.

REFRAIN 1

SHE: I've cut out eggs
  And turkey legs,
  With corned-beef hash I'm all through,
  'Cause I'm getting myself ready for you.
  I never stoop
  To onion soup,
  And pork and beans are taboo,*
  'Cause I'm getting myself ready for you.
  To be sure of being worthy of you, dear, in
    ev'ry way,

**Earlier version of lines 5–7:*
I've ceased to shout
For sauerkraut,
I never cry for ragout.

I'm building a perfect physique,
And besides which, I want you to holler
"Hooray"
When first you see me in my so-to-speak.
If you still feel I need a meal,
I'll risk an olive or two,
But I'm getting myself ready for you.

REFRAIN 2

HE: I'll have some eggs
And turkey legs,
You'll pardon me if I do,
'Cause I'm getting myself ready for you.
But maybe I
Had better try
A dozen oysters or two,
'Cause I'm getting myself ready for you.
To be sure of being worthy of you, dear, in
ev'ry way,
I must have a little to eat.
And besides which, I want you to holler,
"Hooray"
When first I get you in a bridal suite.
And just before we lock the door
I'll take a brandy or two,
'Cause I'm getting myself ready for you!

LOVE FOR SALE

Published November 1930. Sung in the Philadelphia tryout by the vocal trio the Three Girl Friends (June Shafer, Ida Pearson, and Stella Friend). At the New York opening it was sung by Kathryn Crawford and the Three Girl Friends. Because of critical objection to the "taste" of the song, the authors changed the scene in which it was presented from "In Front of Reuben's" to the "Cotton Club, Lenox Avenue, Harlem" and the singer to a "colored girl." Beginning in mid-January, Elizabeth Welch, who went on to a distinguished career as an actress and recording artist in London, replaced Kathryn Crawford. And it was Miss Welch and the Three Girl Friends who sang what Porter frequently referred to as his favorite Porter song. The lyric could not be sung on radio for many years.

VERSE

When the only sound in the empty street
Is the heavy tread of the heavy feet
That belong to a lonesome cop,
I open shop.
When the moon so long has been gazing
down
On the wayward ways of this wayward town
That her smile becomes a smirk,
I go to work.

REFRAIN

Love for sale,
Appetizing young love for sale.
Love that's fresh and still unspoiled,
Love that's only slightly soiled,
Love for sale.
Who will buy?
Who would like to sample my supply?
Who's prepared to pay the price
For a trip to paradise?
Love for sale.
Let the poets pipe of love
In their childish way,
I know ev'ry type of love
Better far than they.
If you want the thrill of love,
I've been thru the mill of love,
Old love, new love,
Ev'ry love but true love.
Love for sale,
Appetizing young love for sale.
If you want to buy my wares
Follow me and climb the stairs,
Love for sale.

THE GREAT INDOORS

Published December 1930. Introduced by Frances Williams and ensemble.

VERSE

When the weekend comes,
All my dearest chums
To the country go tearing off,
To improve their frames
Playing damn-fool games
Such as polo and Tom Thumb golf.
While they're breaking ground,
Biffing balls around,
And perspiring to beat the band,
I am sitting pretty
In the great big city,
With a cool drink in my hand.

REFRAIN

From Saturday until Monday
I'm what the sportsman abhors,
A weekend hater

Thanking my creator
For the great indoors.
While all the others are rushing
From bathing suits to plus fours,
You'll find this mamma's still in her pajamas*
For the great indoors.
The breeze may die,
But what care I,
I've got a big electric fan.
If passing by,
Come in and try
Biting your initial on my artificial tan.
Instead of wrecking my system
By playing games with old bores,
I take no chances,
Sitting on my Frances,
In the great indoors.

*Published version:
I'm glad I own a comf'table kimono

SING SING FOR SING SING

Also titled "Sing Sing." Introduced by Charles King, accompanied by Fred Waring and his Pennsylvanians. The music and lyrics were presumed lost until Waring located a copy of them in 1968 among his personal papers.

VERSE

Come on, you gunmen,
Come on, you con men,
Come on, you grifters and grafters,
Hurry along, boys, we'll have a song,
 boys,
Something that'll reach to the rafters.
Be like the birds in the spring
We'll do it.
Cut out your crabbing and sing.
Go to it.

REFRAIN

Sing sing for Sing Sing,
You sinners, sing, sing, sing.
Lift your loyal voices until the bars on the
 windows ring.
Jailbirds be nightingale birds until the locks are
 forced to spring.
Sing sing for Sing Sing,
You sinners, sing, sing, sing!

TAKE ME BACK TO MANHATTAN

Published December 1930. The Philadelphia opening of *The New Yorkers* was delayed from November 10 to November 12, 1930. To amuse himself and his friends who had come to Philadelphia, Porter wrote "Take Me Back to Manhattan," which replaced "Just One of Those Things" (first version) before the first Newark performance. Introduced by Frances Williams.

VERSE

The more I travel across the gravel,
The more I sail the sea,
The more I feel convinced of the fact
New York's the town for me.
Its crazy skyline is right in my line,
And when I'm far away
I'm able to bear it for several hours,
And then break down and say:

REFRAIN

Take me back to Manhattan,
Take me back to New York,
I'm just longing to see once more
My little home on the hundredth floor.
Can you wonder I'm gloomy?
Can you smile when I frown?
I miss the East Side, the West Side,
The North Side and the South Side,
So take me back to Manhattan,
That dear old dirty town.

LET'S FLY AWAY

Published November 1930. Introduced by Charles King and Hope Williams. Porter struck out "land that's" and substituted "country" (line 6 of refrain) on all surviving manuscripts. The Chrysler Building was New York's tallest until completion of the Empire State Building, May 1, 1931. Noël Coward's parody of this song (done with Porter's blessing) was published in *The Lyrics of Noël Coward* (1967).

VERSE

HE: I've such a hate on Manhattan lately,
 That I'd gladly die.
SHE: Your conversation excites me greatly,
 For so have I.
HE: I'm tired of the telephone always ringing.

SHE: I'm tired of hearing Rudy Vallee singing.
HE: I'm tired of the Paramount's gaudy gilding.
SHE: I'm tired of looking up to the Chrysler Building.
HE: I'm tired of having Texas Guinan greet me.
SHE: I'm tired of having Grover Whalen meet me.
HE: There's only one solution, dear.
SHE: Let's calmly disappear.

REFRAIN

Let's fly away,
And find a land that's warm and tropic;
Where Prohibition's not the topic
All the livelong day.
Let's fly away,
And find a country so provincial
We'll never hear what Walter Winchell
Might be forced to say.
I'll make your life sublime,
Far across the blue,
I'll take up all your time
Compromising you.
Let's not delay,
Make Mother Nature our Messiah;
New York is not for us,
Let's fly away.

I HAPPEN TO LIKE NEW YORK

Published March 1931. The New York *Evening Journal* (December 23, 1930) noted that "Cole Porter has sailed away to Monte Carlo for a vacation. The whole town is whistling and singing the big hit songs in *The New Yorkers* written by Porter and a song which caused Porter to wireless Goetz from mid-ocean when he was two days out at sea, the title being 'I Happen to Like New York.'" It is first listed in the show for the week of January 19, 1931. Introduced by Oscar Ragland.

I happen to like New York.
I happen to like this town.
I like the city air, I like to drink of it,
The more I know New York, the more I think of it.
I like the sight and the sound and even the stink of it.
I happen to like New York.
I like to go to Battery Park
And watch those liners booming in.
I often ask myself, why should it be
That they should come so far
From across the sea?
I suppose it's because they all agree with me,
They happen to like New York.
Last Sunday afternoon
I took a trip to Hackensack
But after I gave Hackensack the once-over
I took the next train back.
I happen to like New York.
I happen to like this burg.
And when I have to give the world
A last farewell
And the undertaker
Starts to ring my funeral bell,
I don't want to go to heaven,
Don't want to go to hell.
I happen to like New York.
I happen to like New York.

JUST ONE OF THOSE THINGS

Published November 1930. Although published, this number was dropped during the Philadelphia performances and replaced by "Take Me Back to Manhattan." Introduced in Philadelphia by Frances Williams. The famous song with the same title but totally different music and lyrics was written for *Jubilee* (1935).

VERSE

Love can make you happy,
Love can make you blue,
Love can make your bitter life sweet,
And your sweet life bitter too.

REFRAIN

If ever I love again
I'll cling to the mem'ry of
The first time I fell in love,
Just one of those things.
If only I'd thought again
I wouldn't have looked! But instead
I lost both my heart and my head,
Just one of those things.
I can't tell you why it started
Or how it evolved,
But when with the dawn we parted
Life seemed to be solved.
I wouldn't have b'lieved it then,
If some gypsy had said to me,

"Your dream will turn out to be
Just one of those things."

THE POOR RICH

Dropped between the Philadelphia tryout and the New York opening. Introduced in Philadelphia by Hope Williams, Eddie Jackson, and Lou Clayton. Incomplete manuscripts survive at Yale and the Porter Trusts office. Alternate titles: "Help the Poor Rich" and "Please Help the Poor Rich."

VERSE

I receive ev'ry morning
A request or a warning
That I help out some fund for the poor.
I admit that big cities
Have to have such committees,
And they're all very worthy, I'm sure.
But why don't they start saying prayers
For poor millionaires?

REFRAIN 1

Have you heard that Missus Burr
Has had to fire her pet masseur?
And you can b'lieve me, baby, that was some
rub.
Have you heard that Billy Boozey
Has given up his fav'rite floozy
And even stopped shooting craps at the Racquet
Club?
Have you heard that Missus Pennell
Has auctioned off her kennel
And all that she has left is one bitch?
Oh, darling Mister Hoover,
Won't you be a sport and please maneuver
To try and find a way to help the poor rich?

REFRAIN 2

Have you heard that Missus Beale
Has lost so much in Hard-Boiled Steel
She can't afford to keep a yacht of her own?
Have you heard the Charlie Skinners,
Who always gave enormous dinners,
Are so hard up that they have to dine all alone?
Have you heard that Missus Baker
Can't pay her French dressmaker
And fit to wear just hasn't a single stitch?
Oh, mighty Lord above us,
If you're not too occupied to love us,
Then try and find a way to help the poor rich.

WE'VE BEEN SPENDING THE SUMMERS WITH OUR FAMILIES

This number, also titled "Opening, Scene 1," was almost certainly dropped before the Philadelphia performance. A number titled "Mona and Her Kiddies" is listed in the Philadelphia program, but it was dropped before the New York opening.

PRINCESS: Good ev'ning, Comte.
COMTE: Good ev'ning, Princess.
COMTESSE: Good ev'ning, Prince.
PRINCE: Good ev'ning, Comtesse.
DUCHESSA: Good ev'ning, Baron.
BARON: Good ev'ning, dear Duchessa.
BARONESS: Good ev'ning, Duca.
DUCA: Good ev'ning, Baronessa.
COMTE & COMTESSE: And where have you been spending
your vacations?
OTHERS: We went abroad to visit our
relations.
COMTE & COMTESSE: And so did we
And we regret to say
That home is not so hot compared
with the U.S.A.

REFRAIN

ALL: We've been spending the summer with
our families,
Sadly sitting on our ancestral seats;
Our ancestral seats would drive you
mad,
The service is simply lousy and the
plumbing is bad.
You've no idea how much we missed
America,
Not to speak of your country's
well-known jack,
So forgive us if we say,
After such a holiday,
COMTE & COMTESSE: Mon Dieu.
DUCA & DUCHESSA: Dio Mio.
PRINCE & PRINCESS: Bozhe moi.
BARON & BARONESS: Gott im Himmel.
ALL: Good God, what a relief to get back.

WHERE CAN ONE POWDER ONE'S NOSE?

Also titled "Opening Reuben's Scene." Music editor Albert Sirmay's pencil score and Porter's holograph lyric for this number (almost certainly unused) were found at Warner Brothers Music warehouse, Secaucus, New Jersey, February 1982.

GIRLS: Where can one powder one's nose?
Tell me darling, where?
BOYS: Take the stairs down one flight,
Then you simply turn to the right.
GIRLS: I hate to ask you, my dear,
But there is no sign that shows
BOYS: The girls today
Have but one thing to say,
"Where can one powder one's nose?"

IT ONLY HAPPENS IN DREAMS

A lyric, but no music, for this number has been in the possession of the Cole Porter Musical and Literary Property Trusts, New York. Music, but no lyrics, was found at the Warner Brothers Music warehouse, Secaucus, New Jersey, February 1982.

VERSE

I dreamed that someone just like you
Appeared one ev'ning from out of the blue,
And being the grandest person I knew,
Suggested a wedding day.
We'd just begun to organize
A happy life under happier skies,
When, damn it, the phone bell opened my eyes,
And you had gone away.

REFRAIN

It only happens in dreams,
It couldn't be true
That I should find you.
Our story only belongs
To Hollywood lovers, in Hollywood songs.
The light that lies in your eyes
Makes me somehow feel,
That you may be there, but you can't be real.
Life couldn't be all it seems,
For it only happens in dreams.

The New Yorkers also included songs not written by Porter, notably special material by Jimmy Durante for Clayton, Jackson, and Durante ("The Hot Patata," "Money!", "Wood!" and "Data!"). "Drinking Song" is noted in the New York programs as having been written by Charles Henderson and Fred Waring. Presumably "The Flit Drill," dropped after the Philadelphia opening, was also theirs.

Porter's "You're Too Far Away," originally intended for *The New Yorkers,* was later included in *Nymph Errant* (1933).

A list of numbers from *The New Yorkers* in Porter's hand, found at the Library of Congress, includes the titles "Louisa," "But He Never Says He Loves Me," and "Why Talk about Sex?" "Louisa" is included with lyrics of *Wake Up and Dream* (1929). "But He Never Says He Loves Me" was introduced in the Philadelphia performances of *The New Yorkers* by Marie Cahill. It was copyrighted as an unpublished song (October 4, 1930). See also note in *Star Dust* (1931) and *Nymph Errant* (1933), under "The Physician." "Why Talk about Sex?" is lost.

At the Library of Congress there are musical sketches but no lyrics for numbers titled "I've Got You on My Mind" (see *Star Dust* and *Gay Divorce,* 1932), "I'm Haunted by You," and "I've Got to Be Psychoanalyzed by You." At Yale there is a music fragment for a number titled "You've Got to Be Hard-Boiled," also apparently intended for *The New Yorkers.*

GAY DIVORCE

1932

"The Gay Divorce," 1932; Claire Luce and Fred Astaire

Tryout: Wilbur Theatre, Boston, November 7, 1932; Shubert Theatre, New Haven, November 21, 1932. Produced by Dwight Deere Wiman and Tom Weatherly at the Ethel Barrymore Theatre, November 29, 1932. 248 performances. Book by Dwight Taylor. Directed by Howard Lindsay. Cast, starring Fred Astaire, included Claire Luce, Luella Gear, Betty Starbuck, Erik Rhodes, Eric Blore, and G. P. Huntley, Jr. Transferred to the Shubert Theatre, New York, January 1933. The film version, known as *The Gay Divorcee* (1934), starring Fred Astaire and Ginger Rogers, included only one Porter song, "Night and Day."

AFTER YOU, WHO?

Published November 1932. Introduced by Fred Astaire. In Porter's June 30, 1953, letter to George Byron he told the following anecdote about "After You, Who?" "I shall always be grateful to 'After You' because I had been engaged by Dwight Wiman for *Gay Divorce.* Our great hope was to persuade Fred Astaire to play the lead. We were living in Paris at the time and I asked Fred over to the house to hear what I had written so far. Once I had played 'After You,' he decided to do the show." The song is known as "After You" and "After You, Who?"

VERSE

Though with joy I should be reeling
That at last you came my way,
There's no further use concealing
That I'm feeling far from gay.
For the rare allure about you
Makes me all the plainer see
How inane, how vain, how empty life without you
would be.

REFRAIN

After you, who
Could supply my sky of blue?
After you, who
Could I love?
After you, why
Should I take the time to try,
For who else could qualify
After you, who?
Hold my hand and swear
You'll never cease to care,
For without you there what could I do?
I could search years
But who else could change my tears
Into laughter after you?

WHY MARRY THEM?

Introduced by Betty Starbuck and ensemble. Not included in the English production of *Gay Divorce,* which opened at London's Palace Theatre, November 2, 1933.

VERSE

BABS: When I see troops of carriages
Go marching to marriages
My heart always bleeds for the bride,
For I know that her honeymoon
Will soon seem a funny moon
When alone she sits nursing her pride.
For all men are polygamous,
At heart at least bigamous,
And when night falls their eyes start to
roam,
So it's pure asininity
To save one's virginity
For a husband who hates to come home.

REFRAIN

ALL: Why marry them?
Why to the altar carry them?
Why not simply keep one or two about
And when you get tired of them throw them
out?
Why humor them, when so many wives
testify
That as lovers they charm, as husbands they
bore,
As lovers they're devoted, as husbands—no
more,
As lovers they love you, and as your
husbands they snore,
So why marry them, why?

SALT AIR

Introduced by G. P. Huntley, Jr., Betty Starbuck, and ensemble.

VERSE

HE: While I'm calmly sitting pretty,
In my office in the city,
Sentimental matters never seem to bother
me.
SHE: You've no need to be heroic,
When in town I'm such a stoic
That I only want a man around to father
me.

HE: Then explain, my dear, why is it,
When I even smell the sea,
I become so damned erotic,
If you knew me you'd agree.
SHE: Do you suffer to surrender
To someone who's sweet and tender?
HE: Yes, I suddenly discover
I was born to be a lover.
SHE: How exciting, how appealing,
I can understand that feeling,
For the ocean has the same effect on me.

REFRAIN 1

Salt air,
Just a whiff of salt air,
And within me somewhere
Voices sing,
"You're all upset, go out and get that thing."
So swear,
To be perfectly square,
If I start a big love affair,
It's nobody's fault,
It's the fault of salt air.

REFRAIN 2

Salt air, it's a fact I can't explain
Just a whiff of salt air goes completely to my brain
And within me somewhere such inflammatory
Voices sing,
"You're all upset, go out and get that thing."
So swear by the dear old Pater's dust,
To be perfectly square, it's an effort but one must.
If I start a big love affair—love affair,
It's nobody's fault,
It's the fault of salt air.

I STILL LOVE THE RED, WHITE AND BLUE

Introduced by Luella Gear. Replaced in the English production by "Where Would You Get Your Coat?," sung originally in *Fifty Million Frenchmen* (1929).

VERSE

A bunch of Bolsheviks, one day,
Were working out an easy way
To make this hellish world a perfect heaven,
And among that thickly bearded clan
To discuss the five-and-ten-cent plan
Was a pure American girl of thirty-seven.
The leader rose and said to them,
"Is this the flag you love?"
As he waved a scarlet banner to and fro,
To which they all, with great success,
Pronounced the Russian word for "Yes,"
Except the American girl, who cried "No."

REFRAIN 1

I still love the red, white and blue,
You may think that I'm funny, but I do,
I cannot understand to what it is owin',
I must be a cross between Betsy Ross and George M. Cohan.
To progress I may be a drag,
But the star-spangled banner is my flag.
Because of Washington, Jefferson, Lincoln, Monroe,
Longfellow, Whittier, Bryant and Poe,
Pershing and Lindbergh and Morgan and Mellon
And Amos and Andy too,
I still love the red, white and blue.

REFRAIN 2

I still love the red, white and blue,
People here think it's crazy, but I do.
We've arranged I should meet that young man Mountbatten
But why should I wait when I got a date with old Manhattan.
Where else could the wild sow an oat
Had that bimbo Columbus missed his boat.
In spite of cyclones and prairie fires, earthquakes and floods,
Luckies, Chesterfields, Camels and Spuds,
Grifters and grafters, con men and gunmen
And men I've been married to,
I still love the red, white and blue.

NIGHT AND DAY

Published November 1932. Introduced by Fred Astaire; danced by Astaire and Claire Luce. Porter's most famous song was also the title of his film biography, which starred Cary Grant as Porter. Porter claimed that the music to "Night and Day" was inspired by a Mohammedan call to worship he had heard in Morocco. He also said he had finished the song on the beach in Newport, Rhode Island. Porter's assertion that the song took a long time to become popular is not true. Less than two months after *Gay Divorce* opened in New York, Leo Reisman on Victor and Eddie Duchin on Brunswick had best-selling recordings of it. And it was one of the six leading sheet-music sellers in New York and Los Angeles for January 1933.

VERSE

Like the beat beat beat of the tom-tom
When the jungle shadows fall,
Like the tick tick tock of the stately clock
As it stands against the wall,
Like the drip drip drip of the raindrops
When the sum'r show'r is through,
So a voice within me keeps repeating
You—You—You.

REFRAIN

Night and day you are the one,
Only you beneath the moon and under the sun,
Whether near to me or far
It's no matter, darling, where you are,
I think of you, night and day.
Day and night, why is it so
That this longing for you follows wherever I go?
In the roaring traffic's boom,
In the silence of my lonely room,
I think of you, night and day.
Night and day under the hide of me
There's an, oh, such a hungry yearning burning
  inside of me,
And its torment won't be through
Till you let me spend my life making love to you
Day and night, night and day.

HOW'S YOUR ROMANCE?

Published December 1932. Sung by Erik Rhodes and ladies of the ensemble in both the New York and London productions. Rhodes also was in the film version.

VERSE

TONETTI: In Italia the signori are so very
    amatory,
  That their passion, a priori, is l'amor.
GIRLS: Is it always l'amor?
TONETTI: Sì sempre l'amore.
  And from Napoli to Pisa,
  Ev'ry man has
  On his knees a
  Little private Mona Lisa
  To adore.
GIRLS: As he once said before,
  It's always l'amore,
TONETTI: The result is, when Italians meet a
    friend who's been away,
  Instead of saying, "How's your health?"
  They say—

REFRAIN

How's your romance?
How is it going?
Waning or growing,
How's your romance?
Does she or not love you an awful lot?
Cold, tepid, warm, or hot,
How's your romance?
Do you from the moment you met her
Never, never, never, forget her?
Do you when she sends you a letter,
Begin to go into a dance,
Break me the news,
I'm with you win or lose,
So tell me how's and who's your romance?

GIRLS: Do you from the moment you met him
  Never, never, never forget him?
  Do you when he wants you to let him
  Begin to go into a dance?
ALL: Break me the news,
  I'm with you win or lose,
  So tell me, how's and who's your
    romance?

WHAT WILL BECOME OF OUR ENGLAND?

Introduced by Eric Blore and ensemble. Not sung in the London production.

VERSE

WAITER: From the ladies dining at the Berkeley
  To the Lizas tippling in the pubs,
  From the girls who frighten
  The kippers down at Brighton
  To the dowagers rippling in their tubs,
  From the girls who b'lieve that life is
    rosy
  To their sisters harder to convince,
  From the gayer set to the glummer
    set,
  From the great soubrettes in London's
    mummer set,
  To the girls even dumber down in
    Somerset,
  They're all in love with the prince.
GIRLS: Oh, we're all so in love with the
    Prince.

REFRAIN 1

WAITER: So what will become of our England
When the Prince of Wales finds a wife?
Who's going to dance with our debutantes,
Who's going to worry our maiden aunts?
What will become of our fair sex
When Prince Charming furls his sails?
What will become of our England?
And what will become of our Prince of Wales?

REFRAIN 2

GIRLS: What will become of our England
When the Prince of Wales finds a wife?
Who's going to dance with our debutantes,
Who's going to worry our maiden aunts?
What will become of our fair sex
When Prince Charming furls his sails?
As a lover he charms, as a husband he'll bore,
As a lover he's devoted, as a husband—no more,
As a lover he loves you, as a husband he'll snore.
So what will become of our Prince of Wales?

I'VE GOT YOU ON MY MIND

Published November 1932. Written earlier and apparently intended first for *The New Yorkers* (1930) and then for the unproduced *Star Dust* (1931). Sung in the New York and London productions by Fred Astaire and Claire Luce.

VERSE

SHE: You can't be much surprised to hear
I think you're sweller than swell,
HE: But granting all your virtues, dear,
You've certain failings as well.
SHE: You don't sing enough, you don't dance enough,
HE: You don't drink the great wines of France enough!
SHE: You're not wild enough,
HE: You're not gay enough,
SHE: You don't let me lead you astray enough.
HE: You don't live enough, you don't dare enough,
You don't give enough,
SHE: You don't care enough,
HE: You don't make my sad life sunny enough.
SHE: Yet, sweetheart, funny enough—

REFRAIN

SHE: I've got you on my mind
Although I'm disinclined,
You're not so hot, you,
But I've got you on my mind.
HE: I'd thank the gods above
If I could only love
Somebody not you
But I've got you on my mind.
SHE: Let my poor upset leisure be
Otherwise my pet treasure be
HE: And arrange to let pleasure be
A bit less refined.
BOTH: For, darling, not until
I get that famous thrill
Will I be resigned.
I've got you on my mind.

MISTER AND MISSUS FITCH

Published February 1954. Porter invented a phony, social-climbing couple, Mr. and Mrs. S. Beech Fitch from Tulsa, Oklahoma. The Fitches had a daughter named Sonia. The pages of the international edition of the New York *Herald Tribune* were filled with invented stories and letters by and about the Fitches, all concocted by Porter and friends. To cap it all, Porter wrote this song, which was first earmarked for *Star Dust* (1931). The spoof was eventually revealed by Walter Winchell and Cholly Knickerbocker. The published version uses "witch" and "son of the rich" for "bitch" and "son of a bitch." Luella Gear, who introduced the song, told me she had an arrangement with the show's drummer to drown out the allegedly offensive words so they could be sung but not heard. The percussion part found in the *Gay Divorce* orchestrations at the Warner Brothers Music warehouse in Secaucus, New Jersey, confirm's Miss Gear's recollection. The part contains explicit instructions to cover "bitch" and "son of a bitch."

VERSE

On a farm far from pleasant,
No pair was more peasant
Than Mister and Missus Fitch.
Their days, each one duller,
Were so lacking in color
They didn't know which was which.

When suddenly tilling the soil
Mister Fitch struck oil.

REFRAIN

Mister and Missus Fitch one day
Hit town, determined to play.
Mister and Missus Fitch were green,
Ambitious, but rich.
And soon the crowd they call "elite"
Were fighting madly to meet
The young, attractive, and rich,
Mister and Missus Fitch.
When they called for champagne,
Champagne arrived.
An aeroplane,
The plane arrived.
A private train,
The train arrived.
But when they called for cash
The Crash arrived.
Now men who once knew Missus Fitch
Refer to her as a bitch.
While the girls who once loved Mister Fitch
Say he always was a son of a bitch.
So love and kisses,
Mister and Missus Fitch.

YOU'RE IN LOVE

Published December 1932. Introduced by Fred Astaire, Claire Luce, and Erik Rhodes.

MIMI: Coffee, Guy?
GUY: Please, Mimi.
MIMI: How many lumps?
GUY: Two.
MIMI: Tonetti, how about you?
TONETTI: No, no, non voglio niente.
Iere sera, ho dovuto mangiare
Qualche cosa che mi ha fatto male.
Non mi sento bene.
GUY: Ah, che disastro.
As far as I go,

VERSE

GUY: I woke today feeling so gay
I don't know what it should be.
MIMI: I too admit I never felt so fit
I wonder what's happened to me*
TONETTI: Do you ask me, do you dare,
Aren't you perfectly aware?

REFRAIN

You're in love.
What a marvelous picture to view.
I congratulate you—you're in love.
You're in love.
It's no wonder that life seems so sweet,
You have the world at your feet.
You're in love.
So adore your love,
Respect your love,
And protect your love from all harm.
Love today is so rare
That it is worth your care.
High above there are angels just dying
To come down out of heaven flying
And go walking with you hand in glove.
You're in love.

Published version:
The reason you both fail to see.

FATE

Dropped before the first Boston performance. Same music as refrain of "Salt Air."

It's fate,
Just a matter of fate
That I met you so late.
What a crime
To think we wasted so much precious time.
Wait,
Maybe, baby, we'll mate,
But if later we separate
Don't blame me, my love,*
It's a matter of fate.

Alternate version:
Don't forget, my love,

A WEEKEND AFFAIR

Written for *Gay Divorce*, but not used. Also titled "The Weekend Affair."

VERSE

HE: It's a curious fact
That during the week
I simply never think of love
But the moment Friday night appears
I begin to.
SHE: Tho' I always have lacked
The courage to speak

About the thing you're talking of
When the weekend comes I feel a longing
To sin too.
HE: Two brains with the same queer complex,
SHE: Two hearts with a single urge,
BOTH: It does seem rather fated that we should
merge.

REFRAIN

Here we are, well matched and unattached,
In a spot beyond compare.
What a staging for engaging
In a weekend affair.
When your system cries for exercise
And you're tired of city air
No distraction has the action
Of a weekend affair.
All through Saturday and Sunday
We can give romance a try
But the moment we awake and see it's Monday,
"Goodbye."
And thereafter, when we meet again,
We'll exchange a stony stare.
What a chic end
To a weekend
Affair.

I LOVE ONLY YOU

Porter wrote three new songs for the London production: "Never Say No," "Waiters v. Waitresses," and "I Love Only You." A fragmentary music sketch of "Never Say No" is in the Porter Collection at Yale (lyrics lost). Music and lyrics for "Waiters v. Waitresses" are lost. The music for "I Love Only You" is included in the piano selection from the London production, a copy of which was given by the late Charles Gaynor to the Porter Trusts. Gaynor wrote the lyric of "I Love Only You" into his copy of the piano selection. A complete version of the music was found recently by Ira Gershwin's musical secretary, Michael Feinstein.

Later productions of *Gay Divorce* added other songs that are almost certainly not by Porter.

Tonight I'm forced to compromise
A radiant blonde with ravishing eyes,
But don't worry, Maria,
I love only you!
Tomorrow night I'm bound to pet
A most disarming charming brunette,
But don't worry, Maria,
I love only you!
Only you could ever put my heart in frenzy,
Only you could ever bring back the spring,
Back in Firenze.
So if I must with all my might
Embrace a different lady each night,
Still don't worry, Maria,
I love only you.

A great deal of material was found for this show, including a complete set of orchestral parts for the 1932 production. Much incidental music also turned up at the Warner Brothers Music warehouse in Secaucus, New Jersey, February 1982, including music, but no lyrics, for songs titled, "Never Give In to Love" and "In Case You Don't Know."

NYMPH ERRANT

1933

"Nymph Errant," 1933; Gertrude Lawrence

Tryout: The Opera House, Manchester, England, September 11, 1933. Produced by Charles B. Cochran at the Adelphi Theatre, London, October 6, 1933. 154 performances. Book by Romney Brent, based on the novel by James Laver. Directed by Romney Brent under the personal supervision of Charles B. Cochran. Cast, starring Gertrude Lawrence, included Iris Ashley, Doris Carson, Walter Crisham, Austin Trevor, David Burns, and Elizabeth Welch.

Nymph Errant was sold to Fox Films (later known as 20th Century–Fox), but no film version was made. The U.S. premiere took place at New York's Equity Library Theater on March 11, 1982.

EXPERIMENT

Published September 1933. Introduced by Moya Nugent; reprised by Gertrude Lawrence. Revised for the unproduced film *Mississippi Belle,* 1943–1944. Both versions appear here.

VERSE

Before you leave these portals
To meet less fortunate mortals,
There's just one final message
I would give to you.
You all have learned reliance
On the sacred teachings of science,
So I hope, through life, you never will decline
In spite of philistine
Defiance
To do what all good scientists do.

REFRAIN

Experiment.
Make it your motto day and night.
Experiment
And it will lead you to the light.
The apple on the top of the tree
Is never too high to achieve,
So take an example from Eve,
Experiment.
Be curious,
Though interfering friends may frown.
Get furious
At each attempt to hold you down.
If this advice you always employ
The future can offer you infinite joy
And merriment.
Experiment
And you'll see.

Revised version for the film MISSISSIPPI BELLE (1943–1944)

VERSE

As I was leaving high school
My pet professor of my school
Said: My dear, one parting message I would give
to you.
By now you've learned reliance
On the sacred teachings of science,
So I hope, through life, you never will decline,
In spite of philistine
Defiance
To do what all good scientists do.

REFRAIN 1 [SAME AS ORIGINAL REFRAIN]

INTERLUDE

And now, each one of you, do
Let me adapt this ditty to you.

REFRAIN 2

Experiment.
Whenever doubtful take a chance.
Experiment
And you'll discover sweet romance.
When in a state of ignorant bliss
Regarding a creature you crave
'Tis folly, my friend, to behave,
Experiment,
Be curious,
And when you've picked a perfect wife,
Get furious
Till she is yours and yours for life.
If this you do (and no cock-and-bull)
In time she may give you a nurs'ry full*
Of merriment.
Experiment
And you'll see.

IT'S BAD FOR ME

Published September 1933. Introduced by Gertrude Lawrence.

VERSE

Your words go through and through me
And leave me totally dazed,
For they do such strange things to me

**Or:*
The future may give you a nurs'ry full

They nearly make me gloomy,
For you, dear, are so clever,
So obviously "the top,"
I wish you'd go on forever,
I wish even more you'd stop.

REFRAIN

For it's bad for me, it's bad for me,
This knowledge that you're going mad for me,
I feel certain my friends would be glad for me,
But it's bad for me.
It's so good for me, so new for me,
To see someone in such a stew for me,
And when you say you'd do all you could for me
It's so good for me, it's bad for me.
I thought I'd been, till you met me,
Completely put on the shelf,
But since you started to pet me
I'm just crazy about myself.
Oh, it's sweet for me, it's swell for me,
To know that you're going through hell for me,
Yet no matter however appealing
I still have a feeling
It's bad for me.

NEAUVILLE-SUR-MER

Porter originally titled this song "Deauville-sur-Mer," after the seaside resort in France. Introduced by Gerald Nodin, Annabel Gibson, Kenneth Ware, and Betty Hare.

Neauville-sur-Mer
Would be a little more delightful
If only while there
The weather wasn't quite so frightful,
But that is the cross we must bear.
Today it is fair
But soon'll come a clap o' thunder
At which, in despair,
We'll go to bed again and wonder
Just what could be glummer than summer at
Neauville-sur-Mer.
For here when the rain comes and drives you
indoors,
It pours and it pours and it pours and it pours
With persistence so wearing, you find yourself
tearing your hair.
And yet though aware
The place is nothing but a washout,
Each August with care
We get the little mackintosh out
And come back to swear
At Neauville-sur-Mer.

THE COCOTTE

Introduced by Queenie Leonard. The music was published in 1933 as part of the piano selection. Porter recorded it for Victor on January 3, 1935.

VERSE

While the lucky ones sit together
With nothing to curse but weather,
Permit me to tell you of my sad fate.
For due to my great discretion
In practicing my profession,
I suddenly wake up to find I date.
When ladies still had propriety,
Women like me were covered with glory,
But now, since these damned society
Women invaded my territory,

REFRAIN 1

A busted, disgusted cocotte am I,
Undesired on my tired little bottom, I,
While those fat femmes du monde
With the men whom once I owned
Splash around like hell-bound hippopotami.
Since only dames with their names on their
checks appeal
To modern men, instead of sex, I now have
ex-appeal.
What will Ma say to me
When she sees I've turned out to be
An annoyed, unemployed cocotte?

REFRAIN 2

A cheated, defeated cocotte am I,
On the page of this age, just a blot am I.
Since the girls known as chic
Have invented new technique,
I'm afraid, in my trade, not so hot am I.
As ladies smart make love's art so delectable,
The boys about won't take me out—I'm too
respectable,
And on my tombstone, I trust,
Will be written: "Excuse the dust
Of a fast but outclassed cocotte."

HOW COULD WE BE WRONG?

Published September 1933. Introduced by Gertrude Lawrence.

VERSE

The moment I saw you
And you looked my way,
That moment of moments
I started to say:
"Could this be my long-lost dream come true?"
The moment we touched, I knew.

REFRAIN

How could we be wrong
When we both are so set on it,
How could we be wrong?
Our love is so strong
I'd be willing to bet on it,
How could we be wrong?
Why should it ever die?
Darling, you and I
Are too wonderfully happy today
To throw it away.
Now, life is a song
If we build a duet on it,
How could we be wrong?

THEY'RE ALWAYS ENTERTAINING

Among the sextet that introduced "They're Always Entertaining" was a young woman named Sheila Marlyn, later and better known as Sheilah Graham.

VERSE

Run, run, run, rush,
Mop, dust, sweep, brush,
Work, work, work until you drop.
All day, all night,
No sleep in sight,
Dio mio, when will it ever stop?
Since the fam'ly of Americans have taken this palazzo,
We work so hard that ev'ryone is practically pazzo,
Yet when we suggest
We need a little rest,
They look at us and laugh at us and say to us,
"Is that so?"

REFRAIN

They're always entertaining,
These Americans who come to town.
Forever entertaining,
It's no wonder we're a bit run down.
Ev'ry day they ask a bunch
Of celebrities for lunch.
If you think that that is all,
Ev'ry night they give a ball,
So excuse us for complaining,
But these Americans are always entertaining.

GEORGIA SAND

Introduced by Doris Carson. Dropped during the London run and replaced by "Cazanova."

VERSE

Georgia Sand was an authoress
Who, all through her life, had great success,
Not only with her books
But also with her looks.
Among the boys who gave her fun
Young Alfred de Musset was the one
That Georgia loved the most,
For he was such a good host.
Ev'ry night that beau of Georgia's
Gave an affair that would scare the Borgias,
French champagne and Russian ballets,
Ellington's band and Rudy Vallee's.
All went well till one fine night
Her favorite of males
Gave a ball and, to shock them all,
Georgia came in tails.

When he saw his best girl in trousers,
Alfred nearly died.
And in front of all those carousers,
Alfred loudly cried:

REFRAIN

Georgia Sand, dressed up like a gent,
Georgia Sand, what do you represent?
Where are your frills
That gave me such thrills?
Where are those undies
That made my Saturday-to-Mondays?
Georgia Sand, can't you understand
Though I worship you,
You're a little too
Plump, I fear,
To pull a Marlene Dietrich, dear.
Georgia Sand, go home and change.

CAZANOVA

Introduced by Doris Carson. Replaced "Georgia Sand" during the London run.

VERSE

Though Mister Cazanova
Was for years a human stove, a
Moment came when he began to cool down.
So like a homing pigeon
Whose abode is its religion,
Back he tottered to Venezia town.
There, nights without number,
He couldn't slumber,
Because a certain gal
Sang in soprano,
And not piano,
This phony canzone across the canal.

REFRAIN

Cazanova, why is it true?
Tell me, why is it true, Cazanova,
So many girls have a weakness for you,
  Cazanova?
Cazanova, give me a clue.
Won't you give me a clue, Cazanova,
What do you do when you do what you do,
  Cazanova?
Why, when they see you pass by,
Do the ladies all try
To discover that red-hot secret you've got?
Cazanova, I'm very blue.
If you've nothing to do, Cazanova,
How would you like to come ova
And—

NYMPH ERRANT

Published October 1933. The title song was added after the Manchester premiere and before the London opening. It replaced "When Love Comes Your Way" (see *Jubilee*, 1935), also introduced by Gertrude Lawrence.

VERSE

Men,
I used to take you
So seriously.
Then,
I dreamed about you
Deliriously.
But now I've gone so far
I know how harmless you are,
So I'm off to follow the voice
That whispers mysteriously.

REFRAIN

Nymph errant, go wandering on,
You've lived and loved*
Your illusions are gone.
Nymph errant, forget your blues,
You've all to gain,
And nothing to lose;
So climb the hill
And cross the dale,
Like the pale moon above
And go sailing gaily on and on,
Forever on and on—
Laughing at love.

RUINS

This number, a quartet, opened Act II. Introduced by Gerald Nodin, Annabel Gibson, Kenneth Ware, and Betty Hare.

VERSE

When we started on this Mediterranean cruise
We were quite prepared to squander ev'ry rupee
On the kind of fun one's clergyman taboos,
That delightful sport that's known as making
  whoopee.
Yet though still athirst for ribald Arabian nights
We're becoming so depressed you wouldn't know
  us,
For whenever we go out to see the sights,
Instead of anything gay—they always show us

REFRAIN

Ruins, ruins, ruins.
Ev'rywhere we go they show us ruins.
We saw a pile in Carthage,
In Rome, another lot,
While here, apart from bugs and fleas,
The only thing they've got
Is ruins, ruins, ruins.
They constitute our daily doin's.
We're off again, thank heaven,
This afternoon at four,
To sail across the water
For Egypt's balmy shore,

*Published version:
You've lived and learned.

And when we get to Luxor
We'll be dragged to see some more
Ruins, ruins, ev'rywhere we go, they show us
Ruins, ruins, ruins.

THE PHYSICIAN

Published September 1933. Originally titled "But He Never Says He Loves Me," it was first presented in the pre-New York performances of *The New Yorkers* (1930). Subsequently, it was earmarked for the unproduced show *Star Dust* (1931). The title change to "The Physician" and a few lyric changes occurred during rehearsals for *Nymph Errant.* Gertrude Lawrence, who introduced it, recorded it on October 18, 1933. Porter recorded it on January 3, 1935.

VERSE

Once I loved such a shattering physician,
Quite the best-looking doctor in the state.
He looked after my physical condition,
And his bedside manner was great.
When I'd gaze up and see him there above me,
Looking less like a doctor than a Turk,
I was tempted to whisper, "Do you love me,
Or do you merely love your work?"

REFRAIN 1

He said my bronchial tubes were entrancing,
My epiglottis filled him with glee,
He simply loved my larynx
And went wild about my pharynx,
But he never said he loved me.
He said my epidermis was darling,
And found my blood as blue as could be,
He went through wild ecstatics,
When I showed him my lymphatics,
But he never said he loved me.
And though, no doubt,
It was not very smart of me,
I kept on a-wracking my soul
To figure out
Why he loved ev'ry part of me,
And yet not me as a whole.
With my esophagus he was ravished,
Enthusiastic to a degree,
He said 'twas just enormous,
My appendix vermiformis,
But he never said he loved me.

REFRAIN 2

He said my cerebellum was brilliant,
And my cerebrum far from N.G.,
I know he thought a lotta
My medulla oblongata,
But he never said he loved me.
He said my maxillaries were marvels,
And found my sternum stunning to see,
He did a double hurdle
When I shook my pelvic girdle,
But he never said he loved me.
He seemed amused
When he first made a test of me
To further his medical art,
Yet he refused
When he'd fix up the rest of me,
To cure that ache in my heart.
I know he thought my pancreas perfect,
And for my spleen was keen as could be,
He said of all his sweeties,
I'd the sweetest diabetes,
But he never said he loved me.

REFRAIN 3

He said my vertebrae were "sehr schöne,"
And called my coccyx "plus que gentil,"
He murmured "molto bella,"
When I sat on his patella,
But he never said he loved me.
He took a fleeting look at my thorax,
And started singing slightly off key,
He cried, "May Heaven strike us,"
When I played my umbilicus,
But he never said he loved me.
As it was dark,
I suggested we walk about
Before he returned to his post.
Once in the park,
I induced him to talk about
The thing I wanted the most.
He lingered on with me until morning,
Yet when I tried to pay him his fee,
He said, "Why, don't be funny,
It is I who owe you money,"
But he never said he loved me.

SOLOMON

Published September 1933. Introduced by Elizabeth Welch, who recorded it on October 18, 1933.

So———olomon had a thousand wives
And being mighty good, he wanted all o' them
To lead contented lives;
So he bought each mamma a plat'num piano,

A gold-lined kimono and a diamond-studded
Hispano.
So———olomon had a thousand wives.

In spite o' all he gave 'em the wives of Solomon
Found their poppa slow,
And for her jazzin' ev'ry wife o' Solomon
Took on a gigolo.
And while they pampered those high-brown
heroes
By bunchin' them and lunchin' them and suppin'
them at Ciro's.
So———olomon hadn't no place to go.

Soon, Sol began to miss those baby dolls o' his
And got his fav'rite eunuch, Rastus Brown,
And when he heard the lowdown on those molls
o' his,
He said, "Go out and hunt the whole darn town
Till you've found your massa a thousand knives,
I'm tired of doin' the treating for a thousand
cheating wives.
So———olomon is gonna cut the whole crop
down."

So So———olomon summoned his thousand
wives,
Then So———olomon pulled out his thousand
knives
And he slashed their gizzards and gashed their
muzzles
Till all that was left of them was a lot of jigsaw
puzzles.
Then slowly mounting his royal dais,
He picked up his microphone and said, "All I
gotta say is
So———olomon no longer has a thousand
wives."

BACK TO NATURE WITH YOU

First slated for Act I, this number was shifted to Act II. Introduced by Gertrude Lawrence and Walter Crisham.

VERSE

SHE: Let's quit this weary world of ours
And live among the birds, the flow'rs,
The butterflies, the crickets and the frogs.
HE: 'Twould be a far more pleasant thing
Than sitting here and witnessing
Our civilization going to the dogs.
SHE: Why, just regard the headlines
In case you haven't read.
HE: "In Bucharest, the bread lines
Have all run out of bread."
SHE: "The pubs throughout Great Britain
Will soon be forced to close."
HE: "Our delegate to Switzerland
Comes home with bloody nose."
SHE: "Ten thousand heads of Chinese bandits
hang high
In the crowded streets of Shanghai."
HE: "Market drops to double zero."
"Gangster made a national hero."
SHE: "Royalists turn Bolshevistic.
Bolsheviks turn Royalistic."
HE: "War in Timbuctoo."
"Snakes escape from London Zoo."
SHE: "No more cows in Channel Islands."
"No more grouse in Scottish Highlands."
HE: "No more cowboys on the prairies."
"In the bushes, no more fairies."
SHE: Ev'ry moment, faster, faster,
Closer, closer, comes disaster.
Darling, if you love me, you'd better take me

REFRAIN

SHE: Back to nature with you.
HE: Back to nature we two.
What a shake-up in life's monotony,
SHE: Dear, to wake up with you and botany.
HE: Other music we'll ban
for the sweet pipes of Pan.
SHE: And when night falls without apology
You can give me a lesson in biology.
HE: For I so want to go when you do,
Back to nature with you.

PLUMBING

Introduced by Walter Crisham.

VERSE

You ask me, dear, to sing you a song?
I never sang a song before, I may go wrong.
So I suppose the wise thing to do
Is to weave an air about
The only thing I care about,
Think about and dream about the whole day
through.

REFRAIN

Plumbing, making life so sweet and so clean,
Plumbing, giving us such moments serene.

When do I miss my little home
At the end of the garden path?
Not when I miss a mother's love,
But when I need a bath.
Plumbing, as the world revolves and revolves,
Plumbing, what a lot of problems it solves,
So why should the critics cry that it's
unbecoming
If I sing of plumbing, modern plumbing.

SI VOUS AIMEZ LES POITRINES

Introduced by Iris Ashley. Listed in the program as "If You Like les Belles Poitrines."

VERSE

Trav'lers I've seen
Say the prettiest poitrines
Are the ones you find in Poona.
Others are these
Say the buxom Balinese
Have the greatest goona-goona.
Spaniards maintain
That the kind you find in Spain
Are so fair that ev'ry man tumbles.
While not long ago
A boy in Eastbourne I know
Simply raves about those on the crumbles.
Ces belles poitrines sau-vage
May be very fair perchance
But why should one voy-age
When the best of them are made in France?

REFRAIN

Si vous aimez les poi-trines
Come to Gay Paree.
Si leur beauté vous a-nime
Come and call on me.
I will show you how di-veene
Parisiennes poi-trines really are,
If you promise me, you naughty boy,
Not to go too far.
Si vous voulez d'la ten-dresse
Et d'la volupté,
Let me give you my ad-dresse
For a rainy day.
And when zat feeling comes a-stealing
You know what I mean?
Mais oui, monsieur,
Come and play wiz me in Gay Paree,
Si vous aimez les poitrines.

YOU'RE TOO FAR AWAY

Published April 1934. Originally intended for *The New Yorkers* (1930), this number was sung in the Manchester performances of *Nymph Errant* by Vladimir Reconenko under the title "I Look at You." After it was dropped from *Nymph Errant*, it was published as an independent song.

VERSE

I read so many tales of love,
I didn't b'lieve them true
Until the day when heav'n above
First let me gaze at you.
So I suppose it's love's revenge
That I should long so much
For one so fair, so rare,
But one I dare not touch.

REFRAIN

I think of you and suddenly start
To sing you the song that's been long in my
heart.
I sing in vain,
You're too far away.
Why should I dream of wonderful nights
When I'm in the depths, dear, and you're in the
heights?
It's all so plain,
You're too far away.
I only pine
To make you mine,
But ev'ry moment it's clearer
That I can't succeed
Till you've agreed
To come just a little bit nearer.
And till we're so close together that we
Can't tell any longer what's you and what's
me,
I'll still maintain
You're too far away.

SWEET NUDITY

Also known as "Nudity, Sweet Nudity," this song was dropped during rehearsals. At one time it was planned as the penultimate number in Act I. It also has an instrumental section in march tempo.

ALL: Oh, nudity, sweet nudity,
In humble reverence we sing to thee,

For from a world of care and strife
Thy hand has led us to the simple life.
GIRLS: No hats to choose, no frocks to tear,
BOYS: No studs to lose and no stiff shirts to wear,
GIRLS: No ladders running up and down our hose,
BOYS: No drawers to open and no drawers to close,
GIRLS: No powder puffs, no further frills,
BOYS: No fights with laundries and no tailor bills,
ALL: So, nudity, sweet nudity,
No wonder, in return, we sing to thee.

FRENCH COLONIAL EXPOSITION SCENE

Intended for Act II. The music was apparently never written. A number called "Bring on the Girls" was not written.

The French Colonial Exposition
Is quite the best we ever saw.
And yet for those of our tradition
It's got one serious flaw.
To any Englishman of standing
The crowd's a little mixed, we fear,
What with so many Frenchmen, Americans and Prussians
So many Spaniards, Italians and Russians,
So damned many aliens here.

ANYTHING GOES

1934

Tryout: Colonial Theatre, Boston, November 5, 1934. Produced by Vinton Freedley at the Alvin Theatre, New York, November 21, 1934. 420 performances. Book by Guy Bolton and P. G. Wodehouse, revised by Howard Lindsay and Russel Crouse. Directed by Howard Lindsay. Cast, starring William Gaxton, Ethel Merman, and Victor Moore, included Bettina Hall, Vivian Vance, and Leslie Barrie. Transferred to the 44th Street Theatre, October 1935. A complete piano-vocal score was published in July 1936.

I GET A KICK OUT OF YOU

Published November 1934. Introduced by Ethel Merman. The Lindbergh kidnapping occurred after "I Get a Kick Out of You" was written for *Star Dust* (1931), so Porter removed the reference to Mrs. Lindbergh and revised the lyric.

It should be noted that any substitutes for the lines that begin "Some get a kick from cocaine" are incorrect, various published versions notwithstanding. "Some like the perfumes of Spain . . . whiff" and "Some like a bop-type refrain . . . riff" are particularly prevalent and equally objectionable.

VERSE

My story is much too sad to be told,
But practically ev'rything leaves me totally cold.
The only exception I know is the case
Where I'm out on a quiet spree
Fighting vainly the old ennui
And I suddenly turn and see
Your fabulous face.

REFRAIN

I get no kick from champagne.
Mere alcohol doesn't thrill me at all,
So tell me why should it be true
That I get a kick out of you?
Some get a kick from cocaine.
I'm sure that if I took even one sniff
That would bore me terrific'ly too
Yet I get a kick out of you.
I get a kick ev'ry time I see
You're standing there before me.
I get a kick though it's clear to me
You obviously don't adore me.
I get no kick in a plane.
Flying too high with some guy in the sky
Is my idea of nothing to do,
Yet I get a kick out of you.

Original version

VERSE

Until the day
You came my way
I got no joy from being alive.
But now that you have given a kick to my life
I know that I'm slated to thrive.

REFRAIN [LAST SIX LINES]

I get a kick when you look at me
And whisper you adore me.
I get no kick in a plane.
I shouldn't care for those nights in the air
That the fair Mrs. Lindbergh goes through,
Yet I get a kick out of you.

BON VOYAGE/THERE'S NO CURE LIKE TRAVEL

This number is known as "Bon Voyage," but the countermelody, called "There's No Cure Like Travel," is also part of the number. Together they make up "Opening, Act I," Scene 2. Ensemble number.

VERSE

MEN: My dear, you're sailing off without me,
Yet you don't seem to give a damn.
GIRLS: I know it's fearful of me not to be
More tearful,
But thank heaven I am.
MEN: You mean to say you're glad to leave me?
Can I believe that's what you mean?
GIRLS: Why, don't be funny, I'm just wild about
you, honey,
But I'm oh so glad, so glad,
It's driving me mad to say goodbye
To all things that typify
The humdrum of my daily routine.

REFRAIN

And there's no cure like travel
To help you unravel
The worries of living today.
When the poor brain is cracking
There's nothing like packing a suitcase and
sailing away.
Take a run 'round
Vienna,
Granada, Ravenna,

Siena and then a-
'Round Rome.
Have a high time, a low time,
And in no time
You'll be singing "Home, Sweet Home."

Bon voyage, I mean "bon voyage."
I hate to say goodbye, sweetheart,
By the seashore, I mean "sur la plage."
I'll sit and watch the sea till you come back to
me.
For my dearie, I mean "ma chérie,"
I'm yours for life, I mean "pour la vie,"
So kiss me, pretty wench,
In English or in French,
Bon voyage—"bon voyage."

ALL THROUGH THE NIGHT

Published November 1934. Introduced by Bettina Hall and William Gaxton. The less familiar additional lines are in the script and in several manuscripts. "All Through the Night," reputedly, was added to the show because Gaxton objected to singing "Easy to Love" (see *Born to Dance,* 1936).

VERSE

The day is my enemy,
The night my friend,
For I'm always so alone
Till the day draws to an end.
But when the sun goes down
And the moon comes through,
To the monotone of the evening's drone
I'm all alone with you.

REFRAIN

All through the night I delight in your love.
All through the night you're so close to me.
All through the night from a height far above,
You and your love bring me ecstasy.
When dawn comes to waken me,
You're never there at all.
I know you've forsaken me
Till the shadows fall,
But then once again I can dream I've the right
To be close to you all through the night.

If I stopped to think twice
I know I'd hurry away,
But it all is so nice
So I'll only think once and stay.
All through the night I delight in your love.
All through the night, oh so close to me.
All through the night, under bright stars above
You and your love will bring ecstasy.
When dawn's overtaken us, we'll sadly say
goodbye,
Till dreams reawaken us and the moon is high.
And then, once again, will I know I was right
Staying close to you, all through the night.

THERE'LL ALWAYS BE A LADY FAIR

Published February 1936. Introduced by the Foursome Quartet (Marshall Smith, Ray Johnson, Dwight Snyder, and Del Porter). Listed in programs as "Sailor's Chantey."

VERSE 1

A sailor's life is supposed to be
A hell of a lot of fun,
But when you're a sailor take it from me
You work like a son of a gun.
They give us jobs of ev'ry kind
And chores of ev'ry sort,
But sweat away, sailor, you don't mind
'Cause you know when you hit port

REFRAIN 1

There will always be a Lady Fair, a Jenny Fair
or a Sadie Fair,
There'll always be a Lady Fair who's waiting
there for you.
There will always be a Lady Fair
To smooth your troubles and to muss your hair,
There'll always be a Lady Fair who's waiting
there for you.

There will always be a woman's charms
To kill your worries and to fill your arms,
There'll always be a Lady Fair who's waiting
there for you.

VERSE 2

When you're three days out, and the time arrives
When you're hankerin' for the dames,
There are always certain passengers' wives
Who will help you further your aims.
So when the moon isn't too damn bright
And the sea isn't too damn rough,

Go up to the boat deck late at night
And you'll find that sure enough

REFRAIN 2

There will always be a Lady Fair, a Jenny Fair,
or a Sadie Fair,
There'll always be a Lady Fair who's waiting
there for you.
There will always be a girl's caress
To change your answer from a no to yes,
There'll always be a Lady Fair who's waiting
there for you.

You will always find a maiden sweet
To cool your temper and to warm your feet,
There'll always be a Lady Fair who's waiting
there for you.

INTERLUDE

That's the reason why you married men,
No matter how much you roam,
Still count your blessings now and then,
'Cause you know you want to go home.

REFRAIN 3

There will always be a Lady Fair, a Jenny Fair
or a Sadie Fair,
There'll always be a Lady Fair who's waiting
there for you.

WHERE ARE THE MEN?

Introduced by Vera Dunn, Houston Richards, and ensemble.

VERSE

1ST SOLO: Officer, we've got something most
important to say.
GIRLS: Listen to them, Officer, we all feel the
same way.
1ST SOLO: The food we get is edible, especially
the apples.
GIRLS: But why bring up apples?
2ND SOLO: The chapel is incredible, the daintiest
of chapels.
GIRLS: If you like chapels.
1ST SOLO: The swimming pool is a beaut!
2ND SOLO: The gymnasium is very cute.
1ST SOLO: The kennels seem to please
My Pekinese.
2ND SOLO: The lounge has cozy nooks in it
And very nice indeed.
1ST SOLO: The library has books in it
That even I can read.
2ND SOLO: The dining room is an outshining
room
And we all like the bar a lot.
1ST SOLO: But unfortunately, Mister Officer,
There's one thing you forgot—

REFRAIN

GIRLS: Where are the men?
Is this a nunnery?
Where are the men?
We want some fun. A re-
Fusal to find some will leave us
completely floored,
And if our wishes are ignored
We swear to jump overboard.
Bring on the boys,
And sentimental boys,
We want the joys of love again.
The moon shines ev'ry night
And we thrill beneath its light
But, Officer, where are the men?

YOU'RE THE TOP

Published November 1934. Introduced by Ethel Merman and William Gaxton. As far as I can tell, refrains 6 and 7 were not sung in the show. Porter and the newspapers were inundated with imitations and parodies. P. G. Wodehouse wrote some of the lyrics for the English production (opened at the Palace Theatre, London, June 14, 1935). The famous parody, often attributed to Porter, is included here, although I am virtually certain he did not write it.

VERSE 1

At words poetic, I'm so pathetic
That I always have found it best,
Instead of getting 'em off my chest,
To let 'em rest unexpressed.
I hate parading
My serenading,
As I'll probably miss a bar,
But if this ditty
Is not so pretty,
At least it'll tell you
How great you are.

REFRAIN 1

You're the top!
You're the Colosseum.

You're the top!
You're the Louvre Museum.
You're a melody from a symphony by Strauss,
You're a Bendel bonnet,
A Shakespeare sonnet,
You're Mickey Mouse.
You're the Nile,
You're the Tow'r of Pisa,
You're the smile
On the Mona Lisa.
I'm a worthless check, a total wreck, a flop,
But if, baby, I'm the bottom
You're the top!

VERSE 2

Your words poetic are not pathetic.
On the other hand, boy, you shine,
And I can feel after every line
A thrill divine
Down my spine.
Now gifted humans like Vincent Youmans
Might think that your song is bad,
But for a person who's just rehearsin'
Well, I gotta say this my lad:

REFRAIN 2

You're the top!
You're Mahatma Gandhi.
You're the top!
You're Napoleon brandy.
You're the purple light of a summer night in
  Spain,
You're the National Gall'ry,
You're Garbo's sal'ry,
You're cellophane.
You're sublime,
You're a turkey dinner,
You're the time
Of the Derby winner.
I'm a toy balloon that is fated soon to pop,
But if, baby, I'm the bottom
You're the top!

REFRAIN 3

You're the top!
You're a Ritz hot toddy.
You're the top!
You're a Brewster body.
You're the boats that glide on the sleepy Zuider
  Zee,
You're a Nathan panning,
You're Bishop Manning,
You're broccoli.
You're a prize,
You're a night at Coney,
You're the eyes
Of Irene Bordoni.
I'm a broken doll, a fol-de-rol, a blop,
But if, baby, I'm the bottom
You're the top!

REFRAIN 4

You're the top!
You're an Arrow collar.
You're the top!
You're a Coolidge dollar.
You're the nimble tread of the feet of Fred
  Astaire,
You're an O'Neill drama,
You're Whistler's mama,
You're Camembert.
You're a rose,
You're Inferno's Dante,
You're the nose
On the great Durante.
I'm just in the way, as the French would say
"De trop,"
But if, baby, I'm the bottom
You're the top.

REFRAIN 5

You're the top!
You're a Waldorf salad.
You're the top!
You're a Berlin ballad.
You're a baby grand of a lady and a gent,
You're an old Dutch master,
You're Mrs. Astor,
You're Pepsodent.
You're romance,
You're the steppes of Russia,
You're the pants on a Roxy usher.
I'm a lazy lout that's just about to stop,
But if, baby, I'm the bottom
You're the top.

REFRAIN 6

You're the top!
You're a dance in Bali.
You're the top!
You're a hot tamale.
You're an angel, you, simply too, too, too diveen,
You're a Botticelli,
You're Keats,
You're Shelley,
You're Ovaltine.
You're a boon,
You're the dam at Boulder,

You're the moon over Mae West's shoulder.
I'm a nominee of the G.O.P.
or GOP,
But if, baby, I'm the bottom
You're the top.

REFRAIN 7

You're the top!
You're the Tower of Babel.
You're the top!
You're the Whitney Stable.
By the river Rhine,
You're a sturdy stein of beer,
You're a dress from Saks's,
You're next year's taxes,
You're stratosphere.
You're my thoist,
You're a Drumstick Lipstick,
You're da foist
In da Irish Svipstick.
I'm a frightened frog
That can find no log
To hop,
But if, baby, I'm the bottom
You're the top!

FINALE, ACT I

RENO: You're the top!
You're my Swanee River.
You're the top!
You're a goose's liver.
You're the boy who dares
Challenge Mrs. Baer's son, Max.
You're a Russian ballet,
You're Rudy Vallee,
MOON: You're Phenolax!!!!
RENO: You're much more,
You're a field of clover—
BILLY: I'm the floor
When the ball is over.

Parody version

You're the top!
You're Miss Pinkham's tonic.
You're the top!
You're a high colonic.
You're the burning heat of a bridal suite in use,
You're the breasts of Venus,
You're King Kong's penis,
You're self-abuse.
You're an arch
In the Rome collection.
You're the starch
In a groom's erection.
I'm a eunuch who
Has just been through an op,
But if, Baby, I'm the bottom
You're the top.

ANYTHING GOES

Published November 1934. Introduced by Ethel Merman and ensemble. The lyric for an earlier version of the first refrain was found in a copyist ink score at Warner Brothers Music warehouse, Secaucus, New Jersey, February 1982. Over the years Porter revised the sequence of the song's three refrains. Presumably, his final thoughts are set down in the version published in *The Cole Porter Song Book* (1959).

VERSE

Times have changed
And we've often rewound the clock
Since the Puritans got a shock
When they landed on Plymouth Rock.
If today
Any shock they should try to stem,
'Stead of landing on Plymouth Rock,
Plymouth Rock would land on them.

REFRAIN 1

In olden days, a glimpse of stocking
Was looked on as something shocking,
But now, God knows,
Anything goes.
Good authors too who once knew better words
Now only use four-letter words
Writing prose,
Anything goes.
If driving fast cars you like,
If low bars you like,
If old hymns you like,
If bare limbs you like,
If Mae West you like,
Or me undressed you like,
Why, nobody will oppose.
When ev'ry night, the set that's smart is in-
Truding in nudist parties in
Studios,
Anything goes.

REFRAIN 2

When Missus Ned McLean (God bless her)
Can get Russian reds to "yes" her,
Then I suppose

Anything goes.
When Rockefeller still can hoard en-
Ough money to let Max Gordon
Produce his shows,
Anything goes.
The world has gone mad today
And good's bad today,
And black's white today,
And day's night today,
And that gent today
You gave a cent today
Once had several châteaux.
When folks who still can ride in jitneys
Find out Vanderbilts and Whitneys
Lack baby clo'es,
Anything goes.

REFRAIN 3

If Sam Goldwyn can with great conviction
Instruct Anna Sten in diction,
Then Anna shows
Anything goes.
When you hear that Lady Mendl standing up
Now turns a handspring landing up-
On her toes,
Anything goes.
Just think of those shocks you've got
And those knocks you've got
And those blues you've got
From that news you've got
And those pains you've got
(If any brains you've got)
From those little radios.
So Missus R., with all her trimmin's,
Can broadcast a bed from Simmons
'Cause Franklin knows
Anything goes.

Earlier version of first refrain

In former times a glimpse of stocking
Was looked on as something shocking,
But now God knows—
Anything goes.
Novelists who once knew better words
Now only use four letter words for their prose—
Anything Goes.
If saying your pr'yers you like,
If green pears you like,
If old chairs you like,
If backstairs you like,
If love affairs you like
With young bears you like,
Why, nobody will oppose.
And every night the set that's smart is
Indulging in nudist parties in studios,
Anything Goes.

PUBLIC ENEMY NUMBER ONE

The opening number of Act II. Introduced by ensemble.

1ST SOLO: Tonight there's going to be some fun
TUTTI: Some fun—o! Some fun—o!
2ND SOLO: For Public Enemy Number One.
TUTTI: Public Enemy Number One—o!
3RD SOLO: Our gallant captain has told the staff
TUTTI: The staff—o!, The staff—o!
3RD SOLO: It's time for killing the fatted calf.
4TH SOLO: As he's throwing a party in behalf
Of Public Enemy Number One.
TUTTI: Public Enemy Number One—o!
1ST SOLO: For since the news has spread
That he prefers to use this company,
2ND SOLO: The company's stock has gone up so far
That it's now nearly par.
3RD SOLO: The president of the line has sent
Congratulations too
4TH SOLO: And to celebrate the big event
He's promised to double the
Wages of the crew.
TUTTI: So, Public Enemy Number One,
Thank thee for ev'rything thou hast done.
Blessings on thee, thou noble chap,
For putting this boat of ours on the map.
Thank thee heartily, holy man,
For boosting shipping American
And henceforth we'll be crowded on ev'ry run
Due to thee, Public Enemy Number One.

BLOW, GABRIEL, BLOW

Published November 1934. Introduced by Ethel Merman and ensemble. Porter's regard for Ethel Merman was so high that when she had some problems with an earlier version, he revised it to make her happier.

VERSE

[TRUMPET CALL]

RENO: Do you hear that playin'?
CHORUS: Yes, I hear that playin'.
RENO: Do you know who's playin'?
CHORUS: No, who is that playin'?
RENO & CHORUS: Why, it's Gabriel, Gabriel playin',
Gabriel, Gabriel sayin',
RENO: "Will you be ready to go when I blow my horn?"

REFRAIN

Oh, blow, Gabriel, blow
Go on and blow, Gabriel, blow!
I've been a sinner, I've been a scamp,
But now I'm willin' to trim my lamp,
So blow, Gabriel, blow!
I was low, Gabriel, low,
Mighty low, Gabriel, low.
But now since I have seen the light,
I'm good by day and I'm good by night,
So blow, Gabriel, blow.
Once I was headed for hell,
Yes, once I was headed for hell;
But when I got to Satan's door
I heard you blowin' on your horn once more,
So I said, "Satan, farewell!"
And now I'm all ready to fly,
Yes, to fly higher and higher!
'Cause I've gone through brimstone and I've been through the fire,
And I've purged my soul and my heart too,
So climb up the mountaintop and start to
Blow, Gabriel, blow.
Go on and blow, Gabriel, blow!
I want to join your happy band
And play all day in the Promised Land,
So blow, Gabriel, blow!

BE LIKE THE BLUEBIRD

Published November 1934. Introduced by Victor Moore. Porter recorded this song for Victor (January 3, 1935).

VERSE

There's an old Australian bush song
That Melba used to sing,
A song that always cheered me when I was blue.
Even Melba said this bush song
Was a helluva song to sing,
So be quiet whilst I render it for you.

REFRAIN

When your instinct tells you that disaster
Is approaching you faster and faster,
Then be like the bluebird and sing
"Tweet tweet tra lalla-la-lalla."
When you know you're headed for the jailer
Don't allow the old face to look paler
But be like the bluebird and sing
"Tweet tweet tra lalla-la-lalla."
Be like the bluebird who never is blue,
For he knows from his upbringing
What singing can do,
And though by other birdies in the boughs, he
May be told that his efforts are perfectly lousy,
He sings on and on till his troubles are through
"Tweet tweet tra lalla-la-lalla."

BUDDIE, BEWARE

Published November 1934. Introduced by Ethel Merman. Dropped after the New York opening and replaced by a reprise of "I Get a Kick Out of You" by the week of December 10, 1934.

VERSE

Since I know such a lot of men
The opinions that I've got of men
Are respected not only by amateurs but by pros.
I'd like to write a book on men
And explain that certain look on men
Which means they're about to propose.
Of course it helps a maiden's pride to be
In the class of somebody's bride-to-be
And the reason that I've escaped this doubtful bliss
Is because a certain fear in me
Wakes the honest pioneer in me
And instead of answering "Yes," I always say this:

REFRAIN 1

Buddie, beware,
Buddie, better take care,
Though at heart I'm a pearl
I'm a difficult girl,
So, Buddie, beware.
When I go to a show
I prefer the first row,
When invited to dine
I can't eat without wine,

So, Buddie, beware.
During Christmas holidays
I develop taking ways
And I'm not at all anti
Pretty things Santy
Brings from Cartier's.
Your devotion I prize
But you must realize, my boy,
Other girls' luxuries
Are my necessities,
So, Buddie, beware.

REFRAIN 2

Buddie, beware,
Buddie, better take care,
Even angels, I'm told,
Are still harping on gold,
So, Buddie, beware.
Somehow I don't feel nice
When I wear a dress twice,
Since the day I was weaned
I'm a caviar fiend,
So, Buddie, beware.
Now and then I like to see
Willie Stewart and Company
'Cause I hear divine voices
When their Rolls-Royces
Come and honk for me.
But if still you insist
And we riddle love's mysteries,
I should hate leaving you
For Wooley Donahue,
But, Buddie, Beware.

REFRAIN 3

Buddie, beware,
Buddie, better take care,
I must warn you that I'm
Simply never on time,
So, Buddie, beware.
When you order a steak
And no supper I'll take,
If you tell me I'm rude
When I play with your food,
Then, Buddie, beware.
I feel I should put you right.
As I lie in bed at night
While the twinkling stars gleam on,
With my cold cream on
I'm a lovely sight.
And another thing too,
When I'm married to you, my sweet,
If to come home you fail,
I'll open all your mail,
So, Buddie, beware.

THE GYPSY IN ME

Published November 1934. Introduced by Bettina Hall and ensemble.

VERSE

SOLO: Long, long ago,
So long ago
I hardly know when,
My great-great-grandmother
Now and then
Stepped out with a gypsy.
GIRLS: The usual alibi.
SOLO: A little bit tipsy
But tipsy, no, no.
Of their love there wasn't a doubt,
So I can't wait to get the stage all set
So I can let the gypsy in me out.

REFRAIN

Hiding away
There's a little bit of gypsy in me
That's never been found,
Waiting its day.
There's a little bit of gypsy in me
Just hanging around
Till the magical night
When the stars by their light
Give mystery to the sleeping lagoon,
While a tinkling guitar
Not too near, not too far,
Gaily strums away,
Hums away
A titillating tune.
When I'm there in that dream
With the one in the world I worship passionately,
At the moment supreme
Will be shown the unknown
Gypsy in me.

WALTZ DOWN THE AISLE

Published November 1934. Dropped before the Boston opening, even though published, along with other numbers from the score. Previously intended for *Ever Yours* (1933–1934), it was later lengthened and considered for *Jubilee* (1935).

PRINCESS: Alone, at last.
ERIC: At last alone,
No radio and no telephone.

In all the world
We couldn't find, I'm sure,
A setting so perfect for a scène d'amour.

PRINCESS: My fondest dream
Has come true,
For at last I'm alone with you.
Do you love me, Eric?

ERIC: I do, I fear;
Though against ev'ry rule of my life, my dear,
But when you are the prize and so much is at stake,
What good's a rule for if it's not to break?

PRINCESS: Will you marry me, Eric?

ERIC: Will I marry you?
It's the one thing on earth I want most to do;
But if I answer "Yes," with a heavy "Heigh-ho!"
It's because weddings always depress me so.
The murky cathedral, the bishop in black,
And those bores who are there just to stare at your back.
The lugubrious music they always must play.

PRINCESS: But why do we have to be married that way,
Why not make the ceremony gay?*
When those bells start to chime,
To commemorate the happy time,
When at last you can trust yourself to me.
For a change I suggest
That our marriage not be like the rest,
But a great deal less long and less gloomy,
For our bridesmaids we'll choose
Only dancers from revues
And only ushers who can turn somersaults
And the old Wedding March, so pretentious and so arch,
Will give way to a lively waltz.

REFRAIN

When we waltz down the aisle,
Won't the papers have the vapors.
When we two start the style
Of a waltz down the aisle,
What a crush,
What a rush.
Delegations of relations
Will be there wearing a smile
When we waltz down the aisle.
Just a moment of delaying,
Then the organ starts to boom.
What is that he's playing?
Why, it's "Here Comes the Bride" and the Groom.
Off we go, to and fro,
To the altar and the halter.
What a treat for the rank and file
When we waltz down the aisle.

*From beginning through "ceremony gay" appears in *Jubilee* version. "When those bells" begins the published verse and refrain from *Anything Goes.*

WHAT A JOY TO BE YOUNG

Listed in the Colonial Theatre program as "To Be in Love and Young," it was sung in Boston by Bettina Hall. It was dropped from the show before the New York opening.

VERSE

A girl of sweet sixteen
Believes every word she hears
When any little boy appears
And plays a love scene.
It would be rather fun
To be sixteen again
And still have faith in men,
But that's all over now,
I'm over twenty-one.

REFRAIN

What a joy to be young,
And to b'lieve ev'ry love song that's sung.
What a blessing to be not so clever,
As to doubt if love can go on forever.
Ev'ry day I am told,
You'll be wiser far when you're old,
But till away the sweet dream has been flung,
What a wonderful joy
To be in love and young.

KATE THE GREAT

An unused song written for Ethel Merman. Madeleine Smith, Porter's secretary, has said that Porter often referred to his mother as "The Great Kate." Other "Kate" creations by Porter include "Katie of the Y.M.C.A." (see page 50), "Katie Went to Haiti" (*Du Barry Was a Lady*, 1939), and, of course, the show title *Kiss Me, Kate* (1948).

Catherine of Russia, that potentate,
Knew that her job was to fascinate.
Some people called her a reprobate,
But still she's known as Kate the Great.
To sessions of Congress she wouldn't go,
Never heckled the crowd on the radio.
She never would mix in affairs of state,
But in affairs of the heart, how Kate was great.
As few
Lovely ladies today,
She knew where woman should stay.
She never laid a five-year plan,
But was there ever such a girl
At laying—a plan—
For a man?
So drink
To that jovial jade
And think of the history she made.
Why, she made the Congress,
She made the Premier,
She made the clergy,
And she made 'em cheer.
She made the butler,
She made the groom,
She made the maid who made the room.
She made the Army,
She made the Marines,
Made some of them princes
And some of them queens.
And when she was still discontent,
Kate'd create a new regiment.
So, beautiful ladies, before too late,
Follow the lead of this potentate,
Give up arranging affairs of state
And stay in the hay like Kate the Great.
Hay-de-hay hay-de-hay hay-de-hay.
Stay in the hay like Kate the Great.

In November 1934, Porter told Lucius Beebe of the New York *Herald Tribune* that his next commitment was to go to Hollywood to write a score for an Eddie Cantor film for producer Samuel Goldwyn. The film was never made.

ADIOS, ARGENTINA

1934-1935

Porter wrote six songs in late 1934 and early 1935 for this unproduced Fox film. The screenplay by Allen Rivkin and producer Lou Brock was at one time titled *Okay, Argentina.*

ADIOS, ARGENTINA

Copyrighted unpublished January 1935. At this time Harms, Porter's publisher, must have known that Max Dreyfus, who had sold his interest in Harms to Warner Brothers, was re-entering the American music-publishing business with a new company, Chappell, an affiliate of the well-known English publisher. It is not surprising that Harms, realizing that Porter, along with Gershwin, Rodgers, and others, would leave to join Dreyfus at Chappell, would copyright unpublished Porter songs.

VERSE

The moon looks down on the pampas
And silhouettes two gauchos in its light,
While their flashing knives
Decide their lives
As they gleam in the dreaming night.
Each moment the battle is more heated
And each second more uncertain the fray
Till one falls dead and defeated
And the other slowly walks away.

REFRAIN

Adios, my fair Argentina,
My Argentina,
My joy, my pride.
Adios,
My beautiful Chena,
Never again can I ride
By your side.
Yet though no more we may meet,
There will ever linger, my sweet,
Memories of rapture complete
When I held you close.
So though goodbye
Those moments will never die,
Argentina, my Argentina,
Adios.

THE CHIRIPAH

Copyrighted unpublished January 1935.

Dancing the Chiripah
Down at the Chacarah,
Chiripah, Chacarah,
Chiripah, Chacarah,
Life seems so sweet
When you tangle your feet
In that Chacarah, Chiripah,
Chacarah, Chiripah!

Once you begin
It gets under your skin
As you trip along, skip along,
Dip along,
Furiously.
So come on, little girl,
And prepare for a whirl
To the Chacarah, Chiripah with me.

The Chiripah,
Ay, ay, ay, ay, what a dance,
The Chiripah!
Give it a try if you sigh for romance,
The Chiripah!
Drives ev'ry gaucho ga-ga,
So one, two, three
And dance with me
The Chi-ri-pi-ri-pah!

DON'T FENCE ME IN

Published October 1944. After the triumphant launching of *Anything Goes* at the Colonial Theatre in Boston on November 5, 1934, Porter signed a contract with Twentieth Century–Fox to provide songs for a film tentatively titled *Adios, Argentina.* The plot concerned the decision of an orphan girl who had inherited a big cattle spread in Texas to ship her four polo-playing cowboy tutors East to challenge the winner of a polo match between teams from the United States and Argentina. At one point the cowhands, unable to find anyone to accept their challenge, were supposed to burst into song to express their loneliness for the life back on the ranch. Hired presumably for his exceptional talent at writing songs with a distinct Latin flavor, Porter was also expected to write the cowboy song required by producer Lou Brock for this nostalgic moment in the film.

A month earlier Brock had received a book of verse from his friend Bob Fletcher, then employed in Helena, Montana, as Plans and Traffic Engineer for the Montana State Highway Department. In response, Brock wrote of the fancy he had taken to having a song entitled "Don't Fence Me In" in *Adios, Argentina* and added, "If I use this, will probably have you write or collaborate on the lyrics for the tune, in which event I would want the chorus to start with the words 'Don't Fence Me In.' "

Fletcher promptly wrote a song. On November 3, Brock wired Fletcher asking him to send a copy of the song care of the Waldorf-Astoria in New York, where Brock was staying in his ultimately successful quest to persuade Porter to write the score for the film. Porter signed with Fox on November 14. One week later, Brock asked Fletcher to send a copy of his song to Porter, whom he described as "one of our very best composers, who is rated as high as anyone on Broadway at the present time. Unlike most of the others, he also writes his own lyrics and does not as a rule have anyone collaborating with him. However, he was very much interested in your stuff, and what kind of a deal I can work out with him I do not know as these are matters to press somewhat delicately with a man of his standing."

On November 24, Fletcher sent Porter the lyrics and music for the refrain of "Don't Fence Me In" and some lyrics for a verse. On December 1, Brock wired Fletcher that "Cole Porter wants to buy right to use title and some characteristic words and phrases from your lyrics. Suggest you quote him price two hundred fifty dollars outright. Account Porter's reputation for always doing his own lyrics, believe impractical for him to give you credit. In any event, please wire him your proposition direct immediately and write me what you have done."

Fletcher complied with Brock's request, and Porter accepted the offer, perhaps for the simple reason that his producer had asked him to do so. Whether Porter was unable to write a satisfactory cowboy song is impossible to know. The primary center of musical-comedy production, however, had shifted from Broadway to Hollywood and the opportunities and money were incomparably greater at the Hollywood sound studios. Porter was hopeful that, should he prove to be a "cooperative" creator, the initial assignment from Fox would lead to more exciting and more lucrative offers from the film capital in the future.

The agreement, dated December 11 and signed by both Porter and Fletcher, gave Porter all of Fletcher's rights to the title and lyrics of "Don't Fence Me In" for the sum of $250. The agreement did not apply to Fletcher's music, which Porter did not use in any way. Porter also promised Fletcher that he would do all in his power to see that Fletcher received recognition for the material he sold to Porter.

On January 7, 1935, Porter, acknowledging Fletcher's Christmas gift of a book of his verse, sent Fletcher a copy of "Don't Fence Me In." Advising Fletcher "to keep it carefully under your hat as the music will not be released until next autumn," Porter also wrote, "I have given you credit under the title. Hope you will be pleased with it. Certainly, I am very grateful to you."

A week earlier Porter had gone to the Brunswick studios, where, with the assistance of baritone Edward Nell, pianist Victor Piemonte, and the *Anything Goes* Foursome Quartet, he had participated as a pianist in recording a complete set of demonstration discs of the six songs he had written for the film: "Adios, Argentina," "The Chiripah," "Don't Fence Me In," "If You Could Love Me," "The Side Car," and "Singing in the Saddle." The records were sent to Lou Brock at the Fox studio in Hollywood, but the picture was never filmed and the score went into the trunk.

Ten years later, "Don't Fence Me In" was pulled off the shelves of Harms, Inc., then owned by Warner Brothers, and used in *Hollywood Canteen,* where it was sung by Roy Rogers. A best-selling record by Bing Crosby and the Andrews Sisters sent it to the top of the Hit Parade. The song, then published, sold over one million copies and a like number of records. The published version did not acknowledge Bob Fletcher. Porter later stated that this was an "oversight" committed without his knowledge, as he was in the hospital at the time.

A story in the January 22, 1945, issue of *Newsweek* implied that Fletcher's contribution ("nothing but the title and a couple of words remained at the finish") was minor indeed. This impression has been reiterated by virtually every Porter biographer and almost every article that has appeared about the song. The story was further confused by the rash statements of Fletcher's friends. One of them, a Montana newspaper publisher, printed an editorial accusing Porter of stealing Fletcher's song. Walter Winchell picked up the item, and his version led to people calling Fletcher an "antediluvian cowboy" trying to cash in on Porter's good fortune. Fletcher, of course, had sold the song to Porter outright and had no further claim to it. Nevertheless, Fletcher was quite justified in his disappointment over not receiving credit in the published copies of the song. Porter later made amends for the oversight of his publishers by signing over a portion of the royalties on the song to Fletcher even though he didn't have to.

Still at issue after thirty-five years is the extent of Fletcher's contribution to Porter's lyric. That question can now be answered. Here is Fletcher's original lyric for the refrain of "Don't Fence Me In":

Don't fence me in.
Give me land, lots of land,
Stretching miles across the West,
Don't fence me in.
Let me ride where it's wide,
For somehow I like it best.
I want to see the stars,
I want to feel the breeze,
I want to smell the sage,
And hear the cottonwood trees.
Just turn me loose,
Let me straddle my old saddle
Where the shining mountains rise.
On my cayuse
I'll go siftin': I'll go driftin'
Underneath those Western skies.
I've got to get where
The West commences,
I can't stand hobbles,

I can't stand fences,
Don't fence me in.

And here is Cole Porters' lyric.

VERSE 1

Wild Cat Kelly, looking mighty pale,
Was standing by the sheriff's side,
And when that sheriff said, "I'm sending you to jail,"
Wild Cat raised his head and cried:

REFRAIN

Oh, give me land, lots of land under starry skies above,
Don't fence me in.
Let me ride thru the wide-open country that I love,
Don't fence me in.
Let me be by myself in the evening breeze,
Listen to the murmur of the cottonwood trees,
Send me off forever, but I ask you, please,
Don't fence me in.
Just turn me loose,
Let me straddle my old saddle underneath the Western skies.
On my cayuse,
Let me wander over yonder till I see the mountains rise.
I want to ride to the ridge where the West commences,
Gaze at the moon till I lose my senses,
Can't look at hobbles and I can't stand fences,
Don't fence me in.

VERSE 2

Wild Cat Kelly, back again in town,
Was sitting by his sweetheart's side,
And when his sweetheart said, "Come on, let's settle down,"
Wild Cat raised his head and cried:

REPEAT REFRAIN

IF YOU COULD LOVE ME

A copyist ink score of the music and lyrics was found at the Warner Brothers Music warehouse, Secaucus, New Jersey, in February 1982. The lyric is only slightly different from the transcription made by Elizabeth Wistar Williams from the Cole Porter–Edward Nell demonstration records made for the film's producer, Lou Brock, at the Brunswick Studio in January 1935.

VERSE

So often in the evening
A vision comes to me,
A dream so utterly beautiful
I don't believe it could ever be.
A fountain plays in a garden,
The stars are dancing above,
And there we are, just the three of us,
You and I and our love.

REFRAIN

If you could love me,
If you could learn to care,
It seems to me
Our life would be
A glorious affair.
If you could love me,
But love me, darling, heart and soul,
My one desire would be
To watch over you,
To worship you my goal.
If you would let me take you
And forever make you all my own,
We would live in heaven together,
Together alone.
But why should I be dreaming
When such a dream could only come true
If you could really love me
As I could love you.

THE SIDE CAR

Copyrighted unpublished January 1935.

VERSE

All through the Argentine
When the long day ends,
All the leading gauchos
And their little lady friends
Are doing the Side Car.
All through the Argentine
Folks are taking trips
To see those gauchos
Gaily glorifying their hips
Doing the Side Car.

REFRAIN

Side Car
Ai, ai, ai,
Ai, ai, ai, ai,
Ai, ai, ai, ai,
Side Car.

SINGING IN THE SADDLE

On one of the demonstration recordings made for producer Brock, "Singing in the Saddle" is sung as a countermelody to "The Cowboy Song" ("Don't Fence Me In").

Au-ra!
Au-ra!
Singing in the saddle,
Singing,
Singing the old refrain.
Swinging in the saddle,
Swinging,
Swinging over the plain.
Dreaming in the saddle,
Dreaming,
Feeling lonesome too.
Still I'm singing in the saddle
Till again my knees you straddle
And I'm singing to you.

JUBILEE

1935

Tryout: Shubert Theatre, Boston, September 21, 1935. Produced by Sam H. Harris and Max Gordon at the Imperial Theatre, New York, October 12, 1935. 169 performances. Book by Moss Hart. Directed by Monty Woolley. Entire production supervised, staged, and lighted by Hassard Short. Cast, starring Mary Boland, included Melville Cooper, June Knight, Derek Williams, May Boley, Charles Walters, Margaret Adams, Mark Plant, and Montgomery Clift.

Most of *Jubilee* was written by Porter and Hart during a Southern Hemisphere cruise around the world of the Cunard Line's *Franconia,* which sailed from New York Saturday, January 12, 1935, and returned on May 31, 1935.

OUR CROWN

Also listed as "National Anthem." Copyrighted unpublished by Harms, September 11, 1935. It was not a common practice at that time for music publishers to copyright complete scores. But Harms, knowing that Porter had agreed to offer his subsequent work to Max Dreyfus' Chappell & Co., took the precaution of copyrighting virtually the entire score of *Jubilee.* Introduced and performed during the show's run by the "entire company."

Oh, glorious crown,
Through "ages" of renown
Our pride, our guiding star,
Forever may
You lead us, night and day,
And shield us, near and far;
Forever bring
Contentment to our king
And annihilate
What enemy may wait
To strike him down;
So heav'n above
May bless the land we love
And the glory of our crown,
Forever bring
Contentment to our king,
So heav'n above
May bless the land we love
And the glory of our crown.

WE'RE OFF TO FEATHERMORE

Copyrighted under the title "Feathermore" in September 1935. Introduced by Mary Boland, Melville Cooper, Margaret Adams, and Charles Walters.

PRINCESS: Feathermore, that old gloomy castle, in
the middle of that old gloomy plain,
PRINCE: Feathermore, where there's nothing to
do all day except listen to the radio or
else turn it off and listen to the rain,
KING: Feathermore, the very thought of those
beds, so hard, so cold, and so
dix-huitième, gives me a feeling of
infinite fatigue not to mention a
distinct pain in the B.T.M.,
QUEEN: Feathermore, where the footmen are so
stuffy and they all have so many
buttons on that I can't see why, instead
of working for simple folks like us,
they don't go to Palm Beach and take
the Edward T. Stotesburys and the
Edward F. Huttons on,
But Fruity says we've got to go,
ALL: So tallyho, tallyho, tallyho—

REFRAIN

We're off, we're off to Feathermore,
That vast nasty castle in the North.
The very thought of Feathermore
Drives us mad as we sadly sally forth.
We'd rather linger here and get together more
With the dear, dear people we adore,
But when royal heads are cautioned to pick up
the royal feet,
Lest the royal guts become the butts of bullets
from the street,
Since there's nothing left to sit on but the royal
country seat,
We've got to weather Feathermore.

WHY SHOULDN'T I?

Published September 1935. Introduced by Margaret Adams. Unlike "Begin the Beguine," this song went unnoticed, receiving only slight attention at the time. Later it became perhaps the third best-known song from the score. The music and lyric of the interlude are part of the copyist ink score found at Warner Brothers Music warehouse in Secaucus, New Jersey, February 1982.

VERSE

All my life I've been so secluded
Love has eluded me,
But from knowing second-hand what I do of it,
I feel certain I could stand a closer view of it.
Till today I studied love discreetly,
But now that I'm completely free,
I must find some kind persona grata
To give me data personally.

REFRAIN

Why shouldn't I
Take a chance when romance passes by?
Why shouldn't I know of love?
Why wait around
When each age has a sage who has found
That upon this earth
Love is all that is really worth
Thinking of.
It must be fun, lots of fun
To be sure when day is done
That the hour is coming when
You'll be kissed and then you'll be kissed
again.
Each debutante says it's good,
And ev'ry star out in far Hollywood
Seems to give it a try—
So why shouldn't I?

INTERLUDE

What kind of man will I discover
When I embark upon my quest?
The ordinary type of lover,
I feel would never pass the test,
For I want a man who's creative,
A man who writes,
A man to his fingertips an artist,
A man who can give a girl Arabian nights,
Nevertheless in pyjamas quite the smartest,
A man sent straight from heaven above to me,
Who will know just when and when not to make
love to me,
A man with that certain subtle flair,
In fact, a man like Eric Dare.

ENTRANCE OF ERIC

Copyrighted under the title "Eric" in September 1935. This vocal ensemble heralded the arrival of the Noël Coward figure, Eric Dare (played by Derek Williams). Coward, who was thoroughly amused by the parody, actually did have a brother named Eric. "Entrance of Eric" was recorded privately by Porter and issued commercially in 1972 on Columbia KS 31456.

SATELLITES: Gone are the days that breed
despair,
Gone are the nights that nourish the
blues,
For back at last from his long world
cruise
Our god comes, Eric Dare!
Back is the author of our fav'rite
plays,
Back is the minstrel of our sweetest
lays,
Back is the idol of our matinees,
Our hero, Eric Dare!
While he was away, the only shows
Were the bastard babies of *Abie's
Irish Rose,*
While he wasn't here to write new
tunes,
We were stuck in the muck Bing
Crosby croons;
And as for actors, the only one
Was Walter Hampden, and that's no
fun;
But now those terrible days are done,
And again we satellites can see the
sun,
But now those horrible days are
done,
And again we satellites can see our
rising sun;
For back is the author of our fav'rite
plays,
Back is the minstrel of our sweetest
lays,
Back is the idol of our matinees,
Our hero, Eric Dare!
Back is the darling of our nights and
our days,
Our hero, Eric Dare!
He said he'd be here at six, yes, six
o'clock was the date,
And you know Eric, Eric is never,
never late.
ERIC: Darlings!
SATELLITES: Our Houdini, our Svengali!
And how are you, wonder man?
ERIC: Just regard the light of my eyes so
bright
And the deep bronze of my tan.
SATELLITES: Weren't there moments out in Bali
When you missed us, entre nous?
ERIC: When I felt that way,
I'd sit down and write a play,
Or dash off a song hit or two.

SATELLITES: We can hardly wait to hear
What you say to the press, my dear,
Will you praise the world, or will you pan it?
ERIC: I shall say it's a sweet little planet.
SATELLITES: And one other question, please—
As you sailed the seven seas
Did you give any maiden your heart?
ERIC: No, that was killed from the start.
SATELLITES: Oh!

THE KLING-KLING BIRD ON THE DIVI-DIVI TREE

Published October 1935. Believed to be the first song composed for *Jubilee* during the world cruise. Completed sometime after a visit to Jamaica less than a week after the voyage started. It was first copyrighted unpublished under the title "The Kling-Kling Bird" in September 1935. Porter's own private recording, issued on Columbia KS 31456, is much more complete than the published version. Introduced in *Jubilee* by Derek Williams, it was one of the most acclaimed songs in the score.

ERIC: For we'd scarcely been a week or two at sea
When we came to Panama town,
So I sought the shade of a divi-divi tree,
Where I lay me daintily down.
I had just assumed a Récamier pose
When a kling-kling bird came along,
Who, disregarding my afternoon doze,
Proceeded to sing this song.
SATELLITES: A kling-kling bird on a divi-divi tree
Proceeded to sing this song.
ERIC: Oh, beware, beware of the ladies fair
In the countries across the sea.
Better follow the advice of the kling-kling bird
On the top of the divi-divi tree.
When about to get in a sweet one's net
Make a graceful excuse and flee.
SATELLITES: Better follow the advice of the kling-kling bird
On the top of the divi-divi tree.
ERIC: For it may be fun to belong to someone
But it's wonderful to be free.
Better follow the advice of the kling-kling bird
SATELLITES: Better follow the advice of the kling-kling bird
On the top of the divi-divi tree!
ERIC: On the top of the divi-divi tree!
We had hardly reached Tahiti
When I met such a pretty little sweetie,
Pure Tahitian by her mother,
And pure French by the missionary's brother.
It was hard for me to say "No,"
When she asked me to visit her volcano,
But suddenly overhead
That bloody little bird appeared and said:
SATELLITES: When suddenly overhead
That blessed little bird appeared and said:
ERIC: Oh, beware, beware of the ladies fair
In the countries across the sea;
Better follow the advice of the kling-kling bird
On the top of the divi-divi tree.
When about to get in a sweet one's net
Make a graceful excuse and flee.
SATELLITES: Better follow the advice of the kling-kling bird
On the top of the divi-divi tree.
ERIC: If I'd gone that night, why, today I well might
Have a tropical family;
But I followed the advice of the kling-kling bird
SATELLITES: Yes, he followed the advice of the kling-kling bird
On the top of the divi-divi tree.
ERIC: On the top of the divi-divi tree.
Then we sailed and sailed for miles and miles
Till we came one day to the Cannibal Isles,
Where I soon enjoyed a great success
With a very broad-minded cannibaless.
We had dallied for a week or more,
When she said, one ev'ning, in front of her door,
"Won't you come inside and make poi?"
Then I heard that bird say, "Listen, little boy!"
SATELLITES: Then he heard that absurd old bird say, "Listen, little boy!"
ERIC: Oh, beware, beware of the ladies fair
In the countries across the sea,

Better follow the advice of the
kling-kling bird
On the top of the divi-divi tree.
When about to get in a sweet one's
net
Make a graceful excuse and flee.

SATELLITES: Better follow the advice of the
kling-kling bird
On the top of the divi-divi tree.

ERIC: If you don't take flight and get out of
her sight,
She'll be serving you up for tea:
So, I followed the advice of the
kling-kling bird

SATELLITES: Yes, he followed the advice of the
kling-kling bird
On the top of the divi-divi tree.

ERIC: On the top of the divi-divi tree.
Next I turned my talents on
For a dancer in Ceylon,
Then I made a hit in Cairo
And a pass in Assuan.
But no matter when I'd start
To portray the lover's part,
That damned oiseau would begin to
crow
In a voice just a bit off key:

SATELLITES: Better follow the advice of the
kling-kling bird
On the top of the divi-divi tree.

ERIC: Every time I'd get in a sweet one's
net
I'd be met with the same old plea;

SATELLITES: Better follow the advice of the
kling-kling bird
On the top of the divi-divi tree.

ERIC: So despite the fact I was often
attacked,
I return to you fancy-free,
'Cause I followed the advice of the
kling-kling bird

SATELLITES: Of that very, very nice little
kling-kling bird
On the top of the divi-divi tree.

ERIC: On the top of the divi-divi tree.

WHEN LOVE COMES YOUR WAY

Published in England as part of the *Nymph Errant* (1933) score in September 1933. Published in the United States in September 1935. Sung in pre-London performances of *Nymph Errant* by Gertrude Lawrence, it was also intended for *Ever Yours* (1933–1934). Introduced in *Jubilee* by Derek Williams and Margaret Adams. It was the fourth most mentioned song in the reviews and was privately recorded by Porter (Columbia KS 31456).

VERSE

If ever to your woe
Love comes to you one day,
Remember what I say:
I've loved, I know.
Love hates the sight of tears,
Love only cares for laughter,
So save your tears till after
Love disappears.

REFRAIN

When love comes your way
Take ev'ry bit of joy you can borrow.
Be carefree, be gay,
Forget the world and say
Goodbye to sorrow.
Simply live for today,
And never think at all of tomorrow,
For just when you are sure that love has
Come to stay—
Then love flies away.

WHAT A NICE MUNICIPAL PARK

Copyrighted unpublished September 1935. Introduced by Jack Whitney and ensemble. Porter's private recording was issued on Columbia KS 31456.

1ST TOURIST: What a nice municipal park,
Not too big and yet not too small.

GUIDES: Yes, 'twas given by the King on his
birthday last year,
And there are no regulations at all.

TOURIST: What a rare municipal park!

GUIDES: You can walk on the grass, you can
picnic anywhere,
When you ride on the switchback
no one ever takes your fare.
And if you're fond of swimming,
there's a pool over there,
Where you can go in absolutely
stark.

TOURISTS: What a nice municipal park!

GUIDES: If a lover of flowers, you can pluck
them at your ease—
In the zoo you can feed the
monkeys anything you please—

And if you find it fun to faire
l'amour beneath the trees,
You don't even have to wait until
it's dark.
TOURISTS: What a swell municipal park!
ALL: What a nice municipal park,
What a rare municipal park,
Where no city ordinances
Kill your chances
When you feel the need of a lark.
What a kindly king he must be,
What a most unselfish monarch,
Who, instead of building castles,
Gives his vassals
Such a nice municipal park—
Such a swell municipal park!

WHEN ME, MOWGLI, LOVE

Copyrighted unpublished September 1935. Introduced by Mark Plant, the Johnny Weissmuller–Tarzan figure. Porter's private recording was issued on Columbia KS 31456.

VERSE

If me, little Mowgli, badly dressed,
Me only born in elephant's nest,
Me only know what elephants know,
So me, little Mowgli, little bit slow.
Me so provincial, me simply lack entire
Knowledge of Winchell and O. O. McIntyre;
Me don't know yet what the set called smart is,
Me never get to Elsa Maxwell's parties.
Me simply play in the jungle hay all day—
Speaking of the hay, say:

REFRAIN

When me, Mowgli, love,
When me, little Mowgli-owgli, fall in love,
The love scene me throw
Is so bold even cold thermometers go
On a spree, when me, Mowgli, love.
When the jungle hear little Mowgli love has
found
All the elephants race to the place and huddle
around
And they stay till the dawn,
Ev'ry guest with his best binoculars on,
Just to see me, Mowgli, love.
And though friend Will Hays
Say that Mowgli's ways
Are the roughest he ever met,
And though Emily Post
Call me hell of a host
In her book on etiquette,
Yet ev'ry star, shining above,
Just dance with glee
When me, Mowgli, love.

GATHER YE AUTOGRAPHS WHILE YE MAY

Added to *Jubilee* during its Boston tryout, this is the only number from the score for which no music is known to survive. The only copy of the lyric was found in Moss Hart's libretto. Introduced by ensemble.

Gather ye autographs while ye may,
Crowd all the corridors,
Block the portals,
Gather ye autographs,
That's the quickest way of meeting
The latest immortals.
We've met Toscanini,
We've met Dizzy Dean,
We've met George F. Baker,
We've met Josephine,
We've met Clarence Darrow,
We've met Edward Reilly,
We've met King Selassie,
Haile, Haile, Haile, Haile.
Once in the lobby of the Waldorf-Astoria
I captured Herbert Marshall,
Sic transit gloria.
Once I even traveled to Bermuda, my dear,
Where I caught Professor Beebe
Singing in his bathysphere,
Singing in his chromium-plated bathysphere.
Most of these autographs are easy to get
But Mowgli's autograph is quite the hardest
yet.
For there's a dirty rumor
That's growing day and night
That Mowgli can barely read
Winnie the Pooh and *Ballyhoo*
And Mowgli doesn't know how to write,
He's too primitive to know how to write.
Gather ye autographs while ye may,
Crowd all the corridors,
Block the portals,
Gather ye autographs,
That's the quickest way of meeting
The latest immortals.

That's the only way of meeting
The latest immortals.

MY LOULOU

Copyrighted unpublished in September 1935, this brief opening to the "Café Martinique Scene" was not listed on programs until October 14, 1935. Yet the number was always a part of the score. Introduced by ensemble.

My Loulou, my Louloulou, la-la,
You've got such a lot of oo-la-la
That you make me want to do, la-la,
Things gentlemen don't do.
And although I know you're true, la-la
To the captain and the crew, la-la,
Still I'd go to Timbuctoo, la-la,
For your oo-la-la, Loulou.

BEGIN THE BEGUINE

Published October 1935. Written during the 1935 world cruise somewhere near the Fiji Islands. Porter later claimed that the first four bars of the musical accompaniment to a native dance he witnessed on the island of Kalabahai inspired the melody of "Begin the Beguine." But he also told people that he went to a public dance hall on the Left Bank in Paris during the 1920s where natives from Martinique danced something called the beguine. Porter said it was similar to the rhumba but faster. He wrote that the beguine was derived from a Martinique native dance called the *bel-air.* It was performed at balls, where the leader would set the rhythm with a drum and then start the dance with the signal "beguine."

The song was first copyrighted as an unpublished number titled "The Beguine" in September 1935. It was introduced by June Knight in the show and danced by Miss Knight and Charles Walters. It actually received more favorable mention than any other song in *Jubilee* from the beginning of the show's life. But it took a long time to become popular because it is so difficult to sing. The earliest recording—and an outstanding one—was by Xavier Cugat for Victor.

The song was not ignored. But it took Artie Shaw's swing version recorded for Victor Bluebird in 1938 to give the song lasting fame. It was first performed in motion pictures in *Broadway Melody of 1940.* The original penultimate line ended "the sweetness of sin."

When they begin the beguine
It brings back the sound of music so tender,
It brings back a night of tropical splendor,
It brings back a memory ever green.
I'm with you once more under the stars
And down by the shore an orchestra's playing,
And even the palms seem to be swaying
When they begin the beguine.
To live it again is past all endeavor
Except when that tune clutches my heart.
And there we are, swearing to love forever,
And promising never,
Never to part.
What moments divine, what rapture serene,
Till clouds came along to disperse the joys we
  had tasted,
And now when I hear people curse the chance
  that was wasted,
I know but too well what they mean.
So don't let them begin the beguine!
Let the love that was once a fire remain an
  ember.
Let it sleep like the dead desire I only remember
When they begin the beguine.
Oh yes, let them begin the beguine, make them
  play!
Till the stars that were there before return above
  you,
Till you whisper to me once more, "Darling, I
  love you!"
And we suddenly know what heaven we're in
When they begin the beguine.

GOOD MORNING, MISS STANDING

Copyrighted unpublished September 1935. Listed in all *Jubilee* programs as "Recitative," but copyrighted under the title "Good Morning, Miss Standing." Introduced by May Boley and ensemble.

SECRETARIES: Good morning, Miss Standing.
EVA: Good morning, my dears.
Am I busy today?
SECRETARIES: Yes, you're up to your ears!
You've so much you won't even
  have time to think.
EVA: Come on—give me my engagements; I'm made of zinc.
SECRETARIES: Well, at ten you're being
  photoed by *Movie Screen.*
At ten, ten, you're being painted
  by Neysa McMein.
KING: And after that, the next thing on
  today's program

Is a date to shoot craps with the King of Siam.
EVA: I just love to shoot craps with the King of Siam.
[*Bell*]
Entrez, entrez!
MESSENGERS: Flowers for Miss Standing!
Flowers for Miss Standing!
SECRETARIES: And when that's done—
EVA: Why, Herbert Swope loves me—isn't it all fun!
SECRETARIES: When that's done, you've got a contract to go on the air
And talk about sex and what the men will wear.
KING: Then you've to get a taxi and rush for the dock
'Cause you're launching a battleship at twelve o'clock.
EVA: I'd adore to launch a battleship at twelve o'clock.
[*Bell*]
Entrez, entrez!
BELLBOYS: Wire for Miss Standing!
Wire for Miss Standing!
SECRETARIES: And then at one—
EVA: Why, Tilly Losch loves me—isn't it all fun!
SECRETARIES: And then at one, you've got to be at the Perroquet, since
You've arranged a lunch of eighty for the Dionne Quints.
KING: And after you've finished your midday meal,
You've got a date to go out walking with your new trained seal.
EVA: I'll look divine walking with my new trained seal!
[*Bell*]
Entrez, entrez!
PROCESS SERVER: Summons for Miss Standing!
Summons for Miss Standing!
SECRETARIES: Then you've got to run—
EVA: Why, the Ritz-Carlton's suing me—isn't it all fun!
SECRETARIES: Then you're due at Elizabeth Arden's place
'Cause she's paying you a thousand to lift your face.
KING: Following that you want to order a new ball gown
'Cause the Sultan of Zanzibar has just hit town!
EVA: What! The Sultan of Zanzibar has just hit town!
[*Buzz, buzz*]
It's the telephone—say I'm out, dear.
1ST SECRETARY: Yes, hello—no—Miss Standing's not here.
It's the Sultan of Zanzibar.
EVA: Give me the phone!
And go on out and have a drink, girls, I want to be alone.
Why, the Sultan of Zanzibar, it's too, too divine!
I've just got to get the Sultan for that party of mine.

MY MOST INTIMATE FRIEND

Copyrighted unpublished September 1935. This spoof of Elsa Maxwell was introduced by May Boley.

VERSE

EVA: Good morning, Highness—
I knew you were due to land.
But don't make any engagements, please,
For I've got everything planned—
You're lunching with me this morning,
On a roof you'll simply adore,
Then I've got such a lot of nice debutantes
To smoke hasheesh with you at four,
And tonight I'm giving a charming dinner for you,
And after that, something entirely new—

REFRAIN

I must warn you in advance
I've arranged a little dance,
Just in case you've any champagne you'd like to send.
Will Grace Vanderbilt appear?
Why, of course she will, my dear,
She's my most intimate friend!
'Twill be new in ev'ry way,
Gershwin's promised not to play,
And Miss Otis thinks she will be able to attend.*

**Earlier version of lines 9–18 of refrain:*
And I've paid Charles Hanson Towne not to attend.
Has Mussolini been invited?
What, Benito? Why, he's delighted,
He's my most intimate friend.
Gertrude Stein will be there of course,
And Tommy Hitchcock's bringing his horse,
You know, I taught him how to play polo, isn't it odd!
And although she's a dreadful person,

Has Jack Barrymore been invited?
What! Jack the Skipper? Why, he's delighted!
He's my most intimate friend.
Sally Rand will be there, of course,
And Tommy Hitchcock's bringing his horse.
You know, I taught him how to play polo when
he was three!
And just as an added factor
I've invited my chiropractor
'Cause he's oh so intimate with me.
Now forgive me if I fly—
It just kills me to say goodbye—
And if I had my way, this talk would never
end.
I don't want to go at all,
But, my dear, I've a hurry call—

KING: From her most intimate friend!

A PICTURE OF ME WITHOUT YOU

Published September 1935. Introduced by June Knight and Charles Walters. Many reviewers compared it unfavorably to "You're the Top." Porter's private recording is available on Columbia KS 31456. The lyric in the published version is rather scanty and has been filled out substantially from Porter's own files and the libretto. The line about Huey Long was altered when Long was assassinated on September 8, 1935.

INTRODUCTION

PRINCE: Can't find a cigarette.
KAREN: They're over there.
PRINCE: Can't find my slippers.
KAREN: They're under the chair.
PRINCE: What time is it, darling?
KAREN: Just two.
PRINCE: You know, it's awful, my lamb,
I'm getting so damned dependent on you.

VERSE

From being merely
A necessary luxury
And someone sympathetic to have about,
Why, now you're nearly
A luxurious necessity
I couldn't imagine ever living without.
I suppose I could somehow struggle through,
But I'd hate to picture myself without you.

REFRAIN 1

Picture Henry Ford without a car,
Picture heaven's firmament without a star,
Picture Fritzy Kreisler without a fiddle,
Picture poor Philadelphia without a Biddle,
Picture good cigars without Havana,
Picture Huey Long less Louisiana,
Mix 'em all together, and what have you got?
Just a picture of me without you.

REFRAIN 2

Picture H. G. Wells without a brain,
Picture Av'rell Harriman without a train,
Picture Tintern Abbey without a cloister,
Picture Billy the Oysterman without an oyster,
Picture Central Park without a sailor,
Picture Mister Lord minus Mister Taylor,
Mix 'em all together, and what have you got?
Just a picture of me without you.

REFRAIN 3

Picture Ogden Nash without a rhyme,
Picture Mr. Bulova without the time,
Picture Staten Island without a ferry,
Picture little George Washington without a
cherry,
Picture brother Cain without his Abel,
Picture Clifton Webb minus Mother Mabel,
Mix them all together and what have you got?
Just a picture of me without you.

REFRAIN 4

Picture Paul Revere without a horse,
Picture love in Hollywood without divorce,*
Picture Barbara Hutton without a nickel,
Picture poor Mister Heinz, my dear, without a
pickle,
Picture City Hall without boondogglin',
Picture Sunday tea minus Father Coughlin,
Mix 'em all together and what have you got?
Just a picture of me without you.

REFRAIN 5

Picture Lily Pons without a throat,
Picture Harold Vanderbilt without a boat,
Picture Billy Sunday without a sinner,

I've invited Aimee MacPherson
'Cause we're both so intimate with God.

**Or:*
Picture Noël Coward without a plot,
Picture Douglas Elliman without a lot.

Picture dear Missus Corrigan without a dinner,
Picture Hamlet's ghost without a darkness,
Picture Mother Yale minus Father Harkness,
Mix 'em all together and what have you got?
Just a picture of me without you!

The following verse preceded refrains 4 and 5 in the original score but was deleted.

MOWGLI: It's mighty mean of you, Butch,
To leave me all alone,
And say goodbye to swimmin' school.
You'll never be happy, Butch,
Just sittin' on a throne,
When you could be splashin' your little Mowgli in a pool,
And as far as I go, I know it's true
That I'm gonna be awful lost without you.

EV'RYBOD-EE WHO'S ANYBOD-EE

Copyrighted unpublished September 1935. This ensemble number announced the arrival of the guests for the costume ball. Porter's private recording is available on Columbia KS 31456.

Ev'rybod-ee who's anybod-ee
Is bound to attend this tremendous part-ee,
Not for enjoyment, but merely to see
Ev'rybod-ee who's anybod-ee!

Ev'rybod-ee is dead with ennui,
And just about breaking from making whoopee,
But to see and be seen is the solemn dut-ee
Of ev'rybod-ee who's anybod-ee.

So ev'rybod-ee, steamed up on brand-ee,
Will gallop about till this rout is fini;
So, when asked who was there, they can answer with glee:
Ev'rybod-ee who's anybod-ee.

APHRODITE'S DANCE

A four-part "Masque" called "The Judgment of Paris" was presented during the costume ball in the closing scene of Act I. Music survives for "The Entrance of Paris," "Hera's Dance," "Pallas Athene," and "Aphrodite's Dance." The only part with a lyric was "Aphrodite's Dance," which was copyrighted unpublished in September 1935.

Aphroditah—Aphrodite (Venus)
Eedoo—Behold
Kalah—Beautiful
Perikalah—The most beautiful
Khariessa Korah—the loveliest
Khroosostefan Aphroditah—Golden crowned Aphrodite
Kootheray—Cythera (another name for Aphrodite)
Miara—harlot
Kakourga—prostitute

MEN: Eedoo, Aphroditah
Aphroditah, Kalah
Aphroditah, perikalah Aphroditah
Kalah, Kalah, Khariessa Korah,
Khroosostefan Aphroditah
Kalah, Kalah, Khariessa Korah,
Kootheray.
WOMEN: Miara, Kakourga
Miara, Kakourga
MEN: Kalah, Kalah, Khariessa Korah
WOMEN: Miara, Kakourga
MEN: Kalah, Kalah, Khariessa Korah
WOMEN: Miara, Kakourga
MEN: Kalah, Kalah,
WOMEN: Miara, Kakourga
MEN: Kalah, Kalah
WOMEN: Miara, Kakourga
MEN: Kalah
WOMEN: Miara
MEN: Kalah
WOMEN: Kakourga
MEN: Kalah
WOMEN: Miara
MEN: Kalah
WOMEN: Kakourga
MEN: Aphroditah
Aphroditah
Aphroditah
Aphroditah
Kootheray
Kalah
Aphroditah
Aphrod*itah*
Aphrod*itah*
MEN & WOMEN: Kalah

SWING THAT SWING

Copyrighted unpublished September 1935. The Act I finale, an ensemble number, was written during rehearsals.

Are you the Queen?
Are you the King?
Whoever you are,
You certainly can swing that swing.
Are you the Prince?
Are you the Princess?
Whoever you are,
You certainly can swing that swing.
Swing it!
Swing it!
Swing it!
King it!
Queen it!
Prince it?
Princess it!
Please, Mercedes!
Are you the Queen?
Are you the King?
Whoever you are,
You certainly can swing that swing.

SUNDAY MORNING BREAKFAST TIME

Copyrighted unpublished September 1935. This ensemble number, which opened Act II, was also known as "Breakfast Time." Porter's privately recorded piano-vocal was issued on Columbia KS 31456.

VERSE

Here's to the piping porridge,
Here's to the biscuits hot,
Here's to the java
Flowing like lava
Out of the coffee pot.
Here's to the eggs and bacon,
Here's to the waffles unique,
And here's and here's
Three rousing cheers
For the best meal of the week!

REFRAIN

For it's Sunday morning breakfast time,
The time all men adore!
Why don't the poets go into rhyme
And rave about it more?
For only then can a man forget
The sweat and the worries of his bane-
Ful lot as he calmly enjoys his toast
And most of Arthur Brisbane.
Breakfast time on other days
Means bolting at fever heat,
But on Sunday morning, there's the time
When a man has time to eat—and eat,
When a man has time to . . .
[*Cakewalk*]
. . . Breakfast is served.

MR. AND MRS. SMITH

Copyrighted unpublished September 1935. This complex octet was added during rehearsals and introduced by the eight principals in the first scene of Act II.

VERSE

QUEEN: When once we get established as a
family of Smiths
I suggest a little journey for a thrill
To America, that magic land of
mysteries and myths
Like Mammoth Cave and Cecil B. De
Mille.
OTHERS: What a mystery, what a thrill,
Mammoth Cave and Cecil B. De Mille.

QUEEN: For months and months I've waited
To know just how it felt
To be N.R.A.-diated
By Mr. Roosevelt.
And now that I can have my way
I want to do my best
To see the unemployed at play
And the government at rest.
KING: Well, if they go, and they go, then,
Katie, why can't I go too?
QUEEN: Nat'rally, my darling, yes, of course you
can, old boy.
ALL: So step on the gas, swing it, take it
away, ship ahoy!

REFRAIN

ALL: Mr. and Mrs. Smith
Will soon be sailing across the water
Sailing gaily with
Four charming friends and of course their
two sons and their daughter.
It's an easy guess

That they will all have a great success.
They're such democratic people that I know the U.S.A.
Will put bells in every steeple to ring out a holiday
For Mr. and Mrs. Smith
And the merry crew they're sailing with.

PATTER

PRINCE: I can hardly wait to buy new trunks and order new initials.
QUEEN: I can hardly wait to meet those charming New York custom officials.
PRINCESS: Think of settling down in some gargantuan hotel where the towers go to heaven
KING: And the service goes to hell.
MOWGLI: I'll take you to Coney Island, Butch, and duck you till you're limp.
EVA: I'll get that nice Mr. Goodyear, dear, to bounce us in his blimp.
KAREN: We'll go to the Park Casino and I'll dance you off your toes
ERIC: And if you're a very good little girl I'll present you to Billy Rose.
ALL: Mumbo jumbo, Billy Rose.
QUEEN: When we get tired of city life and its various vagaries
We'll take a covered wagon for a lovely trek across the prairies.
MOWGLI: California, here I come,*
Right back where I—
QUEEN: Mowgli, no commentaries.
EVA: Once we're in Hollywood, I know that I can lasso
My old friend Greta Garbo, and Dear Dorothy di Frasso.
ERIC: Why, here comes Garbo now.
KING: Why, how very cold she's grown.
KAREN: Go 'way, I'm tired of people, I want to be alone.
PRINCESS: And look who's just appeared, Ma.
QUEEN: Why Diana, I declare,
It's none other than my dream boy,
That fascinating Fred Astaire.
PRINCE: [*Dances*]
There!
ALL: Let's be getting started, let's be on our way.
First we go to Rockwell, then
Ta-rah-rah-boom-de-ay.

REPEAT REFRAIN

**Or:*
Metro-Goldwyn, here I come,

GAY LITTLE WIVES

Copyrighted unpublished September 1935 under the title "Six Little Wives." It was an ensemble number. First titled "Tired Little Wives."

GIRLS: Gay little wives quite enchanted to be
Breathing the bracing air of Rockwell by the sea.
Gay little wives from their duties temporarily released
Taking a look at nature's beauties, for a week or two at least.
That is the reason we each seem to be
Happier than any bird on any tree.
That is the reason we each seem to be
Infinitely happier than any bird on any tree.

TO GET AWAY

Copyrighted unpublished September 1935. Although it was not listed in any *Jubilee* program because it was probably considered part of the immediately preceding "Gay Little Wives," this ensemble piece was copyrighted as a separate number. Lynn Siebert, in her Porter Thematic Catalogue, says that "Gay Little Wives" should be considered the verse and "To Get Away" the refrain of the opening to Act II, Scene 2.

What a pleasure it is to get away
From one's husband for a short holiday.
What a joy, on retiring, not to hear
His interminable snoring in your ear,
And though the place where luck may take you
Is a most plebeian place,
Full of people who may make you
Want to massacre the human race,
Still what a treat nonetheless to get away
From one's husband for a short holiday.
And how nice of one's husband to want to pay
His adoring young wife to stay away.
How nice of him
In town to stay
And pay and pay his little wife to stay far away.

ME AND MARIE

Published September 1935. Widely expected to be the show's hit song, "Me and Marie" received a number of recordings. Introduced by Mary Boland and Melville Cooper. Porter's privately recorded piano-vocal version has been issued on Columbia KS 31456. Actually, this number could be considered a "double" song since the patter is a countermelody to the refrain.

VERSE

On Saturday night when my work is through,
I always call for Marie.
Then we hop on a bicycle built for two
And go scorching down to the sea.
After one or two whirls to the German band
We go strolling under the moon
Till we find a good spot on the silv'ry sand
Then, gee whiz, how we spoon.

REFRAIN

You ought to see little me and Marie
By the old seaside.
By the ocean we set
And we pet and we pet
Till we get swept out by the tide.
You may have been to Paris
And had both of your eyes opened wide,
But you ought to see
Me and Marie
By the old seaside.

PATTER

If you want to see a thing of beauty
You should see me spoonin' with my little cutie
By the old seaside.
For when once we get the proper settin'
We begin a-pettin' and go on a-pettin'
Till we end by gettin' such an awful wettin'
From the tide.
First we talk about that and this a bit,
Then we walk about
And hug and kiss a bit
Till we finally
Find a spot where we
Can hide.
Then until the crowin' of the chickens
Me and my Marie proceed to raise the dickens
By the old seaside.

JUST ONE OF THOSE THINGS

Published October 1935. Written on the Ohio farm of Porter's Yale classmate Leonard Hanna in August 1935. It is an entirely different song from "Just One of Those Things" in *The New Yorkers* (1930). Introduced by June Knight and Charles Walters late in Act II. It was hardly ignored, but did not become a standard until the early 1940s.

VERSE

As Dorothy Parker once said to her boy
friend,
"Fare thee well,"
As Columbus announced when he knew he was
bounced,
"It was swell, Isabelle, swell,"
As Abélard said to Héloïse,
"Don't forget to drop a line to me, please,"
As Juliet cried in her Romeo's ear,
"Romeo, why not face the fact, my dear?"

REFRAIN

It was just one of those things,
Just one of those crazy flings,
One of those bells that now and then rings,
Just one of those things.
It was just one of those nights,
Just one of those fabulous flights,
A trip to the moon on gossamer wings,
Just one of those things.
If we'd thought a bit
Of the end of it,
When we started painting the town,
We'd have been aware
That our love affair
Was too hot not to cool down.
So goodbye, dear, and amen.
Here's hoping we meet now and then,
It was great fun,
But it was just one of those things.

THERE'S NOTHING LIKE SWIMMING

Copyrighted unpublished September 1935. Mary Boland, Mark Plant, and the lifeguards introduced it during the Boston tryout, but it was dropped from the show before the New York opening.

QUEEN: A week ago who'd have prophesied
That ever I should be occupied
In going to swimming school.
BOYS: Hurrah for Butch, going to swimming
school!

QUEEN: But now I've swum such an awful lot
That I've reached a point where I'm
simply not
At home except in a pool.
BOYS: She won't get out of the pool!
QUEEN: Apart from the rather rare delight
Of leading the life of a water sprite,
Swimming along at a dreadful pace,
Madly splashing your friends in the
face,
Giving 'em pinches, giving 'em kicks,
And playing rude underwater tricks,
It has other advantages too,
For it happens to be true—

REFRAIN 1

QUEEN: There's nothing like swimming for
trimming the old physique,
For giving the torso that certain chic;
There's nothing that hustles the muscles
and makes 'em tauter
Than gaily doing your daily dozen with
Neptune's daughter.
My classical bust will, I trust, delight
your eyes,
And look at the perfect taste of my
chaste thighs,
Then kindly observe the curve of my
so-to-speak,
And you'll grant me
There's nothing like swimming for
trimming the old physique.

BOYS: Fair Neptune's daughter, come take a
bow,
For in the water you're simply a wow;
We've never seen on any screen a figure
finer
Than you when you ride the tide like an
ocean liner,
And when you do the Australian crawl, in
all your regalia,
We can hear the sirens cheer from here
to Australia.

REFRAIN 2

BOYS: There's nothing like swimming for
trimming the old physique,
For giving the torso that certain chic;
There's nothing that hustles the muscles
and makes 'em tauter
Than gaily doing your daily dozen with
Neptune's daughter.
So please don't be fussed if your bust we
scrutinize,
And dwell on the perfect taste of your
chaste thighs,
Or even observe the curve of your
so-to-speak,
For they show, Butch,
There's nothing like swimming for
trimming the old physique.
On your mark, get set, dive!

YOURS

Copyrighted unpublished September 1935. Dropped before the Boston opening, this is the same number that was intended for *Ever Yours* (1933–1934). It is not the same song as "I'm Yours" from *You Never Know* (1938).

REFRAIN

I'm yours, only yours,
From the day when I fell,
'Neath the charm of your spell,
I belong to you,
I'm yours.
I may try to insist,
That we never have met,
That you could not exist,
But how can I forget,
Since the moment we kissed,
I'm yours.
You may stay, you may go,
You may drift with each shift of the breeze,
Though you go, still I know,
I'll have memories,
So warm me once more,
With the arms that I miss,
And the kiss I adore,
And remember, sweetheart,
If tonight we must part,
That as long as life endures,
I'm yours, all yours.

SING "JUBILEE"

Copyrighted unpublished September 1935. This Act II finale was dropped before the Boston opening and replaced by "Jubilee Presentation," for which there were no lyrics.

Jubilee featured a good deal of incidental music for which no lyrics were written. For more information on "Waltz Down the Aisle," intended as a duet in *Jubilee* for Margaret Adams and Derek Williams before its deletion, see *Anything Goes* (1934).

Is ev'rybody happy?
Is ev'rybody carefree?
Well, if ev'rybody's happy,
Sing "Jubilee."

Is ev'rybody full of beans,
With a capital B?
Well, if ev'rybody's full of beans,
Sing "Jubilee."

. . .

Would ev'rybody like to raise a little wholesome hell?
Well, such being the situation,
Let freedom ring the bell,
'Cause ev'rybody's happy and ev'rybody's carefree,
And so, since ev'rybody's happy,
Sing "Jubilee."

BORN
TO
DANCE

1936

"Born to Dance," 1936; Frances Langford, Buddy Ebsen,
Eleanor Powell, James Stewart, Una Merkel, Sid Silvers

A film produced by Jack Cummings for M-G-M in 1936. Released in November 1936. Screenplay by Jack McGowan and Sid Silvers, based on an original story by McGowan, Silvers, and B. G. De Sylva. Directed by Roy del Ruth. Cast, starring Eleanor Powell, included James Stewart, Virginia Bruce, Una Merkel, Sid Silvers, Frances Langford, Raymond Walburn, Buddy Ebsen, Georges and Jalna, and Reginald Gardiner. The original title of the film was *Great Guns.*

ROLLING HOME

Published September 1936. Written in March 1936 in Hollywood. Introduced by the male ensemble.

Rolling home, across the bounding blue,
So, boys, give 'er class
And start rubbin' the brass,
We're ro-rolling home.

Rolling home, come on, you lazy crew,
Our whole course is set
To race over the wet,
We're ro-rolling home.

Oh, can't you see the light in your mother's
  eye,
When that son of a gun, her roving son,
Attacks a piece o' pie?
And can't you taste the lips of a certain miss,
When her pride and her joy, her sailor boy,
S-macks her with a kiss?
And can't you hear them cheering on the pier?
So, quick, gobs, get on your jobs and tell the
  engineer
We're rolling home, our chores are nearly
  through,
So step lively, pals,
You'll soon be with the gals,
We're ro-rolling home.

PATTER

Just think of it,
No more hardtack, no more beans,
No more salt horse and canned sardines.
We've sailed all the seven seas, we've crossed all
  the ponds,
From now on it's duck soup and pure platinum
  blondes.
So, no more labor, no more toil,
No more Mothersills and no more castor oil,
No more spending the night aboard instead of
  ashore,
Will we ever do it again?
Quoth the raven, "Never more."

I still could swear
When I think of the fair
Venetian maid I met,
'Neath stars above
She taught me to love,
At least to love spaghett.
But when I tried
To return to her side
And visit her on the Lido,
The chief said "No"
And sent me below
To polish his pet torpedo.

It's the worst of breaks
When the captain makes
You polish his pet torpedo.

I hate romance
When I think of the chance
I missed at Honoloola.
I scanned the beach
And there was a peach
Enjoying a hula-hula.
I could plainly see
Her vitamin D,
And my heart was filled with hope,
But how can you deal
With sex appeal
Through a rusty periscope?
Nope,
You can't even register hope
Through a rusty, dusty periscope.

But now our trials are over,
And happy days are here,
And we've got a date
To celebrate,
So step on it, engineer,
We're rolling home, our chores are nearly
  through,
So step lively, pals,
You'll soon be with the gals,
We're ro-rolling home.
We're rolling home, sweet home.

RAP TAP ON WOOD

Published September 1936. Written in March 1936. Introduced by Eleanor Powell.

VERSE

If you want to ring the bell not once, but twice,
If you want to roll and roll those lucky dice,
If you want to spend your journey's end with
sweet music and love,
If you want to lick this world of men and Mickey
Mice,
Take my advice,

REFRAIN

When you sit down, one day,
Look over yourself and say,
"You're very good,"
Ra-ap tap on wood.

When you have such success
You're conscious that you impress
The neighborhood
Ra-ap tap on wood.

When ev'ry meal you take
Is made of milk and honey,
When ev'ry stock you stake
Is making mints of money,
When ev'ry heart you break
Is such a cinch, it's funny,
Careful, sonny,
Rap-tap, rap-tap, rap-tap-tap, rap-a-tap-tap,

You're knockout, you're good news,
And you'll never, never lose
If you just put on your dancing shoes
And rap-tap on wood.

REFRAIN FOR BUDDY EBSEN [UNUSED]

If, after all we've clowned,
You still wanna hang around
My neighborhood,
Ra-ap tap on wood.

If you admit I'm right
That Mush as a husband might
Be purty good,
Ra-ap tap on wood.

Somehow you seem to be
A femmie, not so silly,
So why pick little me,
I'm just a poor hillbilly.
Still, babe, if you agree
You want me willy-nilly,
Hark ye, filly,
Rap-tap, rap-tap, rap-tap-tap, rap-a-tap-tap.

B'lieve me, this ain't no joke,
I mean ev'ry word I spoke,
So simply show me it's okey-doke
And rap-tap on wood.

HEY, BABE, HEY

Published September 1936. Written no later than May 1936. Also titled "I'm Nuts About You." Introduced by ensemble. The three refrains are countermelodies.

VERSE

1ST SAILOR: I've been around such a lot in
my time,
I know the hairpins by heart.
The way they chase after me, babe,
it's a crime,
And the way I make love, it's an art,
So let's find a corner and start,
What d'ya say?

REFRAIN 1

1ST SAILOR: Hey, babe, hey, babe,
How ya doin', today, babe?
You look sorta shipshape to me,
And I've sighted a few.
Hey, babe, hi, babe,
Why not give me a try, babe,
And maybe I'll make you my babe,
'Cause I'm nuts about you.

REFRAIN 2

2ND SAILOR: Hey, baby, hey, baby,
Whadaya say, baby,
How about bein' my crew?
I need a lookout
To point some shady nook out,
'Cause after seafarin'
I wanta try sharin'
A snug little cottage for two,
So be my pilot
To love's dreamy islet,
'Cause I'm nuts about you.

REFRAIN 3

3RD SAILOR: Pretty baby, pretty baby,
And what might your plans for
today be?
If you're lonesome on your
ownsome,
Well, I haven't a darn thing to do.
People tell me it's the season,

When the dames like huggin' and squeezin',
And for some dumb, goofy reason,
Baby, I'm nuts about you.

ENTRANCE OF LUCY JAMES

Unpublished. Introduced by Raymond Walburn and ensemble. "Entrance of Lucy James" segued immediately into "Love Me, Love My Pekinese." The two numbers, conceived as an entity, were written in May 1936.

LOOKOUTS: Miss Lucy James sighted starboard beam . . .
Miss Lucy James approaching starboard beam . . .
Miss Lucy James nearing starboard beam . . .
Miss Lucy James alongside starboard beam . . .
Miss Lucy James boarding starboard beam . . .
CAPTAIN: For your information, Miss James is a dream,
LOOKOUTS: Miss Lucy James boarding starboard beam.
CAPTAIN: Just a combination of peaches and cream.
CREW: Ahoy, ahoy, Miss Lucy James,
And welcome to our submarine,
Most glorified of dames.

CAPTAIN: Good morning, miss, and how do you do?
LUCY: And how's the captain, not to mention the crew?
CAPTAIN: Why, as far as I know, the crew is all right,
But the captain had a big night last night.
CREW: Yes, yesterday,
He drew his pay,
So the captain had a big night last night.
But don't be cross with the dear old boss,
'Cause he had a very, very big night last night.

CAPTAIN: Now, since you ask me about my crew,
It gives me pleasure to present 'em to you.
Boys, meet Miss . . . oh, I'm so awful at names.
CREW: Why, the name of the lady is Lucy James.
CAPTAIN: Lucy James got another papa!
CREW: You got another papa, but he's bad at names
'Cause he had a very, very big night, Miss James.
LUCY: Now since we all have met, and formalities are through,
May I present my heaven-sent Cheeky-Peeky-Poo.
OTHERS: Who?

LOVE ME, LOVE MY PEKINESE

Published October 1936. Introduced by Virginia Bruce and ensemble.

REFRAIN

SOLO: Love me, love my Pekinese,
'Spite of your antipathies,
If you want to cultivate me,
Gotta love Cheeky.
OTHERS: Howdy, little Cheeky.
SOLO: Cheeky, he's my chaperon,
Never lets me be alone,
So when you invite me to tea,
Gotta have Cheeky.
OTHERS: Nasty little Cheeky.
SOLO: Cheeky barks, Cheeky bites,
Cheeky goes in for neighborhood fights,
Cheeky still thinks gentlemen are all trees.
OTHERS: Cheeky, please!
SOLO: But be warned before you start,
If you want to win my heart
Don't bother to buy me big rings
Or other extravagant things,
Get something chic for Cheeky, my Pekinese.
OTHERS: We love you, Cheeky,
You squeaky little Pekinese.

EASY TO LOVE

Published September 1936. Originally written for William Gaxton to sing in *Anything Goes* (1934). Rewritten for *Born to Dance* on April 13, 1936 (Cole Porter diary). Sung by James Stewart, danced by Eleanor Powell, mimed by Reginald Gardiner, and reprised by Frances Langford. The published, familiar version is a condensation of the original lyric presented here.

VERSE

I know too well that I'm
Just wasting precious time
In thinking such a thing could be
That you could ever care for me.*
I'm sure you hate to hear
That I adore you, dear,
But grant me, just the same,
I'm not entirely to blame, For

REFRAIN 1

You'd be so easy to love,
So easy to idolize, all others above,†
So sweet to waken with,‡
So nice to sit down to eggs and bacon with.
We'd be so grand at the game,
So carefree together that it does seem a shame
That you can't see
Your future with me,
'Cause you'd be, oh, so easy to love.

REFRAIN 2

You'd be so easy to love,
So easy to idolize, all others above,
So worth the yearning for,
So swell to keep ev'ry home fire burning for.
Oh, how we'd bloom, how we'd thrive
In a cottage for two, or even three, four, or
five,
So try to see
Your future with me,
'Cause they'd be, oh, so easy to love.

REFRAIN 3

You'd be so easy to love,
So easy to worship as an angel above,
Just made to pray before,
Just right to stay home and walk the baby for.
I know I once left you cold,
But call me your "lamb" and take me back to
the fold.
If you'll agree,
Why, I guarantee
That I'll be, oh, so easy to love.

*Or:
That you would ever marry me.
†Or:
To take on a honeymoon, all others above,
‡Or:
So sweet to watch the day awaken with,

I'VE GOT YOU UNDER MY SKIN

Published September 1936. Written in April 1936. Introduced by Virginia Bruce and danced by Georges and Jalna.

REFRAIN

I've got you under my skin,
I've got you deep in the heart of me,
So deep in my heart, you're really a part of
me,
I've got you under my skin.

I tried so not to give in,
I said to myself, "This affair never will go so
well."
But why should I try to resist when, darling, I
know so well
I've got you under my skin.

I'd sacrifice anything, come what might,
For the sake of having you near,
In spite of a warning voice that comes in the
night,
And repeats and repeats in my ear,
"Don't you know, little fool, you never can
win,
Use your mentality,
Wake up to reality."
But each time I do, just the thought of you
Makes me stop, before I begin,
'Cause I've got you under my skin.

SWINGIN' THE JINX AWAY

Published September 1936. In his diary Porter mentions playing the song on May 2, 1936, for M-G-M executives. Dropped from the film on May 26, the number was subsequently reinstated. Introduced by Frances Langford and the Foursome Quartet; danced by Eleanor Powell and ensemble.

VERSE

Not . . . so many summers ago
The Land of New Dealin' was feelin' so low
That even folks in darkest Washington
Knew . . . something had to be done.
So they called . . . the country's cleverest
  ginks
To figure some plot out to blot out the jinx,
Yet no one had a mumblin' word to say
'Cept Professor Cab Calloway.
But Cab, the Wise,
Rose and said to these guys,
"If you're fixin' to beat this ole thing,
As a Harlem resident,
Mister President,
I say, 'Give 'em Swing.' "

REFRAIN

Now ev'rybody's happy,
And ev'ryone's gay,
'Cause ev'ry little mammy and pappy
Is swingin' the jinx away.

What is that thing they're all a-singin'?
Why, that's "hidy-hidy-hey,"
'Cause ev'rybody's buckin'-and-wingin',
Swingin' the jinx away.

From fair Niag'ra's fountains
To the far Rocky Mountains
They're swingin', swingin' away.

From the Swanee River
To the home of the flivver
They're swingin', swingin' away.

So ev'rybody's happy,
And ev'rybody's okay,
'Cause you can't be blue
When she's clingin' to you
And you're swingin' the jinx away.

PATTER

Just look at those cowboys gaily swingin' on the
  range,
Watch those brokers on that Stock Exchange,
Go to Hollywood and take time to scan
Ev'ry movie star swingin' the fan.
Drive through Maine and, b'lieve it, babe, or
  not,
You'll see ev'ry Blue Nose gettin' hot.
See how Indiana meets demands,
Hog breeders now are all leaders of bands.
Look at Montana,
Or Louisiana,
Examine Nebraska,
Or even Alaska,
Or visit the pris'ners in Alcatraz,
They're doin' time, but the time is jazz,
So . . .

REPEAT REFRAIN

Other numbers considered for *Born to Dance* included "Who but You?" (see *Red, Hot and Blue,* 1936) and possibly "That's the News I'm Waiting to Hear" (see *Red, Hot and Blue,* 1936). The earliest entries in Porter's oldest surviving notebook, hereafter referred to as "Titles and Ideas," date from 1936.

GOODBYE, LITTLE DREAM, GOODBYE

Published September 1936. This song was written, according to Porter's diary, on March 11, 1936, for Frances Langford to sing in *Born to Dance.* But it was not used in the film. Sung by Ethel Merman during the Boston tryout of *Red, Hot and Blue* (October 7, 1936), it was deemed "too somber" to be her first number in the show (New York *Times,* November 8, 1936) and was deleted. It was then introduced by Yvonne Printemps in the English production of *O Mistress Mine* (St. James Theatre, London, December 3, 1936). (Not to be confused with the 1944 Terence Rattigan play of the same title—called *Love in Idleness* in England.) Mme. Printemps recorded it with the Carroll Gibbons Orchestra on November 25, 1936. In recent years, the song has enjoyed a renaissance.

VERSE

I first knew love's delight,
When presto out of the blue,
A dream appeared one night
And whispered, "How do you do?"
I knew I was tempting fate
But I took it straight to my heart.
My fears were right, and now we must
  part.

REFRAIN

Goodbye, little dream, goodbye,
You made my romance sublime, now it's time to
  fly,
For the stars have fled from the heavens, the
  moon's deserted the hill,
And the sultry breeze that sang in the trees is

suddenly strangely still.
It's done, little dream, it's done,
So bid me a fond farewell, we both had our
fun.

Was it Romeo or Juliet who said when about to
die,
"Love is not all peaches and cream,"
Little dream, goodbye.

RED, HOT AND BLUE

1936

Tryout: Colonial Theatre, Boston, October 7, 1936; Shubert Theatre, New Haven, October 19, 1936. Produced by Vinton Freedley at the Alvin Theatre, New York, October 29, 1936. 183 performances. Book by Howard Lindsay and Russel Crouse. Directed by Howard Lindsay. Cast, starring Ethel Merman and Jimmy Durante, included Bob Hope, Polly Walters, Grace and Paul Hartman, Dorothy Vernon, and Thurston Crane.

In early 1935, Vinton Freedley went to Hollywood to confer with Samuel Goldwyn on a deal for Eddie Cantor to appear in a Broadway musical. On February 6, Freedley announced he had signed Cantor for a new, untitled musical comedy to be written by Howard Lindsay and Russel Crouse with music and lyrics by Cole Porter, who was on a world cruise at the time. In the spring of 1935, Freedley signed Ethel Merman and continued to wait for Cantor to be available. The show was originally planned for the fall of 1935. By August the names of William Frawley, Polly Walters, and Helen Broderick were added to those of Cantor and Merman. By late 1935, Cantor was out of the picture, which was fortunate in a way for Porter—if Cantor had participated, Porter's royalty would have been lower. Along the road to production a number of artists, including Jack Haley, Sid Silvers, Willie and Eugene Howard, Jack Benny, William Gaxton, George Rasely, Adele Dixon, Bert Lahr, and Wendy Barrie, were rumored to be in the show or were actually slated to appear in it. By June 1936, Freedley had signed Bob Hope. After a last try to get Willie Howard, he caught up with and engaged Jimmy Durante, who was vacationing in Capri.

In May 1936, the show's title was *But Millions,* which soon became "—But Millions $" and then was changed to *Wait for Baby.* In late July 1936, it became *Red, Hot and Blue,* which inspired Porter to write a song to fit the new title. In July 1936, dance director George Hale said at a press conference held during auditions that "no bad-looking babies were wanted. . . . Watch me come up with swell-looking bimbos. . . . The hard type is out. . . . So is the languid type. . . . Men like fresh, sweet girls—peppy, talented, and untheatrical." Hale asked the girls he was auditioning to sing "Is It True What They Say About Dixie?"

Porter, meanwhile, was concerned that his work was reaching an audience both too limited and too sophisticated. In an interview, Porter said, "Sophisticated allusions are good for about six weeks. Futile as presenting Sophocles in the original Greek. Audience reaction to Lady Mendl lasted about eight weeks. Sophisticated lyrics are more fun but only for myself and about eighteen other people, all of whom are first-nighters anyway. Polished, urbane, and adult playwriting in the musical field is strictly a creative luxury."

AT YE OLDE COFFEE SHOPPE IN CHEYENNE

Introduced by ensemble.

'Twas at Ye Olde Coffee Shoppe in Cheyenne
Where I first met my sweetheart, Little Nan.
I was soaping my stirrup
When she passed the maple syrup,
And our wild Western romance began.
Now she lies in the graveyard down the trail,
Laid away by little me, Windy Dan.
But though she's dead and gone
The maple syrup lingers on,
At Ye Olde Coffee Shoppe in Cheyenne, in my
Cheyenne.

IT'S A GREAT LIFE

"It's a Great Life" and "Perennial Debutantes" are linked numbers in the show. "Perennial Debutantes" was published in November 1936 in a special limited edition of songs from *Red, Hot and Blue* by Random House. Both numbers introduced by ensemble.

It's a great life, if you don't weaken,
Being a maiden in society today,
But unless you know the proper way to play,
You're always in danger
Of meeting a stranger
In the hay.
It's a grand game, if you're just seekin'
Simple diversion in this age of trouble and strife,
And if you keep the limbs nether
Fairly close together,
It's a damn swell
Racket for raising hell,
Well, it's a damn swell life.

PERENNIAL DEBUTANTES

Perennial debutantes, we come out ev'ry season,
Perennial debutantes, for a very simple reason—
The year when first
As buds we burst
We met so many nice men
We decided there and then
To come out ev'ry autumn all over again.

It's a pretty hard life we lead,
What with all this heavy drinking,
But the terrible rate of speed
At least keeps a girl from thinking.
So if someday
You become passé
And the boys won't
Ahsk you to dahnse,
Better start an intrigue
To join the big league
Of perennial debutantes,
Of perennial debutantes.

OURS

Published October 1936. Introduced by Dorothy Vernon and Thurston Crane; danced by Grace and Paul Hartman and ensemble.

VERSE

HE: The high gods above
Look down and laugh at our love,
And say to themselves, "How tawdry it's grown."
They've seen our cars
In front of so many bars,
When we should be under the stars,
Together, but alone.
Ours is the chance to make romance our own.

REFRAIN 1

HE: Ours, the white Riviera under the moon,
Ours, a gondola gliding on a lagoon,
Ours, a temple serene by the green Arabian Sea,
Or maybe you'd rather be going ga-ga in Gay Paree,
Ours, the silent Sierras greeting the dawn,
Or a sun-spotted Devonshire lawn dotted with flowers.
Mine, the inclination,
Yours, the inspiration,
Why don't we take a vacation
And make it all ours.

PATTER

SHE: Don't say "Venice" to me,
Or suggest that old Riviera,
Those faded hot spots fill me with gloom somehow.
As for a Hindu temple, my pet,
I wouldn't enter one on a bet.
Why, I'd be afraid of being chased by a sacred cow.
Don't expect me to dream
Of the silent Sierras, dear,
Or to love that fattening cream
That they give you in Devonshire.
Don't mention the wilds of Paris,
Or, as you call it, "Gay Paree."
I may not be right,
But New York is quite
Wild enough for me.

REFRAIN 2

SHE: Ours, the glitter of Broadway, Saturday night,
Ours, a box at the Garden, watching a fight,
Ours, the mad brouhaha of the Plaza's Persian Room,
Or, if this fills you with gloom,
We can go and admire Grant's tomb.
Ours, a home on the river facing the east,
Or on one of Park Avenue's least frightening tow'rs.
All the chat you're chattin'
Sounds to me like Latin,
Why don't we stay in Manhattan
And play it's all ours.

DOWN IN THE DEPTHS

Published October 1936. Introduced by Ethel Merman. Added to the show during the Boston tryout, October 15, 1936. In the New Haven program, it was listed as "On the 90th Floor." It replaced "Goodbye, Little Dream, Goodbye."

VERSE

Manhattan—I'm up a tree,
The one I've most adored
Is bored
With me.
Manhattan, I'm awf'lly nice,
Nice people dine with me,
And even twice.
Yet the only one in the world I'm mad about
Talks of somebody else
And walks out.

REFRAIN

With a million neon rainbows burning below me
And a million blazing taxis raising a roar

Here I sit, above the town
In my pet pailletted gown*
Down in the depths on the ninetieth floor.
While the crowds at El Morocco punish the parquet
And at "21" the couples clamor for more,†
I'm deserted and depressed
In my regal eagle nest
Down in the depths on the ninetieth floor.
When the only one you wanted wants another
What's the use of swank and cash in the bank galore?
Why, even the janitor's wife
Has a perfectly good love life‡
And here am I
Facing tomorrow
Alone with my sorrow
Down in the depths on the ninetieth floor.

CARRY ON

Introduced by Thurston Crane and ensemble.

Carry on, carry on,
Till the last ticket is gone,
So that Bob can have his Baby to cherish night and day,
And Baby can have her
ta-ra-ra-ra-boom-boom-de-ay.
Never sleep, never lag,
Till we get a billion in the bag.
On your toes, everyone,
There's dirty work to be done.
Carry on, carry on, carry on.
Come along, you flashy flyers,
Get buyers, buyers, buyers.
You've a job to do, so don't fall down,
Pick up your tickets and go to town.

**Or:*
Here I sit while deep despair
Haunts my castle in the air
†Or:
While the founders at Leon and Eddie's "roll down the mountain"
And the mobs that storm the Stork Club clutter the door,
Or:
While the crowds in all the night clubs punish the parquet
And the bars are packed with couples calling for more,
‡Or:
Why, even the janitor's wife
Has some sentiment in her life

If you want to do your duty
By romance in all its beauty,
Carry on, carry on,
Till the last ticket is gone,
So that Bob can have his Baby to cherish night and day,
And Baby can have her
ta-ra-ra-ra-boom-boom-de-ay.
Never sleep, never lag,
Till we get a billion in the bag.
On your toes, everyone,
There's dirty work to be done.
Carry on, carry on, carry on,
Carry on, carry on, carry on, carry on,
Carry on!

YOU'VE GOT SOMETHING

Published September 1936. Introduced by Bob Hope and Ethel Merman.

VERSE

Ev'ry time I'm near you, ev'ry time we touch,
I know well
I'm under your spell,
And a lot too much.
But there's no resisting, for I'm fully aware,
You somehow possess
A strange wondrousness
That's indefinable, but it's there.

REFRAIN

You've got something, darling, something
That's driving me slowly but surely insane,
Something tempting, something intangible,
Something rare that I never could explain.
So if gladly I admire you,
And madly desire you
All else above,
Please believe me or not,
It's merely because you've got
That certain something I love.

IT'S DE-LOVELY

Published September 1936. The title is sometimes given as "Delovely" or "It's D'lovely." The fifth refrain was found in the Porter Trusts office. It is not in the script.

Porter furnished two accounts of the genesis of "It's De-lovely":

> I took a world tour a couple of years ago, and I was in Java with Monty Woolley and Moss Hart. We'd just been served that famous Eastern fruit—the mangosteen—and were all enjoying it mightily. . . . Moss Hart said, "It's delightful!" I chimed in with "It's delicious." And Monty Woolley said, "It's de-lovely!" and there's the title of the song.
>
> In 1935 when my wife and I and Monty Woolley were approaching the harbor of Rio de Janeiro by boat, it was dawn. My wife and I had risen especially for the event, but Mr. Woolley had stayed up all night to see it and during the night had enjoyed a few whisky-and-sodas. As we stood on the bow of the boat my exclamation was "It's delightful!" My wife followed with "It's delicious!" And Monty, in his happy state, cried, "It's dee-lovely!" This last exclamation gave me the title for the song.

Introduced by Ethel Merman and Bob Hope.

VERSE 1

HE: I feel a sudden urge to sing
The kind of ditty that invokes the spring,
So control your desire to curse
While I crucify the verse.
SHE: This verse you've started seems to me
The Tin-Pantithesis of melody,
So spare me, please, the pain,
Just skip the damn thing and sing the refrain.
HE: Mi, mi, mi, mi,
Re, re, re, re,
Do, sol, mi, do, la, si.
SHE: Take it away.

REFRAIN 1

The night is young, the skies are clear,
So if you want to go walking, dear,
It's delightful, it's delicious, it's de-lovely.
I understand the reason why
You're sentimental, 'cause so am I,
It's delightful, it's delicious, it's de-lovely.
You can tell at a glance
What a swell night this is for romance,
You can hear dear Mother Nature murmuring low,
"Let yourself go."
So please be sweet, my chickadee,
And when I kiss you, just say to me,
"It's delightful, it's delicious,
It's delectable, it's delirious,
It's dilemma, it's delimit, it's deluxe,
It's de-lovely."

VERSE 2

SHE: Oh, charming sir, the way you sing
Would break the heart of Missus Crosby's Bing,
For the tone of your tra la la
Has that certain je ne sais quoi.
HE: Oh, thank thee kindly, winsome wench,
But 'stead of falling into Berlitz French
Just warble to me, please,
This beautiful strain in plain Brooklynese.
SHE: Mi, mi, mi, mi,
Re, re, re, re,
Do, sol, mi, do, la, si.
HE: Take it away.

REFRAIN 2

Time marches on and soon it's plain
You've won my heart and I've lost my brain,
It's delightful, it's delicious, it's de-lovely.
Life seems so sweet that we decide
It's in the bag to get unified,
It's delightful, it's delicious, it's de-lovely.
See the crowd in that church,
See the proud parson plopped on his perch,
Get the sweet beat of that organ, sealing our doom,
"Here goes the groom, boom!"
How they cheer and how they smile
As we go galloping down that aisle.
"It's divine, dear, it's diveen, dear,
It's de-wunderbar, it's de victory,
It's de vallop, it's de vinner, it's de voiks,
It's de-lovely."

REFRAIN 3

The knot is tied and so we take
A few hours off to eat wedding cake,
It's delightful, it's delicious, it's de-lovely.
It feels so fine to be a bride,
And how's the groom? Why, he's slightly fried,
It's delightful, it's delicious, it's de-lovely.
To the pop of champagne,
Off we hop in our plush little plane
Till a bright light through the darkness cozily calls,
"Niag'ra Falls."
All's well, my love, our day's complete,
And what a beautiful bridal suite,

"It's de-reamy, it's de-rowsy,
It's de-reverie, it's de-rhapsody,
It's de-regal, it's de-royal, it's de-Ritz,
It's de-lovely."

REFRAIN 4

We settle down as man and wife
To solve the riddle called "married life,"
It's delightful, it's delicious, it's de-lovely.
We're on the crest, we have no cares,
We're just a couple of honey bears,
It's delightful, it's delicious, it's de-lovely.
All's as right as can be
Till, one night, at my window I see
An absurd bird with a bundle hung on his nose—
"Get baby clo'es."
Those eyes of yours are filled with joy
When Nurse appears and cries, "It's a boy,"
"He's appalling, he's appealing,
He's a pollywog, he's a paragon,
He's a Popeye, he's a panic, he's a pip,
He's de-lovely."

REFRAIN 5

Our boy grows up, he's six feet three,
He's so good-looking, he looks like me,
It's delightful, it's delicious, it's de-lovely.
He's such a hit, this son of ours,
That all the dowagers send him flowers,
It's delightful, it's delicious, it's de-lovely.
So sublime is his press
That in time, L. B. Mayer, no less,
Makes a night flight to New York and tells him he should
Go Hollywood.
Good God! today, he gets such pay
That Elaine Barrie's his fiancée,
"It's delightful, it's delicious,
It's delectable, it's delirious,
It's dilemma, it's delimit, it's deluxe,
It's de-lovely."

CURTAIN, ACT I

MERMAN: It's a failure.
HOPE: It's a fold-up.
MERMAN: It's a fade-away.
HOPE: It's a fare-thee-well.
MERMAN: It's affliction.
DURANTE: It's a flaccus.
HOPE: What does that mean?
DURANTE: Well, don't pin me down.
MERMAN: It's a—(*curtain*)

A LITTLE SKIPPER FROM HEAVEN ABOVE

RED, HOT AND BLUE
1936

Published October 1936. Introduced by Jimmy Durante and ensemble.

VERSE

The raging sou'wester was over,
It was calm and the heavens had cleared,
The sails were gently flapping,
The sailors all a-napping,
When their hero, Captain Cosgrove, appeared.
It was obvious he had been crying,
And he seemed to have lost all his poise
As he stood there, so stark,
And was heard to remark,
"I've got something to say to you, boys"—

REFRAIN 1

I'm about to become a mother,
I'm only a girl, not a boy.
Years ago I disguised as my brother
And went rolling down to Rio, ship ahoy.
Though it hurts me to leave you, my hearties,
Still you must understand, it was love,
And I'm about to give birth
To the sweetest thing on earth,
A little skipper from heaven above.

REFRAIN 2

I'm about to become a mother,
I'm only a girl, not a boy
(Strange as it may seem to you).
Years ago I discovers my brother was a nance,
So I gives him my petticoats and puts on his pants,
Then I finds me a sailor who's lookin' for romance,
Ship ahoy, man the scuppers!
Though this data I gotta may hurt-a
(But believe me, lads),
My name isn't Robert, it's Roberta,
And I'm about to give birth
To the sweetest thing on earth—
A little skipper from heaven,
A little skip, skip, skip, skip, skipper,
A little nip, nip, nip, nip, nipper,
A little dripper from heaven above.

FIVE HUNDRED MILLION

First sung by the Wallace Sisters. After they left the show, but before the New York opening, the song was given to Vivian Vance and Betty Allen.

WALLACE SISTERS: Five hundred million in the dear days of old
Meant half a billion, and half a billion in gold.
DEBUTANTES: Let us shed a little tear
For the gold of yesteryear.
WALLACE SISTERS: With five hundred million
In that age of renown,
Any healthy civilian
Could proceed to go to town.
DEBUTANTES: In that era so sublime
He could really give himself a time.
WALLACE SISTERS: With five hundred million
In those days forever lost
Any hospitable civilian
Could afford to give a big cotillion
In a silk-lined pavilion
Full of dancers Castilian
And music Cuban and Brazilian
Without once thinking of the cost.
DEBUTANTES: His income was so immense
That he could say, "To hell with the expense."
WALLACE SISTERS: But today, what with the fed'ral tax,
The state tax and the process tax,
1ST TWO DEBUTANTES: The unemployment tax and the sales tax,
2ND TWO DEBUTANTES: The corporation tax and the gift tax,
WALLACE SISTERS: The gasoline tax and the liquor tax,
And the taxes still to come,
DEBUTANTES: Why, five hundred million is a very small sum.
WALLACE SISTERS: And so, if we win the prize,
We shall not give a ball,
For we know before the day is o'er
The government will take it all.
DEBUTANTES: Oh, how very wise
To realize
They couldn't give a ball,
For we know before the day is o'er
The President will tell the government
To take it all.
WALLACE SISTERS: The President
Won't be content
Till the government
Has spent it all.

RIDIN' HIGH

Published September 1936. Sometimes referred to as "How'm I Ridin'?" Introduced by Ethel Merman and ensemble.

VERSE

Love had socked me,
Simply knocked me
For a loop.
Luck had dished me
Till you fished me
From the soup.
Now, together,
We can weather
Anything.
So please don't sputter
If I should mutter:

REFRAIN

Life's great, life's grand,
Future all planned,
No more clouds in the sky.
How'm I ridin'? I'm ridin' high.

Someone I love,
Mad for my love,
So long, Jonah, goodbye.
How'm I ridin'? I'm ridin' high.

Floating on a starlit ceiling,
Doting on the cards I'm dealing,
Gloating, because I'm feeling
So hap-hap-happy,
I'm slap-happy.

So ring bells, sing songs,
Blow horns, beat gongs,
Our love never will die.
How'm I ridin'? I'm ridin' high.

PATTER 1

What do I care
If Missus Harrison Williams is the best-dressed woman in town?

What do I care
If Countess Barbara Hutton has a Rolls-Royce
built for each gown?
Why should I have the vapors
When I read in the papers
That Missus Simpson dined behind the throne?
I've got a cute king of my own.
What do I care
If Katie Hepburn is famous for the world's most
beautiful nose,*
Or if I, for my sins,
Don't possess underpins
Like the pegs "Legs" Dietrich shows?
I'm feeling swell,
In fact so well
It's time some noise began,
For although I'm not
A big shot,
Still, I've got my man.

So ring bells, sing songs,
Blow horns, beat gongs,
Our love never will die.
How'm I ridin'? I'm ridin' high.

PATTER 2

What do I care
If Missus Dorothy Parker has the country's
wittiest brain?
What do I care
If little Eleanor Jarrett only swims in vintage
champagne?
Why should I be a-flutter
When Republicans mutter
That Missus R. gets pay to write her day,
If I could write my nights, hey, hey!
What do I care
If fair Tallulah possesses tons and tons of jewels
from gents?
Or if someone observes
That I haven't the curves
That Simone Simon presents?†
I'm doin' fine,
My life's divine,
I'm living in the sun
'Cause I've a big date
With my fate,
So I rate
A-1.

So ring bells, sing songs,
Blow horns, beat gongs,
Our love never will die.
How'm I ridin'? I'm ridin' high.

Or:
If Shirley Temple goes swimming in a pool just brimming
with beaux,

†*Or:*
That the gay Mae West presents?

WE'RE ABOUT TO START BIG REHEARSIN'

"We're About to Start Big Rehearsin' " and "Hymn to Hymen," linked pair of ensemble numbers, opened Act II.

We're about to start big rehearsin'
For the marriage of Baby and Bob,
And it makes our tender hearts throb
When we think of that chap
Taking that rap.
For we know that Nails is the person
That he pets when he gets amorous,
So forgive this "aside,"
But speaking of the bride,
Thank God it's not us.

HYMN TO HYMEN

Hymen, thou phony
God of matrimony,
Humbly we pray, keep away from our door.
Those thou hast mated
Say thou art overrated
And call thee a dated, unmitigated bore.
Why wouldst thou tie us
In wedlock, holy and pious,
Knowing as thou doest
Love is truest when it's free.
So, Hymen, thou phony
God of matrimony,
We say baloney to thee.

WHAT A GREAT PAIR WE'LL BE

Published in the Random House limited edition, November 1936. Introduced by Dorothy Vernon and Thurston Crane; danced by Grace and Paul Hartman and ensemble.

VERSE

HE: Let the modern cynics all laugh at
marriage
And say that it's not worth the fuss,
SHE: But an illegitimate baby carriage
Would never go down with us.
HE: Just the thought we're heading
For a bona fide wedding
Is enough to fill my heart with delight.
SHE: And when once we're mated
And get well domesticated,
We will prove to them all we were
right,
BOTH: Yes, completely prove we were right.

REFRAIN

BOTH: What a great pair we'll be,
What a swell sight to see
When as girl and boy
We taste the full joy
Of sweet matrimony.
SHE: What a lush life to lead,
What a lilting poem to read,
HE: When, with flags unfurled,
We show the whole world
What bliss marriage can be.
SHE: How we'll glory in our story,
How we'll thank the stars we're alive,
HE: How our love will prosper and thrive
SHE: In that cottage for two,
HE: Or three,
SHE: Or four,
HE: Or five.
SHE: And when you've made your pile
And we've grown our own family tree,
HE: What a proud,
Unbearably stuffy,
But terribly great pair we will be.
SHE: What a swell sight to see
When I'm eighty and you're eighty-three,
BOTH: As we scan the years
And chirrup, "Three cheers
For sweet matrimony."

YOU'RE A BAD INFLUENCE ON ME

Published October 1936. Introduced by Ethel Merman. Note the difference between the published and the show versions. Dropped soon after the New York opening.

VERSE

Since first you crossed my horizon
With your load of love charms,
I spend my whole time devisin'
Means to stay in your arms.
There must be some tricky treatment that would
cool my brain,
For to me it's so plain,
And you'll admit the fact that I'm practic'lly
sane.

REFRAIN 1

You're a bad influence on me, sorry,
But you're a bad influence, I must say,
For I get in such a dither
When you use your famous "come hither"
That all thoughts of Hame and Mither
Seem to wither away.
The thing your eyes do to me is such folly,
That I feel sure your middle name must be
Svengali.
Your ev'ry move fills me with fright,
But I beg you, dear, come up tonight*
And be a bad influence on me.

REFRAIN 2

You're a bad influence on me, sorry,
But you're a bad influence, I must say,
For I get in such a dither
When you use your famous "come hither"
That all thoughts of Hame and Mither
Seem to wither away.
When you appear, dear, I want to start
shootin'
'Cause I'm sure you used to say black mass with
Rasputin.
I wish you'd cease singeing my wings,
But before you do, take off your things
And be a bad influence on me.

THE OZARKS ARE CALLIN' ME HOME

Published December 1936. It replaced "You're a Bad Influence on Me" in late November 1936. Introduced by Ethel Merman.

**Published version:*
You throw me way out of my stride,
Still I beg of you, stay by my side

VERSE

Oh, the great big wicked city
Is losin' all its thrill,
And each day finds me feelin' more forlorn,
'Cause I might be sittin' pretty
On a green Missouri hill,
In the Ozark Mountains where I was born.

REFRAIN 1

I've a feelin' the Ozarks are callin',
And I've also a feelin' I'm fallin',
So I'll soon be leavin' town,
'Cause the city has let me down,
And the Ozarks are callin' me home.

I'm already in the kitchen fryin' chicken,
And I hear Paw givin' Maw her daily lickin',
While a-stretchin' on the floor
Is the mule that we all adore,
Oh, the Ozarks are callin' me home.

Why, there's tiny tongue-tied Baby Jane, by
cracky,
Givin' ole Gran'paw a chaw of her tobaccy,
And there's Gran'maw, I declare,
Wrasslin' round with a big black bear,
Oh, the Ozarks are callin' me home.

I can see dear Aunt Eliza in the rocker,
Readin' Andy Gump and Cholly Knickerbocker,
And there's bashful sister Ann
Makin' hay with a travelin' man,
Oh, the Ozarks are callin' me home,
Callin' me home, home, home, sweet home.

REFRAIN 2

I've a feelin' the Ozarks are callin',
And I've also a feelin' I'm fallin',
So I'll soon be leavin' town,
'Cause the city has let me down,
And the Ozarks are callin' me home.

It is April, and the trees are all in blossom,
And in ev'ry single tree I see a possum,
While a-struttin' round there still
Is the rooster we couldn't kill,
Oh, the Ozarks are callin' me home.

I see dear deaf brother Jeff, while his tomata
Plays the "Melody in F" on her potata,
And Aunt Pansy, pink and plump,
Takes a shower beneath the pump,
Oh, the Ozarks are callin' me home.

Why, there's Uncle Ezra sleepin' in the gutter,
He walked forty miles today to borrow butter,
And, hello, here comes those two
Little bastards of sweet Aunt Sue,†
Oh, the Ozarks are callin' me home,
Callin' me home, home, home, sweet home.

RED, HOT AND BLUE

Published October 1936. Introduced by Ethel Merman and ensemble.

VERSE

Due to the tragic lowness of my brow,
All music that's highbrow
Gets me upset.
Each time I hear a strain of Stravinsky's,
I hurry to Minsky's
And try to forget.
I don't like Schubert's music or Schumann's,
I'm one of those humans
Who only goes in for Berlin and Vincent
Youmans.
I'm for the guy that eludes
Bach sonatas and Chopin preludes.
So when some nice man I meet,
I always murmur tout d'suite:

REFRAIN 1

If you want to thrill me and drill me for your
crew,
Sing me a melody that's red, hot and blue.
Before you expand on that grand cottage for two,
Sing me a melody that's Red, Hot and Blue,
I can't take Sibelius,
Or Delius,
But I swear I'd throw my best pal away
For Calloway,
So when we're all set and I get married to you,
Don't let that violin
Start playing *Lohengrin*,
It may be sweet as sin
But it's not red, hot and blue.

REFRAIN 2

If you ask me, toots,
Just what puts
Me in a stew,
Sing me a melody that's red, hot and blue.
If I'm quite correct,
You expect

†*Or:*
Little half-wits of sweet Aunt Sue,

Me to come through,
Sing me a melody that's red, hot and blue.
This craze that's pursuin' me,
May ruin me,
But my Waterloo won't be Wellington
But Ellington.
So if you feel tonight
Like a light
Ev'ning for two,
I've no desire to hear
Flagstad's Brünnhilde, dear,
She waves a pretty spear,
But she's not red, hot and blue.

WHEN YOUR TROUBLES HAVE STARTED

This number was dropped from Act I, Scene I during the show's Boston tryout. It was published in *The Unpublished Cole Porter.*

VERSE

As reporters who interview the Jezebels of crime,
And who've seen them bowed down with care
As they crouch in their cubicles
Waiting for the time
When they can feel the real comfort of the chair,
We have grown so accustomed to the tragedies of
life
That if our own little plans go wrong,
'Stead of asking for arsenic or calling for a knife,
We simply sing this song:

REFRAIN

When your troubles have started,
When your luck has departed,
When you feel so downhearted
That you're ready to curse,
When the blues that you've got-oh
Make you want to get blotto,
Just remember this motto:
"It might be a helluva lot worse."

PATTER

For example—
If your phone is out of order,
If your car is on the fritz,
If you suddenly get the hiccoughs
When you're dining at the Ritz,
If you can't have ev'ning callers
'Cause your pa is such a prude
And he can't prevent your mother
From appearing in the nude,
If you saw a dress at Saks
For which you'd just give up the ghost,
Then you see it being sported
By the girl you hate the most,
If you think your heavy lover
Is about to propose,
But instead he says, "You've got a little
Soot on your nose,"
If your bath starts leaking,
And your bed starts creaking,
If you take your Johnnie walking
And your shoes start squeaking,
If such unimportant matters
Make you think the world's wrong,
Don't rant but simply chant
This song:

REPEAT REFRAIN

BERTIE AND GERTIE

Unused. Dropped during rehearsals.

VERSE

SHE: Oh, gentle stranger, tell me who are you.
HE: Why, I'm Bertie, a bad butterfly.
SHE: It's nice to know that you're an insect too,
'Cause a sad little honeybee am I.
For I find this year, the price of pollen is so
dear
That I don't know what on earth to do with
my life.
HE: Come, my sweet, don't mope,
While there's life there's always hope.
Stick to me and I'll show you the high
life.

REFRAIN

HE: I'm Bertie, a bad little butterfly.
SHE: I'm Gertie, a sad little bee.
My skies aren't so sunny 'cause I'm not in
the money,
And you can't get honey free.
HE: Then come to my bach'lor apartment,
dear,
And I'll open my old eau-de-vie.
SHE: Oh, thank you, sweet Bertie, but now you're
getting dirty.
HE: Why, Gertie, you mad little bee.

PATTER

SHE: They tell me in New York you're very social this year.
HE: Yes, as Cholly Knickerbocker says, "Just hectic, my dear,"
For one mustn't miss the horse show,
And one must attend the fights,
SHE: And one must be there to grin and bear those long op'ning nights.
HE: Then, of course, there's the opera and those boring exhibitions
SHE: And those parties where songwriters play their latest compositions.
What with all my invitations to those great marble halls,
My life is just a series of balls, balls, balls—
SHE: Why, Bertie, you bad little butterfly.
HE: Why, Gertie, you mad little bee.

WHO BUT YOU?

Unused. Also dropped from *Born to Dance* (1936).

VERSE

I suppose my best chances are small,
But ev'ry word I say is sincere.
No one else but you matters at all,
And I couldn't live without you near.
Why not be the high spot in my career?
Listen, dear.

REFRAIN

Who but you
Could ever make me feel as happy as I do?
Who but you?

Who but you
Could cheer me up those moments when I'm, oh, so blue,
Who but you?

Who, apart
From you, panics my heart?

Who else gives my brain the buzz
That my baby does?

And when, one fine day,
I get a cozy hideaway,
Who's got to be there too?
Who but you?

THAT'S THE NEWS I'M WAITING TO HEAR

Unused.

When some fine night with the stars above
You tell me I'm all on earth you love,
That's the news I'm waiting to hear.
When you decide in the early spring
You'd like to wear my engagement ring,
That's the news that's needed to tickle my ear.
Though Mr. Hearst
May do his worst
To give me hot news,
Unless he tells
Of our wedding bells,
Darling, it's not news.
But when you say with a smile sublime
That you could bear me at breakfast time,
That's the news I'm
Waiting to hear.

WHERE?

Unused. No music survives.

Where could there be a more perfect pair
Than you and me?
Where could one find
Such a combination of heart and mind?
How could we fail,
You went to finishing school,
I went to Yale.
So where could there be a more perfect pair
Than you and me?

LONELY STAR

Unused. No music survives.

Lonely star, the astronomers say you're so far,
Yet you seem so near to me,
Lonely star.
Lonely star, I am lonelier far than you are,
For someone so dear to me,
Lonely star.
As you wander the silent night

Through the heavens above,
You've no need for the guiding light
Of requited love.
Lonely star, what a precious example you are,
You've a light of your own,
Lonely star.

There are also a number of lyric fragments that survive from this show.

ROSALIE

1937

"Rosalie," 1937; Eleanor Powell and Nelson Eddy

A film produced by William Anthony McGuire for M-G-M in 1937. Released December 24, 1937. Screenplay by William Anthony McGuire, based on the musical comedy libretto by McGuire and Guy Bolton. Directed by W. S. Van Dyke. Cast, starring Nelson Eddy and Eleanor Powell, included Frank Morgan, Edna May Oliver, Ray Bolger, and Ilona Massey.

WHO KNOWS?

Published September 1937. Introduced by Lois Clements (dubbed by Camille Sorey, later known as Julie Gibson). Reprised by Lois Clements/Camille Sorey and Nelson Eddy. Danced by Eddy and Eleanor Powell.

VERSE

Being here by your side seems somehow so right
That I find myself asking whether
We are merely two ships that pass in the night
Or will we, one day, be docked close together?
All common sense tells me it's not to be,
So why does my heart
Suddenly start
To whisper, "It's got to be"?

REFRAIN

HE: Who knows?
Who knows?
Not even the stars above.
Who knows
But one night
We two
Might fall in love,
Who knows?
I might have success,
You might answer "yes"
When I propose.
Dreams do
So often come true,
But outside of you
Who knows?

SHE: Who knows?
Who knows?
Not even the stars above.
Who knows
But one night
We two
Might fall in love,
Who knows?
You might have success
I might answer "yes"
When you propose.
Dreams do
So often come true,
But outside of you
Who knows?

I'VE A STRANGE NEW RHYTHM IN MY HEART

Published September 1937. Introduced by Eleanor Powell and ensemble.

VERSE

If you've noticed I'm
Doing a time step all the time,
If my walk of late,
Has a syncopated gait,
If I start to swing
The moment the postman gives a ring,
Cease your endless chatter
And I'll tell you what's the matter—

REFRAIN

Since I gazed in someone's eyes,
To my joy I realize
I've a strange new rhythm in my heart.
Perhaps as she (he) seemed to be
A bit more than fond of me
I've a strange new rhythm in my heart.

This beat, beat, beating
I'm talking of
Goes on repeating,
"You're in luck, Lonesome,
You're in love!"

So I'm always dancing now,
For I find that life somehow
Is so-oh much sweeter
Since I found this meter,
This c-razy st-range new rhythm in my heart.

ROSALIE

Published September 1937. Porter wrote several versions of what became the film's title song. Not all of them survive. This final version was introduced by Nelson Eddy and frequently reprised by the ensemble.

First or Serenade Version*

REFRAIN

Rosalie, dear,
You are my guiding star.
Rosalie, near,
Rosalie, near or far,
Why does a radiant halo gleam about you?
Why am I happier when I dream about you?
Oh, Rosalie, rare,
Rosalie, divine,
When can I say "Rosalie, mine"?
When will you be
My Rosalie?

Sixth version

VERSE

Since first you murmured your name to me,
Your name, in heaven designed,
The night no longer is the same to me
For I've only "Rosalie" on my mind.
Why does the sound of it thrill me through and
through?
Is it my Song of Songs
Because it belongs
To

REFRAIN

Rosalie, Rosalie,
I keep repeating "Rosalie,"
Just a name, just a word,
Yet still the sweetest I ever heard.
On I go, never I tire,
For ev'ry syllable sets my heart afire.
What can be
The strange flame
That hallows thy name?
Rosalie, could it be love?

Published version

VERSE

When knighthood was in flow'r
And a man wooed a maid,
Beneath her sacred bow'r
He sang a serenade.
I date,
I suppose,
It's late
Heaven knows,
It blows
And it snows,
But anyway, here goes:

REFRAIN

Rosalie, my darling,
Rosalie, my dream,
Since, one night, when stars danced above,
I'm oh, oh, so much in love.
So, Rosalie, have mercy,
Rosalie, don't decline,
Won't you make my life thrilling,
And tell me you're willing
To be mine, Rosalie, mine.

*The verse for this version is the same as the verse used for the published version.

WHY SHOULD I CARE?

Published September 1937. Introduced by Frank Morgan.

VERSE

Now of late, the daily papers
Say the government's cash is low,
And to keep on cutting capers
They've got to have lots more dough,
But whenever I feel worried,
After reading such news as this,
I hie me back
To my grimy shack,
And my sweetheart gives me a kiss.

REFRAIN

Why should I care
When my sweetheart is there?
Why should I cry
If the taxes go sky high?
Why should I curse
When the Treasury trims my purse?
Why should I care?
I know my sweetheart is there.
Tra, la, la, la,
La, la, la, la, la, la,
Tra, la, la, la,
La, la, la, la, la, la, la.
How can it hurt
If the government takes my shirt?
Why should I care?
I know my sweetheart is still there.

SPRING LOVE IS IN THE AIR

Copyrighted unpublished May 1937. Introduced by Ilona Massey and chorus; danced by the Albertina Rasch Dancers.

SOLO: At last, the winter is over,
And the wind from the northland is still,
The trees have lost
Their garments of frost,
And the snow has gone from the hill.
The sun, no longer a stranger,
Smiles down as one by one the flow'rs appear,
The lamb looks out from his manger,
You're in danger,
Spring love is here.

The spring brooks are laughing,
The spring skies are fair,
The spring breeze
Is wooing the trees,
And spring love is in the air.
Spring flow'rs fill the meadow,
And there's sweet perfume ev'rywhere.
So beware, stranger,
Your heart is in danger,
For spring love is in the air.

ALL: Hi!
Hi!
Hi!
Hi!
SOLO: Stranger, best be wary when you wander,
Stranger, love is waiting just over yonder.
CHORUS: Stranger, lonely stranger,
Spring's here and you're in danger.
SOLO: Lover, better heed the gypsy's warning,
Lover, or you'll curse yourself in the morning.
CHORUS: Lover, run for cover,
Take care,
For there is spring love ev'rywhere.
ALL: Hi!
Hi!
Hi!
Hi!
Hi!
Hi!
SOLO: So beware, stranger,
Your heart is in danger,
For spring love is in the air,
Spring love is in the air,
Spring love,
ALL: Spring love,
SOLO: Spring love is in the air
ALL: Hoopla!

CLOSE

Published September 1937. Intended for Nelson Eddy, but his vocal rendition was deleted from the film, leaving only a background instrumental version.

VERSE

I've longed for this, ever since the day
I lost you just when I'd found you,
A stream, a garden, a night in May,
And you, with my arms around you,
Now it has all come true
And I'm close to you.

REFRAIN

Close
To you, dear,
While the trees moan above,
Close
I can hear
Only our song of love.
Close
To your kiss,
So soft, so sweet, so warm,
Close
To such bliss,
Why should I fear the storm?
All gone
Is the wail
Of the wind through the night,
Dawn
Lifts her veil
On a sea, sparkling bright,
As on,
On we sail
To the land of our dreams,
How lovely life seems
When I'm close to you.

IN THE STILL OF THE NIGHT

Published September 1937. This number, reputed to have made L. B. Mayer cry, was introduced by Nelson Eddy.

In the still of the night,
As I gaze from my window
At the moon in its flight,
My thoughts all stray to you.
In the still of the night,*
While the world is in slumber,
Oh, the times without number,
Darling, when I say to you,
"Do you love me as I love you?
Are you my life-to-be, my dream come true?"
Or will this dream of mine
Fade out of sight
Like the moon
Growing dim
On the rim
Of the hill
In the chill,
Still
Of the night?

IT'S ALL OVER BUT THE SHOUTING

Copyrighted unpublished June 1937. A partial vocal was introduced by the ensemble and Nelson Eddy.

VERSE

EDDY: Well, the Navy's where she should be, in a deep doleful grave,
And I only wish I could be on the crest of the wave,
But I look at that football, and my glee becomes gloom,
To think of it getting dusty in a trophy room.
BOLGER: Fare thee well, little pigskin, fare thee well.

REFRAIN

EDDY: It's all over but the shouting,
Our fighting days are done.
We've played the game,
We've achieved our aim,
For we've won, men, we've won!
You will soon be going your way,
I will soon be going mine,
It's all over but the shouting,
So here's a cheer for Auld Lang Syne.

In Eddy's film vocal, the first five lines are:
In the still of the night,
While I'm drifting and dreaming,
In the still of the night,
My thoughts all stray to you.
By the moon's mellow light,

TO LOVE OR NOT TO LOVE

Copyrighted unpublished July 1937. Introduced by Nelson Eddy, Ray Bolger, and ensemble. Only a portion of the song was used.

VERSE

Love—
My evil curse, my deadly foe,
My bitter pill, my cup of woe,
My sunless vale of tears, my burden of sorrow!

Oh, love—
My greatest good, my dearest friend,
My happy chance, my trouble's end,
My dawn, my light, my life, my rosy tomorrow!

If I leave my heart in your care,
Will my destiny be joy or despair?

REFRAIN

To love or not to love,
That is the question to decide.
To love or not to love,
To brazen the danger or to hide.
To say, as ev'ry cynic says,
"Love had only lonely hours to give."
Or to say, "Sweetheart,
If ever we must part,
Let's die for love and start to live!"

OPENING, ROMANZA SEQUENCE

"Opening, Romanza Sequence" and "Entrance of Prince Paul," both ensemble numbers, were to be performed in sequence. Both songs were unused, although the film's musical cue sheet lists partial use of an instrumental version. "Opening, Romanza Sequence" was copyrighted unpublished July 1937.

1ST GROUP
OF MEN: Oh, the Feast Day of the Saints

Is a day when ev'rybody cheers,
For it's the one day
When Romanza goes gay,
And the whole royal family appears.

2ND GROUP OF MEN: First the King in full-dress regalia,

3RD GROUP OF MEN: Then the Queen with all her paraphernalia,

4TH GROUP OF MEN: And to top them, looking as lovely as can be,
Our highly prized, Americanized Rosalie.

1ST GROUP OF GIRLS: First, in splendor, leading the big parade,
Comes the one we worship the most of all.

2ND GROUP OF GIRLS: We refer to the pet of ev'ry maid,
Our hero, good Prince Paul.

1ST GROUP OF MEN: Make way, the trumpets call,
There go the drums,
Here he comes,
Prince Paul!

ENTRANCE OF PRINCE PAUL

GIRLS: When Prince Paul rides forth, all the girls in town
Bow down, as well they should,
Not because of his rank
Or his infinite swank,
But because Prince Paul is so good.
He's so good to ev'ry maiden he meets
That no wonder we shout when he steps out in the streets—

Hip hooray for good Prince Paul,
Hip hooray for nice Prince Paul,
He may not be, perhaps,
The most reliable of chaps
But he's, oh, so good to us all.
Hip hooray for kind Prince Paul,
Hip hooray for sweet Prince Paul,
He may not be, perhaps,
The most reliable of chaps,
But he's, oh, so good to us all!

PRINCE PAUL: Good morning, Mareea, good morning, Estelle,
Good morning, Sopheea, good morning, Isabel,
Good morning, Amelia, you're looking fine and dandy,
Good morning, Cecelia, and thank you for the candy,
Good morning, Diana, and don't forget to write,
Good morning, fair Susanna, Hannah, good night!

GIRLS: Hip hooray for good Prince Paul,
Hip hooray for nice Prince Paul,
He may not be, perhaps,
The most reliable of chaps,
But he's, oh, so good to us all.
Hip hooray for kind Prince Paul,
Hip hooray for sweet Prince Paul,
He may not be, perhaps,
The most reliable of chaps,
But he's, oh, so good to us all.

DISCONTENTED MALES: We simply can't understand at all
Why all the girls go for *that* Prince Paul.
It can't be money and it can't be brains,
Why, he doesn't know enough to come in when it rains.
We never once heard a single rumor
That he had the slightest sense of humor,
So why *do* the ladies love him such a lot?
What has Prince Paul got
That we haven't got?

GIRLS: Hip hooray for good Prince Paul.
MEN: Not at all, not at all.
Down
GIRLS: Up
MEN & GIRLS: With Prince Paul!

I KNOW IT'S NOT MEANT FOR ME

Copyrighted unpublished June 1937. Published 1975 in *The Unpublished Cole Porter.* Intended for Ray Bolger. Although the cue sheet indicates that a portion of this number was used, I have never heard it in the film.

VERSE

As far as love goes,
Each time I do
The moon above goes,
The lady too.*
Still I continue
Fighting against my fate,
For, oh gee, it certainly must be greater than
great.

REFRAIN

To fall in love, to go insane,
And then to find it wasn't all in vain,
What a joy that would be,
But I know it's not meant for me.
To say, one day, "Perhaps we might
Be married soon," then to your huge delight
Have your sweetheart agree,
But I know it's not meant for me.
Never daunted, ever scheming,
What a fool! Why am I always dreaming
Of that home, sweet home I so desire,
That easy chair before an open fire,
And the missus upon my knee,†
When I know it's not meant for me?

*Or:
The lover too.
†Or:
And a youngster upon each knee,

A FOOL THERE WAS

Copyrighted unpublished June 1936. Earlier that month Porter signed a contract with M-G-M to write songs for the film that became *Rosalie.* This song was not used.

A fool there was, goes the story,
A fool there was not long ago,
Who dreamed of love in all its glory,
He was mad, poor fool, he didn't know.

This fool laid eyes on a maiden,
A maid as dazzling as the dawn,
And, of course, the dunce
Fell in love with her at once,
But she laughed and told him to be gone.

A fool there was, broken-hearted,
To see his dream suddenly die,
Till he woke and said,
"My heart once ruled my head,
But no longer a fool am I."

YOU NEVER KNOW

1938

Tryout: Shubert Theatre, New Haven, March 3, 1938; Shubert Theatre, Boston, March 7, 1938; National Theatre, Washington, March 21, 1938; Forrest Theatre, Philadelphia, March 28, 1938; Nixon Theatre, Pittsburgh, April 18, 1938; Cass Theatre, Detroit, April 24, 1938; Grand Opera House, Chicago, May 1, 1938; Shrine Auditorium, Des Moines, May 22, 1938; English's Theatre, Indianapolis, May 23, 1938; Hartman Theatre, Columbus, May 27, 1938; Erlanger Theatre, Buffalo, May 29, 1938; Bushnell Auditorium, Hartford, September 16, 1938. Produced by Lee and J. J. Shubert, in association with John Shubert, at the Winter Garden Theatre, New York, September 21, 1938. 78 performances. Book adapted by Rowland Leigh from *By Candlelight.* Directed by Rowland Leigh. Cast, starring Clifton Webb, Lupe Velez, and Libby Holman, included Toby Wing, Rex O'Malley, Charles Kemper, and June Preisser.

I AM GASTON

Added to the show during its long pre-Broadway tryout. Introduced by Clifton Webb.

GASTON (IN FRONT OF CURTAIN): Ladies and gentlemen,
I beg of you, throw down
That useless program.
Ladies and gentlemen,
If you wish the lowdown
On just who I am,
I'm Gaston,
The famous Gaston,
A butler-valet so superb at the game
That in the swell set,
The hotter-than-hell set,
Nobody's ever heard my fam'ly name.
You mention Tom,
They know it's Lamont.
You speak of Henry,
It's Henry DuPont.
You're painted by Neysa,
Of course, McMein.
You rave about Dizzy,
They don't say, "Who is he?"
You borrow from Barney,
It must be Baruch.
You hula with Doris,
It's got to be Duke.
And what's the other name of
Cordell?
It's Hull.
And of Gaston? Well, there's a lull.

REFRAIN

For I'm Gaston, Gaston,
A man without a fam'ly name,
I'd gladly filch
The name of Zilch,
Or even sign
As Finkelstein,
But Gaston, Gaston
Will stick when even I have passed on,
And I know in heaven's bar,
Thirsty angels from near and far
Will cry for Gaston, Gaston, take
this—
Gaston, Gaston, bring that—
More drinks, Gaston, Gaston, more
drinks—
Gaston!

CROWD (BEHIND CURTAIN): Gaston!
Gaston!

GASTON: There you are!

AU REVOIR, CHER BARON

This ensemble number was also added to the show during its pre-Broadway tour.

FRENCH GROUP: Au revoir, cher Baron, au revoir.
1ST GUEST: Gaston, good day.
FRENCH GROUP: Ah! Mon dieu, what a chic host you are.
2ND GUEST (TO GASTON): My coat, si'l vous plaît.

ENGLISH GROUP: Toodle-oo, dyeah Baron, toodle-oo.
3RD GUEST: Gaston, my stick.
ENGLISH GROUP: Such a hearty cocktail party, thenks to you.
4TH GUEST (TO GASTON): A taxi, quick.

GERMAN GROUP: Danke, danke, Baron, auf Wiedersehen.
5TH GUEST: Gaston, good night.
GERMAN GROUP: It is wunderbar, the vay you entertain.
6TH GUEST: Gaston, I'm tight.

SPANISH GROUP: Adios, muchacho, you're the last aristocrat.

ITALIAN GROUP: Arrivederci, dear fellow, e che bello, your little flat.

. . .

ONE AMERICAN MAN: Boy, the scotch sure was swell, oh say, Gaston, where's my hat?
I'll see yuh soon.
ITALIANS: Arrivederci,
SPANISH: Adios,
GERMANS: Auf Wiedersehen,
ENGLISH: Toodle-oo,
FRENCH: Au revoir,
BARON & GASTON: And that's that.

MARIA

Published April 1938. Introduced by Clifton Webb and ensemble.

Maria,
You say your name is Maria?

REFRAIN

Maria, oh, what a lovely name,
Maria, it sets my heart aflame.
Your laughter has all the music of a cool summer breeze,
That sings on the hilltop and dances in the trees.
Reply, dear, and say what would you do,
If I, dear, tonight should come to you.
Maria, you say that such a panacea could never be,
Oh, cara mia,
Why can't you learn to love me?
You know, I love you,
Maria, won't you love me?

YOU NEVER KNOW

Two versions of this song exist. The version published in April 1938 was added during the pre-Broadway tour. Introduced by Libby Holman.

VERSE

Love's such a funny thing
Even when you neglect it.
It gives your bell a ring
When you least expect it.
And though I'm, so far, entirely fancy-free,
Still I'm all prepared in case it should call on me.

REFRAIN

For you never know
When love will say hello,
When love, gaily swinging,
Will happen along
And set you to singing
Your favorite love song.
Don't be afraid,
It comes to ev'ry man and to ev'ry maid,
So take my advice
And reserve two tickets to paradise,
For you never know.

Earlier song

VERSE

Once upon a time I was clever,
Smart as could be,
Fancy and free with my love words.
All at once I quit being clever.
You came along,
Something went wrong with my love words.

REFRAIN

You'll never know
Just what you do to me,
You'll never know
How sweet your lips can be.
I'm longing to tell about you
But what can I say?
This wonderful spell about you,
No words could ever convey.
You'll never know
The thrill of all your charms.
Don't let me go
From heaven in your arms.
You'll never know
There's nothing I can do!
You'll only know
That I'm in love with you.

WHAT IS THAT TUNE?

Published October 1938. Added to the show during the pre-Broadway tour. Introduced by Libby Holman and Clifton Webb.

VERSE

GASTON: There's a snatch of a song
I've been singing for days,
MARIA: It is merely a phrase,

GASTON: But it stays and it stays with me all day long,
Though the rest of it's lost to me.
MARIA: It's a phrase I adore,
And it troubles me so
Not to know where I heard it before.

REFRAIN

BOTH: Hm, what is that tune?
MARIA: Hm, I know it so well.
GASTON: Hm, what is that tune?
MARIA: It's so insinuating,
I'm under its spell.
GASTON: Hm,
MARIA: What is that song?
GASTON: Hm, oh, darling, now I realize,
The lost refrain I've been humming
Is the strain the guitars were strumming
The first time I gazed in your eyes.
MARIA: Sweet melody—
That came so suddenly out of the night and gave you to me!
Tormenting refrain—
If it could only bring you back to me again!
BOTH: Hm—

FOR NO RHYME OR REASON

Published March 1938. Also copyrighted unpublished January 1938. This number was shifted from the opening of Act II to the middle of Act I during the extended pre-Broadway tour. Introduced by Toby Wing, Charles Kemper, the Debonairs, and ensemble.

VERSE

HE: Here you are, a total stranger,
Yet so perfectly we blend
That I warn you, you're in danger
Of becoming my greatest friend.
SHE: On the other hand, I'm so happy
That we two should get along,
That I just can't wait
To celebrate
By bursting into song.
HE: But why wait, my pet?
Let's make the song a long lyric duet!
BOTH: Tra, la, la, la, la.

REFRAIN

Why is it (no teasin')
We have such a swell time,
For no rhyme or reason,
For no reason or rhyme?
We could be sizzlin' or freezin',
We'd still feel in our prime,
For no rhyme or reason,
For no reason or rhyme.
We click so
That we must have, I know,
Ev'ry blessing from heaven above,
And by next week
We'll be able to speak
That tricky language of love,
For though it's not yet the season,
I hear wedding bells chime,
For no rhyme or reason,
For no reason or rhyme.

FROM ALPHA TO OMEGA

Published March 1938. Refrains 4 and 5 were added during the show's run at the Shubert Theatre, Boston. Porter's lyric for these refrains is dated March 11, 1938. Introduced by Clifton Webb and Lupe Velez.

VERSE

You're such a ne plus ultra creature
That if I had your photo,
I couldn't pick my fav'rite feature,
I like you so in toto.
In ev'ry way, from ev'ry angle,
You're the bangle I long to dangle,
For from basement to roof,
From Wagner op'ra to op'ra bouffe,

REFRAIN 1

From Alpha to Omega,
From A to Z,
From Alpha to Omega,
You're made for me.
From left hooks by Dempsey to Braddock's uppercuts,*
From Jericho to Kokomo, not to mention from soup to nuts,
From *Journal* until *Mirror*,
From coast to coast,

**Originally:*
From death blows by Dempsey to Schmeling's uppercuts,

From Juliet to Norma Shearer,†
You're what I like the most,
And from morning until evening
In mis'ry I shall pine,
Till from Alpha to Omega you're mine.

REFRAIN 2

From Alpha to Omega,
From A to Z,
From Alpha to Omega,
You're made for me.
From love songs by Schumann to hits by Jerry Kern,
From Sarawak to Hackensack, not to mention from stem to stern,
From dyah Missus Pat Campbell
To sweet Mae West,
You happen to be the mammal
This baby loves the best,
And from morning until evening,
Will you stun yourself with wine?
Certainly, till from Alpha to Omega you're mine.

REFRAIN 3

From Alpha to Omega,
From A to Z,
From Alpha to Omega,
You're made for me.
From Lou Gehrig's home run to Lou Chiozza's bunt,
From Tripoli to Kankakee, not to mention from Lynn to Lunt,
From great eighty-pound codfish
To sardines canned,
You happen to be the odd fish
This lad would love to land,
And will you woo me and pursue me,
With sinker, hook, and line?
Yes, till from Alpha to Omega you're mine.
And will you chase me,‡
And embrace me,
And say that I'm divine?
Till from Alpha to Omega you're mine.

REFRAIN 4

From Alpha to Omega,
From A to Z,
From Alpha to Omega,
You're made for me.
From cotton plowed under
To this year's bumper crop,
From Benzedrine
To Ovaltine,
Not to mention from go to stop.
From corn muffins to Triscuit,
From fat to thin,
From Zev to the young Seabiscuit,
I'll bet on you to win.
And will you brunch me,
And then lunch me,
Then make me stay to dine?
Yes, till from Alpha to Omega you're mine.

REFRAIN 5

From Alpha to Omega,
From A to Z,
From Alpha to Omega,
You're made for me.
From old English sherry
To very French vermouth,
From Mozambique
To Battle Creek,
Not to mention from North to South.
From great eagles to sparrows,
From large to small,
From Austins to big Pierce-Arrows,
Your rumble tops 'em all,
And will you beat me
And maltreat me,
And bend my Spanish spine?
Yes, till from Alpha to Omega you're mine.

FINALE, ACT II

From martinis to brandy,
From East to West,
From Salomey to Sally Randy,
I like your fan the best,
And from morning until ev'ning,
The sun will never shine
Till from Alpha to Omega you're mine.

†*Lines 7–9 originally:*
From Rembrandt to Picasso,
From coast to coast,
From Eve to the fair di Frasso

‡New exit finish to refrain, as requested by Mr. Webb.

DON'T LET IT GET YOU DOWN

Written for the René Clair film *Break the News* (1938) but not sung in it. Added to *You Never Know* during its pre-Broadway tour. Introduced by June Preisser, Dan Harden, the Debonairs, and ensemble.

VERSE

Once a gypsy told me something
That has helped me all my life through.
It will give you zip
When you start to slip,
So I'm handing it on to you.

REFRAIN

When the state of your mind
Is a deep shade of brown,
Always try to remember
Don't let it get you down.
When you wake up and find
You're the laugh of the town,
Go ahead, swear and tear your hair,
But don't let it get you down.
In case your romance
Has been giving you that runaround,
Go into your dance
And you'll still find heap much fun around.
Say hello to a smile,
Say goodbye to a frown,
Give a cheer for this vain world,
This dear old insane world,
It's a mere cellophane world,
So don't let it get you down.

WHAT SHALL I DO?

Published May 1938. Copyrighted unpublished under the title "What Should I Do?" January 1938. For some unexplained reason, the lyric in published copies is credited to Rowland Leigh, although the numerous sketches and drafts confirm that it was a Porter lyric. Introduced by Lupe Velez.

Miss Velez used this song as a springboard for her impersonations of Marlene Dietrich, Katharine Hepburn, Simone Simon, Shirley Temple, Gloria Swanson, Vera Zorina, and Dolores del Rio. I believe that the special material for this song was the part written by Rowland Leigh.

VERSE

I've just read of Cleopatra
The glamorous empire shatt'rer,
Who to Caesar lost her heart as well as her head,
But that early Roman Nazi
Was so mean to his Cleopatsy*
That she fell in love with Marc Antony instead.
To worship two men in turn may be sublime,
But, oh, it's hell when you care for both at the same time.

REFRAIN

What shall I do?
Just imagine what I'm going through,
I love not one, but two,
What shall I do?
I'm in a spot,
Cupid's given me a double shot,
So won't you tell me what
As well as what not shall I do?
Two men appear,
Each a swell Apollo Belvedere,
Each one ideal,
But though I fairly itch to,
I don't know which to hitch to.
I can't marry both,
After all, this isn't Timbuctoo,
That's the reason I appeal to you, and you,
What shall I do?

I'm in a spot,
This young man attracts me quite a lot,
So won't you tell me what
As well as what not I shall do?
My note still unsealed
Also eggs me on to carry through,
In the situation wouldn't you and you?
That's what I'll do!

What shall I do?
Evidently husbands can't be true,
Mine's just like all the crew.
What shall I do?
That blonde cocotte
Has him dancing like a Hottentot,
So won't you tell me what
As well as what not to do?
Wise gods above
Say I'm just a step ahead of love.
Love's lots of fun,
So shall I change my diet
And, on the quiet, try it?
The deah Baron's flow'rs
Also make me want to carry through,
In the situation, wouldn't you and you?
What shall I do?

Lines 4 and 5 originally:
But that stingy old Rotarian
Gave her nothing but one Caesarian,

AT LONG LAST LOVE

Published March 1938. Introduced by Clifton Webb. Porter told an interviewer: "When this horse fell on me, I was too stunned to be conscious of great pain, but until help came I worked on the lyrics for a song called 'At Long Last Love.' " Interestingly, the song was copyrighted as an unpublished number on October 6, 1937, only eighteen days before the accident. But as late as February 18, 1938, it still lacked a verse. The substitution of Granada for Lido in the published copy is only one of many changes Porter made in the lyric.

VERSE

I'm so in love,
And though it gives me joy intense,
I can't decipher
If I'm a lifer,
Or if it's just a first offense.
I'm so in love,
I've no sense of values left at all.
Is this a playtime,
Affair of Maytime,
Or is it a windfall?

REFRAIN 1

Is it an earthquake or simply a shock?
Is it the good turtle soup or merely the mock?
Is it a cocktail—this feeling of joy,*
Or is what I feel the real McCoy?
Have I the right hunch or have I the wrong?
Will it be Bach I shall hear or just a Cole Porter song?
Is it a fancy not worth thinking of,
Or is it at long last love?

REFRAIN 2

Is it the rainbow or just a mirage?
Will it be tender and sweet or merely massage?
Is it a brainstorm in one of its quirks,
Or is it the best, the crest, the works?
Is it for all time or simply a lark?
Is it the Lido I see or only Asbury Park?
Should I say "Thumbs down" and give it a shove,
Or is it at long last love?

REFRAIN 3

Is it a breakdown or is it a break?
Is it a real Porterhouse or only a steak?
What can account for these strange pitter-pats?
Could this be the dream, the cream, the cat's?
Is it to rescue or is it to wreck?
Is it an ache in the heart or just a pain in the neck?
Is it the ivy you touch with a glove,
Or is it at long last love?

REFRAIN (UNFINISHED)

Is it in marble or is it in clay?
Is what I thought a new Rolls, a used Chevrolet?
Is it a sapphire or simply a charm?
Is it ——— or just a shot in the arm?
Is it today's thrill or really romance?
Is it a kiss on the lips or just a kick in the pants?
Is it the gay gods cavorting above,
Or is it at long last love?

Earlier lyrics:

Refrain 1
Line 3: Is it a brainstorm—this feeling of joy?
Lines 5–6: Is it to broadcast or is it to ban?
Is it a bolt from the blue or just a flash in the pan?

Refrain 2
Lines 5–7: Is it by Browning (Swinburne, Byron, Shakespeare) or doesn't it scan?
Is it a bolt from the blue or just a flash in the pan?
Should I say "Amscray" and give it a shove,

Refrain 3
Line 2: Is it a Chateaubriand or only a steak,

YES, YES, YES

Porter completed this lyric before January 29, 1938. Introduced by Toby Wing and ensemble.

VERSE

IDA: If I rattle with clips from Flato's,
If I battle with frocks from France,
It's because I mind my own potatoes
When it comes to love and romance,
For when I was only a tot
Mother said to me

ATTENDANT OF LADIES' ROOM: Your mamma said what?

REFRAIN

IDA: Baby, life's so short
And you want happiness,
So be smart and learn to say,
"Yes, yes, yes."

When a boy pays court
To that "nyah" you possess,

Merely murmur, right away,
"Yes, yes, yes."
ATTENDANT: "Yes, yes, yes."

IDA: If you once say, "No,"
In this ever-lovin' nation,
You will lose your beau,
What's more, ruin your reputation.

But at springtime sport
You can howl with success
If you answer, night and day,
"Yes, Yes, Yes."
ATTENDANT: "Yes, Yes, Yes."
IDA: "Yes, Yes, Yes."
ATTENDANT: Yowsah!
IDA: Yes, indeedy, yes!

GOOD EVENING, PRINCESSE

Completed by February 16, 1938. Introduced by Clifton Webb and Lupe Velez.

COUPLET 1

HE: Good evening, Princesse.
SHE: Good evening, dear Marquis.
HE: If by some good chaunce
You have not this daunce,
Will you try a little shag with me?
SHE: I'd be delighted, Marquis.

COUPLET 2

SHE: And tell me, Marquis,
Your wife, just where is she?
HE: Why, she left today
To be gone till May,
So I hope you'll let me come to tea.
SHE: Oh, naughty, naughty Marquis!

COUPLET 3

HE: Then tell me, Princesse,
If tea for two with you won't do,
Will you come to dine
Tomorrow night at nine,
And I'll show you all my etchings too?
SHE: You will show me all your etchings too?
I'm afraid, Marquis,
You're insulting me,
I never heard such outrageous parlez-vous!

COUPLET 4

HE: Then tell me, Princesse,
If dinner caunt be done,
Would it keep you up
If I came to sup,
Say, tomorrow night at haulf paust one?
SHE: I'd be enchaunted, Marquis,
If you'll stay to breakfast with me!

I'LL BLACK HIS EYES

Completed by February 18, 1938. Dropped during the pre-Broadway tour.

VERSE

BALTIN: The one I adore in a bachelor's apartment!
CROWD: Yes, yes, your wife is keeping a rendezvous tonight!
BALTIN: I never before knew what torture of the heart meant,
But now that I do, the Baron's got to fight!
CROWD: Hurrah! A fight!
BALTIN: He little guesses
He's about to suffer
A series of chosen blows entirely new to him.
CROWD: The Paris press says
You're an awful bluffer,
Let down your hair,
Whadayuh dare
Do to him?
BALTIN: What'll I do?
CROWD: Yes, what'll you do, new to him?

REFRAIN

I'll black his eyes,
I'll punch his nose,
I'll twist his ears,
I'll stomp on his toes,
And if he still wants to take a chance,
As a gift,
He'll get a swift
Kick in the pants.
I'll knock him out,
And when he's down,
My running jump'll plump a big bump
On his crown,
And if he still wants to fight, well then,
I'll stand him up and start it all over again.

. . .

BALTIN: I'll black his eyes,
CROWD: He'll black his eyes,
BALTIN: I'll punch his nose,
CROWD: He'll punch his nose,
BALTIN: I'll twist his ears,
CROWD: He'll twist his ears,
BALTIN: I'll stomp on his toes,
CROWD: He'll stomp on his toes,
BALTIN: And if he still wants to take a chance,
CROWD: To take a chance,
BALTIN: As a gift,
He'll get a swift
Kick in the pants,
CROWD: Kick in the pants.
BALTIN: I'll knock him out,
CROWD: He'll knock him out,
BALTIN: And when he's down,
CROWD: And when he's down,
BALTIN: My running jump'll plump a big bump
On his crown,
CROWD: Bump, bump, bump, bump, bump, bump
on his crown,
BALTIN: And if he still wants to fight, well then,
CROWD: Well, then,
BALTIN: I'll stand him up and start it all over
again.
CROWD: He'll black his eyes,
BALTIN: I'll punch his nose,
CROWD: He'll twist his ears,
BALTIN: I'll stomp on his toes,
CROWD: He'll knock him out, and when he's
down, well then,
BALTIN: I'll stand him up and do it all over
again,
CROWD: Again, again, again, again, again, an'
again, an' again, an' again, an' again!

ALL: Again, again, again, again,
An' again, an' again, an' again!
Again, again, again, again,
An' again, an' again, an' again!
TENORS: Again, again, an' again!
BASSES: An' again!
TENORS: An' again, an' again, an' again!
BASSES: An' again,
An' again,
An' again!

I'M YOURS

There are two versions of this song, which was revised in March 1938, then dropped during the pre-Broadway tour. Sung in the tryout by Libby Holman.

I'm yours, only yours,
Since the moon high above
Saw the birth of our love,
I belong to you, I'm yours.
I may try to insist
That we never have met,
That you could not exist,
But how can I forget,
Since the moment we kissed,
I'm yours?
You may stay, you may go,
You may drift with each shift of the breeze,
Though I go, still I know
I shall have memories—melodies
That will sing evermore
Of the moon high above and the love that we
swore,
For, remember, sweetheart,
If today we must part,
That as long as life endures,
I'm yours,
Helplessly,
Hopelessly
Yours.

Later version

I'm yours, only yours,
Since the moment divine
When your eyes first met mine,
I belong to you, I'm yours.
I should ask, with alarm,
Why so quickly I fell in the spell of your charm,
But all fear I'm above,
I'm in heav'n, I'm in love,
I'm yours!
You may stay, you may go,
You may drift with each shift of the breeze,
If you go, still I know
I shall have memories—melodies
That will sing, ever sweet,
Of the joy that I knew when we two chanced to meet,
So remember, sweetheart,
If you stay or depart,
Still as long as life endures,
I'm yours,
Helplessly,
Hopelessly
Yours.

WHAT A PRICELESS PLEASURE

Completed February 24–25, 1938. Listed as "The Waiters" in the Boston and other pre-Broadway programs. Introduced by ensemble. Dropped before the New York opening.

ALL: What a priceless pleasure,
you'll agree,
To prepare whatever breed of
birdie
For a famous gourmet such as
he.
We refer to his nibs, Baron
Ferdie.
After serving such a lot of
rummies
It's indeed a gift from heav'n
above
To titillate and slightly inflate
the tummies
Of the Baron and his lady love.
BASSES: After serving so many rummies
TENORS: What a kick to tickle the
tummies
BASSES: Of such epicurean chummies
TENORS: As the Baron and his lady love,
ALL: His joy, his hope, his life, his
love!
MAÎTRE D'HÔTEL: Ah, good ev'ning, men of mine.
WAITERS: Hearty welcome, maître d'hôtel.
MAÎTRE D': Is the supper super-fine?
WAITERS: Yes, it's très, très swell.
MAÎTRE D': Let me taste the consommé,
1ST WAITER
(TO 2ND WAITER): Have a care, don't let it jostle.
MAÎTRE D': As dear Hollywood would say,
It's terrific, it's colossal!
2ND WAITER: Would you like to see the
pheasant?
3RD WAITER: And the bread crumbs?
4TH WAITER: And the jelly?
MAÎTRE D': What a very fitting present
For Lucius Beebe's belly.
ALL WAITERS: Oh, a spectacle so pleasant,
Would inspire Keats or Shelley,
An entire roasted pheasant
In Lucius Beebe's belly.
MAÎTRE D': Now the salad—
5TH WAITER: Yes, the salad.
6TH WAITER: Where's the salad?
7TH WAITER: Here's the salad!
MAÎTRE D': What a salad, what a salad!
It's an Irving Berlin ballad!
8TH WAITER: And this cheese you will adore.
MAÎTRE D': Well, I hate to be detract'ry,
But it carries me once more
To the old glue fact'ry,
ALL WAITERS: To the old glue fact'ry,
Oh, so far, far away,
To that doomed, perfumed fact'ry
Where he first saw the light of
day.
MAÎTRE D': Is the coffee well distilled?
1ST WAITER: Sir, I gave it all the workin's.
MAÎTRE D': And the champagne, is it
chilled?
ONE WAITER: Yes, it's colder than Ma
Perkins!
ALL WAITERS
(SHIVERING): Brrr—Ma Perkins!
MAÎTRE D': Then we need no more
preparin',
Kindly stand just back of me
And we'll tell the noble Baron,
That his supper is servi.
WAITERS
(WITH MAÎTRE D'
CONDUCTING): Oh, most noble, gracious Baron,
If for bang-up food you're
carin',
Please excuse us for declarin'
Supper is servi.
Supper is servi!

JUST ONE STEP AHEAD OF LOVE

Written in late March 1938, revised in early April, and added to the show during the Philadelphia performances, where it was listed as "One Step Ahead of Love" and sung by Libby Holman. It was dropped before the New York opening.

VERSE

MADAM
BALTIN: Since long months, my maties,
Are my Lares and Penates,
Well, I mean I'm all settled down.
But last week I fell u-
Pon a high-yelluh fortune-telluh,
Just in from Harlem town.
She took a look at me and rolled her eyes,
And then proceeded to state
To my great
Surprise—

REFRAIN

MADAM BALTIN: You're just one step ahead of love, baby,
Miss one step and you're bound to fall.
There's someone you'll be dreaming of, baby,
So slip not
Or you got
No chance at all.
Those wise gods
Are betting you'll soon be in his arms,
Giving big odds
In heaven above.
So, baby,
Don't spoil the fun,
Wrap your heart up and start to run,
Cause you're just one step ahead of love.

PATTER

So, for instance,
Never hear Bing Crosby croon,
Never gaze at the silver moon,
Don't go in for shady nooks,
And above all, don't read hotcha-cha books.
Of hot spices don't get fond,
Don't sing songs by Carrie Jacobs Bond,
As for perfumes, be agin' 'em,
And avoid pictures with Greta Stokowski in 'em,
For the wise gods
Are betting you'll end in his arms,
Giving big odds
In heaven above.
So, baby,
Don't spoil the fun,
Wrap your heart up and start to run,
'Cause you're just one,
Just one-half,
One-quarter,
Just one-eighth,
Just one-sixteenth,
One thirty-second,
These here things can't 'xactly be reckoned,
But at best, you're jest
One,
At best, you're jest one
Step ahead of love.

REPEAT REFRAIN

NEW PATTER

So beware of
Long walks on moonlit nights,
Deep divans and lowered lights,
Sweet music and sugary books,
For unless I'm wrong, by the way it all looks—

REPEAT REFRAIN

VERSE

MADAM BALTIN: I suppose all husbands are quite the same
When it comes to playing the marriage game.
I have no idea if he knew or not,
But, of course, I spotted that blonde cocotte.
I've been so long a slave
Now it's my turn to misbehave.
Was that Harlem fortune-teller right,
When she rolled her eyes and said to me the other night?

PEAT REFRAIN

HA, HA, HA

Also titled "Finale, Act I," this number was completed in late February 1938, but dropped from the show before its New York opening.

BALTIN: Ha, ha, ha, HA, HA, HA,
Ha, ha, ha, HA, HA, HA!
Ha, ha, ha, HA, HA, HA, HA, HA, HA, HA,
(POINTING TO GASTON) I've got the HA, HA on you,
(POINTING TO MARIA) I've got the HA, HA on you,
I'm afraid I'll die
Or at least lose my mind,
If you knew what I
Had expected to find.
GASTON (POINTING TO MARIA): He's got the HA, HA on you!
BALTIN: HA, HA,
MARIA (POINTING TO GASTON): He's got the HA, HA on you!
BALTIN: HA, HA.
GASTON: I fear the joke's on us,
But instead of making a fuss
Let's HA, HA, HA, HA too.
GASTON & MARIA: HA, HA.
BALTIN: Ha, ha, ha, HA, HA, HA, HA, HA, HA,

CROWD: Ha, ha, ha, HA, HA, HA,
HA [*repeated as often as necessary until curtain falls.*]

BY CANDLELIGHT

Porter's version of "By Candlelight," copyrighted unpublished January 1938, was never used in the show.

By candlelight,
So often at night,
I dream of you close to my heart.
By candlelight
The world looks so bright
That we swear we nevermore shall part.
Life seems such perfect bliss,
And so sweet ev'ry kiss,
I know that love like this
Couldn't be true.
And yet so real
It seems that I feel
Fortune beams
On my candlelight dreams
Of you.

I'M BACK IN CIRCULATION

Written in March 1938 for Toby Wing and ladies of the ensemble. I do not know if it was ever sung in the show during its pre-Broadway tour. At any rate, it was dropped before the New York opening.

VERSE

IDA: After spending quite a spell
In one young man's society,
I'll say one young man is swell
But I must have variety.

1ST GIRL: Serge for luncheon,
2ND GIRL: Condé for tea,
3RD GIRL: Doc for dinner,
4TH GIRL: Then Jock to Big Apple me,
ALL GIRLS: Ida is bona fide,
But Ida isn't one to bide-a-wee.
IDA: No, no, that's the reason that

REFRAIN

I'm back in circulation,
My education
Can now go on.
I was so tied, so tied
To a little fireside,
But the fire suddenly died,
So it's time I got back my stride.
Playboys, once more I call you,
As well as all you
Big businessmen!
Any moment you're free
Better cash in on me,
'Cause I'm back in circulation again.

I'M GOING IN FOR LOVE

Written in March 1938 for Libby Holman. I do not know if it was ever sung in the show. It was not performed in New York. Published in *The Unpublished Cole Porter.*

VERSE

MADAM BALTIN: I suppose all husbands are quite the same
When it comes to playing the marriage game.
I have no idea if he knew or not,
But, of course, I spotted that blonde cocotte.
I've been so long a slave
Now it's my turn to misbehave,
So—

REFRAIN

Tell 'em to light all the stars in heaven,
And tell 'em to turn on the moon above.
Maybe it's not done,
But tonight I'm out for fun,
I'm going in for love.
Tell 'em to order the breeze of ev'ning
To start in to sigh like a cooing dove.
Maybe it's absurd,
But in spite of all I've heard,
I'm going in for love.
Love, don't resist, you
Must be sweet to me,
Love, for I've missed you
Oh so long,
So, so long.
So tell 'em to tip off a certain someone,
That someone I've ever been dreaming of,
Warn him to beware,
For the spring is in the air
And I'm going in for love,
Love,
I'm going in for love.

IT'S NO LAUGHING MATTER

Not used.

It's no laughing matter
When your head begins to whirl
And the drums in your heart start to clatter
'Cause you've suddenly seen that certain girl.
It's no laughing matter
When you offer your heart
And place it on a platter
Before the fairest flow'r that grows,
And she looks at it, but looks at it down her nose.
No, no, it's no time to chatter
About the boundless blessings from heaven above,
For it's no laughing matter
When the lady laughs at your love.

Throughout the life of *You Never Know,* a number of songs by other writers were added to and deleted from the show, which Porter later described as the worst production he had ever been associated with. Yet his gratitude to the Shuberts for helping to get him back to work after his accident was so great that he always tried to ensure that his musicals were booked into Shubert houses.

LEAVE IT TO ME

1938

"Leave It To Me," 1938; Mary Martin

Tryout: Shubert Theatre, New Haven, October 13, 1938; Shubert Theatre, Boston, October 17, 1938. Original title: *Clear All Wires.* Produced by Vinton Freedley at the Imperial Theatre, New York, November 9, 1938. 307 performances. Book by Bella and Samuel Spewack. Cast, starring William Gaxton and Victor Moore, included Sophie Tucker, Tamara, Mary Martin, and Gene Kelly.

HOW DO YOU SPELL AMBASSADOR?

The opening chorus. Introduced by ensemble.

1ST REPORTER: How do you spell *ambassador?*
OTHERS: Can't say.
2ND REPORTER: How do you spell *Moscow,* men?
OTHERS: Too tough, by far.
3RD REPORTER: How do you spell *contributor?*
OTHERS: Won't play.
4TH REPORTER: How do you spell *administration,* then?
OTHERS: Just put F.D.R.
5TH REPORTER: How do you spell *Soviet?*
OTHERS: Tain't fair.
6TH REPORTER: How do you spell *Stalin?* I forget.
OTHERS: Don't care

ALL REPORTERS: Why bother to spell these tricky names
And add years to your age
When the paper is only read by dames
Who make the Society Page?

Why bother, therefore?
They only care for
The Society Page.

WE DRINK TO YOU, J. H. BRODY

Introduced by William Gaxton and ensemble.

VERSE

BUCK: Your Excellency,
On behalf
Of the members of your numerous publications,
And particularly
Of this staff,
I offer you congratulations.
Your official appointment's due any moment now.
BOYS: Good luck.
BUCK: But till Washington sends it through, here's how!
BOYS: You said it, Buck.

REFRAIN

BUCK: We drink to you, J. H. Brody!
BOYS: Our next Ambassador to Russia, hey, hey!
BUCK: We drink to you in ice-cream sody,
BOYS: The vodka of the U.S.A.
BUCK: Our glasses clink to you, J. H. Brody,
Because we know you're sure
To come through.
The Russian flag is red
But you've got over your head
Forever the Red, White and Blue.
BOYS: With Cordie Hull to back you, Mister Brody,
To the Kremlin you will never have to toady.
BUCK: The Russian flag is red,
But you've got over your head
BUCK & BOYS: Forever the Red, White and Blue.

VITE, VITE, VITE

Opening of Scene 2, Act I. Introduced by ensemble.

PORTERS: Vite, vite, vite,
For the Moscow Express.
Vite, vite, vite,
You give a tip to me, no, yes?
Vite, vite, vite,
Hurry and get your seat
If you want to go to Moscow,
Madame, you better be vite!
1ST GIRL: Oh, I've lost my hatbox.
2ND GIRL: I've lost my sables.
3RD GIRL: I've lost my suitcase—
The one with the beautiful labels!
4TH GIRL: I lost my trav'ler's checks
Only this afternoon.
5TH GIRL: I've still got my
Virginity
But I'm hoping to lose it soon.
LOVERS: Farewell, my sweetheart,

Don't fail to write.
I'm going to miss you
More and more ev'ry night.
While you're away, dear,
From me so far
I shall be waiting for you at the
Ritz, in the bar.

SWEETHEARTS: Farewell, my lover,
Daily I'll write.
I'm going to miss you
More and more ev'ry night.

LOVERS: While you're away, dear,
From me so far
I shall be waiting for you at the
Ritz, in the bar.

PORTERS: Vite, vite, vite,
Hurry and get your seat,
If you want to go to Moscow,
Madame, you better be vite!

I'M TAKING THE STEPS TO RUSSIA

Published November 1938. Also titled "Taking the Steps to Russia." Introduced by Sophie Tucker and ensemble.

VERSE

From what I hear
I greatly fear
For the mujik and his mate.
For the Soviet
Hasn't learned as yet
How to make 'em syncopate.
The Moscovites
Complain that their nights
Are so long they never end,
And so to get 'em in the groove
And prove
That I'm a friend—

REFRAIN

I'm taking the steps to Russia,
I'm showing 'em how to dance,
I'm starting the shag in Moscow,
I'm putting red ants in their pants.
The way they still love Tchaikovsky
I'm sure is not quite the right thing.
I know what's the matter with 'em,
What they need is Harlem rhythm,
So I'm making Communithm
Thwing!

Second version

REFRAIN 1

I'm taking the steps to Russia,
I'm showing 'em how to dance,
I'm starting the shag in Moscow,
I'm putting red ants in their pants.
Instead of those gloomy op'ras
I'll give 'em Bob Crosby and Bing,
Their troubles they'll all forget-ski,
And study the clarinet-ski,
When I make the Soviet-ski
Swing.*

PATTER

The gypsies in the bars,
All over the place,
No more will strum guitars
But slappa the bass.
Each Volga boatman and
Each mountain woodman
Will start to beat the band
Like Benny Goodman.
Those proletari-ats
And agitators
Will all be alley cats
And alley-gators.
The thing to cheer 'em up is jam and
jive,
A Yank attack
Is what they lack,
So to bring 'em back
Alive

REFRAIN 2

I'm taking the steps to Russia,
I'm teaching 'em peckin' talk.
I'll dance the bean off Litvinov,
I'll make the Bear lambeth its walk.
Instead of those corn-fed folk songs,
The latest hot ditties they'll sing,
Old Stalin will hush his gush-a
And strut like a Roxy usher
When I make the steppes of Russia
Swing.

EXIT FINISH

From Asia to eastern Prussia
I'll sweep like a Fuller brush-a
Till I make the steppes of Russia
Swing.

**Last four lines as corrected for publication were the same as the exit finish.*

EXIT LYRIC FOR MISS TUCKER

Our rhythm they all will bow to,
And learn how to flow-dow-dow, too,
When I show the Russians how to
Swing.

EXIT LYRIC FROM SCRIPT

So I'm taking my flock of chickies
To show 'em some brand-new trickies
And we'll make the Bolshevikies
Swing!

GET OUT OF TOWN

Published October 1938. Introduced by Tamara. At one point this was the second number in Act I.

VERSE

The farce was ended,
The curtain drawn,
And I at least pretended
That love was dead and gone.
But now from nowhere
You come to me as before,
To take my heart
And break my heart
Once more.

REFRAIN

Get out of town,
Before it's too late, my love.
Get out of town,
Be good to me, please.
Why wish me harm?
Why not retire to a farm
And be contented to charm
The birds off the trees?
Just disappear,
I care for you much too much,
And when you are near,
Close to me, dear,
We touch too much.
The thrill when we meet
Is so bittersweet
That, darling, it's getting me down,
So on your mark, get set,
Get out of town.

WHEN ALL'S SAID AND DONE

Added to the show during the Boston performances. It replaced "When the Hen Stops Laying." Introduced by William Gaxton, Mary Martin, and ensemble.

VERSE

BUCK: This affair has been so swell,
But we must face the fact
That once it used to ring the bell,
But now it's out of the act.
DOLLY: Dear Buckie, you'll go far!
What a great philosopher you are.

REFRAIN 1

BUCK: When all's said and done,
Though I hate to see you go,
When all's said and done,
I must say it's best.
DOLLY: When all's said and done,
We've had plenty heidy-ho,
It's all been sublime,
But I guess it's time
We gave it a rest.
BUCK: We've had so much pleasure playing,
But there's an old saying,
Oh, so profound,
"You can't have peaches all the year
round."
DOLLY: So long and goodbye,
It's been proven in the past
The real good things never last,
And we've had our fun, baby,
BOTH: When all's said and done.

PATTER 1

DOLLY: We've wandered 'neath the stars together,
And in the rain.
BUCK: We've opened so many bars together
And so much champagne.
DOLLY: How often we did the town together
BUCK: And ended by falling down together.
DOLLY: But now, honey, it's
The end of it all, let's call it quits.
BUCK: So long and goodbye
Without even feeling sad,
Because, heaven knows, we've had
A whole lotta fun, baby,
BOTH: When all's said and done.

REFRAIN 2

ENSEMBLE: When all's said and done,
Though I hate to see you go,

When all's said and done,
I must say it's best.
When all's said and done,
We've had plenty heidy-ho,
It's all been sublime,
But I guess it's time
We gave it a rest.
We've had so much pleasure playing,
But there's an old saying,
So very true,
"The birds fly south when summer is through."
So long and goodbye,
You go your way, I'll go mine,
And someday drop me a line.
We've had so much fun, baby,
When all's said and done.

PATTER 2

DOLLY: Each ev'ning, we'd set sail together
And never stop.
BUCK: We nearly once went to jail together
But you vamped the cop.
DOLLY: How often we meant to sup together
BUCK: And ended by waking up together.
DOLLY: But now duty calls
Me back to my daddy's marble halls.
BUCK: So long and goodbye,
DOLLY: You go your way, I'll go mine,
BUCK: And someday drop me a line.
BOTH: We've had so much fun, baby,
When all's said and done.

EXTRA FINISH

DOLLY: And your bracelet, dear.
BUCK: No, no, keep it just for luck.
And this case,
DOLLY: Oh, thank you, Buck,
I might meet someone, baby,
When all's said and done.

MOST GENTLEMEN DON'T LIKE LOVE

Published October 1938. Introduced by Sophie Tucker and ensemble. Intended originally for *Greek to You* (1937–1938).

VERSE

When Mummy in her sixteenth year
Was dreaming of romance a lot,
She thought that she was Guinevere
And ev'ry boy Sir Launcelot,
But now that Mummy's more mature
And knows her way about,
She doesn't b'lieve in "Vive l'amour"
For Mummy's found out—

REFRAIN 1

Most gentlemen don't like love,
They just like to kick it around,
Most gentlemen can't take love,
'Cause most gentlemen can't be profound.
As Madam Sappho in some sonnet said,
"A slap and a tickle
Is all that the fickle
Male
Ever has in his head,"
For most gentlemen don't like love.
I've been in love,
So I know what I'm talking of
And, oh, to my woe I have found
They just like to kick it around.

REFRAIN 2

Most gentlemen don't like love,
They just like to kick it around,
Most gentlemen don't like love,
'Cause most gentlemen can't be profound.
So just remember when you get that glance,
A romp and a quickie
Is all little Dickie
Means
When he mentions romance,
For most gentlemen don't like love,
They just like to kick it around.

REFRAIN 3

Most gentlemen don't like love,
They just like to kick it around,
Most gentlemen don't like love,
'Cause most gentlemen can't be profound.
In ev'ry land, children, they're all the same,
A pounce in the clover
And then when it's over
"So long and what is your name?"
'Cause most gentlemen don't like love,
They just like to kick it around.

REFRAIN 4

Most gentlemen don't like love,
They just like to kick it around,
Most gentlemen don't like love,
'Cause most gentlemen can't be profound.

So if your boy friend, some fine night, should say
He'll love you forever
And part from you never,
Just push him out of the hay (way),
'Cause most gentlemen don't like love,
They just like to kick it around.

COMRADE ALONZO

Introduced by ensemble. Finale of Act I.

CROWD: 'Tis the final conflict, let each stand in his place,
The International Soviet shall lead the human race,
'Tis the final conflict, let each stand in his place,
The International Soviet shall lead the human race.

DOUBLE QUARTETTE: Comrade Alonzo, we love you, Russia will never forget.
By the deed you have done
You have proved to be one
Of the biggest Bolsheviks yet.
Bill Bullitt at heart was a bourgeois, and Davies played ball with the upper set,
So we thank Topeka, Kan.,
For you, little man,
The Savior of the Soviet,
No, Russia will never forget.
STALIN: Nyet, nyet, nyet, nyet,
DOUBLE QUARTETTE: The greatest ambassador yet,
BUCK: Nyet, nyet, nyet, nyet,
DOUBLE QUARTETTE: Alonzo P. Goodhue, our pet.
GOODHUE: Nyet, nyet, nyet, nyet,
DOUBLE QUARTETTE: The Savior of the Soviet.

THANK YOU

This recitative may have been dropped before the New York opening, as it is not in the libretto.

BUCK: My friends . . . we are gathered here tonight in solemn conclave, to present to you and the world The Goodhue Plan.
My friends . . . is this the world we want to leave our children? This world of plots, politics and pickpockets? No, no, not so, my friend.
CROWD: Buck Thomas, I suppose, felt
He was helping Mister Roosevelt
By calling us all "my friends."
BUCK: No, no, the world of which we dream
Is one where peaches swim in cream.
What do we call this world? "Utopia!"
CROWD: But there ain't no such place, yuh dope, yuh!
BUCK: Ah, yes, it lies so very near
That I invite our comrade here, His Excellency, the United States Ambassador to Moscow, and my silent partner in The Goodhue Plan. And, incidentally, a very great man, and like another great American, *first in the hearts* of his countrymen,
Will now present The Goodhue Plan.

RECALL GOODHUE

This number also may have been dropped before the New York opening.

1ST HALF OF CROWD: Phooey, Goodhue!
2ND HALF OF CROWD: Screwy, Goodhue!
1ST HALF OF CROWD: Applesauce, Goodhue!
2ND HALF OF CROWD: Baloney!
1ST HALF OF CROWD: He's mad, Goodhue!
2ND HALF OF CROWD: He's nuts, Goodhue!
1ST HALF OF CROWD: He's crazy, Goodhue!
2ND HALF OF CROWD: He's a phony!
1ST HALF OF CROWD: Turn him off!
2ND HALF OF CROWD: Throw him out!
1ST HALF OF CROWD: Take him away!
2ND HALF OF CROWD: Send him home!
1ST HALF OF CROWD: Knock him down!
2ND HALF OF CROWD: Muss him up!
1ST HALF OF CROWD: Maul him!
2ND HALF OF CROWD: Recall him!
1ST HALF OF CROWD: Recall him!
2ND HALF OF CROWD: Recall him!
1ST HALF OF CROWD: Recall him!
ALL: Recall, Goodhue!
Recall him!

FROM NOW ON

Published October 1938. During the tryout this number was sung in Act I. Introduced by William Gaxton and Tamara.

VERSE 1

BUCK: A fool there was
And he made his pray'r
To lights that glitter,
Bugs that jitter,
And girls too bitter to care.
But this fool that was
Has suddenly found life solved
Since you appeared,
So, baby, be it resolved—

REFRAIN 1

From now on, no more philand'ring,
No more hot spots, no scatterbrain,
From now on, my fun will be meand'ring
With my darling, down lover's lane.
The old gang will never know me
When they find
I've become the kind
People call "homey."
No more yearn for something new, dear,
My address is you, dear,
From now on.

VERSE 2

COLETTE: I'd like to b'lieve, chéri,
The words that you say to me,
For if I have your love,
Could I ask for anything more?
But, frankly, dites-moi
Exactly, combien de fois,
When the moon shone above
Have you said before—

REFRAIN 2

"From now on, no more philand'ring,
No more hot spots, no scatterbrain,
From now on, my fun will be meand'ring
With my darling, down lover's lane."
I can't b'lieve a word you say, boy,
For you see
You were born to be
Merely a playboy.
So put love back on the shelf, dear,
Be your charming self
From now on.

PATTER

SINGERS: Let's call it a day,
Tough luck,
At the good old Paradise.
BUCK & COLETTE: Child's is cheaper.
SINGERS: Give it up, give it up.
Would you like to take a rest?
M-m, m-m!
Up on Riverside Drive
The brother Elks,
So you're growing a beard?
At the county jail,
Why don't you stop?
Quiet, please
No reprise
From now on.

REFRAIN FOR FINALE, ACT I

BUCK: From now on, no aimless floating,
I see daylight, I've got a plan.
From now on, my job will be promoting
This great hero, this superman!
So don't be surprised (how could you?)
When they name
For the Hall of Fame
Stinky P. Goodhue.
COLETTE: At long last, the skies are blue, dear,
My address is you, dear,
From now on.

I WANT TO GO HOME

Published December 1938. Introduced by Victor Moore.

VERSE

When the sun goes down on the big Red Square,
I dream of Kansas away out there,*
And I get so homesick I swear
I just go silly.
How I long at the drugstore again to sit
And order a double banana split,
And then wash it down with some rare old sars'parilly.
The trouble is with this job
You can't get corn on the cob.

**Published version:*
Ev'ry afternoon when the sun goes down,
I dream of Kansas and my home town,

REFRAIN

I want to go home to old Topeka
And cry "Eureka,
I'm here to stay!"
I want to go home to Middle West land
'Cause that is the best land
In the world today.
When those Cossacks start to sing,
That's when I retire,
Why, they couldn't show a thing
To our Baptist choir.
Topeka to some may seem a hick town,
To me it's a slick town,
And I want to go home.

REFRAIN 2

I want to go home to old Topeka
And cry "Eureka,
I'm here to stay!"
I want to go home to Middle West land
'Cause that is the best land
In the world today.
How I long once more to go
With the folks that we know
To a double-feature show
For a game of "Screeno."
Some bus drivers say Topeka's dirty,
To me it's so purty
And I want to go home.

REFRAIN 3

I want to go home to old Topeka
And cry "Eureka,
I'm here to stay!"
I want to go home to Middle West land
'Cause that is the best land
In the world today.
Often, ev'nings, just for fun,
When I've ceased my labors,
I take pop-shots with my gun
Just to scare the neighbors.
Topeka to you might seem too quiet,
To me it's a riot,
And I want to go home.

REFRAIN 4

And besides her city hall
And her other glories,
There's a pool room where they all
Tell the darnedest stories!
Topeka for you may be the last town,
To me it's a fast town
And I want to go home.

MY HEART BELONGS TO DADDY

Published November 1938. This number launched the Broadway career of Mary Martin.

VERSE

I used to fall
In love with all
Those boys who maul
Refined ladies.
But now I tell
Each young gazelle
To go to hell—
I mean, Hades,
For since I've come to care
For such a sweet millionaire.

REFRAIN 1

While tearing off
A game of golf
I may make a play for the caddy.
But when I do
I don't follow through
'Cause my heart belongs to Daddy.
If I invite
A boy, some night,
To dine on my fine finnan haddie,
I just adore
His asking for more,
But my heart belongs to Daddy.
Yes, my heart belongs to Daddy,
So I simply couldn't be bad.
Yes, my heart belongs to Daddy,
Da-da, da-da-da, da-da-da, dad!
So I want to warn you, laddie,
Tho' I know you're perfectly swell,
That my heart belongs to Daddy
'Cause my Daddy, he treats me so well.
He treats it and treats it,
And then he repeats it,
Yes, Daddy, he treats it so well.

REFRAIN 2

Saint Patrick's Day,
Although I may
Be seen wearing green with a paddy,
I'm always sharp
When playing the harp,
'Cause my heart belongs to Daddy.
Though other dames
At football games
May long for a strong undergraddy,

I never dream
Of making the team
'Cause my heart belongs to Daddy.
Yes, my heart belongs to Daddy,
So I simply couldn't be bad.
Yes, my heart belongs to Daddy,
Da-da, da-da-da, da-da-da, dad!
So I want to warn you, laddie,
Tho' I simply hate to be frank,
That I can't be mean to Daddy
'Cause my Da-da-da-daddy might spank.
In matters artistic
He's not modernistic
So Da-da-da-daddy might spank.

TOMORROW

Published October 1938. Introduced by Sophie Tucker and ensemble.

VERSE

Ladies and gentlemen, when my heart is sick
I've got a remedy that does the trick,
So, ladies and gentlemen, whenever you're blue
I advise you to try
My remedy too,
Just say—

REFRAIN 1

Tomorrow, your troubles'll be done,
Tomorrow, your vict'ry'll be won,
Tomorrow, we're all gonna have fun,
'Cause there ain't gonna be no sorrow, tomorrow.
Tomorrow, when the dawn appears, we all will be
so good,
And so intent on doing just exactly as we should,
That there'll be no double-crossing, even out in
Hollywood,
'Cause there ain't gonna be no sorrow, tomorrow.
Tomorrow, you poor Jerseyites, who got such
awful jars,
When Orson Welles went on the air and made
you all see stars,
I know you'll be relieved to hear we're giving
him back to Mars,
'Cause there ain't gonna be no sorrow, tomorrow.
Tomorrow, plumpish ladies who are heavier than
whales,
Will wake to find that suddenly they're all as
thin as rails,
So little Elsa Maxwell will no longer break the
scales,
'Cause there ain't gonna be no sorrow, tomorrow.
We'll have so much spare time that each of
Maurice Evans' plays
Instead of lasting seven hours will last for days
and days,
And to make all federal projects even bigger, we
propose
To throw out Harry Hopkins and instead hire
Billy Rose.
Tomorrow, this dear world will be so beautiful a
place,
And such a happy hunting ground for all the
human race,
That you'll even see John L. Lewis with a smile
upon his face,
'Cause there ain't gonna be no sorrow, tomorrow.

REFRAIN 2

Tomorrow, your troubles'll be done,
Tomorrow, your vict'ry'll be won,
Tomorrow, we're all gonna have fun,
'Cause there ain't gonna be no sorrow, tomorrow.
Yes, yes, tomorrow, it's all gonna be grand,
Tomorrow, you'll start leadin' the band,
Tomorrow, we'll live in a new land
'Cause there ain't gonna be no sorrow, tomorrow.
There ain't gonna be
No tears in your eyes,
You ain't gonna see
No clouds in the skies,
You ain't gonna have
No worries at all,
So why do you fret yourself iller?
You'll feel like a killer-diller.
Tomorrow, you'll wake up and feel swell,
Tomorrow, you'll start ringin' the bell,
Tomorrow, we're all gonna raise hell
'Cause there ain't gonna be no sorrow, tomorrow.
And so why borrow
Even a small cup of sorrow?
Instead, get in your head, mio caro,
There ain't gonna be no sorrow, tomorrow.
No, no there ain't gonna be
No sorrow for you and me
Tomorrow.

REFRAIN 3

Tomorrow, there'll be nothin' but peace—
Tomorrow, we'll all get a new lease,
Tomorrow, your trousers'll all crease,
'Cause there ain't gonna be no sorrow, tomorrow.
Yes, yes, tomorrow, the soldiers and their kits,
Tomorrow, will put war on the fritz,
Tomorrow, and move into the Ritz,
'Cause there ain't gonna be no sorrow, tomorrow.

You girls who adore
New clothes on your backs,
You'll each own a floor
At Gimbels and Saks.
You boys who are blue,
'Cause always it's true
When you see the girls,
You want to ensnare 'em,
You'll each have a Turkish harem.
Tomorrow, your dear hubby, madame,
Tomorrow, who's colder than a clam,
Tomorrow, will start pushin' a pram,
'Cause there ain't gonna be no sorrow,
Tomorrow.

REFRAIN 4

Tomorrow, if blue, laddie, you are,
Tomorrow, 'cause she's gone away far,
Tomorrow, you'll meet Hedy Lamarr,
'Cause there ain't gonna be no sorrow, tomorrow.
Yes, yes, tomorrow, dear lady with gray hair,
Tomorrow, if you'd like an affair,
Tomorrow, Bob Taylor'll be there
'Cause there ain't gonna be no sorrow, tomorrow.
You're sure gonna meet
The one you'll adore,
Your heart's gonna beat
As never before,
It's all gonna change
From darkness to dawn,
So why do you squeal and feel so darn bitter?
You'll score like a Yankee hitter.
Tomorrow, the season'll be spring,
Tomorrow, the birdies'll all sing,
Tomorrow, Dan Cupid'll be king,
So there ain't gonna be no sorrow, tomorrow.
And so why trouble
Each time a pin bursts your bubble?
Just say, when you feel 'way below par, oh,
"There ain't gonna be no sorrow, tomorrow."

CODA

No, no there ain't gonna be
No sorrow for you and me
Tomorrow.

FAR AWAY

Published November 1938. Introduced by William Gaxton and Tamara.

VERSE

Now that there is no question
Of my not becoming your wife,
I've a certain suggestion
As to our married life.
If you only accept it
I shall prove my gratitude.
Go on, spring it,
If possible, sing it,
For I'm in a lyrical mood.

REFRAIN 1

I'm not suggesting to you
A drafty cottage for two
By the side of a wide waterfall,
But you must grant me, sweetheart,
That it would be rather smart
To get away, far away from it all.
I'll make a row if you lease
A tumbling temple in Greece,
Or a hole in the ole China wall,
But when it's all said and done
I'll admit it would be fun
To get away, far away from it all.
What a joy not to fear,
As we wander 'neath the moon,
That some radio near
Will repeat that Berlin tune.
And to be certain, my dear,
That the readers of Heywood Broun
Are far away,
Far, far away,
But me from you
Never too
Far away.

REFRAIN 2

I'm not proposing we get
A tent atop of Tibet,
Or that we cross the sea in a yawl,
But, dear, with me as your mate
You'll agree it would be great
To get away, far away, from it all.
Please don't suggest that we test
The open spaces out West,
In a shack with no back to the hall,
But if we took some nice nook
I could watch you while you cook
And get away, far away from it all.
With the blue skies above,
And a peaceful habitat,
There'll be no danger of
Hearing Franklin give a chat.
And we'll know also, my love,
Grover Whalen and his hat

Are far away,
Far, far away,
But me from you
Never too
Far away.

TO THE U.S.A. FROM THE U.S.S.R.

Also titled "From the U.S.A. to the U.S.S.R." Introduced by Victor Moore, Sophie Tucker, and ensemble.

REFRAIN 1

MRS. GOODHUE: To the U.S.A.
MR. GOODHUE: From the U.S.S.R.
MRS. GOODHUE: Good God, it's far!
From a five-year plan
MR. GOODHUE: To a five-cent cigar,
Jeepers creepers, it's far!
MRS. GOODHUE: Think of any nation so backward,
Any country so doggone slow,
That, instead of Charlie McCarthy,
MR. GOODHUE: Who's the funniest guy I know,
MRS. GOODHUE: They still vote a fellow called
Stalin
Number One on the radio!
Good God, it's far away
BOTH: From the little ole U.S.A.,
From the snappy little,
Happy little
U.S.A.

REFRAIN 2

MRS. GOODHUE: To the U.S.A.
MR. GOODHUE: From the U.S.S.R.
MRS. GOODHUE: Good God, it's far!
From a five-year plan
MR. GOODHUE: To a five-cent cigar,
Jeepers creepers, it's far!
Why, in Russia, if you're
imprisoned
For some government bonds you
stole,
MRS. GOODHUE: Or convicted because, one
morning,
You forgot about self-control
And bumped off your husband's
relations,
Why, you can't even get a parole.
Good God, it's far away
BOTH: From the little ole U.S.A.,
From the snappy little,
Happy little
U.S.A.

WHEN THE HEN STOPS LAYING

Sung in the New Haven tryout by William Gaxton and Mary Martin. Deleted in Boston and replaced by "When All's Said and Done." In Porter's notebook, "Titles and Ideas," there is a 1938 music sketch with the title "Then I'll Stop Crying for You," one line of which is: "When the President stops smiling."

VERSE

DOLLY: Ev'ry time I ask, "Do you love me?"
You begin to clown.
BUCK: If I don't, may heaven above me
Suddenly mow me down,
DOLLY: Very soon I'll wake and discover
You were nothing but a hit-and-run
lover.
BUCK: No, you've got me wrong,
The following ditty is my theme song:

REFRAIN 1

When the hen stops laying
And the cow stops calfing,
When the ass stops braying
And the President stops laughing,
When the cock stops crowing
On getting the welcome news,
When the movies stop making those floperoos,
When the owl stops blinking
And the lamb stops bleating,
When the Irish cease drinking
And the Scotch have begun treating,
When the snake stops crawling
And the tax collector stops calling,
When it's all over and through,
That's when Poppa stops loving you.

REFRAIN 2

When the hen stops laying
And the tree stops leafing,
When the horse stops neighing,
And the Republicans stop beefing,
When the sun stops setting
To signal the day is done,
When the children stop
Paying for Hopkins' fun,
When the dog stops biting

And the bat stops flying,
When Miss Ferber has stopped writing
And dear Eleanor stops trying,
When the Chinks stop suey
And the Tamm'ny Tiger stops Dewey,
When it's all over and through,
That's when Poppa stops loving you.

REFRAIN 3

When the hen stops laying
And the worm stops turning,
When the cat stops straying
And the Communists stop burning,
When the mad duck Donald
Gets over his crazy quirks,
When Benito stops
Giving the wops the works,
When the mouse stops spinning
And the crow stops pecking,
When the Army has stopped winning
And the Navy has stopped necking,
When the debt gets littler
And the heebie-jeebies get Hitler,
When it's all over and through,
That's when Poppa stops loving you.

JUST ANOTHER PAGE IN YOUR DIARY

An unused number written for William Gaxton and Mary Martin. Introduced in 1941 in the revue *Two Weeks with Pay.* There are two versions.

VERSE

DOLLY: Our affair was simply swell
But let's admit the fact
Once it used to ring the bell
But now it's out of the act.
BUCK: Old Dame Fortune signifies
It's time we said our last goodbyes
But, baby, don't make a scene.
After all, what did I mean?

Original version

REFRAIN 1

DOLLY: I was just another page in your diary,
Just another afternoon in your car,
I was just another flow'r in your buttonhole,
Just another double daiquiri at your bar,
I was just another touchdown on your score card,
Just another baby panda to put in your zoo,
Now it's over, dead and done,
Let's admit it was lots of fun,
Well, at least it was fun for you.

REFRAIN 2

I was just another page in your diary,
Just another Christmas toy on your tree,
I was just another tune on your radio,
Just another comfy cushion on your settee,
I was just another breakfast in your boudoir,
Just another dash of pepper to put on your stew,
But before we say farewell
Let's admit it was simply swell,
Well, at least it was swell for you.

Revised Version

REFRAIN 1

BUCK: I was just another page in your diary,
Just another afternoon in your car,
I was just another charm on your bracelet,
Just another double daiquiri at your bar,
I was just another lipstick in your compact,
Just another shot of saccharine in your tea,
Now the whole affair's a bust
But, my dear, I sincerely trust
You will find another just like me.

REFRAIN 2

DOLLY: I was just another page in your diary,
I was just another rose on your path,
I was just another fowl in your barnyard,
Just another dash of lavender in your bath,
I was just another biscuit in your basket,
Just another gift from Santa Claus on your tree,
There are more fish in the pool,
So I'm certain, my sweet, that you'll
Find another little fool like me.

REFRAIN 3

BUCK: I was just another page in your diary,
Just another kind of rouge on your face,
DOLLY: I was just another toy in your playroom,
Just another brand of cigarettes in your case,
BUCK: I was just another breakfast in your boudoir,

Just another barracuda you caught at sea,
BOTH: Now you've got to take the rap
And I know, if you scan the map,
You will find another sap like me.

REFRAIN 4

GIRLS: I was just another page in your diary,
I was just another kiss for your hug,
BOYS: I was just another goose in your duck pond,
Just another boogie-woogie to cut your rug,
GIRLS: I was just another hurdle in your track meet,
BOYS: Just another comfy cushion on your settee,
BOTH: Though I hate to see you go,
You will meet someone else, I know,
But he'll (she'll) never heel-and-toe like me.

REFRAIN 5

DOLLY: I was just another page in your diary,
Just another little bear in your trap,
BUCK: I was just another camp for your trailer,
Just another Pomeranian in your lap,
DOLLY: I was just another touchdown on your score card,
BUCK: Just another cake to make in your bakery,
BOTH: Now it's time to cut the rope,
Still, my dear, I sincerely hope
That you find another dope like me.

INFORMATION, PLEASE

Unused. This was written for Tamara and Victor Moore, but dropped before the tryout.

VERSE 1

COLETTE: You are a man who knows,
I'm very sure,
That certain quelque-chose
They call "l'Amour."
So as a connoisseur
Of its virtue and its vice,
Do me a great faveur
And give me some of your sex-expert advice.
GOODHUE: What kind of advice?

REFRAIN

COLETTE: Information, please,
I love so much
Someone to such
A ga-ga degree.
Information, please,
But sad to tell,
That someone, well—
He doesn't love me.
Shall I stay or just go?
I should say, of all people, you ought to know.
So, on my bended knees,
I beg of you, give me information, please.

VERSE 2

GOODHUE: You are very friendly to seek a
Bit of advice from me.
But a native son of Topeka
Doesn't know about love, you see.
But if, dearie, it calms your heart
To tell me ev'rything,
Just repeat it all from the start,
I like to hear you sing.

REFRAIN 2

COLETTE: Information, please,
I love so much
Someone to such
A ga-ga degree.
Information, please,
As man to man
I ask you, can
He really love me?
Should I buy a trousseau?
You see why, of all people, you ought to know,
So, on my bended knees,
I beg of you, give me information, please.

THERE'S A FAN

Unused.

VERSE

Some girls collect Roman epitaphs,
Some girls collect French china,
Some girls collect baby photographs
Of dear Missus Claire's little Ina,

Some girls collect old radios and primitive Ford sedans,
But I'm such a dainty little minx that I collect fans.

REFRAIN 1

There's a fan that came from Granada,
There's a fan from far off Japan,
There's a fan Du Barry
Always used to carry
When King Louie was her leading man.
There's a fan that cooled Cleopatra
When her Marc
Used to park
Upon her knee,
But the fan I call
My fav'rite fan of all
Is that little fan my mother gave to me.

REFRAIN 2

There's a fan that came from Calcutta,
And a fan from Greece long ago.
There's a fan of satin
Made in old Manhattan
For an early girlie Shubert show.
There's a fan I found in Chicago
That once fanned
Sally Rand
When she was three.
But of all the lot
The nicest fan I've got
Is that little fan
That a trav'ling man,
Who knew Mother, bequeathed to me.

AS LONG AS IT'S NOT ABOUT LOVE

I found this lyric in the Porter Collection of the Library of Congress, but I do not know if any music survives. Unused.

Tell me tales of Araby,
Tell me stories of mystery.
Even fall into poetry,
As long as it's not about love.
Spin a yarn of pirates bold,
Tell me any tale new or old,
As long as it's not about love.
For once I had a love affair
But it, presto,
Went West, oh.
You don't know my despair,
So what you tell I don't much care
As long as it's not about love.

WHY CAN'T I FORGET YOU?

Also located in the Library of Congress. No music survives.

Why can't I forget you,
Why must I regret you,
And miss you so?
Why can't I simply erase
The time and the place
I met you?
When will the moonlight lose its glow?
Why, ever since, has the night meant
A thrill of excitement
When I gaze above?
Why, darling, can't I forget you
And merely remember I was once in love?

"Wild Wedding Bells" (see *Greek to You*, page 194) was considered for *Leave It to Me* in the summer of 1938.

BROADWAY MELODY OF 1940

1939

I have placed the lyrics from this film here because the score was written in the summer of 1939 before Porter started work on *Du Barry Was a Lady.* Produced by Jack Cummings for M-G-M in 1939. Released February 9, 1940. Screenplay by Leon Gordon and George Oppenheimer, based on a book by Jack McGowan and Dore Schary. Directed by Norman Taurog. Cast, starring Fred Astaire and Eleanor Powell, included George Murphy, Frank Morgan, Douglas McPhail, and Carmen D'Antonio and her vocal group.

PLEASE DON'T MONKEY WITH BROADWAY

Published January 1940. Copyrighted unpublished September 1939. Written in August 1939. Introduced by Fred Astaire and George Murphy.

VERSE

Due to landscape gard'ners gifted
Father Knickerbocker's face is being lifted
So much
That you hardly know it as such.
All the streets are being dressed up,
So before they ruin Broadway, I suggest up
You go
To the City Fathers and say:
Whoa!

REFRAIN 1

Glorify Sixth Avenue,
And put bathrooms in the zoo,
But please don't monkey with Broadway.
Put big floodlights in the park,
And put Harlem in the dark,
But please don't monkey with Broadway.
Though it's tawdry and plain,
It's a lovely old lane,
Full of landmarks galore and memories gay,
So move Grant's tomb to Union Square
And put Brooklyn anywhere,
But please, please,
I beg on my knees,
Don't monkey with old Broadway.

REFRAIN 2

Plant trees in the Polo Grounds,
And put Yorkville out of bounds,
But please don't monkey with Broadway.
Close those Village honky-tonks,
Suppress cheering in the Bronx,
But please don't monkey with Broadway.
Think what names used to dance
On this road of romance!
Think what stars used to stroll along it all day!
Make City Hall a skating rink,
And push Wall Street in the drink,
But please, please,
I beg on my knees,
Don't monkey with old Broadway.

BETWEEN YOU AND ME

Published December 1939. Copyrighted unpublished August 1939. Introduced by George Murphy; danced by Murphy and Eleanor Powell.

VERSE

As you sail your glorious way
Like a shining star,
You don't know what havoc you play,
And how upsetting you are,
For so near you seem,
At night when I dream,
But when I waken, how far!

REFRAIN

Between you and me,
You're something spectacular,
Between you and me,
You're a prize,
Between you and me,
To use the vernacular,
You've got what they call "oomph" in your eyes.
Till I make you mine,
Your heart I'll bombard to get,
No matter how hard to get
It may be.
So why not combine
And chuck the formality
Between love and
Between you and
Me.

I'VE GOT MY EYES ON YOU

Published December 1939. Copyrighted unpublished August 1939. Introduced by Fred Astaire; danced by Astaire and Eleanor Powell.

VERSE

I don't want you to feel
When you go out for a meal
With my rivals in town
That I mean to track you down,
Or that when out you sail
For a date down in the dale
There's a Dictaphone
Under ev'ry stone
And a bloodhound on your trail.
However—

REFRAIN

I've got my eyes on you,
So best beware where you roam,
I've got my eyes on you,
So don't stray too far from home.
Incidentally
I've set my spies on you,
I'm checking on all you do
From A to
Z.
So, darling, just be wise,
Keep your eyes
On
Me.

I CONCENTRATE ON YOU

Published December 1939. Copyrighted unpublished August 1939. Written no later than July 1939. Intended originally for Fred Astaire, but introduced by Douglas McPhail; danced by Astaire and Eleanor Powell.

Whenever skies look gray to me
And trouble begins to brew,
Whenever the winter winds become too strong,
I concentrate on you.
When Fortune cries, "Nay, nay!" to me
And people declare, "You're through,"
Whenever the blues become my only song,
I concentrate on you,
On your smile so sweet, so tender,
When at first my kiss you decline,
On the light in your eyes when you surrender
And once again our arms intertwine.
And so when wise men say to me
That love's young dream never comes true,
To prove that even wise men can be wrong,
I concentrate on you,
I concentrate
And concentrate
On you.

I HAPPEN TO BE IN LOVE

Published December 1939. Copyrighted unpublished September 1939. This number, intended for Eleanor Powell, was dropped from the film before it was released.

INTRODUCTION

BOYS: Good morning, Lady Hard-to-Get,
And tell us, how are you?
SOLO: Well, frankly, I'm a bit upset,
You don't know what I've been through.
BOYS: This wild expression in your eyes
Fills all our hearts with pain.
SOLO: How charming of you to sympathize,
I'll endeavor to explain.

VERSE

SOLO: Keep it quiet, keep it dark,
But last ev'ning in the park,
Pardon me if I remark,
I met my doom.
When he stopped and said hello
I knew Cupid drew his bow,
'Cause my heart began to go
Skiddle-di-ak,
Biddle-di-ak,
Boom!

REFRAIN 1

SOLO: Oh, please don't take offense
If I suddenly don't make common
sense,
I happen to be in love.
It's really not my fault
If I suddenly turn a somersault,
I happen to be, but hopelessly, in love.
And ever since love in its glitt'ring
glory
Set my heart aflame,
I'm just a bit weak in the upper story,
Isn't it a shame!
So please don't make a scene
If I suddenly, you know what I mean,
I happen to be
Terrifically
In love.

REFRAIN 2

BOYS: So if she can't make common sense,
Well, it wouldn't be jake to take
offense,
She happens to be in love.

And if she turns a somersault,
Well, it wouldn't be kind to find a fault,
She happens to be, but hopelessly, in
love.
And ever since love in its glitt'ring
glory
Set her heart awhirl,
She's just a bit weak in the upper story,
Poor little girl!
So if she starts to swing and sway,
Well, there's nothing for you to do but say:
Unfortunately
She happens to be
Terrifically
In love.

I'M SO IN LOVE WITH YOU

Copyrighted unpublished September 1939. Either this was the original lyric set to the music of "I've Got My Eyes on You," or some thought was given to using the same music with two different lyrics, or Porter wrote two lyrics and the choice was made to use "I've Got My Eyes on You." This version was not used.

VERSE

I don't want you to feel
If you go out for a meal
With my rivals in town
That I'll let it get me down,
Or that if out you sail
For a date down in the dale
I shall close up shop,
Call myself a flop
And proceed to take the veil.
However—

REFRAIN

I'm so in love with you
I can't tell sunshine from rain,
I'm so in love with you
I don't know pleasure from pain.
Confidentially,
Whenever you appear
And tell me you're riding high,
Why am I
Blue?
You know the answer, dear,
I'm so in love with you.

DU BARRY WAS A LADY

1939

"Dubarry Was a Lady," 1939; Bert Lahr and Ethel Merman

Tryout: Shubert Theatre, New Haven, November 9, 1939; Shubert Theatre, Boston, November 13, 1939; Forrest Theatre, Philadelphia, November 27, 1939. Produced by B. G. De Sylva at the 46th Street Theatre, December 6, 1939. 408 performances. Book by Herbert Fields and B. G. De Sylva. Directed by Edgar MacGregor. Cast, starring Bert Lahr and Ethel Merman, included Betty Grable, Benny Baker, Charles Walters, and Ronald Graham.

WHERE'S LOUIE?

The opening to Act I. Introduced by ensemble.

Where's Louie?
Where's Louie?
Oh, what a big break!
He's living on cake.
He got the only ticket that could win the sweepstake,
And we want to show
Him how to spend his dough.
If he'll buy my old car
I'll present him to Bar-
B'ra Hutton.
I can sell him Grant's tomb
If he needs some more room
For struttin'.
Here's a very nice blonde
Who's for sale, if he's fond
Of mutton.
Well, anyhoo,
The man that we
Have simply got to see
Is Lou-ie, Lou-ie,
Louie, Louie, Louie, Lou-ie,
That damned lucky old Lou.

EV'RY DAY A HOLIDAY

Published January 1940. This is an entirely different song from "Make Every Day a Holiday" in *Greenwich Village Follies* (1924). Introduced by Charles Walters, Betty Grable, and ensemble.

VERSE

HE: What a life we'll lead
When at least we're agreed
That we two would be better as one.
SHE: Famous ev'rywhere
As the happiest pair
Of true lovers under the sun.
BOTH: Oh, but, baby, won't we have fun!

REFRAIN

We'll make ev'ry day a holiday,
We'll make ev'ry night a sweet dream,
We'll make ev'ry hour a fabulous flow'r,
And ev'ry moment extra extreme.
And in time, Mamma
Will give Papa
A replica
From heaven above.
We'll make ev'ry day a holiday,
Dedicated to love.

PATTER

SHE: All day long I'll wait for you
Till from work you're back.
SINGERS: In a cottage built for two
By the side of the railroad track.
HE: I'll work, oh so hard, my dear,
That in time we'll thrive.
SINGERS: Wait till all those bills appear
And the babies start to arrive.
SHE: Oh, my love for you will never sway.
SINGERS: Fifteen bucks a week, yes, that's his pay.
BOTH: We'll make ev'ry day a holiday
Dedicated to
Love.

IT AIN'T ETIQUETTE

Porter wrote fragments for a different lyric titled "It Ain't Etiquette," possibly intended for Jimmy Durante in *Red, Hot and Blue* (1936). The *Du Barry* "Etiquette" was introduced by Bert Lahr and Jean Moorhead.

VERSE

LOUIE: Missus Emily Post,
Who they tell me is most
Reliable,
VI: Yes, my man of all men.
LOUIE: For a helluva sum
Wrote a book that's become
My Bi-able.
VI: So you read now and then,
LOUIE: And if only you look
At that etiquette book
Of dear Emily's,

VI: Yes, but how many looks?
LOUIE: You can cohabitate
With America's great
Families.
Now, for instance, Snooks,
It ain't smart,
It ain't chic,
It ain't etiquette.

REFRAIN 1

If you meet J. P. Morgan while playing golf
With the Long Island banking set,
Don't greet him by tearing your girdle off,
It ain't etiquette.
When invited to hear from an op'ra box
Rigoletto's divine quartet,
Don't bother your neighbors by throwing rocks,
It ain't etiquette.
When you're asked up to dine by some mean old minx,
And a meatball is all you get,
Never say to your hostess,
"This dinner stinks,"
It ain't smart,
It ain't chic,
It ain't etiquette.

REFRAIN 2

On arriving at one of those White House balls,
While you're touching up your toilette,
Don't write smutty jokes on the bathroom walls,
It ain't etiquette.
When the Chinese Ambassador's wife unfurls
After three drinks of anisette,
Don't ask if it's true about Chinese girls,
It ain't etiquette.
If you thought you were gypped at the Fair last year
And that Grover is just all wet,
Don't suggest what he do with the Perisphere,
It ain't smart,
It ain't chic,
It ain't etiquette.

REFRAIN 3

If a very proud mother asks what you think
Of her babe in the bassinet,
Don't tell her it looks like the missing link,
It ain't etiquette.
If you're asked up to tea at Miss Flinch's school
By some shy little violet,
Don't pinch poor Miss Flinch in the vestibule,
It ain't etiquette.
If you're swimming at Newport with some old leech
And he wrestles you while you're wet,
Don't call him a son of a Bailey's Beach,

WHEN LOVE BECKONED

Published November 1939. Alternate title: "When Love Beckoned in (on) Fifty-second Street." Introduced by Ethel Merman.

VERSE

I don't mean to cause a shock in the house,
But I'd like to know, is there a doc in the house
Who will give first aid
To the most confused maid in town?
I had, oh, such sweet suburban ideas,
You know what I mean, Deanna Durbin ideas,
Till one fatal night when suddenly somebody spoke
And broke 'em all down.

REFRAIN 1

I used to dream
Of a star-lighted stream
Where my man and I would first meet,
So try to surmise
My terrific surprise
When love beckoned
In Fifty-second Street.
I thought a breeze
Would appear in the trees
And sing something tender and sweet,
But how could it sing
With a band playing swing,
When love beckoned
In Fifty-second Street?
Now, when we want to coo
Country lanes are taboo
And old West Fifty-two
Is our favorite beat
(When we're on our feet).
So you can bet
I shall never forget
That mad second
When I first reckoned
That love beckoned
In Fifty-second Street!

REFRAIN 2

I used to dream
Of a star-lighted stream

Where my man and I would first meet,
So try to surmise
My terrific surprise
When love beckoned
In Fifty-second Street.
I thought a breeze
Would appear in the trees
And sing something tender and sweet,
But how could it sing
With a band playing swing,
When love beckoned
In Fifty-second Street?
Now when we're full of youth
Country lanes seem uncouth
And old West Fifty-two-th
Is our favorite cup
(When we're out and up).
So you can bet
I shall never forget
That mad second
When I first reckoned
That love beckoned
In Fifty-second Street!

SECOND ACT REPRISE

MIDDLE

Now when moi et mon vieux
Want to play juste un peu
La belle rue cinquante-deux
Is our street favorite,
Ooh-la-la, oui, oui!

FINISH

When love beckoned
Dans la cinquante-deuxième rue.

COME ON IN

Published January 1940. Introduced by Ethel Merman and ensemble.

VERSE

Down in Forty-second Street,
Where fun is fun and heat is heat,
There's a barker man I know
Who barks for a burlesque show.
When he starts to sell his wares
As eight o'clock arrives,
Lovers leave their love affairs
And husbands chuck their wives,
To hear him hollering once again:
"Gentlemen,
Gentlemen,
Pardon me if I call you gentlemen,

REFRAIN 1

"Come on in and see the show tonight,
Our girls are dynamite,
They'll raise your Fahrenheit,
Come on in and see the show.
Come on in and view our chicken farm,
Each chick's so full o' charm
She'll ring your fire alarm.
Come on in and see the show,
There's a slant-eyed doll
Called Tokyo Moll,
She was last year's Miss Japan,
And when her hips
Do Nipponese nips
Can she wave her fan?
Yes, she can.
Come on in and give the girls a glance,
And if you take a chance
They'll show you, when they dance,
They've all been made in France,
Come on in,
Come on in,
Come on in and see the show!"

COUPLETS FOR GIRLS IN DANCE REFRAIN

If you go for apples, boss,
Why don't you try my applesauce?

If you go for pie, sweetheart,
Why don't you try my cherry tart?

If you go for candy, Judge,
Why don't you try my homemade fudge?

REFRAIN 2 (MIDDLE)

There's a Cuban queen
Who does a routine
In a single-breasted shawl,
And when that dinge
Starts shaking her fringe
Does the market fall?
Don't we all?

REFRAIN 3 (MIDDLE)

There's a Southern find
Who does a slow grind
That will break you right in two!
She keeps it clean,

If you know what I mean,
But when she's all through,
So are you!

DREAM SONG

Introduced by ensemble.

Dear Louie promptly went to sleep
After getting the Mickey Finn,
Yes, Louie promptly went to sleep
And while in a state of slumber deep,
He dreamed what he might have been,
He dreamed what he might have been.
So we hope that you will not complain
And say that we've suddenly gone insane,
If we take you now into Louie's brain,
A helluva place to be!

MESDAMES ET MESSIEURS

Introduced by ensemble.

Mesdames et Messieurs, écoutez-vous,
Pardon us if into French we fall,
But King Louie's fav'rite beauty *nous*
Invite to a *très* French ball.
Down in *cher* Versailles she's throwing it,
People say it is sure to be great,
And in case you feel like going, it
Won't be *difficile* to crash the gate.
You'll meet *comtesses*
And haughty *duchesses,*
If one undresses,
It's *pour l'Amour de la France.*
You'll see Du Barry
Still raising old Harry,
So *pourquoi* tarry?
Let's hurry on and join *la danse.*
If your style is eighteenth century,
Come and gaze at the days gone by,
If you're one who likes adventure, e-
Lect this opportunity to visit Versailles.
With a tirra-lirra-lay and a tirra-lirra-loo,
With a tirra and a lirra and a lah-dee-dah, too.
With a hidy-hidy-ho and a hody-hody-hi,
Elect this opportunity to see Versailles.

BUT IN THE MORNING, NO

Published November 1939. Copyrighted unpublished September 1939. This song could not be sung on the air for many years. Introduced by Ethel Merman and Bert Lahr. My aim was to achieve as complete a version of the lyric as possible, utilizing every version of all the various refrains Porter essayed.

VERSE

HE: Love affairs among gentility
Hit the rocks with great agility
Either because of income or incompatibility.
SHE: We've adjusted our finances,
You run mine and I run France's,
So there's only one question that's hot,
Will we have fun or not?

REFRAIN 1

SHE: Are you fond of riding, dear?
Kindly tell me, if so.
HE: Yes, I'm fond of riding, dear,
But in the morning, no.
SHE: Are you good at shooting, dear?
Kindly tell me, if so.
HE: Yes, I'm good at shooting, dear,
But in the morning, no.
When the dawn's early light
Comes to crucify my night,
That's the time
When I'm
In low.
SHE: Are you fond of wrestling, dear?
Kindly tell me, if so.
HE: Yes, I'm fond of wrestling, dear,
But in the morning, no, no—no, no,
No, no, no, no, no!*

REFRAIN 2

HE: Do you like the mountains, dear?
Kindly tell me, if so.
SHE: Yes, I like the mountains, dear,
But in the morning, no.
HE: Are you good at climbing, dear?
Kindly tell me, if so.
SHE: Yes, I'm good at climbing, dear,
But in the morning, no.
When the light of the day
Comes and drags me from the hay,
That's the time

*This refrain, with "boxing" substituted for "wrestling," was the only published refrain from the song.

When I'm
In low.
HE: Have you tried Pike's Peak, my dear?
Kindly tell me, if so.
SHE: Yes, I've tried Pike's Peak, my dear,
But in the morning, no, no—no, no,
No, no, no, no, no!

REFRAIN 3

SHE: Are you fond of swimming, dear?
Kindly tell me, if so.
HE: Yes, I'm fond of swimming, dear,
But in the morning, no.
SHE: Can you do the crawl, my dear?
Kindly tell me, if so.
HE: I can do the crawl, my dear,
But in the morning, no.
When the sun through the blind
Starts to burn my poor behind
That's the time
When I'm
In low.
SHE: Do you use the breast stroke, dear?
Kindly tell me, if so.
HE: Yes, I use the breast stroke, dear,
But in the morning, no, no—no, no,
No, no, no, no, no!

REFRAIN 4

HE: Are you fond of Hot Springs, dear?
Kindly tell me, if so.
SHE: Yes, I'm fond of Hot Springs, dear,
But in the morning, no.
HE: D'you like old Point Comfort, dear?
Kindly tell me, if so.
SHE: I like old Point Comfort, dear,
But in the morning, no.
When my maid toddles in
With my orange juice and gin,
That's the time
When I'm
In low.
HE: Do you like Mi-ami, dear?
Kindly tell me, if so.
SHE: Yes, I like your-ami, dear,
But in the morning, no, no—no, no,
No, no, no, no, no!

REFRAIN 5†

SHE: Are you good at football, dear?
Kindly tell me, if so.
HE: Yes, I'm good at football, dear,
But in the morning, no.
SHE: Do you ever fumble, dear?
Kindly tell me, if so.
HE: No, I never fumble, dear,
But in the morning, yes.
When I start with a frown
Reading Winchell upside down,
That's the time
When I'm
In low.
SHE: Do you like a scrimmage, dear?
Kindly tell me, if so.
HE: Yes, I like a scrimmage, dear,
But in the morning, no, no—no, no,
No, no, no no, no!

REFRAIN 6

HE: D'you like Nelson Eddy, dear?
Kindly tell me, if so.
SHE: I like Nelson Eddy, dear,
But in the morning, no.
HE: D'you like Tommy Manville, dear?
Kindly tell me, if so.
SHE: I like Tommy Manville, dear,
But in the morning, no.
When my maid says, "Madame!
Wake 'em up and make 'em scram,"
That's the time
When I'm
In low.
HE: Are you fond of Harvard men?
Kindly tell me, if so.
SHE: Yes, I'm fond of Harvard men,
But in the morning, no, no—no, no,
No, no, no, no, no!

REFRAIN 7

SHE: Are you good at figures, dear?
Kindly tell me, if so.
HE: Yes, I'm good at figures dear,
But in the morning, no.
SHE: D'you do double entry, dear?
Kindly tell me, if so.
HE: I do double entry, dear,
But in the morning, no.
When the sun on the rise
Shows the bags beneath my eyes,
That's the time
When I'm
In low.
SHE: Are you fond of business, dear?
Kindly tell me, if so.
HE: Yes, I'm fond of business, dear,

†Cole wrote refrains 5 and 6 to satisfy the objections of some of the critics as well as the complaints of Boston censors.

But in the morning, no, no—no, no,
No, no, no, no, no!

REFRAIN 8

HE: Are you in the market, dear?
Kindly tell me, if so.
SHE: Yes, I'm in the market, dear,
But in the morning, no.
HE: Are you fond of bulls and bears?
Kindly tell me, if so.
SHE: Yes, I'm fond of bears and bulls,
But in the morning, no.
When I'm waked by my fat
Old canary, singing flat,
That's the time
When I'm
In low.
HE: Would you ever sell your seat?
Kindly tell me, if so.
SHE: Yes, I'd gladly sell my seat,
But in the morning, no, no—no, no,
No, no, no, no, no!

REFRAIN 9

SHE: Are you fond of poker, dear?
Kindly tell me, if so.
HE: Yes, I'm fond of poker, dear,
But in the morning, no.
SHE: Do you ante up, my dear?
Kindly tell me, if so.
HE: Yes, I ante up my dear,
But in the morning, no.
When my old Gunga Din
Brings the Bromo Seltzer in,
That's the time
When I'm
In low.
SHE: Can you fill an inside straight?
Kindly tell me, if so.
HE: I've filled plenty inside straight,
But in the morning, no, no—no, no,
No, no, no, no, no!

REFRAIN 10

HE: Are you fond of Democrats?
Kindly tell me, if so.
SHE: Yes, I'm fond of Democrats,
But in the morning, no.
HE: Do you like Republicans?
Kindly tell me, if so.
SHE: Yes, I like Republi-cans,
But in the morning, no.
When my pet Pekinese
Starts to cross his Q's and P's,
That's the time
When I'm
In low.
HE: Do you like third parties, dear?
Kindly tell me, if so.
SHE: Yes, I love third parties, dear,
But in the morning, no, no—no, no,
No, no, no, no, no!

DO I LOVE YOU?

Published November 1939. Introduced by Ronald Graham and Ethel Merman.

VERSE

After that sweet summer afternoon
When for the first time I saw you appear,
Dreaming of you, I composed a tune,
So will you listen to it, dear?

REFRAIN

Do I love you, do I?
Doesn't one and one make two?
Do I love you, do I?
Does July need a sky of blue?
Would I miss you, would I,
If you ever should go away?
If the sun should desert the day,
What would life be?
Will I leave you never?
Could the ocean leave the shore?
Will I worship you forever?
Isn't heaven forevermore?
Do I love you, do I?
Oh, my dear, it's so easy to see,
Don't you know I do?
Don't I show you I do?
Just as you love me?

DU BARRY WAS A LADY

This elaborate ensemble number brought Act I to its conclusion.

STARLETS: Poor man of sorrow,
Forget tomorrow
And relax.
HARRY &
QUARTET: Till tomorrow,

When we give you the ax.
STARLETS: Picture tomorrow
When to our sorrow
You are dead.
QUARTET: That's tomorrow
When we chop off your head.
Chop, chop, chop, etc.
STARLETS: All our eyes will pop, pop, pop,
All our tears will drop, drop, drop,
All our hearts will stop, stop, stop,
When tomorrow
HARRY & QUARTET: Tomorrow
STARLETS: Tomorrow
HARRY & QUARTET: Tomorrow
TOGETHER: Tomorrow we see 'em chop off your head—
Tomorrow you see 'em chop off your head
HARRY & QUARTET: Chop, chop
STARLETS: Off your head,
TOGETHER: Chop, chop off your head,
Chop, chop off your head,
Chop, chop, chop, chop, chop,
Chop off your head.

CHOISEUL: Silence, his most royal Majesty.
LOUIE: I found him, the writer,
And now he's on the spot,
I found him, the blighter,
When other men could not!

GIRLS: All our eyes will pop, pop, pop,
All our tears will drop, drop, drop,
All our hearts will stop, stop, stop,
When tomorrow we see 'em chop off your head.
MEN: Chop, chop, chop, chop, etc.
When tomorrow we see 'em chop off your head.

ALEX: Do I love you, do I?
Would I die for you, my France?
Do I love you, do I,
Land of beauty and great romance?
Do I love you, do I?
Oh, my homeland, ma chère patrie!
Don't you know I do?
Don't I show that I do?
Just as you love me.
MAY: Oh, I'm getting tired of this song and dance,
So set him free again, Lou.
This poor poet obviously worships France
And, baby, France means you.
ENSEMBLE: Too true, too true,
France means Lou.
LOUIE: No, I won't agree till I hear him try
To sing that shameful ballad he wrote.
MAY: You can't force the pris'ner to testify
Against himself.
LOUIE: Then I will sing it.
Mimimimi, mimimimi, mi
Mimimimi, mimimimi, mi
Pardon my throat,
Mesdames et Messieurs.

Du Barry was a lady
Who brought King Louie to shame,
Du Barry was a lady
Who was the person to blame,
A viper, vile and shady,
A vulture in high finance,
Du Barry was a lady
Who caused the ruin of France.

MAY: Du Barry was a lady.
Who brought King Louie to shame?
ENSEMBLE: Who brought King Louie to shame?
MAY: Du Barry was a lady.
Who was the person to blame?
ENSEMBLE: Who was to blame?
MAY: A viper, vile and shady,
A vulture in high finance.
MAY: Du Barry was a lady.
MAY & ENSEMBLE: Who caused the ruin of France, of France?
You caused the ruin of France!

GIVE HIM THE OO-LA-LA

Published January 1940. Written during the Boston tryout when everyone connected with the show felt that Ethel Merman needed an additional song.

REFRAIN 1

Say you're fond of fancy things,
Diamond clips and em'rald rings.
If you want your man to come through,
Give him the Oo-la-la.
When your car is asked to stop
By some handsome traffic cop,
'Less you want a ticket or two,
Give him the Oo-la-la.
If poor Napoleon at Waterloo-la-la
Had had an army of debutantes,
To give the British the well-known Oo-la-la,
He'd have changed the hist'ry of France.
When your fav'rite Romeo

Grabs his hat and starts to go,
Don't reveal the fact you are blue,
Don't break down and start to boohoo,
There's but one thing for you-la-la,
To-la-la
Do-la-la,
Dance a hula
And give him the Oo-la-la!

REFRAIN 2

If the tax man calls one day
And insists you pay and pay,
Just to cut your taxes in two,
Give him the Oo-la-la!
If your rich old uncle Ben,
Starts to make his will again,
Just before his lawyer is due,
Give him the Oo-la-la!
If Mr. Roosevelt desires to rule-la-la,
Until the year nineteen forty-four,
He'd better teach Eleanor how to Oo-la-la!
And he'll be elected once more.
If your bridegroom at the church,
Starts to leave you in the lurch,
Don't proceed to fall in a faint,
Don't run wild and crack up a saint,
There's but one thing for you-la-la,
To-la-la
Do-la-la,
Go Tallulah
And give him the Oo-la-la!
La-la, la-la, la-la,
The Oo-la-la,
The Oo-la-la,
The Oo-la-la, Oo-la-la,
Oo-la-la, Oo-la-la,
Oo-la-la!

WELL, DID YOU EVAH!

Published January 1940. Later, when Porter was seeking ideas for a song for Bing Crosby and Frank Sinatra in the film *High Society* (1956), he recalled and revised this song's lyric. The revised version was published in August 1956. Introduced in *Du Barry* by Betty Grable and Charles Walters.

VERSE

HE: When you're out in smart society
And you suddenly get bad news,
You mustn't show anxiety
SHE: And proceed to sing the blues.
HE: For example, tell me something sad,
Something awful, something grave,
And I'll show you how a Racquet Club lad
Would behave.

REFRAIN 1

SHE: Have you heard the coast of Maine
Just got hit by a hurricane?
HE: Well, did you evah!
What a swell party this is.
SHE: Have you heard that poor, dear Blanche
Got run down by an avalanche?
HE: Well, did you evah!
What a swell party this is.
It's great, it's grand.
It's Wonderland!
It's tops, it's first.
It's DuPont, it's Hearst!
What soup, what fish.
That meat, what a dish!
What salad, what cheese!
SHE: Pardon me one moment, please,
Have you heard that Uncle Newt
Forgot to open his parachute?
HE: Well, did you evah!
What a swell party this is.
SHE: Old Aunt Susie (Miss Pringle) just came back
With her child and the child is black.
HE: Well, did you evah!
What a swell party this is.

REFRAIN 2

HE: Have you heard it's in the stars
Next July we collide with Mars?
SHE: Well, did you evah!
What a swell party this is.
HE: Have you heard that Grandma Doyle
Thought the Flit was her mineral oil?
SHE: Well, did you evah!
What a swell party this is.
What daiquiris!
What sherry! Please!
What Burgundy!
What great Pommery!
What brandy, wow!
What whiskey, here's how!
What gin and what beer!
HE: Will you sober up, my dear?
Have you heard Professor Munch
Ate his wife and divorced his lunch?
SHE: Well, did you evah!
What a swell party this is.
HE: Have you heard that Mimsie Starr
Just got pinched in the Astor Bar?
SHE: Well, did you evah!
What a swell party this is!

REFRAIN 3

SHE: Have you heard that poor old Ted
Just turned up in an oyster bed?
HE: Well, did you evah!
What a swell party this is.
SHE: Lily Lane has lousy luck,
She was there when the light'ning struck.
HE: Well, did you evah!
What a swell party this is.
It's fun, it's fine,
It's too divine.
It's smooth, it's smart.
It's Rodgers, it's Hart!
What debs, what stags!
What gossip, what gags!
What feathers, what fuss!
SHE: Just between the two of us,
Reggie's rather scatterbrained,
He dove in when the pool was drained.
HE: Well, did you evah!
What a swell party this is.
SHE: Mrs. Smith in her new Hup
Crossed the bridge when the bridge was up.
HE: Well, did you evah!
What a swell party this is!

REFRAIN 4

HE: Have you heard that Mrs. Cass
Had three beers and then ate the glass?
SHE: Well, did you evah!
What a swell party this is.
HE: Have you heard that Captain Craig
Breeds termites in his wooden leg?
SHE: Well, did you evah!
What a swell party this is.
It's fun, it's fresh,
It's post-Depresh.
It's Shangri-la.
It's *Harper's Bazaar!*
What clothes, quel chic!
What pearls, they're the peak!
What glamour, what cheer!
HE: This will simply slay you, dear,
Kitty isn't paying calls,
She slipped over Niagara Falls.
SHE: Well, did you evah!
What a swell party this is.
HE: Have you heard that Mayor Hague
Just came down with bubonic plague?
SHE: Well, did you evah!
What a swell party this is.

Revised lyric for HIGH SOCIETY (1956)

VERSE

MIKE: When you're out in smart society
And you suddenly get bad news,
You mustn't show anxiety
And proceed to sing the blues.

REFRAIN 1

DEXTER: Have you heard, among this clan,
I am called "The Forgotten Man"?
MIKE: Well, did you evah?
What a swell party this is!
DEXTER: Have you heard the story of
Dexter boy being gypped by love?
MIKE: Well, did you evah?
What a swell party this is!
What frails, what frocks!
What furs, what rocks!
DEXTER: What gaiety!
It's all too exquis!
MIKE: That French champagne!
DEXTER: So good for the brain!
MIKE: That band, it's the end!
DEXTER: Kindly don't fall down, my friend.
MIKE: Have you heard? Professor Munch
Ate his wife and divorced his lunch.
DEXTER: Well, did you evah?
What a swell party this is!
Have you heard? The Countess Krupp
Crossed the bridge when the bridge was up.
MIKE: Well, did you evah?
BOTH: What a swell party this is!

REFRAIN 2

MIKE: Have you heard that Mimsie Starr
Just got pinched in a sailor's bar?
DEXTER: Well, did you evah?
What a swell party this is!
Have you heard that Uncle Newt
Forgot to open his parachute?
MIKE: Well, did you evah?
What a swell party this is!
It's great, it's grand!
DEXTER: It's Wonderland!
MIKE: What soup, what fish!
DEXTER: That beef, what a dish!
MIKE: That grouse, so rare!
DEXTER: That old Camembert!
MIKE: That Baba au Rhum!
DEXTER: Will you please move over, chum?
MIKE: Have you heard that poor dear Blanche
Got run down by an avalanche?
DEXTER: Well, did you evah?

What a swell party this is!
Have you heard? It's in the stars
Next July we collide with Mars.
MIKE: Well, did you evah?
BOTH: What a swell party this is!

Published version of HIGH SOCIETY lyric

Verse

HE: When you're out in smart society
And you suddenly get bad news,
You mustn't show anxiety
SHE: And proceed to sing the blues.
HE: For example, tell me something sad,
Something awful, something grave,
And I'll show you how a Racquet Club lad
Would behave.

REFRAIN 1

SHE: Have you heard, it's in the stars
Next July we collide with Mars.
HE: Well, did you evah!
What a swell party this is!
Have you heard that poor dear Blanche
Got run down by an avalanche?
SHE: Well, did you evah!
What a swell party this is!
HE: What frails, what frocks!
SHE: What furs, what rocks!
HE: What gaiety!
SHE: It's all too exquis!
HE: That French champagne!
SHE: So good for the brain!
HE: That band, it's the end!
SHE: Kindly don't fall down, my friend.
Have you heard that Missus Krupp
Crossed the bridge when the bridge was up?
HE: Well, did you evah!
What a swell party this is!
Have you heard? Professor Munch
Ate his wife and divorced his lunch.
SHE: Well, did you evah!
BOTH: What a swell party this is.

REFRAIN 2

SHE: Connie's all burned up because
She found out what a third rail was.
HE: Well, did you evah!
What a swell party this is.
Fannie isn't paying calls,
She slipped over Niagara Falls.
SHE: Well, did you evah!
What a swell party this is.
HE: It's great, it's grand!
SHE: It's Wonderland.
HE: What soup, what fish!
SHE: That beef, what a dish!
HE: That grouse, so rare!
SHE: That old Camembert!
HE: That Baba au Rhum!
SHE: Kindly don't fall over, chum.
Have you heard that Grandma Doyle
Thought the Flit was her min'ral oil?
HE: Well, did you evah!
What a swell party this is.
Have you heard that Mimsie Starr
Just got pinched in the Astor Bar?
SHE: Well, did you evah!
BOTH: What a swell party this is.

IT WAS WRITTEN IN THE STARS

Published November 1939. Originally intended for Act I, but shifted to Act II when *Du Barry* played Philadelphia. Introduced by Ronald Graham and ensemble.

VERSE

Though the world may try its best
To keep us far apart,
We can always face the test
Because we know, sweetheart,

REFRAIN

It was written in the stars
That our love would be born,
It was written in the stars,
We'd meet early one morn,
So when first I saw you appear,
As the night left the sea,
This was no coincidence, dear,
It was fated to be.
In the heavens high above
Where dreams flourish and flow'r,
It was written that our love
Would grow stronger each hour,
So remember when at last you are mine,
And Venus is mated to Mars,
It was written
Always written in the stars.

KATIE WENT TO HAITI

Published November, 1939. Introduced by Ethel Merman and ensemble.

REFRAIN 1

Katie went to Haiti,
Stopped off for a rest.
Katie met a natie,
Katie was impressed.
After a week in Haiti
She started to go away,
Then Katie met another natie,
So Katie prolonged her stay.
After a month in Haiti
She decided to resume her trip,
But Katie met still another natie
And Katie missed the ship.
So Katie lived in Haiti,
Her life there, it was great,
'Cause Katie knew her Haiti
And practically all Haiti knew Katie.

REFRAIN 2

Katie stayed in Haiti
Spending all her pay.
Katie met a natie
Ev'ry other day.
Katie would tell the natie
That Katie was out for thrills.
Each natie got a few for Katie
And Katie, she got the bills.
After a year in Haiti
She decided she should really go
But Katie had lived at such a ratie
That Katie had no dough.
So Katie stuck to Haiti
Delighted with her fate,
'Cause Katie still had Haiti
And practically all Haiti had Katie.

REFRAIN 3

Katie looked at Haiti
Feeling rather tired.
Katie met a natie,
Katie was inspired.
After another natie
She sat down and wrote a book,
A guidebook for visitors to Haiti
Called "Listen, Stop, and Look!"
After the book by Katie
Had been published in the U.S.A.
The ratie of tourist trade in Haiti
Got bigger ev'ry day.
When Katie died at eighty
They buried her in state,
For Katie made her Haiti
And practically all Haiti made Katie.

FRIENDSHIP

Published December 1939. Introduced by Bert Lahr and Ethel Merman.

REFRAIN 1

HE: If you're ever in a jam, here I am.
SHE: If you ever need a pal, I'm your gal.
HE: If you ever feel so happy you land in jail,
I'm your bail.
BOTH: It's friendship, friendship,
Just a perfect blendship.
When other friendships have been forgot,
Ours will still be hot.
Lahdle—ahdle—ahdle—dig, dig, dig.

REFRAIN 2

SHE: If you ever lose your way, come to May.
HE: If you ever make a flop, call for Pop.
SHE: If you ever take a boat and get lost at sea,
Write to me.
BOTH: It's friendship, friendship,
Just a perfect blendship.
When other friendships have been forgit,
Ours will still be it,
Lahdle—ahdle—ahdle—chuck, chuck,
chuck.

REFRAIN 3

HE: If you're ever down a well, ring my bell.
SHE: If you ever catch on fire, send a wire.
HE: If you ever lose your teeth and you're out
to dine,
Borrow mine.
BOTH: It's friendship, friendship,
Just a perfect blendship.
When other friendships have ceased to jell
Ours will still be swell.
Lahdle—ahdle—ahdle—hep, hep, hep.

REFRAIN 4

SHE: If they ever black your eyes, put me wise.
HE: If they ever cook your goose, turn me loose.
SHE: If they ever put a bullet through your
brr-ain,

I'll complain.

BOTH: It's friendship, friendship,
Just a perfect blendship.
When other friendships go up in smoke
Ours will still be oke.
Lahdle—ahdle—ahdle—chuck, chuck, chuck.
Quack, quack, quack,
Tweet, tweet, tweet,
Push, push, push,
Give, give, give,
Gong, gong, gong,
Cluck, cluck, cluck,
Woof, woof, woof,
Peck, peck, peck,
Put, put, put,
Hip, hip, hip.

ENCORES

REFRAIN 5

HE: If you ever lose your mind, I'll be kind.
SHE: If you ever lose your shirt, I'll be hurt.
HE: If you're ever in a mill and get sawed in half,
I won't laugh.
BOTH: It's friendship, friendship,
Just a perfect blendship.
When other friendships have been forgate,
Ours will still be great.
Lahdle—ahdle—ahdle—goof, goof, goof.

REFRAIN 6

SHE: If they ever hang you, pard, send a card.
HE: If they ever cut your throat, write a note.
SHE: If they ever make a cannibal stew of you,
Invite me too.
BOTH: It's friendship, friendship,
Just a perfect blendship.
When other friendships are up the crick,
Ours will still be slick,
Lahdle—ahdle—ahdle—zip, zip, zip.

WHAT HAVE I?

Dropped during rehearsals. Intended for Bert Lahr.

VERSE

In spite of the fact
I have always lacked
The power to keep 'em awake,
The ladies I see
Are so kind to me
And, oh, so on the make.
I wonder what it is,
Dear Professor Quiz.

REFRAIN 1

What have I, what have I
That makes the girls all glow?
What have I, what have I
That ladies love me so?
Could it be my classic nose
Or my famous lower lip?
Could it be my stately pose
When I stand, hand on hip?
Is it perchance my lovely voice
When a serenade I sing?
Or just because I own a Rolls-Royce?
Hell, there ain't no such thing!
Then what have I, what have I?
Oh, prithee tell me what.
What have I, what have I
That other men have not?
What have I, what have I?
Well, what haven't I, after all!

REFRAIN 2

Could it be my royal stride,
When I tread my privy path?
Could it be my perfumed hide,
That is, after a bath?
Why do they always wail and weep
Ev'ry time I leave the place?
Is it because I won the Irish Sweep?
Hell, there ain't no such race!
Then what have I, what have I?
That makes the girls all fall?
What have I, what have I?
Well, what haven't I, after all?

REFRAIN 3

Could it be my fairy feet
When I trip the light gavotte?
Or the contour of my seat
When to battle I trot?
Is it the subtle sighs I've learnt
That could cause their hearts to thump?
Or do they know I now own half the jernt?
Hell, there ain't no such dump!
Then what have I, what have I?
Oh, prithee tell me what.
What have I, what have I,
That other men have not?

REFRAIN 4

Could it be my flashing eyes,
When I plan a maiden's doom?
Could it be my hefty thighs
As we race 'round the room?
They always pant, "Oh, kiss me quick!"
Ev'ry time I start to kid.
Do they suppose I've got a special trick?
No, not that, God forbid!
Then what have, what have I?
What could it be, perchance?
What have I, what have I?
Well, haven't I la France?

IN THE BIG MONEY

This number, intended for Ethel Merman, was slated for Act II. It was replaced by "Give Him the Oo-la-la." In Porter's notebook, "Titles and Ideas," there is a 1940 title: "It's the Big Money That Gets Me."

VERSE

No matter what's your creed in life,
You may be high church or low,
But if you want to succeed in life,
Take it from me—I know.

REFRAIN

Go out and start your career, honey.
It's time you made your bed,
But if you get in the big money,
Don't lose your head.
Go out and learn all the smart rackets,
Go out and play your hand,
But if you get in the top brackets,
Don't get too grand.
As you sit there on your lofty shelf,
The envy of all the town,
Ev'ry once in a while just say to yourself,
"Everything that goes up—must come down."
I know your life will be so sunny,
'Cause all your cards are good,
But if you get in the big money,
Don't go Hollywood.

MISCELLANEOUS

1930s

WHAT'S MY MAN GONNA BE LIKE?

Porter wrote this song for Evelyn Hoey in 1930 while he was traveling in the Far East. Miss Hoey introduced it in the second act of *The Vanderbilt Revue.* Her piano accompanists were Jacques Fray and Mario Braggiotti. *The Vanderbilt Revue* opened at the Vanderbilt Theatre on November 5, 1930, and closed after 13 performances.

VERSE

I suppose a life of marriage
With the usual baby carriage
Is the logical career for me.
But before its consummation
I should welcome some indication
As to who my other half will be.
I've seen so many wiser girls blund'ring
That no wonder I'm so busy wond'ring

REFRAIN 1

What's my man gonna be like?
What's the match I'm fated to strike?
Will he be the chief of some clan,
Or just an uninspired, tired businessman?
Will he wear a fancy mustache
Or hide behind a thick Vandyke?
As a fiancée
I'm dying to play,
But what's my man gonna be like?

REFRAIN 2

What's my man gonna be like?
What's the match I'm fated to strike?
Will I be a queen with a suite,
Or just another mother down in Mulberry Street?
Will we grow a family tree
Or only have a bob-tailed tyke?
As a blushing bride
I want to be tried,
But what's my man gonna be like?

STAR DUST, 1931

In 1931 Porter completed the score for a musical titled *Star Dust.* The producer was to be E. Ray Goetz. The book was by Herbert Fields. The star was to be Peggy Wood. It was never produced. Porter told one of his biographers, Richard Hubler, author of *The Cole Porter Story* (1965), that the show was not produced because a large cigarette company, which was going to put up the money, backed out when an extra tax was levied on cigarettes.

A complete list of the songs Porter intended for *Star Dust* does not exist, but the score was to have included such previously discarded numbers as "I Worship You" (see *Fifty Million Frenchmen,* 1929) and "But He Never Says He Loves Me" (see note at the end of *The New Yorkers,* 1930, and "The Physician" in *Nymph Errant,* 1933).

Three numbers intended for *Star Dust* appeared in *Gay Divorce* (1932). They are: "I've Got You on My Mind," "Mister and Missus Fitch," and "I Still Love the Red, White and Blue."

Star Dust's most famous casualty was "I Get a Kick Out of You," later used in *Anything Goes* (1934).

The lyrics printed here are those which did not appear in other productions. I am not including the lyric for "Die Schöne Wirtstochter," which is mostly in German and probably not by Porter, although the music is almost certainly Porter's.

AUF WIEDERSEH'N

Lynn Siebert's Thematic Catalogue of Porter's music notes that the music to "Auf Wiederseh'n" is almost identical to the music for "The Old-Fashioned Waltz" *(Hitchy-Koo of 1922).* Notations on manuscript copies indicate that "Auf Wiederseh'n" might also have been intended for the unproduced Porter show titled *Ever Yours* or *Once Upon a Time* (1933–1934).

VERSE

Somewhere I read
A poet who said
That parting was such a sweet sorrow.
I, too, can say
As you leave me today
That my sorrow is sweet
If tomorrow we meet.

REFRAIN

Auf Wiederseh'n,
Auf Wiederseh'n,
So fare thee well till we meet again,
For though we part,
We know, sweetheart,
Our love could not be in vain.
You'll trust in me,
I'll trust in you,
And soon we'll live in a dream come true.

So please don't cry,
It's not goodbye,
It's only Auf Wiederseh'n.

MYSTERIOUSLY

As Lynn Siebert notes, this song reappears with new lyrics and new title, "I'm Yours," in *You Never Know* (1938). However "Yours" (see *Jubilee*, 1935) is different musically. Note that the "mysteriously/deliriously" rhyme turns up in the verse of the title song of *Nymph Errant* (1933). The phrase "on and on" appears near the close of "Nymph Errant" 's refrain.

It all seems a dream,
But I dream with delight
Of the wonderful night when you came to me,
Mysteriously.
I still hear the sighs
Of the breeze in the trees,
As we strolled 'neath the skies
And you told me you loved me
And gazed in my eyes,
So seriously.
The moon through the mist
Wound a pale silver veil 'round our happiness,
As we kissed
And we kissed,
Deliriously.
And now you are gone,
And the moon looks so cold and so old, and so wan,
But the music divine
Of your heart next to mine
Ever throbs, and throbs and throbs,
On and on,
Mysteriously.

PICK ME UP AND LAY ME DOWN

Published 1975 in *The Unpublished Cole Porter.* This song was rediscovered by David Koslow (Yale 1971) and sung in his revue *The Coeducated Cole Porter,* which was first presented in New Haven.

VERSE

A certain yearning
That's burning me up
I never felt before.
Ideas within me
Are churning, concerning
Returning to nature once more.
I want to study the pea, the bean, the beet,
From omega to alpha,
And get acquainted with corn and oats and wheat,
Not to mention alfalfa.
So—

REFRAIN

Pick me up and lay me down
On a sleepy farm.
Where the cares that weigh me down
Can do no more harm.
Let the sun behind the hill
Be my cue to yawn,
Let me rival the rooster
As a booster
Of the dawn.
I want to gaze at
Gardens of green,
I want to hoe potatoes,
I want to learn the diff'rence between
Tomahtoes and tomatoes.
If you know of such a spot
Not too far from town,
Pick me up and lay me,
Lay me down.

EVER YOURS, 1933–1934

An article in the Indianapolis *Star,* January 21, 1934, said that Porter was working on a musical for Gilbert Miller. It was to be based on a play called *The Spell,* by Lili Hatvany. The musical was known variously as *Yours, Ever Yours,* and *Once Upon a Time.* Porter's surviving music manuscripts use the title *Once Upon a Time.*

By early 1934 Guy Bolton had written the script of a musical called *Ever Yours.* A copy of Bolton's script was located in the Theater Collection of Lincoln Center's Library for the Performing Arts by Betty Wharton. The show was never produced.

GYPSY SONG

This is the first number in Act I of Bolton's script. Not a conventional opening chorus, it was to have been sung by a musician. It is known as "Gypsy (Gipsy) Song" or "Beware, Gypsy, Beware."

The second number noted in the script (Act I, p. 16) is "Ilsa's Song." From the script it appears to be a song of reminiscence. It is lost.

VERSE

At last the winter is over,
And the voice of the wind is still,
The trees have lost,
Their garments of frost,
And the snow has gone from the hill.
The sun, no longer a stranger,
Smiles down as one by one the flowers appear,
The lamb looks out of his manger,
You're in danger,
Spring is here.

REFRAIN

Beware, Gypsy, beware,
The buds again on the branch are swinging.
Beware, Gypsy, take care,
The brooks once more are happily singing,
The bluebirds, too, build their little nests anew,
Knowing that the time is due
For a love affair.
So start watching your leaping heart,
The spring is in the air.

THE NIGHT OF THE BALL

Intended as a duet for Michael and Ilsa (Bolton, Act I, pp. 48–50).

VERSE

Disguised as a young canary,
I shall never feel the same
As that big night we met at the Opera Ball.
Dressed up like a dainty fairy,
I can still recall my shame
When I found you thought that I represented
Saint Paul.
The amount of good champagne we drank
Was enough to have emptied France.
And we only had ourselves to thank
When we started to do that dance.

REFRAIN 1

'Twas the night of the ball.
We were tight, that was all.
When we rolled on the floor,
It was only for fun, nothing more.
If we rolled and we rolled
Till the p'lice threw us out in the cold.
It was not really our fault at all,
'Twas the fault of the Opera Ball.

INTERLUDE

Although we knew it was late,
We were both still in such a delightful mood
That we ran through the streets till we came to
the great
Frau Sacher's, and cried, "Food!"

REFRAIN 2

'Twas the night of the ball.
We were tight, that was all.
When we broke all those plates,
We were just crazy inebriates.
If we broke such a lot
That it cost all the cash that we'd got,
It was not really our fault at all,
'Twas the fault of the Opera Ball.

INTERLUDE

'Twas already day,
When those dirty so-and-sos
Ejected us from Sacher's,
But we felt so gay
That you summoned one of those
Now obsolete fiacres.
I didn't know where we were going next
Till you suddenly shouted, "Hark!
The spring is here, I love you, dear—
Driver, to the park."

REFRAIN 3

'Twas the night of the ball.
We were tight, that was all.
When we swam in the brook,
We'd no idea how naked we'd look.
If the end of the tale
Was a shak'ning awak'ning in jail,
It was not really our fault at all,
'Twas the fault of the Opera Ball.

ONCE UPON A TIME

Intended for Margrit (Bolton, Act I, pp. 36–37).

Once upon a time,
Lived a poor princess,
Poor because the prince she loved
Loved her less and less.
He'd become the vassal
Of a witch extremely old
Who promised him a castle
If he'd sell his heart for gold.
Picture our princess
Rueing her position
Till her fairy guardian came
And called his great magician,
Who took her on his magic carpet for a journey sublime.
That was once upon a time.

IT ALL SEEMS SO LONG AGO

Intended as a duet for Margrit and Ferrari (Bolton, Act II, pp. 14–15).

VERSE

It must have been in June,
When first we met by the Tuileries,
For already the chestnut trees were so green.
'Twas a Sunday afternoon
And I remember so well you wore
By far the cleanest pinafore I'd ever seen.
Your nurse and my nurse decided to have a talk,
So both their young charges proceeded to take a walk.

REFRAIN

It all seems so long ago,
So very, very long ago.
I remember the joy I knew
To be there all alone with you.
Your kiss was so warm, so sweet,
When suddenly our lips chanced to meet.
You told me you loved me, I somehow believed it was so.
It all seems so long ago.

COFFEE

Intended for Ilsa and the Girls (Bolton, Act III, p. 6).

VERSE

Coffee, what a gift heaven-sent,
Coffee, what a blessed event,
Coffee was the drink Homer meant,
When he sang about nectar of the gods.
Coffee, putting jangled nerves in tune,
Coffee, what a comfort, what a boon,
For though you've had an awful night
You know that very soon
There'll be coffee, so what the odds?

REFRAIN

In the morning when you wake up,
And you think you're heading for a break-up,
It's amazing what a good cup of coffee can do.
When you're trembling and you're feeling,
That immediate death would be appealing,
It's amazing what a good cup of coffee can do.
The doctors all say disaster it brings,
And reformers try to suppress it,
It's supposed to be full of horrible things,
But even if it is, God bless it,
For though battered, simply shattered by the night
You've just been through,
It's amazing what one good cup of coffee can do.

IT'S PROBABLY JUST AS WELL

Although not listed in the Bolton script, "It's Probably Just as Well" was almost certainly intended for this score, since the lyric was typed on the same stationery that most of the other surviving lyrics were (the address is "4 Whitehall Court, London, S.W.1"). The music has not survived.

It's probably just as well,
When I proposed,
You didn't seem disposed
To think it swell.

It's probably just as well
We didn't attempt to dwell
In one of those fetid
Underheated
Cottages in the dell.

Whenever the husbands tell
About their wives,
It's plain their married lives
Are simply hell.

. . .

And if we two had ever wed,
Today I'd be potty and you'd be dead,
So though we're only friends instead
I thoroughly trust
The evidence must
Convince you it's just
As well.

"When Love Comes Your Way," dropped from *Nymph Errant* (1933), was intended as an Act I duet in *Ever Yours* (Bolton, pp. 23–24) for characters named Viola and George. It was used in *Jubilee* (1935). "Yours," (Bolton, Act I, pp. 33–34), a solo for Margrit, was later considered for *Jubilee* and can be found with the lyrics from that production. "When We Waltz Down the Aisle," also earmarked originally for *Ever Yours* (Bolton, pp. 59–60), as a duet for George and Margrit, was revised and dropped from both *Anything Goes* (1934) and *Jubilee.*

"Ballet Music" (Bolton, Act I, p. 52) survives, but music for "The Polka Mazurka" (Bolton, Act II, pp. 2–3) does not.

It is possible that "Thank You" (Bolton, Act II, pp. 25–26), for Ilsa, became "Thank You So Much, Missus Lowsborough-Goodby" (see page 194), but there is no evidence to substantiate that conjecture.

Act III of Bolton's script lists a song titled "Success" (Bolton, p. 16), for Michael, Ilsa, Margrit, and George, but no music or lyric for that title is known to exist.

In Bolton's script, six numbers are reprised: "Yours," "Once Upon a Time," "When Love Comes Your Way," "It All Seems So Long Ago," "Gypsy Song," and "Waltz Down the Aisle."

Music for "Lead Me On" and "Fox Trot" survives, but not the lyrics. "Ballet Music" and "Fox Trot" use the same music. Music survives for a song titled "Technique," but the lyric is lost.

Porter told Richard Hubler (*The Life of Cole Porter,* p. 28) that he and Gilbert Miller christened *The Spell* as *The Smell.*

MISS OTIS REGRETS

Published April 1934. Porter wrote this as a parody of a country and western song, and dedicated it to Elsa Maxwell. Monty Woolley suggested the title to Porter, which he accompanied with a wager that Porter could not write a song to fit the title. It was first performed on stage by Douglas Bing in the London production of *Hi Diddle Diddle* that opened on October 3, 1934.

Miss Otis regrets she's unable to lunch today,
Madam,
Miss Otis regrets she's unable to lunch today.
She is sorry to be delayed,
But last evening down in lovers' lane she strayed,
Madam,
Miss Otis regrets she's unable to lunch today.
When she woke up and found
That her dream of love was gone,
Madam,
She ran to the man
Who had led her so far astray,
And from under her velvet gown
She drew a gun and shot her lover down,
Madam,
Miss Otis regrets she's unable to lunch today.
When the mob came and got her
And dragged her from the jail,
Madam,
They strung her upon
The old willow across the way,
And the moment before she died
She lifted up her lovely head and cried,
Madam,
"Miss Otis regrets she's unable to lunch today."

THANK YOU SO MUCH, MRS. LOWSBOROUGH-GOODBY

Published December 1934. A typescript of the lyric was found among the unused lyrics of *Anything Goes,* indicating that Porter might have contemplated using it in the show. Another possibility is that this is the song titled "Thank You" listed in the Guy Bolton script for *Ever Yours* (1933–1934). Porter recorded a piano-vocal version of it for Victor (Vic 24766) on October 26, 1934.

VERSE

Mrs. Lowsborough-Goodby gives weekends
And her weekends are not a success,
But she asks you so often
You finally soften
And end by answering "Yes."
When I left Mrs. Lowsborough-Goodby's
The letter I wrote was polite
But it would have been bliss
Had I dared write her this,
The letter I wanted to write:

REFRAIN

Thank you so much, Mrs. Lowsborough-Goodby,
Thank you so much.

Thank you so much for that infinite weekend
with you.
Thank you a lot, Mrs. Lowsborough-Goodby,
Thank you a lot,
And don't be surprised if you suddenly should be
quietly shot
For the clinging perfume
And that damp little room,
For those cocktails so hot
And the bath that was not,
For those guests so amusing and mentally
bracing
Who talked about racing and racing and
racing,
For the ptomaine I got from your famous tin
salmon,
For the fortune I lost when you taught me
backgammon,
For those mornings I spent with your dear but
deaf mother,
For those evenings I passed with that bounder,
your brother,
And for making me swear to myself there and
then
Never to go for a weekend again.
Thank you so much, Mrs. Lowsborough-Goodby,
Thank you, thank you so much.

BREAK THE NEWS, 1937

A film produced by René Clair for Monogram Pictures, England, 1937. Released in England in 1938; United States release, 1941. Screenplay by Geoffrey Kerr. Directed by René Clair. Cast headed by Maurice Chevalier, Jack Buchanan, and June Knight.

IT ALL BELONGS TO YOU

Published May 1938. While on his 1937 summer holiday in Europe after completing the songs for *Rosalie,* Porter was asked by E. Ray Goetz to write two songs for a René Clair film to be titled *The Laugh of the Town.* Porter completed the songs during August 1937 and sent them to Clair: "It All Belongs to You" and "Don't Let It Get You Down." The latter, which bore the subtitle "The Laugh of the Town," was not used in the film but was later used in the show *You Never Know* (1938). "It All Belongs to You" was introduced by Maurice Chevalier, Jack Buchanan, and ensemble.

VERSE

Why the tears, little one,
What's the matter?
Why the woebegone look in your eyes?
Why this air so distressed,
How on earth can you dare be depressed?
Don't you realize

REFRAIN

There are stars dancing in the heavens,
It's a fine night, the moon is new,
A fragrant breeze is fresh'ning the trees,
It all belongs to you.

There's a brook laughing in the valley,
There are rare flow'rs of every hue,
The whippoorwill is haunting the hill,
It all belongs to you.

Each time today's troubles confound you,
Just for fun, little one,
Look, look around you.
It's a swell planet,
If you take time to scan it,
And it all belongs to you.

GREEK TO YOU, 1937–1938

A story in the New York *Herald Tribune,* September 26, 1937, announced that Vinton Freedley was planning to produce a musical, *Greek to You,* based on an "original talking motion picture comedy" by William Jordan Rapp and Lowell Brentano. The show was to star Clifton Webb. The book was to be by Howard Lindsay and Russel Crouse and the songs by Porter. An outline of the book survives, but the project was never finished.

When Porter returned from his European vacation in early October 1937, Lindsay and Crouse were still deeply involved in completing *Hooray for What?* (music by Harold Arlen, lyrics by E. Y. Harburg), a musical that opened at the Winter Garden, December 1, 1937. On October 24, 1937, Porter was severely injured in the riding accident that altered his life drastically and eventually necessitated more than thirty operations to save his legs from amputation.

While Porter was recovering from surgery, Clifton Webb arranged with the Shuberts to ask Porter to write the score for a musical version of *By Candlelight,* which became *You Never Know.* On June 27, 1938, the *Herald Tribune* announced that Freedley had abandoned *Greek to You.*

GREEK TO YOU

Published in *The Unpublished Cole Porter.*

VERSE

Ev'ry hour, ev'ry place,
I'm pursued by your haunting face,
And though there's none other such,
It's omnipresence is nearly too much.
In each cloud, in each flow'r,
In my slumber and in my show'r,
Yours is the one face I find,
And I'm gradually losing my mind—

REFRAIN

It may be
Greek to you and Greek to me
That you should so seem unique to me.
There may be no why or wherefore,
But you're the one I tear my hair for.
I can't explain at all, this big windfall,
This personal call from heaven above.
It may be Greek to you
And Greek to me,
But it may be, baby, just love.

MELOS, THAT SMILING ISLE

In Porter's notebook, "Titles and Ideas," under 1938, the following notation occurs:

Idea for opening of 2nd act of "Greek to You"

Melos is an obscure island belonging to Greece. It's devoid of interest except for the fact that life here is charming because there are

(1) No John L. Lewises,
(2) No ——— etc. and not a Roosevelt in the place.

On the em'rald-green Aegean,
Lies Melos, that smiling isle.
Melos may be too plebeian
For the av'rage European,
But to us each hour is laden
With pure joy, what with a boy for every maiden,
And the boys don't need persuadin'
To come up and stay a while,
In Melos, that beguiling, smiling isle.

WILD WEDDING BELLS

In "Title and Ideas," 1938, the following titles appear: "I Can't Hear Those Wedding Bells Any More" and "Do I Hear Wedding Bells?" On a typed lyric dated June 9, 1938, there is a reference to *Clear All Wires,* an earlier title of *Leave It to Me* (1938), indicating that Porter briefly considered using this song in the show that became *Leave It to Me.*

Why is it, dear,
When you're around
I always hear
The sound
Of wild wedding bells?
It's such a thrill
When you are there
Because you fill
The air
With wild wedding bells.
It's very queer
And yet it's true,
That I can hear them chime
Only when I'm with you.
So all the while
Close to me cling,
Till down the aisle
We swing
To the ding-ding-a-ding-dong-ding,
Of those wild, wild, wild wedding bells.

IT NEVER ENTERED MY HEAD

No music survives.

It never entered my head
What love could do
Till, darling, you
Entered the room.
. . .

It never entered my head
That love could take
A desert and make
A garden in bloom.

Now I'm so much wiser,
I believe in miracles,
For I know that you and I
Couldn't live or die apart.

It never entered my head
Such dreams came true
Till you
Entered my heart.

RIVER GOD

Published June 1938. On March 18, 1938, Porter received a script by Guy Bolton and Pat Wallace titled *River of Stars*, based on some West African stories by Wallace's father, Edgar. The authors asked Porter to write a song for a spot where the protagonist prepares to set out on a journey up the Congo. The result, "River God," was introduced by Todd Duncan. The show, retitled *The Sun Never Sets,* opened at the Drury Lane, London, on June 9, 1938. Porter had completed the lyric on April 4, 1938. It was during 1938 that Porter's secretary began to make it a regular practice to date copies of his lyrics.

River God, good River God,
The night is dark, the stars don't shine,
And there's no moon to see
In the tall tamarind tree,
River God, watch over me and mine.
River God, great River God,
The song of the breeze has changed to a
  whimpering whine,
And the mist hangs so low
There's trouble ahead, I know,
River God, watch over me and mine.
You watch over the jackal,
You watch over the lion,
You shepherd the leopard from sundown to dawn,
And you keep all her cubs from cryin'.
When the big storm breaks
You shelter the snakes
And you quiet the chimpanzee,
You smile all the while
On the crocodile,
So smile on mine and me.
Oh, River God, mighty River God,
Won't you hear my pray'r, and give me some
  sign
That you'll grant my request,
You watch over all the rest,
So, River God, watch over me and mine,
River God,
Watch over me and mine.

WHAT AM I TO DO?

George S. Kaufman and Moss Hart asked Cole Porter to write a Noël Coward–type song for their play *The Man Who Came to Dinner.* Produced by Sam H. Harris at the Music Box Theatre, it starred Monty Woolley as Sheridan Whiteside and featured John Hoysradt as Beverly Carlton. Hoysradt introduced "What Am I to Do?" in Act II. On his manuscript of the song, Porter listed the author as "Noël Porter."

VERSE

Off in the nightfall
I think I might fall
Down from my perilous height;
Deep in the heart of me,
Always a part of me,
Quivering, shivering light.
Run, little lady,
Ere the shady
Shafts of time
Barb you with their winged desire,
Singe you with their sultry fire.
Softly a fluid druid meets me,
Olden and golden the dawn greets me:
Cherishing, perishing, up to the stairs I climb.

REFRAIN

What am I to do
Toward ending this madness,
This sadness,
That's rending me through?
The flowers of yesteryear
Are haunting me,
Taunting me,
Darling, for wanting you.
What am I to say
To warnings of sorrow
When morning's tomorrow
Greets the dew?
Will I see the cosmic Ritz
Shattered and scattered to bits?
What not am I to do?

AT LAST IN YOUR ARMS

This number was written for the M-G-M film *Balalaika*, but was not used. Copyrighted unpublished September 1939. The film starred Nelson Eddy and Ilona Massey.

At last in your arms,
Where I've wanted so long to be,
At last in your arms,
Promise never to set me free,
For now I can make
My sacrifice to paradise above.
You are mine tonight,
And my heart's as light
As the white wings of a dove,
And at last, at last,
You hold me fast,
In the arms of love,

JAVA

No music survives for this song, which cannot be dated precisely.

Why don't they change that old N.R.A
To an S.O.S.?
We Europeans are far more gay
And we worry less.
But instead of their sending a few emergency
calls,
When we mention Europe they always say,
"That's all."

Balls this season
In London for no reason
Are great.
Balls in Berlin
Have ev'ry man whirlin'
His mate.
Balls in France
Prove romance
Isn't utterly through.
Balls in Italy
Go over prettily.

Too many men in the U.S.A.
Work like maniacs,
Trying to keep up their wives and pay
For their Cadillacs,
So when they admit life in ev'ry way
Is a mess,
Then why don't make that old N.R.A. S.O.S.?

HOW DO THEY DO IT?

No music survives.

How do they do it?
Put on all this swank?
How do they do it
Without a penny in the bank?
You've seen the butler
And admired his tails,
He's the only British subject who still
Cuts the Prince of Wales.

The maids are all French, they say,
And imported from the Chabanais.
The footmen have so many buttons on
They ought to take the Huttons on.
So how do they do it?
I'm asking you
'Cause I want to go home and do it too.

MAYBE YES, MAYBE NO

No music survives.

VERSE

I'm nearly positive I care for you,
But to my sorrow, dear, I find,
One day I simply tear my hair for you,
Next day, I'm otherwise inclined.
Somehow I can't make up my mind.

REFRAIN

Maybe yes, maybe no,
Do I love you? Maybe so.
Is my love for you burning hot?
Maybe, baby, and maybe not.
If the great day you should fix
Would I jump the rainbow, would I nix?
Are you ev'rything I long to possess?
Maybe no and, then again, maybe yes.

THE UPPER PARK AVENUE

No music survives.

VERSE

In town the other night,
I saw, to my delight,
The blue bloods of high finance
Doing a new dance.
It made them all relax
And forget the income tax.
It was a treat
To see 'em back again on their feet.

REFRAIN

If of late you haven't kicked up,
And the blues are chasing you,
Try this little new step I picked up
Up on upper Park Avenue.
It's the type of syncopation
That would please a child of two,
That's the reason it spells *sensation*
Up on upper Park Avenue.
The smart set, the swank set,
The heap-big-pile-in-the-bank set,
The fast set, the hot set,
The 'way-down-South-on-the-yacht set,
The night set, the tight set,
The right set, but not quite set,
The picnic, party and ball set,
Start this and they're all set.
So if you need action, sister,
Do what all the Gotrocks do,
Try this little old ankle-twister
Called the Upper Park Avenue.

DRESSING DAUGHTER FOR DINNER

No music survives. This appears to have been written for one of the fashion magazines in the mid-1930s, possibly *Harper's Bazaar.*

Come, awake, fair daughter,
Here's the Coty toilet water,
And the Perstick which your boy friends love so
much.
Bring along that little jar a'
Velva cream, the Winx mascara,
Your new Ne-Tebs and of course your Baby
Touch.

My, your lids look bad, oh,
Where's the Bleu Corbeau eye shadow
And the Kiss-proof rouge to add to your success?
Oh, I know it's hard to waken
But your side-car has been shaken
And it's time that Mother's pet should start to
dress.

Wear your peach-blush Pantasys
(I love these modern fantasies).
Is that a Kneelast or a Belle-sharmeer?
Your effect should be fantastic
In that pistache Perfolastic
And they're sure to like your cute Cup Form
brassière.

Why not try those Pedemode shoes,
Not the browns, the Eleanor blues,
And that sexy Airplane bustle, just for show.
In your watermelon Bendel
You will shatter Lady Mendl,
And I know your mink Gills collar
Will make Mona simply holler.
Are your ear clips firmly on?
Dear, you look a little wan,
Why not add a bit more Tre-jur
And, to give your mother pleasure,
Pause a moment and rehearse
How to swing your Zipperpurse,
And, darling, don't forget
To attach your new Changette.
Wear your eggplant velvet gloves
(That's the color Mother loves)
And your Moonglow muskrat muff.
Are you sure you're warm enough?
Where's your dinner? In the eighties?
Then you'd better wear your Gaytees.
Now you're forty minutes late, it's time to go.

PANAMA HATTIE

1940

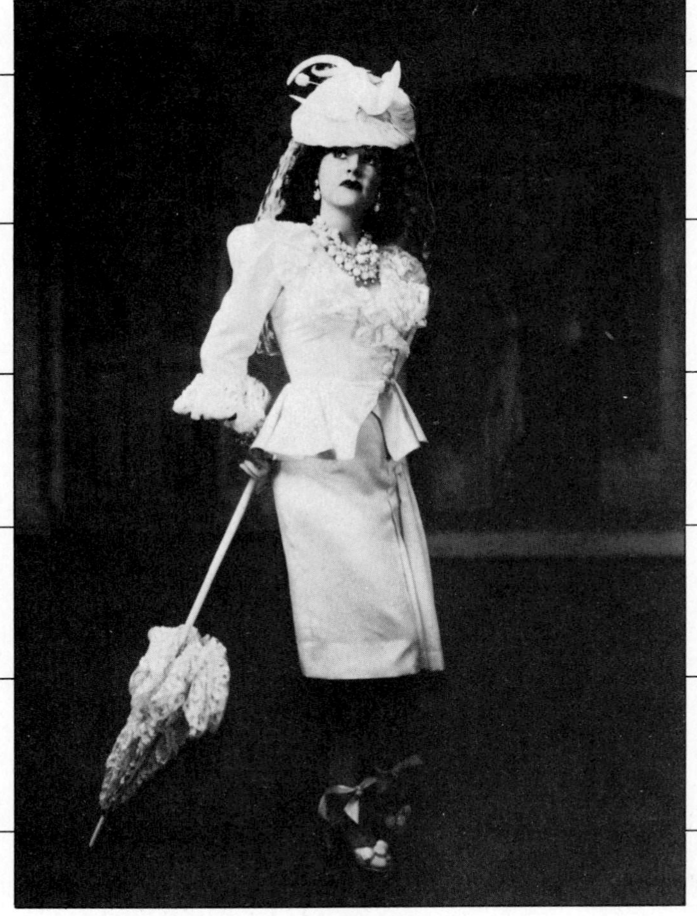

"Panama Hattie," 1940; Ethel Merman

Tryout: Shubert Theatre, New Haven, October 3, 1940; Shubert Theatre, Boston, October 8, 1940. Produced by B. G. De Sylva at the 46th Street Theatre, New York, October 30, 1940. 501 performances. Book by Herbert Fields and B. G. De Sylva. Staged by Edgar MacGregor. Cast, starring Ethel Merman, included Arthur Treacher, Betty Hutton, James Dunn, Phyllis Brooks, Jean Carroll, Rags Ragland, Pat Harrington, Frank Hyers, Janis Carter, and Lipman Duckat (Larry Douglas).

A STROLL ON THE PLAZA SANT' ANA

Also titled "Opening, Act I, Scene 1" and "Opening, Santa Ana Market." Introduced by ensemble.

SINGING GIRLS: A stroll on the Plaza Sant' Ana,
Is better even than a
Promenade in Central Park,
You meet ev'ry rank, ev'ry
station,
And what a combination
Of the white meat and the dark.
So many pretty girls you see,
And if a stranger you should be,
They're so polite
They all invite
You home to stay.
So try a little stroll on the Plaza
Sant' Ana,
Don't wait until mañana,
Make it right away.

BOOTBLACKS: Shoe shine, shoe shine.
Who want shoe shine?
You want shoe shine?
Me shine-a your shoe.
Shoe shine,
Shoe shine,
Shoe shine,
Me shine-a your shoe.

FLOWER GIRLS: Flores frescas, gardenias,
Flores frescas, camelias,
Claveles y rosas muy bellas.
Señor, cuanto, cuanto quiere dar?
Flores frescas, plumerias,
Flores frescas, orquideas,
Flores frescas, flores frescas,
Quien quiere comprar?
Quien,
Quien,
Quien,
Quien quiere comprar?

JOIN IT RIGHT AWAY

Introduced by Rags Ragland, Pat Harrington, Frank Hyers, and ensemble.

VERSE

SCAT &
WINDY: When some goofy guy,
Some two left-legged creature,
Asks us, "Where can I
Locate a dancing teacher?"
We say, "Bo,
Why waste your dough
On a course in carpet-cuttin'?
Take a trip
On a battleship
And you'll get lessons for nuttin'."

REFRAIN

Boy, if you're a dancin' fool,
Join the Navy.
Don't waste time at dancin' school,
Join the Navy.
When you're dressed in Navy blue
The hot totsies go for you,
So join the Navy,
Get the gravy.
If to bounce a babe about
You're a demon,
No one ever sits it out
With a seaman.
Ev'ry puss who plays the Navy will back me
when I say,
"Join it,
Join it,
Join it right away."

PATTER

You can learn new bumps
In the Hindoo dumps
With the Kootch girls of Bombay.
All the dancin' stars
Of the tango bars
Will escort you about B.A.
Ev'ry native chief
Will go on relief
When you touch East Africa.
And Egyptian frails
Will start waivin' their veils
When you land in Alexandria.
When you hit Natal
Ev'ry Zulu gal
Will throw out her fav'rite Zulu.
And you'll head the class

When you cut the grass
On the outskirts of Honolulu.
Ev'ry girl you meet
Who has exercised the fleet
Will agree when I
Say for steppin' high
American sailors can't be beat,
So—

REPEAT REFRAIN

VISIT PANAMA

Published November 1940. Introduced by Ethel Merman and ensemble.

VERSE

I felt so glum,
So deadly dumb,
That I'd become
Completely blah,
Until I read
A sign that said,
"Before you're dead,
Visit Panama."

Arriving there,
I took the air,
Though it was fair-
Ly late,
Then in the mob,
I spied a gob
And ob-
Viously a date!

It wasn't hard
To play my card,
As it was Mard-
I Gras,
We met, et
Cetera—
I visited Panama!

REFRAIN

If away you long to steal
To a real Shangri-la,
If your heart you wish to heal,
Visit Pa-na-na-na-na-ma,
If 'neath the stars you long to dance,
And to a fancy orchestra,
If you're in need of new romance,
Grab your chance
And scan
Pan-
Ama.
Visit Panama,
Visit Panama,
Grab your chance and scan Panama.
Olé!

PATTER

HATTIE: If you want to see the city, well let's embark.
On the right is the sight-seers' fav'rite park,
You can see even more sights after dark.
FAMILY: We've got a bigger one back home.
HATTIE: This church on the left is many years old,
There's an altar inside all made of gold,
It's the best church to go to if you want to catch cold.
FAMILY: We've got a bigger one back home.
MAN: And what's that ruined old portico?
HATTIE: Ah, to hear about that you hanker?
Well, it was ruined by Morgan years ago,
I mean the buccaneer, not the banker.
CHILD: And look at that broken-down house, Mama,
And that poor old lady, so lame!
HATTIE: That's the oldest ruin in Panama,
I mean the domicile, not the dame.
MAN: What's that?
HATTIE: That's the Tivoli.
MAN: Holy smoke!
HATTIE: It's a hotel for so-called gentlefolk,
You can go in free but you'll come out broke.
FAMILY: We've got a bigger one back home.
WIFE: Just look at those girls all covered with paint,
What a curious district, isn't it quaint?
HATTIE: This district is restricted and I'll bet you ain't
Got a bigger one back home.

REPEAT REFRAIN

MY MOTHER WOULD LOVE YOU

Published October 1940. Introduced by Ethel Merman and James Dunn.

VERSE

Oh, I'll be ridin' high
That perfect day
When you and love and I
Go sailing away
And I take you back home with me
To meet my fav'rite family,
They're the best family yet
And I'm certain, if you met,

REFRAIN 1

My mother would love you
And so would my sister Sue,
My brother would think the world of you
And you'd make gran'pappy
Slap-happy
Too.
My dozens of cousins
Would all start singin'
If we went swingin'
By.
My mother would love you
And, come to think of it, so do I.

REFRAIN 2

My mother would love you
And so would my uncle Lou,
My brother would make a god of you
And you'd win my dizzy
Aunt Lizzie
Too.
My balmy gran'mommy
Would start rug cuttin'
If we went struttin'
By. (Yoo-hoo!)
My mother would love you
And, oh, to hell with it (incidentally), so
do I.

REPRISE

The mater would hate her,
The pater would just leave town.
My sister, who's quite an arm-twister,
In the bath would lock her
And knock her
Down.
At table, Aunt Mabel
Would throw pie at her
And sing "Poor Batter-
Fly."
The mater would simply hate her,
And when she throttles me,
So do I.

I'VE STILL GOT MY HEALTH

Published October 1940. Introduced by Ethel Merman and ensemble. There are several typescripts of this song that had to be reconciled. My aim, was to make the song as complete as possible with maximum fidelity to Porter's original intentions.

VERSE 1

I wasn't born to stately halls
Of alabaster,
I haven't given many balls
For Missus Astor,
But all the same, I'm in the pink,
My constitution's made of zinc
And you never have to give this goil
Oil castor.

REFRAIN 1

I'm always a flop at a top-notch affair,
But I've still got my health, so what do I care!
My best ring, alas, is a glass solitaire,
But I've still got my health, so what do I care!
By fashion and fopp'ry
I'm never discussed,
Attending the op'ry,
My box would be a bust!
When I give a tea, Lucius Beebe ain't there,
Well, I've still got my health, so what do I
care!

VERSE 2

In spite of my Lux movie skin
And Brewster body,
I've never joined the harem in
Scheherazade,
But, if so far, I've been a bust,
I'm stronger than the Bankers Trust
And you never have to give *this* one
Hunyadi.

REFRAIN 2

No rich Vanderbilt gives me gilt underwear,
But I've still got my health, so what do I care!
I've never been dined by refined L.B. Mayer,
But I've still got my health, so what do I care!
When Barrymore, he played
With his wife of yore,
The lead Missus B played,
But I played Barrymore,

She chased me a block for a lock of my hair,*
Well, I've still got my health, so what do I care!

REFRAIN 3

I haven't the face of Her Grace, Ina Claire,
But I've still got my health, so what do I care!
I can't count my ribs, like His Nibs, Fred
Astaire,
But I've still got my health, so what do I care!
Once I helped Jock Whitney
And as my reward,
I asked for a Jitney—
In other words, a Ford,
What I got from Jock was a sock, you know
where,
Well, I've still got my health, so what do I care!

REFRAIN 4

When I'm in New York, I'm the Stork Club's
despair,
But I've still got my health, so what do I care!
No radio chain wants my brain on the air,
But I've still got my health, so what do I care!
At school I was noted
For my lack of speed,
In fact I was voted
"Least likely to succeed,"
My wisecracks, I'm told, are like old Camembert,
Well, I've still got my health, so what do I care!

REFRAIN 5

ENSEMBLE: She never will have that Park Avenue
air,
HATTIE: But why should I weep?
Or toss in my sleep.
'Cause, I've still got my health, so
what do I care!

VERSE 3

When Broadway first reviewed this wench,
The Press was catty,
They all agreed I'd even stench
In Cincinnati.
But if I laid an awful egg,
I'm still as hot as Mayor Hague,
So in case you want to start a fire,
Wire Hattie.

REFRAIN 6

The hip that I shake doesn't make people stare,
But I've still got my health, so what do I care!
The sight of my props never stops thoroughfare,
But I've still got my health, so what do I care!
I knew I was slipping
At Minsky's one dawn,
When I started stripping,
They hollered, "Put it on!"
Just once Billy Rose let me pose in the bare,
Well, I've still got my vitamins A, B, C, D,
E, F, G, H,
I
Still have my
Health.

Alternate line:
Elaine kicked me out, with a clout, you know where,

FRESH AS A DAISY

Published October 1940. Introduced by Betty Hutton, Pat Harrington, and Frank Hyers.

VERSE

I was a sunken soufflé,
A shirt still looking for starch,
I was a ballroom, after the ball,
I was a fallen arch,
I was a frozen asset,
A burlesque without a tease,
Then suddenly
From over the sea
Came—well just look at me, please,
I'm—

REFRAIN 1

Fresh as a daisy,
Hard as a rock,
Fit as a fiddle,
Proud as a cock,
Bright as a button,
Sly as a fox,
Shy as a violet,
Strong as an ox,
Light as a feather,
Blind as a bat,
Mad as a hatter
And nervous as a cat,
Sharp as a razor,
Smooth as a glove,
That means, Mister, I'm in love.

REFRAIN 2

Fresh as a daisy,
Tough as a steak,
Mean as a miser,

Low as a snake,
Scared as a rabbit,
Small as a mite,
Gay as a meadowlark,
High as a kite,
Wild as a tiger,
Drunk as a fool,
Sour as a lemon
And stubborn as a mule,
Sweet as a cookie,
Pure as a dove,
That means, Mister, I'm in love.

REFRAIN 3

Fresh as a daisy,
Quick as a flash,
Slow as a tortoise,
Mixed as a hash,
Fierce as a lion,
Meek as a lamb,
Hot as a poker
And cold as a clam,
Dead as a doornail,
Dumb as a dolt,
Spry as a kitten
And frisky as a colt,
Good as an angel
In heaven above,
That means, Mister, I'm in love.

WELCOME TO JERRY

Introduced by ensemble

SINGERS: Welcome chiquita Geraldina,
Welcome, bonita angelina,
Welcome, la linda filadelfiana,
Welcome en musica gitana.
Bienvenida, señorita Geraldina,
Bienvenida, muchachita superfina,
Aquí, te invitamos a morar.
So welcome, Jerry, a tu nuevo hogar.

LET'S BE BUDDIES

Published October 1940. Original title was "What Say, Let's Be Buddies." Introduced by Ethel Merman and Joan Carroll.

VERSE

HATTIE: I get awful gloomy,
JERRY: You mean, *very* gloomy,
HATTIE: *Very* gloomy, now and then, in this town,
'Cause it's always so hard
To find a real pard
Who'll play in your yard
When you're down.
But since the talk you and me,
I mean, you and *I* have had,
I've got a good friend, I see.
JERRY: Well I'm not so very bad.

REFRAIN

What say, let's be buddies,
What say, let's be pals,
What say, let's be buddies,
And keep up each other's morales.
I may never shout it,
But many's the time I'm blue,
What say, how's about it,
Can't I be a buddy to you?

PATTER

JERRY: Yes, with certain reservations.
HATTIE: Will you try your best to go for this moll?
JERRY: Hattie, what are you talking about?
HATTIE: If you do, I'll buy a new dress for your doll.
JERRY: But please let *me* pick it out.
HATTIE: And I'll take you to hear the big cathedral bells.
JERRY: Oh, I hate those noisy old chimes.
HATTIE: Well, instead then we'll go to see *Gone With the Wind.*
JERRY: But I've already seen it four times.
HATTIE: Would you like a big box of chocolate creams?
JERRY: No, for candy I never did care.
HATTIE: Then will you let me get you a cute little dog?
JERRY: Would you mind making it a bear?
HATTIE: Say, Jerry, old kid, you're a tough proposition.
Are you sure your lid is in a healthy condition?
Are you feelin' good, Jerry?
JERRY: What me? Why, very.
HATTIE: Well, whether you are or not—

VERSE (PUBLISHED VERSION)

If you're on the town,
If you're on your own,

Well, I'm sort a down
And sick of being alone,
Do you ever spend your ev'nings with the blues?
'Cause if you do, my friend,
We're both in the same shoes.

THEY AIN'T DONE RIGHT BY OUR NELL

Introduced by Betty Hutton and Arthur Treacher.

VERSE

SHE: You couldn't realize
How blue I have been,
You never could surmise
The spot I've been in,
I used to have, let's say,
Twelve lovers a year,
But, darn it all, today
They never appear.
HE: Oh, love is to touch not,
Love is to try not,
Love doth the heart destroy, so why not
Get thee to a nunnery, dear?
SHE: What's this I hear?

REFRAIN 1

SHE: Ev'ry girl in town who's over three
Has a boy friend who's keeping her company,
Ev'ry girl in town excepting poor me,
They ain't done right by our Nell.
HE: Who's Nell?
SHE: When the sun goes down and ev'ning comes
And the cricket his beautiful love song hums,
I sit all alone and twiddle my thumbs,
They ain't done right by our Nell.
HE: Who is this Nell?
SHE: No, they ain't done right,
HE: They ain't done right,
SHE: No, they ain't done right,
HE: They ain't done right,
SHE: So no wonder I
Just cry and cry
'Cause it's h—
HE: Cultivated ladies never say "hell."
SHE: I can still recall my first affair,
He was rich, he was smart, he went ev'rywhere,
Well, he did until he went to the chair,
They ain't done right by our Nell.

REFRAIN 2

SHE: No, they ain't done right,
HE: They ain't done right.
SHE: No, they ain't done right,
HE: They ain't done right,
SHE: No wonder I
Just cry and cry
'Cause it's h—
HE: Cultivated ladies never say "hell."
SHE: Of my next affair, the mem'ry clings,
He was very well-bred and he liked nice things,
Well, he must have, 'cause he stole all my rings.
They ain't done right by our Nell.
HE: Obviously!
SHE: They ain't
HE: They ain't
SHE: Done
HE: Ain't done
SHE: Right by our Nell.
BOTH: Poor little Nell.

REFRAIN 3

SHE: Ev'ry girl in town who's over three
Has a boy friend who's keeping her company,
Ev'ry girl in town excepting poor me,
They ain't done right by our Nell.
HE: What again?
SHE: When the sun goes down and eve'ning comes
And the cricket his beautiful love song hums,
I sit all alone and twiddle my thumbs,
They ain't done right by our Nell.
HE: Damn little Nell!
SHE: No, they ain't done right!
HE: They ain't done right,
SHE: No, they ain't done right,
HE: They ain't done right,
SHE: So, no wonder I
Just cry and cry
'Cause it's h—
HE: I told you twice already, never say "hell."
SHE: To a senator I once was drawn
'Cause he had such a lovely loose collar on,
Well, he did until they hung him at dawn,
Oh, they ain't done right by our Nell.
HE: Obviously,
SHE: They ain't
HE: They ain't
SHE: Done
HE: Ain't done

SHE: Right by our Nell.
BOTH: Poor little Nell!

I'M THROWING A BALL TONIGHT

Introduced by Ethel Merman and ensemble. Published in *The Unpublished Cole Porter.*

VERSE

My life was simply hellish,
I didn't stand a chance,
I thought that I would relish
A tomb like General Grant's,
But now I feel so swellish,
So Elsa Maxwell-ish,
That I'm giving a dance.

REFRAIN

I feel like a million dollars,
I feel simply out o' sight,
So come on down, come on down,
I'm throwing a ball tonight.
I'm full of the old paprika,
I'm loaded with dynamite,
So come on down, come on down,
I'm throwing a ball tonight.
A certain person just brought some news,
And wow, was it great!
So I'm rehearsin' my dancin' shoes
'Cause now, I can celebrate.
I feel like a million dollars,
I feel simply out o' sight,
So come on down, come on down,
I'm throwing a ball tonight.

PATTER 1

I invited Wendell Willkie,
I invited F.D.R.,
And for photographs,
I asked the staffs
Of *Life, Look, Peek, Pic, Snap, Click,* and
Harper's Bazaar.
I invited Monty Woolley
And of course I asked Cliff Odets,
But to my surprise
Ev'ry one of those guys
Tendered his regrets.
And so I
Feel like a million dollars,
I feel simply out o' sight,
So come on down, come on down,
I'm throwing a ball tonight.

PATTER 2 (1ST VERSION)

I invited Gov'nor Lehman,
And Commishner Valentine,
And to do their stunts
I asked the Lunts
And Grace Moore, Bert Lahr, Mae West, and
Father Divine.
I invited Gracie Allen
And of course I asked Fanny Brice.
But to all my bids
Ev'ry one of those kids
Wired back,
"No dice!"

PATTER 2 (2ND VERSION)

I've arranged a rhumba contest,
Just to make the party chic
And the winning ones
Will get two tons
Of Lux, Ponds, Teel, Squibbs, Mum, Zip, and
Campho-phenique.
I invited Johnnie Walker
And Haig and Haig I asked twice,*
But to all my bids
Ev'ry one of those kids
Wired back,
"No dice!"
And so I
Feel like a million dollars,
I feel simply out o' sight,
So come on down, come on down,
Come on down,
Come on down,
Come on down,
I'm feeling magnific,
I'm throwing a turr-ific
Ball . . . tonight.

WE DETEST A FIESTA

Also listed as "Opening Act II, Scene 1." Introduced by ensemble.

This is our fiesta!
This is our fiesta!

**Earlier version:*
I invited all the Dionnes
And the Morgan twins I asked twice,

This is our fiesta!
This is our fiesta!

Like all the people here in Panama,
We like an awful lot of hoop-la-la,
But after sev'ral weeks of Mardi Gras
We detest a
Fiesta!

These native dancers have so much éclat,
When pirouetting to an orchestra,
But as we suffer from insomnia,
We detest a
Fiesta!

We detest,
We detest,
We detest,
We detest,
We detest a
Fiesta!

WHO WOULD HAVE DREAMED?

Published October 1940. Introduced by Janis Carter and Lipman Duckat (Larry Douglas).

VERSE

No wonder it's true
I'm as dazed as can be,
For I know I love you
And I know you love me.
Just to think, dear, that fate
Such a fairy tale could weave!
Why, it's almost too great,
Too unreal,
Too ideal
To believe.

REFRAIN

Who would have dreamed
That we'd know love in all its glory?
Who would have dreamed that I'd
Ever rock on a rainbow with you by my
side?
Who would have dared
Foretell so utterly swell a story?
Who would have dreamed
That such a sweet dream could
Come true!

MAKE IT ANOTHER OLD-FASHIONED, PLEASE

Published October 1940. Introduced by Ethel Merman.

VERSE

Since I went on the wagon, I'm
Certain drink is a major crime,
For when you lay off the liquor
You feel so much slicker,
Well, that is, most of the time.
But there are moments,
Sooner or later,
When it's tough, I've got to say,
Not to say:
Waiter,

REFRAIN 1

Make it another old-fashioned, please,
Make it another double old-fashioned, please,
Make it for one who's due
To join the disillusioned crew,
Make it for one of love's new
Refugees.
Once, high in my castle, I reigned supreme,
And oh! what a castle built on a heavenly dream,
Then quick as a lightning flash,
That castle began to crash,
So make it another old-fashioned, please.

REFRAIN 2

Make it another old-fashioned, please,
Make it another double old-fashioned, please,
Make it for one who's due
To join the disillusioned crew,
Make it for one of love's new
Refugees.
Once I owned a treasure, so rare, so pure,
The greatest of treasures, happiness safe and
secure,
But like ev'ry hope too rash,
My treasure, I find, is trash,
So make it another old-fashioned, please.
Leave out the cherry,
Leave out the orange,
Leave out the bitters,
Just make it a straight rye!

ALL I'VE GOT TO GET NOW IS MY MAN

Published December 1940. Introduced by Betty Hutton and ensemble.

VERSE

If I'm in a high
State of jitter,
If I typify
Glow and glitter,
If you wonder why
I'm touring heaven with the swallows,
Then hark ye
And mark ye
What follows.

REFRAIN

Got the gown, got the veil,
Got the ring, it's a whale,
Got the crowd in the church,
Got the minister on his perch,
All I've got to get now is my man.
Picked the house, not too far,
Open fire, open bar,
Second floor, what a treat,
Such a beautiful bridal suite,
All I've got to get now is my man,
Yes, all I've got to get now is my man,
Yes, all I've got to get now is my man,
'Cause ev'rything is set now,
I've got a complete layette now
And all I've got to get now is my man.
Ev'rything's set now,
Got the layette now,
All I gotta get now
Is my man.

COUPLET FOR ENCORE REFRAIN:

I'm tired of always chumming
With plumbers who don't like plumbing,
So all I've got to get now is my man.

YOU SAID IT

This number developed out of a song Porter was working on titled "One Hundred Years from Today." Introduced by Ethel Merman, Arthur Treacher, Rags Ragland, Pat Harrington, and Frank Hyers.

VERSE

HATTIE: Hello, brethren, howdy do!
BOYS: Sister, we've been looking' for you,
We've got a question to ask yuh, see?
HATTIE: Hurry up, brethren, shoot it to me.

REFRAIN 1

BOYS: What do you think of reducing diets?
HATTIE: What do I think of reducing diets?
BOYS: Yes, what do you think of reducing diets?
HATTIE: This is what I think of reducing diets!
I just had one and what a bore,
But one thing about it I adore,
Fannie doesn't live here any more!
BOYS: You said it, sister!
Yes, you said it!
BUDD: Who said it?
BOYS: She said it.
BUDD: Oh, I thought Fannie said it.
HATTIE: No, I said it,
So give me full credit,
'Cause you wish you'da said it too.
BOYS: Yea, verily, yea, verily,
HATTIE: With a siss, boom, ah,
And a double rah-rah,
ALL: Yea, verily, very verily,
BOYS: We wish we'da said it too,
HATTIE: You wish you'da said it too.

REFRAIN 2

BOYS: What do you think of summer theayters?
WOOZY: What do I think of summer theayters?
BOYS: Yes, what do you think of summer theayters?
WOOZY: This is what I think of summer theayters!
Actresses are made there, more and more,
Still there's nothing new along that score,
Girls have been made in barns before.
BOYS: You said it, brother!
Yes, you said it!
BOYS: Who said it?
BOYS: He said it.
BUDD: Oh, I thought *she* said it.
WOOZY: No, I said it,
So give me full credit,
'Cause you wish you'da said it, too.
BOYS: Yea, verily, yea, verily,
WOOZY: With a hip-hooray,
And a double play-play,
ALL: Yea, verily, very verily,
BOYS: We wish we'da said it too.
WOOZY: You wish you'da said it too.

REFRAIN 3

BOYS: What do you think of winter cruises?
BUDD: What do I think of winter cruises?
BOYS: Yes, what do you think of winter cruises?
BUDD: This is what I think of winter cruises!
Winter cruises are, oh, so gay
They never make your bed up night or day,
But you meet such a lot of nice people that way.
BOYS: You said it, brother!
Yes, you said it!
BUDD: Who said it?
BOYS: Thee said it,
BUDD: Oh, I thought *he* said it.
Well, I said it,
So give me full credit,
'Cause you wish you'da said it too.
BOYS: Yea, verily, yea verily,
BUDD: With a sweet young chick
And a double quick-quick,
ALL: Yea, verily, very verily,
BOYS: We wish we'da said it too.
BUDD: You wish you'da said it too.

REFRAIN 4

BOYS: What do you think of the amusement tax?
WINDY: What do I think of the amusement tax?
BOYS: Yes, what do you think of the amusement tax?
WINDY: This is what I think of the amusement tax!
I met my girl and we had a long chat,
It got so late that she stayed in my flat,
Can they charge an amusement tax for that?
BOYS: You said it, brother!
Yes, you said it!
BUDD: Who said it?
BOYS: He said it.
BUDD: Oh, I thought *he* said it.
WINDY: No, I said it,
So give me full credit,
'Cause you wish you'da said it too.
BOYS: Yea, verily, yea, verily,
WINDY: With a dress from Saks
And a double tax-tax,
ALL: Yea, verily, very verily,
BOYS: We wish we'da said it too.
WINDY: You wish you'da said it too.

REFRAIN 5

BOYS: What do you think of this thing called sex?
SCAT: What do I think of this thing called sex?
BOYS: Yes, what do you think of this thing called sex?
SCAT: This is what I think of this thing called sex!
According to what the experts say,
Sex is a myst'ry in ev'ry way,
But whatever it is, it's here to stay!
BOYS: You said it, brother!
Yes, you said it!
BUDD: Who said it?
BOYS: He said it.
BUDD: Oh, I thought *he* said it.
SCAT: No, I said it,
So give me full credit,
'Cause you wish you'da said it too.
BOYS: Yea, verily, yea, verily,
SCAT: With a rose in bloom
And a double room-room,
ALL: Yea, verily, very verily,
BOYS: We wish we'da said it too.
SCAT: You wish you'da said it too.

REFRAIN 6

BOYS: What do you think of conscription weddings?
HATTIE: What do I think of conscription weddings?
BOYS: Yes, what do you think of conscription weddings?
HATTIE: This is what I think of conscription weddings!
A man who does that is an awful fool,
He's holding himself up to ridicule,
But it's better than necking an army mule.
BOYS: You said it, sister!
Yes, you said it!
BUDD: Who said it?
BOYS: She said it.
BUDD: Oh, I thought I said it.
HATTIE: No, I said it,
So give me full credit,
'Cause you wish you'da said it too.
BOYS: Yea, verily, yea, verily,
HATTIE: With a date first-class
And a double pass-pass,
With a moonlight walk,
And a double talk-talk,
With an extra cup
And a double up-up,
ALL: Yea, verily, very verily,
BOYS: We wish we'da said it too.
HATTIE: You wish you'da said it too.

GOD BLESS THE WOMEN

Introduced by Rags Ragland, Pat Harrington, and Frank Hyers.

VERSE

1ST SAILOR: As Shakespeare once wrote—
2ND SAILOR: He's been playin' with books.
1ST SAILOR: As Shakespeare once wrote—
3RD SAILOR: Aw, snap out of it, Snooks.
1ST SAILOR: As Shakespeare once wrote—
2ND SAILOR: Go ahead, cut his throat.
1ST SAILOR: Well, as I was sayin' . . .
ALL: As Shakespeare once wrote—

REFRAIN 1

ALL: God bless the women,
The wonderful, terrible women.
WINDY: They may stroke your hair,
And vow to be true,
SCAT: But then you discover they stroke the crew.
ALL: Still God bless the women,
Again and again and again.
WOOZY: A seafarin' man may be clever and brave,
WINDY: He knows how the wind and the weather behave,
SCAT: Well, he does 'til he's hit by a permanent wave.
ALL: God bless the women
And God help the men.

REFRAIN 2

ALL: God bless the women,
The wonderful, terrible women.
SCAT: The secrets they know
Mean nothing to them,
WINDY: You might as well publish 'em in *P.M.*
ALL: Still God bless the women,
Again and again and again.
WOOZY: You wine 'em and dine 'em and buy 'em bouquets,
SCAT: And beautiful bonnets from Lily Daché's,
And they want you to think it's the woman that pays.
ALL: God bless the women
And God help the men.

REFRAIN 3

ALL: God bless the women,
The wonderful, terrible women.
We know they're not worth
The money we spend,
But they keep on gettin' us—in the end.
Still God bless the women
Again and again and again.
I once was engaged to a girl named Clarice,
I caught her embracin' the chief of police
And I would end up in jail for disturbin' the peace.
God bless the women
And God help the men.

ENCORE REFRAIN 1

ALL: God bless the women,
The wonderful, terrible women.
They turn down the lights,
They turn on the charm,
And then when you squeeze 'em they break your arm.
Still God bless the women,
Again and again and again.
I fell for a girl by the name of Marie,
An innocent wench and as shy as could be,
So I chased her around till she caught up to me.
God bless the women
And God help the men.

ENCORE REFRAIN 2

ALL: God bless the women,
The wonderful, terrible women.
They're devils or saints,
You never can tell.
They take you to heaven and give you hell.
Still God bless the women,
Again and again and again.
Whatever you do they're just one step ahead,
They read a man's thoughts like a book, so it's said,
What a pity they don't do more reading in bed.
God bless the women
And God help the men.

HERE'S TO PANAMA HATTIE

Dropped during rehearsals. The last revised lyric was dated September 26, 1940. Intended for James Dunn and ensemble as an opening to Act II, Scene 3.

VERSE

BOYS &
GIRLS: Thanks, Nick, for a corking afternoon,
Thanks, Nick, we'll see you very soon,
Thanks, Nick, thanks,
We're sorry we've got to breeze,
The cocktails were simply great.
NICK: Wait a moment, please,
I have something to say, before you all go,
I'm about to get me a wife.
GIRLS: Oh, what a crime!
NICK: For finally Hattie has stopped saying no
And agreed to be mine for life.
BOYS: That's a mighty long time!
NICK: So fill your glasses once more
And drink to the girl I adore.

REFRAIN

NICK: Here's to Panama Hattie,
My darling future bride.
Here's to Panama Hattie,
My love, my joy and my pride.
Soon we're going to marry
And live in our fav'rite flat,
So here's to Panama Hattie
And her man in a Pan-ama hat.

BOYS &
GIRLS: Here's to Panama Hattie,
Your darling future bride.
Here's to Panama Hattie,
Your love, your joy and your pride.
Soon you're going to marry
And live in your fav'rite flat,
So here's to Panama Hattie,
And her man in a Pan-ama hat.
That's that.

AMERICANS ALL DRINK COFFEE

Unused. Intended for Arthur Treacher.

VERSE

Oh, Americans and Englishmen,
How far they are from each other!
For England's child has gone so wild
That she's even wilder than her mother.
Yet they still have in common one quality, I find,
And 'twould take a mastermind to top it,
They're both too tolerant,
Both too kind,
But they both know when to say
"Stop it!"

REFRAIN 1

Americans all drink coffee,
Englishmen all drink tea,
When Englishmen say "'Pon my word!"
Americans say "Oh, gee!"
Americans love their sunshine,
Englishmen love their fogs,
While Englishmen eat cold roast beef,
Americans eat hot dogs.
Yet when some dictator threatens
Johnny Bull or Uncle Sam,
An American
And an Englishman
Both say "Scram!"

REFRAIN 2

Americans all drink coffee,
Tea is for English chaps,
When Englishmen are shooting grouse,
Their cousins are shooting craps.
Americans don't like cricket,
Englishmen hate baseball,
The English love their ladies blonde,
Americans love them all.
Yet they're so alike in one way,
When a goat against 'em butts,
An American
And an Englishman
Both say "Nuts!"

REFRAIN 3

Americans all drink coffee,
England drinks tea a lot,
The English like their music sweet,
Americans like it hot.
Americans all drink cocktails,
Whiskey's what England drinks,
The English say a play is bad,
Americans say it stinks.
Yet they're so alike in one way,
When a mad dog comes to town,
An American
And an Englishman
Both say "Down!"

REFRAIN 4

Americans all drink coffee,
Tea is what England tries,

While England's making dreadful puns,
America's throwing pies.
America has its heat waves,
England by cold is cursed,
While England reads Lord Beaverbrook,
Americans still read Hearst.
Yet they're so alike in one way,
When encountered by a lout,
An American
And an Englishman
Both say "Out!"

REFRAIN 5

Americans all drink coffee,
Tea is an English sin,
What England calls a one-pound note,
America calls a fin.
America's sold on football,
England's a soccer fan,
While England's got its good King George,
America's got her man.
But when any fake magician
Tries to play them dirty tricks,
An American
And an Englishman
Both say "Nix!"

REFRAIN 6

Americans all drink coffee,
Englishmen tea prefer,
When Englishmen say "What a gel!"
Americans say "Get *her!*"
Americans all play poker,
Englishmen, solitaire,
When Englishmen their molars lose,
Americans lose their hair.
Yet they're so alike in one way,
When confronted by a rat,
An American
And an Englishman
Both say "Scat!"

ENCORE REFRAIN 1

Americans all drink coffee,
Tea is what England picks,
While England has her provinces,
America has her sticks.
America's palsy-walsy,
England's a trifle smug,
While England does the stately waltz,
America cuts a rug.
But when any boasting bully
Tries to tell them what to do,
An American
And an Englishman
Both say "Screw!"

ENCORE REFRAIN 2

Americans all drink coffee,
Englishmen tea approve,
When England's feeling too divine,
America's in the groove.
Americans ride in streetcars,
Englishmen ride on trams.
What Englishmen call lovely legs
Americans call nice gams.
But when any goofy gangster
Starts to tread on either's toe,
An American
And an Englishman
Both say "Blow!"

YOU'LL NEVER GET RICH

1941

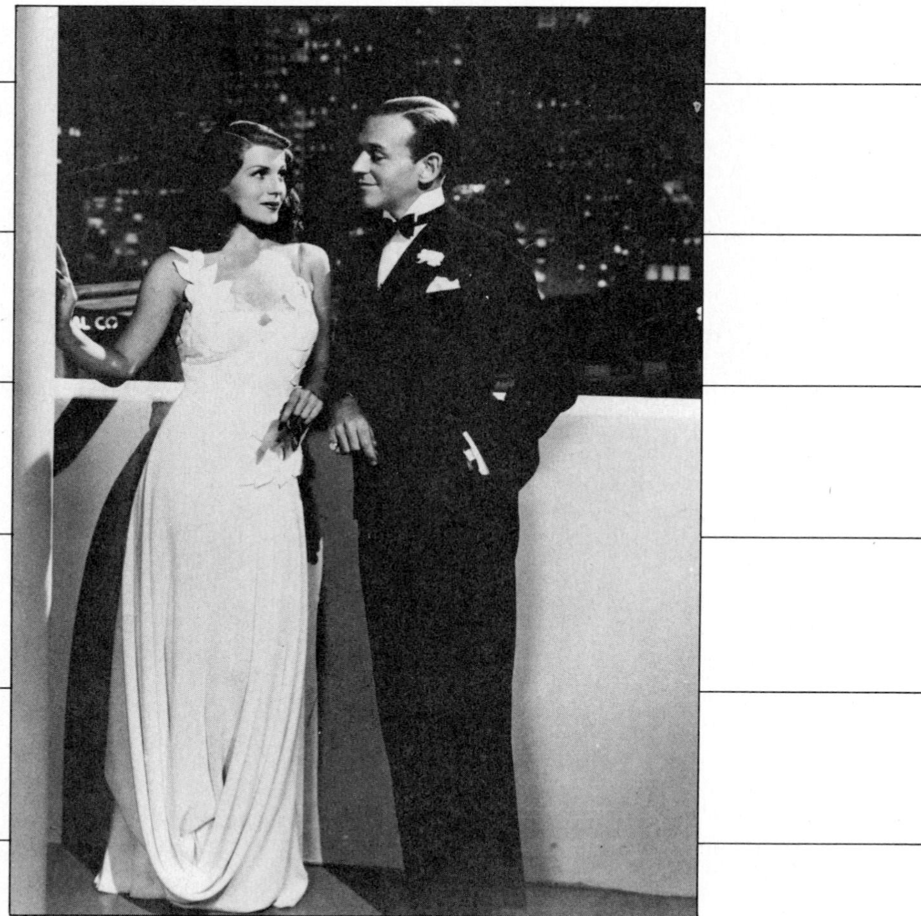

"You'll Never Get Rich," 1941; Rita Hayworth and Fred Astaire

A film produced by Samuel Bischoff for Columbia Pictures in 1941. Released October 23, 1941. Screenplay by Michael Fessler and Ernest Pagano. Directed by Sidney Lanfield. Cast, starring Fred Astaire and Rita Hayworth, included Robert Benchley, Martha Tilton, and the Delta Rhythm Boys.

Porter signed a contract on February 28, 1941, to write seven songs for a film tentatively called *He's My Uncle.* The title was later changed to *You'll Never Get Rich.* Two of the numbers turned out to be instrumentals: "A-stairable Rag" and "Boogie Barcarolle" (published July 1941).

DREAM-DANCING

Published July 1941. Danced by Fred Astaire and Rita Hayworth. The vocal was deleted during production.

VERSE

When shades enfold
The sunset's gold
And stars are bright above again,
I smile, sweetheart,
For then I know I can start
To live again, to love again.

REFRAIN

When day is gone
And night comes on,
Until the dawn
What do I do?
I clasp your hand
And wander through slumberland,
Dream-dancing with you.
We dance between
A sky serene
And fields of green,
Sparkling with dew.
It's joy sublime
Whenever I spend my time
Dream-dancing with you.
Dream-dancing,
Oh, what a lucky windfall!
Touching you, clutching you, all
The night through,
So say you love me, dear,
And let me make my career
Dream-dancing,
To paradise prancing,
Dream-dancing with you.

SHOOTIN' THE WORKS FOR UNCLE SAM

Published July 1941. Introduced by Fred Astaire and ensemble. This and the other numbers in the film were written during April and May 1941.

VERSE

Tell me why
So many men are marchin' by?
Uncle Sam is in a jam
And that's the reason why.

REFRAIN

The doctor drops his pills,
The dentist stops his drills,
The tenor forgets his tantrums
And the actor, his tailor bills.
Though not a one
Has ever seen a gun
They're shootin' the works for Uncle Sam.
The yokel quits the sticks,
The boss, his politics,
The dandy forgets his diet
And the butler, his parlor tricks.
As patriots
Who never pull their shots
They're shootin' the works for Uncle Sam.
North, South, East, West,
All the boys are hep
To do their damndest (darndest)
To defend Miss Liberty's rep,
So cheer 'em, Bo, for even though they're slightly out o' step,
They're shootin' the works,
They're shootin' the works,
Yes, ma'am, they're shootin' the works for Uncle Sam.

GIRLS: Farewell, our hero,
Slave driver sublime,
Don't be like Nero
And fiddle away your time.
If ever you're lonely,
Just remember this, please do,
You're the best of rookies
And your sweet cookies
Are proud of you.

ASTAIRE: Thank you, thank you,
Why, I'm completely floored.

TRAINMAN: All aboard, all aboard,
All—aboard!

ASTAIRE: Goodbye, dear friends of mine,
My dancing troupe divine,
Suzetta, you should be next to Jean,

Janetta, you're not in line.
To go I hate,
But, girls, I've got a date,
I'm shootin' the works for Uncle
Sam.
No crying, Marge and Myrt,
You need a girdle, Gert,
And promise me, please, to write,
Louise,
And give me the latest dirt.
I'm off, my queens,
To learn some new routines,
I'm shootin' the works for Uncle
Sam.

GIRLS: North, South, East, West,
All the boys are hep
To do their damndest (darndest)
To defend Miss Liberty's rep.
So cheer 'em, Bo, for even though
they're slightly out o' step,
They're shootin' the works,
They're shootin' the works,
Yes, ma'am, they're shootin' the works
for Uncle Sam.

BOYS &
GIRLS: From the palms of Pensacola
To the pine-pierced Oregon sky,
From the air so brisk-o
Of December in Frisco,
To the scent of Jersey City in July,
From the hills of old New Hampshire
To the beaches where the film stars
play,
Ev'ry Yankee Doodle
Has but one thought in his noodle,
It's "God bless the U.S.A.!"

SINCE I KISSED MY BABY GOODBYE

Published July 1941. Introduced by the Delta Rhythm Boys; danced by Fred Astaire.

VERSE

Oh, what nights, glory be,
When my baby and me
Used to ramble lovers' lane
From sundown to dawn.
Then a voodoo, I guess,
Put the jinx on our happiness,
And the mockin'bird's refrain
Is done dead and gone.

REFRAIN

Evenin', creepin' down the mountain,
Wakes up Mister Firefly,
Bullfrog, settin' there,
Starts a-croakin', but I don't care,
Since I kissed my baby goodbye.
South wind shakes the ole magnolia,
Moon-man lights the dingy sky,
Stars start sprinklin' gold
On the river, but still I'm cold
Since I kissed my baby goodbye.
Since my baby and me
Parted company,
I can't see what's the diff if I live or I die.
Oh, Lawd, I'm takin' such a beatin',
I'm no good, even cheatin',
Since I kissed my baby goodbye.

SO NEAR AND YET SO FAR

Published July 1941. Sung by Fred Astaire; danced by Astaire and Rita Hayworth.

VERSE

I so often dream
We might make a team,
But so wild a scheme
I must banish,
For each time I start
To open my heart
You vanish.
We might find some isle
Where lotuses smile
And our time beguile
Going native,
But how can we go
Unless you are co-
Operative?

REFRAIN

My dear, I've a feeling you are
So near and yet so far,
You appear like a radiant star,
First so near, then again so far.
I just start getting you keen on clinches galore
with me,
When fate steps in on the scene and mops up the
floor with me.
No wonder I'm a bit under par,
For you're so near and yet so far.

My condition is only so-so,
'Cause whenever I feel you're close, oh,
You turn out to be, oh, so
Far.

THE WEDDING CAKEWALK

Published July 1941. Sung by Martha Tilton; danced by Fred Astaire, Rita Hayworth, and ensemble.

VERSE

Well, here comes the bride, no less,
It's hot stuff, that fluffy dress!
I must admit
Though she's lit,
She looks a bit
Sweet.*

No wonder her Romeo
Begins shoutin' "Hidy-ho!"
As his bride
Starts to stride
To a boogie beat—

REFRAIN

There's a big increase in marriages
Due to a tune, they say—
The Wedding Cakewalk
Is the roundelay.
When newlyweds in fancy carriages
Leave that reception gay,
The Wedding Cakewalk
Sends 'em on their way.
Pasty choirs in tasty churches
Give it all they've got,
Prudish old preachers on their perches
Say, "A-men, it's hot!"
All those bridal suites at Claridge's
Have radios that play
The Wedding Cakewalk
Night and day!

* *Or:*
From where I sit
I'll admit
She looks a bit
Sweet.

LET'S FACE IT

1941

"Let's Face It," 1941; Danny Kaye, Eve Arden, Edith Meiser, Vivian Vance, Benny Baker, Jack Williams

Tryout: Colonial Theatre, Boston, October 6, 1941. Produced by Vinton Freedley at the Imperial Theatre, New York, October 29, 1941. 547 performances. Book by Herbert and Dorothy Fields. Staged by Edgar MacGregor. Cast, starring Danny Kaye, included Eve Arden, Benny Baker, Mary Jane Walsh, Edith Meiser, Vivian Vance, Sunnie O'Dea, Nanette Fabray, and Jack Williams. The show included special material for Danny Kaye by his wife, Sylvia Fine Kaye.

MILK, MILK, MILK

Opening, Act I, Scene 1. At one time the show's opening number was to be called "Steak and Potatoes." Introduced by ensemble.

ALL SINGERS: This picture may seem
To you, when first you spy it,
An outdoor hareem
Of ladies running riot,
But such is not the case,
So don't be too inquiet,
We're here
Because we're mere-
Ly on a diet.
3 SINGERS: And what a diet!
1ST SINGER: Oh, for some Colony mayonnaise,
2ND SINGER: Oh, for a Plaza demitasse,
3RD SINGER: Oh, to be back
With Charlie and Jack
4TH SINGER: In those plush rooms,
Eating mushrooms
Under glass!
5TH SINGER: Oh, for some broccoli Hollandaise
6TH SINGER: And those other dear dishes of that ilk.
ALL SINGERS: This cure, so they state,
Will make a girl reduce her weight,
But, brudder,
Why flood 'er
With milk?

DANCERS: Milk—at eight o'clock,
Milk—at ten o'clock,
Noon—and then a clock
Strikes—and we get some more milk,
Milk—at two o'clock,
Milk—at four o'clock,
Six—once more a clock
Strikes—and we get some more milk,
And what do you think
They give us to drink
When we settle in our sheets of silk?
Milk, milk, milk, milk,
Big bumpers of milk!

A LADY NEEDS A REST

Lyric dated September 16, 1941. Introduced by Eve Arden, Vivian Vance, and Edith Meiser.

VERSE

I'm tired, I'm pooped,
I'm ready to drop,
I'd gladly cut my throat, I feel so bad.
For some unanswered reason,
This year, the social season
Has been the most
Overdosed
Season we ever had.

REFRAIN 1

Life is very far from easy
For a lady nowadays,
What with closing all the hot spots
And opening all the plays,
What with ev'ry day a luncheon,
A dinner date ev'ry night,
What with keeping her children sober
And keeping her husband tight,
What with shopping tours
And manicures
And learning to bowl as well,
What with Philharmonics
And high-colonics
And giving the servants hell,
Add to this her wifely duty
Of letting him play the pest,
No wonder, now and then, a lady needs a rest.

REFRAIN 2

Life is very far from easy
For a lady nowadays,
What with posing for her photo
In all the best cafés,
What with burning up her mattress
With cigarettes she's endorsed,
What with getting her children married
And getting herself divorced,
What with fashion shows
And rodeos
And plugging for Billy Conn,

What with paying taxes
To beat the Axis,
And spraying her stockings on,
What with trying all the doodads
That *Harper's* and *Vogue* suggest,
No wonder, now and then, a lady needs a rest.

REFRAIN 3

Life is very far from easy
For a lady nowadays,
What with buying stocks in Woolworth's
And shopping at Cartier's,
What with eating only pot cheese
For fear of becoming stout,
What with keeping her children in nights
And keeping her husband out,
What with paying calls
And giving balls
And living beyond her means,
What with portrait sittings
And girdle fittings
And christening submarines.
Add to that a Latin boy friend
She keeps in a private nest,
No wonder, now and then, a lady needs a rest.

REFRAIN 4

Rip Ra-Ti-Ra-Ti-Ra
Life is very far from easy
For a lady nowadays,
What with benefits unending
And charity matinees,
What with rooting for the Russians
Without being called a Red,
What with trying to read the *Tribune*
And doing her nails instead,
Whata witha frocks to fit
And socks to knit
For the Britishers overseas,
What with art collections,
Hormone injections,
And walking her Pekinese,
Add to this her constant worry
Of keeping her friends impressed,
No wonder, now and then, a lady needs a—
Lady needs a—
Lady needs a rest cure
Now and then a lady needs a rest—sure
Now and then a lady needs a rest.

JERRY, MY SOLDIER BOY

Published January 1942. Introduced by Mary Jane Walsh.

VERSE

People tell me, "Never mold your
Life around a soldier,
Never let yourself get too warm
And go loony for a uniform."
So no one else is to blame
If I'm playing the Army game,
His name is—

REFRAIN 1

Jerry,
My Jerry!
Does his touch
Thrill me much?
Yes, very.
Does he beat the band
At makin' me feel well-manned?
Yes, he's, oh, so sweet,
Ev'ry time we meet
I could eat right out of his hand,
The hand of Jerry,
My rookie,
My sweet cookie,
My bundle full of joy,
And though now and then he lets me down,
I'm savin' my wedding gown,
For Jerry, my soldier boy.

REFRAIN 2 (ENDING)

And even though he stalls and stalls,
I'm savin' Niag'ra Falls
For Jerry, my soldier boy.

REFRAIN 3 (ENDING)

The hand of Jerry,
My Jerry—
Mrs. Jerry Walker, if you please.
But if he tries to do me in
I'm savin' a Mickey Finn
For Jerry, my soldier boy.

LET'S FACE IT

Introduced by Tommy Gleason and the Royal Guards.

REFRAIN

ALL: Let's face it, it's not so bad
Wearing a uniform.
Let's face it, girls all go mad
Each time their hearts we storm.
Why, when we attack
And give 'em a smack,
Do they give it back?
Yes, ma'am!
So let's face it, it's not so tough
Roughing it for Uncle Sam.

PATTER 1

ALL: Besides all these chances to pet
Just think of the presents we get!
1ST SOLDIER: My girl gave me a Ford coupé.
2ND SOLDIER: My girl gave me a breakfast tray.
3RD SOLDIER: My girl gave me a great big sled.
4TH SOLDIER: My girl gave me a Simmons folding bed.
5TH SOLDIER: My girl gave me the poems of Keats.
6TH SOLDIER: My girl gave me some crêpe-de-Chine sheets.
7TH SOLDIER: My girl gave me a barrel of fun.
8TH SOLDIER: And my girl gave me a little son of a gun!

REPEAT REFRAIN

PATTER 2

1ST SOLDIER: My girl gave me a Paisley shawl.
2ND SOLDIER: My girl gave me a cannonball.
3RD SOLDIER: My girl gave me a Frigidaire.
4TH SOLDIER: My girl gave me her daddy's Croix de Guerre.
5TH SOLDIER: My girl gave me her last movie test.
6TH SOLDIER: My girl gave me her bulletproof vest.
7TH SOLDIER: My girl gave me a weekend sublime.
8TH SOLDIER: What my girl gave me, gave me a hell of a time!
ALL: But let's face it, it's not so tough
Roughing it for Uncle Sam,
Let's face it for Uncle Sam.

FARMING

Published October 1941. Introduced by Danny Kaye, Benny Baker, Jack Williams, Sunnie O'Dea, Nanette Fabray, and ensemble. In Porter's notebook, "Titles and Ideas," June 17, 1941, there is the following reference: "Hollywood. Romantic cows Milky / All give cream Willkie. Elsa —— tattle / Well-goosed dehorning cattle." Editing this lyric was problematic because Porter shifted portions of the lyric around from refrain to refrain. This version is the most complete and comprehensive and includes all known variants.

VERSE

Here's a bit of news that's quite a shocker,
Proving Mother Nature still has charm,
Quoting Mister Cholly Knickerbocker,
"Get in the swim and buy a farm."
Acres of alfalfa, fields of clover
Suddenly enchant our top "Who's Who,"
So the moment all this row is over
What say if we go hayseed too?
For—

REFRAIN 1

Farming, that's the fashion,
Farming, that's the passion
Of our great celebrities of today.
Kit Cornell is shellin' peas,
Lady Mendl's climbin' trees,
Dear Mae West is at her best in the hay.
Stomping through the thickets,
Romping with the crickets,
Makes 'em feel more glamorous and more gay.
They tell me cows who are feeling milky
All give cream when they're milked by Willkie,
Farming is so charming, they all say.

REFRAIN 2

Farming, that's the fashion,
Farming, that's the passion
Of our great celebrities of today.
Monty Woolley, so I heard,
Has boll weevils in his beard,
Michael Strange has got the mange, will it stay?
Mussing up the clover,
Cussing when it's over,
Makes 'em feel more glamorous and more gay.
The natives think it's utterly utter
When Margie Hart starts churning her butter,
Farming is so charming, they all say.

REFRAIN 3

Farming, that's the fashion,
Farming, that's the passion
Of our great celebrities of today.
Fannie Hurst is haulin' logs,
Fanny Brice is feedin' hogs,

Garbo-Peep has led her sheep all astray.
Singing while they're rakin',
Bringing home the bacon,
Makes 'em feel more glamorous and more gay.
Miss Elsa Maxwell, so the folks tattle,
Got well-goosed while dehorning her cattle,
Farming is so charming, they all say.

REFRAIN 4

Farming, that's the fashion,
Farming, that's the passion
Of our great celebrities of today.
Don't inquire of Georgie Raft
Why his cow has never calfed,
Georgie's bull is beautiful, but he's gay!
Seeing spring a-coming,
Being minus plumbing,
Makes 'em feel informal and dégagé.
When Cliff Odets found a new tomater
He plowed under the Group Theaytre,
Farming is so charming, they all say.

REFRAIN 5

Farming, that's the fashion,
Farming, that's the passion
Of our great celebrities of today.
Steinbeck's growing Grapes of Wrath,
Guy Lombardo, rumor hath,
Toots his horn and all the corn starts to sway.
Racing like the dickens,
Chasing after chickens,
Makes 'em feel more glamorous and more gay.
Liz Whitney has, on her bin of manure, a
Clip designed by the Duke of Verdura,
Farming is so charming, they all say.

[*Among the unused lines were the following*]
Farming, that's the fashion,
Farming, that's the passion
Of our great celebrities of today.
Digging in his fertile glen,
Goldwyn dug up Anna Sten,
Fred Astaire has raised a hare and it's gray.
Clowning in their mittens,
Drowning extra kittens,
Makes 'em feel more glamorous and more gay.
Paul Whiteman, while he was puttin' up jelly,
Ate so much he recovered his belly,
Farming is so charming, they all say.

Farming, that's the fashion,
Farming, that's the passion
Of our great celebrities of today.
Missus Henry Morgenthau
Looks so chic behind a plow,
Mrs. Hearst is at her worst on a dray.
Tearing after possum,
Wearing just a blossom,
Makes 'em feel more glamorous and more gay.
Why, Orson Welles, that wonderful actor,
Has Del Rio driving a tractor.
Farming is so charming, they all say.

Farming, that's the fashion,
Farming, that's the passion
Of our great celebrities of today.
Just to keep her roosters keen,
Dietrich, that great movie queen,
Lifts her leg and lays an egg, what a lay.
Going after rabbits,
Knowing all their habits,
Makes 'em feel more glamorous and more gay.
So Harpo Marx, in a moment of folly,
Had his barn repainted by Dali.
Farming is so charming, they all say.

Farming, that's the fashion,
Farming, that's the passion
Of our great celebrities of today.
Lynn Fontanne is brandin' steer,
Sophie Tucker, so I hear,
Rides en masse upon an ass, hip-hooray.
Hoeing new potatoes,
Throwing all tomatoes,
Makes 'em feel more glamorous and more gay.
So Clifton Webb has parked his ma, Mabel,
"Way Down East" in a broken-down stable,
Farming is so charming, they all say.

EV'RYTHING I LOVE

Published October 1941. Introduced by Danny Kaye and Mary Jane Walsh.

VERSE

If I were Lord Byron,
I'd write you, sweet siren,
A poem inspirin',
A killer-diller-oo.
Too bad, I'm no poet,
I happen to know it,
But anyway
Here's a roundelay
I wrote last night about you:

REFRAIN

You are to me ev'rything,
My life-to-be, ev'rything,

When in my sleep you appear,
Fair skies of deep blue appear,
Each time our lips touch again,
I yearn for you, oh, so much again,
You are my fav'rite star,
My haven in heaven above,
You are ev'rything I love.

TAG

And while I'm learnin!
I'll keep the home fires burnin',
You are ev'rything I love.

ACE IN THE HOLE

Published October 1941. Introduced by Mary Jane Walsh, Sunnie O'Dea, Nanette Fabray, and ensemble.

VERSE

WINNIE: If my brain is simply uncanny
When I'm in a spot,
MURIEL
& JEAN: When you're in a spot, it's true,
You always know what to do.
WINNIE: It's because my clever old Granny
Knew, oh, such a lot.
MURIEL
& JEAN: She was older than God,
So it doesn't seem odd
If Granny knew, oh, such a
lot.
WINNIE: To steady me,
And ready me
For the battle of men and mice,
Each night, Grandmummy
Would pat on her tummy
And give me this good advice,
This perfect advice.
MURIEL
& JEAN: How sweet of Granny, how nice!
Repeat your Granny's advice.

REFRAIN

WINNIE: Sad times
May follow your tracks,
Bad times
May bar you from Saks,
Add times
When Satan in slacks
Breaks down your self-control,
Maybe
As often it goes,
Your Abie
May tire of his Rose,
So, baby,
This rule I propose,
Always have an ace in the hole.
MURIEL
& JEAN: Always try to arrive at
Having an ace some place private.
WINNIE: Always have an ace in the hole.

PATTER

If about some boy you're silly
But he won't give in,
Tell him you just talked to Lili
And she's lending you Errol Flynn.
If his head's as thick as mutton
And he just can't get your slant,
Say you talked to Barb'ra Hutton
And she's sending you Cary Grant.
If about this, your heart to bombard
He's still unable,
Then tell him you heard from Carole Lombard
And she's giving you Gable.*
For maybe
As often it goes,
Your Abie
May tire of his Rose,
So, baby,
This rule I propose,
Always have an ace in the hole.
Always try to arrive at
Having an ace some place private,
Always have an ace in the hole.
Just in case, always have an ace
In some secluded but accessible place,
Always have an ace in the hole.

YOU IRRITATE ME SO

Published October 1941. Introduced by Nanette Fabray and Jack Williams. Most of the lyrics from the second refrain are listed in "Titles and Ideas" under 1940. They are crossed out, as it was Porter's practice to cross out an idea after he used it in a song.

**After Carole Lombard's death, during the run of the show, these lines were changed to:*
If he still remains in a state so hypnotic
That your heart is ranklin',
Then tell him that El'nor is so patriotic
She's lease-lending you Franklin.

VERSE 1

SHE: When you first said, "Baby mine,
Let me be your valentine,"
I assumed that phrase meant
You gave your heart to me.
I was sure you'd be so nice,
Just a parcel from paradise,
But to my amazement,
Look what you've turned out to be!

REFRAIN 1

SHE: You're the fly in my ointment,
You're the frog in my throat,
You're the weed in my garden,
You're the leak in my boat,
You're the bats in my belfry,
You're the pebble in my shoe,
You're the bull in my china shop,
You're the mouse in my stew,
You're the knock in my engine,
You're the rust in my gear,
You're the ache in my tummy,
You're the pain in my—
The hurricane in my—
Supersensitive heart, dear.
Still I love you, I know,
And the reason is merely because
You irritate me so!
You fascinate me,
You devastate me,
Because, my dearie, you irritate me so!

VERSE 2

HE: Oh, please explain
Your mad refrain,
For in sentiment I'm just wallowing.
How can I be
Your cup of tea
When you say that I'm also the following!

REFRAIN 2

SHE: One
HE: I'm the fly in your ointment,
SHE: Two
HE: I'm the frog in your throat,
SHE: Three
HE: I'm the weed in your garden,
SHE: Four
HE: I'm the leak in your boat,
SHE: Five
HE: I'm the bats in your belfry,
SHE: Six
HE: I'm the pebble in your shoe,
SHE: Seven
HE: I'm the bull in your china shop
SHE: Eight
HE: I'm the mouse in your stew,
I'm the knock in your engine,
I'm the rust in your gear,
I'm the ache in your tummy,
I'm the pain in your—
The hurricane in your—
Supersensitive heart, dear.
Still you love me, I know,
And the reason is merely because
I irritate you so!
SHE: You fascinate me,
HE: I devastate thee,

HE: Because, my dearie, I irritate thee so!
SHE: Because, my dearie, you irritate me so!

ENCORE

HE: I'm the bee in your bonnet,
I'm the soap in your eye,
I'm the run in your stocking,
I'm the cloud in your sky.
SHE: You're the fall in my arches,
You're the water on my knee,
You're the moth in my cedar chest,
You're the shark in my sea.
HE: I'm the hitch in your zipper,
I'm the crack in your glass,
I'm the tax on your income,
I'm the pain in your—
The hurricane in your—
[*Continue as in previous refrain*]

BABY GAMES

Introduced by Danny Kaye, Eve Arden, Benny Baker, Edith Meiser, Vivian Vance, and Jack Williams.

VERSE

NANCY: Hark ye, children, listen to Mother,
Now that we all know one another,
I've got marvelous news—
We're about to disappear in twos.
So, Cornie, take Frankie, I shall take Eddie,
Maggie of course will stick to her steady.
EDDIE: I don't go for this news
About disappearing in twos.
JERRY: One moment, Ed,
Don't lose your head,
I know how to handle these quails.
I'll calm 'em down,

I'll go to town,
I'll tell 'em some fairy tales.

EDDIE & FRANKIE: What, fairy tales?
JERRY: Yes, fairy tales.
EDDIE & FRANKIE: You said, fairy tales?
JERRY: I said, fairy tales.
BOYS: Come on, you beautiful quail,
You're about to hear a fairy tale.

FRANKIE: One moment, kid,
You're off your lid,
I know how to handle these dames.
We'll wear 'em down,
We'll make 'em clown,
We'll make 'em play baby games.
JERRY & EDDIE: What, baby games?
FRANKIE: Yes, baby games.
JERRY & EDDIE: You said, baby games?
FRANKIE: I said, baby games.
BOYS: Come on, you beautiful dames,
We're about to play baby games!

REFRAIN 1

FRANKIE: Who wanna play hide-and-seek?
JERRY: Me wanna play hide-and-seek.
FRANKIE: Who else wanna play hide-and-seek?
EDDIE: Me wanna play hide-and-seek.
LADIES: We don't wanna play hide-and-seek,
That's a silly game.
BOYS: Don't be that way,
Come on and play
Hide-and-seek all the same.

ALL: With a hidy-ho
And a beedle-um-bo,
"Hide and Seek," that's the game!

REFRAIN 2

[*Same as Refrain 1, substitute "London Bridge" for "hide-and-seek"*]

REFRAIN 3

[*Same as Refrain 1, substitute "piggy-back" for "hide-and-seek"*]

RUB YOUR LAMP

Published October 1941. Introduced by Mary Jane Walsh and ensemble; danced by Mary Parker and Billy Daniel.

VERSE

If about Harlem some night you're gaddin',
Pay a short call on the Princess Aladdin,
All dolled up like Scheherazade,
She tells fortunes for ev'rybody.
People all say she's a mah'rajah's ranee,
Came from Bombay by way of the Swanee,
And if you slip her a buck or two,
The Princess Aladdin whispers to you

REFRAIN

Rub your lamp, if you want health,
Rub your lamp, if you want health,
Rub your lamp, if you want health,
Your vigor will be bigger, if you rub your lamp.
Rub your lamp, if you want wealth,
Rub your lamp, if you want wealth,
Rub your lamp, if you want wealth,
In ermine you'll be squirmin' if you rub your lamp.
Rub your lamp, if you want love,
Rub your lamp, if you want love,
Rub your lamp, if you want love,
On neckin' you can reckon, if you rub your lamp.
Yes, rub your lamp, if you want health,
Rub your lamp, if you want wealth,
And if you're daft and gettin' dafter
'Bout someone you're runnin' after,
If you want a life of love and laughter,
Rub, rub, rub, rub, rub your lamp.

I'VE GOT SOME UNFINISHED BUSINESS WITH YOU

The opening to Act II. Introduced by Mary Jane Walsh, Nanette Fabray, Sunnie O'Dea, Helen Devlin, Betty Moran, Joseph Macaulay, and Fred Irving Lewis.

INTRODUCTION

Frankie, Eddie,
You'd better get ready!

VERSE

You think you're such a smarty
But you're a dud,
And with a certain party
Your name is mud.
I'm willing to retire
But you should be warned
That hell hath no fire
Like a lady scorned,
And—

REFRAIN

Before I crack up from black despair,
Before I go mad and tear my hair,
Before I break down and start to boohoo,
I've got some unfinished business with you.
Before I hang from the willow tree,
Before I swallow some TNT,
Before I leap in the deep ocean blue,
I've got some unfinished business with you.
I've got a certain job that must be done,
So, little one,
Wait till baby gets a gun,
You'll be in heaven when once I get through
That certain unfinished business with you.

LET'S NOT TALK ABOUT LOVE

Published December 1941. Introduced by Danny Kaye and Eve Arden. There is some question as to whether the "Let's Talk About Love" portion of the song was actually performed in the show. It is not in the script. This editor found it among the Tams-Witmark manuscripts for the score. The discarded lyrics included:

Let's curse the superfluity
Of Hollywood's fatuity.

Why don't we go insane
About Marlene and her beau-ity.
(rhyming with) Zanuck's ingenuity

Let's probe the authenticity
Of Garbo's eccentricity.
Have movie stars felicity
Or merely good publicity?
Let's try to be explicit
On illicit domesticity.

VERSE 1

MAGGIE: Relax for one moment, my Jerry,
Come out of your dark monastery,
While Venus is beaming above.
Darling, let's talk about love.

REFRAIN 1

Let's talk about love, that wonderful thing,
Let's blend the scent of Venice with Paris in spring,
Let's gaze at that moon and try to believe
We're Venus and Adonis, or Adam and Eve,
Let's throw away anxiety, let's quite forget propriety,
Respectable society, the rector and his piety,
And contemplate l'amour in all its infinite variety,
My dear, let's talk about love.
Pretend you're Chopin and I'll be George Sand.
We're on the Grand Canal and, oh, baby, it's grand!
Let's mention Walküres and helmeted knights,
I'm beautiful Brünnhilde, You're Siegfried in tights,
Let's curse the asininity of trivial consanguinity,
Let's praise the masculinity of Dietrich's new affinity,
Let's picture Cleopatra saying "Scram" to her virginity,
My dear, let's talk about love.
The weather's so warm and you are so cute,
Let's dream about Tahiti and tropical fruit,
I've always said men were simply deevine
(Did you know that Peggy Joyce was once a pupil of mine?).
Let's gather miscellanea on Oberon's Titania,
Or ladies even brainier who've moved to Pennsylvania
(Bucks County, so I hear, is just a nest of nymphomania),
My dear, let's talk about love.

VERSE 2

JERRY: My buddies all tell me selectees
Are expected by ladies to neck-tease,
I could talk about love and why not?
But believe me, it wouldn't be so hot,
So—

REFRAIN 2

Let's talk about frogs, let's talk about toads,
Let's try to solve the riddle why chickens cross roads,
Let's talk about games, let's talk about sports,

Let's have a big debate about ladies in shorts,
Let's question the synonymy of freedom and
autonomy,
Let's delve into astronomy, political economy,
Or if you're feeling biblical, the book of
Deuteronomy,
But let's not talk about love.
Let's ride the New Deal, like Senator Glass,
Let's telephone to Ickes and order more gas,
Let's curse the Old Guard and Hamilton Fish,
Forgive me, dear, if Fish is your favorite dish.
Let's heap some hot profanities on Hitler's
inhumanities,
Let's argue if insanity's the cause of his inanities,
Let's weigh the Shubert Follies with the Ear-rl
Carroll Vanities,
But let's not talk about love.
Let's talk about drugs, let's talk about dope,
Let's try to picture Paramount minus Bob Hope,
Let's start a new dance, let's try a new step,
Or investigate the cause of Missus Roosevelt's
pep,
Why not discuss, my dee-arie,
The life of Wallace Bee-ery
Or bring a jeroboam on
And write a drunken poem on
Astrology, mythology,
Geology, philology,
Pathology, psychology,
Electro-physiology,
Spermology, phrenology?
I owe you an apology,
But let's not talk about love.

REFRAIN 3

Let's speak of Lamarr, that Hedy so fair,
Why does she let Joan Bennett wear all her old
hair?
If you know Garbo, then tell me this news,
Is it a fact the Navy's launched all her old
shoes?
Let's check on the veracity of Barrymore's
bibacity
And why his drink capacity should get so much
publacity,
Let's even have a huddle over Ha'vard
Univassity,
But let's not talk about love.
Let's wish him good luck, let's wish him more
pow'r,
That Fiorella fella, my favorite flow'r,
Let's get some champagne from over the seas,
And drink to Sammy Goldwyn,
Include me out please.
Let's write a tune that's playable, a ditty
swing-and-swayable
Or say whatever's sayable, about the Tow'r of
Ba-abel,
Let's cheer for the career of itty-bitty Betty
Gra-abel,
But let's not talk about love.
In case you play cards, I've got some right here,
So how about a game o' gin rummy, my dear?
Or if you feel warm and bathin's your whim,
Let's get in the all-together and enjoy a short
swim,
No, honey, ah suspect you-all
Of bein' intellectual
And so, instead of gushin' on,
Let's have a big discussion on
Timidity, stupidity, solidity, frigidity,
Avidity, turbidity, Manhattan, and viscidity,
Fatality, morality, legality, finality,
Neutrality, reality, or Southern hospitality,
Pomposity, verbosity,
You're losing your velocity,
But let's not talk about love.

A LITTLE RUMBA NUMBA

Published October 1941. Introduced by Tommy Gleason and the Royal Guards, Marguerite Benton, Mary Parker, and Billy Daniel. Porter has several notes about "Rhumba Numba" as an idea for a song.

REFRAIN

SOLO: A little rumba numba
Down Argentina way,
Made me forget to slumba
As through a dance she'd sway,
Singing, "Ay, ay, ay,
BOYS: Ay, ay, ay,
GIRLS: Ay, ay, ay,
SOLO: Ay, ay, ay."

That little rumba numba
And I fell so in love
That while the world would slumba
We'd hear the stars above
Singing, "Ay, ay, ay,
BOYS: Ay, ay, ay,
GIRLS: Ay, ay, ay,
SOLO: Ay, ay, ay."

That little rumba numba
Is now my darling wife,
And though we never slumba
We lead a lovely life,
Singing, "Ay, ay, ay,

BOYS: Ay, ay, ay,
SOLO: Ay, ay, ay,
ALL: Ay, ay, ay, ay.
SOLO: Ay, ay,
GIRLS: Ay, ay,
SOLO: Ay, ay,
SOLO: Ay, ay, ay, ay,
ALL: Ay, ay, ay,
Ay, ay, ay, ay,
Ay, ay, ay, ay, ay!"

I HATE YOU, DARLING

Published October 1941. Introduced by Vivian Vance, James Todd, Mary Jane Walsh, and Danny Kaye.

INTRODUCTION

WINNIE: Oh, Jerry, I'm so blue,
And, as always, because of you

REFRAIN

I hate you, darling, my turtledove,
I hate you, darling, all else above,
I hate you, darling, because I love you so.
I should be clever and say, "Goodbye,
Goodbye, forever, my butterfly,"
But why be clever when, darling, I
Need the joy you bring more than anything I know.
I'm in the depths of inferno
Whenever you're far from me, dear,
But when our sweet nights return, oh,
My habitat
Is the strat-
Osphere.
Still I hate you, darling, it's true, my pet,
I hate you, darling, but don't forget
I hate you, darling, and yet
I love you so.

GET YOURSELF A GIRL

Introduced by Tommy Gleason and the Royal Guards. Most of this song appears to have been dropped during the Boston tryout, but the script indicates that at least a few lines were sung in the show.

INTRODUCTION

Little man, little man,
Gee, you are looking bad,
Little man, little man,
If you are feeling sad,

REFRAIN

ALL: Get yourself a girl, a baby doll,
For your morale, get yourself a girl.
Get yourself a girl, it's always best,
When you're depressed, get yourself a girl.
If you long to be consoled in your cold little berth,
We suggest they make the best foot-warmers on earth,
So give yourself a slice of paradise,
And let yourself get yourself a girl.
1ST SOLO: If you're feeling sorry you ever met yourself,
2ND SOLO: If throughout the daytime, you sit and fret yourself,
3RD SOLO: If in your apartment at night you shet yourself,
And so upset yourself
You have to pet yourself,
ALL: Get yourself a girl, a baby doll,
For your morale, get yourself a girl.
Get yourself a girl, it's always best,
When you're depressed, get yourself a girl.
If you long to be consoled in your cold little berth,
We suggest they make the best foot-warmers on earth,
So give yourself a slice of paradise,
Don't fret yourself, upset yourself,
Or regret you ever met yourself,
But get yourself a girl,
Get yourself a girl.

REVENGE

Dropped during rehearsals.

VERSE

MURIEL: I'm so mad I'm out for trouble.
JEAN: I'm so angry I'm seein' double.
MURIEL: Now I'm ready.
JEAN: Now I'm set.
BOTH: And now I'm gonna get—

REFRAIN

BOTH: Revenge, I'm gonna get revenge on that boy,
I'm seein' red and rarin' to start,
Revenge, I'm gonna get, and, oh, with what joy
I'll spoil his lunch and punch holes in his heart.
And so if you're on the jury
When I've killed that pup
Remember hell hath no fury
Like a queen who's been stood up.
That guy is gonna fly with angels above
When I get my sweet revenge on love.
I'm gonna get revenge!
I'm gonna get revenge!
Revenge, revenge!

WHAT ARE LITTLE HUSBANDS MADE OF?

Dropped during rehearsals.

What are little wives made of?
What are little wives made of?
Sugar and spice
And ev'rything nice—
That's what little wives are made of.

What are little husbands made of?
What are little husbands made of?
Grumbling and snoring
And ev'rything boring—
That's what little husbands are made of.

I suppose that one of their major crimes
Is to greet you ev'ry morning from behind the *Times*,
Till they realize suddenly it's time to fly,
So they upset the coffee and peck you goodbye.
They say they want to dine tonight
Promptly at eight,
But you don't flinch when they arrive
At least an hour late.
Then they sit down and grouse about the overdone steak,
And bring up again that old pie that Mother used to make.
You've got your green dress on and you're feeling serene,
Till they look up and say to you, "Must you wear green?"
So you rush up and change into your negligee of blue
And they say, "You know green is more becoming to you."
Then they tell you endless stories of the Stock Exchange type
And go on and on smoking that goddamn pipe,
And when fin'lly you're asleep and feeling totally dead,
They dream about football and kick you out of bed.

So what are little husbands made of?
Well, whatever it is, it ain't hay.

PETS

Dropped during rehearsals. In "Titles and Ideas," there is a title entry for "Pets" on July 18, 1941. The title is followed by the line: "Oh, I'm just a child—wild about pets."

VERSE

Some folks collect paintings,
Some folks collect stamps,
Some are amassers
Of antimacassars
And other Victorian camps.
Some folks collect horses,
Others we know, Reno divorces,
But I, little me,
Well, I just can't wait till you see my—

REFRAIN 1

Pets,
I collect pets,
I collect ev'rything from mice to marmosets,
I've a whirling mouse called Jumbo
And a cockatoo from Colombo
Who tells dirty jokes and smokes cigarettes.
I've a dinner-jacketed penguin who gives me lessons in poise,
And a very sexy old peacock who makes such an int'resting noise,
But the pride of my collection is my bevy of Harvard boys.
I'm like a child,
I'm simply wild
About my pets!

REFRAIN 2

Pets,
I collect pets,

I collect ev'rything from mice to marmosets,
I've a genuine chinchilla
And a rather chichi gorilla,
Who wears negligees and plays minuets.
I've a Persian kitten from Newport who only cares for whipped cream,
And a pair of riotous rabbits, the way they behave is a scream!
And as soon as I've more cages
I'll take over the Dartmouth team.
I'm like a child,
I'm simply wild
About my pets!

REFRAIN 3

Pets,
I collect pets,
I collect ev'rything from mice to marmosets,
I've an acrobatic monkey
And a highly endowed young donkey
Who's played sev'ral shows
And knows Cliff Odets.
I've an op'ra-conscious canary
Who sings so loud that I'm deaf,
And an awf'lly fussy French poodle
(Thank heaven I've got a French chef!).
And whenever Winston's willing
I'm adopting the R.A.F.,
I'm like a child,
I'm simply wild
About my pets!

MAKE A DATE WITH A GREAT PSYCHOANALYST

Unused. Written for Eve Arden. In "Titles and Ideas," June 23, 1941, the following appears: "And then comes Raymond Gram Swing."

VERSE

Listen, girls, last Wednesday, I went to a matinee
And saw Gertrude Lawrence in *Lady in the Dark*, that wonderful play.
You know it was written by that wonder boy called Moss Hart,
And *in* it, Gertie—that's what Ilka Chase calls her—plays the part
Of a magazine editor who knows so little of life
That simply because the boys wouldn't romp with her when she was a child,
She got all mixed up in her love life.
So she goes to see a brain doctor who lets her recline on a sofa
And talk about herself until she gets into such a perfect state of bliss
That—well, in any case—the point of that beautiful
Gertrude Lawrence play was this:

REFRAIN

If you've certain problems that must be solved,
If your love affairs have been involved,
If you're haunted by the way you look,
If your son has just eloped with your fav'rite cook,
Make a date with a great psychoanalyst and lie down.
If at winning at bridge you've lost your touch,
If you dream about Raymond Gram Swing too much,
If of late you're constantly in your cups,
If your Peke's become the mother of poodle pups,
Ring the bell of a swell psychoanalyst and lie down.
If your nights are dreary and your days long
'Cause your boy friend has given you the gate,
Find a fancy doctor with a chaise longue
And wait—simply wait.
If your lawyer's been sent to Alcatraz,
If you just found out that your husband has
Ev'ry day with a gay cutie-pie a tryst,
I suggest it is best that you try a tryst
With some willing, eye-filling psychiatrist
And lie down.

UP TO HIS OLD TRICKS AGAIN

No music survives. Unused. Lyric is dated June 29, 1941.

REFRAIN

Up to his old tricks again,
Oh, what a heel!
Love, I appeal
To thee.
Up to his old tricks again,
I'm in the same fix again,
I'm weeping for him when he should be weeping for me.
But now it's time, my live wire,
You should be warned

That hell had no fire
Like a woman scorned!
This brain o' mine clicks again,
I've got it planned
So you'll never pick
Another trick
Out of your hand.

YOU CAN'T BEAT MY BILL

No music survives. Unused. Lyric is dated July 2, 1941.

REFRAIN

My boy Bill has charming traits
And he'd make quite the best of mates,
But when it comes to breaking dates,
Oh, you can't beat my Bill.
Ev'ry time I go to town,
Planning to wear my wedding gown,
Billy calls up and lets me down,
No, you can't beat my Bill.
Yet he still is my master
Though I'm still not his bride,
It's a major disaster
That I've got him under my hide.
Though his nose I'd gladly plaster,
Yet I don't think I will,
For at making love
No angel above
Could beat my sweet guy Bill.

SOMETHING TO SHOUT ABOUT

1943

A film produced by Gregory Ratoff for Columbia Pictures in 1942. Released in February 1943. Screenplay by Lou Breslow and Edward Eliscu. Directed by Gregory Ratoff. Cast, starring Don Ameche and Janet Blair, included William Gaxton, Jack Oakie, Hazel Scott, Cobina Wright, Jr., and Veda Ann Borg.

Porter signed a contract to write seven songs for a "photoplay" titled *Wintergarden* on March 5, 1942. The number was augmented to nine songs in a revised contract, dated June 27, 1942. The title of the film was eventually changed.

YOU'D BE SO NICE TO COME HOME TO

Published October 1942. Introduced by Janet Blair and Don Ameche. There are several references to this song in "Titles and Ideas":

February 6, 1942: "You Would Be So Wonderful to Come Home To"
February 9, 1942: "Someone to Come Home To"
February 19, 1942: "Something to Keep Me Warm"
March 27, 1942 (Los Angeles): "You'd Be So Nice to Come Home To" (line: And the gods began bombing above)

The refrain was completed April 1, 1942.

April 13, 1942: line from verse ("Home To"): It's not that you reek of that old pre-war chic
April 23, 1942: "Nice"
Verse: It's not that you're rarer
Than asparagus out of season,
No, darling, this is the reason
Why I love you so much.

Porter finished the number on April 30, 1942.

VERSE 1

HE: It's not that you're fairer
Than a lot of girls just as pleasin'
That I doff my hat
As a worshipper at
Your shrine.
It's not that you're rarer
Than asparagus out of season,
No, my darling, this is the reason
Why you've got to be mine:

REFRAIN

You'd be so nice to come home to,
You'd be so nice by the fire,
While the breeze on high
Sang a lullaby,
You'd be all that I
Could desire.
Under stars chilled by the winter,
Under an August moon burning above,
You'd be so nice,
You'd be paradise
To come home to and love.

VERSE 2

SHE: I should be excited,
But, Lothario, why not own up
That you always chase
After ev'ry new face
In town?
I would be delighted
If we two could, some day, be sewn up,
For if you behaved like a grown-up
And could only slow down.

I CAN DO WITHOUT TEA IN MY TEAPOT

A partial instrumental was introduced at the piano by Hazel Scott. In "Titles and Ideas," March 16, 1942, a title appears: " 'I Can Never Do Without You' (Idea: I can do without sugar, tires, etc.)."

VERSE

Till we get our enemies
On their Japo-Nazi knees,
There are certain luxuries
We all must do without,
And since we collided,
My pretty one, I've decided:

REFRAIN 1

I can do without tea in my teapot,
I can do without gas in my car,
I can do without pleats in my sports coat,
I can do without gin in my bar.
When my last raincoat rips,
And my zipper no longer zips,
I can still cheer the dear Red, White and Blue.
I can do without weekends forever,
But, baby, never
Without you.

REFRAIN 2

I can do without tea in my teapot,
I can do without combs in my hair,

I can do without tubes for my lipstick,
I can do without silk underwear.
When the old sugar bowl
Is no more than an empty hole,
I can still cheer the dear Red, White and Blue.
I can do without girdles forever,
But, baby, never
Without you.

REFRAIN 3

I can do without tea in my teapot,
I can do without perfume from France,
I can do without cuffs on my zoot suit,
I can do without two pair of pants,
When I'm tired out, poor thing,
But my bedsprings no longer spring,
I can still cheer the dear Red, White and Blue.
I can do without garters forever,
But, baby, never
Without you.

THROUGH THICK AND THIN

Introduced by Hazel Scott and Janet Blair; danced by Jack Oakie and James "Chuckles" Walker. In "Titles and Ideas," March 26, 1942, the following entry appears:

Through thick and (or) thin
Through rain and (or) snow.

VERSE

The battle of life,
It has always been shown,
Can with trouble be rife
If you fight it alone,
So if all else above,
You desire to come through,
Get someone you love
To sing this ditty with you:

REFRAIN

Through thick and thin, through thin and
  thick,
Together we will always stick.
If harder times we've got to brave,
We'll stride on
Till we ride on
The crest of the wave.
It's me for you and you for me,
So, partner, we're bound to win,
For though fair or stormy weather,
We'll stick together
Through thick and thin.

CODA

Through hot and cold,
Through high and low,
Through young and old,
Through day and night,
Through good and bad,
Through rich and poor,
Through gay and sad,
Through champagne cocktails and bathtub gin,
Together we'll stick and
Through thick and
Thin.

I ALWAYS KNEW

Published November 1942. Introduced by Janet Blair and Jaye Martin; reprised by Blair and Don Ameche. The title is listed in "Titles and Ideas," May 30, 1942.

VERSE

Since that lovely evening
In the twilight's blur,
When the Fates cried "abracadabra,"
And there you were:

REFRAIN

I always knew
You were but the greatest girl (boy) of them all,
I always knew
That in time the whole wide world you'd enthrall,
So now that you are the top card in the pack,*
Don't mind, sweetheart,
If I start
To pat myself on the back,
For since you first burst out of the blue,
My darling, I somehow always knew.

SOMETHING TO SHOUT ABOUT

Published November 1942. Introduced by Janet Blair; reprised at the end by Blair, William Gaxton, Don

**Or:*
And so when you are the top card in the pack,

Ameche, Jack Oakie, Veda Ann Borg, the Bricklayers, and chorus.

VERSE

Just in case I'm found
Leaping 'round
The prairie,
Making sense much less
Than is nec-
Essary,
If I feel so gay
People say
That I'm scary,
If I look like that
Pussycat
That swallowed the fat
Canary—

REFRAIN 1

I've got something to shout about,
Something to spout about,
Something that's tough to land.
I've got something to dream about,
Something to beam about,
Something grander than grand.
For since someone I care about,
Just tear my hair about,
Took me to heaven above,
I've got something to shout about,
Something hot I've gotta give out about,
Something that's known as love.

REFRAIN 2 (AMECHE)

You'll have something to shout about,
Something to spout about,
Something to draw the mob.
You'll have something sensational
Once inspirational
Me turns loose on this job.
I'll write pages so lyrical
You'll see a miracle
Due to my marvelous prose.
You'll have something to shout about,
Something they'll all hail and give out about,
You'll have the show of shows!

REFRAIN 3 (GAXTON—IN OFFICE)

Give me something to shout about,
Something to spout about,
Something that simply whirls.
Give me something uproarious,
Gleaming with glorious
Girls, girls, girls—I mean girls!
Give me something tremendious,
Super-stupendious,
Something that never will close.
Give me something to shout about,
Something hot they've gotta give out about,
Give me the show of shows!

REFRAIN 4 (GAXTON—FINALE)

I've got something to shout about,
Something to spout about,
Something that simply whirls.
I've got something uproarious,
Gleaming with glorious
Girls, girls, girls—I mean girls!
I've got something tremendious,
Super-stupendious,
Something that never will close.
I've got something to shout about,
Something hot I've gotta give out about,
I've got the show of shows!

REFRAIN 5 (OAKIE)

You'll have something to shout about,
Something to spout about
'Cause, baby, you've got me.
I'm the personality
Ev'ry locality
Wears out rubber to see.
I'm so great, so colofissal,
Boy, your box office'll
Boom so it never can close.
You'll have something to shout about,
When my big-time figger I flout about,
You'll have the show of shows!

REFRAIN 6 (AMECHE & OAKIE)

You'll have something to shout about,
Something to spout about
Once I turn loose the press.
When the papers in this city
Print my publicity
You'll just howl with success.
I'm the one personality
Ev'ry locality
Longs for, so this baby knows
You'll have something to shout about
When my big-time figger I flout about,
You'll have the show of shows!

LOTUS BLOOM

Published November 1942. Introduced by Janet Blair; danced by David Lichine, Lily Norwood (Cyd Charisse), and ensemble. The film *Something to Shout About* was unusual because it had no overt references to World War II. It is interesting, therefore, to note the removal of the reference to "the bombs that kill" in Porter's later version of this lyric. May 21, 1942, song list for *Wintergarden* mentions No. 4, "Chinese Lullaby."

Lotus bloom,
Oh, my sleepy little lotus bloom,
Jade shadows loom
'Round the lantern's low gleam,
So rest your head
On the pillow of your trellised bed
And dream, little lotus bloom, dream.

Sail the skies
To the garden where the south wind sighs,
While dragonflies
Kiss the willow-swept stream,
Your heart enthrall
With laughter of the waterfall,
Yes, dream, little lotus bloom, dream.

For there upon the shore
Waits your fairy prince of yore,
Who will give you once more
The ecstasy of love supreme.
This world of gloom
Wasn't meant for you, my lotus bloom,
So dream, little lotus bloom, dream,
Dream,
Dream,
Dream.

Earlier version

Lotus bloom,
Oh, my sleepy little lotus bloom,
The tree trunks loom
By the summer-seared stream,
So cease your sighs,
Close the petals of your drowsy eyes
And dream, little lotus bloom, dream.

Dream away
Of the garden where you used to play
Until that day,
My beloved moonbeam,
Return once more
To the laughter that you heard before,
Yes, dream, little lotus bloom, dream.

For soon our homeless hill
Will again be green and still
And the bombs that kill
No longer through the night will scream.
Till then, my lamb,
Trust in heaven and your Uncle Sam,
And dream,
Dream,
Dream.

HASTA LUEGO

Published November 1942. Introduced by Janet Blair, David Lichine, and ensemble. The original title was "Hasta la Vista." There is mention in a March 1942 song list for the movie of a "Maria Montez–South American number."

VERSE 1

In a small canteena,
On an island far,
Señorita Leena
Sang a song to a hot guitar.
All the ding-dong dandies
Used to gather about,
When the lovely Leena,
La diveena,
Would give in and give out:

REFRAIN

Hasta luego,
Too bad we must part,
Hasta luego,
And here's moocha good luck, sweetheart.

VERSE 2

Señorita Leena
Had no love affairs
Till from Pasadena
Came the last of the millionaires.
After glimpsing Leena,
This tycoon of finance
Felt so full of life, he
Wired his wifey
Back home in the old manse:

REPEAT REFRAIN

VERSE 3

Once they'd married, Leena
And her rich old guy
Moved to Pasadena,
Where the best people go to die,
But when she'd collected
All his Copper Preferred,

Back to her canteena,
Lovely Leena
Went flying as she purred:

REPEAT REFRAIN

CODA Hasta luego,
Too bad we must part,
Hasta luego,
And moocha good luck, sweetheart,
Olé!

IT MIGHT HAVE BEEN

Published December 1942. Written in April 1942, when the film was still titled *Wintergarden*, but the number was dropped during production. The cue sheet indicates background use of a partial instrumental.

It might have been,
It might have been,
A joy akin
To heaven above,
So it seems a shame
That fate ever came
To destroy my beautiful dream of love.
For I dreamed, you see,
You worshipped me
And that skies would be
Forever benign.
So it seems a sin
That fate happened in,
For it might have been
So divine,
That absurd, that completely insane,
Vain
Dream of mine.

COULDN'T BE

Unused. The title appears in "Titles and Ideas," May 4, 1942, and again for May 5, 1942. There is a sketch for the music in a Porter music notebook. Another title for this song is "I Couldn't Be More in Love." The lyric for the refrain is dated May 7, 1942.

REFRAIN

Couldn't be—more delighted,
Here I am, there you are,
Couldn't be—more excited,
Couldn't rate more eight-to-the-bar,
Never was—such an ev'ning,
Never saw—such a sky above,
Couldn't be clearer,
So move a bit nearer
'Cause I couldn't be more in love.

TAKE IT EASY

Not used in the film, but there are several sketches for it in a Porter music notebook. The following appears in "Titles and Ideas," April 23, 1942:

"Take It Easy"
Suggestion lyric:
Take it easy, take it easy
With that fatal charm that you've got,
Take it gently, not so sentiment'ly,
Or, baby, I'll give you everything that I've got,
(And that's a lot)
Suggestion finish:
I'll admit you're the stuff
But I know when enough's enough,
So take it easy or you'll break my heart.

REFRAIN

Take it easy, take it easy,
Play the cold more and stress less the hot,
Take it gently, not so sentiment'lly,
Or I might accident'lly give all that I've got.
Treat me sweetly but discreetly,
Otherwise you and your prize baby must part.
I adore all your stuff,
And I'm sure that you've more than enough,
But take it easy or you'll break my heart.

LET DOCTOR SCHMETT VET YOUR PET

No music survives. The movie called for a radio commercial, and this is what Porter produced. I have no evidence that this number was in the film. A "Pepsipop" commercial (authorship unknown) was used.

If your doggie's lookin' sick,
If your tomcat's lost his kick,
If your goldfish is feelin' all wet,
Let Doctor Schmett vet your pet.
If your donkey starts to balk,
If your parrot talks double-talk,
If your hen by some rooster's upset,
Let Doctor Schmett vet your pet.

. . .

Let Doctor Schmett vet your pet,
Let Doctor Schmett vet your pet,
Let Doctor Schmett vet your pet,
'Cause Doctor Schmett is the best vet yet.
Call up Flatbush three, four five six seven, don't forget.*

**Or:*
Address, two t'ree two T'oid Avenue, and don't forget.

SOMETHING FOR THE BOYS

1943

Tryout: Shubert Theatre, Boston, December 18, 1942. Produced by Michael Todd at the Alvin Theatre, New York, January 7, 1943. 422 performances. Book by Herbert and Dorothy Fields. Staged and lighted by Hassard Short. Cast, starring Ethel Merman, included Paula Laurence, Bill Johnson, Betty Garrett, Betty Bruce, and Allen Jenkins.

The contract for this show, once titled *Jenny, Get Your Gun,* was signed on October 16, 1942.

ANNOUNCEMENT OF INHERITANCE

Also listed as "Prologue—Announcement of Inheritance." Lyric dated December 2, 1942. Introduced by Jed Prouty, Paula Laurence, Allen Jenkins, and Ethel Merman.

CALHOUN: Miss Florence Hart, please get me straight,
I'm the answer to all your prayers.
I'm the lawyer, the attorney, and the advocate
For the Court of Missing Heirs.
I have hunted for you ev'rywhere,
As the head of our legal branch,
For we suddenly discover you're the partial heir
To a tip-top Texas ranch,
So your two distant cousins and you now own,
CHIQUITA: But I haven't any cousins!
CALHOUN: Though to you they're unknown,
Still the words I state are strictly true,
For our expert tracers find that, due
To the death of your long-lost Uncle Lew,
Your distant cousins, not to mention you,
Both rightfully and lawfully have fallen heir to
Four thousand acres in Texas.

CHIQUITA: What, four thousand acres in Texas!
And a third is for this belle?
Well, how'm I doin'?
How'm I doin'?
I'm doin' swell!

CALHOUN: Mister Harry Hart, please get me straight,
I'm the answer to all your prayers,
I'm the lawyer, the attorney, and the advocate
For the Court of Missing Heirs.
I have hunted for you ev'rywhere,
As the head of our legal branch,
For we suddenly discover you're the partial heir
To a tip-top Texas ranch,
So your two distant cousins and you now own,
HARRY: But I haven't any cousins!
CALHOUN: Though to you they're unknown,
Still the words I state are strictly true,
For our expert tracers find that, due
To the death of your long-lost Uncle Lew,
Your two distant cousins, not to mention you,
Both rightfully and lawfully have fallen heir to
Four thousand acres in Texas.

HARRY: What, four thousand acres in Texas!
And a third of it is mine?
Well, how'm I feelin'?
How'm I feelin'?
I'm feelin' fine!

CALHOUN: Miss Blossom Hart, please get me straight,
I'm the answer to all your prayers,
I'm the lawyer, the attorney, and the advocate
For the Court of Missing Heirs.
I have hunted for you ev'rywhere,
As the head of our legal branch,
For we suddenly discover you're the partial heir
To a tip-top Texas ranch,
So your two distant cousins and you now own,
BLOSSOM: But I haven't any cousins!
CALHOUN: Though to you they're unknown,
Still the words I state are strictly true,
For our expert tracers find that, due
To the death of your long-lost Uncle Lew,
Your two distant cousins, not to mention you,
Both rightfully and lawfully have fallen heir to
Four thousand acres in Texas.

BLOSSOM: What, four thousand acres in Texas!
And a third is mine? Oh, my!
Well, how'm I ridin'?
How'm I ridin'?
Put yourself in my place, I'm ridin' high!

SEE THAT YOU'RE BORN IN TEXAS

Published January 1943. Lyric dated October 8, 1942. Introduced by ensemble.

REFRAIN 1

See that you're born in Texas,
Old Texas, the Lone Star State.
See that you're born in Texas,
And you'll grow up to be great.
All babies of both sexes
From Texas in headlines land,
So see that you're born in Texas
And they'll meet you with a big brass band.

PATTER

Just think of the top names that Texas has
offered,
Sam Houston, Steve Austin, Frank Buck, and
Joan Crawford,
And John Nance Garner, oh, what a man!
Say, in a sweater, who looks better than Missus
Sheridan's Ann?
You've got to give credit to Texas for
startin'
Gene Autry, Ken Maynard, and smart Mary
Martin,
Add Bebe Daniels, Peggy Fears, and Joanie
Blondell,
Texas Guinan, Jesse Jones, and Linda
Darnell,
And don't forget our Ginger Rogers, not to
mention our
Great heroes, Nimitz and Eisenhow'r.

REFRAIN 2

See that you're born in Texas,
Old Texas, the Lone Star State.
See that you're born in Texas,
And you'll grow up to be great.
Don't do it in Ohio,
In Iowa or in Maine,
But see that you're born in Texas
And you'll travel on a special train,
On a simply super-duper,
Special
Train.

ENCORE

See that you're born in Texas,
Old Texas, the Lone Star State.
See that you're born in Texas,
And you'll grow up to be great.
Never be popped in Joisey
If, boysie, you want a big name,
But see that you're born in Texas,
And you'll end up in the Hall of Fame.

WHEN MY BABY GOES TO TOWN

Published January 1943. Introduced by Bill Johnson and ensemble. In "Titles and Ideas," October 28, 1942, there are the following suggested "final lines": "And do we—and do we neck?" and "And am I—a total wreck?" The completed lyric is dated October 8, 1942.

VERSE

I'm playin' a local belle,
She's strictly One-A!
Her figure is something swell—why?
She keeps it that way.
Yes, daily, she
Takes a walk
And you should see
Those natives gawk.

REFRAIN 1

When my baby goes to town,
Does my baby knock 'em down!
When she saunters by on Broadway,
Lookin', oh, so serene,
People stare in such an awed way
You'd think she was a queen.
When my baby's had her stroll,
I see her home—God bless her soul—
And in her front parlor, nice and warm,
Does she convince me she's in perfect form!
When my baby goes to town.

REFRAIN 2

When my baby goes to town,
Does my baby knock 'em down!
When she struts along the sidewalk,
Lookin' so full o' beans,
Even though it's quite a wide walk
They're packed in like sardines.
When my baby's done a mile,
I see her home—and stay a while—
And on her settee, do we let go!
And do I often have to holler "Whoa"!
When my baby goes to town.

REFRAIN 3

When my baby goes to town,
Does my baby knock 'em down!
When she shuffles by the hotel,
Where the boys hang about,
Do they gaze at her and gloat? Hell,
A lot of 'em pass out!
When my baby's had her hike,
I ride her home on my old bike
And if to her sofa we retire,
Why do the neighbors always holler "Fire"
When my baby goes to town?

SOMETHING FOR THE BOYS

Published December 1942. Introduced by Ethel Merman and ensemble. Completed lyric dated October 8, 1942. When the working title of the show was *Jenny, Get Your Gun,* Porter had the following notes in "Titles and Ideas": January 26, 1942: "Jenny, Jenny, Are You Getting Any?" and April 23, 1942: "Jenny, Are You Getting Any?" "Titles and Ideas" has specific references to only one performer, Ethel Merman, who was starring in her fifth Porter musical in *Something for the Boys.* The references include:

December 17, 1941 (song title for Merman)
"You're Terrific"

August 24, 1942 "No Dice"
For Merman, line: When you suddenly can say
It's good, it's grand,
It's super-duper nice,
But it's no dice!

The third refrain of "Something for the Boys" was completed on December 8, 1942, and the Act II finale on December 28, 1942.

VERSE

Back in the days of giftie giving
When all God's daddies had greens,
I was but, oh, so busy living
Beyond several gentlemen's means.
I didn't care much where I fluttered,
Long as my bankroll was buttered,
But now my life's completely cluttered
With soldiers,
Sailors,
Not to speak of those big marines,
'Cause

REFRAIN 1

I'm always doing something,
Something for the boys,
I'm always doing something
For our lads
If it adds
To their joys.
So don't tell me it's a rum thing
If I'm out with 'em nightly till three,
'Cause I'm always doing something for the boys
Or they're doing something for me.

REFRAIN 2

I'm always doing something,
Something for the boys,
I'm always doing something
For our lads
If it adds
To their joys.
So don't tell me it's a rum thing
When I plop on some corporal's knee,
'Cause I'm always doing something for the boys
Or they're doing something for me.

REFRAIN 3

I'm always doing something,
Something for the boys,
I'm always doing something
For our lads
If it adds
To their joys.
So don't tell me it's a rum thing
If the W.P.B. gave me an E,
'Cause I'm always doing something for the boys
Or they're doing something for me.

FINALE, ACT II

I'm always doing something,
Something for the boys,
I'm always doing something
For our lads
If it adds
To their joys,
So don't tell me it's a rum thing
If the new year brings happiness plus,
'Cause we'll all be doing something for the boys
While they're doing so much for us.

WHEN WE'RE HOME ON THE RANGE

Introduced by Ethel Merman, Paula Laurence, and Allen Jenkins. Lyric dated October 27, 1942.

VERSE

ALL: Oh, it will seem strange
To be home on the range
In our ranch house far, far away.
CHIQUITA: In our new old home
Where the buff'lo roam,
BLOSSOM: And the graceful swan
Goes a-gliding on—
HARRY: Oh, to hell with that bird!
BLOSSOM: And there seldom is heard
Any four-letter word
All day.

REFRAIN 1

ALL: When we're home on the range,
When we're home on the range,
BLOSSOM: Far away from the city
We'll be happy for a change.
CHIQUITA: I can rest on the slope
Eating wild antelope.
BLOSSOM & HARRY: And if that don't take
You can try a rattlesnake,
ALL: When we're home on the range.

TAG 1

ALL: Let 'er rip
With a yip and a yip and a to-and-fro,
With a yip, yip, yippy, and a do-si-do,
With a swing-your-partners and away we'll go
To our home on the range.

REFRAIN 2

ALL: When we're home on the range,
When we're home on the range,
CHIQUITA: Far away from Diana and her mater, Michael Strange,
HARRY: What if when you retire
I should burn with desire?
BLOSSOM & CHIQUITA: Say instead of ants
You'll have cactus in your pants,
ALL: When we're home on the range.

TAG 2

ALL: Let 'er rip
With a yip and a yip and a big sashay,
With a yip, yip, yippy, say you're gittin' too gay,
With a turn and balance and a breakaway
For our home on the range.

REFRAIN 3

ALL: When we're home on the range,
When we're home on the range,
HARRY: If you don't get the rickets
You at least can get the mange.
BLOSSOM: Every morn when it's clear
I'll go out ropin' steer.
CHIQUITA & HARRY: Say, if that's your plan
Wear a bustle on your can,
ALL: When we're home on the range.

TAG 3

ALL: Let 'er rip
With a yip and a yip, ketch me if you kin
With a kiss, kiss, kiss me and a kiss me agin,
With a stop that kissin' and we'll all fall in
For our home on the range.

ENCORE 1

BLOSSOM: Howdy, Ramrod Kelly,
HARRY: Howdy, Snagtooth Sal,
BLOSSOM: How's about resumin' with your fancy gal?
CHIQUITA: Listen, Ramrod Kelly, I'm your wife, that's true,
And if you don't plug 'er, honey, I'll plug you.

REPEAT TAG 1

ENCORE 2

HARRY: Oh, the mortgage agent says he won't renew,
CHIQUITA: And the train our daughter's on is overdue,
BLOSSOM: Stop your cryin', Mama, looka what I'm worth,
I been playin' poker in an upper berth.

REPEAT TAG 2

ENCORE 3

BLOSSOM: Say, did Dogface Charlie say he'd marry you?

CHIQUITA: Yes, he did.
BLOSSOM: 'Cause Charlie said he'd marry me too.
CHIQUITA & BLOSSOM: Listen, Dogface, to whicha will yuh keep your troth?
HARRY: Come to Salt Lake City an' I'll marry yuh both.

REPEAT TAG 3

COULD IT BE YOU?

Published December 1942. Introduced by Bill Johnson and ensemble. Lyric is dated November 21, 1942.

VERSE

BOYS: The place?
ROCKY: A big shindig in Baltimore.
BOYS: The time?
ROCKY: The clock had just struck eleven.
BOYS: The girl?
ROCKY: A great beauty appeared at the door,
A vision, an angel from heaven.
BOYS: Go on, Rocky, go on!
ROCKY: I knew later when I danced with her
BOYS: What did you know?
ROCKY: That I could love her madly!
BOYS: Because why?
ROCKY: Because my brain was in such a state of blur
That I found myself singing,
BOYS: And not badly.

REFRAIN

Could it be you,
The one I'm fated for?
Could it be you,
The love I've waited for?
For lo, since you came along
And kindled the song in my heart,
Why bother pretending?
The song is unending.
Are you the dream
I always dream about?
Are we the team
I'm on the beam about?
Could be these rev'ries of mine
Are far too divine
To come true,
Or could it be really you?

Published version

VERSE

A white seashore in moonlight immersed,
A silent palm tree swaying,
When out of nowhere you suddenly burst
And I found myself saying:

HEY, GOOD-LOOKIN'

Published December 1942. Introduced by Ethel Merman and Bill Johnson. The following notation appears in "Titles and Ideas": "Hollywood, Cal., March 4, 1942, 'Hey, Good-Looking, Say, What's Cooking.' "

VERSE 1

BLOSSOM: When there's a sun above,
I always find
Romantic thoughts of love
Never enter my mind,
But when the day is done
I find that instead
I just love ev'ryone,
And as Elizabeth Barrett Browning once said:

REFRAIN 1

Hey, good-lookin',
Say, what's cookin'?
Do you feel like bookin'
Some fun tonight?
Hey, hey, hey, hey, good-lookin',
If you're not already tooken,
Could you meet me soon,
In the moon-
Light?
Why don't we two go roamin'
Through the gloamin'
While the stars are combin'
The skies above?
Hey, hey, hey, hey, good-lookin',
Give in and we'll begin cookin'
That delish
Little dish
Called love.

VERSE 2

ROCKY: Your voice, Miss Ovaltine,
Has me impressed,
You're the missing link between
Lily Pons and Mae West.
But I must warn you, ma'm,

If later you're free,
That I'm half wolf, my lamb,
And as the famous Tallulah muttered to me:

REFRAIN 2

Hey, good-lookin',
Say, what's cookin'?
Do you feel like bookin'
Some fun tonight?
Hey, hey, hey, hey, good-lookin',
If you're not already tooken,
Could you meet me soon,
In the moon-
Light?
Why don't we two go roamin'
Through the gloamin'
While the stars are combin'
The skies above?
Hey, hey, hey, hey, good-lookin',
Give in and we'll begin cookin'
That delicious,
That surprising,
That divine,
That so appetizing,
That delightful
Itty-bitty-bite-full
Called love.

HE'S A RIGHT GUY

Published December 1942. Introduced by Ethel Merman.

REFRAIN

I can see
He's happier without me,
It could be
My hopes were too high.
Obviously
He's not mad about me,
But b'lieve you me,
He's a right guy.
Yes, I can tell
He far from adores me,
I know but too well
That wandering eye.
I treat him swell
And still he ignores me,
But, what the hell,
He's a right guy.
They'll tell me I should say,
"Goodbye and good night, guy,
Be on your way,
Just toddle along."
But I know one fine day
He'll prove he's a right guy,
And with a right guy
You can never go wrong.

TAG

Never, never,
Never, never,
Well, hardly ever
Go wrong.

THE LEADER OF A BIG-TIME BAND

Published January 1943. Introduced by Ethel Merman; danced by Bill Callahan and ensemble. In "Titles and Ideas," October 12, 1942, there is a mention of "Be a Guy Who's Got a Band."

VERSE

If a girl in any sector
Makes you feel like the puppy called Hector,
And you're longin' to subject 'er,
To elect 'er your wife and protect 'er,
If she's just as sweet as nectar,
But of your job she's no respecter,
Become a top band
Director and
You never, never will miss.

REFRAIN 1

In the old days, when a maid desired to wed,
Any man who'd foot the bill could fill the bed,
But today the lad who's sure to win her hand
Is the leader of a big-time band.
Even gals who go for wrestlers quit 'em quick
When they meet some guy who sings and swings
a stick,
For of late the only date they long to land
Is the leader of a big-time band.
When they hear Harry James
Make with the lips
The most Colonial dames
Fracture their hips,
So if thee would like to be in great demand,
Be the leader of a big-time band.

REFRAIN 2

In the gilded age, a Wall Street millionaire
Was the answer to a working maiden's prayer,

But today she'd chuck that yearly fifty grand
For the leader of a big-time band.
In the days when Casanova was the tops
All his rivals with the femmes were famous
flops,
But today who's got that extra monkey gland?*
Why, the leader of a big-time band.
When Goodman, champ of champs,
Goes blowin' blue,
Rum-ridden debutramps
Nearly come to,
'Cause there's nothing, when you're out, like
being fanned
By the leader of a big-time band.

REFRAIN 3

In the days when old King Louie held the scene,
Any Jock who had the jack could play the
Queen,
But today who'd come and play that baby grand?
Why, the leader of a big-time band.
When, in Venice, Georgia Sand with Chopin
romped,
Her libido had the Lido simply swamped,
But today who would be buried in the sand?
Why, the leader of a big-time band.
When Dorsey starts to tilt
That horn about,
Dear Missus Vanderbilt
Bumps herself out,
So, if, say, you still can play a one-night
stand,
Be the leader of a big-time band.

REFRAIN 4

When in Reno ladies we know used to clown,
All the chaps who wore the shaps could wear 'em
down,
But today the only rider they demand
Is the leader of a big-time band.
When Salome got John the B. and by the head,
It appears he wasn't kosher in da bed.
But todoy who'd be the goy she'd like to land?
Why, the leader of a big-time band.
When Cugat comes to tea
With Gypsy Rose,
She gets so het up she
Puts on her cloe's,
And she only turns one cheek while being
scanned
By the leader of a big-time, jig-time,
dig-a-dig-time band.

* *Or:*
But today who's got that extra gonad gland?

I'M IN LOVE WITH A SOLDIER BOY

Published January 1943. Introduced by Betty Garrett and ensemble. Added to the show during the Boston tryout.

VERSE

I'm in a terrible spot,
This town is gettin' too hot,
I feel so sad I could cry
Because I've got to kiss my baby goodbye.

REFRAIN

I'm in love with a soldier boy,
So in love with a soldier boy,
I'm in love with an Army man
And can he send me? Yes, he certainly can.
Ev'ry moment that he's away
I just hang on the phone all day
And at last when I get his buzz,
Say, does it rock me? Yes, it certainly does.
Ev'ry ev'ning this lover of mine
Comes and takes me out somewhere to dine,
When he brings me home often he stays
For days and days and days and days.
I'm in love with a soldier boy,
So in love with a soldier boy,
He's the greatest event in my life,
And it's no wonder. After all, I happen to be his
wife.

Published version

VERSE

Oh boy, I'm feeling but bad,
Such blues I never have had,
I'm all mixed up and involved
'Cause here's a problem that has got to be
solved.

REFRAIN

I'm in love with a soldier boy,
So in love with a soldier boy,
I'm in love with an Army man
And can he send me? Yes, he certainly can.
Ev'ry moment that he's away
I just hang on the phone all day
And at last when I get his buzz,
Say, does it rock me? Yes, it certainly does.
Ev'ry ev'ning this hero of mine
Comes and takes me out somewhere to dine,
When he brings me home, after a bit,

We sit and talk and then we just sit.
I'm in love with a soldier boy,
So in love with a soldier boy,
Would you say he's in love with me too?
You know the answer, 'cause the soldier is you.

THERE'S A HAPPY LAND IN THE SKY

Introduced by Ethel Merman, Paula Laurence, Allen Jenkins, William Lynn, and Bill Johnson. In "Titles and Ideas," October 31, 1942, the following reference occurs:

"Happy Land": Mister Peter—
If only Saint Peter will let you in

There are other references to the song in a music notebook: "There's a Happy Ending Bye and Bye," "There's a Happy Island in the Sky," and "There's a Happy Isle High in the Sky."

BLOSSOM: There's a happy land in the sky,
There's a happy land in the sky,
But if now you complain,
You will never get on that train
To the happy land in the sky.
OTHERS: We's a-list'nin'.
BLOSSOM: In that happy land in the sky.
OTHERS: Yass, yass,
BLOSSOM: You'll see millions of cars racin' by,
OTHERS: Yass, yass,
BLOSSOM: For they tell me, alas,
There's an oversupply of gas
In that happy land in the sky.
OTHERS: Lead me to it!

TWITCH: In that happy land in the sky,
OTHERS: Heigh-ho,
TWITCH: With old March the fifteenth drawin' nigh,
OTHERS: Say no,
TWITCH: You just sit and relax
'Cause there ain't any income tax
In that happy land in the sky.
OTHERS: Now your talkin'!

ROCKY: In that happy land in the sky,
OTHERS: What's what?
ROCKY: Only girls like Lamour qualify.
OTHERS: Dear Dot!
ROCKY: You see wonderful sights,
'Cause they never dim out the lights
In that happy land in the sky.
OTHERS: Are you kiddin'?

. . .

CHIQUITA: In that happy land in the sky,
OTHERS: Ho, hum.
CHIQUITA: They eat steak, ev'ry day, plus pork pie,
OTHERS: Yum, yum!
CHIQUITA: And they stop you and say,
"Tell me what *is* a meatless day?"
In the happy land in the sky.
OTHERS: Holy mack'rel!

HARRY: In that happy land in the sky,
OTHERS: What now?
HARRY: They've got so much, too much gin and rye,
OTHERS: Here's how!
HARRY: That the bars never close,
So if you want a bright red rose,
Try that happy land in the sky.
OTHERS: Down the rat hole!

BLOSSOM: On each corner, you meet some rich guy
OTHERS: Some punk.
BLOSSOM: Who for you a mink coat longs to buy,
OTHERS: Or skunk.
BLOSSOM: But their homes are so warm
Only G-strings are in good form,
In that happy land in the sky.
OTHERS: Strip for action!

ALL: There's a happy land in the sky,
There's a happy land in the sky,
BLOSSOM: So don't complain and don't carp,
And you'll, one day, be playin' a harp
In that happy land,
OTHERS: That happy land,
BLOSSOM: That happy land in the sky!
OTHERS: In the sky,
BLOSSOM: In the sky,
OTHERS: Yes, in the sky,
BLOSSOM: Yes, in the sky,
ALL: There's a happy, happy land in the sky!

BY THE MISSISSINEWAH

Published January 1943. Introduced by Ethel Merman and Paula Laurence. In "Titles and Ideas" the following notations occur:

May 12, 1942: "On the Miss-iss-inewa"
March 30, 1942: "It Came from Indiana"
Or: "It Always Comes from Indiana"

VERSE

BOTH: We're two little squaws from Indiana,
Who embarked on a trip for fun,
We're two little squaws who'll sing "Hosanna"
When the doggone trip is done.
No, no more we shall roam
BLOSSOM: From our comfy, cozy Hoosier home!

REFRAIN 1

BOTH: By the Miss-iss-iss-iss-iss-iss-iss-iss-inewah,
BLOSSOM: There's a husband who waits for me,
CHIQUITA: And me!
BOTH: By the Miss-iss-iss-iss-iss-iss-iss-iss-inewah,
BLOSSOM: There he waits in a wigwam built for three,
CHIQUITA: [*spoken*] Me, he, and she!
BLOSSOM: As it's one whole week since from our sheik we've been awah,
We're longing so for our co-papa,
CHIQUITA: Our co-dada!
BOTH: Thank the Lord this trip is brief
So we can leap on our heap-big chief
By the Miss-iss-iss-iss-iss-iss-inewah, wah-wah!
By the Miss-iss-iss-iss-iss-iss-inewah.

PATTER

CHIQUITA: If we tried the Mississippi,
I am certain I'd go dippy.
BLOSSOM: If they moved us to the S'wanee,
I'd take "coke" or smoke "marrawanny."
CHIQUITA: Life would surely be a fluke on
That Alaskan stream, the Yukon.
BLOSSOM: And as for the Rio Grande,
No, its bed is much too sandy!
CHIQUITA: You'll agree that we two dames
Would not be F.F.V. on the James.
BLOSSOM: I could never go to slumberland
On the Kennebec or the Cumberland.
CHIQUITA: Would you like the old "Putomuck?"
BLOSSOM: It would give me a pain in my "stowmuck."
CHIQUITA: Would the Missouri put you in a fury?
BLOSSOM: Why, yuh houri, I'm from Missouri.
CHIQUITA: To the Delaware
I'm well aware
We could never, never move,
BLOSSOM: For beside our stream,
Life is such a sweet dream
That we're strictly in the groove.

REFRAIN 2

BOTH: By the Miss-iss-iss-iss-iss-iss-iss-iss-inewah,
CHIQUITA: There's a husband who waits for me,
BLOSSOM: And me!
BOTH: By the Miss-iss-iss-iss-iss-iss-iss-iss-inewah,
CHIQUITA: There he waits in a wigwam built for three.
BLOSSOM: [*spoken*] It's bigamy!
CHIQUITA: Since no love we've had since from that lad we've been awah,
Back by that stream, we will scream "Hoorah!"
BLOSSOM: Hip, hip, hoorah!
BOTH: Yes, the moment we get in,
We'll blow the top with our pop redskin,
By the Miss-iss-iss-iss-iss-iss-inewah, wahoo!
By the Miss-iss-iss-iss-iss-iss-inewah,
Wah, wah, wah, wah
Wah, wahwah, wah, wah,
Wah!

REFRAIN 3

BOTH: By the Miss-iss-iss-iss-iss-iss-iss-iss-inewah,
There's a husband with whom we thrive *and* jive,
By the Miss-iss-iss-iss-iss-iss-iss-iss-inewah,
There he waits for the day when we arrive, Mister Ten-by-Five,
We're a total loss, since from the boss we've been awah,
'Cause for that Bo, we are so ga-ga, completely blah,
Life will be a dream again
When we can laze in a daisy chain
By the Miss-iss-iss-iss-iss-iss-inewah, without a bra,
By the Miss-iss-iss-iss-iss-iss-inewah,
Wah, wah, wah.

REFRAIN 4

BOTH: By the Miss-iss-iss-iss-iss-iss-iss-iss-inewah,
CHIQUITA: Il m'attend mon charmant joujou,
BLOSSOM: Are you kiddin'?
BOTH: By the Miss-iss-iss-iss-iss-iss-iss-iss-inewah,
CHIQUITA: Il m'attend, dans une veegvam, mon p'tit chou,
BLOSSOM: [*spoken*] Dig me, honey, dig me!
CHIQUITA: Je suis très, très glum since, from mon homme, I've been awah

Et comme, je yearn to return là-bas,
BLOSSOM: Mais, pourquoi pas?
We'll be rootin' pour la France
When in we tucky with our lucky
Alphonse,
CHIQUITA: Sur la Meess-eess-eess-eess-eess-eess-
eenewah!
BLOSSOM: Oo-la-la!
BOTH: Sur la Meess-eess-eess-eess-eess-eess-
eenewah,
Wah, wah, wah,
Wah, wahwah, wah, wah, wah!

REFRAIN 5

BOTH: By the Miss-iss-iss-iss-iss-iss-iss-iss-
inewah,
CHIQUITA: There's a husband who me adore,
BLOSSOM: Me more.
BOTH: By the Miss-iss-iss-iss-iss-iss-iss-iss-
inewah,
CHIQUITA: There he waits in a wigwam built for
four.
BLOSSOM: [*spoken*] Are you expectin' too?
CHIQUITA: Though to sleep I try, since from that
guy I've been awah,
I have such awful insomnia.
BLOSSOM: [*spoken*] Et cetera.
CHIQUITA: Oh, that wigwam will be heaven
When we are one, two, three, four,
BLOSSOM: [*spoken*] Five, six, seven,
BOTH: By the Miss-iss-iss-iss-iss-iss-inewah,
howdy, Ma!
By the Miss-iss-iss-iss-iss-iss-inewah!
Wah, wah, wah,
Wah, wahwah, wah, wah, wah!

Published version

VERSE

I'm a poor little squaw from Indiana,
Who embarked on a trip for fun,
I'm a poor little squaw who'll sing "Hosanna,"
When the doggone trip is done.
No, no more shall I roam
From my comfy, cozy Hoosier home!

REFRAIN 1

By the Miss-iss-iss-iss-iss-iss-iss-iss-inewah,
There's a husband to whom I'm true,
By the Miss-iss-iss-iss-iss-iss-iss-iss-inewah,
There he waits in a wigwam built for two.
Since no love I've had since from that lad I've
been awah,
Back by that stream I will scream "Hoorah!"
Thank the Lord this trip is brief
So I can leap on my heap-big chief
By the Miss-iss-iss-iss-iss-iss-inewah, wah-wah!
By the Miss-iss-iss-iss-iss-iss-inewah!

REFRAIN 2

By the Miss-iss-iss-iss-iss-iss-iss-iss-inewah,
There's a husband to whom I'm true,
By the Miss-iss-iss-iss-iss-iss-iss-iss-inewah,
There he waits in a wigwam built for two.
I'm a total loss since from the boss I've been
awah,
'Cause for that Bo, I am so ga-ga.
Yes, the moment I get in
I'll blow the top with my pop redskin,
By the Miss-iss-iss-iss-iss-iss-inewah, wah-wah!
By the Miss-iss-iss-iss-iss-iss-inewah!

RIDDLE-DIDDLE ME THIS

Dropped from the show during the Boston tryout. Introduced by Ethel Merman and Allen Jenkins.

VERSE

BLOSSOM: Hi, big boy, what's doin' today?
HARRY: I've been lookin' for you, sis,
Do you like guessin' riddles?
BLOSSOM: I'll say.
HARRY: Then, jeez, riddle-diddle me this:

REFRAIN 1

HARRY: Why does a chicken cross the road?
Why does a chicken cross the road?
BLOSSOM: Why does a chicken cross the road?
HARRY: Why, to get on the other side.
BOTH: Ha, ha, ha, ha, ha,
BLOSSOM: You kill me,
BOTH: Ha, ha, ha, ha,
BLOSSOM: You slay me,
BOTH: Ha, ha, ha, ha,
BLOSSOM: You murder me.
Now you riddle-diddle me this:

BLOSSOM: When is a door not a door?
When is a door not a door?
HARRY: When is a door not a door?
BLOSSOM: Why, you big boob, when it's ajar (a
jar).
BOTH: Ha, ha, ha, ha, ha,
HARRY: You kill me,
BOTH: Ha, ha, ha, ha,
HARRY: You slay me,
BOTH: Ha, ha, ha, ha,

HARRY: You murder me.
Now you riddle-diddle me this:

HARRY: When is a finger not a finger?
When is a finger not a finger?
BLOSSOM: When is a finger not a finger?
HARRY: Why, you dumbbell, when it's a thumb.
BOTH: Ha, ha, ha, ha, ha,
BLOSSOM: You kill me,
BOTH: Ha, ha, ha, ha,
BLOSSOM: You slay me,
BOTH: Ha, ha, ha, ha,
BLOSSOM: You murder me.
Now you riddle-diddle me this:

BLOSSOM: What's the best way to make a jacket last?
What's the best way to make a jacket last?
HARRY: What's the best way to make a jacket last?
BLOSSOM: Make the vest and the trousers first.
BOTH: Ha, ha, ha, ha, ha,
HARRY: You kill me,
BOTH: Ha, ha, ha, ha,
HARRY: You slay me,
BOTH: Ha, ha, ha, ha,
HARRY: You murder me,
BOTH: When you riddle-diddle me
You simply kiddle me
When you riddle-diddle me, babe.

REFRAIN 2

BLOSSOM: Why's Lana Turner like a hinge?
Why's Lana Turner like a hinge?
HARRY: Why's Lana Turner like a hinge?
BLOSSOM: She is something to adore (a door).
BOTH: Ha, ha, ha, ha, ha,
HARRY: You kill me,
BOTH: Ha, ha, ha, ha,
HARRY: You slay me,
BOTH: Ha, ha, ha, ha,
HARRY: You murder me.
Now you riddle-diddle me this:

HARRY: When is a spanking like a hat?
When is a spanking like a hat?
BLOSSOM: When is a spanking like a hat?
HARRY: Why, you nitwit, when it's felt.
BOTH: Ha, ha, ha, ha, ha,
BLOSSOM: You kill me,
BOTH: Ha, ha, ha, ha,
BLOSSOM: You slay me,
BOTH: Ha, ha, ha, ha,
BLOSSOM: You murder me.
Now you riddle-diddle me this:

BLOSSOM: What are those little white things that bite?
What are those little white things that bite?
HARRY: What are those little white things that bite?
BLOSSOM: Why, you great big palooka, your teeth.
BOTH: Ha, ha, ha, ha, ha,
HARRY: You kill me,
BOTH: Ha, ha, ha, ha,
HARRY: You slay me,
BOTH: Ha, ha, ha, ha,
HARRY: You murder me.
Now you riddle-diddle me this:

HARRY: How do you keep a fish from smellin'?
How do you keep a fish from smellin'?
BLOSSOM: How do you keep a fish from smellin'?
HARRY: Why, you simply cut off its nose.
BOTH: Ha, ha, ha, ha, ha,
BLOSSOM: You kill me,
BOTH: Ha, ha, ha, ha,
BLOSSOM: You slay me,
BOTH: Ha, ha, ha, ha,
BLOSSOM: You murder me,
BOTH: Ha, ha, ha, ha, ha,
Ha, ha, ha, ha,
Ha, ha, ha, ha, ha.

REFRAIN 3

HARRY: What time is it when the clock strikes thirteen?
What time is it when the clock strikes thirteen?
BLOSSOM: What time is it when the clock strikes thirteen?
HARRY: Why, it's time you got a new clock.
BOTH: Ha, ha, ha, ha, ha,
BLOSSOM: You kill me,
BOTH: Ha, ha, ha, ha,
BLOSSOM: You slay me,
BOTH: Ha, ha, ha, ha,
BLOSSOM: You murder me.
Now you riddle-diddle me this:

BLOSSOM: How d'ya get down from an elephant?
HARRY: How d'ya get down from an elephant?
BLOSSOM: You don't get down from an elephant,
You only get down from a duck.
BOTH: Ha, ha, ha, ha, ha,
HARRY: You kill me,
BOTH: Ha, ha, ha, ha,
HARRY: You slay me,
BOTH: Ha, ha, ha, ha,
HARRY: You murder me.
Now you riddle-diddle me this:

HARRY: Why does a stork stand on one foot?
Why does a stork stand on one foot?
BLOSSOM: Why does a stork stand on one foot?

HARRY: If he'd lift the other foot, he'd fall
down.
BOTH: Ha, ha, ha, ha,
BLOSSOM: You kill me,
BOTH: Ha, ha, ha, ha,
BLOSSOM: You slay me,
BOTH: Ha, ha, ha, ha,
BLOSSOM: You murder me.
Now you riddle-diddle me this:

BLOSSOM: What's the name of the spider that's
black?
HARRY: What's the name of the spider that's
black?
BLOSSOM: I don't know the name of the spider
that's black,
But you'd better pick it off your neck.
BOTH: Ha, ha, ha, ha, ha,
HARRY: You kill me,
BOTH: Ha, ha, ha, ha,
HARRY: You slay me,
BOTH: Ha, ha, ha, ha,
HARRY: You murder me,
BOTH: Ha, ha, ha, ha, ha,
Ha, ha, ha, ha,
Ha, ha, ha, ha, ha.

SO LONG, SAN ANTONIO

Dropped from the show during the Boston tryout. The same music with a different lyric became "So Long," intended for *Mississippi Belle,* a film score begun in 1943 and abandoned in 1944. In "Titles and Ideas," November 3, 1942, there is the following reference to this song:

> "So Long, San Antonio":
> Pray for my baby and me,
> Tell him I shall miss him so
> When he must go
> Over the sea.

VERSE

Why, y'all seem to be
So darn gay
At the thought of leaving this town,
But when it comes to me,
I must say
That it's got me definitely down.
Yes, it does seem a crime,
I was having such a swell time.

REFRAIN 1

So long, San Antonio,
Too bad we had to part,
Please tell Private . . . well, you know,
To take good care of my heart.
Remind him of that simply grand
Reunion we planned
Under the moon.
So long, San Antonio,
And please see that he
Comes home to me
Soon.

REFRAIN 2

So long, San Antonio,
I knew right off it was too good to be true.
Doggone, why did they have to close this
place?
It was so good getting to see him every night.
How do I know where he'll be going from
here?
How do I know when I'll be seeing him
again?
Remind him of that simply grand
Reunion we planned
Under the moon
So long, San Antonio
And please see that he
Comes home to me
Soon.

WASHINGTON, D.C.

Dropped from the show during rehearsals.

VERSE

ROCKY & BOYS: Welcome to San Antonio,
ROCKY: And how d'you like it,
Melanie?
MELANIE: To answer I feel afraid,
I'm trav'ling without my maid
And she knows all the answers,
not me.
BOYS: Get Melanie!
MELANIE: But as your guest
I'll do my best
And say it's a major thrill!
ROCKY & BOYS: And were you glad
Or were you sad
To leave your dad
On Capitol Hill?
MELANIE: Oh, heavens, no.

REFRAIN 1

MELANIE: It's just a joy to be
Far from Washington, D.C.,
What a joy supreme!
To be rushed by all you dear men,
Not by those run-down dollar-a-year
men.
No more I'll wheeze and freeze
At those air-conditioned teas
Where brass hats for war prepare.
Oh, what a joy to be
Far from Washington, D.C.,
Now that Av'rell's there.

REFRAIN 2

ALL: Oh, what a joy to be
Far from Washington, D.C.,
What a joy supreme!
MELANIE: To be somewhere really racy
ROCKY: And not at home with Hopkins and
Macy.
ALL: Oh, what an awful spot
Where a girl's a patriot
If she's got a cot to share.
Oh, what a joy to be
Far from Washington, D.C.
MELANIE: Now that all those—
ROCKY: What do you call those—
MELANIE &
OTHER BOYS: Aide-de-camp followers are there!
ALL: Aide-de-camp followers are there!

OH, HOW I COULD GO FOR YOU

Unused. In "Titles and Ideas," September 14, 1942, there is the following title: "I Could Go for You." There is a music sketch in a notebook for "Oh, How I Could Go for You." The lyric for the refrain is dated September 29, 1942. There is no completed piano-vocal for this song, although one could be extracted from Porter's notebook.

REFRAIN

If the scene were a green South Sea Island
And you came like a flame from the blue,
Yes, if there I should find you,
With a moon just behind you,
Oh, how I could go—for you.
In the calm of the palm-covered highland,
We would rest in our nest, made of sweet
bamboo,
And from seven to seven,
In the hush of our homemade heaven,
Oh, how I could go—for you.
But we're not on that hot South Sea island
And we've got no trick bungalow for two,
But if that day should come
And you felt you could take it, chum,
Oh, how I could go—for you.

TEXAS WILL MAKE YOU A MAN

Unused. No music survives. Lyric is dated September 9, 1942. Perhaps this was a forerunner of "See That You're Born in Texas."

Try Texas right away, son,
And we'll show you how to lick the Huns,
For from Corpus Christi
To the mountains misty
There are guns, guns, guns, guns, guns!
If you love the U.S.A., son,
But at fighting you're an also-ran,
Get the sock of Texas
In your solar plexus,
And Texas will make you a man.

WELL, I JUST WOULDN'T KNOW

Unused. No music survives. In "Titles and Ideas," September 14, 1942, the following entry occurs:

"Well, I Just Wouldn't Know":
In a uniform I like your looks,
But the way you'd look in mufty, snooks—

REFRAIN 1

SHE, TO 1ST BOY: I've a hunch that you'd be
good to get
As a possible Romeo,
But as long as we have merely
met,
Well, I just wouldn't know.
SHE, TO 2ND BOY: You appear to be so big and
strong

And your vitamins fairly glow,
But until you prove I'm right
or wrong,
Well, I just wouldn't know.
SHE, TO 3RD BOY: I like your mouth
From north to south,
I love your brow so noble,
Those massive ears
Are perfect dears
And your eyes are so big
they're global.
SHE, TO 4TH BOY: And I think that I could go for
you
And believe it, Toots, I can go,
But unless you make a pass or
two
Well, I just wouldn't know,
No, no, no,
I just wouldn't know.

REFRAIN 2

SHE, TO 5TH BOY: I've a hunch that I could like
you too,
As a possible Romeo,
But until I see much more of
you,
Well, I just wouldn't know.
SHE, TO 6TH BOY: I've a feeling I could learn to
care,
If you ever should will it so,
But until, kid, you let down
your hair,
Well, I just wouldn't know.
6TH BOY, TO HER: Your clothes are cute,
Your hat's a beaut,
And right smart I find you.
7TH BOY, TO HER: Your shapely props
Are simply tops,
Not to mention those bumps
behind you.
8TH BOY, TO HER: Do you think you'd like to take
a look
At an elegant bungalow?
SHE, TO 8TH BOY: Gee, unless, kid, you know
how to cook,
Well, I just wouldn't know,
No, no, no,
I just wouldn't know.

WOULDN'T IT BE CRAZY?

Unused. No music survives. In "Titles and Ideas," October 1, 1942, there is the following entry:

"Wouldn't It Be Funny (or Crazy)?
Wouldn't it be strange, a laugh, a riot,
etc.

Last lines: Wouldn't it be lovely,
If a son, an heir, would appear,
Wouldn't it be crazy, dear?

REFRAIN

Wouldn't it be crazy,
Wouldn't it be strange,
If we fell in love one of these days?
Wouldn't it be just a riot
If, one morning, on the quiet,
You became my better half?
Ha, ha, ha, ha, what a laugh!
Wouldn't it funny, if we settled down
In a cottage sunny, far away from town?
And if later, maybe, a baby should appear,
Wouldn't it be cuter than cute,
Wouldn't it be simply a beaut?
And wouldn't it be crazy, dear?

CARBORUNDUM

Also known as "Opening, Act I, Scene 5," "Bomber Scene," or "Assembly-Line Song." It is more recitative than song.

1ST GIRL: First I do this,
2ND GIRL: Then I do that,
3RD GIRL: Then I do this,
4TH GIRL: Then I do that,
5TH GIRL: Then I do this,
6TH GIRL: Then I do that,
BLOSSOM: Then I polish it off with
carborundum!

1ST GIRL: First I do this,
2ND GIRL: Then I do that,
3RD GIRL: Then I do this,
4TH GIRL: Then I do that.
HARRY: But what if she falls on her love
seat where she sat?
BLOSSOM: Then I polish it off with
carborundum!

MARY-FRANCES: In the late afternoon,
We cook dinner, hand and glove,
Then our husbands come soon
Take us out and make us love,
HARRY: But what if the moon isn't bright
enough above?
BLOSSOM: Then I polish it off with
carborundum!

MISSISSIPPI BELLE

1943-1944

An unproduced musical film written for Warner Brothers in 1943 and abandoned in 1944. Porter signed the contract on December 28, 1942. The lyrics are printed in alphabetical order.

AMO AMAS

The music is dated April 14, 1943. The lyric is dated April 15, 1943. Porter advised Warner Brothers that "Amo Amas" was adapted from a late-eighteenth-century drinking song entitled "Amo Amas." The original lyric appears in *Early Songs of Uncle Sam,* compiled by George Sturtevant Jackson (published by Bruce, Humphries, Inc., Boston, 1933). All songs not otherwise noted are original Porter songs.

VERSE 1

SOLO: Amo Amas,
I love a lass,
As a cedar tall and slender.
Sweet cowslip grace
Is her nominative case,
And she's of the feminine gender.

REFRAIN

ALL: Rorum corum,
Sunt divorum,
Haram scarum,
Divo!
Tag rag merry derry, periwig,
Hic, hoc, horum, genitivo!

VERSE 2

SOLO: Can I decline
This nymph divine?
Her voice as a flute is dulcis;
Her oculis bright,
Her manus white,
And soft when I tacto her pulse is.

VERSE 3

SOLO: And this puella,
Oh, oh, so bella,
I'll kiss, saecula, saeculorum,
For one day, she
My wife will be,
O dies benedictorum!

CLOSE TO ME

No music survives. The lyric, the earliest completed for the film, dates from February 4, 1943.

Close to me, stay close to me,
Through the calm, through the storm,
Close to me, stay, oh, so close to me
And keep the fire within me ever warm,
Yes, nestle near
And say, "I love you, dear,
I love you, dear, as never before,"
And promise me
You will be close to me,
Darling, forevermore,
Darling, forever
And ever-
More.

HIP, HIP, HOORAY FOR ANDY JACKSON

The music is dated June 24, 1943.

Hip, hip, hooray for Andy Jackson!
Join in and sing his praise!
Hip, hip, hooray for Andy Jackson,
Who will bring back the good old days.
Give a rousing cheer
For the day that's drawing near
When hard times will come to an end,
With a hip, hip, hooray for Andy Jackson,
Old Hick'ry, the people's friend!
Come on, all you men,
Come on and do it again—
Hip, hip, hooray for Andy Jackson!
Join in and sing his praise!
Hip, hip, hooray for Andy Jackson,
Who will bring back the good old days.
Give a rousing cheer
For the day that's drawing near
When hard times will come to an end,
With a hip, hip, hooray for Andy Jackson,
Old Hick'ry, the people's friend!
Old Hick'ry, the people's friend!

I LIKE PRETTY THINGS

Dated June 26, 1944. Published in *The Unpublished Cole Porter.*

VERSE

When some Lothario
Asks me to marry-o,
I'm always fair to him
And coyly declare to him:
I'd give my hide to be
Your blushing bride-to-be,
But before I say yes to you,
I've one little weakness to confess to you.

REFRAIN 1

I like pretty things,
As, for example, sparkling rings,
I could simply dote
On even one chinchilla coat.
For cash I don't care
But I could face lace underwear.
If you wed me I know you'll find
I'm not one bit the mercenary kind,
But I warn you, son, before the deal is signed
That I like pretty things.

REFRAIN 2

I like pretty things
Including great big pearls in strings,
I find full of charm
A row of bracelets on each arm.
I'm not of that ilk
That can't relax in sheets of silk,*
So if you think you really care
And wish to take me for your Lady Fair,
Well, I hope for your sake you're a millionaire,
As I like pretty things.

REFRAIN 3

I like pretty things
Such as a house with sev'ral wings,
I would gladly drive
A coach and four or even five,
I'd wear, on a dare,
A diamond brooch most anywhere,
And when we're on our honeymoon
From night till morning we will sing love's tune,
But I'll take you shopping ev'ry afternoon,
'Cause I like pretty things.

*Or:
That can't repose in sheets of silk,

I'M NOT MYSELF AT ALL

The music is dated March 8, 1943.

I'm like the charmed night
That shrouds the Emerald Isle,
I'm like the stilled lizard on the wall,
For since the starlight
Revealed your heavenly smile,
My darlin', I'm not myself at all.

I'm like the wild loon
Who knows not whither he flies,
I'm like the mad mountain waterfall,
For since the clear moon
Disclosed your devilish eyes,
My darlin', I'm not myself at all.

And till at your shrine,
You let me worship, my sweet,
And in my arms, you finally fall,
Yes, till you're all mine,
Forgive me if I repeat,
My darlin', I'm not myself at all,
At all, at all, at all, at all,
Not myself at all.

IN THE GREEN HILLS OF COUNTY MAYO

The music is dated March 8, 1943, and April 20, 1943. Porter wrote Warner Brothers that "the melody of this is adapted from the melody of Dobbins' 'Flowery Vale,' a traditional Irish air which I found in *Irish Country Songs:* second volume published by Boosey and Company, London, edited by Herbert Hughes."

VERSE 1

PADDIES: Where are the fields of corn, arrah,
Where are the fields of corn?
Where are the fields of corn
Of which they talked from night to morn?
SOLO: If you want to see a field of corn,
Go back to the bow'r where you were born,
For there, there, there, arrah,
There is a field of corn.

VERSE 2

PADDIES: Where are the streets of gold, arrah,
Where are the streets of gold?

Where are the streets of gold
Of which we always have been told?
SOLO: Hurry back to Erin, climb a tree
And look at the sunset on the sea,
For there, there, there, arrah,
There is a street of gold.

REFRAIN 1

PADDIES: Oh why, oh why,
Mother, tell me why
Did you ever let your goslin' go
From the darlin' dell
Where I used to dwell
In the green hills
Of County Mayo?
MORE PADDIES: Oh why, oh why,
Mother, tell me why
Did you ever let your goslin' go
From the darlin' dell
Where I used to dwell
In the green hills
Of County Mayo?

VERSE 3

PADDIES: Where are the maidens fair, arrah,
Where are the maidens fair?
Where are the maidens fair
Of which they told us ev'rywhere?
SOLO: If a maiden fair you hope to find
Go back to the love you left behind,
For there, there, there, arrah,
There is a maiden fair.

REFRAIN 2

PADDIES: Oh why, oh why,
Mother, tell me why
Did you ever let your goslin' go
From the darlin' dell
Where I used to dwell
In the green hills
SOLO: The sweet, serene hills*
Of County Mayo,
Mayo, Mayo!

KATHLEEN

The music is dated March 24, 1943.

VERSE

The stars that dance
On the gleaming glade
Suggest romance
And a serenade,
So mi' amore, mon amour,
Hark without scorn
To your love-torn
Troubadour.

REFRAIN

Kathleen, you are all I adore,
Kathleen, you are divine,
Kathleen, I'll be yours evermore
If only you will be mine.
Oh, hear my pray'r
For, dear, I swear
Your peer anywhere
Ne'er have I seen.
So say you'll be mine, I implore,
Kathleen, Kathleen, Kathleen.

LOADING SONG

The music is dated April 20, 1943. Porter wrote Warner Brothers that scattered couplets of this song could be found in *American Ballads and Folk Songs*, by John A. Lomax and Alan Lomax. The couplets were all attributed to anonymous authors.

2 ROUSTERS: Up sack!
Hanh!
Yo' gone!
1ST ROUSTER (RECEIVING SACK): Hanh!
2 ROUSTERS: Up sack!
Hanh!
Yo' gone!
2ND ROUSTER (RECEIVING SACK): Hanh!
2 ROUSTERS: Up sack!
Hanh!
Yo' gone!
3RD ROUSTER (RECEIVING SACK): Hanh!
2 ROUSTERS: Up sack!
Hanh!
Yo' gone!
4TH ROUSTER (RECEIVING SACK): Hanh!

*Or:
The calm, serene hills

. . .

CROWD: Wake up, niggah, hold up yo' head,
Better start workin' or yo'll wake up dead.
1ST ROUSTER: Ef I feels tomorrow like I felt dis mawn,
Call my name and I'll be gone.
CROWD: Git up dere, don't yo' hear de whistle blow?
Ef yo' trip dis time, you'll trip no mo'.
2ND ROUSTER: I git up in de mornin' so doggone soon,
Can't see nothin' but de stars and moon.
CROWD: Come on, yo' ole rouster,
De captain's on de deck,
So hurry up, niggah, or yo'll cotch it in de neck.
3RD ROUSTER: Jest can't wait till ma money come,
Throw up de job and go on de bum.
CROWD: Git under dat sack an' stop a-walkin' lame,
Or you'll get a number instead of a name.
4TH ROUSTER: De reason ah likes dis Lightning Line trade,
Ah walk and talk wid de chambermaid.

MAMIE MAGDALIN

The music is dated March 25, 1943. The note on "Loading Song" applies here too.

VERSE 1

SOLO: Only thing ah evah done wrong,
CHOIR: Mamie Magdalin,
SOLO: Ah stayed down ribber one day too long,
CHOIR: Mamie Magdalin,
SOLO: Ah was settin' dere lak a sleepy ole toad,
CHOIR: Mamie Magdalin,
SOLO: When a heavy-hipped woman struts down de road,
CHOIR: Mamie Magdalin.

VERSE 2

SOLO: When ah seen dat baby all dressed in red,
CHOIR: Mamie Magdalin,
SOLO: Ah done fergit dat mah wife ain't dead,
CHOIR: Mamie Magdalin,
SOLO: When she gave me chitlins an' some jelly roll,
CHOIR: Mamie Magdalin,
SOLO: She stole mah heart an' de debbil, mah soul,
CHOIR: Mamie Magdalin.

VERSE 3

SOLO: De las' time ah seen 'er, she was in de shade,
CHOIR: Mamie Magdalin,
SOLO: Countin' all de good money dat ah done made,
CHOIR: Mamie Magdalin,
SOLO: But soon as ah kin git some mo' dough,
CHOIR: Mamie Magdalin,
SOLO: Ah's gwine down ribber and do wrong once mo',
CHOIR: Mamie Magdalin.

REFRAIN

CHOIR: Yass,
SOLO: Mamie Magdalin,
CHOIR: Yass,
SOLO: Mamie Magdalin,
CHOIR: Yass,
SOLO: Mamie Magdalin,
CHOIR: Yass,
SOLO: Ah's comin' down,
CHOIR: Yass, yass, yass,
SOLO: Mamie Magdalin,
CHOIR: Yass,
SOLO: Mamie Magdalin,
CHOIR: Yass,
SOLO: Ah's comin' back agin,
ALL: Yass,
Mamie Magdalin Brown,
SOLO: Ah's comin' back agin,
CHOIR: Comin' back agin,
SOLO: Mamie Magdalin,
CHOIR: Mamie Magdalin
ALL: Brown,
Mamie Magdalin Brown.

MISSISSIPPI BELLE

The lyric is dated June 30, 1943; the music is dated July 7, 1943. Published in *The Unpublished Cole Porter.*

VERSE

On a filigreed balcony
Stood a Southern maid,
While below her, imploringly,
Sang a love-stung young blade,
And as listening stars looked down
On her lover there,
They all wished him success
When he warbled, more or less,
This air:

REFRAIN

Mississippi Belle,
Along the levee,
Scent of jasmine is heavy
And the fireflies glow.
Mississippi Belle,
The night's enthralling
And the mockin'bird's calling,
"Come along, let's go!"
'Neath the mellow moon,
In all her glory,
There's a certain love story
I'm a'pinin' to tell.
And, my honey, while
Our lips are blending,
You'll be guessin' the ending,
Mississippi Belle!

MY BROTH OF A BOY

The music is dated March 17, 1943. According to Porter, the lyrics were adapted from the lyrics of a song entitled "Lullaby" in an old volume, *Songs of Erin*, published by Boosey and Company, London.

VERSE 1

I will give you, my broth of a boy, a nest,
A nest in the Slumber Tree,
And I'll rock you there to rosy rest
Where you so peaceful will be.

REFRAIN 1

"Hush-o," will sing the leaves,
The leaves in the Slumber Tree,
"Hush-o," will sing the leaves
Till ev'rything that hurts or grieves
From my broth of a boy must flee.

VERSE 2

I will give you, my broth of a boy, a boat,
A boat on the Slumber Shore,
And you'll dream that through the seas you
float
Like your forefathers of yore.

REFRAIN 2

"Yo-ho," the wind will hum,
The wind from the Slumber Shore,
"Yo-ho," the wind will hum
Till you wake and find, be gob, you've become
Just a broth of a boy once more.
"Hush-o,"
Just a broth of a boy once more.

SCHOOL, SCHOOL, HEAVEN-BLESSED SCHOOL

The music and lyrics are dated April 16, 1943.

ALL: School, school, heaven-blessed school,
Of knowledge our fountain, of
learning our pool,
Where only taught
Is virtuous thought
And constant kindness is the rule.
We love, revere
And hold most dear,
Our heaven-blessed school,
Our heaven-blessed school.
TEACHER: Now, once again.
KATHLEEN: School, school, horrid old school,
Of knowledge not my fountain, of
learning not my pool,
Where having fun
Is strictly not done
And boring study is the rule.
I shall not grieve
When I can leave
This horrid old school,
This vastly ghastly, horrid old
school.

SO LONG

This is a revision of "So Long, San Antonio" (see *Something for the Boys*, 1943). The music is dated April 5, 1944.

VERSE

Ev'ry time I gaze in your eyes
As we murmur goodbyes
And you depart,
Ev'ry time I fail to protest
These words unexpressed
Rest in my heart:

REFRAIN

So long as the radiant rose
Gives out a scent divine,
So long as December snows
Hush, hush the slumbering pine,
So long as the stars appear
And dance with delight, the night through,
So long will you love me, dear?
For so long will I love you.

WHEN A WOMAN'S IN LOVE

The music is dated April 27, 1943. Published in *The Unpublished Cole Porter.* Porter wrote that the source of the lyrics of "When a Woman's in Love" is the poem "Oh, Say No Woman's Love Is Bought," in George Sturtevant Jackson's *Early Songs of Uncle Sam,* (1933).

They say a woman's love can be bought
With any vain, tawdry treasure,
They say a woman's heart can be caught
By any inane, passing pleasure,
They say, especially if she be fair,
That, like a bee, the lea she ranges,
Pursuing flow'rs, more sweet and more rare,
As her fancy changes.
I say that when a woman's in love,
From her one love she wanders never,
I say that when a woman's in love, alackaday,
She loves forever.

WHEN MCKINLEY MARCHES ON

No music survives. But a perusal of the lyric should reveal that the words are set to the music of "When Johnny Comes Marching Home."

Come, all, and sing the Jubilee, hurrah, hurrah,
McKinley is our nominee, hurrah, hurrah.
With Roosevelt on for second place,
No Popocrat can win the race
And we'll all feel gay when McKinley marches
in.

He's sound upon the money plan, hurrah, hurrah,
The friend of every workingman, hurrah, hurrah,
The bus'nessmen all know he's great,
From Maine way out to the Golden Gate,
And we'll all feel gay when McKinley marches
in.

Then wave our starry banner high, hurrah, hurrah,
For McKinley and sound money cry, hurrah, hur-
rah,
How the men will cheer and the boys will shout,
The Popocrats torn inside out
And we'll all feel gay when McKinley marches on.

WHEN YOU AND I WERE STRANGERS

The music is dated April 2, 1943.

When you and I were strangers,
Our fates at opposite ends,
In sadness, bowed,
The moon wore a cloud,
Then you and I became friends.

When you and I were friends, dear,
The moon grew brighter above
And less depressed,
In stardust she dressed,
Then you and I fell in love.

Now you and I are lovers,
And, my beloved, life has just begun
And 'twixt us twain,
The moon will never wear a cloud again
When you and I become one,
When you and I become one.

WHO'LL BID?

The music is dated May 20, 1943, but on May 5, 1943, Porter wrote Warner Brothers that "for your file my song 'Who'll Bid?' is adapted from 'The Female Auctioneer,' page 58 in the book *Americans and Their Songs* by Frank Luther, published by Harper Brothers."

VERSE 1

Be quiet, please, you ask me why?
The reason let me tell,
A lady auctioneer am I
With something rare to sell,
Yes, something rare to sell, my dears,
But not for vulgar pelf,
For unlike other auctioneers
I'm auct'ning off myself.

REFRAIN 1

KATHLEEN: Who'll bid?
1ST MAN: I'll bid!
KATHLEEN: Who'll bid?
2ND MAN: I'll bid!
KATHLEEN: Is it Jo, is it Jack, is it John?
3RD MAN: It's Algernon!
KATHLEEN: Who'll bid?
4TH MAN: I'll bid!
KATHLEEN: Who'll bid?
5TH MAN: I'll bid!
KATHLEEN: Am I going, going, going, or gone?

VERSE 2

Dear gentlemen, I look at you,
But pray don't think me rude,
Nor rate me as a scold or shrew,
A coquette or a prude,
My heart and hand I offer fair,
And should you buy the lot
I'm sure we'll make a happy pair
When someone ties the knot.

REFRAIN 2

KATHLEEN: Who'll bid?
6TH MAN: I'll bid!
KATHLEEN: Who'll bid?
7TH MAN: I'll bid!
KATHLEEN: Is it Dan, is it Dick, is it Don?
8TH MAN: It's Jock, hoot mon!
KATHLEEN: Who'll bid?
9TH MAN: I'll bid!
KATHLEEN: Who'll bid?
10TH MAN: I'll bid!
KATHLEEN: Am I going, going, going, or gone?

VERSE 3

Though some may call me pert, no doubt,
The thought cuts like a knife,
Pray tell me, where's a girl about
Who'd not become a wife?
Ah yes, to wed I really would,
In spite of all alarms,
Won't some dear bach'lor be so good
And take me in his arms?

REFRAIN 3

KATHLEEN: Who'll bid?
11TH MAN: I'll bid!
KATHLEEN: Who'll bid?
12TH MAN: I'll bid!
KATHLEEN: Is it Carl, is it Ken, is it Con?
13TH MAN: Es yo, Don Juan!
KATHLEEN: Who'll bid?
14TH MAN: I'll bid!
KATHLEEN: Who'll bid?
15TH MAN: I'll bid!
KATHLEEN: Am I going, going, going?
ALL MEN: You're gone!
KATHLEEN: I'm gone!

MEXICAN HAYRIDE

1944

Tryout: Shubert Theatre, Boston, December 29, 1943. Produced by Michael Todd at the Winter Garden Theatre, New York, January 28, 1944. 481 performances. Book by Herbert and Dorothy Fields. Entire production staged and lighted by Hassard Short. Cast, starring Bobby Clark, included June Havoc, George Givot, Wilbur Evans, Luba Malina, Corinna Mura, Paul Haakon, Edith Meiser, and Sergio DeKarlo.

Porter signed the contract for this show on July 28, 1943.

ENTRANCE OF MONTANA

Opening chorus, Act I. Introduced by ensemble.

PART 1

SINGERS: Beware, Montana, that bull's a devil, beware,
Beware!
Oh, what a pass and what a turn!
You're there, Montana, yes, on the level, you're there,
You're there!
Just look at his eyes, they fairly burn,
O-lé,
Oh, but what grace and what skill,
O-lé, o-lé,
Get yourself set for the kill,
Montana!
(FIRST TIME) Look at him going ga-ga,
(SECOND TIME) Look at him stagger about,
Montana!
(FIRST TIME) Hurrah, hurrah!
(SECOND TIME) He's down, he's out.

PART 2

SINGERS: What a treat, divine Montana,
Senorit' Americana,
We know why ev'ry bull
(FIRST TIME) Offers you his ear,
(SECOND TIME) Gives you his ear,
You're such a dear!
Aren't you proud as 'round he flounders,
While the crowd, including founders
Of the S.P.C.A.,
Cry, "O-lé, o-lé, o-lé, o-lé, o-lé,
Montana, o-lé!"

SING TO ME, GUITAR

Published February 1944. Introduced by Corinna Mura and ensemble.

Sing to me, guitar,
From my dearest of all
I am parted,
And I live in a thrall,
Heavy-hearted,
So sing to me, guitar.
Sing to me, guitar,
Into melody burst
And take me roaming
To the moment we first
Met in the gloaming.
Oh, sing to me, guitar,
Sing to me of that evening divine
By the moonlit lagoon in the mist,
Sing to me of his lips pressed to mine
As we kissed and we kissed and we kissed.
Sing to me of the love that we swore
By the light of the bright morning star,
Sing to me of the day when we will meet once more,
Sing to me,
Sing to me,
Sing to me.
But why so suddenly
Do you sing to me in a minor key?
Guitar
Explain to me,
Guitar.*

THE GOOD-WILL MOVEMENT

Published December 1943. Introduced by Wilbur Evans and ensemble.

VERSE

Rumor says, while a-seeking solace
For his woes, Vice-a-Pres'dent Wallace

**Published version:*
Sing to me, guitar,
Yes, sing to me of the love that we swore
By the light of the bright morning star,
Sing to me of the day when we will meet once more,
Sing to me,
Sing to me,
Guitar.

Wowed the Washington scene
By inventing a dance routine.
It's a dance to promote back-pattin'
'Twixt ourselves and our neighbors Latin.
F.D.R., when he saw Hal swaying,
Rushed a wire to Camacho saying,
"On the border I'll order a special floor
If you launch it, fella,
With Ella-
Nor."

REFRAIN 1

A super-step
Is the Good-Will Movement,
It's in that pep,
Pan-American mood.
It's hyper-hep
But with this improvement,
It's got that rum-tum
"Here's to yuh, chum,"
"Salud, amigo, salud."
The music's "Oklahoma"
Plus a rumba beat,
"La Paloma"
But in Basin Street.
If you approve
Of the Good-Will Movement,
Get in the groove
And let the good will flow.

TRIO 1

Cuernavaca,
Meet Wahoo,
Hey, Oaxaca,
Meet Kalamazoo,
Indianapolis,
Meet Tehaucán,
Dear Minneapolis,
Meet Mazatlán,
Manzanillo,
Meet Duluth,
Hermosillo,
Meet Mobile, dat's in de South,
Hello, Bill from Bunker Hill,
In case you feel the urge,
Meet the Clara Luce of Vera Cruz
And merge, America, merge.

REFRAIN 2

A super-step
Is the Good-Will Movement,
It's in that pep,
Pan-American mood.
It's hyper-hep
But with this improvement,
It's got that rum-tum
"Here's to yuh, chum,"
"Salud, amigo, salud."
You'll soon see spics and gringos
In the dicty sumps,
Mixin' lingos,
Not to mention bumps!
If you're a pal
Of the Good-Will Movement,
Then grab your gal
And let the good will flow.

REFRAIN 3 [LAST 8 LINES]

The music's muy catchy
If you care for corn,
Mariachi
Plus a Harlem horn.
If you can click
To the Good-Will Movement,
Then case your chick
And let the good will flow.

TRIO 2

Massachusetts,
How's my girl?
Georgia, you sets
My heart all awhirl.
Howdy, Maryland,
You're lookin' good.
Hail, Queen of Fairyland,
How's Hollywood?
Minny Sota, please step forth,
Dear Dakota, are you South or are you North?
You're a pip, Miss Mississipp,
How's ev'ry little thing?
Arkansas sublime, you're just in time,
With your permission, we'll sing:

REFRAIN 4 [LAST 8 LINES]

The rhythm comes from Taxco,
But the tune's Berlin,
Hot Tabasco
Mixed with saccharine.
If you consent
To the Good-Will Movement,
Then jive your gent
And let the good will flow.

I LOVE YOU

Published December 1943. Introduced by Wilbur Evans. Monty Woolley reportedly wagered Porter he could not write a song with such an obvious title. Original title was "It All Belongs to You and Me."

On February 4, 1944, Mike Todd sent Cole Porter the following telegram: "Dear Cole: Bing Crosby is recording 'I Love You' a week from today. I love you." By late April, the Bing Crosby recording (John Scott Trotter Orchestra, Decca 18595) was, according to *The Billboard*, the best-selling retail record in America, while the song itself was second in nationwide sheet-music sales and number one on the Lucky Strike Hit Parade (CBS, April 29, 1944).

VERSE

If a love song I could only write,
A song with words and music divine,
I would serenade you ev'ry night
Till you'd relent and consent to be mine.
But alas, just an amateur am I,
And so I'll not be surprised, my dear,
If you smile and politely pass it by
When this, my first love song, you hear:

REFRAIN

"I love you,"
Hums the April breeze.
"I love you,"
Echo the hills.
"I love you,"
The golden dawn agrees
As once more she sees
Daffodils.
It's spring again
And birds, on the wing again,
Start to sing again
The old melody.
"I love you,"
That's the song of songs,
And it all belongs
To you and me.

THERE MUST BE SOMEONE FOR ME

Published January 1944. Introduced by June Havoc.

VERSE

If you're a maid men always quit
And with such velocity
That you're getting ready to commit
A ferocatrocity,
If you're blue because in each love affair,
You have wound up on the shelf,
Simply learn this little old nurs'ry air
And repeat it to yourself:

REFRAIN 1

There's a boy cat for ev'ry girl cat,
There's a boy bat for ev'ry girl bat,
There's a boy rat for ev'ry girl rat,
So there must be someone for me.
There's a boy snail for ev'ry girl snail,
There's a boy quail for ev'ry girl quail,
There's a boy whale for ev'ry girl whale,
So there must be someone for me.
For each lassy hippo in the riverbed,
Say the rhymes of Mother Goose,
There's a laddie hippo she will shortly wed,
So why in hell should I reduce?
There's a boy mouse for ev'ry girl mouse,
There's a boy grouse for ev'ry girl grouse,
There's a boy louse for ev'ry girl louse,
So there must be someone for me.

REFRAIN 2

There's a boy lamb for ev'ry girl lamb,
There's a boy clam for ev'ry girl clam,
There's a boy ham for ev'ry girl ham,
So there must be someone for me.
There's a boy trout for ev'ry girl trout,
There's a boy lout for ev'ry girl lout,
There's a Boy Scout for ev'ry Girl Scout,
So there must be someone for me.
Mister Charlie Chaplin, simply look at him,
He'll be sixty-three today,
Yet whenever Charlie's feeling full of vim
He gets another protégée.
There's a boy tot for ev'ry girl tot,
There's a boy hot for ev'ry girl hot,
There's no boycott on any girl cot,
So there must be someone for me.

REFRAIN 3

There's a boy chick for ev'ry girl chick,
There's a boy tick for ev'ry girl tick,
There's a boy hick for ev'ry girl hick,
So there must be someone for me.
There's a boy moose for ev'ry girl moose,
There's a boy goose for ev'ry girl goose,
There's a pa-poose for ev'ry ma-poose,
So there must be someone for me.
Mister John L. Lewis I could not begin
To imagine as my spouse,
Yet a lot of girls would love to slumber in
The bushes of his eyebrows.
There's a boy loon for ev'ry girl loon,
There's a boy prune for ev'ry girl prune,

There's a boy goon for ev'ry girl goon,
So there must be someone for me.

CARLOTTA

Published January 1944. Introduced by Corinna Mura and ensemble.

VERSE 1

SOLO: When Carlotta and Max'milian
Were Chapultepec's royal pair,
A misguided young civilian
Fell in love with the Empress fair.
SINGERS: Disregarding poor Max'milian,
A misguided young civilian
Fell in love with the Empress fair.
SOLO: And when Lotta, so decorative,
On her balcony would parade,
That enchanted little native
Would warble this serenade,
SINGERS: Yes, to Lotta, decorative,
That enchanted little native
Would warble this serenade:

REFRAIN

SOLO: Oh, Carlotta,
Carlotta, so fair to see,
Oh, Carlotta,
Why can't you be fair to me?
It's foolish to slight
So romantic a night,
For ne'er were the stars so bright above.
Oh, Carlotta,
Come out and I'll give you my love.

VERSE 2

SOLO: There's a sequel to the story
Though Chapultepec's days are o'er
And Carlotta, in her glory,
On the balcony stands no more.
SINGERS: There's a sequel to the story
Though Carlotta, in her glory,
On the balcony stands no more,
SOLO: Though our singer upon his pillow
Many years in the ground has lain,
Near the palace there's a willow
That whispers still his refrain,
SINGERS: Though our singer's on his pillow,
Near the palace there's a willow
That whispers still his refrain:

REPEAT REFRAIN

GIRLS

Published March 1944. Introduced by Bobby Clark and ensemble.

VERSE

HUMPHREY: An old gypsy prophesied when I was three
GIRLS: And what did she tell our little star?
HUMPHREY: That one day a lady-killer I would be.
GIRLS: And now, dear, you certainly are.
HUMPHREY: Yes, now when I dash along the boulevard,
GIRLS: Continue, O man we love!
HUMPHREY: I'm always escorted by a bodyguard
Consisting entirely of

REFRAIN 1

HUMPHREY: Girls to the right of me,
Girls to the left of me,
Girls in front of me,
Girls behind,
Girls all over me,
I don't mind.
Oh, what a rogue am I,
So much in vogue am I,
Simply smothered in kisses and curls,
By the girls, girls, girls, girls, girls!

PATTER 1

HUMPHREY: What do all men sin for?
GIRLS: Girls!
HUMPHREY: What is Errol Flynn for?
GIRLS: Girls!
HUMPHREY: What are girdles geared for?
GIRLS: Girls!
HUMPHREY: And what are falsies brassiered for?
GIRLS: Girls!
HUMPHREY: What should heav'n be thanked for?
GIRLS: Girls!
HUMPHREY: What was *Esquire* spanked for?
GIRLS: Girls!
HUMPHREY: What are kisses, my child, for?
GIRLS: Girls!
HUMPHREY: And wow, wow, what am I wild for?

REFRAIN 2

Girls to the right of him,
Girls to the left of him
Girls in front of him,
Girls behind,
Girls all over him,

We don't mind.
Oh, what a rogue is he,
So much in vogue is he,
Simply smothered in kisses and curls,
By the girls, girls, girls, girls, girls!

PATTER 2

HUMPHREY: I go to the office and they're waiting there,
I go to the barber shop, they trim my hair,
I go to the tailor's and they fit my clo'es,
I go to the rest room and they powder my nose,
I go to my club to have a game of gin
But ah, here's the rub, they simply follow me in.
And though a hot-water bottle I
Tonight will take to bed,
Tomorrow morning, what'll I
Find instead?

WHAT A CRAZY WAY TO SPEND SUNDAY

Introduced by ensemble. Unpublished but included in the Decca original-cast recording (Decca 23339).

PART 1

BOYS & GIRLS: What a crazy way to spend Sunday,
Having lunch with the bunch on a barge,
And a lunch consisting of no less
Than garlic soup, goat's milk, and frijoles.
What a crazy way to spend Sunday,
With a band on a hand-painted scow,
And our thoughts all roam
To the folks back home
And to what they are doing now.

PART 2

BOYS & GIRLS: Father is reading the funnies,
Mother is reading what to wear,
Aunt Isabella
Is reading Luella
While Gran'ma and Winchell make a pair,
SOLO: Such a happy pair.
BOYS & GIRLS: Sister is doing the crossword,
Brother is reading about the fight,
While here we are
From home so far
That there's not a Sunday paper in sight!
SOLO: Not one in sight.

REPEAT PART 1

ABRACADABRA

Published March 1944. Introduced by June Havoc and ensemble.

VERSE

Little boys, there's a thing called love*
That will, one day, drive you insane,
But lest you don't know what I am talking of,
Pay attention to what I explain:

REFRAIN 1

SOLO: Your heart's lost its quiver,
Your life's a bore,
You say, "Lord deliver
Poor me from more,"
A jump in the river
You're thinking of
Then Abracadabra!
And you're in love.
Your troubles are over,
For night and day
You're living in clover,
Hey, hey, hey hey!
With joy and Jehovah
You're hand in glove,
It's Abracadabra!
And you're in love,
It's Abracadabra
And you're in love,
BOYS: And you're in love,
SOLO: It's Abracadabra!
And you're in love,
BOYS: And you're in love.
SOLO: Then, presto, one day
His kisses away

**Published version:*
Boys and girls, there's a thing called love

You shove,
BOYS: His kisses away you shove,
SOLO: 'Cause Abracadabra!
You're out of love,
BOYS: You're out of love,
SOLO: Yes, Abracadabra!
You're out of love,
BOYS: You're out of love,
SOLO: Yes, Abracadabra!
You're out of love,
BOYS: You're out of love.
SOLO: Then presto one night
He turns out the light
Above,
BOYS: He turns out the light above,
SOLO: And Abracadabra! You're back in love,
BOYS: You're back in love!

PATTER

For instance,
You meet a boy Monday,
You fall in love like that,
You meet again Tuesday,
What's more, you meet in his flat.
Through Wedn'sday and Thursday
Life is pure delight,
You marry him Friday
And you push him out the window Saturday night.

REFRAIN 2

SOLO: 'Cause Abracadabra, you're out of love,
BOYS: You're out of love,
SOLO: Yes, Abracadabra, you're out of love,
BOYS: You're out of love,
SOLO: Then somebody new
Appears like a coo-
Ing dove,
BOYS: Appears like a cooing dove,
SOLO: And Abracadabra you're back in love,
BOYS: And you're back in love,
SOLO: Yes, you're back in love,
BOYS: Yes, you're back in love,
SOLO: Then you're out of love,
BOYS: Then you're out of love,
SOLO: Yes, you're back in love,
BOYS: Yes, you're back in love.

COUNT YOUR BLESSINGS

Published January 1944. Introduced by June Havoc, Bobby Clark, and George Givot.

VERSE

MONTANA: Ev'ry time I've trouble
And I'm in despair
'Cause I've been crossed-double
By a love affair,
When I feel so blue
That I'm in the dumps
'Cause I just had the flu
And I'm getting the mumps,
When I'm in such a jam
That I can't relax
'Cause I just paid my goddamn
Income tax,
When my temper's too short
And my face is too long,
My favorite sport
Is to sing this song:

REFRAIN 1

MONTANA: Count your blessings,
Count your blessings,
Count your blessings, honey chile,
LOMBO & HUMPHREY: Honey chile,
MONTANA: If today you're not in clover,
Your woes will soon be over,
So count your blessings and smile,
LOMBO & HUMPHREY: Count your blessings!

MONTANA: And smile,
LOMBO & HUMPHREY: And smile,
MONTANA: And smile,
LOMBO & HUMPHREY: And smile,
MONTANA: All your troubles will be over in a little while,
LOMBO & HUMPHREY: In a little while,

MONTANA: You'll forget life's barbs and brambles
When they date you up at Campbell's,
LOMBO: You'll forget your sad palaver
When they're cooling your cadaver,
HUMPHREY: You'll be happier when you own a
Pretty pickled pine kimona,
ALL: So count your blessings and smile.

REFRAIN 2

[First 14 lines of refrain 1]

MONTANA: You'll forget you had the dropsy
When they finish your autopsy,

LOMBO: You'll forget you had the measles
When you're nibbled by the weasels,
HUMPHREY: You'll forget you had the willies
When you're fertilizing lilies,
ALL: So count your blessings and smile.
[*Lines 9–14 refrain 1*]

MONTANA: You will soon have lots of good lawn
Growing over you in Woodlawn,
LOMBO: Yes, you'll soon be sitting pretty
When you move to Marble City,
HUMPHREY: All your past will seem more comic
When you've stink-weed on your stomick
ALL: So count your blessings and smile.

REFRAIN 3

[*First 14 lines of refrain 1*]

MONTANA: You'll forget this gal from Tucson
When the hot seat puts the juice on,
LOMBO (TO HUMPHREY): On the slab, no more, they'll shelve you
When they ship your brains to Bellevue,
HUMPHREY (TO LOMBO): When your box, with locks, is plastered
I'll forget I met a bastard,
ALL: So count your blessings and smile.

ENCORE 1

[*First 14 lines of refrain 1*]

MONTANA: You will find in many ways, ease,
When you're pushing up the daisies,
LOMBO: You won't feel so mediocre
When you're stiffer than a poker,
HUMPHREY: Yes, you'll be a lot more docile
When you're nothing but a fossil,
ALL: So count your blessings and smile.
[*Lines 9–14 of refrain 1*]

MONTANA: You'll no longer be a sulker
When you're pushed in your sepulcher,
LOMBO: When you're in your mausoleum
There'll be rats but you won't see 'em,
HUMPHREY: When with ants your grave's infected
You won't care who's re-elected.
ALL: So count your blessings and smile.

ENCORE 2

[*First 14 lines of refrain 1*]

MONTANA: All your blues will seem less solemn
When you make the obit column,
LOMBO: 'Stead of cursing fate, you'll thank it
When you're sewn up in a blanket,
HUMPHREY: Meatless days won't make you grumble
When your skull begins to crumble,
ALL: So count your blessings and smile.
[*Lines 9–14 of refrain 1*]

MONTANA: Wordly cares no more will kill you
When the termites start to drill you,
LOMBO: When your coffin's full of crickets
You won't need your ration tickets,
HUMPHREY: When those hungry worms have et you
Mr. Morgenthau can't get you,
ALL: So count your blessings and smile.

HEREAFTER

A duet for June Havoc and Bobby Clark that was dropped from the show during its Boston tryout.

VERSE

MONTANA: Come on, you sheik,
You've got to speak,
The mike is standing there.
HUMPHREY: I quite agree,
But b'lieve you me
I've never been on the air.
MONTANA: Say something silky
Like Wendell Willkie,
Or down the river they'll sell you.
HUMPHREY: To sockeroo 'em
What shall I say to 'em?
MONTANA: Repeat what I tell you.

REFRAIN

MONTANA: Hereafter, hereafter,
HUMPHREY: Hereafter, hereafter,
MONTANA: Hereafter it's a happy holiday,
HUMPHREY: Hereafter it's a happy holiday,
MONTANA: Hereafter the lid's off,
HUMPHREY: Hereafter the lid's off,
MONTANA: So, kids, off for an old-time breakaway,
HUMPHREY: For an old-time breakaway.
MONTANA: Let's all forget for days and days
We're gentlemen and ladies.

HUMPHREY: Let's all forget and start to raise
What the Hays office calls
"Hades."
MONTANA: Hereafter just laughter,
HUMPHREY: Hereafter just laughter,

MONTANA: Hereafter ev'rybody gay!
HUMPHREY: Ev'rybody gay!
BOYS: Hereafter,
GIRLS: Hereafter,
BOYS: Hereafter,
GIRLS: Hereafter,
Hereafter it's a happy holiday,
BOYS: Hereafter it's a happy holiday.
GIRLS: Hereafter,
BOYS: Hereafter,
GIRLS: The lid's off,
BOYS: The lid's off,
GIRLS & BOYS: So, kids, off, for an old-time
breakaway.
Let's all forget for days and days
We're gentlemen and ladies,
Let's all get set and start to raise
What the Hays office calls
"Hades."
Hereafter, hereafter,
Just laughter,
Just laughter,
Hereafter,
Ev'rybody gay!

IT MUST BE FUN TO BE YOU

Published December 1943. Sung during the Boston tryout by Sergio DeKarlo, Wilbur Evans, and June Havoc. Dropped before the New York opening. Entries in "Titles and Ideas," September 30, 1943: "It Can't Be Fun to Be Bill," and October 9, 1943: "It Must Be Fun to Be You."

VERSE 1

DAVID: I hear, in affairs romantic,
You drive all your victims frantic,
For, as they explain,
You're as fickle as a weather vane.
MIGUEL: I know from the ones who grumble
That you, like the bees that bumble,
Change from hour to hour
The name and address of your favorite
flow'r.

REFRAIN 1

DAVID & MIGUEL: It must be fun to be you,
And play with love as you do,
To treat each new romance
As merely one more dance
Or just another book to glance through.
It must be fun to acquire
Whatever heart you desire,
And when you're bored with it
To tear it in two,
It must be fun to be you.

INTERLUDE 1

MONTANA: Hush your chatter, I implore you,
Or you'll kill my success.
DAVID & MIGUEL: What's the matter? We adore you,
But, Montana, nevertheless

REFRAIN 2

DAVID & MIGUEL: It must be fun to be you,
PAGE: Perdone, Meess M., telefono.
DAVID & MIGUEL: And play with love as you do,
MONTANA: Who is it? It's Peppy? Why, hello!
DAVID & MIGUEL: To treat each new romance
MONTANA: What?
DAVID & MIGUEL: As merely one more dance
MONTANA: Rot!
DAVID & MIGUEL: Or just another book to glance through.
MONTANA: Not true? Why, darling, there's no one
I love but you.
DAVID & MIGUEL: It must be fun to acquire
MONTANA: I'm sorry but, Pepps, I shan't be in,
DAVID & MIGUEL: Whatever heart you desire,
MONTANA: I'm dining tonight with Errol Flynn.
DAVID & MIGUEL: And when you're bored with it
MONTANA: What's that?
DAVID & MIGUEL: To tear it in two,
MONTANA: You know what you can do!
DAVID & MIGUEL: It must be fun to be you.
MONTANA: Thank heaven, that's through!

INTERLUDE 2

MONTANA: In spite of that telephone call
And this crazy game I was playing,

I'm really not fickle at all,
And I'm tired of hearing you saying

REFRAIN 3

MONTANA: It must be fun to be you,
And play with love as you do,
To treat each new romance
As merely one more dance
Or just another book to glance
through.

MONTANA, DAVID, MIGUEL, BOYS, & GIRLS: It must be fun to acquire
Whatever heart you desire
And when you're bored with it
To tear it in two,
It must be fun to be you.

HERE'S A CHEER FOR DEAR OLD CIRO'S

Opening of Act I, Scene 3. Dropped from the show during the Boston tryout. Sung there by Larry Martin and ensemble.

BOYS: Here's a cheer for dear old
Ciro's
And for its host, A. C.
Blumenthal,
He is one of our greatest
heroes
And Mexico's fav'rite rose of
them all,
Though his dinner checks
have far too many zeros,
Ev'ry meal at least is like a
feast of Nero's,
So here's a cheer for dear old
Ciro's
And for you, A. C.
Blumenthal.

GIRLS: Blumey, Blumey,
Where can he be?
Blumey, Blumey!

A. C. BLUMENTHAL: Did anybody ask for me?

BOYS & GIRLS: Blumey, Blumey, Blumey,
Blumey, Blue-mey!

A. C. BLUMENTHAL: My friends, to see you sitting
there
Is a cosa exquisita,
And now to sing to you, ladies
fair,
May I present the heaven-sent
Lolita!

ALL: Lolita, Lolita,
Go to it, Lolitita

TEQUILA

At the end of "Ciro's," Corinna Mura entered and sang "Tequila," which was also dropped during the Boston tryout.

VERSE

While you're here in Mexico
Some big hombre, sweet and low,
May upset your status quo
Terrifically.
Now the night he fails to call,
Don't consider a wailing wall,
Find a bar nearby
And get a supply
Of our national remedy.

REFRAIN

SOLO: Tequila,
Nothin' like tequila,
The right drink,
When you want to be gay.
Why tarry
If a torch you carry?
Let tequila
Wash your blues away.
When first love started,
You were so light-hearted,
Then love departed
Like the dying day.
But hark ye, dearie,
'Stead of hara-kiri,
Let tequila
Wash your blues away.

INTERLUDE

Now get some salt and half a lime,
And I'll show you how to drink the drink of all
time.

PATTER

SOLO: First you take some salt,
SINGERS: First you take some salt,
SOLO: Then you sip a bit,
SINGERS: Then you sip a bit,
SOLO: Then you squeeze your lime,

SINGERS: Then you squeeze your lime,
SOLO: To kill the taste of it,
SINGERS: To kill the taste of it.

SOLO: Then you take some salt,
SINGERS: Then you take some salt,
SOLO: And you drink the rest,
SINGERS: And you drink the rest,
SOLO: Then you squeeze your lime,
SINGERS: Then you squeeze your lime,
SOLO: Now there's hair on your chest,
SINGERS: Now there's hair on your chest.

SOLO: Then you take some salt,
SINGERS: Then you take some salt,
SOLO: Try another one,
SINGERS: Try another one,
SOLO: Then you squeeze your lime,
SINGERS: Then you squeeze your lime,
SOLO: Now you're havin' fun,
SINGERS: Now you're havin' fun.

SOLO: Then you order a third,
SINGERS: Then you order a third,
SOLO: Now you're gettin' tight,
SINGERS: Now you're gettin' tight,
SOLO: When you've drunk your fourth,
SINGERS: When you've drunk your fourth,
SOLO: You're as high as a kite,
SINGERS: You're as high as a kite,
SOLO: When you've had your fifth, you let 'er rip,
And you try to do a double flip,
But you suddenly find that you're flat on the floor,
Hollerin', "Waiter, por favor, more."

REPEAT REFRAIN

CODA

SINGERS: Wash, wash, wash, wash,
SOLO: Wash your blues away,
SINGERS: Wash, wash, wash, wash, wash, wash, wash, wash,
SOLO: Wash your blues away, away, away,
SINGERS: Wash all your blues away.

WE'RE OFF FOR A HAYRIDE IN MEXICO

This was the original opening number of the show, but it was dropped during rehearsals. It is the nearest thing the show had to a title song.

8 LADY TOURISTS: We're off for a hayride,
A joy ride, a gay ride,
A happy holiday ride,
We're off for Mexico.
We're off for a hot time,
A b'lieve-it-or-not time,
So, ladies, if you've got time
You really ought to go.

SOLO LADY TOURIST: Ev'ry Mexicano chico
Likes to prove he's muy rico,
And for girls who go for Clicquot
It's a lucky thing to know,

8 LADY TOURISTS: We're off for a hayride,
A joy ride, a gay ride,
A happy holiday ride,
Goodbye, we've got to blow!
We're off, we're off, we're off, we're off
For a hayride in Mexico.

GAVOTTE

MOTHER: Will you miss Brooklyn, daughter?
8 DAUGHTERS: Mush, Mama!
MOTHER: Have you your Pluto Water?
8 DAUGHTERS: Hush, Mama!
MOTHER: What are those steps you're doing?
8 DAUGHTERS: Struts, Mama.
MOTHER: What are those things you're chewing?
8 DAUGHTERS: Nuts, Mama.
MOTHER: In Mexico, you beware!
8 DAUGHTERS: Why, Mama?
MOTHER: Errol Flynn is down there.
8 DAUGHTERS: My, Mama!
MOTHER: Will you all be good girls?
8 DAUGHTERS: Swell, Mama!
MOTHER: And you?
1 DAUGHTER: I'm gonna raise hell, Mama!

INTERLUDE

4 PORTERS: Madame, ah guess y'ull
Have to get alive,
Mexico Special
Leavin' Track Five.
ALL: We're (They're) off for a hayride,
A joy ride, a gay ride,
A happy holiday ride,
We're (They're) off to Mexico.
We're (They're) off for a hot time,
A b'lieve-it-or-not time,

So, ladies, if you've got time
You really ought to go.

SOLO LADY TOURIST: Very shortly, all we lasses
Will be crossing mountain passes
On our itty-bitty asses
From the highland to the low,

ALL: We're (They're) off for a hayride,
A joy ride, a gay ride,
A happy holiday ride,
Goodbye, we've (they've) got to blow!
We're (They're) off, we're (they're) off,
we're (they're) off, we're (they're) off
For a hayride
To Mex-i-co,

4 PORTERS: Off for a gay ride,
A happy holiday ride,
A hayride in Mexico.

HE CERTAINLY KILLS THE WOMEN

Slated for the conclusion of Act I, Scene 4. It was to have been sung by Edith Meiser. The number was dropped during rehearsals. In "Titles and Ideas" there is the following entry for August 5, 1943: "But He Kills the Women."

VERSE

Speaking of men in Mexico,
At love, not being so good,
I worry about that man Lombo
Much more than I should.

REFRAIN 1

That man who's got me mystified
Has all the ladies looking starry-eyed,
The cause of his wallop I cannot decide
But he certainly kills the women!
Is he well-read? No, not one bit.
Is he amusing? He's the opposite,
If he had more brains, he'd be a quarter-wit,
But he certainly kills the women!
At giving the girlies the razzle-dazz,
That fellow somehow never flops,
I can't understand what the rascal has
But whatever it is, it's tops!
The clothes he wears when out of doors
Are ev'rything the Well-Dressed Man abhors,
Of course, I've not seen him in his flannel
drawers,
But he certainly kills the women!

REFRAIN 2

He'll never be a dancing king,
I doubt if ever has he heard of swing,
He still thinks the Charleston is the latest thing,
But he certainly kills the women!
At playing bridge, he's such a heel
That when invited for a game genteel
He'll only accept if he can always deal,
But he certainly kills the women!
Wherever he goes, such success is his,
No wonder his rivals he irks,
They all want to know what his secret is,
'Cause whatever it is, it works!
Shall we refer to his physique?
I hardly think you'd call it classic Greek,
So far I've not caught him in his so-to-speak,
But he certainly kills the women!

REFRAIN 3

If you go out with him to dine
You always get imported German wine,
It must be imported since we wrecked the Rhine,
But he certainly kills the women!
An English girl who'd just been bombed
Wired him for cash, he answered, "You be
domned,"
He's got the first penny that he ever palmed,
But he certainly kills the women!
Wherever he wanders, the ladies trot,
As if he were from Hollywood,
I can't quite make out what the scoundrel's got,
But whatever it is, it's good!
He's not a champ at water sports
Yet when he dives, why, ev'ry matron snorts,
It must be the color of his nylon shorts,
'Cause he certainly kills the women!

A HUMBLE HOLLYWOOD EXECUTIVE

Unused. Also possibly intended for Edith Meiser.

REFRAIN 1

A humble Hollywood executive
At Bar X
Taught me for sev'ral weeks consecutive
About sex,
Though I was still a saplin'
And barely old enough.
He used to cast for Chaplin,
So he knew his stuff.

As day by day we slowly walked about,
He'd explain,
Well, matters people never talked about
In Fort Wayne,
And if the facts of life I know
All the credit should clearly go
To a humble Hollywood executive
At Bar X.

REFRAIN 2

A helpful Hollywood executive
At Bar X
Taught me for sev'ral weeks consecutive
About sex.
He told me of that dipsy
Queen Helen and her boy,
I'd believe it of Poughkeepsie
But, to think, in Troy!
He had a print of Aphrodite on
A settee
Receiving guests without a nightie on
And no G,
And when we played games later on,
I'd be Leda and who, the swan?
Why, a helpful Hollywood executive
At Bar X.

REFRAIN 3

A hefty Hollywood executive
At Bar X
Taught me for sev'ral weeks consecutive
About sex.
We'd meet at old Mount Lookout,
Where no one's ever nigh,
And when he'd take his book out
How the time would fly!
By clarifying all the mystery
Of romance,
He made me love the naughty history
Of old France.
If Louie's Queen could live again
She would drop the King in the Seine
For a hefty Hollywood executive
At Bar X.

REFRAIN 4

A hectic Hollywood executive
At Bar X
Taught me for sev'ral weeks consecutive
About sex.
They called that ranch the best cure
For folks not feeling well,
It wasn't quite a rest cure
But it sure was swell!
His tales of life in Santa Monica
Were a scream,
A place that's close to Lake Veronica,
It would seem.
Oh yes, I dwelt in heav'n above
While I studied that thing called love
'Neath a hectic Hollywood executive
At Bar X.

IT'S A BIG NIGHT

Intended as the opening of Act I, Scene 6, this ensemble number, if it had been used, would have preceded "Carlotta."

It's a big night at Chapultepec,
If a big night is your dish,
For it gives to ev'rybody
An opportunity to toddy
To amigo Humphrey Fish.
Every guest up to the President
Will be dressed up to the ears,
And you're simply social lepers
If you're not among the steppers
At the biggest brawl in years.
Yes, you're simply social lepers
If you're not among the steppers
At the biggest brawl in years.

IT'S JUST LIKE THE GOOD OLD DAYS

An unused duet written for June Havoc and Bobby Clark. Porter acknowledged receiving lyric ideas for this song from William Endrich.

VERSE

How's it back in the homeland, Buzz?
I feel so far away.
Things are quite as they used to wuz,
In fact, I'm sure you would say:

REFRAIN 1

It's just like the good old days,
Our country's just the same,
It's just like the good old days,
We're still playing the game.
The landmarks we always loved

Haven't changed their charming ways,
The pet of the networks is still Major Bowes,
Durante is still being paid through the nose,
Missus Harrison Williams is still wearing clo'es,
It's just like the good old days.
Miss Garbo remains as the Hollywood Sphinx,
Monty Woolley's still bathing his beard in his
drinks,
P.M. still assures us that ev'rything stinks,
It's just like the good old days,
Just like the good old days.

REFRAIN 2

It's just like the good old days,
Our country's just the same,
It's just like the good old days,
We're still playing the game.
The landmarks we always loved
Haven't changed their charming ways,
Drew Pearson still worries the President most,
Walter Lippmann still ruins your coffee and toast,
Martin Dies still refuses to give up the ghost,
It's just like the good old days.
At dear Wanamaker's the organ still plays,
At Morocco, it still is the woman who pays,
When Cornell doesn't jell there is still Helen
Hayes,
It's just like the good old days,
Just like the good old days.

REFRAIN 3

It's just like the good old days,
Our country's just the same,
It's just like the good old days,
We're still playing the game.
The landmarks we always loved
Haven't changed their charming ways,
The subway is still the most popular place,
George Nathan's still writing and so's Ilka Chase,
At the Met they do *Carmen* and still in whiteface,
It's just like the good old days.
On the air, Maxwell Coffee is still a big name
And Jell-O continues in radio fame
But in spite of Jack Benny it still tastes the
same,
It's just like the good old days,
Just like the good old days.

REFRAIN 4

It's just like the good old days,
Our country's just the same,
It's just like the good old days,
We're still playing the game.
The landmarks we always loved
Haven't changed their charming ways.
Tommy Manville still pays 'em by certified check,
"21" still provides you with Pommery Sec,
The Hope diamond still bruises poor Evalyn's
neck,
It's just like the good old days.
Doris Duke still tells Cromwell she won't pay the
price,
Bertrand Russell still preaches the virtue of vice,
Pa Divine is still God and and so everything's
nice,
It's just like the good old days,
Just like the good old days.

REFRAIN 5

It's just like the good old days,
Our country's just the same,
It's just like the good old days,
We're still playing the game.
The landmarks we always loved
Haven't changed their charming ways,
Louie Bromfield is still raising Cain with his
crops,
Miss Dietrich is still raising hell with her props,
The gangsters are still raising dough with the
cops,
It's just like the good old days.
Dick Tracy still runs his habitual risk,
Bing Crosby still costs you a nickel a disc,
Polly Adler still tells me that business is brisk,
It's just like the good old days,
Just like the good old days.

IT'S JUST YOURS

There is a sketch for this song in a Porter music notebook on a page headed May 17, 1943. The lyric is dated September 23, 1943. It is possible that this was one of many numbers Porter wrote for Bobby Clark that he either wouldn't or couldn't sing. But Wilbur Evans was another likely candidate. It was published in *The Unpublished Cole Porter.*

REFRAIN 1

Your charm is not like the still of ev'ning, dear,
Your glamour not like the sky when stars appear,
Your warmth is not like the moonlight on the
moors,
It's just yours, it's just yours, it's just yours.
Your touch is not like the summer breeze, oh no!
Your sweetness, not like a song of long ago,
Your smile is not like the sun a-shine

But, darling, like this heart of mine,
It's just yours, it's just yours, it's just yours.

REFRAIN 2

Your walk is not like a graceful young gazelle's,
Your style is not what the chic Mainbocher sells,
Your voice is not Gracie Fields' or Gracie
Moore's,
It's just yours, it's just yours, it's just yours.
Your charm is not that of Circe's with her swine,
Your brain would never deflate the great
Einstein,
Your laughter's not like a babbling brook,
But my love, believe me, Snook,
It's just yours, it's just yours, it's just yours.

REFRAIN 3

Your mouth is not like a rosebud on the wall,
Your neck is not like a swan's, oh, not at all,
Your nose is not early Greek like Dot Lamour's,
It's just yours, it's just yours, it's just yours.
Your skin is not like the virgin winter snow,
Your figure hardly excels Blondell's, oh no!
Your smile is not like the sun a-shine
But, lambkin, like this heart of mine,
It's just yours, it's just yours, it's just yours.

OCTET

This appears to be a discarded Act II finale. Intended for June Havoc, Luba Malina, Edith Meiser, Corinna Mura, Bobby Clark, Wilbur Evans, George Givot, and Sergio DeKarlo.

VERSE

MIGUEL: I came for a gay vacation
From the Mexican Embassy,
But sad to tell
I fell in her spell,
And look what happened to me!

LOLITA: A maiden from Sevilla,
I came here on a spree,
But I took my guitar
To Ciro's bar,
And look what happened to me!

MONTANA: Defeated in the bull ring
I knew I'd never be,
But I lost my head
To a wolf instead,
And look what happened to me!

. . .

DAVID: I never thought of marriage
In Washington, D.C.,
Then, Lord Hosanna,
I met Montana,
And look what happened to me!

DAGMAR & EADIE: Two unattached young ladies,
We came here full of glee,
But we met that heel
That spic schlemiel,
And look what happened to we!

LOMBO: For a guy from far Chihuahua
I was doing fine, you see,
Then I made a chum
Of a gringo bum,
And look what happened to me!

HUMPHREY: My life was like a poem,
I was happy and carefree
Till I tried to get rich
With that son of a Chihuahua,
And look what happened to me!

REFRAIN

ALL: The moral of our story
Must be clear to ev'ryone,
If you stay, old pard,
In your own back yard,
A risk you never will run.
Yes, the moral of our story
Must be clear to ev'ryone,
But if you never roam
From your home, sweet home
You miss an awful lotta fun.
Yes, the moral of our story
Must be clear to ev'ryone:
If you never roam
From your home, sweet home
You miss an awful lotta fun,
LADIES: You miss a helluva lot,
MEN: You miss a helluva lot,
LADIES: You miss a helluva lot,
MEN: You miss a helluva lot,
LADIES: You miss a helluva lot,
MEN: You miss a helluva lot
Of fun,
LADIES: Of fun,
MEN: Of fun,
LADIES: Of fun,
ALL: You miss a helluva lot,
You miss a helluva lot,
You miss a helluva lot,
You miss a helluva lot,
You miss, you miss a helluva lot,
You miss, you miss a helluva lot,

Of fun, of fun,
An awful lotta fun.
Go for it or notta
But we've gotta lotta data,
So do notta getta hotta
If we tell you what is whatta.
You'll be safer if you squatta
On the spotta that you gotta
But if off you never trotta
You will miss a lotta fun,
You'll miss a helluva lot,
You'll miss a helluva lot
Of fun,
Of fun,
Of fun.

PUT A SACK OVER THEIR HEADS

This unused number was intended for Bobby Clark to sing in Act II, Scene 3. A note in "Titles and Ideas," September 18, 1943, lists the title "Put a Sack over Their Heads and They're All Sisters."

VERSE

There are fifty-seven varieties of pickles,
There are sixty-seven varieties of pearls,
There are over a thousand different kinds of roses,
But I'd be an ass if I
Tried to classify
Girls.

REFRAIN 1

Put a sack over their heads and they're all sisters,
Put a sack over their heads and they're all the same.
To take a gal to sup somewhere
You nearly break your neck,
She brings along a billionaire
But it's you who pays the check.
Put a sack over their heads and they'll all take you
For so fast a ride it would put Paul Revere's to shame.
I understand what Caesar meant
When he said, "A gent is often not a gent,
But a dame is always a dame!"

REFRAIN 2

Put a sack over their heads and they're all sisters,
Put a sack over their heads and they're all the same.
They'll tell you you're the only guy
And tell you till you're deaf
But one fine night you happen by
And you meet the R.A.F.
Put a sack over their heads and they'll all kid you
Till you start to think Casanova's your middle name,
But just when you are getting warm
Let a husky enter in a uniform
And a dame is always a dame!

A SIGHTSEEING TOUR

Unused. Intended for George Givot, Bobby Clark, Jean Cleveland, Eric Roberts, William A. Lee, Lois Bolton, and ensemble.

SECTION 1

LOMBO: Shall I show you more of Mexico?
OTHERS EXCEPT ADAMSONS: Yes, show us more of Mexico.
MRS. ADAMSON: How about you, son? How about you, Gus?
JUNIOR: It's oke with me and so it's oke with us.
LOMBO: Then kindly hop aboard my private bus.
HUMPHREY: It's the biggest one I ever saw!

SECTION 2

LOMBO: The Bellas Artes now you view,
LYDIA: Whaty-yuh-mean?
LOMBO: That's the Opry House to you,
Inside there's a curtain all made of glass.
MR. ADAMSON: Don't it break when they drop it?
MRS. ADAMSON: Oh, shut up, you ass!
LOMBO: As an op'ra, has it not got mucho class?
HUMPHREY: It's the biggest one I ever saw!

SECTION 3

LOMBO: Our great cathedral now you see,
She was built in fifteen seventy-three,
Just admire those tow'rs and that preety dome.
MRS. DUNCAN: It's exactly like Saint Peter's church in Rome.

TILLIE: Why, it's bigger than the Baptist church back home,
It's the biggest one I ever saw!

SECTION 4

LOMBO: On the left you see a pyramid.
JUNIOR: So what?
LOMBO: Señor, will you choke that kid?
It is made of rock, yes, ev'ry bit.
TILLIE: Why, the top looks pointed here from where I sit!
JUNIOR: Would you like to take a climb and sit on it?
HUMPHREY: It's the biggest one I ever saw!

SECTION 5

LOMBO: Now before you the statue of an Aztec struts.
MRS. DUNCAN: What's that?
LOMBO: Cuauhtemoc.
MRS. DUNCAN: Aw nuts!
It is made of bronze and not of stone.
TILLIE: It's the spittin' image of our Franchot Tone.
LOMBO: And the head, it weighs at least two tons alone.
HUMPHREY: It's the biggest one I ever saw!

SECTION 6

LOMBO: Do you see that flow'r there in the sand?
That's the leetlest flow'r in all the land,
But the Mexican man, he love it much,
'Cause when that flow'r in your hand you clutch,
You've a feeling that your sweetheart's cheek you touch.
HUMPHREY: It's the biggest one I ever saw!

THAT'S WHAT YOU MEAN TO ME

Unused. There are references to this number in a Porter music notebook under the title "U Mean."

REFRAIN

You mean my farewell to sorrow,
That's what you mean to me.
You mean no more joy need I borrow,
That's what you mean to me.
You mean the fun
Of falling in love,
You mean my helicopter to heaven above,
For you mean my life, my tomorrow,
That's what you mean to me.

TRIO

HE: I feel the moment near
When you decide, my dear,
With me to cast your lot,
I see a chapel gleaming
And a parson beaming
As he ties the knot.
I see our love a-blooming
In some unassuming
Yet poetic spot.
Just a cottage small
SHE: Or a palace cool
HE: By a waterfall
SHE: Or a swimming pool.

I'M AFRAID I LOVE YOU

Unused. In "Titles and Ideas," July 5, 1943, there is the entry: "I'm Afraid I Love You." The lyric is dated August 25, 1943. This is not the same song as "I'm Afraid, Sweetheart, I Love You" (see *Kiss Me, Kate,* 1948).

I'm afraid I love you,
Win or lose, right or wrong.
I'm afraid that of you
I am doomed to dream my life long.
When you're near, my dear, I'm so light-hearted,
But the moment we're parted,
Oh, am I blue!
I'm afraid I love you
And I'm afraid you're afraid too.

I'M SO GLAHD TO MEET YOU

An unused duet for June Havoc and Bobby Clark. Dated October 5, 1943. No piano-vocal of the song survives. There is a music sketch in a Porter notebook.

VERSE

MONTANA: You villain, you viper,
You rascal, you wretch,
I thought by now, baby,
You'd be doing a stretch.
Why are you down here,
As a matter of fact?
HUMPHREY: Hush, the whole crowd's watching,

Let's put on an act.

REFRAIN 1

HUMPHREY: I'm so glahd to meet you,
It thrills me no end,
I'm so glahd to meet you
And I trust you're feeling well, my friend.
MONTANA: This moment delightful
Is long overdue
And I hope, while hyah,
HUMPHREY: Why, of course, my dyah,
BOTH: I can see a little more of you.

PATTER

MONTANA: Isn't Mexico enchanting?
HUMPHREY: Yes, for people who are banting,
As one simply cawnt face the bill o' fare.
MONTANA: Aren't you pleased the weather's warmah?
HUMPHREY: Yes, espec'lly at the Reforma,
Where they only could put me up in the Frigidaire.
MONTANA: If you'd like to meet Lupescu
I shall ahsk her quick to esk you
To a pahty.
HUMPHREY: Are you shoo-a it'll be smaht?
MONTANA: Oh, you rogue, you're being clevah,
Now I've got to fly, howevah,
I must tell you once again before we paht:

REFRAIN 2

MONTANA: I'm so glahd to meet you,
It thrills me no end,
I'm so glahd to meet you
And I trust you're feeling well, my friend.
HUMPHREY: This moment delightful
Is long overdue
And I hope that soon
MONTANA: No, you don't, you goon,
BOTH: I can see a little more of you.

Other titles possibly intended for *Mexican Hayride* include "I've Got the Bull by the Horns" ("Titles and Ideas", August 4, 1943), "Never You Mind" (notebook), and "Oh, What a Night for Love" (notebook).

SEVEN LIVELY ARTS

1944

Tryout: Forrest Theatre, Philadelphia, November 24, 1944. Produced by Billy Rose at the Ziegfeld Theatre, New York, December 7, 1944. 183 performances. Book by Moss Hart, George S. Kaufman, Robert Pirosh, Joseph Schrank, Charles Sherman, and Ben Hecht. Staged and lighted by Hassard Short. Cast, starring Beatrice Lillie, Bert Lahr, Benny Goodman, Alicia Markova, and Anton Dolin, included Teddy Wilson, Red Norvo, Bill Tabbert, Nan Wynn, Jere McMahon, Dolores Gray, Billie Worth, Paula Bane, Mary Roche and, in her Broadway debut, Helen Gallagher.

BIG TOWN

Introduced by Nan Wynn, Jere McMahon, Paula Bane, Billie Worth, Mary Roche, Bill Tabbert, Dolores Gray, and ensemble.

REFRAIN

Big Town, what's before me,
Fair weather or stormy?
Big Town, will I hit the heights
And see my name in electric lights?
Big Town, will I blunder,
Fall down and go under
Or will I rise and rise
Till I scrape your skies?
Big Town,
Wise old town,
What's the lowdown on me?

VERSE 1

NAN WYNN: From an Indiana farm, green and flow'ry,
I've come on here to show you I can paint.
After weeks I found a room in the Bow'ry
And it's everything my room at home ain't.
Yes, my life you'd hardly call "Ritzy-Tow'ry,"
But I work so, I'm bound to get ahead,
And the day when I prove
I'm a painter in the groove
I'm gonna paint
The town red.

VERSE

JERE MCMAHON: At a school in Lansing,
I've been taking dancing
And if you'll give me one glance,
You'll compare Ray Bolger
To a dancing wooden soldier
When I go into my dance.

VERSE 3

PAULA BANE: If Ginny Simms and Georgia Carroll
And Dinah Shore and Eileen Farrell
And Mildred Bailey
Can, night-and-daily,
Impress the public so,
Then I too
From Wahoo
Can sing on the radio.

VERSE 4

BILLIE WORTH: Cain't cook,
Cain't sew,
Cain't plow,
Cain't hoe,
So Maw says,
"On a train you get
And join the ballet at the Met."

VERSE 5

MARY ROCHE: When exactly three was my age
I longed to be on the stage
As I watched Miss Cornell
From the preacher's perch
When she played *Dishonored Lad-Y* in our Baptist church,
So here's new talent, Big Town,
And I beg you, don't let me down,
For I can't face my folks back in Rye
Till a Broadway star am I.

VERSE 6

BILL TABBERT: From the hills of Arkansaw
I'm a playwright in the raw,
And when writin' great plays I start,
You will soon be hootin'
That man Van Druten
And that highfalutin
Moss Hart.

VERSE 7

DOLORES GRAY: L. B. May'r said, "My pet,
You're not ripe for pictures yet,
Go to New York and get
Into a play.

In the movies, to hop
From the bottom to the top,
You must first be a flop
On Broadway."

IS IT THE GIRL (OR IS IT THE GOWN)?

Published November 1944. Introduced by Dolores Gray and ensemble.

VERSE

Mister Romeo,
Say you're at some show
But each girl so far
Has been under par
When, lo and behold, stage center,
You see a perfect Juliet enter.
She so drives you mad
That you wish you had
Just a cottage cool
By a swimming pool
With her waiting there for Daddy.
Well, before you grow fonder,
Stop and ponder, laddie.

REFRAIN

Is it the girl or is it the gown?
Which one of the two do you love?
Is it her hair that makes her so fair?
Is it her lips you long to caress
Or is it that exquisite dress?
Is she the dream of all you desire
Or is it her frock
That happens to knock you down?
Is it the girl you love so dearly
Or is it merely her beautiful gown?

2ND ENDING

Oh, the gown may be swell,
But you know very well it's the girl!

EV'RY TIME WE SAY GOODBYE

Published November 1944. Introduced by Nan Wynn. A Porter music notebook contains sketches for the opening (dated May 16, 1944) and the ending of the refrain. Entry in "Titles and Ideas," May 31, 1944: "Ev'ry Time We Say Goodbye I Die a Little Bit."

VERSE

We love each other so deeply
That I ask you this, sweetheart,
Why should we quarrel ever,
Why can't we be enough clever
Never to part?

REFRAIN

Ev'ry time we say goodbye
I die a little,
Ev'ry time we say goodbye
I wonder why a little,
Why the gods above me
Who must be in the know
Think so little of me
They allow you to go.
When you're near there's such an air
Of spring about it,
I can hear a lark somewhere
Begin to sing about it.
There's no love song finer
But how strange
The change
From major to minor
Ev'ry time we say goodbye,
Ev'ry single time we say goodbye.

ONLY ANOTHER BOY AND GIRL

Published November 1944. Introduced by Mary Roche and Bill Tabbert.

VERSE

SHE: To be in love is so new to me
It's difficult to believe
That it hasn't been
An original sin
Since the days of Adam and Eve.
HE: I can't explain what you do to me
But I know that now we've combined
Ev'ry hour is, oh, so breathtaking,
So soul-shaking, so epoch-making
That it's mighty hard to bear in mind:

REFRAIN 1

BOTH: We're only another boy and girl,
We're only two kids in love,
Folks who've been through the mill
Say our chances are nil
But we'll still climb our hill
Hand and glove.
HE: We're only another spring romance
SHE: But, baby, we'll see it through,
BOTH: We're only another boy and girl
HE: But we'll God bless our break,
SHE: Take a lot more pains than our elders take
BOTH: And make love's young dream come true.

REFRAIN 2
[*First 9 lines of refrain 1*]

SHE: We'll God bless our break,
HE: Take a lot less gin than our elders take
BOTH: And make love's young dream come true.

REFRAIN 3
[*First 9 lines of refrain 1*]

HE: But we'll God bless our break,
SHE: Shake a lot less hip than our elders shake
BOTH: And make love's young dream come true.

WOW-OOH-WOLF!

Published March 1945. Introduced by Nan Wynn, Dolores Gray, and Mary Roche.

INTRODUCTION

So this is the road to success!
Shall we answer no or yes?

VERSE

People tell us New York is simply full uff
A brand-new type of wool-uff,
The kind who's only out to find giddy gur-ulls
With hay seed still in their cur-ulls.
So, to keep out-of-town girls from temptation,
We think the police should station
A lady cop in ev'ry rooming house
And say to you this: Miss Country Mouse,

REFRAIN 1

If you're with the mob
Looking for a job
And a hair-raising howl you hear
"Wow-ooh-wolf!"
And a billy goat
In a camel coat
Says he'll help you with your career
"Wow-ooh-wolf!"
He may disarm you,
Completely charm you
When you behold the gold in his pouch,
But later, when you
Are in his den, you
Will be asked to sign on the dotted couch.
If he says his wife
Leads a sep'rate life,
Better run for the door, my dear.
"Wow-ooh,
Wow-ooh,
Wow-ooh,
Wow-ooh-wolf!"

2ND ENDING

"Wolf,
Wolf,
Wolf,
Wolf,
Wolf, wolf,
Wolf, wolf,
Wolf!"

REFRAIN 2

When the lights are low
And the servants go
And it's champagne instead of beer,
"Wow-ooh-wolf!"
When you see his eyes
Shrink to half their size
And he's grinning from ear to ear,
"Wow-ooh-wolf!"
When he comes closer
Don't cry, "No, no, sir,"
And start to scold the old roustabout,
But when he pounces
Upon your flounces
Simply clout the clown till he's down and out.
Then drink up his wine
While you write a line
Saying, "So long and sorry, dear,
Wow-ooh,
Wow-ooh,
Wow-ooh,
Wow-ooh,
Wolf!
Wolf,
Wolf,
Wolf,
Wolf, wolf,

Wolf, wolf,
Wow-ooh-wolf!"

SOLO 1

Mister Wolf, you're too old,
So may I be so bold
As to give this advice to you?
Take Errol Flynn along to howl for you
Then get Vic Mature
To make l'amour
For you too.

SOLO 2

So you are a wolf, ha-ha!
And tonight you decided to try me,
So you are a wolf, papa!
I regret but you don't terrify me,
For my mother wrote saying, "Have no fear,
In a city of so many millions,
Not all men are wolves, my dear
Only sailors, soldiers and civilians."

SOLO 3

You can't scare me, Mister Louie Shurr,
Though you're Hollywood's best-known agent.
Just why should I let you handle me, sir?
You're a much too famous-in-the-hay gent.
For all your gifts, Mister Louie Shurr,
I'll forever be your debtor,
But why did you send me that rabbit fur
When I know you like bare skin better?

DRINK

Introduced by Bert Lahr and ensemble.

PROLOGUE

SOLO: Hey there, in the halyards,
Hey there, in the head,
Hey there, in the scuttlebutt,
Hey there, in bed,
We've a nor'-wester, blast 'er,
And unless we travel faster
We're facing disaster.
MEN'S CHOIR: What do you mean master?

VERSE

SOLO: I just received a wire from Lord
Nelson,
The enemy is eastward bound,
And when they attack,
Since we can't attack back,
We will all be definitely drowned.
So, lads, before to Davy Jones's
locker we sink,
How's about just one little drink?
MEN'S CHOIR: Aye aye aye, sir, aye aye aye, sir,
aye aye aye, sir,
Just one little drink before we die,
sir.

REFRAIN 1

SOLO: Drink, drink, drink,
While we live, let us live in clover,
Drink, drink, drink,
When we're dead, we'll be dead all over,
So up with the cup, hip, hip, hip, hoorah!
To quaff is to laugh, ha, ha, ha, ha!
Yes, drink, drink, drink,
Drink, drink, drink,
Drink, drink, drink, drink,
Drink,
Drink,
Drink!

PATTER 1

Drink to our man-o'-war, so slick and sleek,
Drink to her bottom, may she never leak,
Drink to our pleasure when her decks we scrub
And drink to the members of the Racquet Club.
Drink to the flag that we so proudly hail,
Drink to our Alma Mater, Eli Yale,
Drink to the glory of the King's Navee
And drink to the members of the Souse family.
Drink to October ale and pink champagne,
Drink to the 7-Up we got in Maine,
Drink to me only with thine eyes
And whoopsy-boo! you'll get a big surprise.
Drink to the joy of gin and orange juice,
Drink to the Masons, Eagles, Elks and Moose,
Roll out the barrel, roll in the jug
And glug, glug, glug, glug, glug, glug, glug, glug.
Drink to our Secretary Morgenthau,
Drink to Miss Perkins, beg your pardon, Maw,
Drink to our Eleanor, so heaven-sent,
"I'd rather be right than President."
Drink to the land we love, away so far,
Drink even faster to the Astor Bar,
Drink, drink to drink, my hearties, one and all,
"United we stand, dee-vided we fall."
Drink to the *Desert Song* and *Rose Marie*,
Drink to Moselle, to hell with Burgundy,
Drink to Sigmund Romberg, our greatest prize,
But "Don't fire before you see the whites of his
eyes."

Drink to the *Student Prince,* that show sublime,
And please, don't forget Jeanette in *Blossom Time,*
Drink to Nelson Eddy before you faint
And here's to J. J. Shubert, our patron saint.

REFRAIN 2

SOLO: Drink, drink, drink,
While we live, let us live in clover,
SOLO & MEN'S CHOIR: Drink, drink, drink,
When we're dead, we'll be dead all over,
So up with the cup, hip, hip, hip, hoorah!
To quaff is to laugh, ha, ha, ha,
Yes, drink, drink, drink,
MEN'S CHOIR: Drink, drink, drink,
Drink, drink, drink, drink,
SOLO & MEN'S CHOIR: Drink,
SOLO: Drink to ev'rything including the kitchen sink.

PATTER 2

Drink to the little wife for whom I pant,
Drink to the illness of my rich old aunt,
Here's to the memory of my dear old ma,
I don't mean that mama down in Panama.
Drink to my angel of a moth'r-in-law,
Drink to the day I sock her right on the jaw,
Drink to my brother once a boy so fine,
Who suddenly became Sweet Adeline.
Drink to the ladies whether young or old,
Drink to the ladies whether hot or cold,
Drink to the ladies whether rich or poor,
Vive la France, also Vive l'Amour!
Drink to the ladies who insist we pay,
Drink to the nights when it's the other way.
Landlord, the tankards, landlord, the bowl,
And skoal, skoal, skoal! And down the ole rat hole.

FINISH

Yes, drink, drink, drink, drink,
Drink, drink, drink,
Drink, drink, drink till you stink,
Drink,
Drink,
Drink,
Drink,
Drink, drink,
Drink, drink,
Drink, drink, drink, drink,
Drink, drink, drink, drink,
Drink,
Drink,
Hoorah!

WHEN I WAS A LITTLE CUCKOO

Published February 1945. Introduced by Beatrice Lillie. Entry in "Titles and Ideas," June 21, 1944: "When I Was a Little Cuckoo."

VERSE

Last year down in dear Miami
I picked up such a sweet Hindu swami,
And as by the sea we'd gaily stroll
He'd talk of the transmigration of the soul.
I found since the world's beginning,
I'd had many an outing and inning,
I'd been ev'ry sort of person and ev'ry kind of thing,
But my greatest success was as a bird on the wing.

REFRAIN 1

When I was a little cuckoo
Was I full of mischief? Oh boy!
Flitting hither and thither
Far from mither and fither,
I lived in a dither
Of joy.
Each night meant a new flirtation,
Each dawn another fond goodbye,
And if my wings became singed
And my tail, a bit fringed,
Just a little cuckoo was I.

TRIO 1

Singing, "Cuckoo,
Cuckoo,"
As I soared through the heavens of blue.
Singing, "Cuckoo,
Cuckoo,
Cuckoo, cuckoo,
And how are you?"

To return to the soul and its trick transmigrations,
Let us now make a list of my many incarnations:

PATTER

I first lived on earth as a crab-apple tree
And Adam and Eve used to romp under me.
I soon reappeared as Methuselah's wife
And slowly but certainly shortened his life.
Next, in Troy, I pursued a more frivolous course
As a fly on the tail of a big wooden horse.
As a royal snake charmer I made Egypt gasp
When I struck Cleopatra for kicking my asp.
And when Rome caught on fire I wasn't dismayed
For I was the G-string on which Nero played.
In days medieval I had lots of sport
As a cute little cockroach in King Arthur's Court.
As Catherine of Russia I never once guessed
That I'd one day appear on the stage as Mae
  West.
And under Napoleon I was more glamorous
As a tiny jade button on the Emperor's truss.

REFRAIN 2

But
When I was a little cuckoo
Was I full of mischief? Oh boy!
Flitting hither and thither
Far from mither and fither,
I lived in a dither
Of joy.
There was Bob White, Tom-Tit, Cock Robin,
And Bertie, what a dirty old jay!
And if you think I was wrong
To be had for a song,
Just a little cuckoo was Ay.

TRIO 2

Singing, "Cuckoo,
Cuckoo,"
As I sailed through the heavens of blue,
Singing, "Cuckoo,
Cuckoo,
Cuckoo, cuckoo,
And how are you?"

FRAHNGEE-PAHNEE

Published November 1944. Introduced by Bill Tabbert and ensemble.

VERSE

To a bamboo drum persistent
In a monotone,
To the bursting fire of a distant
Volcano's cone,
To a tense group in a dark'ning glade
A story was being told
By jingling ankles bedecked in jade
And fingers of gleaming gold.
As the crowd grew frenzied and began to yell
And I watched you weaving your bewitching
  spell
I knew
I could never leave you,

REFRAIN

Frahngee-Pahnee,
How exciting you were to see,
How my heart was entranced
When my way first you glanced
As you danced
Under the banyan tree.
Frahngee-Pahnee,
Oh, how tender you were to me
When the others had gone
And we stayed on and on
Till the dawn
Under the banyan tree.
I can still see you there,
Glist'ning flow'rs in your hair
Like the stars studding the skies above you,
I can still feel you near,
I can still hear you, dear,
Whisp'ring low, "Look in my eyes, I love
  you."
Oh, Frahngee-Pahnee,
What a poem each hour will be
Once the knot has been tied
And through life we can hide,
Side by side,
Under the banyan tree.

CODA

Side by side,
Under the banyan tree.

DANCIN' TO A JUNGLE DRUM (LET'S END THE BEGUINE)

Introduced by Beatrice Lillie. Before Porter finished "Let's End the Beguine," it had evolved into "Dancin' to a Jungle Drum." In this edition, I have combined the "Beguine" lyric with "Dancin' to a Jungle Drum."

INTRODUCTION

A broken-down Oriental dancer am I,
So take out your 'kerchiefs, children, and prepare to cry:

VERSE

If you ask me, as a dancer,
Why my life can't last for long
I can quickly give the answer,
I've been wrecked by a Broadway song.
For wherever I'm seen
Some orchestra guy
Begins the Beguine
Accompanied by
Drums,
Those jungle drums.
When I left my home in Bali
For a show in N.Y.C.
Some cheroot in Tin Pan Alley
Wrote this song espeshly for me.
So wherever I'm seen
Some orchestra guy
Begins the Beguine
Accompanied by
Drums,
Those jungle drums.

REFRAIN

I've a twisted neck and a twisted back
And a crack in my sacroiliac.
What from?
How come?
From dancin' to a jungle drum.
On this hand no more can I wear a glove,
Just regard the sad expression of
That thumb.
How come?
From dancin' to a jungle drum.
How I'd love to do a polka to violins
And without these bangles bruisin' my little shins,
Yes, the jungle's more than I can take,
I'm so muscle-bound I can hardly shake
My tum.
How come?
From dancin' to a jungle drum.

PATTER

Due to that Beguine, I detest those songs
Where the groaners go for calico sarongs.
Due to that Beguine, I resent each tune
That involves an actor with an acter-oon.
I hate grass skirts, I hate grass huts,
I hate palm trees and as for cocoa, nuts!
In a Bob Hope picture, I hate that scene
Where a finished baritone begins the Beguine.
I'm tired of *not* seein' that old rope trick
And the mammal called a camel makes me slightly sick.
When I hear those off-key temple bells,
"Hell's bells" is what ah yells.
I resent pineapples as a form of dress,
I detest bananas even more—or less.
Why doesn't dear Dorothy Lamour relax
And exchange that diaper for a pair of slacks?
How I hate to sleep in the bright moonlight
With a lizard on my gizzard through the perfumed night,
But the thing that leaves me completely numb
Is the beat, beat, beat,
And the tick, tick, tock,
And the drip, drip, drip,
Of a jungle drum,
Oh, those drums!
[*Drums*]
Those jungle drums!
[*Drums*]
Those boring drums!
[*Drums*]
Those dreadful drums!
[*Drums*]
Those bloody drums!
[*Drums*]
Oh, those bim-bam
Flim-flam,
Slim-slam,
Jim-jam,
[*Drums*]
Beg your pardon, ma'm,
Goddamn drums!

HENCE IT DON'T MAKE SENSE

Published December 1944. Introduced by Nan Wynn, Mary Roche, Dolores Gray, Billie Worth, and Jere McMahon.

VERSE

When we use words like scat, cat,
Skin, fin, reet, pleat,
The squares want to give up the heat-seat
For the jive we talk today.
But when I hear those hicks talk
That straight-from-the-sticks talk,
It don't make sense, I say,

When they use the slang of yesterday,
In the following way:

REFRAIN 1

Now a girl is a babe
And a babe is a chick
And a chick is a bird
And a bird is a fowl
And a fowl is a ball
And a ball is a great big dence,
But a girl ain't a great big dence,
Hence it don't make sense.

EXTRA REFRAINS

Now a skirt is a gal
And a gal is a doll
And a doll is a dear
And a deer is a buck
And a buck is a man
And a man is a pair of pents,
But a skirt ain't a pair of pents,
Hence it don't make sense.

Now a skunk is a fur
And a fur is a fleece
And a fleece is a theft
And a theft is a sin
And a sin is taboo,
And Tabu is perfume from France,
But a skunk ain't perfume from France,
Hence it don't make sense.

Now a jerk is a pull
And a pull is a tug
And a tug is a craft
And a craft is a trick
And a trick is a gal
And a gal is a big romence,
But a jerk ain't a big romence,
Hence it don't make sense.

Now a bra is a lift
And a lift is a boost
And a boost is a plug
And a plug is a stop
And a stop is a block
And a block is a good defense,
But a bra ain't a good defense,
Hence it don't make sense.

Now a virgin's a miss
And a miss is a strike
And a strike is a blow
And a blow is a toot
And a toot is a jag
And a jag is a big expense,
But a virgin ain't a big expense,
Hence it don't make sense.

THE BAND STARTED SWINGING A SONG

Published January 1945. Introduced by Nan Wynn. Either this number was added to the show soon after the New York opening or it was inadvertently omitted from the New York opening-night program.

VERSE

It's strange how a song you first heard
With someone you used to adore
May hide in your heart for many a year
Then, all of a sudden, reappear
And you're just as much in love as you were
before.

REFRAIN

Last night, while I
Was stepping high,
The band started swinging a song,
But in that dive
Of gin and jive
Its theme didn't seem to belong.
Then through the smoke
Sweet mem'ries woke
And brought back an old Broadway show
And again I was there
And again you were there
When the band started swinging
And my heart started singing
Our song of long ago.

THE BIG PARADE / YOURS FOR A SONG

This number appears to have been the musical elaboration of the Act I finale skit, "Billy Rose Buys the Metropolitan Opera." But the number might have been dropped, as there is no reference to it in the programs. Other sections of the finale were quotations from grand opera.

The Big Parade

Hold your hoss, here they come,
Rat-tat-tat goes the drum,
The circus is on parade.
See the clown falling down,
It's the best show in town,
The circus is on parade.
See the monk climb the rope,
Hear the steam calliope,
Buy me a lemonade.
Look-a-here, look-a-there,
Throw your hats in the air,
For the big parade.

Yours for a Song

Yours for a song, for a song of romance,
Yours for a song, if romance has a chance.
I've seen New York,
And I've seen the Fair.
No one but you
Could top the wonders there.
I'm yours in the glow,
Of the low-hanging moon,
Trading my heart for a time.
Thrill me until
The moon is out of sight,
I'm yours for a song tonight.

PRETTY LITTLE MISSUS BELL

Introduced by Beatrice Lillie in the Philadelphia tryout, but dropped from the show before the New York opening.

INTRODUCTION

SOLO: Have you heard the tale they tell
Of the pretty little Missus Bell?

VERSE 1

SOLO: Now pretty little Missus Bell
Was a bride in Happy Harbor
And she felt she'd married very well
When she got Bill Bell, the barber.
(In the town of Happy Harbor
Mister Bell was quite a barber.)

REFRAIN 1

SOLO: On Sunday nights, he'd take his bride
For a stroll around the city,
And how he'd gloat when people cried,
"Gee whitakers, ain't she pretty!"
No wonder ev'rybody fell
When she came to Happy Harbor,
For a nifty chick was Missus Bell,
Married to Mister Bell, the barber.
CHOIR: Yes, married very well
Was the pretty little Missus Bell.

VERSE 2

SOLO: Missus Bell, one day on the beach, was out
For her daily dozen rehearsal
When along came a Hollywood talent scout
From a firm called Universal.
Cried the scout from Universal,
"What a juicy little mersel!"

REFRAIN 2

SOLO: Then he said he'd put her on the screen,
And he swore from next October on
She'd be famous as a cross between
Patsy Kelly and Lady Oberon.
So as soon as she could leave the sand,
Quite forgetting her rehearsal,
She divorced Bill Bell, the barber, and
Married the scout from Universal.
CHOIR: Yes, headed straight for hell
Was the former little Missus Bell.

VERSE 3

SOLO: To the coast with him she quickly ran
But his heart became another's,
So she found herself a cam'ra man
From a firm called Warner Brothers.
(All the stars at Warner Brothers
Much preferred him to the others.)

REFRAIN 3

SOLO: He was such a master of his craft,
This magician of magicians,
That she soon was being photographed
And in several new positions.
When she left his big projection room
Full of, oh, such cozy corners,
She divorced the talent scout and voom!
Married the cam'raman from Warners.
CHOIR: Getting closer still to hell
Was the former little Missus Bell.

VERSE 4

SOLO: Up the ladder now she thought she'd go
But he started to neglect her,

So one night she told her tale of woe
To a Paramount director.
(As a Paramount director
He immediately necked her.)

REFRAIN 4

SOLO: Then he ordered wine and he ordered more,
And it proved such a soothing ointment
That she stood next day at his office door
With a Chippendale couch appointment.
And when he said his only wish
Was to help her and protect her
She divorced the cam'raman and swish!
Married the Paramount director.
CHOIR: At the very gates of hell
Was the former little Missus Bell.

VERSE 5

SOLO: When he found she had no temp'rament
He proceeded to vamoose her.
Then she chanced to meet a perfect gent
Called an M-G-M producer.
(As an M-G-M producer
He was qualified to goose her.)

REFRAIN 5

Then he promised he would make her life
Even greater than Greer Garson's,
And he said if she would be his wife
He'd show her Louella Parsons.
So as soon as he had ceased to spank
Her derrière, entre nous, sir,
She divorced the Paramountebank
And married the M-G-M producer.
CHOIR: So they stoked the fires in hell
For the former little Missus Bell.

VERSE 6

SOLO: To be starred she never ceased to beg,
So in self-defense he starred her,
But our glamour girl laid such an egg
Even Mike Romanoff barred her.
(And when Mike Romanoff scrams you
It definitely damns you.)

REFRAIN 6

SOLO: Then she got divorced and, if you please,
Hurried back to Happy Harbor,
And you'll all be glad to hear that she's
Just been remarried to the barber.
She's back in Happy Harbor,
Remarried to the barber.
Thus ends the tale they tell
Of the pretty, itty, bitty Missus Bell,
CHOIR: Of the pretty, itty, bitty Missus Bell.

DAINTY, QUAINTY ME

Unused. The date on the lyric (November 28, 1944) suggests that Porter was trying to write another song for Bert Lahr even after the show had opened its pre-Broadway engagement in Philadelphia. But Lahr, according to his son John in his superb biography of his father (*Notes on a Cowardly Lion,* 1970), said that he rejected "Dainty, Quainty Me" because he wouldn't sing a song that rhymed "cinema" with "enema."

VERSE

I was such a fragile precocious little elf
When we still had a family tree
That my nanny taught me to call my little self
"Dainty, Quainty Me."
And although today I am sixty-two
And I soon'll be sixty-three,
I continue always to think about myself
As "Dainty, Quainty Me."

REFRAIN 1

I'm "Dainty, Quainty Me,"
And from care completely free.
You may ask me how I can still feel gay,
Why, by merely ignoring the world of today.
I never answer the telephone,
For a phone, I refuse to own.
So like the lark, I'm as happy as can be,
I'm "Dainty, Quainty Me."

PATTER

In the morning, after taking a bath,
Not a shower, I put on dear Grandpapa's dressing gown
And have a breakfast consisting of one coddled egg
And a cup of very weak jasmine tea;
Then after dusting my jades and writing a letter
To the *Times,* I embark
On a long walk in Gramercy Park.
My favorite flowers are sweetheart roses,
White violets, petunias, forget-me-nots, jack-in-the-pulpits,
And baby's breath;
As for tiger lilies they frighten me to death.

I lunch every day at Schrafft's on chicken broth,
A green salad and a Triscuit,
And pistachio ice cream when I dare risk it.
I never accept an invitation to dinner unless
I can dine in a room that has pastel shades, with
  Adam furniture,
Queen Anne silver, Dresden china,
Georgian candlesticks and the finest of damask
  napery;
I shun everything Dorothy Drapery.
In contrast to the paintings of Botticelli,
I consider the works of Picasso,
Van Gogh, Cézanne, Renoir, Matisse, Manet and
  Monet
So much balonay.
When people talk about those columnists,
Such as Walter Winchell, Ed Sullivan, Westbrook
  Pegler,
Hedda Hopper, Dorothy Thompson,
Dorothy Kilgallen and that frightfully
Vulgar girl they all call "Elsa,"
I take a Bromo Seltza.
When anyone mentions Martha Raye, Carmen
  Miranda,
Lana Turner, Anita Louise, Joan Davis, Betty
  Hutton,
Gregory Ratoff, Red Skelton, Monty Woolley,
  Don Ameche,
Jack Oakie, Sir Cedric Hardwicke and other stars
  of the cinema,
I have to take an inema.

REFRAIN 2

I'm "Dainty, Quainty Me,"
And from care completely free.
You may ask me how I can still feel gay,
Why, by merely ignoring the world of today.
Whene'er I feel like misbehaving
I go out and buy a French engraving,
So like the lark, I'm as happy as can be,
Little old "Dainty, Quainty Me."

PATTER

As against those currently popular women
  novelists,
Such as Edna Ferber, Fannie Hurst, Kathleen
  Norris and
Lillian Smith (you know her book
Strange Fruit has recently been banned in
  Boston),
Give me Jane Austen.
Though such poets as Archibald MacLeish,
Edna St. Vincent Millay, Gertrude Stein, Ogden
  Nash
And Dorothy Parker may be wiser and wittier,
Give me John Greenleaf Whittier.
On Sunday, when everybody else is following
  Dick Tracy,
Terry and the Pirates, Flash Gordon, Superman,
The Gumps, Barney Google, Joe Palooka, Popeye,
  Lil' Abner
And all those other menaces,
I'm reading either Deuteronomy, Leviticus,
  Exodus or Genesis.
I far prefer hearing a string quartet by Bach,
  Beethoven,
Mozart, Haydn or Handel
Than listening to Lady Mendl.
When I dine alone, I prefer the Brevoort, the
  Lafayette,
The Murray Hill Hotel or the Union (that's my
  one New York Club),
To dining at the Stork Club.
Last night I had a sick headache
While I was standing in the graveyard of Trinity
  Church
Looking at the steeple, but I wasn't afraid,
Because I always carry with me Lydia Pinkham's
  Pink
Pills for Pale People.
Those magazines like the *Cosmopolitan,*
The Red Book, The New Yorker, Collier's,
  McCall's, True Detective,
True Love Stories and *True Confessions,*
I consider trash infernal,
Personally, I only read *The Ladies' Home Journal.*
As for the womenfolk, rather than spend an
  evening
With those advanced girls such as Nancy Astor,
  Anne Morgan,
Helen Gahagan and Clare Boothe Luce,
That green-eyed leopardess, I'd much rather
  climb some
Arcadian hill and dally with a shepherdess.
The *Times* is my favorite newspaper.
I also like the *Tribune* and the *Sun.*
I tolerate the *World-Telegram.*
But somebody should certainly condemn
The *News,* the *Mirror,*
The *Journal-American,* the *Post,* and for Marshall's,
If not for heaven's sake, *P.M.*

I WROTE A PLAY

Written in September 1944. Unused. This song might have been intended for Bill Tabbert.

I wrote a play
And it took me many a day,

It took me many a month, hear, hear!
It took me many a hungry year,
Yet I still thrill when I say
That I wrote a play.

When I finished my play
I said to myself one day,
"It must have a title with sweep and swirl."
Then I suddenly thought of it, "Boy Loves Girl,"
So "Boy Loves Girl" right away
Became the name of my play.

Then I packed my play
And carried it quick to Broadway,
Where I dug up a millionaire friend of mine,
Who took Gilbert Miller somewhere to dine
And filled the great gourmet so full of feed
That finally Gilbert agreed to read,
Without a moment's delay,
"Boy Loves Girl," my pearl of a play.

A year passed and a day,
Then Gilbert phoned me to say,
"I think your play is excellent stuff,
But hardly European enough,
Yet with slight alterations it ought to go far,
So it's being rewritten by Shaw and Molnár
And I'm changing the title from 'Boy Loves Girl'
To 'Hungarian Princess Loves British Earl.' "
So I went to his office that day
And stole my pretty play away.

I next took my play
To the Theatre Guild, heigh, heigh!
They read it and said, "It's charming stuff,
But, of course, for the Guild not long enough,
So Eugene O'Neill will rewrite the whole thing
And when it's longer than Wagner's Ring
We'll start rehearsing your play at once
As we've simply got to revive the Lunts,
But as 'Boy Loves Girl' doesn't quite fit in,
We have changed the title to 'Alfred Loves
Lynn.' "
So I rushed to their office that day
And snatched my darling play away.

Then heavy-hearted I trod
With my play to Michael Todd.
He read it and said, "It's terrifical stuff,
But for Broadway it ain't big and dirty enough,
Still I'm gonna produce it, just for a lark,
I'm taking the Mall in Central Park,
It's being rewritten by Gypsy Rose,
I'm hiring a nudist to do the clo'es,
The cast will consist of Man Mountain Dean
And a boatload of babes from the Argentine,
And I've changed the title, so help me God,
To 'The Love Life of Michael Todd.' "
So I ran to his office that day
And plucked my precious play away.

Then I sent to the coast my play,
And Sam Goldwyn phoned me to say,
"Hello, my boy, and au revoir,
Now listen slowly and have a cigar.
Your lousy play is a stinkeroo,
I just read part of it all the way through,
But I like the title extremely much,
Somehow 'Boy Loves Girl' has the Goldwyn touch.
Now I've bought a play that was tough to get
Called 'Romeo and Juliet,'
But if the title was 'Boy Loves Girl'
What a helluva picture for Milton Berle!
And if you'll sell me that title, by heck,
I'll wire you at once a blanket check."
So I sold him the title that day
And that's what became of my play,
Yes, that's what became of my play.

IF I HADN'T A HUSBAND

Unused. The lyric is dated August 17, 1944. The melody was later used for "Should I Tell You I Love You?" (*Around the World*, 1946).

REFRAIN

SHE: If I hadn't a husband
HE: And I hadn't a wife
BOTH: Around we'd cruise
And bruise our shoes
In kicking the blues out of life.
I'm not sure that you're perfect
But one thing I certainly sav,
If it only were not
For that goon that I've got
What a hell of a time we'd have.

WHERE DO WE GO FROM HERE?

A duet for Beatrice Lillie and Bert Lahr that was not used.

VERSE

HE: I loves yuh, lady, 'cause you're so refeened,
It musta been on champagne that you was
weaned,

I loves yuh 'cause you're crammed fulla blood that's blue.
SHE: Strangely, sir, I loves yuh too,
Your Grecian nose I simply idolize,
I adore the lack of distance between your eyes,
It's just another case, let's face it, chum,
Of the lady,
HE: Such a lady!
BOTH: Of the lady and the bum.

REFRAIN 1

SHE: Where do we go from here?
Oh, where do we go from here?
I'm tired of supper with the upper set,
So where do we go from here?
HE: Oh, not very far from here,
No, not very far from here.
I know a beanery behind the Met,
BOTH: So that's where we go from here.

REFRAIN 2

SHE: And what do we do while there?
Oh, what do we do while there?
HE: We'll both play footsie and forget to eat,
SHE: So that's what we do while there?
HE: But where do we go from there?
Oh, where do we go from there?
SHE: To a burlesque show on Forty-second Street,
BOTH: So that's where we go from there?

REFRAIN 3

HE: And what do we do while there?
Oh, what do we do while there?
SHE: We'll go romantic
While we watch 'em strip,
HE: So that's what we'll do while there?
SHE: But where do we go from there?
Oh, where do we go from there?
HE: To Jimmy Kelly's and we'll let 'er rip,
BOTH: So that's where we go from there?

REFRAIN 4

SHE: And what do we do while there?
Oh, what do we do while there?
HE: I'll let you treat me to a quart of gin,
SHE: So that's what we do while there?
HE: But where do we go from there?
Oh, where do we go from there?
SHE: To Chinatown and see a bit of sin,
BOTH: So that's where we go from there?

REFRAIN 5

HE: And what do we do while there?
Oh, what do we do while there?
SHE: We'll just relax and kick the gong around,
HE: So that's what we do while there?
SHE: But where do we go from there?
Oh, where do we go from there?
HE: An open hack and we'll be Harlem bound,
BOTH: So that's where we go from there?

REFRAIN 6

SHE: And what do we do while there?
Oh, what do we do while there?
HE: We'll boogie-woogie till the world is ours,
SHE: So that's what we do while there?
HE: But where do we go from there?
Oh, where do we go from there?
SHE: To my apartment at the Waldorf Tow'rs,
BOTH: So that's where we go from there?

CODA

HE: So that's where we go?
SHE: Yes, that's where we go,
And I've got some blue
Pajamas for you,
HE: Don't that take the cake?
A bum gets a break!
SHE: But just one thing more,
I'm bolting my door.
HE: And where do I sleep?
SHE: Outside, on the floor,
So that's where we go from there,
HE: What?
BOTH: That's where we go from here.

CAFÉ SOCIETY STILL CARRIES ON

Intended for Bert Lahr. Not used. No music survives.

REFRAIN 1

And in spite of the fact there's no imported Camembert,
In spite of no more Beluga caviar,
In spite of the fact some ass
Has limited all the gas
So even a gent
Is forced to rent
A car,

In spite of the dearth of decent dancing
shoes,
We manage to lope about from dark to dawn,
And in spite of the constant cuts
From these people who say we're nuts,
Café Society still carries on.

REFRAIN 2

In spite of the frightful service in the supper
clubs,
And lately I find, no matter where I sup,
The waiter who serves your food
Is either extremely rude
Or else he's so old
You have to hold
Him up.
In spite of the vodka shortage at the Colony
(I happen to know it's practically gone)
And in spite of those daily cracks
That we're headed to get the ax,
Café Society still carries on.

AROUND THE WORLD IN EIGHTY DAYS

1946

Tryout: Boston Opera House, Boston, April 28, 1946; Shubert Theatre, New Haven, May 7, 1946; Shubert Theatre, Philadelphia, May 14, 1946. Produced by Orson Welles as a Mercury Theatre Production at the Adelphi Theatre, New York, May 31, 1946. 75 performances. Book adapted by Orson Welles from the Jules Verne novel. Directed by Orson Welles. Cast, starring Orson Welles, included Arthur Margetson, Mary Healy, Julie Warren, Larry Laurence (Enzo Stuarti), and Victoria Cordova.

LOOK WHAT I FOUND

Published April 1946. Introduced by Julie Warren, Larry Laurence, and ensemble. There is a penciled, undated title listed in "Titles and Ideas": "And Look What I Found."

VERSE

So wrong seemed the world
I faced it with rage,
While hopeless I whirled
Like a mouse in a cage,
Till you came in range.
Not that life was worth!
Then presto change!
I'm the happiest girl
On earth.

REFRAIN

Flow, sweet music,
Flow in rippling sound.
Flow, sweet music,
Look, look, look what I found.
Sing, you songbird,
Make the hills resound,
Sing higher, oh, songbird,
Look, look, look what I found.
From nights of care
And dismal despair
With days only lonely in view
I woke to see
How sweet life could be,
That great big moment when I found you.
So chime, gay joy-bells,
Chime the world around,
Chime, all the time, joy-bells,
Look, look, look,
Look, look, look,
Look, look, look, look what I found.

THERE HE GOES, MR. PHILEAS FOGG

Published June 1946. Introduced by Arthur Margetson and Larry Laurence.

VERSE

PHILEAS: You will wake me at eight each morning
To the toll of St. James's chimes
With tea and toast
But important most,
A heated copy of the *Times.*
PAT: A slightly undone
Copy of the London
Times.
PHILEAS: At nine thirty-two, hot water
For me shaving, if you please,
And be more than sure
That its temperature
Is exactly eighty-eight degrees.
PAT: Fahrenheit or Centigrade, sir?
PHILEAS: That last word at once retrench!
Centigrade
Was Napoleon-made.
Fahrenheit
Is Britain's own right,
Let us have no truck with the French.
PAT: Yes, sir,
Not one truck with the French.
PHILEAS: And while I make me toilet
You'll prepare me clothes for me,
So at ten fifty-four
When I open that door
The following things I see:
My pantaloons,
PAT: Your coat and vest,
PHILEAS: They're marked each according to date.
They should all be brushed but never pressed,
A horrid Amèrican trait!
PAT: Your shirt, your shoes, a 'kerchief clean,
PHILEAS: And of woolen socks two pair,
PAT: A collar and tie
PHILEAS: And naturally my
Red flannel underwear.
PAT: Down to where?
PHILEAS: Down to there,
PHILEAS & PAT: My (His) red flannel underwear.
PHILEAS: At eleven twenty-nine, precisely
I depart for my club each day,
So your orders are, Pat,
To be positive that
I am dressed in an elegant way,

For although 'tis of no interest to me
If I please either damsel or dame,
'Tis a matter of pride
As the streets I stride,
To hear all the ladies exclaim,
PAT: To hear the dear ladies all exclaim:

REFRAIN

PHILEAS: There he goes, Mister Phileas Fogg,
Setting ev'ry girlie agog,
Wouldn't he make a marvelous mate?
Never early, never late!
There he goes, that smart Mister
Phileas,
In his clo'es so Picca-dicca-dilly-ous.
What a dude, what a dapper old dog!
There he goes, Mister Phileas Fogg,
There he goes,
There he goes,
There he goes.

MEE-RAH-LAH

Introduced by ensemble.

Azure-eyed Mee-rah-lah, how lovely you are.
Ne'er a fairer flow'r ever grew.
Iv'ry-limbed Mee-rah-lah, Auriga's great star
Never shone as brightly as you.
Cooling as the song of the evening breeze,
Warming as the sun on the morning sea,
Oh, Allah, Allah, Allah, my hunger appease,
Give, oh, give Mee-rah-lah to me.

SEA CHANTEY

Introduced by ensemble.

Roamin' home, ahoy,
Roamin' over the foamin' sea,
Yes, I'm roamin' home, ahoy,
So goodbye, my shy little chickadee.
From now on, my sweet,
You can roll the rest o' the fleet,
But you'll never again roll me,
For I'm roamin' home, ahoy,
Roamin' over the foamin' sea.

SHOULD I TELL YOU I LOVE YOU?

Published April 1946. Introduced by Mary Healy. In "Titles and Ideas," July 29, 1942, there is the following entry:

Did I tell you I love you?
Line for finish: Or did you tell it to me?
Or: And when will you tell it to me?

see Aug. 1946 "Should I Tell You etc."

VERSE

Too often, my dear,
With good-night time drawing near,
I ask myself, I fear,
As we part,
Should now I reveal
The longing for him I feel
Or still conceal
The secret in my heart?

REFRAIN

Should I tell you I love you,
Should I say how much I do?
Should I tell you how of you
I dream away, all the day through?
Should I tell you what paradise
Together our life would be?
Should I tell you I love you,
Or wait till you tell me?

INTERLUDE

'Tis strange that, oh, such a short while ago
I thought my days were done,
But now, dear great-hearted trav'ler, I know
My life has only begun.

PIPE DREAMING

Published April 1946. Introduced by Larry Laurence.

On this lonely night
When my pipe I light,
Through the rings of white
You're there as before.
As I see you, dear,
All my hopes reappear,

For again I am near
The one I adore.
Once our lips have met
I completely forget
All the sundown-till-dawn
Heartaches I've gone
Through.
Love is life sublime,
Ev'ry moment that I'm
Only wasting my time
Pipe dreaming of you,
Pipe dreaming of you,
Faraway you,
Faraway you,
Precious you,
Precious you,
Faraway you,
Faraway you.
You,
You.

IF YOU SMILE AT ME

Published April 1946. Introduced by Victoria Cordova, reprised by Julie Warren.

VERSE

One night in Mexico
Too long I lingered, I fear,
When someone whispered low
This little song in my ear.

REFRAIN

If you smile at me, I smile at you.
If you smile twice at me, I smile twice at you.
If you flirt with me, I flirt with you.
If you make love to me, I make love to you.
If you long for me, I long for you.
If you are sweet to me, I am sweet to you.
If you are true to me, I am true to you.
If you forget me, I forget you.

WHEREVER THEY FLY THE FLAG OF OLD ENGLAND

Published May 1946. Introduced by Arthur Margetson and ensemble. The Marine hymn, "The Halls of Montezuma," is sung as a countermelody to the refrain.

VERSE

Stop! Is there a British consul present?
No? Then I beg of you, gentlemen, don't be fools.
This game of yours is not only most unpleasant
But quite against the Marquis of Queensberry
Rules.
Alas, if you'd only been
Born on British land
Ruled by our gracious Queen
The more readily you'd understand:

REFRAIN

Wherever they fly the flag of old England,
Wherever they wear the old school tie,
Wherever a fox would never chase a foxhound,
Wherever a steak and a kidney make a pie,
Wherever they're certain that
The Derby's not a hat,
Wherever to ice your drink is still a sin,
Wherever the air is full
Of old John Bull,
Whatever is not cricket can't win.

MISSUS AOUDA

Sung by Alan Reed and ensemble during the pre-Broadway tryout. When Orson Welles replaced Reed out of town, the song was deleted.

INTRODUCTION

Oh, bear with me (and I know you shall)
If my program include a
Short hist'ry of a Bengal gal
Known as Missus Aouda.

Now Missus Aouda when a child of two
Though a b'liever in Buddha
Became engaged to a rich Hindu
Known as Mister Aouda.

Now he belonged to a Hindu sect
That in marriage deems it quite correct
Should the husband die and his wife
survive
She must be burned alive.

Still bear with me (and I know you shall)
If my program include a
Short hist'ry of that Bengal gal
Known as Missus Aouda.
. . .

And now, esteemed gentlemen, I'd
Be delighted to show you the first
lantern slide.

SOLO: First we see the bride and groom elect,
Both members of that Hindu sect.
Will the groom survive his bride of five
Or will his wife be burned alive?
CHORUS: Missus Aouda,
Missus Aouda,
Missus Aouda,
Will she be burned alive?

SOLO: Next, Mister Aouda out of luck
Having et some putrid Bombay duck.
Will a stomach pump, in time, arrive,
Or will his wife be burned alive?
CHORUS: Missus Aouda,
Missus Aouda,
Missus Aouda,
Will she be burned alive?

SOLO: We see them next on a hunting trip
And there he is in the tiger's grip.
Can he call off that tiger drive
Or will his wife be burned alive?
CHORUS: Missus Aouda,
Missus Aouda,
Missus Aouda,
Will she be burned alive?

SOLO: We see him next very sportsmanlike
As he coasts downhill on his brand-new bike.
To stop that bike can he contrive
Or will his wife be burned alive?
CHORUS: Missus Aouda,
Missus Aouda,
Missus Aouda,
Will she be burned alive?

SOLO: We see him next he's on a spree
Taking can-can lessons in Gay Paree.
Can he last out—he's sixty-five—
Or will his wife be burned alive?
CHORUS: Missus Aouda,
Missus Aouda,
Missus Aouda,
Will she be burned alive?

SOLO: We next will see that rich old fool
Playing leapfrog in his swimming pool.
Will he ever come up if he takes that dive
Or will his wife be burned alive?
CHORUS: Missus Aouda,
Missus Aouda,
Missus Aouda,
Will she be burned alive?

SOLO: And next he lies in his robes of gold,
A corpse already stiff and cold.
Would you ever say he could revive
Or will his wife be burned alive?
CHORUS: Missus Aouda,
Missus Aouda,
Missus Aouda,
Will she be burned,
Will she be burned,
Will she be burned alive?

SLAVE AUCTION

No music survives.

Here's Keecha-Kacha-Coocha from Baluchistan
And valeting rich gentlemen is her trade.
It's easy quite to find a gentleman's gent
But how about a gentleman's gentle maid?
In case you've use of a tip-top masseuse
At May at Bombay take a look.
She has given massages
To all of India's fattest maharajahs,
She also can cook.

SNAGTOOTH GERTIE

Unused.

Snagtooth Gertie, I love but you,
Your eyes they may be flirty but your heart is true.
Snagtooth Gertie, you drive me wild,
You may be fat and furty but you're cute like a child.
Snagtooth Gertie, you are my queen,
Your neck it may be dirty but your soul is clean.
Snagtooth Gertie, will you be mine?
Your tooth it ain't so purty but it's gen-u-ine.

THE PIRATE

1948

A film produced by Arthur Freed for M-G-M in 1948. Released June 11. Screenplay by Albert Hackett and Frances Goodrich, based on S. N. Behrman's play. Directed by Vincente Minnelli. Cast, starring Judy Garland and Gene Kelly, included Walter Slezak, Gladys Cooper, Reginald Owen, and the Nicholas Brothers. Hugh Fordin, in his book *The World of Entertainment,* indicates that the filming of *The Pirate* lasted from February 17 to November 18, 1947. Most of Porter's songs were written in 1946.

MACK THE BLACK

Published March 1948. Copyrighted unpublished July 1946. Introduced by Judy Garland and ensemble.

VERSE 1

There's a pirate known to fame,
Black Macoco was the pirate's name.
In his day the tops was he
'Round the Carib-BE-an or Ca-RIBB-ean sea.

REFRAIN 1

Mack the Black
'Round the Carib-BE-an,
Mack the Black,
Or Ca-RIBB-ean Sea.
Mack the Black
'Round the Carib-BE-bean,
'Round the Carib-BE-bean,
Or Ca-RIBB-ean Sea.

VERSE 2

As a child, his nurse foretold,
Mack was sure to be a pirate,
For when feeding time'd come,
Mack'd have a bottle,
But a bottle o' rum.

REFRAIN 2

Mack the Black,
Mack'd have a bottle,
Mack the Black,
But a bottle o' rum.
Mack the Black,
Mack'd have a bottle,
Mack'd have a bottle,
But a bottle o' rum.

VERSE 3

Mack when only twenty-two
Was the captain of a pirate crew.
If the crew from duty shrank
Mack'd send 'em walkin'
Send 'em walkin' the plank.

REFRAIN 3

Mack the Black,
Mack'd send 'em walkin',
Mack the Black,
Send 'em walkin' the plank,
Mack the Black,
Mack'd send 'em walkin'
Mack'd send 'em walkin',
Send 'em walkin' the plank.

VERSE 4

Ev'ry time he'd raid a town,
Holy mack'rel! How he shook 'em down.
If the blighters dared renege,
Mack'd wave his cutlass
And his cutlass was big.

REFRAIN 4

Mack the Black,
Mack'd wave his cutlass,
Mack the Black,
And his cutlass was big.
Mack the Black,
Mack'd wave his cutlass,
Mack'd wave his cutlass,
And his cutlass was big.

VERSE 5

When he'd made his daily rounds,
Gals'd trail him like a pack of hounds.
Ev'ry night he'd have a date,
Ladies go to pieces
Over pieces of eight.

REFRAIN 5

Mack the Black,
Ladies go to pieces,
Mack the Black,
Over pieces of eight.
Mack the Black,
Ladies go to pieces,
Ladies go to pieces
Over pieces of eight.

VERSE 6

Sleep, ma baby, baby sleep,
Time for babe to be in slumber deep.

If yuh wake and cry or laugh
Mack the Black'll whack yuh
And he'll whack yuh in half.

REFRAIN 6

Mack the Black,
Mack the Black'll whack yuh,
Mack the Black,
And he'll whack yuh in half.
Mack the Black,
Mack the Black'll whack yuh,
Mack the Black'll whack yuh,
And he'll whack yuh in half.

VERSE 7

Cobra, cobra, just be calm,
Rest your fangs upon my open palm.
If to bite me you contrive,
Mack the Black'll eat yuh
And he'll eat yuh alive.

REFRAIN 7

Mack the Black,
Mack the Black'll eat yuh,
Mack the Black,
And he'll eat yuh alive.
Mack the Black,
Mack the Black'll eat yuh,
Mack the Black'll eat yuh
And he'll eat yuh alive.

VERSE 8

Mack was ruthless,
Mack was feared,
P'r'aps it's better that he disappeared.
Yet I know
Tho' he was bad
I could fall in love with,
Fall in love with the lad.

REFRAIN 8

Mack the Black,
I could fall in love with,
Mack the Black,
Fall in love with the lad.
Mack the Black,
I could fall in love with,
I could fall in love with,
Fall in love with the lad.

VERSE 9

Evening star, if you see Mack,
Stop his wanderings and guide him back.
I'll be waiting patiently
By the Carib-BE-an or Ca-RIBB-ean sea.

REFRAIN 9

Mack the Black
By the Carib-BE-an,
Mack the Black,
Or Ca-RIBB-ean Sea.
Mack the Black
By the Carib-BE-bean,
By the Carib-BE-bean,
Or in case you're not agreein',
The Ca-RIBB-ean Sea.

NIÑA

Published March 1948. Copyrighted unpublished August 1946. Introduced by Gene Kelly.

VERSE

When I arrive in any town,
I look the ladies up and down,
And when I've picked my fav'rite flame,
This is my patter, no matter her name:

REFRAIN

Niña, Niña, Niña, Niña,
Fascinating Niña,
What a lovely child.
Niña, you enchant me,
Niña, you're so sweet
I mean yuh fairly drive me wild.

Niña, till the moment you hit my heart,
Niña, I was doin' just fine,
But since I've seen yuh,
Niña, Niña, Niña,
I'll be having neurasthenia
Till I make yuh mine!

Niña, Niña, Niña, Niña,
You're the bright gardenia
Of the Spanish Main.
Niña, Niña, Niña, Niña,
Don't be so enticing
Or I'll go insane.

Niña, till alas I gazed in your eyes,
Niña, I was mentally fine,
But since I've seen yah,
Niña, Niña, Niña,

I'll be havin' schizophrenia
Till I make yah—
Till I make yah—
Till I make yah mine!

LOVE OF MY LIFE

Published March 1948. Copyrighted unpublished November 1946. Introduced by Judy Garland. In "Titles and Ideas," April 1, 1946, Porter has an entry which begins:

M-G-M Picture, 1946
Song titles: "The Exception Proves the Rule"
"Niña"
"Love of My Life"
"You Can Do No Wrong"
"I'll Never Feel Anything Again"

VERSE

I lived in a dream, my sweet,
In a dream of you,
My dream was a joy complete,
For you loved me too.
And now I'm no longer afraid of what the future might reveal,
For the stuff that dreams are made of is suddenly real.

REFRAIN

Love of my life, life of my love,
I used to pray and pray you'd hear me.
Love of my life, angels above
Sent you at last, to stay always near me.
Now we are one,
Never to part,
And nevermore need I implore you to miss me.
Come to my arms, come to my heart, kiss me, kiss me.
Come to me, come to me, love of my life, love of my life, love of my life, my life, my love.

YOU CAN DO NO WRONG

Published March 1948. Copyrighted unpublished August 1946. Introduced by Judy Garland. There are a number of undated references to this song in "Titles and Ideas."

REFRAIN

You can do no wrong,
You're as right as the nightingale's song.
You're the nth of perfection,
Of them all you're the star,
When you gaze in my direction,
Life is caviar!
I can barely wait
Till you make me your permanent date,
And from then on, sweet angel,
I shall worship you my life long,
For you can do no wrong.

BE A CLOWN

Published March 1948. Copyrighted unpublished November 1946. Introduced by Gene Kelly, Judy Garland, and ensemble.

VERSE

I'll remember forever,
When I was but three,
Mama, who was clever,
Remarking to me:
If, son, when you're grown up,
You want ev'rything nice,
I've got your future sewn up
If you take this advice:

REFRAIN 1

Be a clown, be a clown,
All the world loves a clown.
Act the fool, play the calf,
And you'll always have the last laugh.
Wear the cap and the bells
And you'll rate with all the great swells.
If you become a doctor, folks'll face you with dread,
If you become a dentist, they'll be glad when you're dead,
You'll get a bigger hand if you can stand on your head,
Be a clown, be a clown, be a clown.

REFRAIN 2

Be a clown, be a clown,
All the world loves a clown.
Be a crazy buffoon
And the demoiselles'll all swoon.
Dress in huge, baggy pants
And you'll ride the road to romance.

A butcher or a baker, ladies never embrace,
A barber for a beau would be a social disgrace,
They all'll come to call if you can fall on your face,
Be a clown, be a clown, be a clown.

REFRAIN 3

Be a clown, be a clown,
All the world loves a clown.
Show 'em tricks, tell 'em jokes
And you'll only stop with top folks.
Be a crack jackanapes
And they'll imitate you like apes.
Why be a great composer with your rent in arrears,
Why be a major poet and you'll owe it for years,
When crowds'll pay to giggle if you wiggle your ears?
Be a clown, be a clown, be a clown.

REFRAIN 4

Be a clown, be a clown,
All the world loves a clown.
If you just make 'em roar
Watch your mountebank account soar.
Wear a painted mustache
And you're sure to make a big splash.
A college education I should never propose,
A bachelor's degree won't even keep you in clo'es,
But millions you will win if you can spin on your nose.
Be a clown, be a clown, be a clown.

REFRAIN 5

Be a clown, be a clown,
All the world loves a clown.
Be the poor silly ass
And you'll always travel first-class,
Give 'em quips, give 'em fun,
And they'll pay to say you're A-1.
If you become a farmer, you've the weather to buck,
If you become a gambler, you'll be stuck with your luck,
But jack you'll never lack if you can quack like a duck
(Quack, quack, quack, quack).
Be a clown, be a clown, be a clown.

VOODOO

Published March 1948 (I have never seen a printed copy). Copyrighted unpublished August 1946. Although Judy Garland recorded this number, it was dropped from the film during production.

VERSE

On my native strip by the Trinidad sea,
On the topmost tip of a tamarind tree
Dwelt a voodoo god called Jim,
For a god how odd of him.
And on ev'nings dark when shadows grew thick,
We would always hark when a woebegone chick
Started singing through the dim
To the dee-i-tee in the tamarind tree called Jim,
To the odd little god known as Jim:

REFRAIN

Voodoo, whisper low from above,
Voodoo, what's this myst'ry called love?
Voodoo, folks keep tellin' me of
Love's allure, love's delight,
June or January, noon or night.
Voodoo, if this love's all that they say,
Voodoo, for one favor I pray,
Voodoo, won't you send it my way?
Voodoo, do, do, do.

MANUELA

Unused. Copyrighted unpublished August 1946. Published in *The Unpublished Cole Porter.*

VERSE

Stop all other music!
I've just met a maid
As cute as a kitten
Who's got me so smitten
I've written a serenade,
So here's to my libido,
With a mi, mi, mi, re, re, re, mi, do (let's go).

REFRAIN

You're a dream, Manuela,
You're supreme, Manuela,
You're divine Manuela, you're as fine
As a wine, sweet and mella.
I'm so sad, Manuela,
Going mad, Manuela,
For my heart beats only for you.

Manuela, tell a fella what to do.

MARTINIQUE

Unused. The music is lost. The title is noted in "Titles and Ideas" (no date).

In Martinique
It still is chic,
It's very chic
To walk (go) around in y'r so-to-speak.
In Kingston (London) town
Y'r friends would frown,
But it still is chic
In Martinique.

In Martinique
It still is chic
To spend your time playing hide-and-seek.*
[*Line missing*]
They'd think you mad,
It's very bad, it's considered bad,
But it still is chic
In Martinique.

To take a bath
More than once a week
In Washington
It isn't done,
But it still is chic
In Martinique.

In case you should to a stranger speak,
To neglect your brain for a good physique,
The folks'd frown
In Boston town,
It isn't done
In Washington,
But it still is considered very smart in Martinique,
For boys and girls to marry once a week,†
But it still is very chic and very smart
In Martinique,
It still is very smart and very chic
In Martinique.

**Or:*
When boys and girls play at hide-and-seek.
†*Or:*
Where boys and girls remarry once a week,

KISS ME, KATE

1948

Tryout: Shubert Theatre, Philadelphia, December 2, 1948. Produced by Saint Subber and Lemuel Ayers at the New Century Theatre, New York, December 30, 1948. 1,077 performances. Book by Sam and Bella Spewack, inspired by and based loosely on Shakespeare's *Taming of the Shrew*. Production staged by John C. Wilson. Cast, starring Alfred Drake, Patricia Morison, Harold Lang, and Lisa Kirk, included Annabelle Hill, Lorenzo Fuller, Harry Clark, and Jack Diamond. The complete vocal score was published June 1951.

ANOTHER OP'NIN', ANOTHER SHOW

Published February 1949. Introduced by Annabelle Hill and ensemble.

Another op'nin', another show
In Philly, Boston or Baltimo',
A chance for stage folks to say hello,
Another op'nin' of another show.
Another job that you hope, at last,
Will make your future forget your past,
Another pain where the ulcers grow,
Another op'nin' of another show.
Four weeks, you rehearse and rehearse,
Three weeks, and it couldn't be worse,
One week, will it ever be right?
Then out o' the hat, it's that big first night!
The overture is about to start,
You cross your fingers and hold your heart,
It's curtain time and away we go!
Another op'nin',
Just another op'nin' of another show.

WHY CAN'T YOU BEHAVE?

Published November 1948. Introduced by Lisa Kirk; danced by Harold Lang.

Why can't you behave?
Oh, why can't you behave?
After all the things you told me
And the promises that you gave,
Oh, why can't you behave?
. . .
Why can't you be good?
And do just as you should?
Won't you turn that new leaf over
So your baby can be your slave?
Oh, why can't you behave?

There's a farm I know near my old home town,
Where we two can go and try settlin' down.
There I'll care for you forever,
Well, at least 'til you dig my grave.
Oh, why can't you behave?

TAG

HE: Gee, I need you, kid.
SHE: I always knew you did,
But why can't you behave?

WUNDERBAR

Published November 1948. Introduced by Patricia Morison and Alfred Drake. At one time during the creation of *Kate* this was intended as the show's opening number.

VERSE

Gazing down on the Jungfrau
From our secret chalet for two,
Let us drink, Liebchen mein,
In the moonlight benign,
To the joy of our dream come true.

REFRAIN

Wunderbar, wunderbar!
What a perfect night for love.
Here am I, here you are,
Why, it's truly wunderbar!
Wunderbar, wunderbar!
We're alone and hand in glove,
Not a cloud near or far,
Why, it's more than wunderbar!
SHE: Say you care, dear,
HE: For you madly,
SHE: Say you long, dear,
HE: For your kiss,
SHE: Do you swear, dear?
HE: Darling, gladly,
SHE: Life's divine, dear!
HE: And you're mine, dear!
BOTH: Wunderbar, wunderbar!
There's our fav'rite star above.
What a bright, shining star,
Like our love, it's wunderbar!

SO IN LOVE

Published November 1948. Introduced by Patricia Morison; reprised by Alfred Drake.

Strange, dear, but true, dear,
When I'm close to you, dear,
The stars fill the sky,
So in love with you am I.
Even without you
My arms fold about you.
You know, darling, why,
So in love with you am I.
In love with the night mysterious
The night when you first were there,
In love with my joy delirious
When I knew that you could care.
So taunt me and hurt me,
Deceive me, desert me,
I'm yours 'til I die,
So in love,
So in love,
So in love with you, my love, am I.

WE OPEN IN VENICE

Published February 1949. Introduced by Alfred Drake, Patricia Morison, Lisa Kirk, and Harold Lang. The song is subtitled "Opening, Padua Street Scene."

VERSE

A troupe of strolling players are we,
Not stars like L. B. Mayer's are we,
But just a simple band
Who roams about the land
Dispensing fol-de-rol frivolity.
Mere folk who give distraction are we,
No Theatre Guild attraction are we,
But just a crazy group
That never ceases to troop
Around the map of little Italy.

REFRAIN 1

We open in Venice,
We next play Verona,
Then on to Cremona.
Lotsa laughs in Cremona.
Our next jump is Parma,
That dopey, mopey menace,
Then Mantua, then Padua,
Then we open again, where?

REFRAIN 2

We open in Venice,
We next play Verona,
Then on to Cremona.
Lotsa bars in Cremona.
The next jump is Parma,
That beerless, cheerless menace,
Then Mantua, then Padua,
Then we open again, where?

REFRAIN 3

We open in Venice,
We next play Verona,
Then on to Cremona.
Lotsa dough in Cremona.
Our next jump is Parma,
That stingy, dingy menace,
Then Mantua, then Padua,
Then we open again, where?

REFRAIN 4

We open in Venice,
We next play Verona,
Then on to Cremona.
Lotsa quail in Cremona.
Our next jump is Parma,
That heartless, tartless menace,
Then Mantua, then Padua
Then we open again, where?
In Venice.

TOM, DICK OR HARRY

Published February 1949. Introduced by Lisa Kirk, Harold Lang, Edwin Clay, and Charles Wood.

VERSE

GREMIO: I've made a haul in all the leading rackets
From which rip-roarin' rich I happen to be,
And if thou wouldst attain the upper brackets,
Marry me, marry me, marry me.

LUCENTIO: My purse has yet to know a silver lining,
Still lifeless is my wifeless family tree,
But if for love unending thou art pining,

Marry me, marry me, marry me.

HORTENSIO: I come to thee a thoroughbred
 patrician
Still spraying my decaying family
 tree.
To give a social goose to thy position,
Marry me, marry me, marry me.
Marry me!

GREMIO & LUCENTIO: Marry me!
HORTENSIO: Marry me!
GREMIO & HORTENSIO: Marry me!
LUCENTIO: Marry me!
GREMIO: Marry me!
3 SUITORS: Marry me!

REFRAIN 1

BIANCA: I'm a maid who would marry
And will take with no qualm
Any Tom, Dick or Harry,
Any Harry, Dick or Tom,
I'm a maid mad to marry
And will take double-quick
Any Tom, Dick or Harry,
Any Tom, Harry or Dick.

REFRAIN 2

GREMIO: I'm the man thou shouldst marry.
BIANCA: Howdy, Pop!
GREMIO: Howdy, Mom.
LUCENTIO: I'm the man thou shouldst marry.
BIANCA: Art thou Harry, Dick or Tom?
HORTENSIO: I'm the man thou shouldst marry.
BIANCA: Howdy, pal!
HORTENSIO: Howdy, chick!
BIANCA: Art thou Tom, Dick or Harry?
HORTENSIO: Call me Tom, Harry or Dick.

REFRAIN 3

BIANCA & SUITORS: I'm (She's) a maid who would marry
And would no longer tarry,
I'm (she's) a maid who would marry,
May my hopes not miscarry!
I'm (she's) a maid mad to marry
And will take double-quick
Any Tom, Dick or Harry,
Any Tom, Harry or Dick,
A dicka dick,
A dicka dick,
A dicka dick,
A dicka dick,
A dicka dick,
A dicka dick.

I'VE COME TO WIVE IT WEALTHILY IN PADUA

Published February 1949. Introduced by Alfred Drake and ensemble.

I've come to wive it wealthily in Padua,
If wealthily then happily in Padua.
If my wife has a bag of gold,
Do I care if the bag be old?
I've come to wive it wealthily in Padua.

I've come to wive it wealthily in Padua.*
I heard you mutter, "Zounds, a loathsome lad
 you are."
I shall not be disturbed one bit
If she be but a quarter-wit,
If she only can talk of clo'es
While she powders her goddamned nose,
I've come to wive it wealthily in Padua.

I've come to wive it wealthily in Padua.*
I heard you say, "Gadzooks, completely mad you
 are!"
'Twouldn't give me the slightest shock
If her knees now and then should knock,
If her eyes were a wee bit crossed,
Were she wearing the hair she'd lost,
Still the damsel I'll make my dame,
In the dark they are all the same,
I've come to wive it wealthily in Padua.

I've come to wive it wealthily in Padua.*
I heard you say, "Good gad, but what a cad you
 are!"
Do I mind if she fret and fuss,
If she fume like Vesuvius,
If she roar like a winter breeze
On the rough Adriatic seas,
If she scream like a teething brat,
If she scratch like a tiger cat,
If she fight like a raging boar,
I have oft stuck a pig before,
I've come to wive it wealthily in Padua.
With a hunny, nunny, nunny,
And a hey, hey, hey,
Not to mention money, money

*In the show, this line was sung by the ensemble as: "He's come to wive it wealthily in Padua."

For a rainy day,
I've come to wive it wealthily in Padua.

I HATE MEN

Published December 1948. Introduced by Patricia Morison.

REFRAIN 1

I hate men.
I can't abide 'em even now and then.
Than ever marry one of them, I'd rest a virgin rather,
For husbands are a boring lot and only give you bother.
Of course, I'm awfly glad that Mother had to marry Father,
But I hate men.
I hate 'em all, from modern man 'way back to Father Adam,
He sired Cain and Abel though the Lord above forbade 'em,
I'd hate both Cain and Abel though Betty Grable had 'em,
Oh, I hate men!*

REFRAIN 2

I hate men.
They should be kept like piggies in a pen.
You may be wooed by Jack the Tar, so charming and so chipper,
But if you take him for a mate, be sure that you're the skipper,
For Jack the Tar can go too far. Remember Jack the Ripper?
Oh, I hate men.*
Of all the types I've ever met within our democracy,
I hate the most the athlete with his manner bold and brassy,
He may have hair upon his chest but, sister, so has Lassie.
Oh, I hate men!

REFRAIN 3

I hate men.
Their worth upon this earth I dinna ken.
Avoid the trav'ling salesman though a tempting Tom he may be,
From China he will bring you jade and perfume from Araby,
But don't forget 'tis he who'll have the fun and thee the baby,
Oh, I hate men.
If thou shouldst wed a businessman, be wary, oh, be wary.
He'll tell you he's detained in town on business necessary,
His bus'ness is the bus'ness which he gives his secretary,
Oh, I hate men!

REFRAIN 4

I hate men.
Though roosters they, I will not play the hen.
If you espouse an older man through girlish optimism,
He'll always stay at home at night and make no criticism,
Though you may call it love, the doctors call it rheumatism.
Oh, I hate men.
From all I've read, alone in bed, from A to Zed, about 'em.
Since love is blind, then from the mind, all womankind should rout 'em,
But, ladies, you must answer too, what would we do without 'em?
Still, I hate men!

*The last four lines of Refrain 1 and the first six lines of Refrain 2 were deleted in the final version.

WERE THINE THAT SPECIAL FACE

Published November 1948. Introduced by Alfred Drake and ensemble.

VERSE

I wrote a poem
In classic style.
I wrote it with my tongue in my cheek
And my lips in a smile.
But of late my poem
Has a meaning so new,
For to my surprise
It suddenly applies
To my darling—to you.

REFRAIN

Were thine that special face
The face which fills my dreaming,

Were thine the rhythm'd grace,
Were thine the form so lithe and slender,
Were thine the arms so warm, so tender,
Were thine the kiss divine,
Were thine the love for me,
The love which fills my dreaming,
When all these charms are thine
Then you'll be mine, all mine.

I SING OF LOVE

Published February 1949. Introduced by Lisa Kirk, Harold Lang, and ensemble.

I sing of love,
I sing only of love,
Ye gods above,
May I never sing of anything but love.
For love is the joy
Of ev'ry girl and boy,
As love, later on,
Keeps 'em going 'til they're gone.
Yes, love is the theme
Of all people who dream,
So love, let's confess,
Is ev'rybody's business.
Oh, ye gods above,
May I never sing of anything but love,
Sweet love.*

PATTER 1

I won't sing a song about battle,
I won't sing of babies who prattle.
I get no glee
From songs about the sea
Or cowboy songs about cattle.
I won't waste a note of my patters
On socially significant matters.
I sing of one thing and I adore it,
Thank heaven for it!

PATTER 2

I loathe all the songs about rivers,
From spring songs I get the cold shivers.
My nerves grow tense
When radios commence
Commercial songs to flush livers.
My hands always get a bit clammy
When Jolson revives his ole mammy.

*In the script, "I" was changed to "we" in this section.

Of what do I sing if you request it?
This time, you guessed it.

KISS ME, KATE

Finale of Act I. Copyrighted unpublished January 1949. Introduced by Alfred Drake, Patricia Morison, and ensemble.

PETRUCHIO: So kiss me, Kate,
Thou lovely loon,
E'er we start
On our honeymoon.
Oh, kiss me, Kate,
Darling devil divine,
For now thou shall ever be
mine.
KATE: I'll never be thine
PETRUCHIO & OTHERS: So kiss me (him), Kate,
KATE: No!
PETRUCHIO & OTHERS: Thou lovely loon,
KATE: Go!
PETRUCHIO & OTHERS: E'er we (you) start
KATE: Nay!
PETRUCHIO & OTHERS: On our (your) honeymoon.
KATE: Away!
PETRUCHIO & OTHERS: Oh, kiss me (him), Kate,
KATE: Fred!
PETRUCHIO & OTHERS: Darling devil divine,
KATE: Kindly drop dead!
PETRUCHIO: For now thou shall ever
be
KATE: Now I shall never be
PETRUCHIO & MEN: Now thou shall ever be
KATE & GIRLS: Now I shall (thou shall)
never be thine,
PETRUCHIO: Yes, mine.
KATE: Not thine.
PETRUCHIO: Yes, mine.

KATE: You swine.
PETRUCHIO: Yes, mine.
KATE: You swine.

PETRUCHIO & SINGERS: She called
PETRUCHIO: Yes, mine.
PETRUCHIO & SINGERS: Him a swine.

PETRUCHIO: So kiss me, Kate.
KATE: I'll crack your pate.
PETRUCHIO: Oh, please don't pout.
KATE: I'll knock you out.
PETRUCHIO: My priceless prize!
KATE: I'll black your eyes.

PETRUCHIO: Oh, kiss me quick!
KATE: Your rump I'll kick.
PETRUCHIO & OTHERS: Oh, kiss me (him)!
KATE: Bounder!
OTHERS: He's not her dish, he's not her dish.
PETRUCHIO & OTHERS: Oh, kiss me (him)!
KATE: Flounder!
OTHERS: A type of fish she would not wish.
PETRUCHIO & OTHERS: Oh, kiss me (him)!
KATE: Dastard!
OTHERS: What's that we heard, what's that we heard?
PETRUCHIO & OTHERS: Oh, kiss me (him)!
KATE: Bastard!
OTHERS: Oh, Katie, that's a naughty word.
PETRUCHIO & GIRLS: Oh, kiss me (him).
MEN & GIRLS: Kiss him.
PETRUCHIO & GIRLS: Kiss me (him).
MEN & GIRLS: Kiss him.
PETRUCHIO, GIRLS & BASSES: Kiss me (him).
MEN & GIRLS: Kiss him.
KATE: Never! [*Repeated 17 times*]
PETRUCHIO & OTHERS: Kiss me (him), kiss me (him). Kate, kiss me (him).
Kiss me (him), Kate, kiss me (him).
Kiss me (him), Kate, kiss me (him).
Kiss me (him), Kate, kiss me (him).
Kiss me (him), Kate.
Kiss me (him), Kate.
Kiss me (him), Kate.
Kiss me (him), Kate.
Kiss me (him), Kate.
Kiss me (him), Kate.
Kiss me (him), Kate.
Kiss me (him), Kate.
Kiss
KATE: [*Screams*]
PETRUCHIO & OTHERS: Me (him),
KATE: [*Screams*]
PETRUCHIO & OTHERS: Kate!

TOO DARN HOT

Published January 1949. Introduced by Lorenzo Fuller, Eddie Sledge, and Fred Davis.

VERSE 1

It's too darn hot,
It's too darn hot.
I'd like to sup with my baby tonight,
And play the pup with my baby tonight.
I'd like to sup with my baby tonight,
And play the pup with my baby tonight,
But I ain't up to my baby tonight,
'Cause it's too darn hot.

It's too darn hot,
It's too darn hot.
I'd like to stop for my baby tonight,
And blow my top with my baby tonight.
I'd like to stop for my baby tonight,
And blow my top with my baby tonight,
But I'd be a flop with my baby tonight,
'Cause it's too darn hot.

It's too darn hot,
It's too darn hot.
I'd like to fool with my baby tonight,
Break ev'ry rule with my baby tonight,
I'd like to fool with my baby tonight,
Break ev'ry rule with my baby tonight,
But, pillow, you'll be my baby tonight,
'Cause it's too darn hot.

REFRAIN 1

According to the Kinsey Report
Ev'ry average man you know
Much prefers to play his favorite sport
When the temperature is low,
But when the thermometer goes 'way up
And the weather is sizzling hot,
Mister Adam
For his madam,
Is not,
'Cause it's too, too,
Too darn hot,
It's too darn hot,
It's too darn hot.

VERSE 2

It's too darn hot,
It's too darn hot.
I'd like to call on my baby tonight,
And give my all to my baby tonight,
I'd like to call on my baby tonight,
And give my all to my baby tonight,
But I can't play ball with my baby tonight,
'Cause it's too darn hot.

It's too darn hot,
It's too darn hot.

I'd like to meet with my baby tonight,
Get off my feet with my baby tonight,
I'd like to meet with my baby tonight,
Get off my feet with my baby tonight,
But no repeat with my baby tonight,
'Cause it's too darn hot.

It's too darn hot,
It's too darn hot.
I'd like to coo with my baby tonight,
And pitch some woo with my baby tonight,
I'd like to coo with my baby tonight,
And pitch some woo with my baby tonight,
But, brother, you bite my baby tonight,
'Cause it's too darn hot.

REFRAIN 2

According to the Kinsey Report
Ev'ry average man you know
Much prefers to play his favorite sport
When the temperature is low,
But when the thermometer goes 'way up
And the weather is sizzling hot,
Mister Gob
For his squab,
A marine
For his queen,
A G.I.
For his cutie-pie
Is not,
'Cause it's too, too,
Too darn hot,
It's too darn hot.
It's too, too, too, too darn hot.

WHERE IS THE LIFE THAT LATE I LED?

Published February 1949. Introduced by Alfred Drake.

VERSE

Since I reached the charming age of puberty
And began to finger feminine curls,
Like a show that's typically Shuberty
I have always had a multitude of girls,
But now that a married man, at last, am I,
How aware of my dear, departed past am I.

REFRAIN 1

Where is the life that late I led?
Where is it now? Totally dead.
Where is the fun I used to find?
Where has it gone? Gone with the wind.
A married life may all be well,
But raising an heir
Could never compare
With raising a bit of hell,
So I repeat what first I said,
Where is the life that late I?

PATTER 1

In dear Milano, where are you, Momo,
Still selling those pictures of the Scriptures in the
Duomo?
And, Carolina, where are you, Lina,
Still peddling your pizza in the streets o'
Taormina?
And in Firenze, where are you, Alice,
Still there in your pretty, itty-bitty Pitti Palace?
And sweet Lucretia, so young and gay-ee?
What scandalous doin's in the ruins of Pompeii!

REFRAIN 2

Where is the life that late I led?
Where is it now? Totally dead.
Where is the fun I used to find?
Where has it gone? Gone with the wind.
The marriage game is quite all right,
Yes, during the day
It's easy to play,
But, oh, what a bore at night,
So I repeat what first I said,
Where is the life that late I?

PATTER 2

Where is Rebecca, my Becki-weckio,
Again is she cruising that amusing Ponte
Vecchio?
Where is Fedora, the wild virago?
It's lucky I missed her gangster sister from
Chicago.
Where is Venetia, who loved to chat so,
Could still she be drinkin' in her stinkin' pink
palazzo?
And lovely Lisa, where are you, Lisa?
You gave a new meaning to the leaning tow'r of
Pisa.

REFRAIN 3

Where is the life that late I led?
Where is it now? Totally dead.
Where is the fun I used to find?
Where has it gone? Gone with the wind.
I've oft been told of nuptial bliss,

But what do you do,
A quarter to two,
With only a shrew to kiss?
So I repeat what first I said,
Where is the life that late I led?

ALWAYS TRUE TO YOU IN MY FASHION

Published December 1948. Introduced by Lisa Kirk.

VERSE

Oh, Bill,
Why can't you behave,
Why can't you behave?
How in hell can you be jealous
When you know, baby, I'm your slave?
I'm just mad for you,
And I'll always be,
But naturally

REFRAIN 1

If a custom-tailored vet
Asks me out for something wet,
When the vet begins to pet, I cry "Hooray!"
But I'm always true to you, darlin', in my fashion,
Yes, I'm always true to you, darlin', in my way.
I enjoy a tender pass
By the boss of Boston, Mass.,
Though his pass is middle-class and notta Backa Bay.
But I'm always true to you, darlin', in my fashion,
Yes, I'm always true to you, darlin', in my way.
There's a madman known as Mack
Who is planning to attack,
If his mad attack means a Cadillac, okay!
But I'm always true to you, darlin', in my fashion,
Yes, I'm always true to you, darlin', in my way.

REFRAIN 2

I've been asked to have a meal
By a big tycoon in steel,
If the meal includes a deal, accept I may.
But I'm always true to you, darlin', in my fashion,
Yes, I'm always true to you, darlin', in my way.
I could never curl my lip
To a dazzlin' diamond clip,
Though the clip meant "let 'er rip," I'd not say "Nay!"
But I'm always true to you, darlin', in my fashion,
Yes, I'm always true to you, darlin', in my way.
There's an oil man known as Tex
Who is keen to give me checks,
And his checks, I fear, mean that sex is here to stay!
But I'm always true to you, darlin', in my fashion,
Yes, I'm always true to you, darlin', in my way.

REFRAIN 3

There's a wealthy Hindu priest
Who's a wolf, to say the least,
When the priest goes too far east, I also stray.
But I'm always true to you, darlin', in my fashion,
Yes, I'm always true to you, darlin', in my way.
There's a lush from Portland, Ore.,
Who is rich but sich a bore,
When the bore falls on the floor, I let him lay.
But I'm always true to you, darlin', in my fashion,
Yes, I'm always true to you, darlin', in my way.
Mister Harris, plutocrat,
Wants to give my cheek a pat,
If the Harris pat
Means a Paris hat,
Bébé, Oo-la-la!
Mais je suis toujours fidèle, darlin', in my fashion,
Oui, je suis toujours fidèle, darlin', in my way.

REFRAIN 4

From Ohio Mister Thorne
Calls me up from night 'til morn,
Mister Thorne once cornered corn and that ain't hay.
But I'm always true to you, darlin', in my fashion,
Yes, I'm always true to you, darlin', in my way.
From Milwaukee, Mister Fritz
Often moves me to the Ritz,
Mister Fritz is full of Schlitz and full of play.
But I'm always true to you, darlin', in my fashion,
Yes, I'm always true to you, darlin', in my way.
Mister Gable, I mean Clark,
Wants me on his boat to park,
If the Gable boat
Means a sable coat,
Anchors aweigh!
But I'm always true to you, darlin', in my fashion,
Yes, I'm always true to you, darlin', in my way.

BIANCA

Published December 1948. Introduced by Harold Lang and ensemble. Verse 2 was written for the published version of the song.

VERSE 1

While rehearsing with Bianca
(She's the darling I adore),
Offstage I found
She's been around
But I still love her more and more;
So I've written her a love song
Though I'm just an amateur.
I'll sing it through
For all of you
To see if it's worthy of her.
Are yuh list'nin'?

REFRAIN

Bianca, Bianca,
Oh, baby, will you be mine?
Bianca, Bianca,
You'd better answer yes or Poppa spanka.
To win you, Bianca,
There's nothing I would not do.
I would gladly give up coffee for Sanka,
Even Sanka, Bianca, for you.

VERSE 2

In the street called Tin Pan Alley
I have suffered endless wrongs,
For I'm the dog
Who writes incog.
All of Cole Porter's Broadway songs.
Here's a new one to Bianca,
Bless her heart and bless her soul.
I'll sing it through
For all of you
Then take it away, Cole.

BRUSH UP YOUR SHAKESPEARE

Published February 1949. Introduced by Harry Clark and Jack Diamond.

VERSE

The girls today in society
Go for classical poetry,
So to win their hearts one must quote with ease
Aeschylus and Euripides.
One must know Homer and, b'lieve me, Bo,
Sophocles, also Sappho-ho.
Unless you know Shelley and Keats and Pope,
Dainty debbies will call you a dope.
But the poet of them all
Who will start 'em simply ravin'
Is the poet people call
The bard of Stratford-on-Avon.

REFRAIN 1

Brush up your Shakespeare,
Start quoting him now.
Brush up your Shakespeare
And the women you will wow.
Just declaim a few lines from "Othella"
And they'll think you're a helluva fella.
If your blonde won't respond when you flatter 'er
Tell her what Tony told Cleopaterer,
If she fights when her clothes you are mussing,
What are clothes? "Much Ado About Nussing."
Brush up your Shakespeare
And they'll all kowtow.

REFRAIN 2

Brush up your Shakespeare,
Start quoting him now.
Brush up your Shakespeare
And the women you will wow.
With the wife of the British embessida
Try a crack out of "Troilus and Cressida,"
If she says she won't buy it or tike it
Make her tike it, what's more, "As You Like It."
If she says your behavior is heinous
Kick her right in the "Coriolanus."
Brush up your Shakespeare
And they'll all kowtow.

REFRAIN 3

Brush up your Shakespeare,
Start quoting him now.
Brush up your Shakespeare
And the women you will wow.
If you can't be a ham and do "Hamlet"
They will not give a damn or a damnlet.
Just recite an occasional sonnet
And your lap'll have "Honey" upon it.
When your baby is pleading for pleasure
Let her sample your "Measure for Measure."
Brush up your Shakespeare
And they'll all kowtow.

REFRAIN 4

Brush up your Shakespeare,
Start quoting him now.
Brush up your Shakespeare
And the women you will wow.
Better mention "The Merchant of Venice"

When her sweet pound o' flesh you would
menace.
If her virtue, at first, she defends—well,
Just remind her that "All's Well That Ends
Well."
And if still she won't give you a bonus
You know what Venus got from Adonis!
Brush up your Shakespeare
And they'll all kowtow.

REFRAIN 5

Brush up your Shakespeare
Start quoting him now.
Brush up your Shakespeare
And the women you will wow.
If your goil is a Washington Heights dream
Treat the kid to "A Midsummer Night's Dream."
If she then wants an all-by-herself night
Let her rest ev'ry 'leventh or "Twelfth Night."
If because of your heat she gets huffy
Simply play on and "Lay on, Macduffy!"
Brush up your Shakespeare
And they'll all kowtow,
We trow, and they'll all kowtow.

GRAND FINALE

Brush up your Shakespeare,
Start quoting him now.
Brush up your Shakespeare
And the women you will wow.
So tonight just recite to your matey,
"Kiss me, Kate, kiss me, Kate, kiss me, Katey."
Brush up your Shakespeare
And they'll all kowtow.

I AM ASHAMED THAT WOMEN ARE SO SIMPLE

Published December 1948. Introduced by Patricia Morison. The words by Shakespeare (Act V, Scene 2, lines 161–79) were slightly altered by Porter.

I am ashamed that women are so simple
To offer war where they should kneel for peace,
Or seek for rule, supremacy, and sway
When they are bound to serve, love and obey.
Why are our bodies soft and weak and smooth,
Unapt to toil and trouble in the world,
But that our soft conditions and our hearts
Should well agree with our external parts?
So, wife, hold your temper and meekly put
Your hand 'neath the sole of your husband's foot,
In token of which duty, if he please,
My hand is ready,
Ready,
May it do him ease.

FINALE, ACT II

Introduced by Alfred Drake, Patricia Morison, and the ensemble.

PETRUCHIO: So kiss me, Kate,
KATE: Caro!
PETRUCHIO: And twice and thrice,
KATE: Carissimo!
PETRUCHIO: Ere we start
KATE: Bello!
PETRUCHIO: Living in paradise.
KATE: Bellissimo!
PETRUCHIO & OTHERS: Oh, kiss me (him), Kate,
KATE: Presto!
PETRUCHIO & OTHERS: Darling angel, divine!
KATE: Prestissimo!
PETRUCHIO: For now thou shall ever be
KATE: Now thou shall ever be
PETRUCHIO & MEN: Now thou shall ever be
KATE & GIRLS: Now thou shall ever be
PETRUCHIO: Mine,
KATE: Mine,
PETRUCHIO & KATE: Darling mine,

KATE: And I am thine, and I am
thine
PETRUCHIO & OTHERS: And I am (she is) thine, and
I am (she is) thine,

ALL: All
Thine!

IT WAS GREAT FUN THE FIRST TIME

Unused. Dropped during rehearsals. At one point it was intended to be the second number in the show.

VERSE

Remember Chez Tony
When we first went out to dine?
The old macaroni

And the new California wine!
We had painted the town so
By the time we said goodbye
That the night was gone
And we watched the dawn
Gaily painting, painting the sky.

REFRAIN 1

It was great fun the first time,
And the second time even more,
It was great fun the third time,
Not to underrate date number four,
It was still fun the last time—
Then what happened? The laughter was through.
It was great fun the first time
But the next time it's up to you.

PATTER

SHE: Who was the first to misbehave?
HE: Who was the first to rant and rave?
It was you, my pretty.
SHE: It was you, my cute.
HE: It was you, you devil.
SHE: It was you, you brute.
HE: Who of the two should take the blame?
SHE: You of the two should die of shame.
HE: Why, how dare you, you hothead, you spitfire, you cat!
SHE: You cheater, you rotter, you rascal, you rat!
HE: I hate you!
SHE: I loathe you!
HE: You monster!
SHE: You mess!
BOTH: Nevertheless—

REFRAIN 2

It was great fun the first time,
And the second time even more,
It was great fun the third time,
Not to underrate date number four,
It was still fun the last time—
Then what happened? How strange love can be!
It was great fun the first time
And the next time just wait and see.

WE SHALL NEVER BE YOUNGER

Unused. Intended for Lilli (Patricia Morison). The music of the release is the same as that of the release of "No Lover" (see *Out of This World*, 1950). Copyrighted unpublished March 1955.

VERSE

I'm not depressed because I can't forget
The words you murmured on the night we met
Or that not so long ago
I inspired your Romeo.
To take the trouble I should never try
To stop your recent indecent wandering eye.
No, I'm far too worldly-wise
But do you realize—

REFRAIN

We shall never be younger,
Father Time goes gaily ticking along.
We shall never be younger,
Soon the spring will tire of singing her song.
The bee needs the flower,
The flower the bee,
Just as I need my darling
And my darling might even need me.
So why let love die of hunger?
We shall never be younger
Than we are today.

A WOMAN'S CAREER

Unused. At one point during rehearsals it was to have been sung in Act II.

VERSE

SHE: The female of the species,
Though supposed to be more frail,
Can aspire to fame
With as sure an aim
As her rival, the male.
HE: But the female of the species,
Though success from her may ooze,
Has a weakness bad
That she always has had
And, alas, never, never will lose.

REFRAIN 1

SHE: A woman's career, ev'rybody agrees,
Can equal the best with the greatest of ease.
HE: She can vanquish the earth, she can conquer the seas,

Can milady match mi-laddie? Yes, she can!
SHE: She can vie with the masters of science and art,
In the merry U.N. she can even take part,
HE: But her life is a failure, at least in her heart,
If she can't hold her man,
BOTH: If she can't hold her man.

REFRAIN 2

SHE: She can make such a fortune she reaches the top,
With a house in Palm Beach and a box at the Op.
HE: But she knows well she's only a fash'nable flop
If she can't, if she can't hold her man.
SHE: She can act on the screen and be starred in big lights,
She can take home an Oscar to Hollywood Heights,
HE: But to live with an Oscar won't liven her nights
If she can't hold her man,
BOTH: If she can't hold her man.

WHAT DOES YOUR SERVANT DREAM ABOUT?

Unused. Another number intended for Act II.

VERSE 1

ALL: What does your servant dream about
The whole day long?
What does your servant dream about
The whole day long?
LACKEYS: Wine, women and song,
CURTIS: Wine, men and song,
ALL: That's what your servant dreams about
The whole day long.

VERSE 2

ALL: What does your servant dream about
The whole night through?
What does your servant dream about
The whole night through?
LACKEYS: Dirt, garbage and you,
CURTIS: Dirt, slop and you,
ALL: Pew!
That's what your servant dreams about
The whole night through.

REFRAIN

ALL: So no wonder that your servant
Has a cockeyed point of view
For he (she) dreams all day
Of ev'rything gay
But he (she) dreams the whole night through
LACKEYS: Of dirt, garbage and you,
CURTIS: Dirt, slop and you,
ALL: Pew!
That's what your servant dreams about
The whole night through.

I'M AFRAID, SWEETHEART, I LOVE YOU

Unused. Not the same song as "I'm Afraid I Love You" (see *Mexican Hayride*, 1944). Published in *The Unpublished Cole Porter.*

I'm afraid, sweetheart, I love you,
I'm afraid that's what is wrong,
I'm afraid, sweetheart, that of you
I'm doomed to dream away
Ev'ry day
Long.
When you smile, life's a rollicking melody,
When you frown, then the music goes blue,
I'm afraid, sweetheart, I love you,
I'm even afraid you love me too.

IF EVER MARRIED I'M

Unused. Intended for Bianca (Lisa Kirk). Dropped during rehearsals.

If ever married I'm,
And the wedding bells no longer gaily chime,
Will the honeymoon be humdrum
Or will I quick to the heavens climb?
If ever married I'm.

If ever married I'm,
Will I vegetate in grandeur or in grime?

Will my groom become a pauper
Or will he buy out Guggenheim?
If ever married I'm.

If ever married I'm,
Will my husband give me happiness sublime
Or will he bore me till I brain 'im
And make the cover of *Life* and *Time?*
If ever married I'm.

At one point before September 1948 the running order of *Kiss Me, Kate* was as follows:

Act I

"Wunderbar"
"It Was Great Fun the First Time"
"Why Can't You Behave?"
"Another Op'nin', Another Show"
"We Shall Never Be Younger"
"We Open in Venice"
"If Ever Married I'm"
"I Sing of Love"
"I've Come to Wive It Wealthily in Padua"
"Were Thine That Special Face"
"Tom, Dick or Harry"
"Kiss Me, Kate"

Act II

"Too Darn Hot"
"What Does Your Servant Dream About?"
"Always True to You in My Fashion"
"Where Is The Life That Late I Led?"
"A Woman's Career"
"Brush Up Your Shakespeare"
"I Am Ashamed That Women Are So Simple"
"Finale"

"So in Love," "I Hate Men," and "Bianca" were not yet part of the score. "So in Love" appears to have been composed as late as September 1948.

MISCELLANEOUS

1940s

SO LONG, SAMOA

This number was completed on February 25, 1940, aboard the *Kungsholm* during a cruise to the South Seas. Alternate title: "Samoa, Samoa." The same music was later used for the song "Farewell, Amanda," sung in the film *Adam's Rib* (1949).

VERSE 1

Mrs. Lundbeck is in despair,
Mrs. Bunting is tearing her hair,
Mrs. Stowell is out of step.
Why, even Mrs. Browning is losing her pep.
And as for me
I'm as gloomy as can be.
Oh

REFRAIN

So long, Samoa,
Lovely land so sweet, so serene,
So long, Samoa,
I've got to go back to the old routine.
But when the next time they tell me
That my income tax is overdue
'Stead of cursing F.D.R. as befoa,
Sweet Samoa, I'll return to you.

VERSE 2

Mrs. Travers is in a fog,
Mrs. Samuels is biting her dog,
All the menfolks have gone insane.
Why, even Mr. Nolan is buying champagne.
Those girls in huts
Drove 'em all completely nuts!
Oh

GLIDE, GLIDER, GLIDE

Published April 1943. Written no later than August 1942.

VERSE

An old-fashioned bluebird was sailing the sky,
When a big fancy new bird flew silently by.
It seemed, to the bluebird, a strange sort of thing
When the rider of that glider, beside 'er, started to sing:

REFRAIN

Glide, glider, glide,
Over mountain, valley and sea,
Glide, glider, glide,
'Round the map
Till we trap
Ev'ry Jap-
Anee.
Glide, glider, glide,
Till the skies of Deutschland we roam
And when the job is done,
Then glide me, little one,
Back to home, sweet home!

SAILORS OF THE SKY

Published January 1943. Written for the Navy, which found Porter's lyric a bit too suggestive. In a telegram to him, the following line appears: "Only factor preventing our exploitation of song is Washington's frown on reference to girls in lyric."

REFRAIN

We're the Navy's aviators,
We're the sailors of the sky.
Day and night, hot or cold,
On our bright wings of gold,
Even when we're flyin' low, we're flyin' high.
With the girls we rank first-raters,
And they all cheer when we sail by,
So our foes overseas
Are the only enemies
Of the sailors of the sky.*

PATTER

So beware, you Huns,
Whether Japanese or German,
'Cause we've got guns
For exterminatin' vermin.
Beware, beware,
We warn you, beware,
Better run, you rats
From the wildcats
Of the air.

REPEAT REFRAIN

**Or:*
And we'll tell you the reason why.
As the eyes of the fleet,
We can spot 'em if they cheat
On the sailors of the sky.

THE GOLD DUSTERS SONG

Written during the Christmas holidays, 1946, for the Vassar singing group the Gold Dusters, of which a relative of Porter's was a member.

We're doin' fine
In the class of forty-nine,
For the Gold Dusters are we,
The Gold Dusters are we.
We dust off the gold
From songs new and old,
Then we melt it down into sweet harmony,
Harmony.
For the not-too-bad,
So we're told,
Not-too-hot however not-too-cold
(Guh, guh, guh) Gold Dusters are we,
Yes siree!

I GAZE IN YOUR EYES

No music survives.

I gaze in your eyes
And to my joy I find
That every fear
Which used to be near
Has gone, gone from my mind.
I gaze in your eyes
And find even when you depart
That every care
Which used to be there
Has gone, gone from my heart.
So give me your love,
The love I shall always prize,
That I may gaze
The rest of my days,
Just gaze and gaze and gaze
In your eyes.

FAREWELL, AMANDA

Published September 1949. Introduced by David Wayne in the film *Adam's Rib* (1949). It has the same music as "So Long, Samoa."

VERSE

I loved you madly, you know it well,
Which makes my story too tough to tell,
So why not forget it all,
Just leave it unsaid,
And I'll merely sing to you instead:

REFRAIN

Farewell, Amanda,
Adios, addio, adieu.
Farewell, Amanda,
It all was great fun but it's done, it's through.
Still now and then, fair Amanda,
When you're stepping on the stars above,
Please recall that wonderful night on the
veranda,
Sweet Amanda, and our love.

OUT OF THIS WORLD

1950

Tryout: Shubert Theatre, Philadelphia, November 4, 1950; Shubert Theatre, Boston, November 28, 1950. Produced by Saint Subber and Lemuel Ayers at the New Century Theatre, New York, December 21, 1950. 157 performances. Book by Dwight Taylor and Reginald Lawrence. Entire production staged by Agnes de Mille. Cast, starring Charlotte Greenwood, included William Eythe, Priscilla Gillette, William Redfield, Barbara Ashley, Janet Collins, George Jongeyans (George Gaynes), Ray Harrison, and David Burns.

PROLOGUE

Introduced by William Redfield.

Ladies and gentlemen,
This costume may strike you as odd,
But how can you wonder why
If bizarrely dressed am I,
I'm a god, I'm a god, I'm a god!
My name is Mercury,
The son of Jupiter and Juno, his wife,
And though seas are never calm
Since I shipped with Pop and Mom,
Still, at least, I lead an int'resting life.
Now as Mercury
I beg of thee,
Ev'ry now and then to chortle
At the crazy tale
We're about to unveil,
'Tis the tale of my sire
And his sudden desire
For a fair American mortal.
He's getting mighty impatient today;
Just listen to what he has to say:

I JUPITER, I REX

Written in July 1949. Copyrighted unpublished August 1949. The show, based on the Amphitryon legend, was titled *Amphitryon* at that time. Introduced by George Jongeyans and ensemble. This number is also titled "I Jupiter" or "Opening, Act I, Scene 1." "Brek-ek, co-ek" is a Yale cheer. Porter also used it in "I Want to Row on the Crew" (*Paranoia*, 1914).

JUPITER: I, Jupiter,
I, Rex,
I, Jupiter,
Am positively teeming with sex.

SINGERS: Brek, ek, co-ek, co-ex,
Brek, ek, co-ek, co-ex,
Brek, ek, co-ek, co-ek, co-ek, co-ek,
co-ek, co-ex.

JUPITER: But I, Jupiter,
I, Jove,
I, Jupiter,
Would like a brand-new dish on my
stove.
SINGERS: Brek, ek, co-ek, co-ove
Brek, ek, co-ek, co-ove,
Brek, ek, co-ek, co-ek, co-ek, co-ek,
co-ek, co-ove.

JUPITER: I'm tried of blasé goddesses
With bustin'-out-all-over bodices,
I crave a merry mortal with a sassy
air
And a baby-blue thirty-two brassière.
SINGERS: Brassière, boom!

JUPITER: I, Jupiter,
I, Rex,
I, Jupiter Rex,
Am positively teeming
SINGERS: He's positively teeming
JUPITER: Yes, positively screaming for sex.
SINGERS: Brek-ek, co-ek, co-ek, Sex!
JUPITER: Sex!
SINGERS: Brek-ek, co-ek, co-ek, Sex!
JUPITER: Sex!
JUPITER & SINGERS: Brek-ek, co-ek, co-ek, co-ek,
Co-ek, co-ek, co-ek, Sex!

JUPITER: I'm tired of blasé goddesses
With bustin'-out-all-over bodices,
I crave a pretty mortal with a merry
air
And a not-too-plump, bump-to-bump
derrière.
SINGERS: Derrière, boom!

TOGETHER: I (He) Jupiter, I (he) Rex, I (he)
Jupiter Rex,
Am (Is) positively teeming,
SINGERS: He's positively teeming
JUPITER: Yes, positively steaming with sex.
SINGERS: Brek-ek, co-ek, co-ek, Sex!
Brek-ek, co-ek, co-ek, Sex!
Brek-ek, co-ek, co-ek, Sex!
Brek-ek, co-ek, co-ek, Sex!
Brek-ek, co-ek, co-ek, Sex!
JUPITER & SINGERS: Brek-ek, co-ek, co-ek, co-ek,
Co-ek, co-ek, co-ek, Sex!

USE YOUR IMAGINATION

Published September 1950. Copyrighted unpublished August 1949. Introduced by William Redfield and Priscilla Gillette.

VERSE

What is, what is this song?
What can it be?
I wonder why
It seems to apply
To me.

REFRAIN

Use your imagination,
Just take this motto for your theme
And soon ev'ry night
Will be crowded with delight
And ev'ry day will be a dream.
Use your imagination,
You'll see such wonders if you do.
Around you there lies
Pure enchantment in disguise
And endless joys you never knew.
Behind ev'ry cloud
There's a so lovely star,
Behind ev'ry star
There's a lovelier one by far,
So use your imagination,
Just take this motto for your theme
And soon you will dance
On the road to sweet romance
And ev'ry day will be a dream.

2ND ENDING

And ev'ry day will be a perfect dream.

IN ROAD TO ATHENS SCENE

MERCURY: Use your imagination,
You've just been married, you're in love.
The big city's noise
Might disturb your bridal joys,
So try this inn I told you of.
Here, in the silent mountains,
The stars will guide you with their gleam.
If this you will try
Mighty Jupiter, on high,
Will make your honeymoon a dream.

HAIL, HAIL, HAIL

Introduced by Peggy Rea, William Redfield, and ensemble. In the Tams-Witmark piano-vocal score, this number is broken down into two segments: "Juno's Ride" and "Entrance of Juno." "Entrance of Juno" was copyrighted unpublished January 1951.

JUNO'S RIDE

ALL: Regard Mother Juno
In heaven's aerodrome,
Beware, Father Jupiter,
She's coming back home,
GIRLS: She's coming back home,
BOYS: She's coming back home,
ALL: She's coming back, coming back,
Coming back home.
She's nearing Pluto,
She's passing Pluto,
She's nearing Neptune,
She's passing Neptune,
She's nearing Uranus,
She's passing Uranus,
She's nearing Saturn,
She's passing Saturn,
She's just passed Mars,
She's rounding the Moon,
She's on the home stretch,
She'll be here soon.
Come on, Ma, come on, Ma,
Come on, Ma, come on, Ma!
MERCURY: She's down!

ENTRANCE OF JUNO

ALL: Hail to thee, Juno, our Mother,
Hail, hail to thee!
Empress of the Universe, Queen of the Heavens,
Protectress of the Earth,
Hail, hail to thee!
Juno, the Mother of all creation, that is to say,
Mother of all things living beneath the sky
And of all things living within the sea,
Hail, hail to thee!
CHORUS: Hail! Hail! Hail!
MERCURY: Hail! Hail! Hail!
CHORUS: Hail! Hail! Hail!
Hail! Hail! Hail! Hail!
Hail! Hail! Hail!
Hail! Hail! Hail! Hail!
Hail! Hail! Hail! Hail!
Hail! Hail! Hail! Hail!
Hail! Hail! Hail! Hail! Hail!

I GOT BEAUTY

Introduced by Charlotte Greenwood and ensemble. Copyrighted unpublished January 1951.

VERSE

JUNO: Me and he,
Jupiter,
ENSEMBLE: Jupiter!
JUNO: Me and he,
Your dad!
ENSEMBLE: Da-da-da-dad!
JUNO: Me and he,
Jupiter,
ENSEMBLE: Jupiter!
JUNO: Were not doin' so bad,
ENSEMBLE: Brek-ek co-ek co-ad,
Brek-ek co-ek co-ad,
Brek-ek co-ek co-ek co-ek co-ek co-ek co-ad.
JUNO: But now your daddy, Jupiter,
ENSEMBLE: Jupiter;
JUNO: For some American siren is hot,
ENSEMBLE: Too darn hot!
JUNO: And so I say,
"Jupiter,
ENSEMBLE: "Jupiter,
JUNO: What has she got
ENSEMBLE: What has she got
JUNO: What has she got
ENSEMBLE: What has she got
JUNO: What has she got
ENSEMBLE: What has she got
JUNO: That I ain't got?"

REFRAIN 1

JUNO: I got beauty,
I got grace,
I got figger,
I got face,
I got glamour,
I got flash,
I got plenty
Cash, cash, cash.
I got breeding,
Take one look,
I can make a bed,
I can cook,
I got hoopla,
Oui, oui, oui!
I got ev'rything
'Cept my he.

TRIO 1

JUNO: So I gotta get, gotta get, gotta get back my he,
Yes, I gotta get, gotta get, gotta get back my he,
So just giddy-ap, giddy-ap, giddy-ap, haw and gee,
'Cause I gotta get, gotta get, gotta get back my he.

REFRAIN 2

ENSEMBLE: She got beauty,
She got grace,
She got figger,
She got face,
She got glamour,
She got flash,
She got plenty
Cash, cash, cash.
She got breeding,
Take one look,
She can make a bed,
She can cook,
She got hoopla,
Oui, oui, oui!
JUNO: I got ev'rything
'Cept my he.

TRIO 2

ENSEMBLE: So she gotta get, gotta get, gotta get back her he,
Yes, she gotta get, gotta get, gotta get back her he,
So just giddy-ap, giddy-ap, giddy-ap, haw and gee,
'Cause she gotta get, gotta get, gotta get, gotta get,
Gotta get, gotta get, gotta get, gotta get,
Gotta get, gotta get, gotta get, gotta get,
Gotta get, gotta get, gotta get, back her
He!

MAIDEN FAIR

Introduced by ensemble.

VERSION 1

CHLOE: Maiden fair, maiden fair,
Best beware, best beware,

Keep thy charms well out of sight,
Lock thee in thy chamber tight,
For this is Midsummer Night,
Jupiter is coming down,
Jupiter is coming,
GIRLS: Jupiter is coming,
ALL: Jupiter is coming down.
SOPRANOS: Beware,
ALTOS: Beware,
SOPRANOS: Beware,
ALTOS: Beware,
CHLOE: And lock thee tonight
In thy chamber tight.
SOPRANOS: Beware,
ALTOS: Beware,
SOPRANOS: Beware,
ALTOS: Beware,
CHLOE: For Jupiter is coming,
GIRLS: Jupiter is coming,
CHLOE: Jupiter is coming down,
GIRLS: Jupiter is coming down,
ALL: Boo!

VERSION 2

NICKY: Maidens fair, drop that frown,
Jupiter may be comin' down,
But thank your lucky stars,
I say,
That you don't live in the
U.S.A.,
Where, month by month and day
by day,
Taxes are a-goin' up, up,
Taxes are a-goin',
CHLOE & GIRLS: Taxes are a-goin',
ALL: Taxes are a-goin' up.
CHLOE & GIRLS: Thank heaven,
NICKY: Thank heaven,
CHLOE & GIRLS: Thank heaven,
NICKY: Thank heaven
That we are far away
From the U.S.A.,
CHLOE & GIRLS: For there,
NICKY: For there,
CHLOE & GIRLS: They say
NICKY: They say
That, on accounta taxes,
Nobody relaxes,
CHLOE & GIRLS: Nobody relaxes, night or day.
NICKY: Thank heaven I'm so far away.
ALL: Wow!

WHERE, OH WHERE?

Published September 1950. Copyrighted unpublished August 1949. The second refrain was not sung in the show. Introduced by Barbara Ashley and ensemble.

VERSE

I often ask
Because I feel
I've ev'ry right to ask,
"Will time take on the task
To reveal,
Yes or no,
My beau
Ideal?"
For even though,
When I'm abed,
I dream he holds me tight,
Awake, I never light
On the man
I plan
One day to wed.

REFRAIN 1

Where, oh where
Is that combination so rare,
A cute knight in armor,
Completely a charmer
Who'd still be a millionaire?
Where, oh where
Is that combination so rare,
A youth who is able
To wrap me in sable
Who'd still be a love affair?
I could accept a cottage small
By a roaring waterfall,
Yet I'd much prefer a castle cool
By a marble swimming pool.
But where, oh where
Is that combination so rare,
A highly admissible, kissable boy
To fill me with, practic'lly kill me with joy
Who'd still be a millionaire?
Tell me where,
Oh where,
Oh where.

REFRAIN 2

Where, oh where
Is that combination so rare,
A swain even sweller
Than John Rockefeller
Who'd still be a love affair?
Where, oh where

Is that combination so rare,
A God's-gift-to-women,
With passion a-brimmin'
Who'd still be a millionaire?
If I should own a castle cool
By a marble swimming pool,
I might often miss that cottage small
By a roaring waterfall.
So where, oh where
Is that combination so rare,
A tip-top tycoon, silver-spoon sort of egg,
Who's batty for dresses by Hattie Carneg,
Who'd still be a love affair?
Tell me where,
Oh where,
Oh where.

I AM LOVED

Published September 1950. Copyrighted unpublished August 1949. Introduced by Priscilla Gillette.

VERSE

Yesterday was a dull day,
Yesterday was a gray day,
But, oh, today,
Today is a gay day.
You ask me, darling, why?
And I answer:

REFRAIN

I am loved,
I am loved
By the one I love in ev'ry way.
I am loved,
Absolutely loved,
What a wonderful thing to be able to say.
I'm adored,
I'm adored
By the one who first led my heart astray.
I'm adored,
Absolutely adored,
What a wonderful thing to be able to say.
So ring out the bells
And let the trumpets blow
And beat on the drums,
For now I know, I know
I am loved,
I am loved,
What a wonderful thing,
What a glorious thing,
What a beautiful thing to be able to say.

THEY COULDN'T COMPARE TO YOU

Copyrighted unpublished January 1951. Introduced by William Redfield and ensemble.

VERSE

MERCURY: Oh, what a bevy of beauties,
Oh, what a school of fish,
Oh, what a covey of cuties,
Oh, what a dish delish!
I've known but litters of minxes,
All of 'em fun for a while,
Yet now, for the nonce, what methinks is,
You've got 'em
GIRLS: We've got 'em
ALL: Beat a mile.

REFRAIN 1

MERCURY: They couldn't compare to you,
They couldn't compare to you,
Although I've played
Many, many a maid,
They couldn't compare to you.
I've thoroughly pitched the woo,
From the heights of Valhalla to Kalamazoo,
And though they all
Had a lot on the ball,
They couldn't compare to you.
Of ladies fair,
I've loved more than my share,
And strange but true,
I hereby declare,
From tiptoe to hair,
They could not compare
To you.

PATTER

MERCURY: After playing the local sirens
Who resided in my environs,
I decided to learn the art of Cupid's trickery,
So, at once, I started cruising,
Found the Muses so amusing
That I even got a kick outa Terpsichore.
After her, I met Calypso,
Who was definitely a dipso,
Then I fled to big Brünnhilde, she was German.
After snitching Eve from Adam,

I attended *Call Me Madam*
And shortly began to nestle Essel
Merman.
I admired the silken body
Of the chic Scheherazade,
Then of Lady Godiva I became the
lord.
After that I staged an orgy
For some friends o' Lucretia Borgie,
And ended up at the Stork with Fanny
Ward.
After having had a party
With Phoenicia's goddess Astarte,
Well, I raised a bit of hell with
Penelope.
After quieting all my urgin's
For several Vestal Virgins,
I put on a strip for Gypsy Rose Lee.
Though I liked the Queen of Sheba,
She was mentally an amoeba.
As for Beatrice d'Este,
She was a pest and far too chesty.
As for the passionate wife of Nero,
My reaction was frankly zero.
As for that sorceress known as Circe,
She was so hot I hollered for mercy!

GIRLS: So hot he hollered for mercy!

MERCURY: There was Galatea,
And mean Medea,
And Sappho, one of the best.
There was Nefertiti,
A perfect sweetie,
And gay Mae West.
I was a helluva fella
With Cinderella
And Isabella of Spain.
And I used to caress
Both Lola Montez
And that damn Calamity Jane.
When betwixt Nell Gwyn
And Anne Boleyn
I was forced to make my choice,
I became so confused
I was even amused
And abused by Peggy Joyce.
There was Mélisande,
A platinum blonde
(How I loved to ruffle her locks).
There was bright Aurora,
Then Pandora,
Who let me open her box!

REFRAIN 2

GIRLS: They couldn't compare to us,
MERCURY: They couldn't compare to you,
GIRLS: Although he's played
Many, many a maid,
MERCURY: They couldn't compare to you.
I've thoroughly pitched the woo,
From Galli-pippo-lippy to Tippecanoe.
GIRLS: And though they all
Had a lot on the ball,
MERCURY: They couldn't compare to you.
Of ladies fair,
I've loved more than my share,
GIRLS: And strange but true,
MERCURY: I hereby declare,
From tiptoe to hair,
GIRLS: From hep cat to square,
MERCURY: From dressed-up to bare,
They could not compare,
To you.

WHAT DO YOU THINK ABOUT MEN?

Copyrighted unpublished May 1955. Introduced by Charlotte Greenwood, Priscilla Gillette, and Barbara Ashley.

VERSE

HELEN & JUNO: What do you think about men?
CHLOE: What do I think about men?
Oh, men are dreamy, men are
sweet,
They simply knock me off my
feet,
They're so enchanting, so much
fun,
And I just can't wait until I
marry one—
That's what I think about men.
HELEN & JUNO: That's what you think about
men.
CHLOE & JUNO: What do you think about men?
HELEN: What do I think about men?
Oh, men are only naughty boys
And we to them are merely toys,
They're always up to some new
prank
And I know of one that Mama'd
love to spank—
That's what I think about men.
CHLOE & JUNO: That's what you think about
men.
HELEN & CHLOE: What do you think about men?
JUNO: What do I think about men?
Oh, men are just a pair of pants,
They're always after fresh
romance,

In search of fun they run about
And they don't come home until they're all run out—
That's what I think about men.
HELEN & CHLOE: That's what you think about men.

REFRAIN 1

ALL: We are absolutely certain
As to what we think of men,
But when night doth draw her curtain
And the hour approacheth ten,
When the moon is o'er the mountain
And there's mischief in the glen,
No matter what we think about men,
We think about men.

REFRAIN 2

ALL: When the moon is o'er the mountain
And there's mischief in the glen,
No matter what we think about men,
We think about men,
Men, men, men, men, men, men,
Men, men, men, men, men,
JUNO: We think about men.

I SLEEP EASIER NOW

Copyrighted unpublished January 1951. This number was added to the show for Charlotte Greenwood during the pre-Broadway tryout. It is dated November 20, 1950.

VERSE

Poets always speak of youth
With such admiration,
But we all must face the truth,
Age has many a compensation.

REFRAIN 1

When I was younger,
When I was younger,
For night life I used to hunger,
I sleep easier now.
When I was cuter,
When I was cuter,
Each night meant another suitor,
I sleep easier now.
In the olden days at ten p.m.
I'd be neckin' in a hack,
But this evening when it's ten p.m.
You will find me hittin' the sack.
When I was snappier,
When I was snappier,
I made lotsa boy friends happier;
I sleep easier now,
I sleep easier now.

REFRAIN 2

When I was greener,
When I was greener,
For late parties I was keener,
I sleep easier now.
When I was smaller,
When I was smaller,
I sure entertained a caller,
I sleep easier now.
In the olden days at ten p.m.
I'd be prancin' ev'ryplace,
But this evening when it's ten p.m.
I'll be puttin' grease on my face.
When I was prettier,
When I was prettier,
In bed I did not read Whittier,
I sleep easier now,
I sleep easier now.

REFRAIN 3

When I was thrilling,
When I was thrilling,
I said "no" but I was willing,
I sleep easier now.
When I was hopin',
When I was hopin',
I left all the doors wide open,
I sleep easier now.
In the olden days at ten p.m.
I'd be at some huge affair,
But this evening when it's ten p.m.
There'll be bobby pins in my hair.
When I was dreamier,
When I was dreamier,
I supped with an old French premier,
I sleep easier now,
I sleep easier now.

REFRAIN 4

When I was speedy,
When I was speedy,
Was I naughty? Yes indeedy,
I sleep easier now.
When I was nattier,
When I was nattier,
My girl friends were all much cattier,
I sleep easier now.

In the olden days at ten p.m.
I'd be leaping like the frogs,
But this evening when it's ten p.m.
I'll be up there, coolin' my dogs.
When I was racier,
When I was racier,
The nightgowns I wore were lacier,
I sleep easier now,
I sleep easier now.

CLIMB UP THE MOUNTAIN

Published November 1950. Introduced by Charlotte Greenwood, David Burns, and ensemble. Its original title was "Lay Your Burden Down."

REFRAIN 1

Climb up the mountain,
Climb up the mountain,
Climb up the mountain
And lay your burden down.
Yes, yes, yes.
Here where the gods receive,
You'd think that each night was New Year's Eve.
Oh, climb up the mountain
And lay your burden,
Lay your burden
Down,
Lay it down.

INTRODUCTION

JUNO: Stop
Whoe'er ye be,
Stop, look and listen to me!

VERSE

JUNO: I've got an invite for everyone,
SINGERS: Climb up the mountain.
JUNO: If you've a hanker to have some fun,
SINGERS: Climb up the mountain.
JUNO: 'Stead of beginnin' to beef an' bawl,
'Stead of frequentin' the wailin' wall,
On gay Mount Olympus just pay a call,
SINGERS: Climb up the mountain.

REFRAIN 2

JUNO: Climb up the mountain,
Climb up the mountain,
Climb up the mountain
And lay your burden down.
SINGERS: Yes, yes, yes.
JUNO: Here in this lovely land,
Cupie and whoopee go hand in hand.
Oh, climb up the mountain
And lay your burden down.
SINGERS: Yes, yes, yes.
JUNO: Here's where a husband thrives,
How can you two-time a thousand
wives?
Oh, climb up the mountain
And lay your burden,
Lay your burden
Down,
ALL: Lay it, lay it, lay it
Down.

REFRAIN 3

SINGERS: Climb up the mountain,
Climb up the mountain,
Climb up the mountain
And lay your burden down.
Yes, yes, yes.
JUNO: Here if he'd stay a while.
Old John L. Lewis might even smile.*
SINGERS: Oh, climb up the mountain
And lay your burden down.
Yes, yes, yes.
JUNO: Here when we try to please,
Falsies are unknown necessities.
ALL: Oh, climb up the mountain
And lay your burden,
Lay your burden
Down,
Lay it, lay it, lay it,
Lay it, lay it, lay it, lay it
Down.

NO LOVER

Published September 1950. Copyrighted unpublished August 1949. Introduced by Priscilla Gillette. The original title was "No Lover for Me." The phrase "out of this world" occurs in this lyric.

REFRAIN 1

No lover,
No lover for me,
My husband
Suits me to a T.
No lover,

**Or:*
Even Ed Sullivan'd crack a smile.

No fiddle-dee-dee,
My husband
Is but heavenly.
Since the moment his kisses
Upon me were hurled,
It's been all hits, no misses,
For he's just out of this world.
Yes, my husband
Suits me to a T.
So no, no, no,
No, no, no, no, no,
No
Lover
For me.

VERSE

So many wives I meet today
Complain because their husbands won't play,
So many wives, to catch romance,
Rush off to Paris,
But not for dresses,
But for caresses,
Made in France.
Let them live their lives,
I'm the most contented of wives.

REFRAIN 2

No lover,
No lover for me,
My husband
Suits me to a T.
No lover,
No fiddle-dee-dee,
My husband
Is but heavenly.
There is something about him,
With glamour so glossed,
That each moment without him,
Why, it's just paradise lost.
Yes, my husband
Suits me to a T.
So no, no, no,
No, no, no, no, no,
No
Lover
For me.

CHERRY PIES OUGHT TO BE YOU

Published October 1950. Introduced by William Redfield, Barbara Ashley, Charlotte Greenwood, and David Burns. Not all of the Mercury-Chloe refrains were sung in the show.

VERSE

MERCURY: Oh, by Jove and by Jehovah,
You have set my heart aflame.
CHLOE: And to you, young Casanova,
My reactions are the same.
MERCURY: I would sing you tender verses
But the flair, alas, I lack.
CHLOE: Oh, go on, try
To versify
And I'll versify back.

REFRAIN 1

MERCURY: Cherry pies ought to be you,
CHLOE: Autumn skies ought to be you,
MERCURY: Mister Pulitzer's prize ought to be you,
CHLOE: Romeo in disguise ought to be you.
MERCURY: Columbine ought to be you,
CHLOE: Sparkling wine ought to be you,
MERCURY: All of Beethoven's nine ought to be you,
CHLOE: Ev'ry Will Shakespeare line ought to be you.
MERCURY: You are so enticing, I'm starting to shake,
CHLOE: You are just the icing to put on my cake.
MERCURY: To continue,
Whistler's ma ought to be you,
CHLOE: Elliott's pa ought to be you,
MERCURY: Ev'rything hip-hoorah ought to be you.
CHLOE: Ought to be you,
MERCURY: Ought to be you,
CHLOE: Ought to be you,
MERCURY: Ought to be you,
CHLOE: Ought to be you,
MERCURY: Ought to be you,
CHLOE: Ought to be you,
BOTH: Ought to be
You!

REFRAIN 2

CHLOE: French perfumes ought to be you,
MERCURY: Texas booms ought to be you,
CHLOE: Early Egyptian tombs ought to be you,
MERCURY: Super Chief drawing rooms ought to be you.
CHLOE: Hot Don Juan ought to be you,
MERCURY: Rita Khan ought to be you,
CHLOE: Cupid with nothing on ought to be you,
MERCURY: Leda without her swan ought to be you.
CHLOE: You may come a cropper, you're losing your breath,

MERCURY: Were I not so proper, I'd squeeze you to death.
CHLOE: To continue,
Cary's chin ought to be you,
MERCURY: Hepburn's grin ought to be you,
CHLOE: Ev'rything sure to win ought to be you.
MERCURY: Ought to be you,
CHLOE: Ought to be you,
MERCURY: Ought to be you,
CHLOE: Ought to be you,
MERCURY: Ought to be you,
CHLOE: Ought to be you,
MERCURY: Ought to be you,
BOTH: Ought to be
You!

REFRAIN 3

CHLOE: 'Rabian nights ought to be you,
MERCURY: Brooklyn Heights ought to be you,
CHLOE: Joe DiMaggio in lights ought to be you,
MERCURY: Garbo in Grable's tights ought to be you.
CHLOE: Bergen's doll ought to be you,
MERCURY: Parsons Loll ought to be you,
CHLOE: India's Taj Mahal ought to be you,
MERCURY: Fibber McGee's pet moll ought to be you.
CHLOE: You have so much talent, you should be in shows,
MERCURY: Were I not so gallant, I'd rip off your clo'es.
CHLOE: To continue,
Heaven's blue ought to be you,
MERCURY: Heaven too ought to be you,
CHLOE: Ev'rything super-do ought to be you.
MERCURY: Ought to be you,
CHLOE: Ought to be you,
MERCURY: Ought to be you,
CHLOE: Ought to be you,
MERCURY: Ought to be you,
CHLOE: Ought to be you,
MERCURY: Ought to be you,
BOTH: Ought to be
You!

REFRAIN 4

MERCURY: Asphodels ought to be you,
CHLOE: Orson Welles ought to be you,
MERCURY: Ankles like Kit Cornell's ought to be you,
CHLOE: Towels from Ritz hotels ought to be you.
MERCURY: Sweet Snow White ought to be you,
CHLOE: Ambrose Light ought to be you,
MERCURY: Eleanor, wrong or right, ought to be you,
CHLOE: Errol Flynn, loose or tight, ought to be you.
MERCURY: You are so exciting, I can't even laugh,
CHLOE: If you're fond of biting, I'll bite you in half.
MERCURY: To continue,
Truman's Bess ought to be you,
CHLOE: His success ought to be you,
MERCURY: All except Truman's press ought to be you.
CHLOE: Ought to be you,
MERCURY: Ought to be you,
CHLOE: Ought to be you,
MERCURY: Ought to be you,
CHLOE: Ought to be you,
MERCURY: Ought to be you,
CHLOE: Ought to be you,
BOTH: Ought to be
You!

REPRISE 1

NIKI: Shooting pains ought to be you,
JUNO: Addled brains ought to be you,
NIKI: Florida, when it rains, ought to be you,
JUNO: Pinchers in subway trains ought to be you.
NIKI: Withered grass ought to be you,
JUNO: Lethal gas ought to be you,
NIKI: Sour old applesass ought to be you,
JUNO: Gabby old Balaam's ass ought to be you.
NIKI: You, you look so fearful,
You give me de joiks.
JUNO: Kid, if you're not keerful,
I'll give you de woiks.
NIKI: To continue,
Horsemeat steak ought to be you,
JUNO: Pickled snake ought to be you,
NIKI: Ev'rything I can't take ought to be you.
JUNO: Ought to be you,
NIKI: Ought to be you,
JUNO: Ought to be you,
NIKI: Ought to be you,
JUNO: Ought to be you,
NIKI: Ought to be you,
JUNO: Ought to be you,
BOTH: Ought to be
You!

REPRISE 2

NIKI: Corn that's tough ought to be you,
JUNO: In the rough ought to be you,
NIKI: Ev'ry old powder puff ought to be you,
JUNO: Ev'rything not enough ought to be you.
NIKI: No one's bride ought to be you,
JUNO: No one's pride ought to be you,

NIKI: Just an old chicken fried ought to be you,
JUNO: Cyanide, on the side, ought to be you.
NIKI: That's the darndest get-up
That I've seen in years.
JUNO: Kid, if you don't shet up,
I'll pull off your ears.
NIKI: To continue,
No one's girl ought to be you,
JUNO: Milton Berle ought to be you,
NIKI: Salad with castor erl ought to be you.
JUNO: Ought to be you,
NIKI: Ought to be you,
JUNO: Ought to be you,
NIKI: Ought to be you,
JUNO: Ought to be you,
NIKI: Ought to be you,
JUNO: Ought to be you,
BOTH: Ought to be
You!

HARK TO THE SONG OF THE NIGHT

Published September 1950. Introduced by George Jongeyans.

VERSE

Come out, oh, my beloved, come out.
Come out, oh, my beloved, come out.
Come out, oh, my beloved,
Myriad stars sing in the skies.
Come out, oh, my beloved,
That I may gaze in your eyes
While you hark,
Hark:

REFRAIN

Hark to the song of the night, sweetheart,
Oh, hark to the song of the night.
'Tis a soft serenade
And the words all are true,
For they tell of my love
And my longing for you,
So hark to the song of the night, sweetheart,
And yield me your infinite charms
Lest the song die away
Ere you whisper, "I swear to stay
Forevermore in your arms,
Forevermore,
Forevermore,
In your arms."

NOBODY'S CHASING ME

Published October 1950. Copyrighted unpublished August 1949. Introduced by Charlotte Greenwood and ensemble. Greenwood told many people she felt this was the show's theme song.

REFRAIN 1

The breeze is chasing the zephyr,
The moon is chasing the sea,
The bull is chasing the heifer,
But nobody's chasing me.
The cock is chasing the chicken,
The pewee, some wee pewee,
The cat is taking a lickin',
But nobody's taking me.
Nobody wants to own me,
And I object.
Nobody wants to phone me,
Even collect.
The leopard's chasing the leopard,
The chimp, some champ chimpanzee,
The sheep is chasing the shepherd,
But nobody's chasing me.
Nobody,
Nobody's chasing me.

REFRAIN 2

The flood is chasing the levee,
The wolf is out on a spree,
The Ford is chasing the Chevy,
But nobody's chasing me.
The bee is chasing Hymettus,
The queen is chasing the bee,
The worm is chasing the lettuce,
But nobody's chasing me.
Each night I get the mirror
From off the shelf.
Each night I'm getting queerer,
Chasing myself.
Ravel is chasing Debussy,
The aphis chases the pea,
The gander's chasing the goosey,
But nobody's goosing me.
Nobody,
Nobody's chasing me.

REFRAIN 3

The rain's pursuing the roses,
The snow, the trim Christmas tree,
Big dough pursues Grandma Moses,
But no one's pursuing me.
While Isis chases Osiris,
And Pluto, Proserpine,

My doc is chasing my virus,
But nobody's chasing me.
I'd like to learn canasta
Yet how can I?
What wife without her masta
Can multiply?
The clams are almost a-mixin',
The hams are chasing TV,
The fox is chasing the vixen,
But nobody's vixin' me.
Nobody,
Nobody's chasing me.

REFRAIN 4

The llama's chasing the llama,
Papa is chasing Mama,
Monsieur is chasing Madame,
But nobody's chasing moi.
The dove, each moment, is bolda,
The lark sings, "Ich liebe dich,"
Tristan is chasing Isolda,
But nobody's chasing mich.
Although I may be Juno,
B'lieve it or not,
I've got a lot of you-know,
And you know what!
The snake with passion is shakin',
The pooch is chasing the flea,
The moose his love call is makin'
[*Sung with head cold*]
But dobody's baki'd be.
Dobody [*sneeze*],
Nobody's chasing me.

WE'RE ON THE ROAD TO ATHENS

This number, written for Mercury (William Redfield) and ensemble, was dropped from the show during its pre-Broadway tryout. Had it remained, it would have followed "I Got Beauty" in Act I.

VERSE

Onward, onward,
Never stopping,
Onward, onward,
Nearly dropping,
Tried one house
Which had no guest room,
We need rest
But where in hell is a rest room?

REFRAIN

We're on the road to Athens,
To look it up and down.
We've heard so much about it
That we're all goin' to town.
Our firm determination
Will never, never cease
Until we're gazing at
The glory that
Was Greece.

PATTER

Spite o' the nits,
Spite o' the gnats,
Spite o' the skunks,
Spite o' the bats,
Spite o' the flies,
Spite o' the fleas,
Spite o' the ants,
Doin' a dance
In your B.V.D.s,
Spite o' the cold,
Spite o' the heat,
Spite o' the rain,
Spite o' the sleet,
Spite o' the mud,
Spite o' the dust,
We'll scamper on,
Do a marathon
To the Parthenon
Or bust!

FROM THIS MOMENT ON

Published September 1950. Inexplicably, this song, which became the show's best-known song—a bona fide hit—was dropped during the tryout. It was sung in Philadelphia by William Eythe (Art) and Priscilla Gillette (Helen) during Act I just before "They Couldn't Compare to You." Tams-Witmark, which licenses the show, still has piano-vocal and conductor scores that include the song. It was also sung on the road in the show's finale and during curtain calls. Why was it cut? Porter told columnist Ward Morehouse on November 8, 1950, that "two of my best songs went out to help the book along" (the other was "You Don't Remind Me"). George Abbott apparently wanted "From This Moment On" out (he was brought in to help out on the direction) in order to streamline and shorten Act I. It must be noted that not a single Philadelphia critic singled it out for praise. Some people close to the production claim, off the record, that it was not sung very well. Usually, or frequently, songs from a show are not published until the show begins its road tour, but several songs, including "From This Moment On," from *Out of This World* were published at least a month before the pre-Broadway tour began. Later, of course, it became famous through numerous recordings and was finally introduced in a production in the film version of *Kiss Me, Kate* (1953) by Ann Miller and Tommy Rall.

VERSE

Now that we are close,
No more nights morose,
Now that we are one,
The beguine has just begun.
Now that we're side by side,
The future looks so gay,
Now we are alibi-ed
When we say:

REFRAIN

From this moment on,
You for me, dear,
Only two for tea, dear,
From this moment on.
From this happy day,
No more blue songs,
Only whoop-dee-doo songs,
From this moment on.
For you've got the love I need so much,
Got the skin I love to touch,
Got the arms to hold me tight,
Got the sweet lips to kiss me good night.
From this moment on,
You and I, babe,
We'll be ridin' high, babe,
Ev'ry care is gone
From this moment on.

INTERLUDE

My dear one,
My fair one,
My sunbeam,
My moonbeam,
My bluebird,
My lovebird,
My dreamboat,
My cream puff,
My ducky,
My wucky,
My poopsy,
My woopsy,
My tootsy,
My wootsy,
My cooky,
My wooky,
My piggy,
My wiggy,
My sugar,
My sweet,
No wonder we rewonder,
We rewonder,
We repeat:

REPEAT REFRAIN

YOU DON'T REMIND ME

Published October 1950. Copyrighted unpublished August 1949. Introduced in the pre-Broadway tryout by George Jongeyans and then deleted for reasons as difficult to explain or justify as the removal of "From This Moment On."

VERSE

I have tried my best sweet words to combine
To tell you all I feel,
And you must believe me, dearest mine,
That my love is entirely real,
So bear with me when I say
In my poor poetic,
Apologetic
Way:

REFRAIN

You don't remind me
Of the iris in spring,
Or of dawn on the mountain
When the bluebird starts to sing.
You don't remind me
Of the breeze on the bay,
Or of stars in the fountain
Where the silver fishes play.
To the moonglow in September
You reveal no resemblance,
Of the first snow in November
You've not even a semblance.
No, you don't remind me
Of the world around me or behind me,
For so much does my love for you blind me
That, my darling, you only remind me
Of you,
Of you,
Of you.

HUSH, HUSH, HUSH

Copyrighted unpublished August 1949. Dropped during the pre-Broadway tryout from its place late in Act I. It was sung on the road by William Redfield, Charlotte Greenwood, Barbara Ashley, and Ray Harrison.

SECTION 1

CHLOE: Hush, hush, hush, hush,
In there, a bride and groom are
dreaming,
GIRLS: In there, the light of love is gleaming,
ALL: So hush, hush, hush, hush.
GIRLS: In there, the rose of love is blooming,
CHLOE: In there, the groom his bride is
grooming,
ALL: So
ALL: Quiet!
Hush, hush, hush, hush.

SECTION 2

CHLOE: Hush, hush, hush, hush,
In there is blessed matrimony,
ONE GIRL: In there, "qui mal y pense soit honi,"
ALL: So hush, hush, hush, hush.
GIRLS: In there, the nuptial knot is tight'ning,
CHLOE: In there, the thunder meets the
lightning,
ALL: So
ALL: Quiet!
Hush, hush, hush, hush.

SECTION 3

CHLOE: Hush, hush, hush, hush,
And shall I listen at the keyhole?
GIRLS: Oh, do, do listen at the keyhole.
ALL: So hush, hush, hush, hush.
GIRLS: And is their love, each moment, tenser?
CHLOE: Oh, goodness gracious, get the censor!
ALL: But hush, hush, hush,
Hush, hush, hush,
Hush!
ALL: Quiet!

AWAY FROM IT ALL

Unused. Written for Priscilla Gillette and ensemble, it bears a great musical similarity to "You Don't Remind Me."

HELEN: Away from it all in the high
hills above
I'll explore Mother Nature with
the only one I love,
Away
SINGERS: Far away
HELEN: From it all
SINGERS: From it all
HELEN: In the high
SINGERS: In the high
HELEN: Hills above
SINGERS: Hills above
HELEN: I'll adore
SINGERS: You'll abhor
HELEN: Mother Nature
SINGERS: Mother Nature
HELEN: With the only one I love,
SINGERS: With the only one you love,
HELEN: In the hills where we're going
GIRL SINGERS: There's a cold wind a-blowing,
BOYS: There's a cold wind a-blowing.
HELEN: Little lambs will be bleating,
GIRLS: There is no central heating,
BOYS: There is no central heating.
HELEN: Busy bees will be humming,
GIRLS: There is no modern plumbing,
BOYS: There is no modern plumbing.
HELEN: And like babes we'll sleep ev'ry
night,
ALL: Till the bedbugs begin to bite,
HELEN & SINGERS: Away from it all in the high
hills above
HELEN: I'll adore
SINGERS: You'll abhor
HELEN & SINGERS: Mother Nature with the only
one
HELEN: I love.
SINGERS: You love.
HELEN: Away from it all
I can hear Nature call:
Come away
SINGERS: You'll be sorry!
HELEN: Come away,
Come afar,
SINGERS: You'll be sorry!
HELEN: Come afar,
Come away, come afar,
SINGERS: Better stay where you are,
HELEN: Come away,
SINGERS: Better stay,
HELEN: Come away,
SINGERS: Better stay,
HELEN: Come away, come away,
SINGERS: Better stay, better stay,
HELEN: Come away, come away, come
away, come away, come away,
Come away, come away,
SINGERS: Better stay, better stay
ALL: *Away!*

MIDSUMMER NIGHT

Unused. Written for William Redfield and ensemble, it was considered as a possible opening for Act II and later as a possible duet for Redfield and Barbara Ashley.

MERCURY: This is not next Sunday night,
This is not last Monday night,
This is not convention or election night,
Halloween or anti-vivisection night,
This is not the Dodgers' night,
This is not Richard Rodgers night,
This is a hum-dinger, ding-hummer night,
This is Midsummer Night.

MERCURY & SINGERS: Midsummer Night,
When lads and lassies get together,
Midsummer Night,
When love is hot no matter what the weather,
Midsummer Night,
When no one stops to question whether
MERCURY: A little ole romp is wrong or right
ALL: On Midsummer,
Midsummer,
Midsummer

ALL: This is not next Sunday night,
This is not last Monday night,
MERCURY: This is not Beethoven or Stravinsky night,
Robeson night or even Vi-vi-shinsky night,
ALL: This is not Yom Kippur night,
MERCURY: This is not Jack the Ripper night,
ALL: This is a hum-dinger, ding-hummer night,
This is Midsummer Night,
Summer Night
This is Midsummer Night.

OH, IT MUST BE FUN

Unused. Published in *The Unpublished Cole Porter.*

VERSE

Ev'ry girl I know,
Has her dashing, smashing beau,
Ev'ry girl but me,
Has her builder-uppa cup o' tea.
Ev'ry other quail,
Has her trailing, wailing male,
So I tell a tragic tale,
For I'm all alone, by no telephone.

REFRAIN

Oh, it must be fun,
When your day is done,
To be with the one,
With the one you love.
Oh, it must be great
To have a nightly date,
And linger much too late,
With the one you love.
I like to laze a lot beneath the trees,
So I know you-know-what 'bout the birds and the bees.
Therefore I repeat,
Oh, it must be sweet,
To turn on the heat,
With the one you love.

TO HELL WITH EV'RYTHING BUT US

Unused. Its verse was the germinal idea for "From This Moment On," the number which replaced it in the show. It even had the same interlude.

VERSE

SHE: From this moment on,
Ev'ry care is gone,
HE: There will only be,
Joy for you and me.
SHE: Dreaming side by side,
Forever and a day,
HE: We'll be justified if we say:

REFRAIN 1

BOTH: To hell with ev'rything but us,
To hell with ev'rything but us,
There's one exception, to be sure,
C'est l'amour, c'est l'amour, c'est l'amour!
ARTHUR: I hear that John L. Lewis*
May start another scrap,
HELEN: It may be

**Or:*
Michael Quill.

But, baby,
Do we give a rap?
BOTH: Let other people fret and fuss,
Long as you love me
The way you do,
And I know
That you know
I worship you,
To hell,
To hell,
To hell,
To hell,
To hell with ev'rything but us.

INTERLUDE

My dear one, my fair one,
My sunbeam, my moonbeam,
My bluebird, my lovebird,
My dreamboat, my cream puff,
My ducky, my wucky,
My poopsy, my woopsy,
My tootsy, my wootsy,
My cooky, my wooky,
My piggy, my wiggy,
My sugar, my sweet,
No wonder we rewonder,
We rewonder we repeat:

REFRAIN 2

BOTH: To hell with ev'rything but us,
To hell with ev'rything but us,
There's one exception, to be sure,
C'est l'amour, c'est l'amour, c'est
l'amour!
HELEN: I hear that Princess Marg'ret†
Is on another toot,
ARTHUR: It may be,
But, baby,
Do we give a hoot?
BOTH: Let other people fret and fuss,
Long as you love me
The way you do,
And I know
That you know
I worship you,
To hell,
To hell,
To hell,
To hell,
To hell with ev'rything but us.

†*Or:*
Sarah Churchill.

TONIGHT I LOVE YOU MORE

Unused. Copyrighted unpublished August 1949.

Tonight I love you more
Than ever before,
Tonight I want you more
Than ever before,
Tonight I'll fill your heart
With mem'ries to store,
For tonight I love you more,
More than ever before,
So hold me, hold me near,
For far too soon will come the dawn,
And always remember, dear,
I shall only live from now on
To love you, love you more
Than ever before,
To love you, love you more,
Even more than ever,
Than ever before.

WHY DO YOU WANTA HURT ME SO?

Listed as published September 1950 (I have never seen a published copy). It was an unused Act I number written for Charlotte Greenwood. Porter later wrote "I Sleep Easier Now" for her.

VERSE

I'm blue,
Black and blue,
And I fear, my dear, it's entirely due to you.

REFRAIN 1

Why do you wanta hurt me so?
Why do you wanta hurt me so?
You used in your arms to wrap me,
But now in the face you slap me,
Why do you wanta hurt me so?
Why do you fill my nights with gloom?
Why do you lock me in my room?
With orchids you used to bunch me,
But now in the nose you punch me,
Why do you wanta hurt me so?
Life was so merry,
In the old cemetery,
By the vault where we'd halt each night.

You'll admit you misled me,
But since Paw pulled a gun and you wed me,
You are suddenly, oh, so impolite.
Why do you wanta hurt me so?
Lover o' mine, I pine to know,
Oh, why did you ever pick me,
In the middle o' my career to kick me?
Why do you wanta hurt me so,
Daddy, baddy,
Why do you wanta hurt me so?

REFRAIN 2

Why do you wanta hurt me so?
Why do you wanta hurt me so?
You used ev'rywhere to tag me,
But now by the hair you drag me,
Why do you wanta hurt me so?
Why do you never heed my groans?
Why do you only feed me bones?
You used on your lap to rock me,
But now in the jaw you sock me,
Why do you wanta hurt me so?
Life was a fable,
In the old stinkin' stable,
When we'd play in the swaying loft.
Due to me, charming mister,
You've been dropped by the Social Register,
Still you could be a teeny-weeny bit soft.
Why do you wanta hurt me so?
Lover o' mine, I pine to know,
Oh, why did you ever pick me,
In the middle o' Kingdom Come to kick me,
Why do you wanta hurt me so?
Unky, punky,
Why do you wanta hurt me so?

REFRAIN 3

Why do you wanta hurt me so?
Why do you wanta hurt me so?
You used to be mad about me,
But now in the gout you clout me,
Why do you wanta hurt me so?
Why are you, dear, no longer couth?
Why did you pull my fav'rite tooth?
You used to, my love, relax me,
But now with an ax you whacks me,
Why do you wanta hurt me so?
Much kinder you were,
In the old-fashioned sewer,
Where we'd hide when the tide was low.
So I pray, darling Abie,
Though I gave you a two-headed baby,
That you go just an itsy-bitsy bit slow.
Why do you wanta hurt me so?
Lover o' mine, I pine to know,
Oh, why did you ever pick me,
In the middle o' my terrasse to kick me?
Why do you wanta hurt me so?
Poppa, stoppa!
Why do you wanta hurt me so?

In early versions of the script there is a reference to an Act II song for Chloe (Barbara Ashley) and chorus titled "Lock Up Your Chickens." No music survives, but in a script dated April 5, 1950, there are the following lines in Act II, Scene 6 (p. 27):

> Lock up your lambs, here comes Jupiter.
> Lock up your chickens, here comes Jove.
> Lock up your wife behind the garden wall,
> Here comes Jupiter, papa of us all!

This number was supposed to lead directly to the Midsummer Eve number, "Midsummer Night."

There is also a reference in the script, dated April 5, 1950, to a "new song for Mercury and Chloe," a song about the beauties of wedded bliss for everyone but them. No further information is known.

CAN-CAN

1953

Tryout: Shubert Theatre, Philadelphia, March 23, 1953. Produced by Cy Feuer and Ernest Martin at the Shubert Theatre, New York, May 7, 1953. 892 performances. Book and direction by Abe Burrows. Dances and musical numbers staged by Michael Kidd. Cast, starring Lilo and Peter Cookson, included Hans Conried, Gwen Verdon, and Erik Rhodes.

A complete piano-vocal score was published in December 1954. Most of the songs were written during 1952.

MAIDENS TYPICAL OF FRANCE

Opening of Act I, Scene 1. Also titled "We Are Maidens Typical of France." Introduced by ensemble.

INTRODUCTION

Monsieur President,
Monsieur President,
Monsieur President,
Monsieur President:

REFRAIN 1

We are maidens typical of France,
In a convent educated.
From the wicked clutches of romance,
We have all been segregated.
We know how to sew, we know how to knit,
We know how to read—at least a little bit,
We know how to wash, we know how to clean.
If also we know the difference between
A pair o' panties and a pair o' pants,
We are maidens typical of France.

REFRAIN 2*

We are maidens typical of France,
In a convent educated.
From the wicked clutches of romance,
We have all been segregated.
We know how to sweep, we know how to dust,
We know how to stew—a rabbit if we must,
We know how to bake, we know how to fry.
If also we know a tart is not a pie
It is because we had the lucky chance
To be maidens typical of France.

REFRAIN 3

We are maidens typical of France,
In a convent educated.
From the wicked clutches of romance,
We have all been segregated.
We're all very pure, we're all very good,
We all try to do exactly as we should,
We all go to church, we all say our prayers,
And if, when we dance, we show our derrières
It is to show that, even when we dance,
We are maidens

POLICEMEN: They are maidens
ALL: Typical of France.

*Refrain 2 was cut from the published score.

NEVER GIVE ANYTHING AWAY

Published March 1953. Copyrighted unpublished September 1952. Introduced by Lilo.

VERSE

PISTACHE: If I have succeeded in life so far,
'Tis because my mama was my guiding star.
When I was a baby upon her knee,
Mama would so often say this to me:

REFRAIN 1

Never give anything away, away, away,
'Tis very unwise,
Never give anything away, away, away,
Do not compromise,
Be economical, I say, I say, I say,
And you will do well,
Never give anything away, away, away
That you can sell.
Ev'ry night, ev'ry day,
Try to remember, ma belle,
Never give anything away, away, away
That you can sell.

REFRAIN 2

GIRLS: Never give anything away, away, away,
'Tis very unwise,
PISTACHE: Never give anything away, away, away,
Do not compromise.
Madame Du Barry used to say, to say, to say,
So histories tell,

"Never give anything away,
away, away
PISTACHE & GIRLS: That you can sell."
PISTACHE: In Versailles, she would say,
Helping some poor demoiselle,
"Never give anything away,
GIRLS: Away,
PISTACHE: Away,
GIRLS: Away,
PISTACHE: Away,
GIRLS: Away,
PISTACHE: Away
That you can sell."

C'EST MAGNIFIQUE

Published March 1953. Copyrighted unpublished September 1952. Introduced by Lilo and Peter Cookson.

VERSE 1

PISTACHE: Love is such a fantastic affair,
When it comes to call,
After taking you up in the air,
Down it lets you fall,
But be patient and soon you will find,
If you follow your heart, not your
mind,
Love is waiting there again,
To take you up in the air again.

REFRAIN

When love comes in
And takes you for a spin,
Oo-la, lala, c'est magnifi-que.
When, ev'ry night,
Your loved one holds you tight,
Oo-la, lala, c'est magnifi-que.
But when, one day,
Your loved one drifts away,
Oo-la, lala, it is so tragi-que,
But when, once more,
He whispers, "Je t'adore,"
C'est magnifi-que!

VERSE 2

ARISTIDE: When you began of love to speak,
I followed every word,
But when you called love magnifique,
I would have called it absurd,
And when you said it was often
tragique,
I would have said it was always
comique,
So, mad'moiselle, be sweet to me
And kindly do not repeat to me.

REPEAT REFRAIN

COME ALONG WITH ME

Published April 1953. Introduced by Erik Rhodes and Hans Conried.

VERSE

From down to up,
About this town,
I've drunk my cup
From up to down,
But being a connoisseur
And a great social pet,
The circle which I prefer
Is the dilettante set.
Come along, little lambkin, do
Let me show it to you.

REFRAIN 1

If you want to pass through the gilded gates
Where the bourgeois meet the sophisticates
To exchange their views and to compare their
mates,
Come along with me.
If you'd like to sup with a rich cocotte
Where the best bohemians go a lot
'Cause her wine is sparkling though her wit is
not,
Come along with me.
Come along with me, my pretty,
Let me open your eyes,
In this great big wicked city
It is folly not to be wise.
And if any night, baby, you would care
For an intellectual love affair,
I'll improve your mind if you let down your
hair,
Come along, woof, woof,
Come along, woof, woof,
Come along with me,
Woof!

REFRAIN 2

We can go to dine with an old marquise
Who delights in putting her guests at ease

By receiving only in a pink chemise,
Come along with me.
There's a prince whose home has become a
must
For the lower men of the upper crust
'Cause his high-born wife has such a low-cut
bust,
Come along with me.
When you meet these folks, my pretty mate,
You will like them a lot.
All their titles are legitimate
Tho' their children often are not.
And again I say, baby, if you'd care
For an unconventional love affair
Plus a boudoir full of fancy underwear,
Come along, woof, woof,
Come along, woof, woof,
Come along with me,
Come along!

REPRISE

Just be nice to him, baby, never fear,
He's the chic-est critic in Paris, dear.
If you want to help me have a great career,
Go along with him.
He is fond of you, though I must confess
I don't understand it, but nonetheless
If you'd see your Boris as a big success,
Go along with him.
Go along and do your duty
Like the good girl you are,
Go along with him, my beauty,
Go along and don't go too far.
Still if he should try making love, chérie,
Be as cozy with him as you can be,
You can still be technically true to me.
Go along.

HILAIRE: Woof, woof!
BORIS: Go along.
HILAIRE: Woof, woof!
BORIS: Go along with
HILAIRE: Woof!
BORIS: Go along with
HILAIRE: Woof, woof, woof, woof,
Woof, come along with me.
BORIS: C'est la vie!

LIVE AND LET LIVE

Published April 1953. Copyrighted unpublished September 1952. Introduced by Lilo.

VERSE

Since tyranny we overthrew
At the fall of the Bastille,
If you tell a Frenchman what to do
Or if you tell him what not to do
He will only give one look at you,
But the look will be nasty.
For France will always curl her lip
At those who block her way,
And to ev'ry form of censorship
The French will always say,
"Vive la liberté!"

REFRAIN

Live and let live, be and let be,
Hear and let hear, see and let see,
Sing and let sing, dance and let dance.
I like Offenbach, you do not,
So what, so what, so what?
Read and let read, write and let write,
Love and let love, bite and let bite,
Live and let live and remember this line:
"Your bus'ness is your bus'ness and my bus'ness
is mine."

REFRAIN 2

Live and let live, be and let be,
Hear and let hear, see and let see,
Drink and let drink, eat and let eat.
You like bouillabaisse, I do not,
So what, so what, so what?
Pray and let pray, slip and let slip,
Dress and let dress, strip and let strip.
Live and let live and remember this line:
"Your bus'ness is your bus'ness and my bus'ness
is mine."

REFRAIN 3*

Live and let live, be and let be,
Hear and let hear, see and let see,
Sculpt and let sculpt, paint and let paint.
I like lavender, you like blue,
J' m'en fou, j' m'en fou, j' m'en fou!
Cheer and let cheer, shoosh and let shoosh,
Pull and let pull, push and let push,
Live and let live and repeat now and then:
"Tes affair-es sont tes affair-es et mes affair-es
sont—les miennes."

*Not published.

I AM IN LOVE

Published March 1953. Copyrighted unpublished September 1952. Introduced by Peter Cookson. This number originally was intended to conclude Act I.

VERSE

Sit down, mad'moiselle,
And from laughing refrain.
Sit down, mad'moiselle,
And, I beg you, try
To listen while I
Explain.

REFRAIN

I am dejected,
I am depressed,
Yet resurrected
And sailing the crest.
Why this elation,
Mixed with deflation?
What explanation?
I am in love!
Such conflicting questions ride
Around in my brain,
Should I order cyanide
Or order champagne?
Oh, what is this sudden jolt?
I feel like a frighten'd colt
Just hit by a thunderbolt,
I am in love!
I knew the odds
Were against me before,
I had no flair
For flaming desire,
But since the gods
Gave me you to adore,
I may lose
But I refuse to fight the—fire!
So come and enlighten my days
And never depart.
You only can brighten the blaze
That burns in my heart,
For I am wildly in love with you,
And so in need of
A stampede of
Love!

IF YOU LOVED ME TRULY

Published April 1953. Includes material titled "Scene Before 'If You Loved Me Truly.'" Introduced by Hans Conried, Gwen Verdon, Phil Leeds, Robert Penn, Richard Purdy, Mary Anne Cohan, Jean Kramer, and Beverly Purvin.

CLAUDINE: I'm always happy when I am dancing,
I have no cares, I have no ills,
I feel like a bird above the hills,
When dancing, my cup of happiness fills
Right up to the brim.
BORIS: When a woman has a man, listen here,
She should think of nothing but him.
3 GIRLS: Claudine, go on a strike!
3 BOYS: You women are all alike.
CLAUDINE: I'd love to make a career of dancing,
I'd dance so well, I'd go so far,
They'd cheer me from here to Zanzibar
And in ev'ry dance hall I'd be a star,
The belle of the ball!
BORIS: When a woman has a man, her career
Should amount to nothing at all.
3 GIRLS: Go out and get your fame!
3 BOYS: You women are all the same.
2ND & 3RD GIRLS: If you could have a career, Claudine,
The world would be at your feet.
1ST GIRL: If you could have a career, Claudine,
Mon dieu, the men you could meet!
2ND GIRL: A member of the Ministère,
1ST GIRL: A South African millionaire,
3RD GIRL: Our newly elected president,
1ST GIRL: I hope he isn't impotent!
2ND GIRL: A viscount who's filthy rich,
1ST GIRL: A Rothschild, no matter which,
3RD GIRL: The Nizam of Hyderabad,
1ST GIRL: The Prince of Wales can still be had!
BORIS: Shut up, shut up!
3 GIRLS & BORIS: Shut up, yourself, you dirty pup!
2ND GIRL: The dear Duc d'Anjou
Would give you a bike built for two.
1ST GIRL: The Rajah of Mysore
Would give you a bed for three or four.
3RD GIRL: The Earl of Athlone
Would give you a bathtub of your own.
1ST GIRL: And good King Leopold
Would give you a toothpick.
CLAUDINE: Give me a toothpick?
1ST GIRL: Made of gold!
BORIS: Stop, stop this insane, this endless hullabaloo
While I explain a sculptor's point of view:

Praxiteles was a sculptor. *He* had a girl,
She didn't want to be a dancer.
Michelangelo was a sculptor. *He* had a girl,
She didn't want to be a dancer.
And I, the greatest sculptor of them all, *I* have a girl,
Does *she* want to be a dancer?
CLAUDINE: Yes is the answer!
3 GIRLS: Yes is the answer!
CLAUDINE: I want to be a dancer and kick up my heels.
BORIS: But if you're a dancer, who'll cook my meals?
CLAUDINE: I want to be a dancer and wear pretty frocks.
3 BOYS: But if you're a dancer, who'll darn his socks?
3 GIRLS: You're just as bad as he is!
3 BOYS: You're just as mad as she is!
3 GIRLS: You're just as bad!
3 BOYS: You're just as mad!
3 GIRLS: You're just as bad!
3 BOYS: You're just as mad!
CLAUDINE: But not as sad as I,
Boris, you know why.

VERSE

SHE: You don't love me, 'tis clear to see.
HE: *I* don't love *you?* You don't love *me!*
SHE: You only think of *your* life, never of *mine.*
HE: *I* only think of *my* life? What a line!
SHE: If you loved me,
HE: If *you* loved me!
SHE: If you loved me,
HE: If *you* loved me!
SHE: If you
HE: If you
SHE: If you
HE: If you
SHE: If
HE: If
SHE: If
HE: If
SHE: If
HE: If

REFRAINS 1, 2, AND 3

SHE: If you loved me truly, if you loved me truly,
Then you would not, should not, could not
So selfish be.
HE: If you loved me truly, you must, you must agree
That you would not, should not, could not
Say that to me.
SHE: (1) You freak, you fool!
(2) You pig, you pill!
(3) You scourge, you scum!
HE: (1) You molecule!
(2) You imbecile!
(3) You vacuum!
BOTH: Nonetheless, I love you, love you truly, truly,
Nonetheless, I love you, love you truly, truly.

MONTMART'

Published April 1953. Copyrighted unpublished September 1952. Introduced by ensemble. During the Philadelphia tryout it was sung by Lilo and ensemble.

VERSE

SOLO: What is the spot where you long to be?
ALL: Montmart'.
SOLO: Where do you not take your family?
ALL: Montmart'.
SOLO: But if your auntie
Wants to be a bacchante,
Where should she start?
Where do you go for fun, where do you go for play?
ALL: Montmart'.
SOLO: Where is the moon the sun, where is the night the day?
ALL: Montmart'.
SOLO: Where is it ev'ry man can
Look at a lovely can-can?
Up on Montmart'!

REFRAIN 1

Montmart', Montmart',
Where the throngs and the songs continue,
Montmart', Montmart',
Where Paree on a spree gets in you,
Montmart', Montmart',
BOYS: Where the quail never fail to win you
When they say, "Oop-la,
Where are you going, papa?"
ALL: Montmart', Montmart'!

REFRAIN 2*

Montmart', Montmart',
Where the throngs and the songs continue,

*Refrains 2 and 3 are not in the published piano-vocal score.

Montmart', Montmart',
Where Paree on a spree gets in you,
Montmart', Montmart',
GIRLS: Where the men murmur when they win you,
"I adore you, dear,
Buy me a bottle o' beer!"
ALL: Montmart', Montmart'!

REFRAIN 3

Montmart', Montmart',
Where the throngs and the songs continue,
Montmart', Montmart',
Where Paree on a spree gets in you,
Montmart', Montmart',
BOYS: Where the quail never fail to win you
When they say, "Shall we
Fiddle-dy, diddle-dy, dee?"
ALL: Montmart', Montmart'!

ALLEZ-VOUS-EN

Published March 1953. Introduced by Lilo.

VERSE

Since the moment when first
Like a rocket you burst
In my hitherto tranquil skies,
I am startled to find
I am not color blind
When I view the hue of your eyes.
Therefore please do not take me to task
If the following favor I ask:

REFRAIN

Allez-vous-en, allez-vous-en, monsieur,
Allez-vous-en, go away.
Allez-vous-en, allez-vous-en, monsieur,
I have no time for you today.
Do be a dear, just disappear, monsieur,
Bid me goodbye, do, do, do.
Allez-vous-en, please go away, monsieur,
Or I may go away with you.

NEVER, NEVER BE AN ARTIST

Opening of Act II. Completed January 1953. Copyrighted unpublished December 1953. Introduced by Hans Conried, Phil Leeds, Richard Purdy, and Pat Turner.

VERSE

Some think an artist's life could never be sad,
Some think an artist's life could only be bad.
When people ask about la vie de bohème,
What do we, what do we say to them?

REFRAIN 1

Never, never be an artist
If you think you can make one cent.
Never, never be an artist
If you've no one to pay your rent.
Never, never be an artist
If you like roast beef called "prime."
Never, never be an artist
Unless you want to have a marvelous time,
Unless you want to have a marvelous time.

PATTER 1

You can think what you please,
You can state what you please,
You can like what you please,
You can hate what you please,
You can taste what you please,
You can try what you please,
You can do ev'rything but buy what you please.
You can date what you please,
You can please what you please,
You can charm what you please,
You can tease what you please,
You can land what you please,
You can trick what you please,
You can give to or get from a chick what you please.

REFRAIN 2

Never, never be an artist
If you think you can make one cent.
Never, never be an artist
If you've no one to pay your rent.
Never, never be an artist
If a pauper's grave you fear.
Never, never be an artist
Unless you want to have a happy career,
Unless you want to have a happy career.

PATTER 2

You can wake when you please,
You can sleep when you please,
You can laugh when you please,
You can weep when you please,

You can laze when you please,
Or be spry when you please,
You can do ev'rything but die when you please.
You can wash when you please,
You can shave when you please,
Be discreet when you please,
Misbehave when you please,
You can flirt when you please,
Take a chance when you please
You can put on or take off your pants when you
please.

REFRAIN 3

Never, never be an artist
If you think you can make one cent.
Never, never be an artist
If you've no one to pay your rent.
Never, never be an artist
If you're faithful to your wife.
Never, never be an artist
Unless you want to have a wonderful life,
Unless you want to have a wonderful life,
Unless you want to have a wonderful life,
Unless you want to have a wonderful life,
Unless you want to have a wonderful life,
Unless you want to have a wonderful life,
Wonderful life!

IT'S ALL RIGHT WITH ME

Published March 1953. Completed just prior to the Philadelphia tryout. Introduced by Peter Cookson.

It's the wrong time and the wrong place,
Though your face is charming, it's the wrong
face,
It's not her face but such a charming face
That it's all right with me.
It's the wrong song in the wrong style,
Though your smile is lovely, it's the wrong smile,
It's not her smile but such a lovely smile
That it's all right with me.
You can't know how happy I am that we met,
I'm strangely attracted to you.
There's someone I'm trying so hard to forget,
Don't you want to forget someone too?
It's the wrong game with the wrong chips,
Though your lips are tempting, they're the wrong
lips,
They're not her lips but they're such tempting
lips
That if some night you're free,
Dear, it's all right,
It's all right
With me.

EV'RY MAN IS A STUPID MAN

Added to the show during the Philadelphia tryout. The lyric is dated April 16, 1953. Copyrighted unpublished December 1953. Introduced by Lilo.

VERSE

The more I see of men,
The more I respect them less,
But I understand
Why they're so in demand,
For a woman must confess,
Yes!

REFRAIN 1

Ev'ry man is a stupid man, stupid man, stupid
man,
Ev'ry man is a stupid man
Except the man you love.
Ev'ry man is an awful fool, awful fool, awful
fool,
Ev'ry man is an awful fool
Except the fool you love.
Good or bad men,
Gay or sad men,
Young or old men,
Hot or cold men,
Poor or rich men,
No matter which men,
They are all the same!
Ev'ry man is a nincompoop, nincompoop,
nincompoop,
Ev'ry man is a nincompoop
Except . . . the poop you love.

REFRAIN 2

Ev'ry man is a stupid man, stupid man, stupid
man,
Ev'ry man is a stupid man
Except the man you love.
Ev'ry man is a silly goose, silly goose, silly goose,
Ev'ry man is a silly goose
Except the goose you love.
Good or bad men,
Gay or sad men,
Young or old men,
Hot or cold men,

Poor or rich men,
No matter which men,
They are all the same!
Ev'ry man's simply terribull, terribull, terribull,
Ev'ry man's simply terribull
Except . . . the bull you love.

REFRAIN 3

Ev'ry man is a stupid man, stupid man, stupid man,
Ev'ry man is a stupid man
Except the man you love.
Ev'ry man is a crazy loon, crazy loon, crazy loon,
Ev'ry man is a crazy loon
Except the loon you love.
Good or bad men,
Gay or sad men,
Young or old men,
Hot men, cold men,
Poor or rich men,
No matter which men,
They are all the same!
Ev'ry man is a perfect ass, perfect ass, perfect ass,
Ev'ry man is a perfect ass
Except . . . the man you love.

Piano-vocal score

REFRAIN 2

Every man is ridiculous, ridiculous, ridiculous,
Every man is ridiculous
Except the louse you love.
Every man is a silly goose, silly goose, silly goose,
Every man is a silly goose
Except the goose you love.
Big or little,
Soft or brittle,
Quick or lazy,
Sane or crazy,
Thin or pudgy, even a judgy,
They are all the same.
Every man is a perfect ass, perfect ass, perfect ass,
Every man is a perfect ass
Except . . . the man you love.

I LOVE PARIS

Published March 1953. Copyrighted unpublished September 1952. Introduced by Lilo.

VERSE

Ev'ry time I look down
On this timeless town,
Whether blue or gray be her skies,
Whether loud be her cheers
Or whether soft be her tears,
More and more do I realize

REFRAIN

I love Paris in the springtime,
I love Paris in the fall,
I love Paris in the winter, when it drizzles,
I love Paris in the summer, when it sizzles,
I love Paris ev'ry moment,
Ev'ry moment of the year.
I love Paris,
Why, oh, why do I love Paris?
Because my love is near.

CAN-CAN

Published March 1953. Copyrighted unpublished September 1952. Porter biographer George Eells (*The Life That Late He Led,* 1966) said that Porter worked on this song in Peru, Indiana, while his mother was dying. She died on August 3, 1952.

VERSE

Ev'rybody,
Chic or shoddy,
Ev'rybody loves to dance
Since that big dance,
Infra-dig dance
Called the "can-can" captivated France.
Why does it kill ev'ry care?
Why is it done ev'rywhere?

REFRAIN 1

There is no trick to a can-can,
It is so simple to do,
When you once kick to a can-can,
'Twill be so easy for you.
If a lady in Iran can,
If a shady African can,
If a Jap with a slap of her fan can,
Baby, you can can-can too.
If an English Dapper Dan can,
If an Irish Callahan can,
If an Afghan in Afghanistan can,*
Baby, you can can-can too.

*Or:
If in Cannes ev'ry tan courtesan can,

REFRAIN 2

If in Deauville ev'ry swell can,
It is so simple to do,
If Debussy and Ravel can,
'Twill be so easy for you.
If the Louvre custodian can,
If the Guard Republican can,
If Van Gogh and Matisse and Cézanne can,
Baby, you can can-can too.
If a chief in the Sudan can,
If the hefty Aga Khan can,
If the camels in his caravan can,
Baby, you can can-can too.

REFRAIN 3

Takes no art to do a can-can,
It is so simple to do,
When you start to do a can-can,
'Twill be so easy for you.
If a slow Mohammedan can,
If a kilted Scottish clan can,
If in Wagner a Valkyrian can,
Baby, you can can-can too.
If a lass in Michigan can,
If an ass in Astrakhan can,
If a bass in the Saskatchewan can,
Baby, you can can-can too.

REFRAIN 4

If the waltz king Johann Strauss can,
It is so simple to do,
If his gals in *Fledermaus* can,
'Twill be so easy for you.
Lovely Duse in Milan can,
Lucien Guitry and Réjane can,
Sarah Bernhardt upon a divan can,
Baby, you can can-can too.
If a holy Hindu man can,
If a gangly Anglican can,
If in Lesbos, a pure Lesbian can,
Baby, you can can-can too.

REFRAIN 5

If an ape gargantuan can,
It is so simple to do,
If a clumsy pelican can,
'Twill be so easy for you.
If a dachshund in Berlin can,
If a tomcat in Pekin can,
If a crowded sardine in a tin can,
Baby, you can can-can too.
If a rhino with a crash can,
If a hippo with a splash can,
If an elm and an oak and an ash can,
Baby, you can can-can too.

THE LAW

Dropped during the Philadelphia tryout. Copyrighted unpublished September 1952. There were at least two versions. Originally intended for Peter Cookson, C. K. Alexander, and David Thomas, it was sung in Philadelphia by Peter Cookson and Lilo.

VERSE

ARISTIDE: Since the time, not so far,
When admitted to the bar,
I've maintained, once 'tis made,
That the law must be obeyed.
So if these girls overrode
And defied the legal code,
They have broken the law
And I can't condone this flaw.
PAUL: But to imprison them
Would be deplorable!
ARISTIDE: They have broken the law.
PRESIDENT: But each is such a gem
And so adorable!
ARISTIDE: I adore even more the law.

REFRAIN

ARISTIDE: The law is my life, the law is my wife,
For the law I was fated, to the law I am mated.
You can show me the beauty of the fairest woman you ever saw,
To the beauty of her, I would absolutely prefer
The beauty, the beauty, the beauty of the law,
For so much I love the beauty of the law.
ALL OTHERS: The law is your life, the law is your wife,
For the law you were fated,
ARISTIDE: To the law I am mated.
So a lady can write me quite the warmest letter you ever saw,
To the letter from her, I would positively prefer
The letter, the letter, the letter of the law,
For so much I love,
ALL OTHERS: So much you love

ARISTIDE: The letter of
ALL OTHERS: The letter of
ARISTIDE: The law
ALL OTHERS: The law.

Earlier version

VERSE

JUDGE: I shall always respect
Any maid who is correct
But I will have no truck
With a maid who runs amuck.
Let my colleagues lose their heads
Over far from thoroughbreds,
I am wed to my work,
Thus I never go bersérk.
CLERK: The word is bérserk, your honor,
Not bersérk.
JUDGE: I stand corrected, Mister Clerk.
OTHERS: The word is bérserk, your honor,
Not bersérk.
JUDGE: Thus I never go—bérserk.

I SHALL POSITIVELY PAY YOU NEXT MONDAY

Copyrighted unpublished October 1952. Dropped from Act I during the Philadelphia tryout, it was listed in Philadelphia programs as "I Will Positively Pay You Next Monday." Sung there by Lilo, Phil Leeds, Robert Penn, Kayton Nesbitt, and ensemble.

VERSE

1ST CREDITOR: You owe me five francs, Miss.
2ND CREDITOR: You owe me five more.
3RD CREDITOR: You owe me ten francs, Miss.
4TH CREDITOR: And me, a louis d'or.
5TH CREDITOR: You owe me for the rent, Miss.
6TH CREDITOR: You owe me for the gas.
PISTACHE: Listen to me,
Listen to me,
Listen to me, en masse.

REFRAIN 1

PISTACHE: Though I have not a single sou
In my stocking or my shoe,
I shall positively pay you next Monday.
Though not a centime I possess
In the bodice of my dress,
I shall positively pay you next Monday.
If but look you will
At my empty till,
Ev'ry eye will fill with tears,
So run along and take a stroll,
Though I have to sell my soul,
I shall positively pay you next Monday.

REFRAIN 2

BOYS: Though she has not a single bean,
m-m-m,
In her garden once so green, m-m-m,
PISTACHE: I shall positively pay you next
Monday.
BOYS: Though she has nothing left to eat,
m-m-m,
But an old petite marmite, m-m-m,
PISTACHE: I shall positively pay you next
Monday.
Though to smile I try,
From starvation, I
Am about to die, my dears.
BOYS: So go away and please behave,
Though she may be in her grave,
m-m-m,
PISTACHE: I shall positively pay you next
Monday,
Or Tuesday,
BOYS: Or Wednesday,
Or Thursday,
PISTACHE: Or one day,
BOYS: Maybe Doomsday,
PISTACHE: One of these years,
BOYS: One of these years.
6 CREDITORS: Goodbye, little one,
4 CREDITORS: Goodbye, little one,
2 CREDITORS: Do not cry, little one,
1 CREDITOR: Do not cry, little one,
BOYS: Well done, little one, well done,
little one,
PISTACHE
& BOYS: Hip, hip, hip, hooray, three cheers!

A MAN MUST HIS HONOR DEFEND

Dropped from Act II during the Philadelphia tryout, where it was sung by Hans Conried, Phil Leeds, Robert Penn, and Kayton Nesbitt.

BORIS: I've been grossly insulted by a cowardly lout
And the lout must be dealt with in a duel,
no doubt,
Though the reason for this I do not at all
comprehend.
BOYS: A man must his honor defend.

. . .

BORIS: When I think of a bullet running 'round in my brain,
In a brain so creative that my rivals complain,
'Stead of fighting Jussac, maybe I should make him my friend.
BOYS: A man must his honor defend.

BORIS: If this blood-curdling battle I am fated to lose,
It is tragic to know I'll not be able to use
All the money Claudine on my lovely casket will spend.
BOYS: A man must his honor defend.

BORIS: I can picture my fun'ral, quite the greatest in years,
All the gentlemen in frock coats, all the ladies in tears,
But I'll snub that Jussac if he has the nerve to attend.
BOYS: A man must his honor defend.

BORIS: I'm too charming to die, I'm too handsome to rot
In the family plot which my family has not,
I'm so popular here, ev'ryone loves me so!
BOYS: No, no, no, no—no, no, no, no,
If you're doomed to go, then you're doomed to go.
BORIS: Well, if this be your answer and the deed must be done,
Please produce my opponent and procure me a gun,
I am ready for action no matter what be the end,
A man must his honor defend.
BOYS: A man must his honor defend
BORIS: A man must his honor de, de, de, de, de, de, de, defend.
BOYS: Defend!

NOTHING TO DO BUT WORK

Unused.

INTRODUCTION

Work, work, work, work,
Work, work, nothing, nothing to do but work.

RONDEAU

Work, little laundress, work away,
No more pleasure and no more play.
All other girls, when work is done,
Have their frolic and have their fun.
Stop, little laundress, thinking of
Making merry and making love.
Work, work,
Nothing, nothing to do but work.

LAUNDRY SCENE

Unused.

ALL: Rub, rub, rub, rub,
Rub, rub, rub, rub,
Rub, rub, rub, tear!
1ST SOLO: Take a look at Papa's flannel underwear!
ALL: Rub, rub, rub, rub,
Rub, rub, rub, rub,
Rub, rub, rub, rip!
2ND SOLO: Who would like some bloomers for her wedding trip?
3RD SOLO: Oh, what a hanky
To wave at a Yankee!
4TH SOLO: This corset cover
Would scare any lover!
5TH SOLO: Oh, what a towel
To drape 'round a bowel!
6TH SOLO: Dieu Almighty,
What a naughty nightie!
ALL: Rub, rub, rub, rub,
Rub, rub, rub, rub,
Rub, rub, rub, scrub,
Would you like to join our little singing club?
Whether laund'ring the linen and the lingerie
Or doing a gentleman's duds,
A washerwoman's mind
Can face the daily grind
By singing, singing in the suds.
Whether laund'ring the linen and the lingerie
Or doing a gentleman's duds,
Us washerwomen get
Relief from getting wet
By singing, singing in the suds,
In the suds, in the suds,
In the slinky, stinky suds,
Tra, la, la, la, la, tra,
La, la, la, la, la, la, la, tra,
La, la, la, la, la, la, la, tra,
La,
In the suds.
Voilà!

HER HEART WAS IN HER WORK

Unused. Copyrighted unpublished September 1952.

REFRAIN 1

Little Fifi making bonnets,
In a hat shop would not stop,
Till she pleased the hat-shop owner so much
That he let her call him "Pop."
Little Fifi still makes bonnets,
And she also owns the shop.
Her heart was in her work.
Arabella sang in op'ra,
Though her voice was on the rocks,
Yet the man who backed the op'ra
Gratefully gave her bonds and stocks.
She has ceased to sing in op'ra,
But she has an op'ra box.
Her heart was in her work.
So I say to you, young lady,
As you start on your career,
When a job you find, to your boss be kind,
And I promise you, my dear,
You will soon be so successful
They will cry when you appear,
"Her heart was in her [*gesture*]!"

REFRAIN 2

Pure Cecilia lived on Saint Street
In a room too small by far,
Till she met a big dressmaker, one day,
And became his model star.
She no longer lives on Saint Street,
Now she lives on caviar.
Her heart was in her work.
Sweet Marie was just a runner
In a bank extremely swank,
But the charming old bank president thought
She deserved a higher rank.
If no more she is a runner,
'Tis because she runs the bank.
Her heart was in her work.
So I say to you, young lady,
If of marble halls you dream,
When a job you get, be the boss's pet,
And you yet may reign supreme.
How the other girls will holler,
As you enter Chez Maxim,
"Her heart was in her [*gesture*]!"

REFRAIN 3

When Babette was in the ballet and the "Dying Swan" did do,
Mister Pinch, the ballet manager, gave her a nightly rendezvous.
Since the "Dying Swan" continues, Mister Pinch is dying too.
Her heart was in her work.
In a turkish bath, Yolanda gave massage for twenty per,
Till the rich Khedive of Egypt arrived and became her customer.
Now that he has bought the bathhouse, the Khedive massages her.
Her heart was in her work.
So I say to you, young lady, if you wish for great éclat,
Follow my advice, to your boss be nice
And, in time, believe you moi,
When they see your open carriage, they will yell, "Hip, hip hurrah!
Her heart was in her [*gesture*]!"

REFRAIN 4

Widow Martin did the cleaning in a hotel quaint and prim,
Till her dear employer noticed, one night, that her form was firm and trim.
She has ceased to do the cleaning, now that she is cleaning him.
Her heart was in her work.
Leaping Lulu, in the circus, riding bareback on her hoss,
Made her boss feel, oh, so happy each night, for she never took a toss,
And today she has her baby riding bareback on her boss.
Her heart was in her work.
So I say to you, young lady, lest your chances do decrease,
To your boss you should be forever good
Till the day of your release,
When they write upon your tombstone as, at last, you rest in peace,
"Her heart was in her [*gesture*]!"

EXTRA LYRICS

Bernadette once played the organ in the Church of Cherubim,
Till a chic eccentric purchased that church just to satisfy a whim.
Bernadette still plays the organ though the church belongs to him.
Her heart was in her work.

When Clarissa was a waitress in a rest'rant, as it were,
Monsieur Dupont, her proprietor, jumped ev'ry time she called him "Sir."

Now that she is Madame Dupont, Monsieur Dupont waits on her.
Her heart was in her work.

Miss Lautrec, the secretary of a senator of note,
Was so apt at writing speeches for him that he never lost a vote.
Though his sal'ry is a small one, you should see her sable coat!
Her heart was in her work.

WHO SAID GAY PAREE?

Unused. Copyrighted unpublished September 1952. Possibly intended for Peter Cookson. Published in *The Unpublished Cole Porter.*

REFRAIN

Who spread the rumor Paris was fun?
Who had such fantasy?
Who never knew
Paris minus you?
Who said Gay Paree?
Who said, of all towns under the sun,
All lovers here should be?
Who failed to add
Paris could be sad?
Who said Gay Paree?
I thought our love, so brightly begun,
Would burn through eternity.
Who told the lie,
Love can never die?
Who said Gay Paree,
Who said Gay Paree?

WHAT A FAIR THING IS A WOMAN

Unused. Copyrighted unpublished September 1952.

VERSE

PAINTER: Oh, woman, thy name is mischief,
And, mischief, thy name is dame,
For as sweethearts or as wives
You complicate our lives,
Yet we love you all the same.

REFRAIN 1

PAINTER: What a fair thing is a woman,
What a perfect work of art,
What a rare thing is a woman,
Ev'ry pose of her, ev'ry part.
How the sweet smile of a woman
Can erase, from your face, a frown,
What a joy is she
And especially
When her husband is out of town!

REFRAIN 2

ARCHITECT: What a fair thing is a woman,
What a temple to l'Amour,
What a rare thing is a woman,
Like a Doric shrine, oh, so pure!
What a true friend is a woman,
What a dear to be near through life,
Even more so when,
Ev'ry now and then,
She permits you to see your wife!

REFRAIN 3

SCULPTOR: What a fair thing is a woman,
In her beauty and her grace,
What a rare thing is a woman,
What a Vict'ry of Samothrace!
How alluring is a woman,
When she coos and you lose your head,
You have fun galore
Till the clock strikes four,
And your wife sends her home to bed!

REFRAIN 4

POET: What a fair thing is a woman,
What a sonnet super-fine,
What a rare thing is a woman,
Each nuance of her, ev'ry line.
How enchanting is a woman
On a sweet, indiscreet weekend,
You are both carefree
And especially
When her husband's your wife's best friend.

ALTERNATE REFRAIN

MUSICIAN: What a fair thing is a woman,
What a soul-inspiring song,
What a rare thing is a woman,
So Mozartian, never wrong.
[*Last 5 lines of refrain 4*]

AM I IN LOVE?

Unused. A forerunner of the song "I Am in Love." The music does not survive.

REFRAIN

Someone fills my heart with tenderness—
Am I in love?
Someone makes me long for her (his) caress—
Am I in love?
Why is this yearning
More and more returning?
I suppose I might as well confess,
I am in love,
Oh, yes, yes, yes,
I am in love.

TO THINK THAT THIS COULD HAPPEN TO ME

Unused. Copyrighted unpublished September 1952. Written for Peter Cookson as a replacement for "Am I in Love?" Published in *The Unpublished Cole Porter.*

REFRAIN

To think that this could happen to me,
To think that this could happen to me—
I pitied the romantic rover
In search of the one four-leaf clover,
I laughed at love till, lately, I knew
The marvel of electrical you,
So now all my laughter at love is over,
To think that this could happen to me.

I DO

Unused. Copyrighted unpublished September 1952. The same music with a new lyric became "Who Wants to Be a Millionaire?" (see *High Society,* 1956).

REFRAIN 1

HE: I delight in art, do you?
SHE: I do.
HE: Do you care for music too?
SHE: I do.
HE: Tell me, are you fond of sport?
SHE: What sort?
HE: Outdoor.
SHE: A bore.
HE: Indoor?
SHE: Much more.
HE: Some night, would you like to meet
SHE: Why not?
HE: Someone who could make it sweet?
SHE: And hot?
HE: Do you feel that to someone you could be true?
SHE: I do.
HE: Me too,
BOTH: But only to you.

REFRAIN 2

SHE: I enjoy good food, do you?
HE: I do.
SHE: Chicken makes the best ragout.
HE: A stew.
SHE: Which part gives you most delight?
HE: To bite?
SHE: The neck?
HE: No touch.
SHE: The breast?
HE: Too much.
SHE: I am very shy, you know.
HE: And pure?
SHE: You may find me rather slow.
HE: But sure.
SHE: Do you think, as a sweetheart, you could be true?
HE: I do.
SHE: Me too,
BOTH: But only to you.

REFRAIN 3

HE: Animals I love, do you?
SHE: I do.
HE: Then of course you know the zoo.
SHE: I do.
HE: Did you see the chimpanzees?
SHE: With fleas.
HE: The snakes?
SHE: One glance!
HE: The wolves?
SHE: In pants.
HE: Ere we say adieu, sweet miss,
SHE: Farewell?
HE: What if I should steal a kiss?
SHE: And tell?
HE: Do you think public kissing should be taboo?
SHE: I do.
HE: Me too,
BOTH: But never with you.

REFRAIN 4

SHE: I adore to read, do you?
HE: I do.
SHE: So you like good writers too?
HE: I do.
SHE: Which gives you the greatest boost?
HE: Not Proust.
SHE: Baudelaire?
HE: I'm shocked.
SHE: Karl Marx?
HE: Gute Nacht!
SHE: I could weather any storm,
HE: You boast?
SHE: Had I you to keep me warm.
HE: As toast.
SHE: Do you think as a spouse that you could come through?
HE: I do.
SHE: Me too,
BOTH: And also with you.

WHEN LOVE COMES TO CALL

Unused. Possibly a forerunner of "C'est Magnifique." Published in *The Unpublished Cole Porter.*

I'm keeping steady—
No nonsense at all—
So I'll be ready
When love comes to call.

No wines too heady,
No highballs too tall,
'Cause I'm preparing the time
When love comes to call.

But when that certain he,
That super-sweetheart-to-be,
Says hello to me,
Hallelujah, will I give a ball.

A gypsy told me
I'm fated to fall,
And how I'll make hay that beautiful day
When, my love, you come to call.

I LIKE THE LADIES

Unused. No music survives. The lyric was found in the Music Division, Library of Congress.

REFRAIN 1

I like the ladies, yea, yea!
I like the ladies who play.
They can be tough or be tender,
I love that ole-time feminine gender.
I like with ladies to bout
Until the ladies knock me out.
Though they make my life half heaven and half Hades,
I must confess, oh, yes, yes, yes,
I like the ladies.

REFRAIN 2

I like the ladies, yea, yea,
Those gracious ladies who pay.
I find their kindness just topping
Espeshly when they take me out shopping.
A gen'rous lady I know
Has just arrived from Chicago.
She has diamonds even bigger than Jim Brady's.
Oh, yes, 'tis true, I do, do, do,
Do like the ladies.

REFRAIN 3

I like with ladies to drink
Whose furs are sable, *not* mink.
Their savoir-faire comes in handy,
Therefore they always buy the best brandy.
I like with ladies to dine
In any rest'rant foul or fine,
So I off'n confuse old mutton with old maidies.
Yet be they curved or just preserved,
I like the ladies.

REFRAIN 4

I like a lady to talk
As down the av'nue we walk.
Her talk may be pure flapdoodle
But it distracts me when curbing her poodle.
A girl named Sadie Fouquet
Received French sailors in Marseille,
Now the whole French fleet say nothing can beat Sadies.
The French navee agree with me,
They like the ladies.

There is also music—but no lyrics—for a number titled "If Only You Could Love Me."

SILK STOCKINGS

1955

Tryout: Shubert Theatre, Philadelphia, November 26, 1954; Shubert Theatre, Boston, January 4, 1955; Shubert Theatre, Detroit, February 1, 1955. Produced by Cy Feuer and Ernest Martin at the Imperial Theatre, New York, February 24, 1955. 477 performances. Book by George S. Kaufman, Leueen MacGrath, and Abe Burrows. Directed by Cy Feuer. Dances and musical numbers staged by Eugene Loring. Cast, starring Don Ameche and Hildegarde Neff, included Gretchen Wyler and Julie Newmar.

TOO BAD

Copyrighted unpublished March 1955. Introduced by Harry Lascoe, Leon Belasco, David Opatoshu, and ensemble. The opening number of Act I. When this song was integrated into the script, it was substantially shortened and altered.

VERSE

1ST RUSSIAN: Here's to our duty, to do one's duty
is just
2ND & 3RD RUSSIANS: When, brother, for the Motherland!
1ST RUSSIAN: We'll rough it in Paris if rough it in
Paris we must,
ALL: But on the other hand:

REFRAIN

ALL: Too bad we can't go back to
Moscow,
No wonder we frown,
Too bad we've got to consent
To stay in this decadent town, ai!
yai! yai!
Too bad we can't go back to
Moscow.
Lenin, pity us, do!
1ST RUSSIAN: Instead of countin' chickens on
each farm ev'rywhere,
2ND RUSSIAN: In case a party member has a
chicken to spare,
3RD RUSSIAN: You'll see us countin' chickens at
the Folies Bergère,
ALL: Too bad, ai!
Too bad, ai!
Too good to be true, hai! hai! hai!

REFRAIN 2

ALL: Too bad we can't go back to
Moscow,
No wonder we frown,
Too bad we have to be stashed
Away in this brain-unwashed town,
ai! yai! yai!
Too bad we can't go back to
Moscow.
Lenin, pity us, do!
1ST RUSSIAN: Instead of singin' sacred songs to
Stalin divine
2ND RUSSIAN: (At home, unless you sing 'em,
you're sent off to a mine)
3RD RUSSIAN: You'll hear us at the Ritz Bar
singin' "Sweet Adeline,"
ALL: Too bad, ai!
Too bad, ai!
Too good to be true, hai! hai!

REFRAIN 3

GIRLS: Too bad zey can't go back to
Moscou,
No wonder zey frown,
3 RUSSIANS: Too bad they force us to see
This Duchess of Windsory town, ai!
yai! yai!
GIRLS: Too bad zey can't go back to
Moscou.
Lenin, pity zem do!
1ST RUSSIAN: We've got to do some night work
on the next Five-Year Plan,
2ND RUSSIAN: At home we did our night work in
the old Kremlin can,
3RD RUSSIAN: But here we'll do our night work in
the Bal Tabarin.
ALL: Too bad, ai!
Too bad, ai!
Too good to be true, hai! hai!

JAIL VERSION

ALL: Too bad we can't remain in
Moscow,
Too bad we can't stay.
Goodbye, you U.S.S.R.,
We're off to the far U.S.A.
Too bad we can't remain in
Moscow.
Lenin, pardon us, do.
NINOTCHKA: I now can have big ev'ning gowns
with big open backs,
MARKOVITCH: And I can have big blondes in all
my big Cadillacs.
CANFIELD: You'll also have an item called a
big income tax.
ALL: Too bad,
Too bad,
Too good to be true!

FINALE

ALL: Too bad we couldn't stay in Moscow,
Moscow, it's goodbye.
Down with the Emma. V.D.,
And up with the Effa. B.I.
Too bad we couldn't stay in Moscow.
Lenin, pardon us, do.
NINOTCHKA: Instead of being locked up if we
mention our cares,
MARKOVITCH: Or sent to far Siberia to become
bait for bears,
CANFIELD: You'll all be sent to Wall Street to
become billionaires.
ALL: Too bad,
Too bad,
Too good to be true!

PARIS LOVES LOVERS

Published November 1954. Introduced by Don Ameche and Hildegarde Neff.

VERSE

Gaze on those glist'ning lights
Below and above,
Oh, what a night of nights
For people in love.
No city but this, my friend,
No city I know
Gives romance
Such a chance
To grow and grow.

REFRAIN 1

Paris loves lovers,
For lovers it's heaven above.
Paris tells lovers,
"Love is supreme,
Wake up your dream
And make love!"
Only in Paris one discovers,
The urge to merge with the splurge of the spring.
Paris loves lovers,
For lovers know that
Love is
Ev'ry-
Thing.

REFRAIN 2

HE: Paris
SHE: Capitalistic,
HE: Loves lovers,
SHE: Characteristic,
HE: For lovers
SHE: Sensualistic,
HE: It's heaven above.
SHE: They should be atheistic.
HE: Paris
SHE: Imperialistic,
HE: Tells lovers,
SHE: I'm pessimistic,
HE: "Love is supreme,
Wake up your dream
And make love!"
SHE: That's anti-communistic.
HE: Only in Paris
SHE: Militaristic,
HE: One discovers
SHE: You're optimistic.
HE: The urge to merge
With the splurge
Of the spring.
SHE: Bourgeois propaganda!
HE: Paris
SHE: Unrealistic,
HE: Loves lovers,
For lovers know that
Love
SHE: Is individualistic.
HE: Is ev'-
SHE: And not at all collectivistic.
HE: Ry thing.
SHE: But a low totalitarianistic thing!

STEREOPHONIC SOUND

Published April 1955. Written during January 1955 and added to the show during its pre-Broadway tour (in Boston). Introduced by Gretchen Wyler.

REFRAIN 1

Today to get the public to attend a picture show,
It's not enough to advertise a famous star they
know.
If you want to get the crowds to come around
You've got to have glorious Technicolor,
Breathtaking Cinemascope and
Stereophonic sound.
If Zanuck's latest picture were the good
old-fashioned kind,
There'd be no one in front to look at Marilyn's
behind.
If you want to hear applauding hands resound
You've got to have glorious Technicolor,

Breathtaking Cinemascope and
Stereophonic sound.
The customers don't like to see the groom
 embrace the bride
Unless her lips are scarlet and her bosom's five
 feet wide.
You've got to have glorious Technicolor,
Breathtaking Cinemascope or
Cinerama, VistaVision, Superscope or Todd-A-O
 and
Stereophonic sound,
And stereophonic sound.

REFRAIN 2

You all remember Lassie, that beloved canine
 star.
To see her wag her tail the crowds would come
 from near and far,
But at present she'd be just another hound
Unless she had glorious Technicolor,
Breathtaking Cinemascope and
Stereophonic sound.
I lately did a picture at the bottom of the sea—
I rassled with an octopus and licked an anchovee,
But the public wouldn't care if I had drowned
Unless I had glorious Technicolor,
Breathtaking Cinemascope and
Stereophonic sound.
If Ava Gardner played Godiva riding on a mare
The people wouldn't pay a cent to see her in the
 bare
Unless she had glorious Technicolor,
Cinecolor or
Warnercolor or
Pathécolor or
Eastmancolor or
Kodacolor or
Any color and
Stereophonic sound,
And stereophonic,
As an extra tonic,
Stereophonic sound.

IT'S A CHEMICAL REACTION, THAT'S ALL

Published December 1954. Introduced by Hildegarde Neff. Before the New York opening, "All of You" preceded it in the show.

When the electromagnetic of the he-male
Meets the electromagnetic of the female,
If right away she should say, "This is *the*
 male!"
It's a chemical reaction, that's all.
And though you Fascists may answer with
 hisses,
The same applies when your misters and
 misses
Hey-diddle-diddle with middle-class kisses,
It's a chemical reaction, that's all.
Say in love with you I fall
And in love with me you also fall,
Though the uninstructed faction
Calls it mutual attraction,
It's a chemical reaction, that's all.

PATTER

As in the case of invertebrates Cambrian,
As in the case of fishes Devonian,
As in the case of amphibians Permian,
As in the case of reptiles, Triassic or Jurassic,
Merely read in the book by Kamichev which has
 now become a classic.

REFRAIN

When the electromagnetic of the he-male
Meets the electromagnetic of the female,
If right away, she should say, "Come and be
 male,"
It's a chemical reaction, that's all.

ALL OF YOU

Published November 1954. Introduced by Don Ameche. In "Titles and Ideas," May 8, 1944, there is the following entry:

The eyes of you
The smile of you
The touch of you
The kiss of you

A lyric (in progress) dated August 15, 1953, shows the many changes Porter was making to perfect this song.

VERSE

After watching your appeal from ev'ry angle,
There's a big romantic deal I've got to
 wangle,
For I've fallen for a certain luscious lass
And it's not a passing fancy or a fancy pass.

REFRAIN

I love the looks of you, the lure of you,
I'd love to make a tour of you,*
The eyes, the arms, the mouth of you,
The east, west, north, and the south of you.
I'd love to gain complete control of you,
And handle even the heart and soul of you,
So love, at least, a small percent of me, do,
For I love all of you.

In reprise of refrain, line 2 is:
I'd love to make quite sure of you,

SATIN AND SILK

Published December 1954. Introduced by Gretchen Wyler. This was at least the third song written for this spot in the show.

VERSE

Since my trips have been extensive ev'rywhere
I've become a much wiser gal,
For I've noticed that expensive underwear
Can improve a gal's morale.

REFRAIN 1

It is strange how lovely lingerie
Can affect a gal's false modesty
If she's wearing silk and satin,
Satin and silk.
Though she knows that boys are evil imps
Yet she yearns to give those boys a glimpse
If she's wearing silk and satin,
Satin and silk.
You cannot expect a lady to exert that certain pull
If she's wearing cotton stockings and her bloomers are made of wool,
But a woman's woes are at an end
And she's all prepared to make a friend
If she's wearing silk and satin,
She's for pettin' and for pattin'
If she's wearing silk and satin, satin and silk.

REFRAIN 2

It is strange what undergarments do
To convert a maiden's point of view
If she's wearing silk and satin,
Satin and silk.
She will never say her pride was hurt
Should a breeze blow by and lift her skirt
If she's wearing silk and satin,
Satin and silk.
You cannot expect a debutante to show she's full o' pep
If her slip is made of cotton and her panties are made of rep,
But she feels much more self-confident
And will dine alone with any gent
If she's wearing silk and satin,
Give her broccoli au gratin,
If she's wearing silk and satin, satin and silk.

REFRAIN 3

Though a gal may have been born a prude
She can quite reverse her attitude
If she's wearing silk and satin,
Satin and silk.
With attractive trimmin's 'neath her dress,
She can shake like hell and spell success
If she's wearing silk and satin,
Satin and silk.
You cannot expect a burlesque queen to cherish further hope
If her bra is made of buckram and her G-string is made of rope,
But she knows 'cause she has traveled miles
She can always lay 'em in the aisles
If she's wearing silk and satin,
She can flatten Lord Mountbatten,
If she's wearing silk and satin, satin and silk.

WITHOUT LOVE

Published November 1954. Introduced by Hildegarde Neff.

VERSE

How little I knew
Until very lately
You altered so greatly
My point of view,
You opened my eyes
To joys which had missed me
And since you kissed me
To my surprise,
Yes, since you kissed me
I realize,
I realize—

REFRAIN

Without love, what is a woman?
A pleasure unemployed.

Without love, what is a woman?
A zero in the void.
But with love, what is a woman?
Serene contentment, the perfect wife,
For a woman to a man is just a woman,
But a man to a woman is her life.

2ND ENDING

But a man to a woman,
Yes, a man to a woman is her life.

HAIL BIBINSKI

Copyrighted unpublished March 1955. In early versions of the show's music layout, "Hail Bibinski" is not listed. This would indicate that it was written just before *Silk Stockings* began its tryout. Introduced by Henry Lascoe, Leon Belasco, David Opatoshu, and ensemble.

SECTION 1

Hail Bibinski,
Hail Bibinski,
Hail Bibinski,
Our brilliant star!
Hail Bibinski,
Hail Bibinski,
The greatest hero of the U.S.S.R.!

SECTION 2

Crowds parading,
Serenading
You, Bibinski, you, Bibinski!
When you're nearing,
All are cheering
You, Bibinski, you, you!
Swords are clanking,
Tanks are tanking,
Drums are thumping,
Trumpets trumping,
Planes are zooming,
Guns are booming,
Bells are ringing,
Ev'rybody singing:

SECTION 3

Hail Bibinski,
Hail Bibinski,
Hail Bibinski,
Our brilliant star!
Hail Bibinski,
Hail Bibinski,
The greatest hero of the U.S.S.R.!

SECTION 4

Cars you're given,
Chauffeur-driven,
You, Bibinski, you, Bibinski!
Hands you're shaking,
Speeches making,
You, Bibinski, you!
Children petting,
Medals getting,
You're our grandest
Propagandist,
You're a god-ka,
Full of vodka,
You are reckoned
Karl Marx the Second!

SECTION 5 (CODA)

Hail—Bibinski,
Hail—our brilliant star!
Hail—Bibinski,
The greatest hero of the U.S.
S.R.!
You are,
You are,
You are,
You are!
You are, you are, you are, you are, you are!
Bibinski!

AS ON THROUGH THE SEASONS WE SAIL

Published November 1954. Introduced by Don Ameche and Hildegarde Neff. Not used in the film score. First written as "If Ever We Get Out of Jail." The authors, wanting to make the show lighter, like the film *Ninotchka*, on which it was based, thought a more conventional love song was appropriate. A typed version of "Jail" has the title "When Over the Rainbow We Sail" penciled in on top of it. Later, "Jail" was contemplated as a reprise of "Sail" during Act II's penultimate scene, but it was dropped during rehearsals.

VERSE

HE: Love me, darling?
SHE: Love you, darling,
With all my soul I guarantee.
HE: Will you, darling,

Marry me, darling?
SHE: I'll marry you so willingly!
HE: Baby—

REFRAIN

I love you, oh, I do,
And this I'll prove to you
As on through the seasons we sail.
Remote from crazy crowds,
We'll float above the clouds
As on through the seasons we sail.
When we are man and wife,
I swear to make our life
A revolutionary fairy tale.
How happy we will be*
Once we are one, two or three
As on through the seasons we sail.

JOSEPHINE

Published February 1955. Introduced by Gretchen Wyler and ensemble. Originally intended as the opening to Act II. The lyric was substantially changed during rehearsals.

JOSEPHINE: Jo-o-o-o-osephine,
Commonly called Jo,
SINGERS: Josephine
JOSEPHINE: Was a throbbin' robin, poor but chic,
Born in ultry-sultry Martinique,
Yet she rose to reach the highest peak,
SINGERS: And why so?
'Cause she had
JOSEPHINE: Agitating eyes,
Titillating thighs,
Lubricating lips,
Undulating hips,
A figure simply swell,
Plus other good points as well.
ALL: Man, she was real cool and low!

JOSEPHINE: Jo-o-o-o-osephine,
Commonly called Jo,
SINGERS: Josephine
JOSEPHINE: Tripped away one day to Paris, France,
In her ye olde Creole fancy pants,
Where she rocked Napoleon at a dance
SINGERS: And why so?
'Cause she had
JOSEPHINE: Agitating eyes,
SINGERS: What eyes,
JOSEPHINE: Titillating thighs,
SINGERS: What thighs,
JOSEPHINE: Lubricating lips,
SINGERS: What lips,
JOSEPHINE: Undulating hips,
SINGERS: What hips,
JOSEPHINE: A figure simply swell
Plus other good points as well.
SINGERS: Man, she was real cool and low!

JOSEPHINE: Why did the great Napoleon fall
For her hot gavotte?
What did the doll have on the ball
Other dolls had not?
Why did the mighty man succumb
To this curvy wench?
Why did he make this little bum
SINGERS: Empress of the French?
'Cause she had
JOSEPHINE: Agitating eyes
SINGERS: Agitating eyes,
JOSEPHINE: Titillating thighs,
SINGERS: Titillating thighs,
JOSEPHINE: Lubricating lips,
SINGERS: Lubricating lips,
JOSEPHINE: Undulating hips,
SINGERS: Undulating hips,
JOSEPHINE: A figure simply swell,
SINGERS: A figure simply swell,
JOSEPHINE: Plus other good points as well.
SINGERS: Man, she was real cool and low!

SINGERS: Why did the great Napoleon fall
For her hot gavotte,
What did the doll have on the ball
Other dolls had not?
Why did the mighty man succumb,
To this curvy wench,
Why did he make this little bum,
Empress of the French?
'Cause she had
JOSEPHINE: Agitating eyes,
SINGERS: Agitating eyes,
JOSEPHINE: Titillating thighs,
SINGERS: Titillating thighs,
JOSEPHINE: Undulating hips,
SINGERS: Undulating hips,
JOSEPHINE: A figure simply swell,
SINGERS: Figure simply swell,
JOSEPHINE: Plus other good points as well.
ALL: Man, she was real cool, yes,

**In the script and the original cast record:*
How sweet our song will be
Once we're in close harmony
As on through the seasons we sail.

Last lines of reprise:
As on through the seasons
As on through the seasons we sail.

Real cool, yes, real cool,
Real cool, and low!

"War and Peace" version

Jo-o-o-o-osephine,
Lost in the deep snow,
As the winter wind blows on and on
And by wolves I may be set upon,
I'm an empress rather woebegone,
And why so?
'Cause there is snow ev'rywhere,
Snow in my hair,
Snow in my clo'es
And snow up my nose.
Poor Josephine,
Lost in the snow!

SIBERIA

Published December 1954. Introduced by Henry Lascoe, Leon Belasco, and David Opatoshu. This song troubled Porter enough for him to seek the help of his friend Noël Coward, who furnished some refrains.

REFRAIN 1

When we're sent to dear Siberia,
To Siberi-eri-a,
When it's cocktail time 'twill be so nice
Just to know you'll not have to phone for
ice.
When we meet in sweet Siberia,
Far from Bolshevik hysteria,
We'll go on a tear,
For our buddies all are there
In cheery Siberi—a.

REFRAIN 2

When we're sent to dear Siberia,
To Siberi-eri-a,
Where they say all day the sun shines bright,
And they also say that it shines all night,
The aurora borealis is
Not as heated as a palace is.
If on heat you dote
You can shoot a sable coat
In cheery Siberi—a.

REFRAIN 3

When we're sent to dear Siberia,
To Siberi-eri-a,
Where the labor laws are all so fair
That you never have unemployment there,*
When we meet in sweet Siberia
To protect us from diphtheria,
We can toast our toes
On the lady Eskimos
In cheery Siberi—a.

REFRAIN 4

When we're sent to dear Siberia,
To Siberi-eri-a,
Since the big salt mines will be so near,
We can all have salt to put in our beer,†
When we meet in sweet Siberia,
Where the snow is so superia
You can bet, all right
That your Christmas will be white
In cheery Siberi—a.

SILK STOCKINGS

Published November 1954. Introduced by Don Ameche.

VERSE

So the dream was doomed to die,
So it's over, dear,
And you sent a sweet goodbye
With a souvenir,
What a heart-warming souvenir,
For again you are there
On the smiling night
When to my delight,
I first saw you dare
Wear

REFRAIN

Silk stockings,
I touch them and find
The joys that remind
Me of you.
Silk stockings
That give me again
Your shy laughter when
They were new.
Silk stockings,

**Script and record:*
There's a most delicious bill of fare,
You must try out filet of polar bear.

†When the salt air makes us feel so fine,
It is fresh salt air from our own salt mine,

What bliss* they recall
When love promised all
Forevermore.
A pair of silk stockings,
So soft and so sheer,
The dear silk stockings
You wore.

THE RED BLUES

Copyrighted unpublished March 1955. This ensemble number was a late addition to the score, during rehearsals.

SECTION 1

1ST GROUP: We got the red blues,
We got the red blues,
We got the red blues,
We got the red blues,
We got the red blues,
We got the red blues,
We got the red, red,
Red, that's what we said,
Red blues.

SECTION 2

2ND GROUP: Why not the white blues?
1ST GROUP: No!
2ND GROUP: Why not the black blues?
1ST GROUP: No!
2ND GROUP: Why not the gray blues?
1ST GROUP: No!
2ND GROUP: Why not the brown blues?
1ST GROUP: No!
2ND GROUP: Why not the green blues?
1ST GROUP: No!
2ND GROUP: Why not the blue blues?
1ST GROUP: No!
We got the red, red,
Red, that's what we said,
Red blues.
2ND GROUP: They got the red, red,
Red, that's what we said,
Red blues.

SECTION 3

1ST GROUP: Forget the white blues,
2ND GROUP: And the yellow blues,
1ST GROUP: Forget the black blues,
2ND GROUP: And the purple blues,
1ST GROUP: Forget the gray blues,
2ND GROUP: And the silver blues,
1ST GROUP: Forget the brown blues,
2ND GROUP: And the copper blues,
1ST GROUP: Forget the green blues,
2ND GROUP: And the olive blues,
1ST GROUP: Forget the blue blues,
2ND GROUP: And the baby blues,
ALL: We got the red, red,
Red, that's what we said,
Red blues.

SECTION 4

ALL: Red blues,
Red blues,
Red blues,
Red blues,
Red blues,
Red blues,
We all got those
Not so
Hot, that's what we said,
Red blues!
Red blues!
Red blues!
Red blues!

ART

Dropped during the pre-Broadway tryout. Originally intended as the first song in Act I.

REFRAIN 1

MARKOVITCH: Art must only please the masses.
BOYS: Masses.
MARKOVITCH: Why are other classes asses?
BOYS: Asses.
MARKOVITCH: I don't know, though judging art is my biz.
Art, whatever the hell that is!
BOYS: That is, that is, that is.
MARKOVITCH: Is George Gershwin epicurean
BOYS: Curean.
MARKOVITCH: More than hotcha Khachaturian?
BOYS: Turian.
MARKOVITCH: I don't know, though I'm a cultural whiz.
Art, whatever the hell that is!
BOYS: That is, that is, that is.
MARKOVITCH: We don't allow degenerate Western pictures.
BOYS: Ah—oh—

*Ameche sings "days" instead of "bliss."

MARKOVITCH: Degenerate Western pictures give me strictures.
BOYS: Ah—oh—
MARKOVITCH: Degenerate Western art must take a beating.
BOYS: Ah—oh—
MARKOVITCH: So we don't even allow the art
Of degenerate Western eating!
BOYS: Why?
MARKOVITCH: I don't know, though I'm supposed to be smart.
Art,
Whatever the hell is art?
BOYS: Whatever the hell is art?

REFRAIN 2

MARKOVITCH: Art is only for the party.
BOYS: Party.
MARKOVITCH: When is party art too arty?
BOYS: Arty.
MARKOVITCH: I don't know, though judging art is my biz.
Art, whatever the hell that is!
BOYS: That is, that is, that is.
MARKOVITCH: Why is not "Swing Low, Sweet Chariot"
BOYS: Chariot.
MARKOVITCH: For the Russian proletariat?
BOYS: Tariat.
MARKOVITCH: I don't know, though I'm a cultural whiz.
Art, whatever the hell that is!
BOYS: That is, that is, that is.
MARKOVITCH: We don't allow degenerate Western writing.
BOYS: Ah—oh—
MARKOVITCH: Degenerate Western writing's too exciting.
BOYS: Ah—oh—
MARKOVITCH: Degenerate Western art we're all for wrecking.
BOYS: Ah—oh—
MARKOVITCH: So we don't even allow the art
Of degenerate Western necking!
BOYS: Why?
MARKOVITCH: I don't know, though I'm supposed to be smart.
Art,
BOYS: Whatever the hell,
MARKOVITCH: Art,
BOYS: Whatever the hell,
MARKOVITCH: Art, whatever the hell,
Whatever the hell,
BOYS: Whatever the hell,
MARKOVITCH: Is art?
BOYS: Ain't art?
MARKOVITCH: Is art?
BOYS: Ain't art?
ALL: Is art?

THERE'S A HOLLYWOOD THAT'S GOOD

Dropped during the pre-Broadway tryout and replaced by "Stereophonic Sound."

VERSE

You ask me about Hollywood,
I shall not lie.
You ask me about Hollywood,
And I reply:

REFRAIN 1

There's a Hollywood that's good,
There's a Hollywood that's bad.
As in any other town,
There's the up and the down,
The hyper-happy and the super-sad.
But if one becomes a queen
Of the ever-wider screen,
One can say sincerely that*
When you clear per year a million flat,
"There's a Hollywood that's good,
Darn
Good."

REFRAIN 2

There's a Hollywood that's good,
There's a Hollywood that's bad.
As in any burg perhaps
There are all breeds of chaps,
The sanely sober and the mainly mad.
But if one becomes much richer
As does Bogie with each "pitcher,"
One can say aboard one's yawl,
"Since I deduct this and Miss Bacall,
There's a Hollywood that's good,
Darn
Good."

REFRAIN 3

There's a Hollywood that's good,
There's a Hollywood that's bad.

**Alternate lines 6–8:*
But if one can share the throne
With Columbia's Harry Cohn,
One can say like Rita that

In their real synthetic pearls,
There are all kinds of girls,
The over-dressy and the under-clad.
But if one can work for Darryl
In a show in no apparel,
One can say like Miss Monroe,
Since she struck out Joe DiMaggio,†
"There's a Hollywood that's good,
Darn
Good."

REFRAIN 4

There's a Hollywood that's good,
There's a Hollywood that's bad.
As in any town of size,
There are all sorts of guys,
The can-be-frigid and the can-be-had.
But if one becomes a star
With a chauffeurized Jaguar,
One can say like Old King Clark,
Who can bench a wench in any park,
"There's a Hollywood that's good,
Good,
Darn
Good."

GIVE ME THE LAND

Unused. Originally intended as a trio for Hildegarde Neff, Don Ameche, and George Tobias late in Act II. It was replaced by a reprise of "Too Bad." Published in *The Unpublished Cole Porter.*

VERSE

I admit that France is big-time,
I admit that Spain is grand,
And I had a swell week
On a shaky but chic peak in Switzerland.
I adored the Ritz in London
And the catacombs in Rome,
But I'm just an American hick, sick for home,
sweet home.

REFRAIN 1

Give me the land
Of malted milk and honey,
Give me the land
Where life is still a joke.
Give me the land
Where ev'ryone makes money,
Give me the land
Where ev'ryone is broke.
Give me her prairies,
Give me her valleys,
Give me her mountains
And her little ole soda fountains.
Give me the land
Where ev'rything's okay,
Give me
My pet country,
Give me the U.S.A.

REFRAIN 2

Give me the land
Of dough and B. O. Plenty,
Give me the land
Of Lux and Listerine.
Give me the land
Where no one's over twenty,
Give me the land
Of bop and Bishop Sheen.
Give me Jack Benny,
Give me Bob Hope,
Give me Fred Allen
And that little ole Kil-kilgallen.
Give me the land
Where ev'rything's okay,
Give me
Publicity,
Give me the U.S.A.

REFRAIN 3

Give me the land
Of chili-burgers juicy,
Give me the land
Of frozen orange juice.
Give me the land
Where people all love Lucy,
Give me the land
Where *Time* and *Life* love Luce.
Give me my clambake,
Give me my fishball,
Give me my chowder,
And my little old room called "powder."
Give me the land
Where ev'rything's okay
Give me
Acidity,
Give me the U.S.A.

†*Alternate lines 6–9:*
But if one can be a gem
In the crown of M-G-M,
One can say, like Cyd Charisse,
Who is Tony Martin's pet release,

REFRAIN 4

Give me the land
Where rooms are overheated,
Give me the land
Where influenza grows.
Give me the land
Where men are not conceited,
Give me the land
Of lovely Billy Rose.
Give me Chicago,
Give me El Paso,
Give me Savannah
And some little ole marijuana.
Give me the land
Where ev'rything's okay.
Give me
Delinquency,
Give me the U.S.A.

REFRAIN 5

Give me the land
Where singers get big sal'ries,
Give me the land
Of Ezio and Bing.
Give me the land
Where people count their cal'ries,
Give me the land
Of chicken à la king.
Give me her forests,
Soothing and silent,
Where robins nestle
Far from little ole Georgie Jessel.
Give me the land
Where ev'rything's okay,
Give me
Variety,
Give me the U.S.A.

IF EVER WE GET OUT OF JAIL

Unused. See note for "As on Through the Seasons We Sail."

VERSE

HE: Love me, darling?
SHE: Love you, darling,
With all my soul, I guarantee.
HE: Worried, darling?
SHE: Terribly, darling.
HE: Then you must put your trust in me,
Baby—

REFRAIN

HE: I love you, oh, I do,
And this I'll prove to you
BOTH: If ever we get out of jail.
HE: Remote from crazy crowds,
We'll float above the clouds
BOTH: If ever we get out of jail.
HE: When we are man and wife,
I swear to make our life
A revolutionary fairy tale.
How happy we will be
When we are one, two or three
BOTH: If ever we get out of jail.
HE: When we are man and wife,
I swear to make our life
A revolutionary fairy tale.
How happy we will be
When we are one,
SHE: Two or three
BOTH: If ever we get out,
HE: If ever we're let out
BOTH: Of jail.

LET'S MAKE IT A NIGHT

Unused. The lyric is dated November 5, 1953.

REFRAIN 1

ALL: Let's make it a night,
Let's make it a night,
MOTHER: Let's go out
And snoop about
For ev'ry forbidden sight.
RUSSIANS: Let's make it a night
MOTHER: To end all nights,
ALL: Let's, let's, let's, let's!
Let's go out and see
Things we never saw,
MOTHER: Let's try not
To miss one spot
That's strictly against the law.
RUSSIANS: Let's make it a night
MOTHER: To end all nights,
ALL: Let's, let's, let's, let's!
RUSSIANS: We know a joint where [*whisper*]
MOTHER: No!
RUSSIANS: We know a joint where [*whisper*]
MOTHER: No!
I know a joint where [*whisper*]
RUSSIANS: So?

MOTHER: [*whisper*]
RUSSIANS: So?
So?
Can't wait to go there!
ALL: Let's make it a night,
A fabulous night,
MOTHER: Let's make it a night, tonight,
ALL: To end all nights,
Let's, let's, let's, let's,
Let's, let's, let's let's,
Let's, let's, let's, let's,
Let's make it a night!

REFRAIN 2

ALL: Let's make it a night,
A major event,
MOTHER: Let's contrive
To dig some dive
That ladies do not frequent.
RUSSIANS: Let's make it a night
MOTHER: To end all nights,
ALL: Let's, let's, let's, let's!
Let's drink in low bars
Where tragedy starts,
MOTHER: Let's go bugs
And meet nice thugs
Who cut out their sweethearts'
hearts.
RUSSIANS: Let's make it a night
MOTHER: To end all nights,
ALL: Let's, let's, let's, let's!
RUSSIANS: We know a dump where [*whisper*]
MOTHER: No!
RUSSIANS: We know a dump where [*whisper*]
MOTHER: No!
I know a dump where [*whisper*]
RUSSIANS: So?
MOTHER: [*whisper*]
RUSSIANS: So?
So?
Can't wait to go there!
ALL: Let's make it a night,
A fabulous night,
MOTHER: Let's make it a night tonight,
ALL: To end all nights,
Let's, let's, let's,.let's,
Let's, let's, let's, let's,
Let's, let's, let's, let's,
Let's make it a night!

THE PERFUME OF LOVE

Unused. Replaced by "Satin and Silk."

REFRAIN

Do you know the perfume they label "Beware"?
Do you know the "Joy" of a "Private Affair"?
Would you mind, "Beloved," were I "Indiscreet"?
Would this be "Tabu" and a "Scandal," my sweet?
Would you call me "Shocking" if I should begin
To spray "Aphrodisia" and give you "My Sin"?
Will you share the "Fragrance" that I'm fondest of?
It's known as the perfume of love.

UNDER THE DRESS

Unused. Replaced first by "The Perfume of Love" and finally by "Satin and Silk."

VERSE

In her garden, Mother Eve
Wore a fig leaf, we believe,
But as this was no success
She went out and bought a dress.
Then, the weather turning cold,
Mother Eve, so we are told,
To resist the wintry air
Bought herself some underwear.
From then on, the gals their pretty bodies
bolstered
Till a lady wasn't dressed, she was upholstered.

REFRAIN

In the olden days, a gal, Lord love 'er,
Wore a corset and a corset-cover
And of petticoats quite a few
And a pair of panties too,
For not yet had gals arranged it to wear less
Under the dress.
Later on, though, petticoats they wore 'em
And they still wore panties for decorum,
Any corset became taboo,
Yes, the corset it was through,
For the gals had now arranged it to wear less
Under the dress.
Very soon even staid maiden aunties
Had discarded their panties for scanties,
So today when scanties have departed,
If the gals all seem a bit downhearted,
Can you wonder that this be true?
They have nothing left to do,
For no more can they arrange it to wear less
Under the dress,
Under the dress,
Under the dress.

WHAT A BALL

Unused. Intended for Hildegarde Neff and ensemble. It was replaced by "The Red Blues." According to a note by Porter in "Titles and Ideas," it was based on a song sketch titled "Play the Boston" (1949).

NINOTCHKA & RUSSIANS: Oh, remember that waltz,
So delightfully schmaltz!
What a night to recall
When we whirled at the high
society ball.
NINOTCHKA: With my love
I was there,
RUSSIANS: There were half-naked girls
ev'rywhere,
NINOTCHKA: With the one
I adore,
RUSSIANS: There was champagne and
champagne galore,
NINOTCHKA: How we danced
And romanced!
RUSSIANS: How we drank
Till we stank!
NINOTCHKA & RUSSIANS: We had no troubles at all
When we whirled at the high
society ball,
What a ball, what a ball, what a ball!
Oh, remember that waltz,
So delightfully schmaltz!
What a night to recall
When we whirled at the high
society ball.

NINOTCHKA: Oh, my Steve,
I implore,
RUSSIANS: Never drank so much brandy
before!
NINOTCHKA: Can't we meet
Once again?
RUSSIANS: Vive l'amour à la Parisienne!
NINOTCHKA: Oh, the bliss
Of your kiss!
RUSSIANS: Were we oiled?
We were boiled!
NINOTCHKA & RUSSIANS: We had no troubles at all
When we whirled at the high
society ball,
What a ball, what a ball, what a ball!
We had no troubles at all
When we whirled at the high
society ball.
NINOTCHKA & GIRL SINGERS: Ah, Paree, far Paree!
RUSSIANS & BOY SINGERS: And that party where brandy and
champagne were free!
NINOTCHKA & GIRL SINGERS: What a joy to be there!
RUSSIANS & BOY SINGERS: With those beautiful half-naked
girls ev'rywhere!
NINOTCHKA & GIRL SINGERS: What a chance for romance!
RUSSIANS & BOY SINGERS: For those communist ants in your
pants, what a dance!
ALL: We (You) had no troubles at all
When we (you) whirled at the high
society ball,
What a ball, what a ball, what a
ball, what a ball,
What a ball, what a ball, what a
ball, what a ball,
What a ball, what a ball, what a
ball, what a ball, what a ball!

WHY SHOULD I TRUST YOU?

Unused. Originally intended for Act II, Scene 2, this trio was dropped in late 1954 and replaced by "Siberia," which appears to have been completed about November 8, 1954, or less than three weeks before the first public performance in Philadelphia. The numbers in the lyric (1,2,3) refer to the three Russians.

REFRAIN 1

1: I cannot trust darling Mama,
I cannot trust darling Papa,
So I ask you this, entre nous,
Why should I trust you?
2: I cannot trust Olga, my aunt,
And my uncle Boris I can't,
So I ask you this, entre nous,
Why should I trust you?
3: Though I do trust dear cousin Serge,
Since the Soviet gave him a purge,
Yet I ask you this, entre nous,
Why should I trust you?
2 & 3: But, comrade, comrade, comrade,
We must stick together like glue.
1: Well, if you'll trust me,
However tough it may be,
Then I'll trust you.
2 TO 3: He's a crook.
3: Very true.

3 TO 1: He's a crook
1: And you are too.
ALL: But if you'll trust me,
However tough it may be,
Then I'll, comrade, trust, comrade, you.

REFRAIN 2

2: I cannot trust Nina, my niece,
Since she told my past to the p'lice,
So I ask you this, entre nous,
Why should I trust you?
3: I cannot trust Misha, my son,
Since the party gave him a gun,
So I ask you this, entre nous,
Why should I trust you?
1: Though I do trust Nadya, my nurse,
Since they sent her home in a hearse,
Yet I ask you this, entre nous,
Why should I trust you?
3 & 1: But, comrade, comrade, comrade,
We must stick together like glue.
2: Well, if you'll trust me,
However tough it may be,
Then I'll trust you.
3 & 1: He's a rat.
1: Very true.
1 TO 2: He's a rat.
2: And you are too.
ALL: But if you'll trust me,
However tough it may be,
Then I'll, comrade, trust, comrade,
you.

REFRAIN 3

3: I cannot trust Sonya, my sis,
Since Malenkov slipped her a kiss,
So I ask you this, entre nous,
Why should I trust you?
1: I cannot trust small brother Pete,
Since he gave me ars'nic to eat,
So I ask you this, entre nous,
Why should I trust you?
2: Though I do trust Laska, my pup,
Since my grandpapa ate her up,
Yet I ask you this, entre nous,
Why should I trust you?
1 & 2: But, comrade, comrade, comrade,
We must stick together like glue.
3: Well, if you'll trust me,
However tough it may be,
Then I'll trust you.
1 TO 2: He's a louse.
2: Very true.
2 TO 3: He's a louse.
3: And you are too.
ALL. But if you'll trust me,
However tough it may be,
Then I'll, comrade, trust, comrade, you.

BÉBÉ OF GAY PAREE

Unused. The music does not survive.

REFRAIN

I'm Bébé of Gay Paree,
I love men and they love me,
When across the street I trot
There's a traffic jam and why not?
I am Bébé of Gay Paree!
I am Bébé of Gay Paree,
I hate women and they hate me,
When I enter chez Maxim
How I gloat when all of them scream.
I am Bébé of Gay Paree!
I am Bébé of Gay Paree,
I hate men and they hate me,
So if you are not above being pixilated by love,
I am Bébé of Gay Paree,
In this cité de joie,
C'est moi, c'est moi, it's me,
Bé-bé, Bébé of little ole Gay Paree.

"Keep Your Chin Up" and "I'm the Queen Thamar" (or "I'm the Queen That Goes Too Far") were left unfinished (manuscripts in the Music Division, Library of Congress). No music survives for either.

FILM VERSION, 1957

The film version of *Silk Stockings* was in production from November 1956 to January 1957 and was released in July 1957. Two new Porter songs were written for the film, which starred Fred Astaire and Cyd Charisse.

FATED TO BE MATED

Published May 1957. Copyrighted unpublished October 1956. This song replaced "As On Through the Seasons We Sail." Introduced by Fred Astaire.

REFRAIN

We were fated to be mated,
We were slated to be tied—
Me as the burning bridegroom,
You as the yearning bride.
We were spotted to be knotted
And allotted a glorious life—
Me as the wonder husband,
You as the wonderful wife.
So why not have a fling with a wedding ring,
Trusting ev'rything to the gods above?
For we were fated to be mated
And forever and ever in love.

THE RITZ ROLL AND ROCK

Published May 1957. Copyrighted unpublished November 1956. Introduced by Fred Astaire.

The rock and roll is dead and gone,
For since the smart set took it on,
Because they found it much too tame,
They jazzed it up and changed its name.
And all they do around the clock
Is the ritz, roll and rock.
You see big bucks togged out in tails,
Wingdingin' with expensive quails,
While dowagers and diplomats
Behave like bally alley cats.
And all they do around the clock
Is the ritz, roll and rock.
These fancy fops and fillies
Throw swell affairs,
And make those hick hillbillies
Look like squares.
It's been at least a year, they say,
Since any of them hit the hay.
And all they do around the clock
Is the ritz, roll and rock.

HIGH SOCIETY

1956

"High Society," 1956; Bing Crosby, Grace Kelly, Frank Sinatra

A film produced by Sol C. Siegel for M-G-M in 1956. Released August 1956. Based on Philip Barry's stage play *The Philadelphia Story.* Screenplay by John Patrick. Directed by Charles Walters. Cast, starring Bing Crosby, Grace Kelly, and Frank Sinatra, included Celeste Holm, John Lund, Louis Calhern, Sidney Blackmer, and Louis Armstrong.

HIGH SOCIETY CALYPSO

Published December 1956. Copyrighted unpublished December 1955. Introduced by Louis Armstrong and band.

ARMSTRONG: Just dig that scenery floatin' by,
We're now approachin' Newport,
Rhode I.
We've been, for years, in *Variety,*
But, Cholly Knickerbocker, now
we're goin' to be
ALL: In High, High So-,
High So-ci-,
High So-ci-ety.
ARMSTRONG: I wanna play for my former pal—
He runs the local jazz festival.
His name is Dexter and he's good
news,
But sumpin' kinda tells me that he's
nursin' the blues
ALL: In High, High So-,
High So-ci-,
High So-ci-ety.
ARMSTRONG: He's got the blues 'cause his wife,
alas,
Thought writin' songs was beneath
his class,
But writin' songs he'd not stop, of
course,
And so she flew to Vegas for a
quicky divorce
ALL: In High, High So-,
High So-ci-,
High So-ci-ety.
ARMSTRONG: To make him sadder, his former wife
Begins tomorrow a brand-new life.
She started lately a new affair
And now the silly chick is gonna
marry a square
ALL: In High, High So-,
High So-ci-,
High So-ci-ety.
ARMSTRONG: But, brother Dexter, just trust your
Satch,
To stop that weddin' and kill that
match.
I'll toot my trumpet to start the fun,
And play in such a way that she'll
come back to you, son,
ALL: In High, High So-,
High So-ci-,
High So-ci-ety.

I LOVE YOU, SAMANTHA

Published May 1956. Copyrighted unpublished December 1955. Introduced by Bing Crosby.

VERSE

Samantha, you're all
I'll ever adore,
So forgive me, do,
If I say to you
What I've said so often before.

REFRAIN

I love you, Samantha,
And my love will never die.
Remember, Samantha,
I'm a one-gal guy.
Together, Samantha,
We could ride a star and ride it high.
Remember, Samantha,
I'm a one-gal guy.
And if some distant day
You decided to say,
"Get along, go away, goodbye!"
Remember, Samantha,
I'm a one-gal guy.

LITTLE ONE

Published May 1956. Copyrighted unpublished October 1955. Introduced by Bing Crosby.

VERSE

Little one, what should I do?
I just can't make any headway with you.

REFRAIN

Little one, I was so gloomy,
Felt that life sure would undo me,
Till, one night, you happened to me,

My little one.
Little one, no controversy,
You're my downfall, you're my Circe,
I'm a good guy, show me mercy,
My little one.
I have such love for you
Our future could be
Heaven above for you
And paradise for me.
Little one, fate might miscarry,
Little one, why do you tarry?
Little one, when may I marry you,
My little one?

WHO WANTS TO BE A MILLIONAIRE?

Published October 1956. Copyrighted unpublished October 1955. Introduced by Frank Sinatra and Celeste Holm.

VERSE

HE: Who has an itch
To be filthy rich?
SHE: Who gives a hoot
For a lot of loot?
HE: Who longs to live
A life of perfect ease?
SHE: And be swamped by necessary luxuries?

REFRAIN 1

HE: Who wants to be a millionaire?
SHE: I don't.
HE: Have flashy flunkeys ev'rywhere?
SHE: I don't.
HE: Who wants the bother of a country estate?
SHE: A country estate
Is something I'd hate!
HE: Who wants a fancy foreign car?
SHE: I don't.
HE: Who wants to tire of caviar?
SHE: I don't.
HE: Who wants a marble swimming pool too?
SHE: I don't.
HE: And I don't,
BOTH: 'Cause all I want is you.

REFRAIN 2

SHE: Who wants to be a millionaire?
HE: I don't.
SHE: Who wants uranium to spare?
HE: I don't.
SHE: Who wants to journey on a gigantic yacht?
HE: Do I want a yacht?
Oh, how I do not!
SHE: Who wants to wallow in champagne?
HE: I don't.
SHE: Who wants a supersonic plane?
HE: I don't.
SHE: Who wants a private landing field too?
HE: I don't.
SHE: And I don't,
BOTH: 'Cause all I want is you.

REFRAIN 3

HE: Who wants to be a millionaire?
SHE: I don't.
And go to ev'ry swell affair?
HE: I don't.
Who wants to ride behind a liv'ried chauffeur?
SHE: A liv'ried chauffeur
Do I want? No, sir!
HE: Who wants an op'ra box, I'll bet?
SHE: I don't.
And sleep through Wagner at the Met?
HE: I don't.
Who wants to corner Cartier's too?
SHE: I don't.
HE: And I don't,
BOTH: 'Cause all I want is you.

TRUE LOVE

Published May 1956. Copyrighted unpublished October 1955. Introduced by Bing Crosby and Grace Kelly.

VERSE

Sun-tanned, wind-blown
Honeymooners at last alone,
Feeling far above par,
Oh, how lucky we are
While

REFRAIN

I give to you and you give to me
True love, true love.
So on and on it will always be
True love, true love.
For you and I
Have a guardian angel on high
With nothing to do

But to give to you and to give to me
Love forever true.

YOU'RE SENSATIONAL

Published May 1956. Copyrighted unpublished October 1955. Introduced by Frank Sinatra. Verse 2 and refrain 2 were not used.

VERSE 1

A thorough knowledge I've got about girls,
I've been around.
And after learning a lot about girls,
This is the important fact I found:

REFRAIN 1

I've no proof
When people say you're more or less aloof,
But you're sensational.
I don't care
If you are called "The Fair Miss Frigid Air,"
'Cause you're sensational.
Making love is quite an art,
What you require is the proper squire to fire
your heart,
And if you say
That one fine day you'll let me come to call,
We'll have a ball,
'Cause you're sensational,
Sensational,
That's all, that's all, that's all.

VERSE 2

A thorough knowledge I've got about boys,
I've been around.
And after learning a lot about boys,
This is the important fact I found:

REFRAIN 2

I've no proof
When people say you're more or less aloof,
But you're sensational.
I don't care
If you are known as "Mister Frigid Air,"
'Cause you're sensational.
Making love is quite an art,
What you should meet is a maiden sweet to heat
your heart.
And if you say
That one fine day you'll like to come and call,
We'll have a ball,
'Cause you're sensational,
Sensational,
That's all, that's all, that's all.

NOW YOU HAS JAZZ

Published June 1956. Copyrighted unpublished November 1955. Introduced by Bing Crosby and Louis Armstrong.

VERSE

Gentlefolk of Newport,
Or should I say "hats and cats,"
Please lend an ear
That ye all may hear
Some shimmering sharps and flats.
For those cozy virtuosi,
Known as "hipsters" to the trade,
Wish to show you now
Precisely how
Jazz music is made.

REFRAIN

Take some skins,
Jazz begins,
Take a bass
Steady pace,
Take a box,
One that rocks,
Take a blue horn New Orleans-born.
Take a stick
With a lick,
Take a bone,
Dixie-grown,
Take a spot,
Cool and hot,
Now you has jazz jazz jazz, jazz jazz.

Now you has,
Now you has,
Now you has,
Now you has,
Now you has,
Now you has,
Now you has jazz, jazz, jazz, jazz, jazz, jazz,
Now you
Has,
Now you
Has,
Now you

Has,
Now you has jazz, jazz, jazz, jazz, jazz.

Jazz,
Jazz,
Jazz,
Jazz,
Jazz,
Jazz,
Now you has jazz,
Now you has jazz,
Now you has jazz.

EXTRA REFRAIN

If you sail
Over the sea,
Take my tip,
They're all molto hip
In Italy.
As for France,
B'lieve it or not,
Frenchmen all
Prefer what they call
"Le Jazz Hot."
Take a plane,
Go to Siam,
In Bangkok
Today, 'round the clock,
They have a jam.
Indians on
The Amazon
Beat one bar
And all of 'em are
Gone, man, gone.
From the Equator
Up to the Pole,
Through the air
You hear ev'rywhere
Rock and roll.
From the East
Out to the West,
Jazz is king,
'Cause jazz is the thing
Folks
Dig
Best.

MIND IF I MAKE LOVE TO YOU?

Published May 1956. Copyrighted unpublished October 1955. Introduced by Frank Sinatra.

REFRAIN

In the heavens, stars are dancing
And the mounting moon is new,
What a rare night for romancing,
Mind if I make love to you?
Since the dear day of our meeting
I've wanted to tell you all I long to do,
Dawn is nearing, time is fleeting,
Mind if I make love to you?
If you let me, I'll endeavor
To persuade you I'm your party for two
And from then on, you will never mind
If I make love to you.

CAROLINE

Unused. Copyrighted unpublished October 1955. Dropped during production and replaced by "Little One."

VERSE

Caroline,
Forgive me, do,
If I dedicate
This song to—

REFRAIN

Caroline, you send me,
Caroline, you end me.
Caroline, I'm blissful but blue,
'Cause I'm so doggone gone about you.
In despair, you get me,
Then up in the air you jet me,
Oh, Caroline, won't you let me make you mine?
When and where, Caroline?

LET'S VOCALIZE

Unused. Copyrighted unpublished October 1955. Dropped during production. Intended for Frank Sinatra, Grace Kelly, and Bing Crosby.

MIKE: To celebrate these happy times,
Let's play a game of nurs'ry rhymes,
But before we start this exercise,
C'mon, let's vocalize,
ALL: Come on and vocalize, go!

TRACY: Well, Jack and Jill went up the hill,

A pail of water for to fill
DEXTER: And they stayed till Jill to Jack got wise.
ALL: C'mon, let's vocalize,
Voh doh dee, oh doh doh, next!

DEXTER: Oh, little Miss Muffet sat, they say,
On a tuffet eating curds and whey
MIKE: Till a spider made Miss Muffet rise.
ALL: C'mon, let's vocalize,
Booh boopa, doop doop doop, next!

MIKE: Oh, Peter, Peter, pumpkin eater,
He had a wife and couldn't keep her,
TRACY: She got fed up makin' pumpkin pies.
ALL: C'mon, let's vocalize,
Hatcha cha, cha cha cha, next!

TRACY: When I was going to Saint Ives
I met a man with seven wives.
DEXTER: They musta been tough to subsidize,
ALL: C'mon, let's vocalize,
Beedle dee, um bum bum, next!

DEXTER: Oh, little Tommy Tittlemouse,
He lived in a tiny little house
MIKE: Till a TV quiz gave him first prize.
ALL: C'mon, let's vocalize,
C'mon, let's vocalize,
Let's all co-op,
C'mon, let's harmonize
Sweet barber shop,

MIKE & DEXTER: Oh, pussycat, pussycat, where've you been?
TRACY: I've been to London to see the Queen
And the Queen she said, to my surprise,
"C'mon,
ALL: Let's vo-cal-ize,
Let's vo-cal-ize."

SO WHAT?

Unused. Also titled "Why Not?"

REFRAIN

MIKE: Woman is a perfect thing.
DEXTER: Virtue is its own reward.
MIKE: Woman is the touch of spring.
DEXTER: The pen is mightier than the sword.
MIKE: Woman is the sunset's gold.
DEXTER: Might makes right, so I've been told.
MIKE: So what?
DEXTER: So what?
How's about a little shot?
MIKE: Why not?

REFRAIN 2

MIKE: Woman is the spice of life.
DEXTER: Heaven gives to him who hath.
MIKE: Ev'ry man must have a wife.
DEXTER: An answer soft away turns wrath.
MIKE: Love will always find a way.
DEXTER: Haste makes waste, Confucius say.
MIKE: So what?
DEXTER: So what?
How's about a little shot?
MIKE: Why not?

REFRAIN 3

MIKE: Woman, sacred is thy name.
DEXTER: Rome was not built in a day.
MIKE: Ev'ry Dick should have a dame.
DEXTER: When the cat's away the mice will play.
MIKE: Woman has a form divine.
DEXTER: And a stitch in time saves nine.
MIKE: So what?
DEXTER: So what?
How's about a little shot?
MIKE: Why not?

REFRAIN 4

MIKE: Woman is from heaven sent.
DEXTER: Unto thine own self be true.
MIKE: Woman is the great event.
DEXTER: You can't have your cake and eat it too.
MIKE: Woman makes the world go 'round.
DEXTER: Practice makes perfect, I have found.
MIKE: So what?
DEXTER: So what?
BOTH: How's about a little shot?
Why not?
Why not?
Why not? Why not?
Why not? Why not?
Why not? Why not?
Why not? Why not?

WHO HAS?

Unused. Two pages of sketches are in a Porter music notebook. No other music survives.

REFRAIN

Who has the look I love so much?
Who has the hair I love to touch?

Who has the lips of eiderdown?
Who has the arms that go to town?
Who has the classic thirty-six?
Who has the only kiss that clicks?
Who has a lover, trusting and true?
No other one but you.

HOW COULD I?

Unused. A one-page sketch is in a Porter music notebook. No other music survives.

REFRAIN

Your eyes are an item
To drive men mad ad infinitum,
How could I look at anyone but you?
A point incidental,
Your body's strictly continental,
How could I look at anyone but you?
As we stroll arm in arm,
I'm so toasted by your charm
It's a fire five-alarm
Raging for two.
So how could I, why should I,
Why would I, when I've such a good eye,
Look at anyone
But you?

For the lyric of "Well, Did You Evah!" sung in the film by Frank Sinatra and Bing Crosby, see *Du Barry Was a Lady* (1939).

Sketches for an unfinished number titled "Hey, Sexy" or "Hi, Sexy" are at the Porter Collection, Yale. Music sketches and an unfinished lyric are in a Porter notebook. Other material in the notebook includes the following titles: "Wonderland" (1 page), "Why Is It?" (1 page), and "Hello Sadness, Bonjour Tristesse" (2 pages).

LES GIRLS

1957

A film produced by Sol C. Siegel for M-G-M in 1957. Released in November 1957. Associate producer, Saul Chaplin. Screenplay by John Patrick. Directed by George Cukor. Cast starred Gene Kelly, Mitzi Gaynor, Kay Kendall, and Taina Elg.

LES GIRLS

Published September 1957. Copyrighted unpublished October 1956. Lyric dated July 24, 1956. Introduced by Gene Kelly.

VERSE

'Round the map I've been a dancer
From New Jersey to Japan,
And if not a perfect prancer
I'm at least a tip-top travelin' man.
Yes, I've played ad infinitum
Ev'ry mountain, ev'ry coast,
For each country has the item
That I enjoy the most.

REFRAIN

Les Girls, Les Girls,
There's no doubt about it,
I just love Les Girls!
Les Girls, Les Girls,
No wonder I shout it,
I worship Les Girls!
Ah, what charms they disclose
From their hats to their hose,
From the tips of their toes up to their curls.
I simply adore,
And ev'ry day more,
Les Girls,
Les Girls,
Les Girls.

REFRAIN (FRENCH VERSION)

ALL: Les Girls, Les Girls,
KELLY: Ah, comme je les aim-e!
GIRLS: How he loves The Girls!
ALL: Les Girls, Les Girls,
KELLY: J'les trou-ve suprêm-es!
GIRLS: He worships Les Girls!
KELLY: De la plant-e des pieds
A la racine des ch'veux,
GIRLS: From the tips of their toes up to their curls.
KELLY: J'ador-e, mais oui,
GIRLS: But most of all, me,
KELLY: Les Girls
ALL: Les Girls,
Les Girls.

REFRAIN (SPANISH VERSION)

ALL: Les Girls, Les Girls,
KELLY: Que siempre he amado!
GIRLS: How he loves Les Girls!
ALL: Les Girls, Les Girls,
KELLY: Soy su enamorado!
GIRLS: He worships Les Girls!
KELLY: De las puntas del pie
A los rizos del pelo,
GIRLS: From the tips of their toes up to their curls.
KELLY: Adoro por sí,
GIRLS: But most of all, me,
KELLY: Les Girls
ALL: Les Girls,
Les Girls.

REFRAIN (ITALIAN VERSION)

ALL: Les Girls, Les Girls,
KELLY: Ah, co-me le amo!
GIRLS: How he loves Les Girls!
ALL: Les Girls, Les Girls,
KELLY: Io tanto le acclamo!
GIRLS: He worships Les Girls!
KELLY: Dalla punta dei piedi
A cappelli si belli,
GIRLS: From the tips of their toes up to their curls.
KELLY: Adoro, sì, sì,
GIRLS: But most of all, me,
KELLY: Les Girls
ALL: Les Girls,
Les Girls.

YOU'RE JUST TOO, TOO

Published September 1957. Copyrighted unpublished December 1956. Lyric dated July 18, 1956. Introduced by Gene Kelly and Kay Kendall.

REFRAIN 1

HE: You're just too charming!
SHE: You're just too great!
HE: You're just too faultless!
SHE: You're just too first-rate!
HE: Of all fair damsels 'tis thee I toast!
SHE: Oh, thank you, Casanova,

'Cause you're just the most!
HE: You're just too darling,
Too very, very nice!
SHE: You're just too dreamy
You're super-paradise!
BOTH: And it's no wonder
I love you as I do,
For I've got to say,
In ev'ry way,
You're just too, too!

REFRAIN 2

HE: You're just too brilliant!
SHE: You're just too bright!
HE: You're just too perfect!
SHE: You're just too top-flight!
HE: To win you, sweetheart,
Is all I wish!
SHE: Then try it, popsy-wopsy,
'Cause you're just my dish!
HE: You're just too luscious,
Too very, very sweet!
SHE: You're just too sexy
When you turn on the heat!
BOTH: But let's get started,
It's time to bill and coo,
For it's clear to me,
From A to Z,
You're just too, too!

ÇA, C'EST L'AMOUR

Published September 1957. Copyrighted unpublished October 1956. Lyric dated June 30, 1956. Introduced by Taina Elg.

REFRAIN

When suddenly you sight
Someone for whom you yearn,
Ça, c'est l'amour.
And when to your delight
She loves you in return,
Ça, c'est l'amour.
Then dawns a dreary day,
Your darling goes away
And all is over, you are sure.
But, oh, when she returns
And loves you as before,
You take her in your lonely arms
And want her even more,
Ça, c'est l'amour,
Ça, c'est l'amour.

LADIES-IN-WAITING

Copyrighted unpublished October 1956. Recorded but not published. Lyric dated July 31, 1956. Introduced by Mitzi Gaynor, Kay Kendall, and Taina Elg.

VERSE

ALL: We're ladies-in-waiting,
In waiting to the King,
As ladies-in-waiting
We're on the spot
Because we've got
To give the King
Ev'rything.

REPEAT VERSE

REFRAIN 1

1ST GIRL: I give him his breakfast,
Served in royal state.
2ND GIRL: I give him his soda
Bicarbonate.
3RD GIRL: And when he wants funsy-wunsy,
When he wants funsy-wunsy—
1ST & 2ND GIRLS: Pray, what do you give him?
3RD GIRL: I give him the gate!

REFRAIN 2

2ND GIRL: I give him his haircut
In his golden chair.
3RD GIRL: I give him his wig 'cause
There ain't no hair.
1ST GIRL: And when he wants candy-wandy,
When he wants candy-wandy—
2ND & 3RD GIRLS: Pray, what do you give him?
1ST GIRL: I give him the air!

REPEAT VERSE

REFRAIN 3

3RD GIRL: I carry his snuffbox
When he gives a dance.
1ST GIRL: I shoulder his gun when
He fights for France.
2ND GIRL: And when he wants tiddly-widdly,
When he wants tiddly-widdly—
1ST & 3RD GIRLS: Pray, what do you give him?
2ND GIRL: A kick in the pants!

REPEAT VERSE

REFRAIN 4

1ST GIRL: I give him his diet
When too fat he grows.
2ND GIRL: I tighten his corset
When still it shows.
1ST GIRL: And when he wants foodle-doodle,
When he wants foodle-doodle,
Pray, what do you give him?
2ND GIRL: A punch in the nose!

REPEAT VERSE

REFRAIN 5

2ND GIRL: I fill him with brandy
When the weather's raw.
1ST GIRL: I sober him up
When it starts to thaw.
2ND GIRL: And when he wants nizzle-nozzle,
When he wants nizzle-nozzle,
Pray, what do you give him?
1ST GIRL: A sock in the jaw!

WHY AM I SO GONE (ABOUT THAT GAL)?

Published October 1957. Copyrighted unpublished December 1956. Lyric dated November 19, 1956. Introduced by Gene Kelly.

VERSE

I've always had both feet on the ground before,
But lately I've been foolish enough to fall
For a doll I only wish I did *not* adore,
'Cause she isn't my type at all.

REFRAIN 1

I'm crazy for a baby that I can't forget,
This baby is a blonde, I like 'em jet-brunette—
Oh, why am I so gone about that gal?
I go for hair that's curly, hers is strictly
straight,
The color of her lipstick is my fav'rite hate—
Oh, why am I so gone about that gal?
To ask her out to dinner I'd be more inclined
But she's got one terrible flaw—
She eats a lot of veg'tables of ev'ry kind
And all of 'em raw!
Her body is a poem when she does a dance
But not for anybody seekin' hot romance—
Oh, why am I so gone about that gal?

REFRAIN 2

Each time I say hello, she always says goodbye,
She wants to be alone, I want to multiply—
Oh, why am I so gone about that gal?
To sit with her and neck with her would be so
nice
If only I could find a way to melt the ice—
Oh, why am I so gone about that gal?
Her clo'es at any supper club are much too plain,
I'm for fancy satin and silk,
And when I ask the waiter for his best champagne,
She hollers for milk!
Yet ev'ry time she's near me I begin to ache,
Espeshly if she socks me when I'm on the make—
Oh, why am I so gone about that gal?

DRINKING SONG

Unused. Lyric dated November 26, 1956. Copyrighted unpublished December 1956. Intended for Kay Kendall, Mitzi Gaynor, and Taina Elg.

REFRAIN

3 GIRLS: So here's to you,
Our friend tried and true,
We love you rain or shine,
And here's three cheers
For happy future years
With a bottoms up to Auld Lang Syne.

2ND ENDING

JOY: With a bottoms up,
ANGELE: And an oo-la-la,
SYBIL: And a cheerio
3 GIRLS: To Auld Lang Syne!

VERSE 1

ANGELE: Remember when the Riviera train went
off the track,
So we rode to Monte Carlo on a truck?
JOY: Where you let us play roulette till we
were absolutely broke,
Then you generously gave us each a buck.
SYBIL: Don't forget our op'ning night in West
Berlin,
When I disappeared because the stage
fell in.

VERSE 2

ANGELE: Remember how the audience adored us
in Seville,

Well, that is to say, until the lights went out?
JOY: And remember in Granada how delightfully you danced
When a bat flew in and batted you about?
SYBIL: And the bullfight in Madrid, how wonderful,
When you helped that great bullfighter catch the bull!

VERSE 3

ANGELE: Remember in Verona how we loved that old hotel,
Though the bath was in another part of town?
JOY: And remember, dear, in Venice when you dropped in that canal?
It was shallow, so our hero didn't drown.
SYBIL: And I never shall forget your perfect tact
When a drunk walked on and tried to join the act.

VERSE 4

ANGELE: Remember when the orchestra they gave us in Marseille
Was so awful that we couldn't dance at all?
JOY: And remember, dear Angele, the night your costume split in two
And they liked it so, you got a curtain call?
SYBIL: Not forgetting, in Vienna, my disgrace
When I took a bow and landed on my face.

HIGH-FLYIN' WINGS ON MY SHOES

Unused. Lyric dated October 31, 1956. Copyrighted unpublished January 1957. Intended for Gene Kelly. Published in *The Unpublished Cole Porter.*

VERSE

With your looks so attractive
And your charm so radioactive,
You're my dream supreme in ev'ry way.
So I long to possess you,
To be close to you and caress you,
Twenty-four hours per day.

REFRAIN

Whenever, darling, by chance,
Together we dance,
Although I've been battling the blues,
You give me stars in my eyes,
Love in my heart
And high-flyin' wings on my shoes.
I so adore you, my dear,
That when you appear,
No matter what moment you choose,
You give me stars in my eyes,
Love in my heart
And high-flyin' wings on my shoes,
So if you care for me,
I guarantee
Our life could be
Forever good news,
Including stars in our eyes,
Love in our hearts
And high-flyin' wings on our shoes.

I COULD KICK MYSELF

Unused. Dated October 29, 1956.

I was so happy when first I found you,
Now I'm constantly blue.
I could kick myself
For being in love with you.
I wove a wonderful dream around you,
One that didn't come true.
I could kick myself
For being in love with you.
I'm so overcome by loneliness
When I gaze at your photograph,
I'm almost in tears, I must confess,
But I only can shed a laugh.
Once on a throne in my heart I crowned you,
Then you broke it in two.
I could kick myself, kick myself,
For being in love,
Wildly in love with you.

MY DARLING NEVER IS LATE

Unused. Dated August 11, 1956. No music survives.

REFRAIN

I'm just gloating,
Fairly floating,
'Cause I'm facing
A super date
With my darling,
A little ole darling,
And my darling
Never is late.
Yes, I'm heading
For a wedding
That I'm racing
To celebrate
With my darling,
A little ole darling,
And my darling
Never is late.
And once we're welded to each other,
Mighty gone for one another,
When I tell her that as a mother
She'd be great,
She'll promptly give me
A little new darling,
'Cause my darling
Never is late.

MY LITTLE PIECE O' PIE

Unused. Dated August 27, 1956. Only a musical fragment survives in a Porter notebook.

REFRAIN

Sorry, can't be late,
Sorry, time to fly,
'Cause I got a date
With my little piece o' pie.
Pip, pip, toodle-oo,
Just must say goo-bye,
Got a rendezvous
With my little piece o' pie.
She's not my plum pie,
She's not my mince pie,
She's not my peach pie,
She's not my quince pie,
She's not my cherry pie,
Or my huckleberry pie,
She's not my cream pie,
She's my dream pie!
Sorry, can't be late,
Sorry, time to fly,
'Cause I got a date
With my,
My,
My little piece o' pie.

WHAT FUN

Unused. Dated August 18, 1956.

VERSE

To see you and know you, dear Granada,
Why ever did I never take the botha?
The silent Alhambra tries to slumba
While crickets in the thickets chirp a
rumba.
I always had dreamed of getting tipsy
On very heavy sherry with a gypsy
And now at last, we are here,
So, cam'raman, please appear
And give us a super souvenir!

REFRAIN

What fun to be photoed together,
What luck for a break so opportune.
Oh, what a lark
To be posed in the park
Underneath the adolescent crescent of the moon.
What fun after years close together
And this night we revive the mem'ry of.
Oh, how we'll laugh
And say when again we see this photograph,
"What fun to be still in love!"

YOU'RE THE PRIZE GUY OF GUYS

Unused. Dated July 18, 1956.

REFRAIN (ORIGINAL VERSION)

I've been doing a lot of scheming
Since that moment we met,
'Cause you're the prize
Guy of guys,
Baby, that I'se
Got to get.
With such passionate love I'm teeming
My blood count is upset,
'Cause you're the prize
Guy of guys

Baby, that I'se
Got to get.
Please won't pretty papa propose
To his mama?
Better do it or heaven knows
She'll go gaga.
It's no wonder I wake up screaming,
Dreaming of you, my pet,
'Cause you're the prize
Guy of guys,
Baby, that I'se
Got to get.

2ND ENDING

Got to get,
Got to get,
'Cause you're that vitamin shot
I'se got to get.

REFRAIN (KELLY VERSION)

I don't mind if for me you're scheming
Since that moment we met,
'Cause I'm the prize
Guy of guys,
Baby, but I'se
Hard to get.
When you say that with love you're teeming
I'm not over-upset,
'Cause I'm the prize
Guy of guys,
Baby, but I'se
Hard to get.
Though I'm daffy for demoiselles
With parlor tricks,
When they talk about wedding bells
I cry, "Nix, nix!"
It's no wonder you wake up screaming,
Dreaming of me, my pet,
'Cause I'm the prize
Guy of guys,
Baby, but I'se
Hard to get.

2ND ENDING

Hard to get,
Hard to get,
Yes, jes' like any top card,
I'se hard to get.

There are sketches (music only) for "Per Favore" and "Is It Joy?" and a few untitled musical ideas in a Porter notebook.

ALADDIN

1958

Produced by Richard Lewine for CBS-TV's *DuPont Show of the Month* on February 21, 1958. Book by S. J. Perelman. Directed by Ralph Nelson. Cast, starring Cyril Ritchard and Dennis King, included Sal Mineo, Anna Maria Alberghetti, Basil Rathbone, Una Merkel, and George Hall.

TRUST YOUR DESTINY TO YOUR STAR

Published January 1958. Lyric dated October 5, 1957. Introduced by Dennis King.

VERSE

Gaze at the stars when at night you're alone
And from out of the blue select one for your
own.

REFRAIN

If you want your purse to be lined with gold,
Trust your destiny to your star.
If you long for glory and fame untold,
Trust your destiny to your star.
When for someone's lips you have yearned and
yearned
But you live without hope so far,
You will soon discover your love is returned
If you trust,
And you must
Trust your destiny to your star.

ALADDIN

Published January 1958. Copyrighted unpublished November 1957. Lyric for verse dated October 12, 1957; refrain dated August 31, 1957. Introduced by Anna Maria Alberghetti and ensemble.

ALADDIN'S VERSE

Oh princess, fair Princess, though I know it
could never be,
I saw you in a dream and you were saying to me:

PRINCESS'S VERSE (PUBLISHED)

They told me that such an unheard-of event
Could never but never occur,
Yet all of a sudden, as if heaven sent,
My darling, there you were!

REFRAIN

Aladdin,
Aladdin,
How could you such love inspire?
Aladdin,
You madden
A maiden with deep'ning desire.
I sadden
And sadden,
Each moment we spend apart.
Aladdin,
Aladdin,
Come and gladden your home in my heart.

COME TO THE SUPERMARKET IN OLD PEKING

Published February 1958. Lyric dated September 21, 1957. Introduced by Cyril Ritchard.

REFRAIN 1

If you want a fancy fan
Or a turkey born in Turkey-stan
Or a slave that's awf'lly African
Or a teapot early Ming,
Come to the supermarket in old Peking.

If you want to buy a kite
Or a pup to keep you up at night
Or a dwarf who used to know Snow White
Or a frog who loves to sing,
Come to the supermarket in old Peking.

Sunflow'r cakes, moonbeam cakes
Gizzard cakes, lizard cakes,
Pickled eels, pickled snakes,
Fit for any king,

If you want a bust of jade
Or an egg that's more or less decayed
Or in case you care to meet a maid
For a nice but naughty fling,

Come to the supermarket,
If you come on a pony, you can park it,
So come to the supermarket

And see
Pe-
King.

REFRAIN 2

If you want a gong to beat
Or a rickshaw with a sassy seat
Or a painting slightly indiscreet
That is simply riveting,
Come to the supermarket in old Peking.

If you want some calico
Or a gentle water buffalo
Or a glowworm guaranteed to glow
Or a cloak inclined to cling,
Come to the supermarket in old Peking.

Bird's-nest soup, seaweed soup,
Noodle soup, poodle soup,
Talking crows with the croup,
Almost anything.

If you want to buy a saw
Or a fish delicious when it's raw
Or a pill to kill* your moth'r-in-law
Or a bee without a sting,

Come to the supermarket,
If you come on a camel, you can park it,
So come to the supermarket
And see
Pe-
King.

I ADORE YOU

Published January 1958. Copyrighted unpublished November 1957. Lyric for first version dated September 7, 1957; lyric for second version dated September 14, 1957. Introduced by Sal Mineo and Anna Maria Alberghetti.

REFRAIN

Since I gazed at you so temptingly near,
I adore you.
There could never be a love more sincere,
I adore you.
So the day may dawn when I might appear
And implore you†
To repeat the words I hunger to hear,
"I adore you, dear."

*Or "still" instead of "kill." I much prefer "kill." [Porter's note.]

†*Second version, lines 5–6:*
And the day has dawned when no more I fear
To implore you

MAKE WAY FOR THE EMPEROR

Published February 1958. Lyric dated October 5, 1957. Introduced by George Hall. Also titled "Make Way."

REFRAIN 1

Make way for His Majesty
And her Oh So Serene Highness.
Make way for the Emperor
And his daughter, the pretty Princess.
Don't add to the traffic jam,
Let the royal parade progress,
Make way for the Emperor
And his daughter, the pretty Princess.
Show your devotion to
Your protector and his daughter
Or be condemned to stew
In a bath of boiling water.
Monarchs can be merciful,
They can also be merciless,
So make way for the Emperor
And his daughter, the pretty Princess.

REFRAIN 2

Make way for His Majesty
And her Oh So Serene Highness.
Make way for the Emperor
And his daughter, the pretty Princess.
Don't add to the traffic jam,
Let the royal parade progress,
Make way for the Emperor
And his daughter, the pretty Princess.
Bow to the Mighty Chang
And his offspring so forgiving,
Or be prepared to hang
Till you're not among the living.
Monarchs can be merciful,
They can also be merciless,
So make way for the Emperor
And his daughter, the pretty Princess.

NO WONDER TAXES ARE HIGH

Published February 1958. Lyric dated October 5, 1957. Introduced by Cyril Ritchard and ensemble.

REFRAIN 1

The Emperor is fond of marble dragons,
So he ordered tons and tons of marble dragons,
His extravagance nobody can deny,
No wonder taxes are high.

In ev'ry room he wants a golden Buddha
And it takes a lot of gold to make a Buddha,
Though to estimate the cost we wouldn't try,
No wonder taxes are high.

Yet we work, work, work
Till our bones are all cracked,
We don't even have a Workmen's Compensation
Act.

His Majesty delights in throwing parties,
So we have to furnish food for all his parties.
When your monarch is a social butterfly,
No wonder taxes are high,
Oh me, oh my!
No wonder taxes are high.

REFRAIN 2

His Grace can only sleep on yellow satin,
Ev'ry night he has a change of yellow satin,
Though we want him to enjoy his hushabye,
No wonder taxes are high.

He likes to juggle emeralds and rubies,
So he cornered all the emeralds and rubies,
His collection is a knockout to the eye,
No wonder taxes are high.

Yet we work, work, work
For a minimum fee,
We don't even get a break to take midmorning
tea.

Our master loves to ogle pretty dancers,
He already has a thousand pretty dancers,
But today he commandeered a new supply,
No wonder taxes are high,
Oh me, oh my!
No wonder taxes are high.

REFRAIN 3

He likes to look at fireworks in the ev'ning,
So we're forced to shoot off fireworks ev'ry ev'ning,
And so many that they clutter up the sky,
No wonder taxes are high.

He drinks a foreign drink that's known as brandy,
So a caravan arrived and brought him brandy.
It's too bad his royal throat is always dry,
No wonder taxes are high.

Yet we work, work, work
Till we're covered with grime,
But he wouldn't think of paying us for overtime.

His Highness fairly reeks of heavy perfume
And his concubines adore his heavy perfume.
It's a shame the way they splash it on the guy,
No wonder taxes are high,
Oh me, oh my!
No wonder taxes are high.

OPPORTUNITY KNOCKS BUT ONCE

Published January 1958. Copyrighted unpublished November 1957. Lyric dated October 12, 1957. Introduced by Cyril Ritchard and ensemble.

VERSE

When I was a baby a-playing,
Sweet Grandmama said, "My pet,
There's an ancient Mongolian saying
That you never, never should forget."

REFRAIN 1

Opportunity knocks but once—at thuh door,
Opportunity knocks but once—at thuh door,
Opportunity won't knock twice—
Or thrice—
Or any more,
Opportunity knocks but once—at thuh door.
So when it knocks, don't hesitate, don't pause,
But grab it quick because, because, because,
because
Opportunity knocks but once,
When for happiness someone hunts,
Opportunity knocks but once—at thuh door.

REFRAIN 2

SOLO: Opportunity knocks but once—at thuh
door,
OTHERS: At, at thuh door,
SOLO: Opportunity knocks but once—at thuh
door,

OTHERS: At, at thuh door,
SOLO: Opportunity won't knock twice—
Or thrice—
Or any more,
Opportunity knocks but once—at thuh door,
OTHERS: At, at thuh door.
SOLO: So when it knocks, don't hesitate, don't pause,
OTHERS: Don't pause,
SOLO: But grab it quick because, because, because, because,
OTHERS: 'Cause, because, because, because, 'cause
SOLO: Opportunity knocks but once,
When for happiness someone hunts,
Opportunity knocks but once—at thuh door,
OTHERS: Where?
SOLO: At thuh door,
OTHERS: Where?
SOLO: At thuh door,
As I said before,
ALL: At thuh door.

WOULDN'T IT BE FUN

Published February 1958. Subtitled "The Emperor's Song." Lyric dated November 5, 1957. Introduced by Basil Rathbone. This is the last song Porter wrote. (There is no lyric for the music titled "Genie's Theme.")

REFRAIN 1

Wouldn't it be fun not to be famous,
Wouldn't it be fun not to be rich!
Wouldn't it be pleasant
To be a simple peasant
And spend a happy day digging a ditch!
Wouldn't it be fun not to be known as an important V.I.P.,
Wouldn't it be fun to be nearly anyone
Except me, mighty me!

PATTER

Yesterday I had to endure a kite-flying match
And rushed to an execution downtown,
Then I gave a luncheon for some horrible hectic Huns
Who proceeded to drink too much and fall down.
After lunch I went to inspect a slave-labor camp
And opened a new wing in my dungeon keep,
Then I gave a feast for a lofty lama from Tibet
And he stayed so late I never got to sleep,
So help me Buddha!

REFRAIN 2

Wouldn't it be fun not to be wealthy,
Wouldn't it be fun not to be great!
How I'd love it dearly
To be a beggar merely
And not be bored to death living in state!
Wouldn't it be fun not to have always deadly diplomats for tea,
Wouldn't it be fun to be nearly anyone
Except me, mixed-up me!

INDEX

This is an alphabetical index of song titles and first lines of Porter's lyrics. It includes individual song copyright information.

Early in his career Porter was grateful to anyone willing to publish his songs. His first Broadway show, *See America First* (1916), was published by G. Schirmer. By the 1920s Porter, like his younger colleagues George and Ira Gershwin, Vincent Youmans, Richard Rodgers, and Lorenz Hart, became one of Max Dreyfus' "boys" at Harms, Inc., which was sold in 1929 to Warner Brothers when sound came to the cinema. In 1935 Dreyfus began Chappell in the United States and Porter, along with his colleagues, continued his association with Dreyfus. Porter's songs were published by Chappell beginning with the 1936 film score, *Born to Dance,* through his final work in 1957 for the television production *Aladdin.* By the late 1940s, after the success of *Kiss Me, Kate,* Porter frequently held song copyrights in his own name, giving publication and distribution rights to Chappell. In 1961 he established the Cole Porter Musical and Literary Property Trusts. After his death in 1964 the executor of his estate, John F. Wharton, the eminent theatrical attorney, became trustee of the Porter Trusts. Wharton, as trustee, registered many unpublished Porter songs. Following Wharton's death in 1977, Robert H. Montgomery, Jr., who had worked closely with Porter since the early 1950s, succeeded Wharton as trustee and has continued the practice of registering the copyrights of unpublished Porter songs.

All rights are reserved on all Porter song copyrights. The following copyright information should be added to individual notices according to the corresponding numbers:

1 Assigned to John F. Wharton, Trustee of the Cole Porter Musical & Literary Property Trusts. Chappell & Co., Inc., Publisher. International Copyright Secured. All Rights Reserved.

2 Assigned to Robert H. Montgomery, Jr., Trustee of the Cole Porter Musical & Literary Property Trusts. Chappell & Co., Inc., Publisher. International Copyright Secured. All Rights Reserved.

3 Chappell & Co., Inc., owner of publication and allied rights throughout the world. International Copyright Secured. All Rights Reserved.

4 Used by Permission of Warner Brothers Inc., and Robert H. Montgomery, Jr., as Trustee of the Cole Porter Musical & Literary Property Trusts. All Rights Reserved.

5 Assigned to G. Schirmer, Inc., 1944. All Rights Reserved.

Publishing rights outside the United States and Canada for the vast majority of Cole Porter's songs are controlled by Chappell & Co. Ltd.

A broken-down Oriental dancer am I, 367
A bunch of Bolsheviks, one day, 152
A busted, disgusted cocotte am I, 159
A certain yearning, 271
A fiddler was fiddling a wonderful tune, 137
A fool there was, 223, 243
A girl of sweet sixteen, 175
A lonely young student once loved, they say, 73
A sailor lost in the jungle wild, 83
A sailor's life is supposed to be, 168
A super-step, 344
A thoro'ly roaring reckless lot in us you see, 42
A thorough knowledge I've got about girls, 456
A troupe of strolling players are we, 388
A week ago who'd have prophesied, 194
ABRACADABRA, 347 Copyright © 1944 by Chappell & Co., Inc. Copyright Renewed.[1]
ABSINTHE, 29 Copyright © 1983 by Robert H. Montgomery, Jr., as Trustee.
ABSINTHE DRIP, 29 Copyright © 1983 by Robert H. Montgomery, Jr., as Trustee.
According to the Kinsey Report, 393
ACE IN THE HOLE, 303 Copyright © 1941 by Chappell & Co., Inc. Copyright Renewed.[1]
Across the Rio Grande, 80
ADIOS, ARGENTINA, 178 © 1935 (Renewed) Warner Bros. Inc.
AFTER ALL, I'M ONLY A SCHOOLGIRL, 112 Copyright © 1966 by John F. Wharton, as Trustee.
After hunting all over for pleasure, 137
After spending quite a spell, 235
After that sweet summer afternoon, 261
After watching your appeal from ev'ry angle, 440
AFTER YOU, WHO? 151 © 1932 (Renewed) Warner Bros. Inc.
AGUA SINCOPADA TANGO (no lyrics), 116
AH FONG LO, 77 Copyright © 1983 by Robert H. Montgomery, Jr., as Trustee.
Ah there! Fascinating females, 49
ALADDIN, 468 Copyright © 1957 by Cole Porter.[3]
ALL ALONE, *See* ALONE WITH YOU.
ALL I'VE GOT TO GET NOW IS MY MAN, 289 Copyright © 1940 by Chappell & Co., Inc. Copyright Renewed.[1]
All my life I've been so secluded, 184
ALL OF YOU, 440 Copyright © 1954 by Cole Porter. Copyright Renewed.[2]
All through the Argentine, 180
ALL THROUGH THE NIGHT, 168 © 1934 (Renewed) Warner Bros. Inc.
ALLEZ-VOUS-EN, 427 Copyright © 1952 by Cole Porter. Copyright Renewed.[2]
ALMIRO, 94 © 1928 (Renewed) Warner Bros. Inc.
Alone, at last, 174
ALONE WITH YOU, 71 Copyright 1918 by Herman Darewski Music Pub. Co. Copyright renewed by Cole Porter.
ALPINE ROSE, 97 © Registered in the name of M.E. Sayag, 1928. Copyright Renewed.[4]

ALTOGETHER TOO FOND OF YOU (music by Porter), 71
ALWAYS TRUE TO YOU IN MY FASHION, 394 Copyright © 1948 by Cole Porter. Copyright Renewed.[1]
AM I IN LOVE? 435 Copyright © 1983 by Robert H. Montgomery, Jr., as Trustee.
AMERICAN EXPRESS, THE, 118 Copyright © 1983 by Robert H. Montgomery, Jr., as Trustee.
AMERICAN PUNCH, THE, 78 © 1922 (Renewed) Warner Bros. Inc.
AMERICANS ALL DRINK COFFEE, 292 Copyright © 1967 by John F. Wharton, as Trustee.
AMO AMAS, 335 Copyright © 1969 by John F. Wharton, as Trustee.
An old-fashioned bluebird was sailing the sky, 401
An old gypsy prophesied when I was three, 346
And in spite of the fact that there's no imported Camembert, 373
And that's why Chinks do it, Japs do it, 101
And there's no cure like travel, 167
And though we live in the grandest kind of style, 68
And when they ask us how dangerous it was, 70
ANNABELLE BIRBY, *See* ANTOINETTE BIRBY.
ANNOUNCEMENT ENSEMBLE, *See* LADY I'VE VOWED TO WED, THE.
ANNOUNCEMENT OF INHERITANCE, 320 Copyright © 1983 by Robert H. Montgomery, Jr., as Trustee.
ANOTHER OP'NIN', ANOTHER SHOW, 387 Copyright © 1949 by Cole Porter. Copyright Renewed.[1]
ANOTHER SENTIMENTAL SONG, 65 © 1919 (Renewed) Warner Bros. Inc.
ANTOINETTE BIRBY, 8 Copyright © 1971 by John F. Wharton, as Trustee.
ANYTHING GOES, 171 © 1934 (Renewed) Warner Bros. Inc.
ANYTIME, 17 Copyright © 1977 by John F. Wharton, as Trustee.
Anytime you're feeling lonely, 17
APHRODITE'S DANCE, 191 © 1935 (Renewed) Warner Bros. Inc.
Are you fond of riding, dear?, 259
Are you the Queen?, 192
ART, 445 Copyright © 1966 by John F. Wharton, as Trustee.
Art must only please the masses, 445
As a buyer for a firm that deals in ladies' fur coats, 120
As a cloak room girl befitting, 105
As a painting you must have heard a lot about me, 132
As a Romeo I'm a wonder, 128
As a waiter, 115
As Dorothy Parker once said to her boy friend, 194
As far as love goes, 223
AS I LOVE YOU, 29 Copyright © 1977 by Robert H. Montgomery, Jr., as Trustee.
As I was leaving high school, 158
AS LONG AS IT'S NOT ABOUT LOVE, 250 Copyright © 1983 by Robert H. Montgomery, Jr., as Trustee.
As long as "spoon" rhymes with "night in June," 65
AS ON THROUGH THE SEASONS WE SAIL, 442 Copyright © 1954 by Cole Porter. Copyright Renewed.[2]
As reporters who interview the Jezebels of crime, 214
As Shakespeare once wrote, 291
As we drip, drip, drip, drip, drip along, 29
As we're poor pioneers, in a bad financial fix, 110
As you sail away, 91
As you sail your glorious way, 252
ASSEMBLY-LINE SONG, *See* CARBORUNDUM.
A-STAIRABLE RAG (no lyrics), 295
At boarding school I was always taught, 123
At evening, when night starts to fall, 113
AT LAST IN YOUR ARMS, 278 Copyright © 1939 by Chappell & Co., Inc. Copyright Renewed.
At last, the winter is over, 220, 272
AT LONG LAST LOVE, 229 Copyright © 1938 by Chappell & Co., Inc. Copyright Renewed.[1]
AT LONGCHAMPS TODAY, 120 Copyright © 1977 by John F. Wharton, as Trustee.
AT THE DAWN TEA, 26 Copyright © 1983 by Robert H. Montgomery, Jr., as Trustee.
AT THE RAINBOW, 18 Copyright © 1976 by John F. Wharton, as Trustee.
At words poetic, I'm so pathetic, 169
AT YE OLDE COFFEE SHOPPE IN CHEYENNE, 205 Copyright © 1983 by Robert H. Montgomery, Jr., as Trustee.
AU REVOIR, CHER BARON, 225 Copyright © 1983 by Robert H. Montgomery, Jr., as Trustee.
AUF WIEDERSEH'N, 270 Copyright © 1966 by John F. Wharton, as Trustee.
Au-ra!, 181
AWAY FROM IT ALL, 417 Copyright © 1967 by John F. Wharton, as Trustee.
Azure-eyed Mee-rah-lah, how lovely you are, 377

BABY GAMES, 304 Copyright © 1983 by Robert H. Montgomery, Jr., as Trustee.
BABY, LET'S DANCE, 98 © Registered in the name of M.E. Sayag, 1928. Copyright Renewed.[4]
Baby, life's so short, 230
Baccia mi, baccia mi con passione, 113
Back in the days of giftie giving, 322
Back in the days when Greece was mighty, 125
BACK TO NATURE WITH YOU, 163 © 1933

(Renewed) Warner Bros. Inc.
BAD GIRL IN PAREE, 106 Copyright © 1983 by Robert H. Montgomery, Jr., as Trustee.
BADMEN, 42 Copyright © 1983 by Robert H. Montgomery, Jr., as Trustee.
BALLET MUSIC (no lyrics), 274
BAND STARTED SWINGING A SONG, THE, 368 Copyright © 1945 by Chappell & Co., Inc. Copyright Renewed.[1]
BANDIT BAND, THE, 80 © 1922 (Renewed) Warner Bros. Inc.
BANJO THAT MAN JOE PLAYS, THE, 110 © 1929 (Renewed) Warner Bros. Inc.
BARCELONA MAID, 16 Copyright © 1941 by Chappell & Co., Inc. Copyright Renewed.
BE A CLOWN, 383 Copyright © 1946 by Chappell & Co., Inc. Copyright Renewed.[1]
BE LIKE THE BLUEBIRD, 173 © 1936 (Renewed) Warner Bros. Inc.
Be quiet, please, you ask me why?, 341
BEAUTIFUL, PRIMITIVE INDIAN GIRLS, 49 Copyright © 1983 by Robert H. Montgomery, Jr., as Trustee.
BÉBÉ OF GAY PAREE, 451 Copyright © 1983 by Robert H. Montgomery, Jr., as Trustee.
Before I crack up from black despair, 306
Before you leave these portals, 158
BEGIN THE BEGUINE, 188 © 1935 (Renewed) Warner Bros. Inc.
Being here by your side seems somehow so right, 218
BELLBOYS, 18 Copyright © 1976 by John F. Wharton, as Trustee.
Belle en-chan-te-ress-e!, 59
BERTIE AND GERTIE, 214 Copyright © 1966 by John F. Wharton, as Trustee.
BETWEEN YOU AND ME, 252 Copyright © 1939 by Chappell & Co., Inc. Copyright Renewed.[1]
BEWARE, GYPSY, BEWARE, *See* GYPSY SONG.
Beware, Montana, that bull's a devil, beware, 343
BEWARE OF THE SOPHOMORE, 27 Copyright © 1983 by Robert H. Montgomery, Jr., as Trustee.
BIANCA, 394 Copyright © 1948 by Cole Porter. Copyright Renewed.[1]
BICHLORIDE OF MERCURY (lost), 42
BIG PARADE, THE, 368 Copyright © 1977 by John F. Wharton, as Trustee.
BIG TOWN, 361 Copyright © 1980 by Robert H. Montgomery, Jr., as Trustee.
BINGO ELI YALE, 5 © 1910 (Renewed) Warner Bros. Inc.
Birds do it, bees do it, 101 footnote
BLOW, GABRIEL, BLOW, 172 © 1934 (Renewed) Warner Bros. Inc.
BLUE BOY BLUES, THE, 132 Copyright © 1922 by Chappell and Co., Ltd. Copyright Renewed.
BLUE HOURS, 96 © Registered in the name of M.E. Sayag, 1928. Copyright Renewed.[4]
BOMBER SCENE, *See* CARBORUNDUM.
BON VOYAGE, 167 © 1936 (Renewed) Warner Bros. Inc.
BOOGIE BARCAROLLE (no lyrics), 295
BOULEVARD BREAK, 97 Copyright © 1983 by Robert H. Montgomery, Jr., as Trustee.
Boy, if you're a dancin' fool, 281
BOYFRIEND BACK HOME, THE, 129 Copyright © 1977 by Robert H. Montgomery, Jr., as Trustee.
Boys and girls, there's a thing called love, 347
BREAKFAST TIME, *See* SUNDAY MORNING BREAKFAST TIME.
BRIDGET MCGUIRE, 4 Copyright © 1971 by John F. Wharton, as Trustee.
BRING ME A RADIO (lost), 88
BRING ME BACK MY BUTTERFLY, 65 © 1919 (Renewed) Warner Bros. Inc.
BRING ON THE GIRLS (not written), 165
BRITTANY, 85 © 1924 (Renewed) Warner Bros. Inc.
BROADCAST A JAZZ, 86 Copyright © 1983 by Robert H. Montgomery, Jr., as Trustee.
BRUSH UP YOUR SHAKESPEARE, 395 Copyright © 1949 by Cole Porter. Copyright Renewed.[1]
BUDDIE, BEWARE, 173 © 1934 (Renewed) Warner Bros. Inc.
BULL DOG, 6 Copyright © 1971 by John F. Wharton, as Trustee.
BUT HE NEVER SAYS HE LOVES ME, *See* THE PHYSICIAN.
BUT IN THE MORNING, NO, 259 Copyright © 1939 by Chappell & Co., Inc. Copyright Renewed.[1]
But it's awfully hard when Mother's not along, 22
BUTTERFLIES, 133 Copyright © 1983 by Robert H. Montgomery, Jr., as Trustee.
BUY HER A BOX AT THE OPERA, 58 Copyright © 1916 G. Schirmer, Inc. Copyright Renewed.[5]
BY CANDLELIGHT, 235 Copyright © 1938 by Chappell & Co., Inc. Copyright Renewed.
By the fire, 132
BY THE MISSISSINEWAH, 327 Copyright © 1943 by Chappell & Co., Inc. Copyright Renewed.[1]

ÇA, C'EST L'AMOUR, 462 Copyright © 1956 by Chappell & Co., Inc.
CABLEGRAM (lost), 11
CAFÉ SOCIETY STILL CARRIES ON, 373 Copyright © 1983 by Robert H. Montgomery, Jr., as Trustee.
CAN-CAN, 429 Copyright © 1952 by Cole Porter. Copyright Renewed.[2]
CARBORUNDUM, 333 Copyright © 1983 by Robert H. Montgomery, Jr., as Trustee.
CARLOTTA, 346 Copyright © 1944 by Chappell & Co., Inc. Copyright Renewed.[1]

CAROLINE, 457 Copyright © 1955 by Chappell & Co., Inc. Copyright Renewed.
CARRY ON, 207 Copyright © 1983 by Robert H. Montgomery, Jr., as Trustee.
Catherine of Russia, that potentate, 176
CAZANOVA, 161 Copyright © 1977 by Robert H. Montgomery, Jr., as Trustee.
C'EST MAGNIFIQUE, 423 Copyright © 1952 by Cole Porter. Copyright Renewed.[2]
CHAPERONS, 26 Copyright © 1983 by Robert H. Montgomery, Jr., as Trustee.
CHARITY, 15 Copyright © 1983 by Robert H. Montgomery, Jr., as Trustee.
Cheer, cheer for Eli today, 5
CHERRY PIES OUGHT TO BE YOU, 412 Copyright © 1950 by Cole Porter. Copyright Renewed.[1]
CHINA DOLL, 68 Copyright © 1983 by Robert H. Montgomery, Jr., as Trustee.
CHIRIPAH, THE, 178 © 1935 (Renewed) by Warner Bros. Inc.
CINCINNATI, 39 Copyright © 1971 by John F. Wharton, as Trustee.
CLEVELAND, 70 Copyright © 1971 by John F. Wharton, as Trustee.
CLIMB UP THE MOUNTAIN, 411 Copyright © 1950 by Cole Porter. Copyright Renewed.[1]
CLOSE, 220 Copyright © 1937 by Chappell & Co., Inc. Copyright Renewed.
CLOSE TO ME, 335 Copyright © 1983 by Robert H. Montgomery, Jr., as Trustee.
COCKTAIL TIME, 131 Copyright © 1922 by Chappell and Co., Ltd. Copyright Renewed.
COCOTTE, THE, 159 © 1933 (Renewed) Warner Bros. Inc.
COFFEE, 273 Copyright © 1969 by John F. Wharton, as Trustee.
Come, all, and sing the Jubilee, hurrah, hurrah, 340
COME ALONG WITH ME, 423 Copyright © 1953 by Cole Porter. Copyright Renewed.[2]
Come, awake, fair daughter, 279
Come, baby, wake up, 98
Come on and take your places, 121
Come on down to Mory's, 5
COME ON IN, 258 Copyright © 1940 by Chappell & Co., Inc. Copyright Renewed.[1]
Come on you, 86
Come on, you gunmen, 146
Come on, you poor ungodly sinners, 97
Come on, you sheik, 349
Come out, oh, my beloved, come out, 414
COME TO BOHEMIA, 17 Copyright © 1983 by Robert H. Montgomery, Jr., as Trustee.
COME TO THE SUPERMARKET IN OLD PEKING, 468 Copyright © 1958 by Cole Porter.[3]
Come with me and waltz once more, 81
COMRADE ALONZO, 242 Copyright © 1974 by John F. Wharton, as Trustee.
CONCENTRATION, 11 Copyright © 1971 by John F. Wharton, as Trustee.
CORA, THE FAIR CHORINE, 12 Copyright © 1983 by Robert H. Montgomery, Jr., as Trustee.
COULD IT BE YOU?, 324 Copyright © 1942 by Chappell & Co., Inc. Copyright Renewed.[1]
COULDN'T BE, 317 Copyright © 1983 by Robert H. Montgomery, Jr., as Trustee.
COUNT YOUR BLESSINGS, 348 Copyright © 1944 by Chappell & Co., Inc. Copyright Renewed.[1]
COWBOY SONG, THE, *See* DON'T FENCE ME IN.
CRAIGIE 404, 39 Copyright © 1983 by Robert H. Montgomery, Jr., as Trustee.
CREW SONG, THE, *See* I WANT TO ROW ON THE CREW.
CURIO SONG, 83 Copyright © 1983 by Robert H. Montgomery, Jr., as Trustee.

DAINTY, QUAINTY ME, 370 Copyright © 1967 by John F. Wharton, as Trustee.
DAMSEL, DAMSEL, *See* WON'T YOU COME CRUSADING WITH ME?
DANCIN' TO A JUNGLE DRUM (LET'S END THE BEGUINE), 366 Copyright © 1966 by John F. Wharton, as Trustee.
DANCING, 17 Copyright © 1983 by Robert H. Montgomery, Jr., as Trustee.
Dancing the Chiripah, 178
DAWN MUSIC (lost, no lyrics), 42
Dear bobby, 114
DEAR DOCTOR, 17 Copyright © 1983 by Robert H. Montgomery, Jr., as Trustee.
Dear Louie promptly went to sleep, 259
DEAUVILLE-SUR-MER, *See* NEAUVILLE-SUR-MER.
DELOVELY, *See* IT'S DE-LOVELY.
DEMOBILIZATION SONG, *See* WHEN I HAD A UNIFORM ON.
DINNER, 48 Copyright © 1983 by Robert H. Montgomery, Jr., as Trustee.
Disguised as a young canary, 272
DIZZY BABY, 105 Copyright © 1966 by John F. Wharton, as Trustee.
DO I LOVE YOU?, 261 Copyright © 1939 by Chappell & Co., Inc. Copyright Renewed.[1]
Do you hear that playin'?, 173
Do you know the perfume they label "Beware"?, 449
DO YOU WANT TO SEE PARIS?, 93 Copyright © 1971 by John F. Wharton, as Trustee.
DOLLYS AND THEIR COLLIES, THE (no lyrics), 88
DON'T FENCE ME IN, 178 © 1944 (Renewed) Warner Bros. Inc.
Don't leave America, 44
DON'T LET IT GET YOU DOWN, 228 Copyright © 1977 by Robert H. Montgomery, Jr., as Trustee.
DON'T LOOK AT ME THAT WAY, 101 © 1928 (Renewed) Warner Bros. Inc.

Don't say it with candy, 143
Don't start the dinner with saying grace, it isn't done, 123
Don't talk loud, 49
DON'T TELL ME WHO YOU ARE, 137 Copyright © 1983 by Robert H. Montgomery, Jr., as Trustee.
Don't you remember, darling, 79
Down by the river, 27
Down by the sea lived a lonesome oyster, 123
Down, down, down, in my lovely submarine, 16
DOWN IN A DUNGEON DEEP, 35 Copyright © 1983 by Robert H. Montgomery, Jr., as Trustee.
Down in Forty-second Street, 258
Down in Santiago town, 29
DOWN IN THE DEPTHS, *Red, Hot and Blue,* 206 Copyright © 1936 by Chappell & Co., Inc. Copyright Renewed.
Down in the depths of the water, 81
DOWN LOVERS' LANE, 37 Copyright © 1983 by Robert H. Montgomery, Jr., as Trustee.
DOWN WITH EVERYBODY BUT US, 126 Copyright © 1977 by Robert H. Montgomery, Jr., as Trustee.
Down with the legislators, 126
DREAM SONG, 259 Copyright © 1977 by John F. Wharton, as Trustee.
DREAM-DANCING, 295 Copyright © 1941 by Chappell & Co., Inc. Copyright Renewed.[1]
DRESDEN CHINA SOLDIERS, 38 Copyright © 1983 by Robert H. Montgomery, Jr., as Trustee.
DRESSING DAUGHTER FOR DINNER, 279 Copyright © 1983 by Robert H. Montgomery, Jr., as Trustee.
DRINK, 364 Copyright © 1977 by Robert H. Montgomery, Jr., as Trustee.
DRINKING SONG, 463 Copyright © 1956 by Chappell & Co., Inc.
DU BARRY WAS A LADY, 261 Copyright © 1983 by Robert H. Montgomery, Jr., as Trustee.
Due to landscape gard'ners gifted, 252
Due to the tragic lowness of my brow, 213
DUODECIMALOGUE, 30 Copyright © 1983 by Robert H. Montgomery, Jr., as Trustee.

Each year, when spring, quite uninvited, 135
EASY TO LOVE, 200 Copyright © 1936 by Chappell & Co., Inc. Copyright Renewed.
Eedoo, Aphroditah, 191
ELI, 5 Copyright © 1971 by John F. Wharton, as Trustee.
EMIGRANTS, THE, *See* ENTRANCE OF EMIGRANTS.
EMPEROR'S SONG, THE, *See* WOULDN'T IT BE FUN.
ENGAGEMENT ENSEMBLE, *See* LADY I'VE VOWED TO WED, THE.
ENTRANCE OF EMIGRANTS, 110 Copyright © 1983 by Robert H. Montgomery, Jr., as Trustee.
ENTRANCE OF ERIC, 184 © 1935 (Renewed) Warner Bros. Inc.
ENTRANCE OF INDIAN MAIDENS, 45 Copyright © 1983 by Robert H. Montgomery, Jr., as Trustee.
ENTRANCE OF JUNO, *See* HAIL, HAIL, HAIL.
ENTRANCE OF LUCY JAMES, 200 Copyright © 1983 by Robert H. Montgomery, Jr., as Trustee.
ENTRANCE OF MONTANA, 343 Copyright © 1983 by Robert H. Montgomery, Jr., as Trustee.
ENTRANCE OF PARIS, THE (no lyrics), 191
ENTRANCE OF PRINCE PAUL, 222 Copyright © 1937 by Chappell & Co., Inc. Copyright Renewed.
ERIC, *See* ENTRANCE OF ERIC.
ESMERELDA (ESMERALDA), *See* AS I LOVE YOU.
Evenin', creepin' down the mountain, 296
EVER AND EVER YOURS, 55 Copyright © 1916 G. Schirmer, Inc. Copyright Renewed.[5]
Ever since that fatal moment, 108
Every law-abiding jurist, 122
Every summery night, 37
Every time that I feel the way of all flesh, 122
Everyone knows, when a maiden is beautiful, 33
Everything's twins, 82
Ev'ry afternoon when the sun goes down, 243 footnote
EV'RY DAY A HOLIDAY, 256 Copyright © 1940 by Chappell & Co., Inc. Copyright Renewed.[1]
Ev'ry girl I know, 418
Ev'ry girl in town who's over there, 286
Ev'ry hour, ev'ry place, 276
EV'RY MAN IS A STUPID MAN, 428 Copyright © 1953 by Cole Porter. Copyright Renewed.[2]
Ev'ry time I ask, "Do you love me?", 247
Ev'ry time I gaze in your eyes, 340
Ev'ry time I look down, 429
Ev'ry time I see you, dear, 140
Ev'ry time I'm near you, ev'ry time we touch, 207
Ev'ry time I've trouble, 348
EV'RY TIME WE SAY GOODBYE, 362 Copyright © 1944 by Chappell & Co., Inc. Copyright Renewed.[1]
EV'RYBOD-EE WHO'S ANYBOD-EE, 191 © 1935 (Renewed) Warner Bros. Inc.
Ev'rybody, / Chic or shoddy, 429
Ev'rybody who's anybody's at Longchamps today, 121
EV'RYTHING I LOVE, 302 Copyright © 1941 by Chappell & Co., Inc. Copyright Renewed.[1]
EXERCISE, 21 Copyright © 1976 by John F. Wharton, as Trustee.
EXPERIMENT, 158 © 1933 (Renewed) Warner Bros. Inc.
EXTRA MAN, THE, 115 Copyright © 1977 by John F. Wharton, as Trustee.

FAIR ONE (lost), 11
FAR AWAY, 246 Copyright © 1938 by Chappell & Co., Inc. Copyright Renewed.[1]
FAR, FAR AWAY, 13 Copyright © 1983 by Robert H. Montgomery, Jr., as Trustee.
FARE THEE WELL, 17 Copyright © 1983 by Robert H. Montgomery, Jr., as Trustee.
FAREWELL, AMANDA, 402 Copyright © 1949 by Chappell & Co., Inc. Copyright Renewed.[1]
FARMING, 301 Copyright © 1941 by Chappell & Co., Inc. Copyright Renewed.[1]
FASCINATING FEMALES, 49 Copyright © 1983 by Robert H. Montgomery, Jr., as Trustee.
FATE, 155 Copyright © 1977 by John F. Wharton, as Trustee.
FATED TO BE MATED, 451 Copyright © 1956 by Chappell & Co., Inc.
FEATHERMORE, *See* WE'RE OFF TO FEATHERMORE.
FINALE, ACT I, *See* HA, HA, HA.
FINALE, ACT I, *See America First,* 51 Copyright © 1983 by Robert H. Montgomery, Jr., as Trustee.
FINALE, ACT II, *Kiss Me, Kate,* 396 Copyright © 1951 by Cole Porter. Copyright Renewed.[2]
FINALE, ACT II, *See America First* (lost), 42
FIND ME A PRIMITIVE MAN, 119 © 1929 (Renewed) Warner Bros. Inc.
First I do this, 333
First select a small canoe, 4
FISH, 95 © Registered in the name of M.E. Sayag, 1928. Copyright Renewed.[4]
FIVE HUNDRED MILLION, 210 Copyright © 1966 by John F. Wharton, as Trustee.
Flow, sweet music, 376
FLOWER MAIDENS, 29 Copyright © 1983 by Robert H. Montgomery, Jr., as Trustee.
FLOWER SONG, *See* LANGUAGE OF FLOWERS, THE.
FOLLIES GIRLS AND THEIR COLLIES, THE, *See* DOLLYS AND THEIR COLLIES, THE.
FOOL THERE WAS, A, 223 Copyright © 1936 by Chappell & Co., Inc. Copyright Renewed.
FOOTBALL KING, A, 6 Copyright © 1983 by Robert H. Montgomery, Jr., as Trustee.
For I presented Mister Morgan to Mister Harjes, 62
For if dear little ermines in Siberia, 120
For I'm Gaston, Gaston, 225
For I'm longing for dear old Broadway, 19
For I'm looking for an old-fashioned boy, 99
For I'm looking for an old-fashioned girl, 98
For I'm the Blue Boy, 132
For I'm unlucky at gambling, 125
For it's Sunday morning breakfast time, 192
FOR NO RHYME OR REASON, 227 Copyright © 1938 by Chappell & Co., Inc. Copyright Renewed.[1]
For you never know, 226
For we'd scarcely been a week or two at sea, 185
For we're such innocent, innocent, innocent, 32
For when Peter Piper picked a peck of peppers, 64
For your thrills, 128
FOUNTAIN OF YOUTH, 99 © Registered in the name of M. E. Sayag, 1928. Copyright Renewed.[4]
FOX TROT (no lyrics), 274
FRAHNGEE-PAHNEE, 366 Copyright © 1944 by Chappell & Co., Inc. Copyright Renewed.[1]
FRENCH COLONIAL EXPOSITION SCENE, 165 Copyright © 1983 by Robert H. Montgomery, Jr., as Trustee.
FRESH AS A DAISY, 284 Copyright © 1940 by Chappell & Co., Inc. Copyright Renewed.[1]
FRIENDSHIP, 266 Copyright © 1939 by Chappell & Co., Inc. Copyright Renewed.[1]
FROM ALPHA TO OMEGA, 227 Copyright © 1938 by Chappell & Co., Inc. Copyright Renewed.[1]
From an Indiana farm, green and flow'ry, 361
From being merely / A necessary luxury, 190
From down to up, 423
FROM NOW ON, 243 Copyright © 1938 by Chappell & Co., Inc. Copyright Renewed.[1]
From Saturday to Monday, 145
From the ladies dining at the Berkeley, 153
FROM THIS MOMENT ON, 415, 418 Copyright © 1950 by Cole Porter. Copyright Renewed.[1]
From what I hear, 239
FUNNY LITTLE TRACKS IN THE SNOW, 32 Copyright © 1983 by Robert H. Montgomery, Jr., as Trustee.

GATHER YE AUTOGRAPHS WHILE YE MAY, 187 Copyright © 1983 by Robert H. Montgomery, Jr., as Trustee.
GAY LITTLE WIVES, 193 © 1935 (Renewed) Warner Bros. Inc.
Gaze at the stars when at night you're alone, 468
Gaze on those glist'ning lights, 439
Gazing down on the Jungfrau, 387
Gee, I'm lucky to get you here, 144
Gee what a place to waste a day in, 19
GENIE'S THEME (no lyrics), 471
Gentlefolk of Newport, 456
GEORGIA SAND, 160 © 1933 (Renewed) Warner Bros. Inc.
GERSHWIN SPECIALTY, 97 Copyright © 1983 by Robert H. Montgomery, Jr., as Trustee.
GET OUT OF TOWN, 240 Copyright © 1938 by Chappell & Co., Inc. Copyright Renewed.[1]
GET YOURSELF A GIRL, 308 Copyright © 1967 by John F. Wharton, as Trustee.
GIBSON GIRLS' ENTRANCE (no lyrics), 89
GIRLS, 346 Copyright © 1944 by Chappell & Co., Inc. Copyright Renewed.[1]
Girls to the right of me, 346
GIVE HIM THE OO-LA-LA, 262 Copyright © 1940 by Chappell & Co., Inc. Copyright Renewed.[1]

GIVE ME THE LAND, 447 Copyright © 1966 by John F. Wharton, as Trustee.
GLIDE, GLIDER, GLIDE, 401 Copyright © registered in the name of Army Air Forces Aid Society 1943. Copyright Renewed.
Glorify Sixth Avenue, 252
GO INTO YOUR DANCE, 143 Copyright © 1977 by Robert H. Montgomery, Jr., as Trustee.
Go out and start your career, honey, 268
GOD BLESS THE WOMEN, 291 Copyright © 1977 by John F. Wharton, as Trustee.
GOLD DUSTERS SONG, THE, 402 Copyright © 1983 by Robert H. Montgomery, Jr., as Trustee.
Gone are the days that breed despair, 184
Gone are the roses that grew down the lane, 87
GOOD EVENING, PRINCESSE, 231 Copyright © 1977 by Robert H. Montgomery, Jr., as Trustee.
Good ev'ning, Comte, 148
Good morning, Highness, 189
Good morning, Lady Hard-to-Get, 253
GOOD MORNING, MISS STANDING, 188 © 1935 (Renewed) Warner Bros. Inc.
Good night! Good night, everyone!, 16
GOODBYE, BOYS, 12 Copyright © 1983 by Robert H. Montgomery, Jr., as Trustee.
GOODBYE, LITTLE DREAM, GOODBYE, 202 Copyright © 1936 by Chappell & Co., Inc. Copyright Renewed.
GOODBYE, MY TRUE LOVE, 27 Copyright © 1983 by Robert H. Montgomery, Jr., as Trustee.
GOOD-WILL MOVEMENT, THE, 343 Copyright © 1943 by Chappell & Co., Inc. Copyright Renewed.[1]
Got the gown, got the veil, 289
GREAT INDOORS, THE, 145 © 1930 (Renewed) Warner Bros., Inc.
GREEK TO YOU, 276 Copyright © 1966 by John F. Wharton, as Trustee.
GREENWICH VILLAGE LADIES' BARBER SHOP (no lyrics), 88
GREETINGS, GENTLEMEN, 43 Copyright © 1983 by Robert H. Montgomery, Jr., as Trustee.
GYPSY IN ME, THE, 174 © 1934 (Renewed) Warner Bros. Inc.
GYPSY SONG, 271 Copyright © 1977 by Robert H. Montgomery, Jr., as Trustee.

HA, HA, HA, 234 Copyright © 1977 by Robert H. Montgomery, Jr., as Trustee.
HA, HA, THEY MUST SAIL FOR SIBERIA, 23 Copyright © 1976 by John F. Wharton, as Trustee.
HAIL BIBINSKI, 442 Copyright © 1955 by Cole Porter. Copyright Renewed.
HAIL, HAIL, HAIL, 405 Copyright © 1951 by Cole Porter. Copyright Renewed.
HAIL TO CYRIL, 39 Copyright © 1983 by Robert H. Montgomery, Jr., as Trustee.
Hail to thee, Juno, our Mother, 405
HAIL TO YALE, 5 Copyright © 1983 by Robert H. Montgomery, Jr., as Trustee.
HAIL, YE MAIDEN INDIANS, 49 Copyright © 1983 by Robert H. Montgomery, Jr., as Trustee.
HANS, 98 © 1928 (Renewed) Warner Bros. Inc.
HAPPY HEAVEN OF HARLEM, THE, 121 © 1929 (Renewed) Warner Bros. Inc.
HARBOR DEEP DOWN IN MY HEART, THE, 81 © 1922 (Renewed) Warner Bros. Inc.
HARK TO THE SONG OF THE NIGHT, 414 Copyright © 1950 by Cole Porter. Copyright Renewed.[1]
Hark ye, children, listen to Mother, 304
HASTA LUEGO, 316 Copyright © 1942 by Chappell & Co., Inc. Copyright Renewed.[1]
Have you ever heard the story of the Sophomore? 27
Have you heard, among this clan, 264
Have you heard that Missus Burr, 148
Have you heard the coast of Maine, 263
Have you heard the tale they tell, 369
HE CERTAINLY KILLS THE WOMEN, 353 Copyright © 1966 by John F. Wharton, as Trustee.
He said my bronchial tubes were entrancing, 162
HEAVEN HOP, THE, 103 © 1928 (Renewed) Warner Bros. Inc.
HEAVEN OF HARLEM, THE, 128, *See also* 86 Copyright © 1983 by Robert H. Montgomery, Jr., as Trustee.
Hello, bretheren, howdy do!, 289
Hello, girls! How d'ye do?, 48
Hello, hello, hello!, 134
Hello, hello, listen to our bellow, 14
Hello, Mabel, how are you?, 73
HELLO, MISS CHAPEL STREET, 11 Copyright © 1971 by John F. Wharton, as Trustee.
HELLO SADNESS, BONJOUR TRISTESSE (unfinished sketch), 459
HELP THE POOR RICH, *See* THE POOR RICH.
HENCE IT DON'T MAKE SENSE, 367 Copyright © 1944 by Chappell & Co., Inc. Copyright Renewed.[1]
HER HEART WAS IN HER WORK, 433 Copyright © 1952 by Cole Porter. Copyright Renewed.
HERA'S DANCE (no lyrics), 191
HERE COMES THE BANDWAGON, 135 © 1929 (Renewed) Warner Bros. Inc.
Here we are, well matched and unattached, 156
Here you are, a total stranger, 227
HEREAFTER, 349 Copyright © 1967 by John F. Wharton, as Trustee.
Here's a bit of news that's quite a shocker, 301
HERE'S A CHEER FOR DEAR OLD CIRO'S, 351 Copyright © 1977 by Robert H. Montgomery, Jr., as Trustee.
Here's Keecha-Kacha-Coocha from Baluchistan, 379
Here's to our duty, to do one's duty is just, 438

HERE'S TO PANAMA HATTIE, 291 Copyright © 1983 by Robert H. Montgomery, Jr., as Trustee.
Here's to the piping porridge, 192
HE'S A RIGHT GUY, 325 Copyright © 1942 by Chappell & Co., Inc. Copyright Renewed.[1]
HEY, BABE, HEY, 199 Copyright © 1936 by Chappell & Co., Inc. Copyright Renewed.
HEY, GOOD-LOOKIN', 324 Copyright © 1942 by Chappell & Co., Inc. Copyright Renewed[1]
HEY, SEXY (HI, SEXY) (unfinished sketch), 459
Hey there, in the halyards, 364
Hi, big boy, what's doin' today?, 329
Hiding away, 174
HIGH SOCIETY CALYPSO, 454 Copyright © 1955 by Chappell & Co., Inc. Copyright Renewed.[2]
HIGH-FLYIN' WINGS ON MY SHOES, 464 Copyright © 1957 by Chappell & Co., Inc.
Hin Hin Hin Hin, 60
HIP, HIP, HOORAY FOR ANDY JACKSON, 335 Copyright © 1969 by John F. Wharton, as Trustee.
Hip hooray for good Prince Paul, 222
HITCHY'S GARDEN OF ROSES, 62 © 1919 (Renewed) Warner Bros. Inc.
Hm, what is that tune?, 227
Hold your hoss, here they come, 369
HOLD-UP ENSEMBLE, 45 Copyright © 1983 by Robert H. Montgomery, Jr., as Trustee.
HOT-HOUSE ROSE, 139 © 1927 (Renewed) Warner Bros. Inc.
HOW COULD I?, 459 Copyright © 1983 by Robert H. Montgomery, Jr., as Trustee.
HOW COULD WE BE WRONG?, 159 © 1933 (Renewed) Warner Bros. Inc.
How dare you issue such an order, 72
HOW DO THEY DO IT?, 278 Copyright © 1983 by Robert H. Montgomery, Jr., as Trustee.
HOW DO YOU SPELL AMBASSADOR?, 238 Copyright © 1974 by John F. Wharton, as Trustee.
How little I knew, 441
How's it back in the homeland, Buzz?, 354
HOW'S YOUR ROMANCE?, 153 © 1932 (Renewed) Warner Bros. Inc.
HUMBLE HOLLYWOOD EXECUTIVE, A, 353 Copyright © 1967 by John F. Wharton, as Trustee.
Humbly begging your pardon, 62
HUSH, HUSH, HUSH, 416 Copyright © 1949 by Cole Porter. Copyright Renewed.
"Hush-o," will sing the leaves, 339
Hyacinth and violet, 37
Hymen, thou phony, 211
HYMN TO HYMEN, 211 Copyright © 1977 by Robert H. Montgomery, Jr., as Trustee.

I admit that France is big-time, 447
I ADORE YOU, 469 Copyright © 1957 by Cole Porter.[3]
I ALWAYS KNEW, 314 Copyright © 1942 by Chappell & Co., Inc. Copyright Renewed.[1]
I AM ASHAMED THAT WOMEN ARE SO SIMPLE, 396 Copyright © 1948 by Cole Porter. Copyright Renewed.[1]
I am dejected, 425
I AM GASTON, 225 Copyright © 1977 by Robert H. Montgomery, Jr., as Trustee.
I AM IN LOVE, 425 Copyright © 1952 by Cole Porter. Copyright Renewed.[2]
I AM LOVED, 408 Copyright © 1949 by Cole Porter. Copyright Renewed.[1]
I came for a gay vacation, 356
I CAN DO WITHOUT TEA IN MY TEAPOT, 313 Copyright © 1977 by Robert H. Montgomery, Jr., as Trustee.
I can see / He's happier without me, 325
I cannot trust darling Mama, 450
I CONCENTRATE ON YOU, 253 Copyright © 1939 by Chappell & Co., Inc. Copyright Renewed.[1]
I COULD KICK MYSELF, 465 Copyright © 1966 by John F. Wharton, as Trustee.
I COULDN'T BE MORE IN LOVE, *See* COULDN'T BE.
I delight in art, do you?, 435
I DO, 435 Copyright © 1952 by Cole Porter. Copyright Renewed.
I don't like men who take you off, 127
I don't love you, dear, 125
I don't mean to cause a shock in the house, 257
I don't mind if for me you're scheming, 466
I don't want you to feel, 253, 254
I DREAM OF A GIRL IN A SHAWL, 112 © 1929 (Renewed) Warner Bros., Inc.
I dreamed that someone just like you, 149
I feel a sudden urge to sing, 208
I feel like a million dollars, 287
I feel so blue, 96
I feel the moment near, 358
I felt so glum, 282
I find that life's not what it used to be, 63
I first knew love's delight, 202
I found romance, 106
I GAZE IN YOUR EYES, 402 Copyright © 1983 by Robert H. Montgomery, Jr., as Trustee.
I GET A KICK OUT OF YOU, 167 © 1934 (Renewed) Warner Bros. Inc.
I get awful gloomy, 285
I get no kick from champagne, 167
I give him his breakfast, 462
I give to you and you give to me, 455
I GOT BEAUTY, 406 Copyright © 1951 by Cole Porter. Copyright Renewed.
I gotta swell idea, 143
I HAPPEN TO BE IN LOVE, 253 Copyright © 1939 by Chappell & Co., Inc. Copyright Renewed.[1]
I happen to be the sister, 97
I HAPPEN TO LIKE NEW YORK, 147 © 1931 (Renewed) Warner Bros. Inc.

I HATE MEN, 390 Copyright © 1948 by Chappell & Co., Inc. Copyright Renewed.[1]
I HATE YOU, DARLING, 308 Copyright © 1941 by Chappell & Co., Inc. Copyright Renewed.[1]
I have tried my best sweet words to combine, 416
I hear, in affairs romantic, 350
I INTRODUCED, 62 © 1919 (Renewed) Warner Bros. Inc.
I JUPITER, I REX, 404 Copyright © 1949 by Cole Porter. Copyright Renewed.[1]
I just received a wire from Lord Nelson, 364
I KNOW IT'S NOT MEANT FOR ME, 222 Copyright © 1937 by Chappell & Co., Inc. Copyright Renewed.
I know too well that I'm, 201
I LIKE PRETTY THINGS, 336 Copyright © 1969 by John F. Wharton, as Trustee.
I LIKE THE LADIES, 436 Copyright © 1983 by Robert H. Montgomery, Jr., as Trustee.
I lived in a dream, my sweet, 383
I LOOK AT YOU, *See* YOU'RE TOO FAR AWAY.
I LOVE ONLY YOU, 156 Copyright © 1983 by Robert H. Montgomery, Jr., as Trustee.
I LOVE PARIS, 428 Copyright © 1952 by Cole Porter. Copyright Renewed.[2]
I love the looks of you, the lure of you, 441
I LOVE YOU, 344 Copyright © 1943 by Chappell & Co., Inc. Copyright Renewed.[1]
I love you, oh, I do, 443, 448
I LOVE YOU, SAMANTHA, 454 Copyright © 1955 by Cole Porter. Copyright Renewed.[2]
I LOVE YOU SO, 23 Copyright © 1976 by John F. Wharton, as Trustee.
I loved a boy from Groton, 35
I LOVED HIM, BUT HE DIDN'T LOVE ME, 109 © 1929 (Renewed) Warner Bros. Inc.
I loved you madly, you know it well, 402
I loves yuh, lady, 'cause you're so refeened, 372
I met a friend of mine a week or two ago, 138
I must be on my way, 131
I must go where you lead me, 55
I must warn you in advance, 189
I NEVER REALIZED, 71 Copyright © 1921 by Leo Feist, Inc. Copyright Renewed.
I often ask, 407
I PRESENTED, *See* I INTRODUCED.
I read so many tales of love, 164
I receive, ev'ry morning, 148
I roam thro' darkest night, 54
I sat in old King Louis' chair one night in sunny France, 83
I SHALL POSITIVELY PAY YOU NEXT MONDAY, 431 Copyright © 1952 by Cole Porter. Copyright Renewed.
I should like you all to know, 114
I simply adorn a secluded corner, 64
I SING OF LOVE, 391 Copyright © 1949 by Cole Porter. Copyright Renewed.[1]
I SLEEP EASIER NOW, 410 Copyright © 1951 by Cole Porter. Copyright Renewed.[2]
I so often dream, 296
I STILL LOVE THE RED, WHITE AND BLUE, 152 Copyright © 1977 by Robert H. Montgomery, Jr., as Trustee.
I still was a dumb child, 136
I suppose a life of marriage, 270
I suppose all husbands are quite the same, 235
I suppose my best chances are small, 215
I think I've gained enough renown, 121
I think of you and suddenly start, 164
I think we'd better go, better go, better go, 81
I think you're great, 101
I used to be the type of mouse, 63
I used to be twice as shy as a lily, 106
I used to dream, 257
I used to fall, 244
I used to mourn, 106
I WANT TO BE A PROM GIRL, 7 Copyright © 1983 by Robert H. Montgomery, Jr., as Trustee.
I WANT TO BE A YALE BOY, 7 Copyright © 1983 by Robert H. Montgomery, Jr., as Trustee.
I WANT TO BE MARRIED (TO A DELTA KAPPA EPSILON MAN), 22 Copyright © 1976 by John F. Wharton, as Trustee.
I WANT TO BE RAIDED BY YOU, 114 © 1929 (Renewed) Warner Bros. Inc.
I WANT TO GO HOME, 243 Copyright © 1938 by Chappell & Co., Inc. Copyright Renewed.[1]
I WANT TO ROW ON THE CREW, 34 Copyright © 1971 by John F. Wharton, as Trustee.
I WANT TWINS (no lyrics), 88
I was a humdrum person, 111
I was a sunken soufflé, 284
I was just another page in your diary, 248
I was mighty blue, 118
I was so happy when first I found you, 464
I was still the mild, money-wild type of child, 65
I was such a fragile precocious little elf, 370
I wasn't born to stately halls, 282
I went to London I met the King, 129
I went to Monte Carlo the other day, 124
I will give you, my broth of a boy, a nest, 339
I will never forget, 106
I woke today feeling so gay, 155
I WONDER WHERE MY GIRL IS NOW, 21 Copyright © 1983 by Robert H. Montgomery, Jr., as Trustee.
I won't sing a song about battle, 391
I WORSHIP YOU, 125 © 1929 (Renewed) Warner Bros. Inc.
I WROTE A PLAY, 371 Copyright © 1967 by John F. Wharton, as Trustee.
I wrote a poem, 390
I'd walk a mile for that schoolgirl complexion, 7
IDYLL, 36 Copyright © 1983 by Robert H.

IDYLL (*continued*)
Montgomery, Jr., as Trustee.
If a custom-tailored vet, 394
If a girl in any sector, 325
If a love song I could only write, 345
If about Harlem some night you're gaddin', 305
If away you long to steal, 282
If ever I love again, 147
IF EVER MARRIED I'M, 398 Copyright © 1966 by John F. Wharton, as Trustee.
If ever to you woe, 186
IF EVER WE GET OUT OF JAIL, 448 Copyright © 1966 by John F. Wharton, as Trustee.
If ever you love again, 143
If I didn't belong to a nation, 129
IF I HADN'T A HUSBAND, 372 Copyright © 1983 by Robert H. Montgomery, Jr., as Trustee.
If I have succeeded in life so far, 422
If I rattle with clips from Flato's, 230
If I were Lord Byron, 302
IF I WERE ONLY A FOOTBALL MAN, 7 Copyright © 1983 by Robert H. Montgomery, Jr., as Trustee.
If I'm in a high, 289
IF IN SPITE OF OUR ATTEMPTS, 46 Copyright © 1983 by Robert H. Montgomery, Jr., as Trustee.
If me, little Mowgli, badly dressed, 187
If my brain is simply uncanny, 303
If of late you haven't kicked up, 279
IF ONLY YOU COULD LOVE ME (no lyrics), 436
If the critics have dominion, 134
If the scene were a green South Sea Island, 332
If you ask me, as a dancer, 367
IF YOU COULD LOVE ME, 180 Copyright © 1983 by Robert H. Montgomery, Jr., as Trustee.
If you look your childhood over, 135
IF YOU LOVED ME TRULY, 425 Copyright © 1953 by Cole Porter. Copyright Renewed.[2]
If you meet J.P. Morgan while playing golf, 257
IF YOU SMILE AT ME, 378 Copyright © 1946 by Chappell & Co., Inc. Copyright Renewed.[1]
IF YOU TAKE ONE PILL, *See* OPERATIC PILLS.
If you want a fancy fan, 468
If you want to pass through the gilded gates, 423
If you want to ring the bell not once, but twice, 199
If you want to thrill me and drill me for your crew, 213
If you want to wed a little girl, 4
If you want your purse to be lined with gold, 468
If your doggie's lookin' sick, 318
If you're a maid men always quit, 345
If you're a reader of the daily news, 66
If you're depressed, 99
If you're ever in a jam, here I am, 266
If you're with the mob, 363
If you've ever been to a night club, 115
If you've got certain problems that must be solved, 310
If you've / Got that pitter-patter in your heart, 82
If you've noticed I'm, 218
I'LL BLACK HIS EYES, 231 Copyright © 1967 by John F. Wharton, as Trustee.
I'll remember forever, 383
I'm a dealer in antiques, 83
I'm a flower that blooms in the winter, 114
I'M A GIGOLO, 114 © 1929 (Renewed) Warner Bros. Inc.
I'm a girl out of fashion, 99
I'm a great success making love on the stage, 134
I'm a maid who would marry, 389
I'm a member very noted, 31
I'm a poor little squaw from Indiana, 329
I'm about to become a mother, 209
I'M AFRAID I LOVE YOU, 358 Copyright © 1966 by John F. Wharton, as Trustee.
I'm afraid I love you, 358
I'M AFRAID, SWEETHEART, I LOVE YOU, 398 Copyright © 1967 by John F. Wharton, as Trustee.
I'm always a flop at a top-notch affair, 283
I'm always doing something, 322
I'm always happy when I am dancing, 425
I'm an Alpine rose, just an Alpine rose, 97
I'M AN ANESTHETIC DANCER (lost), 62
I'm an extra man, an extra man, 115
I'M BACK IN CIRCULATION, 235 Copyright © 1967 by John F. Wharton, as Trustee.
I'm Bertie, a bad little butterfly, 214
I'm blue, / Black and blue, 419
I'm crazy for a baby that I can't forget, 463
I'm Dainty, Quainty Me, 370
I'M DINING WITH ELSA, 138 Copyright © 1983 by Robert H. Montgomery, Jr., as Trustee.
I'm feeling very happy for the future's that's in store for us, 72
I'M GETTING MYSELF READY FOR YOU, 144 © 1930 (Renewed) Warner Bros. Inc.
I'M GOING IN FOR LOVE, 235 Copyright © 1967 by John F. Wharton, as Trustee.
I'M HAUNTED BY YOU (no lyrics), 149
I'm hot-house rose from God knows where, 140
I'm in a terrible spot, 326
I'M IN LOVE, 123 © 1929 (Renewed) Warner Bros. Inc.
I'M IN LOVE AGAIN, 87 © 1925 (Renewed) Warner Bros. Inc.
I'M IN LOVE WITH A SOLDIER BOY, 326 Copyright © 1943 by Chappell & Co., Inc. Copyright Renewed.[1]
I'm in love with the nicest doughboy, 134
I'm just gloating, 465
I'm keeping steady—, 436

I'm like the charmed night, 336
I'm lonesome, 12
I'm nearly positive I care for you, 278
I'm not depressed because I can't forget, 397
I'M NOT MYSELF AT ALL, 336 Copyright © 1969 by John F. Wharton, as Trustee.
I'm not suggesting to you, 246
I'M NUTS ABOUT YOU, *See* HEY, BABE, HEY.
I'm off for New Haven, so long, goodbye, 8
I'm playin' a local belle, 321
I'm so awfully weary, 125
I'm so bored at going to the theatre, 8
I'M SO GLAD TO MEET YOU, 358 Copyright © 1983 by Robert H. Montgomery, Jr., as Trustee.
I'm so in love, 230
I'M SO IN LOVE WITH YOU, 254 Copyright © 1939 by Chappell & Co., Inc. Copyright Renewed.
I'm so mad I'm out for trouble, 308
I'M TAKING THE STEPS TO RUSSIA, 239 Copyright © 1938 by Chappell & Co., Inc. Copyright Renewed.[1]
I'm that charming maiden of Brittany, 85
I'm the Gen., 38
I'M THE VILLAIN, 14 Copyright © 1971 by John F. Wharton, as Trustee.
I'M THROWING A BALL TONIGHT, 287 Copyright © 1966 by John F. Wharton, as Trustee.
I'm tired, I'm pooped, 299
I'M UNLUCKY AT GAMBLING, 124 © 1929 (Renewed) Warner Bros. Inc.
I'M YOURS, 232 Copyright © 1977 by Robert H. Montgomery, Jr., as Trustee.
I'm yours, only yours, 195, 232
IN A MOORISH GARDEN, 94 © Registered in the name of M. E. Sayag 1928. Copyright Renewed.[4]
In a small canteena, 316
IN CASE YOU DON'T KNOW (no lyrics), 156
IN CHELSEA SOMEWHERE, *See* WASHINGTON SQUARE.
In Cincinnati, in Cincinnati, 39
In counting up celebrities, 35
In former times a glimpse of stocking, 172
In four-o-four, 40
In her garden, Mother Eve, 449
IN HITCHY'S BOUQUET, 78 Copyright © 1983 by Robert H. Montgomery, Jr., as Trustee.
IN HITCHY'S GARDEN, *See* HITCHY'S GARDEN OF ROSES, 62
In Italia the signori are so very amatory, 153
In Martinique, 385
In olden days, a glimpse of stocking, 171
In spite of the fact, 267
IN THE BIG MONEY, 268 Copyright © 1967 by John F. Wharton, as Trustee.
IN THE GREEN HILLS OF COUNTY MAYO, 336 Copyright © 1969 by John F. Wharton, as Trustee.
In the heavens, stars are dancing, 457
In the infinite variety, 115
In the land of my heart, 26
IN THE LAND WHERE MY HEART WAS BORN, 26 Copyright © 1983 by Robert H. Montgomery, Jr., as Trustee.
In the morning when you wake up, 273
In the old days, when a maid desired to wed, 325
In the olden days, a gal, Lord love 'er, 449
IN THE STILL OF THE NIGHT, 220 Copyright © 1937 by Chappell & Co., Inc. Copyright Renewed.
In town the other night, 279
INDIAN GIRLS' CHANT, *See* ENTRANCE OF INDIAN MAIDENS.
INDIAN MAIDENS' CHORUS, *See* IF IN SPITE OF OUR ATTEMPTS.
Indian maidens slouching o'er the hills and plains, 45
INFORMATION, PLEASE, 249 Copyright © 1967 by John F. Wharton, as Trustee.
INNOCENT, INNOCENT MAIDS, 32 Copyright © 1983 by Robert H. Montgomery, Jr., as Trustee.
Is ev'rybody happy?, 196
Is it a brainstorm—this feeling of joy? 230
Is it an earthquake or simply a shock? 230
IS IT JOY? (no lyrics), 466
IS IT THE GIRL (OR IS IT THE GOWN)?, 362 Copyright © 1944 by Chappell & Co., Inc. Copyright Renewed.[1]
IT AIN'T ETIQUETTE, 256 Copyright © 1965 by Chappell & Co., Inc.
IT ALL BELONGS TO YOU, 275 Copyright © 1938 by Chappell & Co., Inc. Copyright Renewed.[1]
IT ALL BELONGS TO YOU AND ME, *See* I LOVE YOU.
It all seems a dream, 271
IT ALL SEEMS SO LONG AGO, 273 Copyright © 1977 by Robert H. Montgomery, Jr., as Trustee.
It is Hades, 96
IT ISN'T DONE, 122 Copyright © 1977 by Robert H. Montgomery, Jr., as Trustee.
It may be / Greek to you and Greek to me, 276
IT MIGHT HAVE BEEN, 317 Copyright © 1942 by Chappell & Co., Inc. Copyright Renewed.[1]
It must be a menace to those who play tennis in Venice, 144
IT MUST BE FUN TO BE YOU, 350 Copyright © 1943 by Chappell & Co., Inc. Copyright Renewed.[1]
It must have been in June, 273
IT NEVER ENTERED MY HEAD, 276 Copyright © 1983 by Robert H. Montgomery, Jr., as Trustee.
IT ONLY HAPPENS IN DREAMS, 149 Copyright © 1983 by Robert H. Montgomery, Jr., as Trustee.
IT PAYS TO ADVERTISE, 7 Copyright © 1983 by Robert H. Montgomery, Jr., as Trustee.

IT PUZZLES ME SO, 70 Copyright © 1971 by John F. Wharton, as Trustee.
It seems to me that human history, 64
It was an old-fashioned garden, 64
IT WAS GREAT FUN THE FIRST TIME, 396 Copyright © 1966 by John F. Wharton, as Trustee.
It was just one of those things, 194
IT WAS WRITTEN IN THE STARS, 265 Copyright © 1939 by Chappell & Co., Inc. Copyright Renewed.[1]
ITALIAN STREET SINGERS, 136 Copyright © 1983 by Robert H. Montgomery, Jr., as Trustee.
IT'S A BIG NIGHT, 354 Copyright © 1967 by John F. Wharton, as Trustee.
IT'S A CHEMICAL REACTION, THAT'S ALL, 440 Copyright © 1954 by Cole Porter. Copyright Renewed.[2]
It's a curious fact, 155
IT'S A GREAT LIFE, 205 Copyright © 1978 by Robert H. Montgomery, Jr., as Trustee.
IT'S ALL OVER BUT THE SHOUTING, 221 Copyright © 1937 by Chappell & Co., Inc. Copyright Renewed.
IT'S ALL RIGHT WITH ME, 428 Copyright © 1953 by Cole Porter. Copyright Renewed.[2]
IT'S AWFULLY HARD WHEN MOTHER'S NOT ALONG, 22 Copyright © 1976 by John F. Wharton, as Trustee.
IT'S BAD FOR ME, 158 © 1933 (Renewed) Warner Brothers, Inc.
It's cocktail time!, 131
IT'S DE-LOVELY, 207 Copyright © 1936 by Chappell & Co., Inc. Copyright Renewed.
It's fate, 155
It's just a joy to be / Far from Washington, D.C., 332
IT'S JUST LIKE THE GOOD OLD DAYS, 354 Copyright © 1967 by John F. Wharton, as Trustee.
IT'S JUST YOURS, 355 Copyright © 1966 by John F. Wharton, as Trustee.
IT'S NO LAUGHING MATTER, 236 Copyright © 1966 by John F. Wharton, as Trustee.
It's not 'cause I wouldn't, 140
It's not that you're fairer, 313
IT'S PROBABLY JUST AS WELL, 273 Copyright © 1983 by Robert H. Montgomery, Jr., as Trustee.
It's sex appeal, it's sex appeal, it's sex appeal, that's all, 139
It's strange how a song you first heard, 368
It's strange how lovely lingerie, 441
It's the punch of old George Washington, 79
IT'S THE PUNCHES, *See* THE AMERICAN PUNCH.
It's the wrong time and the wrong place, 428
It's too darn hot, 392
I've a beau, his name is Jim, 140
I've a feelin' the Ozarks are callin', 213
I've a hunch that you'd be good to get, 332
I'VE A SHOOTING BOX IN SCOTLAND, 36 Copyright © 1916 G. Schirmer, Inc. Copyright renewed.[5]
I'VE A STRANGE NEW RHYTHM IN MY HEART, 218 Copyright © 1937 by Chappell & Co., Inc. Copyright Renewed.
I've a twisted neck and a twisted back, 367
I've always had both feet on the ground before, 463
I've been around such a lot in my time, 199
I've been doing a lot of scheming, 465
I've been grossly insulted by a cowardly lout, 431
I've begged all of England's classes, 112
I'VE COME TO WIVE IT WEALTHILY IN PADUA, 389 Copyright © 1949 by Cole Porter. Copyright Renewed.[1]
I've cut out eggs, 144
I've gone afar, 109
I'VE GOT A CRUSH ON YOU, 108 © 1929 (Renewed) Warner Bros. Inc.
I've got a harbor, 81
I've got a table for two, 73
I've got an aeroplane, 94
I'VE GOT AN AWFUL LOT TO LEARN, 48 Copyright © 1916 G. Schirmer, Inc. Copyright renewed.[5]
I've got an invite for everyone, 411
I'VE GOT MY EYES ON YOU, 252 Copyright © 1939 by Chappell & Co., Inc. Copyright Renewed.[1]
I'VE GOT QUELQUE-CHOSE, *See* QUELQUE-CHOSE.
I'VE GOT SOME UNFINISHED BUSINESS WITH YOU, 305 Copyright © 1977 by John F. Wharton, as Trustee.
I'VE GOT SOMEBODY WAITING, 63 © 1919 (Renewed) Warner Bros. Inc.
I've got something to shout about, 315
I've got such a crush on you, 108
I've got the lost liberty blues, 91
I'VE GOT TO BE PSYCHOANALYZED BY YOU (no lyrics), 149
I'VE GOT YOU ON MY MIND, 154 © 1932 (Renewed) Warner Bros. Inc.
I'VE GOT YOU UNDER MY SKIN, 201 Copyright © 1936 by Chappell & Co., Inc. Copyright Renewed.
I've had shooting pains in Scotland (parody), 37
I've just read of Cleopatra, 229
I've longed for this, ever since the day, 220
I've made a haul in all the leading rackets, 388
I've no proof, 456
I'VE STILL GOT MY HEALTH, 283 Copyright © 1940 by Chappell & Co., Inc. Copyright Renewed.[1]
I've such a hate on Manhattan lately, 146
I've wasted years enslaving myself, 125

JAVA, 278 Copyright © 1983 by Robert H. Montgomery, Jr., as Trustee.
Jazz may / Be other folks' diet, 95

JE VOUS COMPRENDS, 59 Copyright © 1983 by Robert H. Montgomery, Jr., as Trustee.
JERRY, MY SOLDIER BOY, 300 Copyright © 1942 by Chappell & Co., Inc., Copyright Renewed.[1]
Joe plays the banjo and plays ev'ry night, 110
JOIN IT RIGHT AWAY, 281 Copyright © 1983 by Robert H. Montgomery, Jr., as Trustee.
JOSEPHINE, 443 Copyright © 1955 by Cole Porter. Copyright Renewed.[2]
JUBILEE PRESENTATION (no lyrics), 195
JUDGMENT OF PARIS, THE, *See* APHRODITE'S DANCE.
JUNGLE ROSE, 83 Copyright © 1983 by Robert H. Montgomery, Jr., as Trustee.
JUNO'S RIDE, *See* HAIL, HAIL, HAIL.
JUST ANOTHER PAGE IN YOUR DIARY, 248 Copyright © 1966 by John F. Wharton, as Trustee.
Just dig that scenery floatin' by, 454
Just in case I'm found, 315
Just look at this miss, 97
JUST ONE OF THOSE THINGS *Jubilee*, 194 © 1935 (Renewed) Warner Bros. Inc.
JUST ONE OF THOSE THINGS *The New Yorkers*, 147 © 1930 (Renewed) Warner Bros. Inc.
JUST ONE STEP AHEAD OF LOVE, 233 Copyright © 1978 by Robert H. Montgomery, Jr., as Trustee.
Just you and me, 66

KATE THE GREAT, 175 Copyright © 1972 by John F. Wharton, as Trustee.
KATHLEEN, 337 Copyright © 1969 by John F. Wharton, as Trustee.
KATIE OF THE Y.M.C.A., 70 Copyright © 1971 by John F. Wharton, as Trustee.
KATIE WENT TO HAITI, 266 Copyright © 1939 by Chappell & Co., Inc. Copyright Renewed.[1]
Keep it quiet, keep it dark, 253
KEEP MOVING, 91 Copyright © 1983 by Robert H. Montgomery, Jr., as Trustee.
Kindly adjust your opera glasses, 32
KISS ME KATE, 391 Copyright © 1949 by Cole Porter. Copyright Renewed.[1]
KLING-KLING BIRD ON THE DIVI-DIVI TREE, THE, 185 © 1935 (Renewed) Warner Bros. Inc.

LA RÊVE D'ABSINTHE (lost), 11
Ladies and gentlemen / I beg of you, throw down, 225
Ladies and gentlemen, if you care for syncopation, 76
Ladies and gentlemen, / This costume may strike you as odd, 404
Ladies and gentlemen, when my heart is sick, 245
LADIES-IN-WAITING, 462 Copyright © 1956 by Chappell & Co., Inc.
LADY FAIR, LADY FAIR, 55 Copyright © 1971 by John F. Wharton, as Trustee.
LADY I LOVE, THE (no lyrics), 116
LADY I'VE VOWED TO WED, THE, 49 Copyright © 1983 by Robert H. Montgomery, Jr., as Trustee.
LADY NEEDS A REST, A, 299 Copyright © 1966 by John F. Wharton, as Trustee.
LANGUAGE OF FLOWERS, THE, 37 Copyright © 1916 G. Schirmer, Inc. Copyright renewed.[5]
Last night, while I / Was stepping high, 368
Last year down in dear Miami, 365
LAUNDRY SCENE, 432 Copyright © 1983 by Robert H. Montgomery, Jr., as Trustee.
LAW, THE, 430 Copyright © 1952 by Cole Porter. Copyright Renewed.
LAY YOUR BURDEN DOWN, *See* CLIMB UP THE MOUNTAIN.
LAZIEST GAL IN TOWN, THE, 140 © 1927 (Renewed) Warner Bros. Inc.
LEAD ME ON (no lyrics), 274
LEADER OF A BIG-TIME BAND, THE, 325 Copyright © 1943 by Chappell & Co., Inc. Copyright Renewed.[1]
LEADERS OF SOCIETY, 16 Copyright © 1983 by Robert H. Montgomery, Jr., as Trustee.
LES GIRLS, 461 Copyright © 1956 by Chappell & Co., Inc.
LET DOCTOR SCHMETT VET YOUR PET, 317 Copyright © 1983 by Robert H. Montgomery, Jr., as Trustee.
Let the modern cynics all laugh at marriage, 212
Let's all go and have a little party in Bohemia, 17
LET'S BE BUDDIES, 285 Copyright © 1940 by Chappell & Co., Inc. Copyright Renewed.[1]
LET'S DO IT, LET'S FALL IN LOVE, 101 © 1928 (Renewed) Warner Bros. Inc.
LET'S END THE BEGUINE, *See* DANCIN' TO A JUNGLE DRUM.
LET'S FACE IT, 301 Copyright © 1977 by Robert H. Montgomery, Jr., as Trustee.
LET'S FLY AWAY, 146 © 1930 (Renewed) Warner Bros. Inc.
Let's live once more the day, 30
LET'S MAKE IT A NIGHT, 448 Copyright © 1966 by John F. Wharton, as Trustee.
LET'S MISBEHAVE, 104 © 1927 (Renewed) Warner Bros. Inc.
LET'S NOT TALK ABOUT LOVE, 306 Copyright © 1941 by Chappell & Co., Inc. Copyright Renewed.[1]
Let's pretend we lived of old, 33
Let's quit this weary world of ours, 163
LET'S STEP OUT, 128 © 1930 (Renewed) Warner Bros. Inc.
Let's talk about love, that wonderful thing, 306
LET'S VOCALIZE, 457 Copyright © 1955 by

Chappell & Co., Inc., Copyright Renewed.
Life at its best is a puzzle, 113
Life is very far from easy, 299
LIFE OF A SAILOR, THE (lost), 89
Life's great, life's grand, 210
Like the beat beat beat of the tom-tom, 153
LIMA, 56 Copyright © 1916 G. Schirmer, Inc. Copyright Renewed.[5]
Listen, girls, last Wednesday, I went to a matinee, 310
Listen here, baby dear, 128
Listen, listen, Mary, 77
Listen, my dearie, 70
Little boys, there's a thing called love, 347
Little fifi making bonnets, 433
Little man, little man, 308
LITTLE ONE, 454 Copyright © 1955 by Cole Porter. Copyright Renewed.[2]
LITTLE RUMBA NUMBA, A, 307 Copyright © 1941 by Chappell & Co., Inc. Copyright Renewed.[1]
LITTLE SKIPPER FROM HEAVEN ABOVE, A 209 Copyright © 1936 by Chappell & Co., Inc. Copyright Renewed.
LIVE AND LET LIVE, 424 Copyright © 1952 by Cole Porter. Copyright Renewed.[2]
LLEWELLYN, 15 Copyright © 1983 by Robert H. Montgomery, Jr., as Trustee.
LOADING SONG, 337 Copyright © 1969 by John F. Wharton, as Trustee.
LOCK UP YOUR CHICKENS (partial lyrics), 420
LOIE AND CHLODO, 24 Copyright © 1976 by John F. Wharton, as Trustee.
LONELY STAR, 215 Copyright © 1983 by Robert H. Montgomery, Jr., as Trustee.
Long, long ago, 87, 174
LONGING FOR DEAR OLD BROADWAY, 19 Copyright © 1971 by John F. Wharton, as Trustee.
LOOK WHAT I FOUND, 376 Copyright © 1946 by Chappell & Co., Inc. Copyright Renewed.[1]
LOOKING AT YOU, 109 © 1929 (Renewed) Warner Bros. Inc.
LOST LIBERTY BLUES, THE, 91 © Registered in the name of M. E. Sayag, 1928. Copyright Renewed.[4]
LOTUS BLOOM, 315 Copyright © 1942 by Chappell & Co., Inc. Copyright Renewed.[1]
LOUISA, *See* MY LOUISA.
Love affairs among gentility, 259
LOVE CAME AND CROWNED ME, 56 Copyright © 1983 by Robert H. Montgomery, Jr., as Trustee.
Love can make you happy, 147
LOVE 'EM AND LEAVE 'EM, 136 Copyright © 1978 by Robert H. Montgomery, Jr., as Trustee.
LOVE FOR SALE, 145 © 1930 (Renewed) Warner Bros. Inc.
Love had socked me, 210
Love is a pure and purple fire, 34
Love is such a fantastic affair, 423
LOVE LETTER WORDS, 80 © 1922 (Renewed) Warner Bros. Inc.
Love me, darling?, 442, 448
LOVE ME, LOVE MY PEKINESE, 200 Copyright © 1936 by Chappell & Co., Inc. Copyright Renewed.
Love—/ My evil curse, my deadly foe, 221
LOVE OF MY LIFE, 383 Copyright © 1946 by Chappell & Co., Inc. Copyright Renewed.[1]
LOVELY HEROINE, THE, 14 Copyright © 1983 by Robert H. Montgomery, Jr., as Trustee.
Lovers are a funny lot, 37
Love's such a funny thing, 226

MA PETITE NINETTE, *See* NINETTE.
MACK THE BLACK, 381 Copyright © 1946 by Chappell & Co., Inc. Copyright Renewed.[1]
MADEMAZELLE, 134 Copyright © 1983 by Robert H. Montgomery, Jr., as Trustee.
MAID OF SANTIAGO, 29 Copyright © 1983 by Robert H. Montgomery, Jr., as Trustee.
MAIDEN FAIR, 406 Copyright © 1983 by Robert H. Montgomery, Jr., as Trustee.
Maiden, maiden, from the first, 30
Maiden, pretty little maiden, 30
Maidens fair, drop that frown, 407
MAIDENS TYPICAL OF FRANCE, 422 Copyright © 1953 by Cole Porter. Copyright Renewed.[2]
MAKE A DATE WITH A GREAT PSYCHOANALYST, 310 Copyright © 1967 by John F. Wharton, as Trustee.
MAKE EVERY DAY A HOLIDAY, 87 © 1924 (Renewed) Warner Bros. Inc.
MAKE IT ANOTHER OLD-FASHIONED, PLEASE, 288 Copyright © 1940 by Chappell & Co., Inc. Copyright Renewed.[1]
MAKE WAY FOR THE EMPEROR, 469 Copyright © 1958 by Cole Porter.[3]
MAMIE MAGDALIN, 338 Copyright © 1969 by John F. Wharton, as Trustee.
MAN MUST HIS HONOR DEFEND, A, 431 Copyright © 1978 by Robert H. Montgomery, Jr., as Trustee.
Manhattan—I'm up a tree, 206
MANUELA, 384 Copyright © 1946 by Chappell & Co., Inc. Copyright Renewed.[1]
Many girls I've met, 71
MARIA, 226 Copyright © 1938 by Chappell & Co., Inc. Copyright Renewed.[1]
Marietta and sweet Babette, 12
MARTINIQUE, 385 Copyright © 1983 by Robert H. Montgomery, Jr., as Trustee.
Mary isn't a youngster, Mary hasn't a bob, 139
MARYLAND SCENE, 76 Copyright © 1983 by Robert H. Montgomery, Jr., as Trustee.
MAYBE YES, MAYBE NO, 278 Copyright © 1983 by

Robert H. Montgomery, Jr., as Trustee.
Me and he, / Jupiter, 406
ME AND MARIE, 193 © 1935 (Renewed) Warner Bros. Inc.
MEE-RAH-LAH, 377 Copyright © 1983 by Robert H. Montgomery, Jr., as Trustee.
MEET ME BESIDE THE RIVER, 27 Copyright © 1983 by Robert H. Montgomery, Jr., as Trustee.
MELOS, THAT SMILING ISLE, 276 Copyright © 1983 by Robert H. Montgomery, Jr., as Trustee.
MEMBER OF THE YALE ELIZABETHAN CLUB, A, 31 Copyright © 1971 by John F. Wharton, as Trustee.
Men, / I used to take you / So seriously, 161
MERCY PERCY (lost), 28
MESDAMES ET MESSIEURS, 259 Copyright © 1983 by Robert H. Montgomery, Jr., as Trustee.
MIDSUMMER NIGHT, 418 Copyright © 1967 by John F. Wharton, as Trustee.
MILITARY MAIDS, 96 © 1928 (Renewed) Warner Bros. Inc.
MILK, MILK, MILK, 299 Copyright © 1977 by Robert H. Montgomery, Jr., as Trustee.
MIND IF I MAKE LOVE TO YOU?, 457 Copyright © 1955 by Chappell & Co., Inc., Copyright Renewed.[2]
MIRROR, MIRROR, 54 Copyright © 1983 by Robert H. Montgomery, Jr., as Trustee.
Miss Antoinette Birby lived way out in Derby, 8
Miss Florence Hart, please get me straight, 320
Miss Lucy James sighted starboard beam, 200
MISS OTIS REGRETS, 274 © 1934 (Renewed) Warner Bros. Inc.
MISSISSIPPI BELLE, 338 Copyright © 1969 by John F. Wharton, as Trustee.
MISSUS AOUDA, 378 Copyright © 1967 by John F. Wharton, as Trustee.
Missus Emily Post, 256
MISTER AND MISSUS FITCH, 154 © 1954 (Renewed) Warner Bros. Inc.
Mister Romeo, 362
Monsieur President, 422
MONTMART', 426 Copyright © 1952 by Cole Porter. Copyright Renewed.[2]
MOON MAN, 31 Copyright © 1983 by Robert H. Montgomery, Jr., as Trustee.
MOON, MOON, 4 Copyright © 1983 by Robert H. Montgomery, Jr., as Trustee.
Moon, moon, silver moon, 16
MORY'S, 5 Copyright © 1983 by Robert H. Montgomery, Jr., as Trustee.
MOST GENTLEMEN DON'T LIKE LOVE, 241 Copyright © 1938 by Chappell & Co., Inc. Copyright Renewed.[1]
Mother Earth would be a charming place, 126
MOTHER PHI (lost), 11
MOTOR CAR, THE, 6 Copyright © 1971 by John F. Wharton, as Trustee.
MR. AND MRS. SMITH, 192 © 1935 (Renewed) Warner Bros. Inc.
Mr. Shubert, J. J., 82
Mrs. Lowsborough-Goodby gives weekends, 274
Mrs. Lundbeck is in despair, 401
MUSIC WITH MEALS (lost), 39
My boy Bill has charming traits, 311
MY BROTH OF A BOY, 339 Copyright © 1969 by John F. Wharton, as Trustee.
MY CARAVAN, *See* WHEN MY CARAVAN COMES HOME.
My childhood's happy hours were spent in ducal towers, 43
MY COZY LITTLE CORNER IN THE RITZ, 64 © 1919 (Renewed) Warner Bros. Inc.
MY DARLING NEVER IS LATE, 464 Copyright © 1983 by Robert H. Montgomery, Jr., as Trustee.
My dear, I have a feeling you are, 296
My dear, you're sailing off without me, 167
My dutiful servants, I come to you, 122
My friends . . . we are gathered here, 242
MY GEORGIA GAL, 31 Copyright © 1983 by Robert H. Montgomery, Jr., as Trustee.
MY HARLEM WENCH, 128 Copyright © 1978 by Robert H. Montgomery, Jr., as Trustee.
MY HEART BELONGS TO DADDY, 244 Copyright © 1938 by Chappell & Co., Inc. Copyright Renewed.[1]
MY HOMETOWN GIRL, 12 Copyright © 1983 by Robert H. Montgomery, Jr., as Trustee.
MY HOUSEBOAT ON THE THAMES, 19 Copyright © 1976 by John F. Wharton, Jr., as Trustee.
My life is done without a doubt, 16
My life was simply hellish, 287
My little Barcelona maid, 16
MY LITTLE PIECE O' PIE, 465 Copyright © 1983 by Robert H. Montgomery, Jr., as Trustee.
My little Salvation Army Queen, 22
MY LONG AGO GIRL, 87 © 1924 (Renewed) Warner Bros. Inc.
MY LONG, LONG AGO GIRL, *See* MY LONG AGO GIRL.
MY LOUISA, 115 Copyright © 1977 by John F. Wharton, as Trustee.
MY LOULOU, 188 © 1935 (Renewed) Warner Bros. Inc.
My mama says that ev'ry girlie, 112
MY MOST INTIMATE FRIEND, 189 © 1935 (Renewed) Warner Bros. Inc.
My mother and father, 126
MY MOTHER WOULD LOVE YOU, 282 Copyright © 1940 by Chappell & Co., Inc. Copyright Renewed.[1]
MY SALVATION ARMY QUEEN, 22 Copyright © 1976 by John F. Wharton, as Trustee.
MY SPANISH SHAWL, 77 Copyright © 1983 by Robert H. Montgomery, Jr., as Trustee.
My story is much too sad to be told, 167
My twilight sweetheart, 15

MYSTERIOUSLY, 271 Copyright © 1972 by John F. Wharton, as Trustee.

NAOMI OF HARTENSTEIN'S RESTAURANT, *See* ANTOINETTE BIRBY.
Naught shall sever us now, 55
NAUGHTY, NAUGHTY, 38 Copyright © 1983 by Robert H. Montgomery, Jr., as Trustee.
NEAUVILLE-SUR-MER, 159 © 1933 (Renewed) Warner Bros. Inc.
NEVER GIVE ANYTHING AWAY, 422 Copyright © 1952 by Cole Porter. Copyright Renewed.[2]
NEVER GIVE IN TO LOVE (no lyrics), 156
NEVER, NEVER BE AN ARTIST, 426 Copyright © 1953 by Cole Porter. Copyright Renewed.[2]
NEVER SAY NO (lyrics lost), 156
NIGHT AND DAY, 152 © 1932 (Renewed) Warner Bros. Inc.
NIGHT CLUB, THE, *See* NIGHT CLUB OPENING.
NIGHT CLUB OPENING, 114 Copyright © 1983 by Robert H. Montgomery, Jr., as Trustee.
NIGHT OF THE BALL, THE, 272 Copyright © 1971 by John F. Wharton, as Trustee.
Night time and day time, 85
NIÑA, 382 Copyright © 1946 by Chappell & Co., Inc. Copyright Renewed.[1]
NINETTE, 12 Copyright © 1983 by Robert H. Montgomery, Jr., as Trustee.
NO LOVER, 411 Copyright © 1949 by Cole Porter. Copyright Renewed.[1]
No matter what's your creed in life, 268
NO SHOW THIS EVENING (lost), 39
No wonder it's true, 288
NO WONDER TAXES ARE HIGH, 470 Copyright © 1958 by Cole Porter.[3]
No wonder that the rose to me's, 139
NOBODY'S CHASING ME, 414 Copyright © 1949 by Cole Porter. Copyright Renewed.[1]
Not . . . so many summers ago, 202
NOTHING TO DO BUT WORK, 432 Copyright © 1967 by John F. Wharton, as Trustee.
Now a girl is a babe, 368
Now a lot of people say, 78
Now a maiden in my station, 22
Now as long as we're united in the bonds of matrimony, 30
Now as Sam was traveling from Harlem to Tennessee, 67
Now before this modern idea had burst, 119
Now Chlodoswinde the fair and I, 23
Now ev'rybody's happy, 202
Now Harry was a Psi U sort of stoic, 22
Now here's some scandal I've just heard, 21
Now I have got a secret for you, my queen, 16
Now I met my girl on a roam through Prussia, 21
Now I'm in an awful condition, 6
Now, I'm the kind of villain that you hear about, 14
Now in every musical show, 26
Now in life there's nought that's lower, 19
Now I've always known that dear Mother was prone, 66
Now of late, the daily papers, 219
Now pretty little Missus Bell, 369
Now since my sweetheart Sal met Miss Elsie de Wolfe, 65
Now since the Allied banners, 63
Now that there is no question, 246
Now that we are close, 416
Now there's a rag that everybody's doin', 15
Now, 'twas late last fall I bought a yawl, 28
Now when I was an infant exceedingly young, 47
Now when I was an undergrad, 17
Now, when I was but a baby, 64
Now when Willie was still an obtuse Montessori-an, 34
NOW YOU HAS JAZZ, 456 Copyright © 1955 by Chappell & Co., Inc. Copyright Renewed.[2]
Now you'd never infer, 19
Nowadays it's rather nobby, 36
NUDITY, SWEET NUDITY, *See* SWEET NUDITY.
NYMPH ERRANT, 161 © 1933 (Renewed) Warner Bros. Inc.

OCTET, 356 Copyright © 1977 by John F. Wharton, as Trustee.
Of European lands effete, 44
Of the sturdy Middle West I am the patriotic cream, 44
Off in the nightfall, 277
Off we go to take a ride, take a ride, take a ride, 6
Officer, we've got something most important to say, 169
Oh, Americans and Englishmen, 292
Oh, bear with me (and I know you shall), 378
Oh, beware of the Sophomore, 27
Oh, Bill, / Why can't you behave, 394
Oh, blow, Gabriel, blow, 173
Oh boy, I'm feeing but bad, 326
Oh boy, that bandit band!, 80
OH, BRIGHT FAIR DREAM, 54 Copyright © 1916 G. Schirmer, Inc. Copyright Renewed.[5]
Oh, bring, oh, bring me back my butterfly, 65
Oh, by Jove and by Jehovah, 412
Oh, Carlotta, 346
Oh, Chlodo, Chlodoswinde, 22
Oh, Cleveland—let's make it Cleveland, 71
Oh gee! It's heaven to be the lovely heroine, 14
Oh, gentle stranger, tell me who are you, 214
Oh, give me land, lots of land under starry skies above, 180
Oh, glorious crown, 183

OH, HONEY, 74 Copyright © 1983 by Robert H. Montgomery, Jr., as Trustee.
OH, HOW I COULD GO FOR YOU, 332 Copyright © 1983 by Robert H. Montgomery, Jr., as Trustee.
Oh, I wonder where my girl is now, 22
Oh, I'll be ridin' high, 283
Oh, I'm so mad about a lad, 101
Oh, I'm the villain, 14
OH, IT MUST BE FUN, 418 Copyright © 1966 by John F. Wharton, as Trustee.
Oh, it really is confusing, 73
Oh, it will seem strange, 323
Oh, it's awfully hard to concentrate at college, 11
Oh, Jerry, I'm so blue, 308
Oh, ladies and gentlemen, 91
Oh, Llewellyn, 15
OH, MARY, 77 Copyright © 1983 by Robert H. Montgomery, Jr., as Trustee.
Oh moon, moon shining up above her, 5
Oh, my gal in Georgia, 31
Oh, nudity, sweet nudity, 164
Oh, please don't take offense, 253
Oh princess, fair Princess, though I know it could never be, 468
Oh, remember that waltz, 450
OH SO SOON, 67 Copyright © 1983 by Robert H. Montgomery, Jr., as Trustee.
Oh, sweet Jungle Rose, 83
Oh, the Feast Day of the Saints, 221
Oh, the great big wicked city, 213
Oh, the wooing words in a love letter, 80
Oh, those funny little tracks in the snow!, 32
Oh, way down in Coontown Alley!, 62
Oh, what a bevy of beauties, 408
OH, WHAT A LONELY PRINCESS, 32 Copyright © 1983 by Robert H. Montgomery, Jr., as Trustee.
OH, WHAT A PRETTY PAIR OF LOVERS, 30 Copyright © 1971 by John F. Wharton, as Trustee.
Oh, what nights, glory be, 296
Oh, what terrible suspense, 38
Oh why, oh why, 337
Oh, woman, thy name is mischief, 434
OLD KING SOLLY, 83 Copyright © 1983 by Robert H. Montgomery, Jr., as Trustee.
OLD RAT MORT, THE, 12 Copyright © 1983 by Robert H. Montgomery, Jr., as Trustee.
OLD-FASHIONED BOY, AN, 99 © 1928 (Renewed) Warner Bros. Inc.
OLD-FASHIONED GARDEN, 64 © 1919 (Renewed) Warner Bros. Inc.
OLD-FASHIONED GIRL, AN, 98 © 1928 (Renewed) Warner Bros. Inc.
OLD-FASHIONED WALTZ, THE, 81 Copyright © 1977 by Robert H. Montgomery, Jr., as Trustee.
OLGA (COME BACK TO THE VOLGA), 131 Copyright © 1922 by Chappell & Co., Ltd. Copyright
OLGA (COME BACK TO THE VOLGA) (*continued*) Renewed.
OMNIBUS, 92 Copyright © 1971 by John F. Wharton, as Trustee.
On a farm far from pleasant, 154
On a filigreed balcony, 339
On my native strip by the Trinidad sea, 384
ON MY YACHT, 28 Copyright © 1983 by Robert H. Montgomery, Jr., as Trustee.
On Saturday night when my work is through, 194
On Sunday nights, he'd take his bride, 369
On the em'rald-green Aegean, 276
ON THE 90TH FLOOR, *See* DOWN IN THE DEPTHS.
On this lonely night, 377
Once a gypsy told me something, 229
Once I loved such a shattering physician, 162
Once there lived a nice young Scampi, 138
ONCE UPON A TIME, 272 Copyright © 1971 by John F. Wharton, as Trustee.
Once upon a time I was clever, 226
ONCE WE'RE WED, *See* WHEN WE'RE WED.
ONE HUNDRED YEARS FROM TODAY, *See* YOU SAID IT.
One night, in Marrakesh, 94
One night in Mexico, 378
ONE STEP AHEAD OF LOVE, See JUST ONE STEP AHEAD OF LOVE.
One summer day I chanced to stray, 64
ONLY ANOTHER BOY AND GIRL, 362 Copyright © 1944 by Chappell & Co., Inc. Copyright Renewed.[1]
Only thing ah evah done wrong, 338
Onward, onward, / Never stopping, 415
OPENING ACT I, *Greenwich Village Follies* (no lyrics), 89
OPENING, ACT I, SCENE 1, *See* STROLL ON THE PLAZA SANT' ANA, A.
OPENING, ACT I, SCENE 1, *See* I JUPITER, I REX.
OPENING, ACT I, SCENE 5, *See* CARBORUNDUM.
OPENING ACT II, SCENE 1, *See* WE DETEST A FIESTA.
OPENING, AMERICAN EXPRESS SCENE, *See* AMERICAN EXPRESS, THE.
OPENING CHORUS TO BOOTLEG SCENE, *See* SAY IT WITH GIN.
OPENING, LONGCHAMPS SCENE, *See* AT LONGCHAMPS TODAY.
OPENING, PADUA STREET SCENE, *See* WE OPEN IN VENICE.
OPENING, RITZ BAR, *See* TOAST TO VOLSTEAD, A.
OPENING, ROMANZA SEQUENCE, 221 Copyright © 1937 by Chappell & Co., Inc. Copyright Renewed.
OPENING, SANTA ANA MARKET, *See* STROLL ON THE PLAZA SANT' ANA, A.
OPENING, SCENE 1, *See* WE'VE BEEN SPENDING THE SUMMERS WITH OUR FAMILIES.
OPERA STAR, 134 Copyright © 1971 by John F. Wharton, as Trustee.

OPERATIC PILLS, 111 Copyright © 1977 by John F. Wharton, as Trustee.
OPPORTUNITY KNOCKS BUT ONCE, 470 Copyright © 1957 by Cole Porter.[3]
Other towns you may boast of, 56
Our affair was simply swell, 248
OUR CROWN, 182 © 1935 (Renewed) Warner Bros. Inc.
OURS, 206 Copyright © 1936 by Chappell & Co., Inc. Copyright Renewed.
OZARKS ARE CALLIN' ME HOME, THE, 212 Copyright © 1936 by Chappell & Co., Inc. Copyright Renewed.

PAGLIACCI, *See* WHEN BLACK SALLIE SINGS PAGLIACCI.
PALLAS ATHENE (no lyrics), 191
PARANOIA, 32 Copyright © 1983 by Robert H. Montgomery, Jr., as Trustee.
PAREE, WHAT DID YOU DO TO ME?, 124 © 1929 (Renewed) Warner Bros. Inc.
PARIS LOVES LOVERS, 439 Copyright © 1954 by Cole Porter. Copyright Renewed.[2]
Peer! Stare! Step slow!, 57
People tell me, "Never mold your, 300
People tell us New York is simply full uff, 363
People who dwell, 132
PER FAVORE (no lyrics), 466
PERENNIAL DEBUTANTES, 205 Copyright © 1936 by Chappell & Co., Inc. Copyright Renewed.
PERFECTLY TERRIBLE (lost), 39
PERFUME OF LOVE, THE, 449 Copyright © 1966 by John F. Wharton, as Trustee.
PETER PIPER, 63 © 1919 (Renewed) Warner Bros. Inc.
PETS, 309 Copyright © 1967 by John F. Wharton, as Trustee.
PHYSICIAN, THE, 162 © 1933 (Renewed) Warner Bros. Inc.
Phooey, Goodhue!, 242
PICK ME UP AND LAY ME DOWN, 271 Copyright © 1966 by John F. Wharton, as Trustee.
Picture Henry Ford without a car, 190
PICTURE OF ME WITHOUT YOU, A, 190 © 1935 (Renewed) Warner Bros. Inc.
Pierrot fondly lingers, 86
PILOT ME, 94 © Registered in the name of M.E. Sayag, 1928. Copyright Renewed.[4]
PIPE DREAMING, 377 Copyright © 1946 by Chappell & Co., Inc. Copyright Renewed.[1]
PITTER-PATTER, 82 Copyright © 1977 by John F. Wharton, as Trustee.
PITY ME, PLEASE, 47 Copyright © 1916 G. Schirmer, Inc. Copyright Renewed.[5]
PLAY ME (US) A TUNE, 79 Copyright © 1983 by Robert H. Montgomery, Jr., as Trustee.
Play on, pipes of Pan, 133
PLEASE DON'T MAKE ME BE GOOD, 125 © 1929 (Renewed) Warner Bros. Inc.
PLEASE DON'T MONKEY WITH BROADWAY, 252 Copyright © 1939 by Chappell & Co., Inc. Copyright Renewed.[1]
PLEASE HELP THE POOR RICH, *See* POOR RICH, THE.
PLUMBING, 163 Copyright © 1977 by Robert H. Montgomery, Jr., as Trustee.
Poets always speak of youth, 410
POKER, 11 Copyright © 1971 by John F. Wharton, as Trustee.
Poor man of sorrow, 261
POOR RICH, THE, 148 Copyright © 1983 by Robert H. Montgomery, Jr., as Trustee.
POOR YOUNG MILLIONAIRE, 137 Copyright © 1971 by John F. Wharton, as Trustee.
PREP SCHOOL WIDOW, THE, 35 Copyright © 1983 by Robert H. Montgomery, Jr., as Trustee.
PRETTY LITTLE MISSUS BELL, 369 Copyright © 1966 by John F. Wharton, as Trustee.
PRITHEE, COME CRUSADING WITH ME, *See* WON'T YOU COME CRUSADING WITH ME?
PROLOGUE—ANNOUNCEMENT OF INHERITANCE, *See* ANNOUNCEMENT OF INHERITANCE.
PROLOGUE, *Out of This World*, 404 Copyright © 1983 by Robert H. Montgomery, Jr., as Trustee.
PUBLIC ENEMY NUMBER ONE, 172 © 1936 (Renewed) Warner Bros. Inc.
PUT A SACK OVER THEIR HEADS, 357 Copyright © 1966 by John F. Wharton, as Trustee.

Queen of my heart, 78
QUEEN OF TERRE HAUTE, THE, 126 © 1929 (Renewed) Warner Bros. Inc.
QUEEN OF THE YALE DRAMAT (lost), 11
QUEENS OF TERPSICHORE, 16 Copyright © 1983 by Robert H. Montgomery, Jr., as Trustee.
QUELQUE-CHOSE, 103 © 1927 (Renewed) Warner Bros. Inc.

RAGTIME PIPES OF PAN, 133 Copyright © 1922 by Ascherberg, Hopwood and Crew, Ltd. Copyright Renewed.
RAP TAP ON WOOD, 198 Copyright © 1936 by Chappell & Co., Inc. Copyright Renewed.
RECALL GOODHUE, 242 Copyright © 1978 by Robert H. Montgomery, Jr., as Trustee.
RECITATIVE, *See* GOOD MORNING, MISS STANDING.
RED BLUES, THE, 445 Copyright © 1955 by Cole Porter; Copyright Renewed.
RED, HOT AND BLUE, 213 Copyright © 1936 by Chappell & Co., Inc. Copyright Renewed.
Regard Mother Juno, 405
Relax for one moment, my Jerry, 306
Remember Chez Tony, 396
Remember when the Riviera train went off the

Remember when the Riviera train (*continued*) track, 463
REVELATION ENSEMBLE, 57 Copyright © 1983 by Robert H. Montgomery, Jr., as Trustee.
REVENGE, 308 Copyright © 1967 by John F. Wharton, as Trustee.
RICK-CHICK-A-CHICK, 27 Copyright © 1983 by Robert H. Montgomery, Jr., as Trustee.
RIDDE-DIDDLE ME THIS, 329 Copyright © 1967 by John F. Wharton, as Trustee.
RIDIN' HIGH, 210 Copyright © 1936 by Chappell & Co., Inc. Copyright Renewed.
Rigid, frigid leaders of society, 16
RITZ ROLL AND ROCK, THE, 452 Copyright © 1957 by Chappell & Co., Inc.
RIVER GOD, 277 Copyright © 1938 by Chappell & Co., Inc. Copyright Renewed.[1]
Roamin' home, ahoy, 377
Roll your bones, 76
ROLLING HOME, 198 Copyright © 1936 by Chappell & Co., Inc. Copyright Renewed.
ROLLING, ROLLING, 13 Copyright © 1983 by Robert H. Montgomery, Jr., as Trustee.
Rorum corum, 335
ROSALIE, 218 Copyright © 1937 by Chappell & Co., Inc. Copyright Renewed.
ROSEBUD, 13 Copyright © 1983 by Robert H. Montgomery, Jr., as Trustee.
'Round the map I've been a dancer, 461
Rub, rub, rub, rub, 432
RUB YOUR LAMP, 305 Copyright © 1941 by Chappell & Co., Inc. Copyright Renewed.[1]
RUINS, 161 Copyright © 1971 by John F. Wharton, as Trustee.
Rumor says, while a-seeking solace, 343
Run, run, run, rush, 160

Sad times, 303
SAILOR'S CHANTEY, *See* THERE'LL ALWAYS BE A LADY FAIR.
SAILORS OF THE SKY, 401 Copyright © 1943 by Chappell & Co., Inc. Copyright Renewed.[1]
SALT AIR, 151 © 1933 (Renewed) Warner Bros. Inc.
Samantha, you're all / I'll ever adore, 454
SAMOA, SAMOA, *See* SO LONG, SAMOA.
SATIN AND SILK, 441 Copyright © 1954 by Cole Porter. Copyright Renewed.[2]
SATURDAY NIGHT, 11 Copyright © 1971 by John F. Wharton, as Trustee.
SAY IT WITH GIN, 143 Copyright © 1983 by Robert H. Montgomery, Jr., as Trustee.
Say you're fond of fancy things, 262
SCAMPI, THE, 138 Copyright © 1971 by John F. Wharton, as Trustee.
SCANDAL, 21 Copyright © 1976 by John F. Wharton, as Trustee.
SCHOOL, SCHOOL, HEAVEN-BLESSED SCHOOL, 339 Copyright © 1969 by John F. Wharton, as Trustee.
SEA CHANTEY, 377 Copyright © 1983 by Robert H. Montgomery, Jr., as Trustee.
SEA IS CALLING, THE, 63 © 1919 (Renewed) Warner Bros. Inc.
SEE AMERICA FIRST, 44 Copyright © 1916 G. Schirmer, Inc. Copyright Renewed.[5]
SEE THAT YOU'RE BORN IN TEXAS, 321 Copyright © 1943 by Chappell & Co., Inc. Copyright Renwed.[1]
SERENADE (lost), 42
SEX APPEAL, 139 Copyright © 1983 by Robert H. Montgomery, Jr., as Trustee.
Shall I show you more of Mexico?, 357
Shawl, though the swallow has taken to wing, 77
SHE WAS A FAIR YOUNG MERMAID, 20 Copyright © 1974 by John F. Wharton, as Trustee.
She's got a black and white dress, a black and white hat, 65
SHOOTIN' THE WORKS FOR UNCLE SAM, 295 Copyright © 1941 by Chappell & Co., Inc. Copyright Renewed.[1]
SHOULD I TELL YOU I LOVE YOU?, 377 Copyright © 1946 by Chappell & Co., Inc. Copyright Renewed.[1]
SI VOUS AIMEZ LES POITRINES, 164 Copyright © 1972 by John F. Wharton, as Trustee.
SIBERIA, 444 Copyright © 1954 by Cole Porter. Copyright Renewed.[2]
SIDE CAR, THE, 180 © 1935 (Renewed) Warner Bros. Inc.
SIGHTSEEING TOUR, A, 357 Copyright © 1967 by John F. Wharton, as Trustee.
SILK STOCKINGS, 444 Copyright © 1954 by Cole Porter. Copyright Renewed.[2]
SILVER MOON, 16 Copyright © 1983 by Robert H. Montgomery, Jr., as Trustee.
SINCE DOLLY'S COME TO TOWN, 5 Copyright © 1983 by Robert H. Montgomery, Jr., as Trustee.
Since first I left my native France, 46
Since first we started out, we've simply run about, 127
Since first you blew in like a boisterous breeze, 119
Since first you crossed my horizon, 212
Since first you murmured your name to me, 219
Since I gazed at you so temptingly near, 469
Since I gazed in someone's eyes, 218
SINCE I KISSED MY BABY GOODBYE, 296 Copyright © 1941 by Chappell & Co., Inc. Copyright Renewed.[1]
Since I know such a lot of men, 173
Since I reached the charming age of puberty, 393
Since I went on the wagon, I'm, 288
SINCE LITTLE BABY BROTHER BECAME A MOVIE STAR, 68 Copyright © 1983 by Robert H.

Montgomery, Jr., as Trustee.
Since long months, my maties, 233
SINCE MA GOT THE CRAZE ESPAGNOLE, 66 Copyright © 1971 by John F. Wharton, as Trustee.
Since my trips have been extensive ev'rywhere, 441
Since that lovely evening, 314
Since the day I succumbed to your fatal charms, 73
Since the moment when first, 427
Since the time, not so far, 430
Since tyranny we overthrew, 424
SINCE WE'VE MET, 20 Copyright © 1976 by John F. Wharton, as Trustee.
SING "JUBILEE," 195 © 1935 (Renewed) Warner Bros. Inc.
SING SING FOR SING SING, 146 Copyright © 1983 by Robert H. Montgomery, Jr., as Trustee.
SING TO ME, GUITAR, 343 Copyright © 1944 by Chappell & Co., Inc. Copyright Renewed.[1]
SINGING IN THE SADDLE, 181 Copyright © 1977 by John F. Wharton, as Trustee.
Sit down, mad'moiselle, 425
SIX LITTLE WIVES, *See* GAY LITTLE WIVES.
SLAVE AUCTION, 379 Copyright © 1983 by Robert H. Montgomery, Jr., as Trustee.
SLOW SINKS THE SUN, 35 Copyright © 1916 G. Schirmer, Inc. Copyright Renewed.[5]
SNAGTOOTH GERTIE, 379 Copyright © 1967 by John F. Wharton, as Trustee.
So here's to you, 463
SO IN LOVE, 388 Copyright © 1948 by Cole Porter. Copyright Renewed.[1]
So kiss me, Kate, 391, 396
SO LET US HAIL, 24 Copyright © 1976 by John F. Wharton, as Trustee.
SO LONG, 339 Copyright © 1969 by John F. Wharton, as Trustee.
So long as the radiant rose, 340
SO LONG, SAMOA, 401 Copyright © 1971 by John F. Wharton, as Trustee.
SO LONG, SAN ANTONIO, 331 Copyright © 1969 by John F. Wharton, as Trustee.
So many wives I meet today, 412
SO NEAR AND YET SO FAR, 296 Copyright © 1941 by Chappell & Co., Inc. Copyright Renewed.[1]
So often in the evening, 180
So the dream was doomed to die, 444
So this is the road to success!, 363
SO WHAT?, 458 Copyright © 1977 by Robert H. Montgomery, Jr., as Trustee.
So what will become of our England, 154
So while I'm counting my tips, 115
So wrong seemed the world, 376
SOCIAL COACH OF ALL THE FASHIONABLE FUTURE DEBUTANTES, THE, 46 Copyright © 1983 by Robert H. Montgomery, Jr., as Trustee.
SOLOMON, 162 © 1933 (Renewed) Warner Bros.

SOLOMON (*continued*)
Inc.
Some folks collect paintings, 309
Some girls collect Roman epitaphs, 249
Some ladies live in extravagant style, 59
Some think an artist's life could never be sad, 427
SOMEBODY'S GOING TO THROW A BIG PARTY, 122 Copyright © 1983 by Robert H. Montgomery, Jr., as Trustee.
Someone fills my heart with tenderness—, 435
SOMETHING FOR THE BOYS, 322 Copyright © 1942 by Chappell & Co., Inc. Copyright Renewed.[1]
SOMETHING TO SHOUT ABOUT, 314 Copyright © 1942 by Chappell & Co., Inc. Copyright Renewed.[1]
SOMETHING'S GOT TO BE DONE, 46 Copyright © 1916 G. Schirmer, Inc. Copyright Renewed.[5]
Somewhere I read, 270
SOON, *See* OH SO SOON.
Sorry, can't be late, 465
Southern belles—We're famous, 76
Speaking of men in Mexico, 353
SPONGE, THE, 81 Copyright © 1922 by Chappell & Co., Ltd. Copyright Renewed.
Spread your wings and start them flapping, 103
SPRING LOVE IS IN THE AIR, 220 Copyright © 1937 by Chappell & Co., Inc. Copyright Renewed.
Step right up to the bar, gentlemen, 118
STEP WE GRANDLY, 58 Copyright © 1983 by Robert H. Montgomery, Jr., as Trustee.
STEPPING OUT, *See* LET'S STEP OUT.
STEREOPHONIC SOUND, 438 Copyright © 1955 by Cole Porter. Copyright Renewed.[2]
Still do I mind me, 36
Stop all other music!, 384
Stop! Is there a British consul present?, 378
Strange, dear, but true, dear, 388
STROLL ON THE PLAZA SANT' ANA, A, 281 Copyright © 1977 by John F. Wharton, as Trustee.
STROLLING, 14 Copyright © 1983 by Robert H. Montgomery, Jr., as Trustee.
Strolling quite fancy free in maiden meditation, 51
SUBMARINE, 16 Copyright © 1983 by Robert H. Montgomery, Jr., as Trustee.
SUCCESS (lost), 274
Such a thriving business, 46
SUNDAY MORNING BREAKFAST TIME, 192 © 1935 (Renewed) Warner Bros. Inc.
Sun-tanned, wind-blown, 455
SWEET ALICE KIRBY, *See* ANTOINETTE BIRBY.
Sweet baby, you're a saint, 105
SWEET NUDITY, 164 Copyright © 1979 by Robert H. Montgomery, Jr., as Trustee.
SWEET SIMPLICITY, 59 Copyright © 1983 by Robert H. Montgomery, Jr., as Trustee.
SWING THAT SWING, 192 © 1935 (Renewed)

Warner Bros. Inc.
SWINGIN' THE JINX AWAY, 201 Copyright © 1936 by Chappell & Co., Inc. Copyright Renewed.
SYNCOPATED PIPES OF PAN, *See* RAGTIME PIPES OF PAN.

TABLE FOR TWO, A, 73 Copyright © 1983 by Robert H. Montgomery, Jr., as Trustee.
Take hold of my hand, baby, 98
TAKE IT EASY, 317 Copyright © 1983 by Robert H. Montgomery, Jr., as Trustee.
TAKE ME BACK TO MANHATTAN, 146 © 1930 (Renewed) Warner Bros. Inc.
Take some skins, 456
TAKING THE STEPS TO RUSSIA, *See* I'M TAKING THE STEPS TO RUSSIA.
TALE OF THE OYSTER, THE, 123 Copyright © 1966 by John F. Wharton, as Trustee.
TALK YOU HEAR AT THE PROM, THE (lost), 39
TECHNIQUE (no lyrics), 274
Tell 'em to light all the stars in heaven, 235
Tell me tales of Araby, 250
Tell me what makes the U.S.A., 78
Tell me why, 295
TEQUILA, 351 Copyright © 1967 by John F. Wharton, as Trustee.
TEXAS WILL MAKE YOU A MAN, 332 Copyright © 1983 by Robert H. Montgomery, Jr., as Trustee.
THANK YOU, *Leave It to Me*, 242 Copyright © 1983 by Robert H. Montgomery, Jr., as Trustee.
THANK YOU, 274
THANK YOU SO MUCH, MRS. LOWSBOROUGH-GOODBY, 274 © 1934 (Renewed) Warner Bros. Inc.
Thanks, Nick, for a corking afternoon, 292
THAT BLACK AND WHITE BABY OF MINE, 65 © 1919 (Renewed) Warner Bros. Inc.
THAT LITTLE OLD BAR IN THE RITZ, 139 Copyright © 1983 by Robert H. Montgomery, Jr., as Trustee.
That man who's got me mystified, 353
THAT ZIP CORNWALL COOCH, 15 Copyright © 1983 by Robert H. Montgomery, Jr., as Trustee.
THAT'S THE NEWS I'M WAITING TO HEAR, 215 Copyright © 1967 by John F. Wharton, as Trustee.
THAT'S WHAT YOU MEAN TO ME, 358 Copyright © 1966 by John F. Wharton, as Trustee.
THAT'S WHY I LOVE YOU, 127 Copyright © 1966 by John F. Wharton, as Trustee.
The battle of life, 314
The breeze is chasing the zephyr, 414
The day is my enemy, 168
The Emperor is fond of marble dragons, 470
The farce was ended, 240
The female of the species, 396
The first time I told him, 68
The French Colonial Exposition, 165
The girl who "comes out," 47
The girls today in society, 395
The gods who nurse, 109
The high gods above, 206
The law is my life, the law is my wife, 430
The moment I saw you, 160
The moon looking down over London town, 77
The moon looks down on the pampas, 178
The moral of our story, 356
The more I see of men, 428
The more I travel across the gravel, 146
The night is young, the skies are clear, 208
The one I adore in a bachelor's apartment!, 231
The place?, 324
The raging sou'wester was over, 209
The rock and roll is dead and gone, 452
The stars that dance, 337
The young fall, the old fall, 135
There are fifty-seven varieties of pickles, 357
There are stars dancing in the heavens, 275
THERE HE GOES, MR. PHILEAS FOGG, 376 Copyright © 1946 by Chappell & Co., Inc. Copyright Renewed.[1]
There is no trick to a can-can, 429
THERE MUST BE SOMEONE FOR ME, 345 Copyright © 1944 by Chappell & Co., Inc. Copyright Renewed.[1]
There once was a staid, 95
There were two little babes in the wood, 86
THERE'LL ALWAYS BE A LADY FAIR, 168 © 1936 (Renewed) Warner Bros. Inc.
There's a big increase in marriages, 297
There's a boy cat for ev'ry girl cat, 345
THERE'S A FAN, 249 Copyright © 1966 by John F. Wharton, as Trustee.
There's a happy heaven of Harlem, 121
THERE'S A HAPPY LAND IN THE SKY, 327 Copyright © 1979 by Robert H. Montgomery, Jr., as Trustee.
THERE'S A HOLLYWOOD THAT'S GOOD, 446 Copyright © 1966 by John F. Wharton, as Trustee.
There's a myth about a maiden called Urania, 31
There's a pirate known to fame, 381
There's a place that I want to G-O, 39
There's a p'liceman on my street, 114
There's a snatch of song, 226
There's a tale of two little orphans who were left in their uncle's care, 85
There's a town in Brittany, 85
There's an old Australian bush song, 173
THERE'S NO CURE LIKE TRAVEL, 167 Copyright © 1977 by John F. Wharton, as Trustee.
THERE'S NOTHING LIKE SWIMMING, 194 © 1935 (Renewed) Warner Bros. Inc.
THEY AIN'T DONE RIGHT BY OUR NELL, 286 Copyright © 1983 by Robert H. Montgomery,

THEY AIN'T DONE RIGHT BY OUR NELL (*continued*) Jr., as Trustee.
THEY ALL FALL IN LOVE, 135 © 1929 (Renewed) Warner Bros. Inc.
(They call her) Cora, the Fair Chorine, 12
THEY COULDN'T COMPARE TO YOU, 408 Copyright © 1951 by Cole Porter. Copyright Renewed.[2]
They say a woman's love can be bought, 340
They told me that such an unheard-of-event, 468
THEY'RE ALWAYS ENTERTAINING, 160 Copyright © 1971 by John F. Wharton, as Trustee.
This affair has been so swell, 240
This is not next Sunday night, 418
This is our fiesta!, 287
This picture may seem, 299
Though Fate demands that I must leave you, 28
Though I have not a single sou, 431
Though it's not quite generally known, 62
Though Mister Cazanova, 161
Though the world may try its best, 265
Though very humbly born I must confess, 113
Though with joy I should be reeling, 151
Though your age, 99
Though you've been around a lot, 124
THROUGH THICK AND THIN, 314 Copyright © 1977 by Robert H. Montgomery, Jr. as Trustee.
Till we get our enemies, 313
Times have changed, 171
TIRED LITTLE WIVES, *See* GAY LITTLE WIVES.
TIRED OF LIVING ALONE, 68 Copyright © 1983 by Robert H. Montgomery, Jr., as Trustee.
'Tis the final conflict, let each stand in his place, 242
To a bamboo drum persistent, 366
TO BE IN LOVE AND YOUNG, *See* WHAT A JOY TO BE YOUNG.
To be in love is so new to me, 362
To celebrate these happy times, 457
To fall in love, to go insane, 223
TO FOLLOW EVERY FANCY, 43 Copyright © 1983 by Robert H. Montgomery, Jr., as Trustee.
TO GET AWAY, 193 © 1935 (Renewed) Warner Bros. Inc.
TO HELL WITH EV'RYTHING BUT US, 418 Copyright © 1967 by John F. Wharton, as Trustee.
TO LOVE OR NOT TO LOVE, 221 Copyright © 1937 by Chappell & Co., Inc. Copyright Renewed.
To see you and know you, dear Granada, 465
To the dear old American Express, 118
TO THE U.S.A. FROM THE U.S.S.R., 247 Copyright © 1974 by John F. Wharton, as Trustee.
TO THINK THAT THIS COULD HAPPEN TO ME, 435 Copyright © 1952 by Cole Porter. Copyright Renewed.
TOAST TO VOLSTEAD, A, 118 Copyright © 1983 by Robert H. Montgomery, Jr., as Trustee.
Today I find / The modern flapper, 98
Today to get the public to attend a picture show, 439
TOM, DICK OR HARRY, 388 Copyright © 1949 by Cole Porter. Copyright Renewed.[1]
TOMORROW, 245 Copyright © 1938 by Chappell & Co., Inc. Copyright Renewed.[1]
TONIGHT I LOVE YOU MORE, 419 Copyright © 1949 by Cole Porter. Copyright Renewed.
Tonight I'm forced to compromise, 156
Tonight there's going to be some fun, 172
TOO BAD, 438 Copyright © 1955 by Cole Porter. Copyright Renewed.
TOO DARN HOT, 392 Copyright © 1949 by Cole Porter. Copyright Renewed.[1]
Too often, my dear, 377
TOY OF DESTINY (lost), 89
Trav'lers I've seen, 164
TRUE LOVE, 455 Copyright © 1955 by Chappell & Co., Inc. Copyright Renewed.[2]
TRUST YOUR DESTINY TO YOUR STAR, 468 Copyright © 1957 by Cole Porter.[3]
Try Texas right away, son, 332
'Twas at Ye Olde Coffee Shoppe in Cheyenne, 205
'Twas the night of the ball, 272
TWILIGHT, 14 Copyright © 1983 by Robert H. Montgomery, Jr., as Trustee.
TWIN SISTERS, 82 Copyright © 1983 by Robert H. Montgomery, Jr., as Trustee.
TWO LITTLE BABES IN THE WOOD, 85 © 1928 (Renewed) Warner Bros. Inc.

Uncle Sam is in a jam, 295
UNDER THE DRESS, 449 Copyright © 1966 by John F. Wharton, as Trustee.
UNDER THE SUMMER MOON, *See* WHEN THE SUMMER MOON COMES 'LONG.
UNDERSTUDIES (no lyrics), 88
UNLUCKY IN GAMBLING, *See* I'M UNLUCKY AT GAMBLING.
Until I came to Paris, 124
Until the day / You came my way, 167
UNTITLED WALTZ (no lyrics), 89
Up at Heaven's happy portals, 103
Up sack!, 337
UP TO HIS OLD TRICKS AGAIN, 310 Copyright © 1983 by Robert H. Montgomery, Jr., as Trustee.
Up to now we've been two shy young things, 128
Up with your hands, do not attempt resistance, 45
UPPER PARK AVENUE, THE, 278 Copyright © 1983 by Robert H. Montgomery, Jr., as Trustee.
USE YOUR IMAGINATION, 405 Copyright © 1949 by Cole Porter. Copyright Renewed.[1]

VENICE, 144 Copyright © 1983 by Robert H.

Montgomery, Jr., as Trustee.
VENUS OF MILO, 73 Copyright © 1983 by Robert H. Montgomery, Jr., as Trustee.
VISIT PANAMA, 282 Copyright © 1940 by Chappell & Co., Inc. Copyright Renewed.[1]
VITE, VITE, VITE, 238 Copyright © 1974 by John F. Wharton, as Trustee.
VIVIENNE, 102 © 1928 (Renewed) Warner Bros. Inc.
VOODOO, 384 Copyright © 1946 by Chappell & Co., Inc. Copyright Renewed.[1]

WAIT FOR THE MOON, 86 © 1924 (Renewed) Warner Bros. Inc.
WAIT UNTIL IT'S BEDTIME, 111 Copyright © 1977 by John F. Wharton, as Trustee.
WAITERS, THE, *See* WHAT A PRICELESS PLEASURE.
WIATERS V. WAITRESSES (lost), 156
WAKE, LOVE, WAKE (lost), 42
WAKE UP AND DREAM, 108 © 1929 (Renewed) Warner Bros. Inc.
WALTZ DOWN THE AISLE, 174 © 1934 (Renewed) Warner Bros. Inc.
WAR SONG, 70 Copyright © 1971 by John F. Wharton, as Trustee.
WASHINGTON, D.C., 331 Copyright © 1967 by John F. Wharton, as Trustee.
WASHINGTON SQUARE, 72 © 1920 (Renewed) Warner Bros. Inc.
WATCHING THE WORLD GO BY, 126 Copyright © 1983 by Robert H. Montgomery, Jr., as Trustee.
Way down, way down in New Haven town, 6
We all know life is short, 87
We are a trio of cantanti, 136
We are absolutely certain, 410
We are Dresden china soldiers, 38
WE ARE MAIDENS TYPICAL OF FRANCE, *See* MAIDENS TYPICAL OF FRANCE.
WE ARE PROM GIRLS, 26 Copyright © 1983 by Robert H. Montgomery, Jr., as Trustee.
WE ARE SO AESTHETIC, 21 Copyright © 1976 by John F. Wharton, as Trustee.
WE ARE THE CHORUS OF THE SHOW, 14 Copyright © 1983 by Robert H. Montgomery, Jr., as Trustee.
We are the queens of Terpsichore, 16
WE DETEST A FIESTA, 287 Copyright © 1977 by John F. Wharton, as Trustee.
WE DRINK TO YOU, J.H. BRODY, 238 Copyright © 1974 by John F. Wharton, as Trustee.
We got the red blues, 445
We love each other so deeply, 362
WE OPEN IN VENICE, 388 Copyright © 1949 by Cole Porter. Copyright Renewed.[1]
WE SHALL NEVER BE YOUNGER, 397 Copyright © 1955 by Cole Porter. Copyright Renewed.
We were fated to be mated, 452
We were simple Europeans, 110
WEDDING CAKEWALK, THE, 297 Copyright © 1941 by Chappell & Co., Inc. Copyright Renewed.[1]
WEEKEND AFFAIR, A, 155 Copyright © 1979 by Robert H. Montgomery, Jr., as Trustee.
Welcome chiquita Geraldina, 285
WELCOME TO JERRY, 285 Copyright © 1983 by Robert H. Montgomery, Jr., as Trustee.
Welcome to San Antonio, 331
WELL, DID YOU EVAH!, *Du Barry Was A Lady*, 263 Copyright © 1940 by Chappell & Co., Inc. Copyright Renewed.[1]
WELL, DID YOU EVAH!, *High Society*, 263 Copyright © 1956 by Chappell & Co., Inc.
Well, here comes the bride, no less, 297
WELL, I JUST WOULDN'T KNOW, 332 Copyright © 1983 by Robert H. Montgomery, Jr., as Trustee.
WELL, IT'S GOOD TO BE HERE AGAIN, 44 Copyright © 1983 by Robert H. Montgomery, Jr., as Trustee.
Well, the Navy's where she should be, in a deep doleful grave, 221
We'll have cocktails at Heublein's, 7
We'll make ev'ry day a holiday, 256
We'll take a trip to Washington Square, 72
WERE THINE THAT SPECIAL FACE, 390 Copyright © 1948 by Cole Porter. Copyright Renewed.[1]
WE'RE A GROUP OF NONENTITIES, 28 Copyright © 1971 by John F. Wharton, as Trustee.
WE'RE ABOUT TO START BIG REHEARSIN', 211 Copyright © 1979 by Robert H. Montgomery, Jr., as Trustee.
We're all alone, 104
We're butterflies, 134
We're doin' fine, 402
We're ladies-in-waiting, 462
WE'RE OFF (lost), 11
WE'RE OFF FOR A HAYRIDE IN MEXICO, 352 Copyright © 1977 by John F. Wharton, as Trustee.
WE'RE OFF TO FEATHERMORE, 183 © 1935 (Renewed) Warner Bros. Inc.
WE'RE ON THE ROAD TO ATHENS, 415 Copyright © 1977 by Robert H. Montgomery, Jr., as Trustee.
We're only another boy and girl, 363
We're suitably attired tonight, 37
We're the Navy's aviators, 401
We're two little squaws from Indiana, 328
WEREN'T WE FOOLS? 140 © 1927 (Renewed) Warner Bros. Inc.
We've a little secret to confess to you, 43
WE'VE BEEN SPENDING THE SUMMERS WITH OUR FAMILIES, 148 Copyright © 1983 by Robert H. Montgomery, Jr., as Trustee.
WHAT A BALL, 450 Copyright © 1966 by John F.

Wharton, as Trustee.
WHAT A CHARMING AFTERNOON, 20 Copyright © 1976 by John F. Wharton, as Trustee.
WHAT A CRAZY WAY TO SPEND SUNDAY, 347 Copyright © 1944 by Chappell & Co., Inc. Copyright Renewed.[1]
WHAT A FAIR THING IS A WOMAN, 434 Copyright © 1952 by Cole Porter. Copyright Renewed.
WHAT A GREAT PAIR WE'LL BE, 211 Copyright © 1936 by Chappell & Co., Inc. Copyright Renewed.
WHAT A JOY TO BE YOUNG, 175 Copyright © 1966 by John F. Wharton, as Trustee.
What a life we'll lead, 256
WHAT A NICE MUNICIPAL PARK, 186 © 1935 (Renewed) Warner Bros. Inc.
What a pleasure it is to get away, 193
WHAT A PRICELESS PLEASURE, 233 Copyright © 1967 by John F. Wharton, as Trustee.
WHAT AM I TO DO?, 277 Copyright © 1971 by John F. Wharton, as Trustee.
WHAT ARE LITTLE HUSBANDS MADE OF?, 309 Copyright © 1977 by Robert H. Montgomery, Jr., as Trustee.
What are little wives made of?, 309
WHAT DO YOU THINK ABOUT MEN?, 409 Copyright © 1955 by Cole Porter. Copyright Renewed.[2]
What do you think of reducing diets?, 289
WHAT DOES YOUR SERVANT DREAM ABOUT?, 398 Copyright © 1967 by John F. Wharton, as Trustee.
WHAT FUN, 465 Copyright © 1977 by Robert H. Montgomery, Jr., as Trustee.
WHAT HAVE I?, 267 Copyright © 1966 by John F. Wharton, as Trustee.
WHAT IS THAT TUNE?, 226 Copyright © 1938 by Chappell & Co., Inc. Copyright Renewed.[1]
What is the spot where you long to be? 426
WHAT IS THIS THING CALLED LOVE?, 111 © 1929 (Renewed) Warner Bros. Inc.
What is, what is this song?, 405
WHAT LOVE IS, 34 Copyright © 1983 by Robert H. Montgomery, Jr., as Trustee.
WHAT SAY LET'S BE BUDDIES, *See* LET'S BE BUDDIES.
What secrets hover, 77
What shadows hover, 113
WHAT SHALL I DO?, 229 Copyright © 1938 by Chappell & Co., Inc. Copyright Renewed.[1]
WHAT SHOULD I DO? *See* WHAT SHALL I DO?
WHAT WILL BECOME OF OUR ENGLAND?, 153 Copyright © 1983 by Robert H. Montgomery, Jr., as Trustee.
WHAT'S MY MAN GONNA BE LIKE?, 270 Copyright © 1983 by Robert H. Montgomery, Jr., as Trustee.
WHAT'S THIS AWFUL HULLABALOO?, 20 Copyright © 1976 by John F. Wharton, as Trustee.
WHEN A BODY'S IN LOVE, 56 Copyright © 1983 by Robert H. Montgomery, Jr., as Trustee.
When a fellow immature, 20
WHEN A WOMAN'S IN LOVE, 340 Copyright © 1970 by John F. Wharton, as Trustee.
WHEN ALL'S SAID AND DONE, 240 Copyright © 1966 by John F. Wharton, as Trustee.
WHEN BLACK SALLIE SINGS PAGLIACCI, 62 Copyright © 1983 by Robert H. Montgomery, Jr., as Trustee.
When Carlotta and Max'milian, 346
When day is gone, 295
When from London I came to Chicago, 113
When Hansel and Gretel had grown up, 98
When I arrive in any town, 382
WHEN I FOUND YOU, 106 Copyright © 1983 by Robert H. Montgomery, Jr., as Trustee.
WHEN I HAD A UNIFORM ON, 63 © 1919 (Renewed) Warner Bros. Inc.
When I left this great big town, 71
When I see troops of carriages, 151
When I started my married career, I confess, 111
WHEN I USED TO LEAD THE BALLET, 19 Copyright © 1916 G. Schirmer, Inc. Copyright Renewed.[5]
When I was a baby a-playing, 470
WHEN I WAS A LITTLE CUCKOO, 365 Copyright © 1945 by Chappell & Co., Inc. Copyright Renewed.[1]
When I was younger, 410
WHEN I'M EATING AROUND WITH YOU, 7 Copyright © 1983 by Robert H. Montgomery, Jr., as Trustee.
When knighthood was in flow'r, 219
WHEN LOVE BECKONED, 257 Copyright © 1939 by Chappell & Co., Inc. Copyright Renewed.[1]
When love comes in, 423
WHEN LOVE COMES TO CALL, 436 Copyright © 1972 by John F. Wharton, as Trustee.
WHEN LOVE COMES YOUR WAY, 186 © 1933 (Renewed) Warner Bros. Inc.
WHEN MCKINLEY MARCHES ON, 340 Copyright © 1983 by Robert H. Montgomery, Jr., as Trustee.
WHEN ME, MOWGLI, LOVE, 187 © 1935 (Renewed) Warner Bros. Inc.
When men declare, 103
When Mummy in her sixteenth year, 241
WHEN MY BABY GOES TO TOWN, 321 Copyright © 1943 by Chappell & Co., Inc. Copyright Renewed.[1]
WHEN MY CARAVAN COMES HOME, 78 © 1922 (Renewed) Warner Bros. Inc.
When my roving caravan, 78
When once we get established as a family of Smiths, 192
When people contend, 65
When Prince Paul rides forth, all the girls in town, 222
When shades enfold, 295

When some fine night with the stars above, 215
When some goofy guy, 281
When some Lothario, 336
When somebody writes you a letter, 80
When suddenly you sight, 462
When that man Joe, 110
When the day's business battle is won, 139
When the electromagnetic of the he-male, 440
WHEN THE HEN STOPS LAYING, 247 Copyright © 1967 by John F. Wharton, as Trustee.
When the little bluebird, 101
When the only sound in the empty street, 145
When the right man comes my way, 81
When the state of your mind, 229
WHEN THE SUMMER MOON COMES 'LONG, 4 Copyright © 1971 by John F. Wharton, as Trustee.
When the sun goes down on the big Red Square, 243
When the time arrives for dinner, 48
When the weekend comes, 145
When there's a sun above, 324
When they begin the beguine, 188
When those bells start to chime, 175
When we started on this Mediterranean cruise, 161
When we use words like scat, cat, 367
When we waltz down the aisle, 175
WHEN WE'RE HOME ON THE RANGE, 323 Copyright © 1979 by Robert H. Montgomery, Jr., as Trustee.
When we're sent to dear Siberia, 444
WHEN WE'RE WED, 18 Copyright © 1983 by Robert H. Montgomery, Jr., as Trustee.
WHEN YOU AND I WERE STRANGERS, 340 Copyright © 1969 by John F. Wharton, as Trustee.
When you feel your heart go pitter-patter, 82
When you find that old man Trouble, 143
When you first said, "Baby mine, 304
When you grumble and sigh, 108
When you sit down, one day, 199
When you think you'd like to float, 19
When your instinct tells you that disaster, 173
WHEN YOUR TROUBLES HAVE STARTED, 214 Copyright © 1966 by John F. Wharton, as Trustee.
When you're out in smart society, 263, 264
Whenever, darling, by chance, 464
Whenever skies look gray to me, 253
WHERE?, 215 Copyright © 1983 by Robert H. Montgomery, Jr., as Trustee.
Where are the fields of corn, arrah, 336
WHERE ARE THE MEN?, 169 © 1936 (Renewed) Warner Bros. Inc.
WHERE CAN ONE POWDER ONE'S NOSE?, 149 Copyright © 1983 by Robert H. Montgomery, Jr., as Trustee.
Where could there be a more perfect pair, 215
WHERE DO WE GO FROM HERE?, 372 Copyright © 1967 by John F. Wharton, as Trustee.
WHERE HAVE YOU BEEN?, 143 © 1930 (Renewed) Warner Bros. Inc.
WHERE IS THE LIFE THAT LATE I LED, 393 Copyright © 1949 by Cole Porter. Copyright Renewed.[1]
WHERE, OH WHERE?, 407 Copyright © 1949 by Cole Porter. Copyright Renewed.[1]
WHERE WOULD YOU GET YOUR COAT?, 120 Copyright © 1966 by John F. Wharton, as Trustee.
WHERE'S LOUIE?, 256 Copyright © 1977 by John F. Wharton, as Trustee.
WHEREVER THEY FLY THE FLAG OF OLD ENGLAND, 378 Copyright © 1946 by Chappell & Co., Inc. Copyright Renewed.[1]
WHICH?, 104 © 1928 (Renewed) Warner Bros. Inc.
WHICH IS THE RIGHT LIFE?, 105 © 1928 (Renewed) Warner Bros. Inc.
While I'm calmly sitting pretty, 151
While rehearsing with Bianca, 395
While tearing off, 244
While the lucky ones sit together, 159
While you're here in Mexico, 351
WHO BUT YOU?, 215 Copyright © 1967 by John F. Wharton, as Trustee.
Who first made my heart stand still?, 102
WHO HAS?, 458 Copyright © 1983 by Robert H. Montgomery, Jr., as Trustee.
Who has an itch, 455
WHO KNOWS?, 218 Copyright © 1937 by Chappell & Co., Inc. Copyright Renewed.
Who on earth was Mr. Pankhurst?, 70
WHO SAID GAY PAREE?, 434 Copyright © 1952 by Cole Porter. Copyright Renewed.
Who spread the rumor Paris was fun? 434
Who wanna play hide-and-seek?, 305
WHO WANTS TO BE A MILLIONAIRE?, 455 Copyright © 1955 by Chappell & Co., Inc. Copyright Renewed.[2]
WHO WOULD HAVE DREAMED, 288 Copyright © 1940 by Chappell & Co., Inc. Copyright Renewed.[1]
WHO'LL BID?, 340 Copyright © 1969 by John F. Wharton, as Trustee.
Why am I / Just as happy as a child?, 88
WHY AM I SO GONE (ABOUT THAT GAL)?, 463 Copyright © 1956 by Chappell & Co., Inc.
WHY CAN'T I FORGET YOU?, 250 Copyright © 1983 by Robert H. Montgomery, Jr., as Trustee.
WHY CAN'T YOU BEHAVE?, 387 Copyright © 1948 by Cole Porter. Copyright Renewed.[1]
Why couldn't I have been Salome, 126
WHY DO YOU WANTA HURT ME SO?, 419 Copyright © 1950 by Cole Porter. Copyright Renewed.[1]
Why does a chicken cross the road?, 329
Why don't they change that old N.R.A., 278
WHY DON'T WE TRY STAYING HOME?, 127 Copyright © 1966 by John F. Wharton, as Trustee.

WHY IS IT? (unfinished sketch), 459
Why is it, dear, 276
Why is it (no teasin'), 227
WHY MARRY THEM?, 151 Copyright © 1979 by Robert H. Montgomery, Jr., as Trustee.
WHY NOT?, *See* SO WHAT?
Why not stay back in Hackensack?, 85
WHY SHOULD I CARE?, 219 Copyright © 1937 by Chappell & Co., Inc. Copyright Renewed.
WHY SHOULD I TRUST YOU?, 450 Copyright © 1966 by John F. Wharton, as Trustee.
WHY SHOULDN'T I?, 183 © 1935 (Renewed) Warner Bros. Inc.
WHY SHOULDN'T I HAVE YOU?, 122 Copyright © 1978 by Robert H. Montgomery, Jr., as Trustee.
WHY TALK ABOUT SEX? (lost), 149
Why the tears, little one, 275
Why, y'all seem to be / So darn gay, 331
WIDOW'S CRUISE, 72 Copyright © 1983 by Robert H. Montgomery, Jr., as Trustee.
Wild Cat Kelly, looking mighty pale, 180
WILD WEDDING BELLS, 276 Copyright © 1978 by Robert H. Montgomery, Jr., as Trustee.
Wise young fellows when they marry, 58
With a million neon rainbows burning below me, 206
With your looks so attractive, 464
WITHOUT LOVE, 441 Copyright © 1954 by Cole Porter. Copyright Renewed.[2]
Woman is a perfect thing, 458
WOMAN'S CAREER, A, 397 Copyright © 1966 by John F. Wharton, as Trustee.
WONDERLAND (unfinished sketch), 459
WOND'RING NIGHT AND DAY, 132 Copyright © 1922 by Chappell & Co., Ltd. Copyright Renewed.
WON'T YOU COME CRUSADING WITH ME?, 33 Copyright © 1916 G. Schirmer, Inc. Copyright Renewed.[5]
WOODLAND DANCE (lost, no lyrics), 42
Work, little laundress, work away, 432
Work, work, work, work, 432
WOULDN'T IT BE CRAZY?, 333 Copyright © 1983 by Robert H. Montgomery, Jr., as Trustee.
WOULDN'T IT BE FUN, 471 Copyright © 1958 by Cole Porter.[3]
WOW-OOH-WOLF!, 363 Copyright © 1945 by Chappell & Co., Inc. Copyright Renewed.[1]
WUNDERBAR, 387 Copyright © 1948 by Cole Porter. Copyright Renewed.[1]

YALE ELIZABETHAN CLUB, THE, *See* MEMBER OF THE YALE ELIZABETHAN CLUB, A.
YANKEE DOODLE, 121 Copyright © 1983 by Robert H. Montgomery, Jr., as Trustee.
Yass, / Mamie Magdalin, 338
YELLOW MELODRAMA, 8 Copyright © 1971 by John F. Wharton, as Trustee.
Yes, I've got an awful lot to learn, girls, 48
YES, YES, YES, 230 Copyright © 1977 by Robert H. Montgomery, Jr., as Trustee.
Yesterday was a dull day, 408
YOU AND ME, *Hitchy-Koo of 1919*, 66 Copyright © 1983 by Robert H. Montgomery, Jr., as Trustee.
YOU AND ME, *La Revue des Ambassadeurs*, 95 © 1928 (Renewed) Warner Bros. Inc.
You are a man who knows, 249
You are to me ev'rything, 302
You ask me about Hollywood, 446
You ask me, dear, to sing you a song?, 163
YOU CAN DO NO WRONG, 383 Copyright © 1948 by Chappell & Co., Inc. Copyright Renewed.[1]
You can't be much surprised to hear, 154
YOU CAN'T BEAT MY BILL, 311 Copyright © 1983 by Robert H. Montgomery, Jr., as Trustee.
You come to Paris, you come to play, 124
You could have a great career, 104
You couldn't realize, 286
YOU DO SOMETHING TO ME, 118 © 1929 (Renewed) Warner Bros. Inc.
You do the boulevard break, 97
YOU DON'T KNOW PAREE, 124 © 1929 (Renewed) Warner Bros. Inc.
You don't love me, 'tis clear to see, 426
YOU DON'T REMIND ME, 416 Copyright © 1949 by Cole Porter. Copyright Renewed.[1]
YOU IRRITATE ME SO, 303 Copyright © 1941 by Chappell & Co., Inc. Copyright Renewed.[1]
YOU MAKE UP, 73 Copyright © 1983 by Robert H. Montgomery, Jr., as Trustee.
You mean my farewell to sorrow, 358
YOU NEVER KNOW, 226 Copyright © 1938 by Chappell & Co., Inc. Copyright Renewed.[1]
You ought to see little me and Marie, 194
You owe me five francs, Miss, 431
YOU SAID IT, 289 Copyright © 1983 by Robert H. Montgomery, Jr., as Trustee.
You see in me an innocent fleur-de-lis, 14
You should buy her a box at the opera, 59
You think you're such a smarty, 306
You villain, you viper, 358
You will wake me at eight each morning, 376
You'd be so easy to love, 201
YOU'D BE SO NICE TO COME HOME TO, 313 Copyright © 1942 by Chappell & Co., Inc. Copyright Renewed.[1]
YOUNGER SONS OF PEERS, 43 Copyright © 1983 by Robert H. Montgomery, Jr., as Trustee.
Your charm is not like the still of ev'ning, dear, 355
Your eyes are an item, 459
Your heart's lost its quiver, 347
Your words go through and through me, 158

YOU'RE A BAD INFLUENCE ON ME, 212 Copyright © 1936 by Chappell & Co., Inc. Copyright Renewed.
You're a dream, Manuela, 384
YOU'RE IN LOVE, 155 © 1932 (Renewed) Warner Bros. Inc.
You're just one step ahead of love, baby, 234
YOU'RE JUST TOO, TOO, 461 Copyright © 1956 by Chappell & Co., Inc.
YOU'RE SENSATIONAL, 456 Copyright © 1955 by Chappell & Co., Inc. Copyright Renewed.[2]
You're such a *ne plus ultra* creature, 227
You're the fly in my ointment, 304
YOU'RE THE PRIZE GUY OF GUYS, 465 Copyright © 1966 by John F. Wharton, as Trustee.
YOU'RE THE TOP, 169 © 1934 (Renewed) Warner Bros. Inc.
YOU'RE TOO FAR AWAY, 164 © 1934 (Renewed) Warner Bros. Inc.
YOURS, 195 © 1935 (Renewed) Warner Bros. Inc.
YOURS FOR A SONG, 368 Copyright © 1977 by John F. Wharton, as Trustee.
YOU'VE GOT SOMETHING, 207 Copyright © 1936 by Chappell & Co., Inc. Copyright Renewed.
YOU'VE GOT THAT THING, 119 © 1929 (Renewed) Warner Bros. Inc.
YOU'VE GOT TO BE HARD-BOILED (fragment), 149

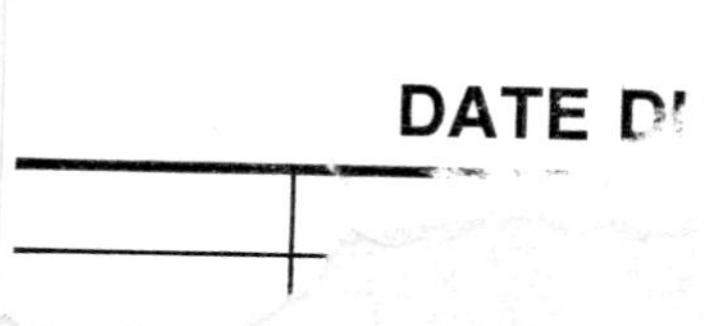